ECONOMICS, SOCIETY, TECHNOLOGY, AND YOU

by Ceslav Ciobanu

Virginia State University

Bassim Hamadeh, CEO and Publisher
Kassie Graves, Director of Acquisitions
Jamie Giganti, Senior Managing Editor
Miguel Macias, Senior Graphic Designer
Amy Stone, Acquisitions Editor
Natalie Lakosil, Licensing Manager
Kaela Martin and Christian Berk, Associate Editors
Kat Ragudos, Interior Designer

BRIEF CONTENTS

CONTENTS

ACKNOWLEDGMENTS

Usually textbooks are created by a team headed by the author, professor, and leading specialist in his or her respective field. It is a collective effort. This book is the result of my own professional experience for more than quarter of century as an academic person and associate professor of political economy in the former USSR at Moscow M. Lomonosov State University (from which I graduated and where I defended my doctoral dissertation) and the Moscow Academy of Oil and Gas. I taught my students in the Academy of Economic Studies of Moldova and in the first private Free International University of Moldova where I served as chair of the Department of Economics and International Relations. I was privileged to teach students in the United States at George Mason University and at Virginia State University for twelve years. This book is also based on my experiences in government as an advisor to former USSR President Mikhail Gorbachev, as an adviser and deputy chief of office to the first President of Moldova, Mircea Snegur, as the first minister of privatization of Moldova, as deputy minister of foreign affairs of Moldova, and as the Moldovan ambassador to the US and Canada. After I accomplished my tour of duty as ambassador, I won public policy awards at the Woodrow Wilson Center for International Scholars, National Endowment for Democracy, and the US Institute of Peace.

This book represents the added value of all my professional experience. I was inspired by my personal meetings with two distinguished American economists and Nobel Prize laureates in Economics, Milton Friedman and Paul Krugman. I am grateful to my VSU colleagues for their support, particularly to Dr. Kwadwo Bawuah, former Department of Economics chair, and Dr. Maxwell Eseonu; to Dr. Cheryl Adeyemi, current Department of Mathematics and Economics chair; Dr. Keith Williamson, dean and professor of College of Engineering and Technology, and Dr. Dawit Haile, associate dean; Dr. Donald Palm, vice president and provost; and to Dr. Makola Abdullah, the new VSU president, all of whom made my work on this textbook possible. I would also like to thank my oldest son, Radu, a graduate of George Mason University and Virginia Tech, who helped me with the graphs, diagrams, and other illustrations. I am grateful to my youngest son, Cristian, a graduate of the University of Virginia and George Washington University, for his sharp comments and remarks.

I was also inspired by the textbooks of such distinguished economists as Bradley Shiller, Robin Bade, Michael Parkin, McConnell Brue, Ben Bernanke, and many others. I hope the book will be a useful and interesting experience for students of Essential Economics as well as for those who are studying other related disciplines, such as International Economics, Economic Development, Transition Economics, History of Economic Thoughts, etc.

The second edition of this book is revised and updated according to comments, suggestions, and recommendations from faculty colleagues and my students. A new chapter (16) on the US and the Global Economy was added, another has been divided into two chapters: Chapter 7: Monopolistic Competition: Quality, Price, and Marketing and Chapter 8: Oligopoly and Game Theory: Strategic Behavior and Decision-Making. Each chapter contains Key Terms, an expanded and updated section on Problems and Application, and a new, concluding section of Review Questions. All graphs and diagrams were revised, simplified, and edited in various colors, which make them more relevant to the book's content and easier to understand. The course materials, problems and applications, and topics for research and presentation are supplemented by references to important websites with many more opportunities for students to adopt an innovative, creative approach to economic issues and categories and apply them in real economic situations. Of course, there is still a window for improvement, and I will be grateful for any constructive comments and suggestions about this new edition of the book.

A NEW APPROACH TO CLASSICS OF ECONOMICS: WHY SHOULD YOU MAJOR IN ECONOMICS?

My dear student, class of the twenty-first century,

You are about to start a fascinating journey into the World of Economics. You are at the gates of the still terra incognita (unknown land) of What, How, and For Whom goods and services are produced; how the market mechanism works through demand and supply; how the US and the world economies are reacting to new challenges, and why they are still facing thrilling ups and downs; what the driving force of economic progress and prosperity is; what the best policy tools for economic recovery are; and why the approval rating of the US President Donald Trump is so sensitive to the state of the economy. And is Professor Ben Bernanke, former chairman of the Fed, to be praised or blamed for the way in which the American economy navigated through the recent financial crisis? These and many, many other questions, notions, categories, and facts will be addressed and discovered in this Economics, Society, Technology, and You.

My first lesson is one I learned from Milton Friedman, one of the most famous American economists and a Nobel Prize laureate, when I visited him in San Francisco in 1994 just a few years after my small, native country in southeastern Europe, Moldova, became independent after the collapse of communism in the Soviet Union. "You are finally 'Free to Choose,'" stressed Dr. Friedman, signing his book for me. From that prospect, I discovered America, a blessed land where the most audacious dreams can become true. And you, my dear student, are about to discover how this great economy and democracy work and why the US is a beacon for the free world and for those who are aspiring to get out of poverty and misery.

This book is different from many others:

First, you, my student, are the subject of Economics; your interests, your choices, your challenges and aspirations are the core of this new approach. I want you to learn how to operate with the economic categories, notions, facts, and statistics, bearing in mind that Economics in its micro- and macrocomposition is not a virtual world, nor is it "the most complex and boring" of disciplines that you have to confront as some of your colleagues might suggest to you. This is the business of your everyday life, an important value added to your career opportunities.

Second, my approach is based on ancient Greek wisdom: everything is cognizable in comparison. To better understand the American way to economic prosperity, it is important to compare how things changed in America itself and in the world: what are the most important market structures, and why is the US Economy identified as a corporate economy; how does the fiscal and monetary policy work or not work, and which one is more efficient in times of crisis and after; why is capitalism triumphing in the West and failing everywhere else as Hernando de Soto stated in his famous book *Mystery of Capital*?

Third, we are living in an interconnected, intertwined world, and challenges to our economy are directly related to global markets as these markets are dependent on what is happening to the American economy. My new approach consists of a critical analysis of Classical Economics in the context of globalization by addressing such questions as: are the Emerging Markets, including those of the BRIC's countries (Brazil, Russia, China, and India), a threat to America's economic power or are they an opportunity; are international trade and global financial markets a benefit or a burden for economic prosperity; is what is good for General Motors still good for America … or for China?

Fourth, this book is focused on critical thinking in search of creative solutions to economic conundrums and is intended as a dialog with you, with the most important factor being the progress of the US economy. Your talent, your skills, and productive work are the keys to your prosperity but also to the prosperity of this great country.

Last, but not least, my course is based on a quarter of a century of experience teaching Economics and Political Economy in different countries and different areas: in Moscow State University from which I graduated and where I defended my doctoral dissertation; in the Moscow Academy of Oil and Gas (Russia); in the Academy of Economic Studies and the Free International University of Moldova, where I served as chair of the International Economics Department; in Virginia State University and some other US universities. Of great importance to this course is also my experience with the government in different positions: as one of the young advisors to Mr. Mikhail Gorbachev in late 1980s and early 1990s, the first and last president of the Soviet Union; as chief economic adviser to the first President of Moldova, Mircea Snegur; as a member of government and the first minister of privatization of Moldova in 1990s, and as Moldovan ambassador to the US in the beginning of the 2000s.

In conclusion, one more remark, inspired by a school poem by my daughter, Ionela:

Love is when you are doing everything well, with fun and satisfaction, and everyone is happy.

I love Economics—the queen of the social sciences and foundation of all financial, business, and other related disciplines. I am passionate about its challenges and puzzles.

My dear student, I have a lot of respect for you and your hard work and dedication, and I wish you good luck in your new and exciting journey to discover *Economics, Society, Technology, And You.*

Ceslav Ciobanu

PhD, Professor of Economics
Coordinator of Economics Programs
VSU Eminent Scholar
Ambassador (ret.)

FOREWORD

RETHINKING ECONOMICS THROUGH KNOWLEDGE AND MODERN TECHNOLOGY

When Dr. Ceslav Ciobanu asked me to write a Foreword to second edition of his book: "Economics, Society, Technology, and You", I immediately accepted because we recently transferred the Economics programs to our College of Engineering and Technology. We made this decision because we felt a solid grounding in economics was as vital as computing and software skills to our modern economy. One only has to look at how computer technology has increased econometric sophistication and is changing the way the world works economically. The first edition of his book was well received by students, and some of the comments about it included the following: "is well-written book with a lot of fundamental content … that allow students to summarize their thoughts and apply the freshly read content to the real world" (Aleceia Howard); "The material on the book is not only great for studying for the tests, but it is interesting material that will enable us to know basic things about our economy as go throughout life" (Brittany White); "I feel as if material is easy to understand and explained in a way in which students such as myself who have no experience in economics can grasp the information and continue on with taking other classes in economics" (Donald Hamilton); "This book helps students see how economics is used in our everyday life and exactly how our choices ultimately affect the economy at a macro and micro level" (Maleik Pride).

Believe the second edition of the book goes even further to help students understand the impact of economics in a global, societal and modern context. I would also emphasize that this new edition is well structured, easy to navigate and rich with real life examples, facts, case studies, and relevant economic analysis. The content is clear, interesting, and enjoyable to read. I believe it is written clearly with a student-centered approach that provides detailed explanation of complex economic notions with relevant and accessible mathematics. The book is focused on improving students' ability to analyze and interpret economic data, to identify and solve applied economics problems. Although the book is designed for introductory economics course, it could be used also as a prerequisite for upper level courses, such as Engineering Economics that involves formulating, estimating, and evaluating the expected economic outcomes and alternatives designed to accomplish a defined purpose. It is also a useful introduction to such courses as intermediate Macro- and Micro-economics, International Economics, and Economics of Development etc. In summary, I am happy to support this book which incorporates nearly three decades of Dr. Ciobanu's teaching experience in different countries, different times, and different economic and political environments. The author's experience in diplomacy and international affairs (Dr. Ciobanu is the former Ambassador of Moldova to the USA and Canada), in working with different governments (he was one of the young consultants for Mikhail Gorbachev, the last President of the Soviet Union; member of the first independent Moldova's Government, Minister of Privatization and Deputy Minister of Foreign Affairs), makes this book even more interesting and appealing.

Sincerely,

Keith Williamson, Ph.D.
Dean and Professor
College of Engineering and Technology Virginia
State University

PREFACE

THE THEORY OF ECONOMICS: A METHOD RATHER THAN A DOCTRINE, AN APPARATUS OF MIND, A TECHNIQUE OF THINKING…

What is Economics about? How can we explain why the American and the World economies recently suffered one of the most painful downturns after the Great Depression of 30s—the global financial crisis of 2007–2009—in spite of all advanced econometric modeling, forecasting, and other new techniques at the disposal of modern economists and governmental institutions? Why did political leaders and economic thinkers fail to predict the recession and to avoid, or at least smooth, its consequences? What is wrong with our economic model that is skidding without producing required growth, jobs, and prosperity? Definitely, we need a new paradigm of growth to address the challenges of today's economy, but, most importantly, we need a new way of economic thinking about market behavior, the role of government, and our place in a future economic order. This is not only about the behavior and prospects of the American, advanced, emerging, or developing economies. This is about the trust in the market mechanism itself, its efficiency in ensuring prosperity and stability with a high standard of living.

As a scholarly discipline, Economics is less than two and a half centuries old although human society dealt with laws and politics of economics from its earliest beginnings. Thus, both testaments of the Bible warn against usury or interest as did Aristotle and St. Thomas Aquinas. Paradoxically, the first important contributions to economic analysis were made not by professional economists but by the philosophers Plato and Aristotle and, later on, John Locke (labor theory of value), David Hume, a philosopher and historian (theory of land rent and inflation stimulus to businesses), John Law, a Scottish adventurer and a scholar (tried to link prosperity with the money creation pump), and even Copernicus, the astronomer (enunciated the quantity theory of money and prices).

The term "economics" has its origin from the Greek word "*oikonomia*," which means "to manage the house." It is used in our discipline along with another term: "Political Economy," which emphasizes the role of politics and social institutions in an economy. The first person who launched this notion was Antoine de Montchrestien, a Frenchman, marquis by birth, duelist and adventurer by character, poet and scientist by chance, who wrote *Traite d'Economie Politique* (*Treatise on Political Economy*) in 1615. But the father and founder of Economics as a special discipline was Adam Smith (1723–1790), Scottish scholar and a full university professor of philosophy at twenty-eight, whose book *An Inquiry into the Nature and Causes of the Wealth of Nations* (universally known as *The Wealth of Nations*), published in 1776, marked the birthday of Economics, the branch of philosophy called in the eighteenth century, "Political Economy." As the Declaration of Independence proclaimed in the same year the freedom of the American colonies from British rule, *The Wealth of Nations* put forth the doctrine of economic freedom.

It was the first attempt of a systematic analysis of how the economy functions, a masterpiece that established the individual as the main object of study and explained an individual's rational behavior in pursuing his or her own self-interest. "The oil of self-interest will keep the gears working in almost miraculous fashion. No one need plan. No sovereign need rule. The market will answer all things." He was a strong believer that the government should have limited interference in the market, leaving people alone to pursue their own self-interest. In such a way, an "invisible hand" of a free market will guide a producer to promote the interest of society "more effectually than when he really intends to promote it." Adam Smith believed in the effectiveness of a system of unregulated markets in maximizing the well-being of society. He advocated the "*laissez faire*" (French for "leave it alone") policy, enumerating in his book countless cases of follies by government through its intervention in business affairs.

The evolution of Economics, like the development of the real economy, which this theory reflects, was never straight and ascendant. The road to hell is paved with good intentions or so the saying goes. Almost a century after *The Wealth of Nations* established the foundations of economic discipline, Karl Marx (1818–1883), a German scholar, wrote the book *Das Kapital* (German for *Capital*) that became the "bible of revolutionaries" for the next century. He was the most outstanding critic of capitalism, believing that the free enterprise system should and inevitably would be replaced by communism, in which the nation's wealth, the main means of production, would be held not by capitalists but by everyone collectively. His core concept—the theory of surplus value defined as the difference between a worker's subsistence wage and the value of its production, explained how capitalists maximize their profit by exploiting workers. Marx, a meticulous, deep thinking but highly controversial economist and revolutionary, came to the conclusion that capitalism would destroy itself, would collapse as a result of class conflict. His famous appeal from the *Communist Manifesto* (1848), written with his friend Friedrich Engels, his benefactor and a successful capitalist, was: "Workers of the world unite! You have nothing to lose but your chains." His theory, an emotional outburst against capitalism's system and market economy, served as the bases for the communist system, under which political dictatorship and inconsistent command economy ruled, at one time, about one-third of the world population, particularly in the former Soviet Union and China. But the most remarkable and surprising statement, which bewildered his followers, was one that Marx made at the end of his life: "I am not a Marxist."

The year when Marx died, John Maynard Keynes (1883–1946), a British phenomenon who revolutionized economics, was born. But while Marx treated capitalism with despair, Keynes, even in the blackest days, looked for explanations, solutions, and hope. Being the most illustrious student of Alfred Marshall (1842–1924), a Cambridge University professor and chair of the Economics Department, the father of microeconomics, Keynes outperformed his teacher, becoming the founder of modern macroeconomics, focusing on overall employment, production, and a new role for government in the years of the Great Depression. He paid tribute to Alfred Marshall's genius, saying, "The master-economist must possess a rare combination of gifts. He must be mathematician, historian, statesman, philosopher … He must be purposeful and disinterested … as aloof and incorruptible as an artist; yet sometimes as near the earth as a politician." John M. Keynes's pathbreaking book, *The General Theory of Employment, Interest and Money,* published in 1936, provided theoretical foundation for government intervention, and the New Deal policy of Franklin D. Roosevelt was its first practical application. At the age of twenty-eight, Keynes became editor of the most prestigious British economic journal, *Economics Journal,* and later on he became a teacher at King's College of Britain, Cambridge University. Keynes was not only a talented scholar and professor but also a successful investor. Under his guidance, a small college fund (30,000 British pounds) was increased ten times. Applying himself for just half an hour each morning—before he got out of bed—he succeeded in making a personal fortune of more than $2 million, speculating in foreign exchange and commodity markets.

The gallery of twentieth century economists is filled with such illustrious names as Milton Friedman, founder of monetarist theory, about whom Paul Samuelson, another Nobel Prize laureate in Economics, said once: "If Milton Friedman had never existed, it would have been necessary to invent him" (Paul A. Samuelson, *Economics.* Tenth edition, McGrow-Hill Kogakusha, Ltd, 1976, p. 848); John Kennett Galbraith, an editor, philosopher, politician, novelist, art connoisseur, ambassador, memoirist, and skier, whose *The Great Crash* (1929) is perhaps one of the best analysis of the Great Depression of the 30s; and, more recently, Joseph Stiglitz, professor at Columbia University, the author of the *Freefall,* an incisive look at the recent global economic crisis; Michael Spence, professor at New York University, with his just published book *The Next Convergence*: *The Future of Economic Growth in a*

Multispeed World; Paul Krugman, a prolific author, columnist and blogger, and professor at Princeton University, whose brilliant book *The Return of Depression Economics* became a cornerstone of the debate over how to respond to the crisis; and many other distinguished economists, notable Nobel Prize winners, a majority of them Americans, whose masterworks inspired the author of this book.

Now we can start by answering a few important questions: What is Economics about? In John Maynard Keynes's words, "The Theory of Economics does not furnish a body of settled conclusions immediately applicable to policy. It is a method rather than a doctrine, an apparatus of mind, a technique of thinking which helps its possessor to draw correct conclusions" (Paul Heyne, Peter Boettke, David Prychitko, *The Economic Way of Thinking.* Prentice Hall, 2006, p. 6).

Why it is important to study Economics? It is important, first of all, because of its major impact on professional and personal applications. At the very least, the following reasons sould also be mentioned:

1. It develops an individual's analytical skills and a better understanding and prediction of the consequences of his or her choices and actions.
2. It enables entrepreneurs to make optimal business decisions.
3. It helps households to make good buying decisions, better employment choices, and intelligent financial investments.
4. It helps governmental officials to elaborate better strategies and programs to deal with unemployment, poverty, and inequality and to manage public finances.

Why is understanding Economics essential for you to become a well-informed citizen? First of all, understanding economic categories and notions will help you to evaluate, for example, how the annual Economic Report of the President of the United States, focused on such important issues as unemployment, inflation, economic growth, taxation, poverty, international trade, health care, pollution, regulation, education, and others, will affect your personal standard of living, your individual economic prospects, and social welfare. At the same time, it should be mentioned that Economics is mainly an academic discipline and not a vocational subject. It examines problems and decisions from a social rather than a personal point of view and is not a study of "how to make money," but once learned it could help you to understand what money is and what are the ways to economize and maximize profit by wisely spending or saving and investing. Economics requires hard work, persistence, and patience, and it will certainly reward the individual and not only with good academic grades and promotions.

Economy is the art of making the most out of life.
—George Bernard Shaw

Introduction of Essential Economic Concepts

CHAPTER 1

BASIC PRINCIPLES, MODELS, AND ECONOMIC SYSTEMS

1. FUNDAMENTAL QUESTIONS OF ECONOMICS

More than fifty years ago, John Kenneth Galbraith in his book *Affluent Society* pointed out that Americans have mostly gone beyond the level of physiological necessity, and consumers often flit from one purchase to another, facing the pressure of fashion and advertising (John Kenneth Galbraith. *The Affluent Society*. Houghton Mifflin, Boston, 1958).

We are living today in a much more affluent society where the family is qualified as poor if it has less than $60 a day, and the average income per person per year is more than $50,000 (a century ago it was $4,000 in today's dollars) for a population of 310 million with over $60 trillion worth of buildings and machinery. Nevertheless, the central problem of the US economy as well as of other economies is that of Scarcity because our unlimited wants exceed our limited recourses. As that famous song by *The Rolling Stones* goes, "You can't always get what you want."

Scarcity is defined as the lack of sufficient resources to satisfy all desired uses of those resources. Everyone, rich or poor, in every society is facing scarcity. Even Bill Gates, or his friend Warren Buffet, the two wealthiest Americans, must choose how to best use their time and wealth.

Because every one of us, every society, is facing scarcity—a limited income (budget constraints), a limited amount of time, or a limited amount of other resources—we all need to make choices. So we can define Economics as the study of choices that people and societies make facing scarcity. Economics is a social science that analyzes the main goals of an economic system.

Any society and any economic systems must confront *three fundamental economic problems:*

1. What goods and services shall be produced and in what quantities; that is, how much and which alternatives and combinations shall be produced;
2. How shall goods and services be produced; that is, by whom and with what resources and technology; and
3. For Whom shall goods and services be produced, or how shall the national product and income to be distributed among different families and individuals?

What, How, and For Whom would not be a problem if resources were unlimited and human wants were fully satisfied. There would be no economic goods, i.e., no goods that are relatively scarce, and there would be no need for any study of economics and "economizing." All goods would be free goods just as pure air is free.

To answer WHAT to produce, or what are our preferences and what should be sacrificed to get what we want, we need to count up our *Economic Resources*—basic inputs necessary to produce goods and services—known as *Factors of Production*. Traditionally, they are classified into four broad categories:

1. **Natural resources**—created by acts of nature and used in the production process (arable land, forests, mineral and water resources, gas and oil, etc.), generally known as Land. They are divided into two big categories: renewable (crops, lakes, forests, clean air, etc.) and nonrenewable (oil, natural gas, coal), which gradually disappear in the process of their intensive use and need to be substituted.
2. **Labor**—human efforts or physical and mental talents of individuals available and usable in producing goods and services. Some economists separate them from Human capital—knowledge and skills acquired by an employee through education and experience and used to manufacture goods and services. They refer to this factor specifically to make a distinction from physical capital; the idea is that "Human capital" requires the willingness to wait during a training period, when the labor does not produce anything, and it increases the productive capacity of the economy.
3. **Physical Capital (capital goods)**—includes all manufactured goods used to manufacture consumer goods and services. The process of producing and purchasing capital goods is known as Investment.

The difference between these two categories—capital goods and consumer goods—resides in the modality of satisfaction of our wants: consumer goods do it directly and capital goods indirectly, being used for production of consumer goods. It is important to make a distinction between the term "capital" used in everyday conversation and referred to regarding financial assets such as common stocks, bonds, bank deposits, or deeds to a house, which are actually financial capital, and the economic notion of "capital," which refers to real capital, such as machinery, tools, computers, factories, and other equipment produced in the past and used to produce goods and services in the present. Take into consideration that money is not capital and is not productive by itself; it is only a paper claim on real (economic) capital.

4. **Entrepreneurship**—the human effort used to coordinate the production process. This is a special human resource distinct from labor and from human capital although very closely related to them. The entrepreneur performs some specific functions: a) Takes the initiative and organizes production, assembling the factors of production (land, labor, and capital) to produce goods and services and seek profit; b) Raises funds and makes business decisions: what goods to produce and how to produce them; c) Takes the risks without any guarantee of profit (in the US about half of new businesses are failing and close within four years); d) Innovates, introducing new products, technology, and other innovations. Take into consideration that invention is the development of new commodities, or a new process to produce them, while innovation is a process of practical application of an invention. The evolution of the US as the first economic power in the world is due, first, to successful entrepreneurs (the French word "*entrepreneur*" means "someone who undertakes" a task), starting with the legendary Thomas Edison and Levy Strauss and continuing with the late Steve Jobs of Apple, with Bill Gates of Microsoft, Larry Page and Sergei Brin of Google, Mark Zuckerberg of Facebook, and many, many others, the majority of them undertaking the risk of innovation in their young years and being rewarded for that with billions of dollars in fortunes in a very short period of time. Jobs, who invented the first Apple computer in the mid-1970s with another colleague, Steve Wozniak, both in their twenties at that time, established the goal "putting a ding in the universe." Under Jobs's first tenure, Apple's innovation premium was 37%, and when he quit the company (1985–98), Apple's innovation premium fell to minus 30%. After he came back to the business, its premium rose to 52%. This is a fascinating role and "premium" for an entrepreneur and an innovator, a premium for a genius (for more details see Clay Christiansen, Jeff Dyer, and Hal Gregersen, *The Innovator's DNA*.).

All these resources combined in the production of goods and services are defined as factors of production, and their owners should be rewarded for their productive uses: rent income and interest income for supplying raw materials and capital equipment, respectively; wages (salaries, bonuses, commissions, and royalties) to those who supply labor and profits; and entrepreneurial income, called "normal profit," for entrepreneurs. Their common characteristic is that factors of production are limited in supply. Their efficient use depends on full employment of all available resources (there are some exceptions—farmland should be allowed to lie fallow periodically). By full production, we understand that all employed resources must be used to provide the maximum possible satisfaction of our economic wants. If we fail to employ all our resources, then they are underemployed. In a market economy, what to produce is determined by the price mechanism—the dollar vote of consumers.

Because of limited resources, we are always facing a dilemma about what to produce, and we always need to make choices, or trade-offs. To illustrate this situation, economists use a model of Production Possibilities. A model is a simplified representation of reality.

The **Production Possibilities** model (table 1.1, figure 1.1) describes the various combinations of goods and services that could be produced with available resources and technology in a given period of time. It is illustrated by a table and graphically by a curve—the Production Possibilities Curve (PPC) or Production Possibilities Frontier, which shows attainable and unattainable combinations of goods.

Output in Year 1	A	B	C	D
Guns (thousand/year)	180	140	80	0
Butter (thousand tons/year)	0	60	100	120
Output in Year 2	A'	B'	C'	D'
Guns (thousand/year)	200	160	100	0
Butter (thousand tons/year)	0	80	120	140

Table 1.1 Production Possibilities Options

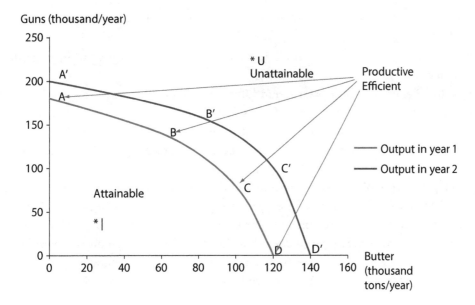

Figure 1.1 Production Possibilities Curve

First, we need to make a few *assumptions*:

1. Fixed resources: their quantity and quality for the given period of time (year) remain unchanged as well as the technology (method) of their use;
2. Full employment of existing resources, which means their productive efficiency: maximum output at least cost;
3. Two types of goods could be produced with available economic resources over the year: a) consumer goods ("bread") and b) military goods ("tanks"); and
4. Some inputs are better adapted to the manufacture of one resource than to the production of the other, and their transfer from one activity to another involves cost and lost output.

Production Possibilities model represents the tradeoffs: how much output (combination of two goods) could be produced with existing recourses: at point A, 180 tanks and 0 bread. If we want more bread, we need to move down the curve to points B and C, or if we want only bread, to point D, reallocating resources from gun production.

During WWII, 12 million Americans served in the armed forces, and 40% of all output consisted of military goods (during the Korean War—14%, Vietnam War—10%). In the last twenty years, and especially after the end of the Cold War, American armed forces were reduced by 600,000 personnel, and the rate of military goods in output was reduced to less than 4%. The simultaneous increase in nonmilitary output represents the gains for nonmilitary (civilian) goods, and it is called the peace dividend.

Conclusion: the PPC shows us:

1. What is attainable and what is not: points outside the curve are not attainable with existing resources and technology;
2. What is efficient and what is not: points on the curve represent productive efficiency, points inside—inefficient use of recourses;
3. What are the trade-offs: there is no possibility to produce more of one good without sacrificing production of another;
4. What is the dilemma between present and future consumption, which is essential for every society and is related to **only one specific combination of output**—optimal at any moment of time that represents the best possible allocation of resources among competing options. To produce this optimal combination of output is the most important goal of economic policy.

To identify this optimal combination, we need to introduce the notion of **Investment**—spending on new capital (factories, technology, or tools) in a given period of time plus changes in business inventories. The investment represents a trade-off between present consumption and future consumption. The option in favor of more investment and less consumption today results in an expansion of production possibilities in the future—an **outward shift in PPC**—and, respectively, an increase in output and **economic growth,** which is the base for increasing the standard of living. The outward shift of the PPC is the result of:

1. Increased quantities of economic resources;
2. Improved quality of economic resources;
3. Advances in technology (computers, communications, and biotechnology); and
4. International trade.

The **Inward shifts in PPC** are possible, as well (the What). For example, the Great Depression of the 30s: one-third of US production was idle, and one-quarter of US workers were unemployed. Economies that experience discrimination based on race and ethnicity operate inside the PPC and do not achieve productive efficiency. Another example is Hurricane Katrina's impact on the national economy, as a whole, and, particularly, on local economies. The consequences of the 9/11 terrorist attack are also an example of inward shift of the curve.

How to produce is not just limited to *getting maximum output from available inputs*. It also involves the issue of *how to make better use of the environment,* searching for an optimal method of producing goods and services. The answer relies on the efficient use of factors of production and adequate safeguards for the environment. We need to make a clear distinction between *productive efficiency*—getting a maximum of output from our limited resources or identification of a least costly way to produce a good, and *allocative efficiency*—to produce a combination of goods and services that society (consumers) wants, assuming that minimum cost production (productive efficiency) is achieved. In a market economy, how things are produced is determined by the price mechanism and competition among producers.

For Whom to produce focuses on *how an economy's output and income are distributed between members of society.* The ideal of communist society was: "from each according to his ability, to each according to his needs." But this principle never materialized. There is no direct link between production and consumption in such a formula, and there are no incentives for efficient use of factors of production. People who work hard are not stimulated properly, and they may decide to exert less effort if they see no tangible reward to working. This is not only a problem of a communist economy. To some extent, welfare programs and benefits face the same kind of problem. As welfare benefits rise, the incentive to work diminishes. If people choose welfare checks over paychecks, total output will decline. Similar problems appear in the tax system. For Whom things are produced is determined also by the price mechanism, that is, by supply and demand for resources and the price of those resources in competitive markets: wages for suppliers of labor, rents for suppliers of land and other resources, interest rates for suppliers of capital, and normal profits (or losses) for entrepreneurs.

2. BASIC ECONOMIC PRINCIPLES

To understand how individuals and societies make choices having limited resources, how these choices interact, and how choices made in each person's self-interest match (or not) with social interest, we need to focus on major principles of economic analysis, or what economists call the economic way of thinking.

RATIONAL (PURPOSEFUL) BEHAVIOR

Economics assumes that human behavior is based on rational self-interest motivated by the scope of maximization of its utility from an action. In other words, you are looking for maximum satisfaction, or pleasure or happiness, from the dollar that you spend. This behavior is directly related to the question, what will be produced and in what quantities? Only those goods and services will be produced that consumers choose to buy. Of course, nobody is guaranteed that his or her choice and decision is the best possible. Nobody is a perfect decision-maker. A rational choice is one that uses the available resources to most effectively satisfy the wants of the person making the choice. Rational choices compare costs and benefits and are made on the margin. Consumers respond to incentives.

MARGINAL ANALYSIS: BENEFIT AND COST

Everything in Economics has a Benefit and Cost. The *Benefit* of an action or from consuming a good is the pleasure or satisfaction that this action or good brings, and it is measured by what you are willing to give up to get it. The *Cost* is what you have to (must) give up to obtain what you want. We always have to check the balance of benefit and cost before being engaged in any exchange, before making any choice, and before we make them on the margin. This is one of the most important principles of economic analysis. Marginal means "a change in," "extra," or "additional." This principle involves comparison of *Marginal Benefit (MB)—the extra benefit resulting from an additional unit increase in an activity, and Marginal Cost (MC)—the extra cost resulting from an additional unit increase in an activity.* As a rational person, you undertake an activity; for example, you buy another unit of a good as long as your marginal benefit exceeds marginal cost. Any rational economic behavior (related to production or consumption) "should be expanded as long as marginal benefit exceeds or equals marginal cost and should be reduced or canceled if marginal cost exceeds marginal benefit.

The optimal amount of the activity occurs where resources are [being efficiently allocated to any product:] *when the marginal benefit and marginal cost of its output are equal (MB = MC)*" *(McConnell, Brue and Flynn 2011).*

How to use the Marginal Principle? Suppose that a student group wishes to rent an auditorium and offers to pay $300, which is the MB for the college. The college should compute the MC: the extra electricity costs is $30, the cleanup costs $80, security costs $110, and $180 is the cost of equipment and other items in this auditorium. So marginal benefit—$300—is less than the marginal cost—$400—and the college administration should not accept this offer. However, what if this college overestimated the cost of renting facilities because it believed that the cost should include some of the fixed costs (that aren't affected by the use of facility) of the college? In that case, the college would miss the opportunity to serve its students.

The economic perspective is always based on marginal analysis. In a world of scarcity, to obtain the marginal benefit associated with some specific action always includes the marginal cost of forgoing something else, which economists call opportunity cost. All costs are opportunity costs with the exception of the so called *sunk cost* that was previously incurred and is irreversible. Once you have incurred a sunk cost, forget about it, and try to maximize your pleasure or satisfaction from your action (good, service).

OPPORTUNITY COST

Opportunity Cost of an item or activity is what you must give up to get this item or to do this activity. It is the amount of other products that must be forgone to obtain one unit of a specific good that you want. In other words, the opportunity cost of something is *what can be sacrificed to get it.* All choices have opportunity costs. Your opportunity costs of attending college include goods and services forgone from paying for tuition and textbooks and the goods and services forgone because you do not have an income from a full-time job. Perhaps one of the highest opportunity costs of a college education was that of Ralph Sampson's at the University of Virginia. He passed up a $1 million contract in the NBA because he wanted a college degree.

The notion of opportunity cost is illustrated by the *Production Possibilities Curve* (figure 1.2). The bowed-out shape of the curve tells us that the more of a product we produce, the bigger its opportunity cost, or, in other words, we have to sacrifice more of another product to increase the amount of the item we want. To measure the opportunity cost of producing one more unit of bread (movement from A to B on the horizontal axis), we must divide the number of tanks forgone (change on vertical axis, $\Delta Y = 40$, Δ is the capital letter "*delta*" for "change in") to the number of tons of bread gained ($\Delta X = 60$).

So, the opportunity cost of producing one more ton of bread is the number of tanks forgone: $\Delta Y/\Delta X$, or 40/60 (moving from A to B); to produce another 40 tons of bread (moving from B to C), we must reduce the production of tanks by another 60 units, and the opportunity cost of bread is: 60/40; and to expand the production of bread by another 20 tons (movement from C to D), we need to reduce tank production by another 80 units; the opportunity cost is 80/20. This example clearly indicates the increased cost of producing the good we want.

The Law of Increasing Opportunity Cost states: the opportunity cost of an additional unit of a good goes up proportionally to the amount a good is produced.

The bowed outward shape of the PPC is also telling us that the resources are not perfectly adaptable for the production of both goods: the workers need to be retrained, technology changed, tools remade, etc.

PROPERTY RIGHTS AND VOLUNTARY EXCHANGE

The property rights assigned to individuals in the form of legal ownership serve as the bases for any exchange in a market economy. They are the most important part of the rules governing the economy and social interaction. The opportunities and wealth of individuals and society, as a whole, could be expanded only on the base of voluntary exchange of legally confirmed and protected property rights. Adam Smith stressed the importance of voluntary exchange when he mentioned that barter, exchange of one thing for another, "… is common to all men, and to be found in no other … animals. Nobody ever saw a dog make a fair and deliberate exchange of one bone for another with another dog" (Adam Smith. *An Inquiry into the Nature of the Wealth of Nations* [First published in 1776; New York: Random House, 1873], Book 1, Chapter 2).

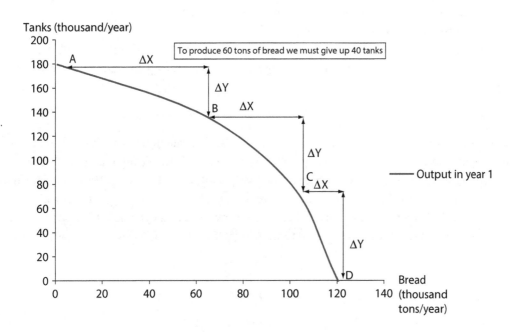

Figure 1.2
Opportunity
Cost

To better understand the importance of this principle on which the market system is based, let's make a reference to Hernando de Soto, the president of the Institute for Liberty and Democracy, headquartered in Peru, who wrote the book *The Mystery of Capital*. He stated:

Imagine a country where nobody can identify who owns what, addresses cannot be easily verified, people cannot be made to pay their debts, resources cannot conveniently be turned into money, ownership cannot be divided into shares, descriptions of assets are not standardized and cannot be easily compared, and the rules that governed property vary from neighborhood to neighborhood or even from street to street. You have just put yourself into the life of a developing country or former communist nation; more precisely, you have imagined life for 80% of its population, which is marked off as sharply from its Westernized elite as black and white South Africans were once separated by apartheid … What you are really living behind when you are traveling to these countries is the world of legally enforceable transactions on property rights" (Hernando de Soto. *The Mystery of Capital. Why Capitalism Triumphs in the West and Fails Everywhere Else.* Basic Books, 2000, p. 15–16).

DIMINISHING RETURNS

This principle of diminishing returns states: that output will increase at a decreasing rate if one input increases while the other inputs remain the same. In the short-run, the only variable input is one whose quantity can be changed (labor), and we can explain it by focusing on the *labor–output relationship*. We have first to introduce two new notions (table 1.2, figure 1.3):

1. Total Product Curve (TPC)—total output of a particular good produced with different quantities of labor, or the relationship between the quantity of labor and the quantity of output.
2. **Marginal Product of Labor (MPL)**. It represents the change in total output generated by change in labor input quantity. In other words, MPL is **the change in the total output resulting from adding one more worker**. The different marginal products brought by additional worker are explained by the structure of the production process.

MPL = change in total product/change in (labor) input

The Law of Diminishing Marginal Returns states that the extra production obtained from an increase in a variable input (labor, in our case) will eventually decline as more of the variable input is used together with the fixed inputs (equipment, tools, etc.). The decline in the Marginal Physical Product (MPP) is explained by the ratio of labor to other factors of production. The relative scarcity of other inputs (capital and land) constrains the marginal product of labor. The only factor that can be varied in the short-run is labor. As more labor is hired, each unit of labor has less capital and land to work with. The MPP can have also a negative sense.

Table 1.2 Diminishing return for production of Pizzas							
Number of Workers	0	1	2	3	4	5	6
Total Pizzas Produced	0	12	18	21	22	21	18
Marginal Product		12	6	3	1	−1	−3

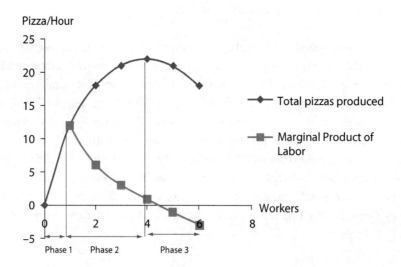

Figure 1.3 Diminishing Returns

The Law of Diminishing Returns determines the manner in which the costs of the firm change as it changes its output in the short-run. As more variable units are added to a fixed resource, beyond some point, the marginal product from each additional unit of a variable resource will decline.

Example: the farmer with a fixed resource of 100 acres planted in corn. Without any cultivation, it will bring 50 bushels per acre; after the first cultivation, 67 bushels; after the second, 71; and after the fourth, 73 bushels. In the nonagricultural sector, the same law functions: the MP of additional workers would decline because there would be more labor in proportion to the fixed amount of capital. We have to mention that the Law of Diminishing Returns assumes that all units of labor are of equal quality. Marginal product diminishes not because successive workers are inferior but because more workers are being used relative to the amount of plant and equipment available (McConnell, Brue and Flynn).

NOW LET'S DISCUSS THE THREE PHASES OF TPC AND MPL CURVES: INCREASING, DECREASING, AND NEGATIVE MARGINAL RETURNS

When TP is increasing at a growing rate, marginal product is rising; when total product is increasing at a decreasing rate, marginal product is falling; and when total product declines, marginal product is negative.

The diminishing returns principle is related to the short-run, a period of time over which one or more factors of production are fixed. And a firm cannot modify it. In the long-run, a firm can change all the factors of production, and this principle is not relevant for long-run decisions.

3. ECONOMIC WAY OF THINKING: MICROECONOMICS VS. MACROECONOMICS

First, there are a number of elements related to the method and logic of economic analysis:

1. The observation of facts;
2. The formulation of hypothesis based upon the facts (explanation of the cause and effect relationship);
3. The testing of the hypothesis against the facts;
4. The acceptance, rejection, or modification of the hypothesis based on these comparisons; and
5. The determination of a theory, law, principle, or model.

Second, terminology, generalizations, **ceteris paribus,** *and abstractions*: we use the terms *"hypothesis"* (needs initial testing), *"theory"* (has been tested but needs more testing), *"law"* or *"principle"* (has provided a strong predictive accuracy), and *"model"* (a combination of principles that reflects simplified reality).

We use *generalizations* in economics. For example, economic principles are described as the habits of typical or average consumers, laborers, or companies. We will use the other-things-being-equal assumption—*ceteris paribus* (Latin)—that all variables are held constant with the exception of those we are considering (example: price and quantity of Pepsi purchased). Economists also use *abstractions*: all economic principles and theories represent simplifications that omit irrelevant facts and circumstances. We will use also *graphical expression* of economic models.

ABSTRACTIONS AND MODELS

Economics is helping us to answer fundamental questions about the economy and to make predictions about how it will evolve, what the implications are of government decisions on market, and how this will influence everyone's economic perspectives and well-being.

Third, economic analysis is divided into two branches: microeconomics and macroeconomics. The terms micro and macro came from the Greek words "*mikro*"— "small" and "*megalos*"— "large."

Microeconomics is focused on choices made by individual participants in economy: individuals, households, businesses, and government organizations. For example, an individual household is interested in opportunities to increase its personal income by making better decisions about jobs and obtaining better mortgage conditions; a business firm is looking for what specific goods and services to produce for the local market and how to price them to maximize its profit; the local government is interested in improving its budget without prejudicing the local business environment, etc. Because of its special preoccupation with prices and trading of goods and services, microeconomics is called *price theory* by some economists. In microeconomics, we are examining the sand, rocks and shells, and not the beach, the trees and not the forest.

Macroeconomics is focused on performance of the nation's economy as a whole, on the "big picture" composed of microeconomic components. It operates with aggregates, such as total national output, total employment, total income, average level of prices, balance of trade, etc. For example, we want to know how the increase by Congress of the level of national debt will affect business perspectives, how the stimulus package promoted by US President Barack Obama's administration will influence job creation and reduce the unemployment, or what determines the business investment and how it will influence the nation's output, etc. In other words, macroeconomics is considering "the beach and not the sand, rocks and shells, the forest and not the trees."

Both macro- and microeconomics are closely interrelated; macroeconomic outcome is influenced by micro behavior, and the behavior of individual participants (micro behavior) depends on macro-outcomes, on the general status of the economy. Many economic situations are characterized by both aspects: micro- and macroeconomics. Both of them are important for understanding how markets work and how they change—to make decisions (personal or managerial), to evaluate public policy debates, and to understand how the government is managing the economy and is promoting economic growth.

Fourth, both branches are operating with the two types of analysis: positive and normative.

Positive or descriptive economics includes description, theory development, and theory testing and relates to facts and cause and effect relationships but avoids value judgments. Positive economics operates with "what is" and makes statements of the "if … then" type. The key consideration is whether the statement is testable and not, whether it is true or false. For example: "If import quotas are imposed, then the price of foreign-produced cars, such as Mercedes, BMW, Lamborghini, etc., for US consumers will increase." "If drinking is prohibited for people less then twenty-one years old, fatal automobiles crashes will be reduced."

Normative economics is about prescriptions and not descriptions or predictions. It attempts to achieve desirable goals through value judgements about recommending policy actions. Normative economics operates with the notion of "what ought to be." For example: "Families of four with incomes below $25,000 per year should be exempted from federal income taxes." Positive statement: "If tuition is increased, college enrollment will fall." Normative: "College tuition should be lowered by 50% so more students can obtain an education." It's certain that these value-based policy questions cause many disagreements between economists.

4. ECONOMICS AS SOCIAL SCIENCE: ECONOMIC POLICY AND ECONOMIC GOALS

Economics is one of the most important tools to formulate economic policies—courses of action based on economic principles and intended to resolve specific economic problems. The main steps in the elaboration of *Economic Policy* are:

1. Identification of an economic goal that must be *specific* ("full employment," for example).
2. Elaboration of various policies to achieve the goal and examination of the eventual effects of each policy option (full employment could be achieved by using fiscal policy or monetary policy or training policy or a combination of all of them).
3. Implementation of the chosen policy and evaluation of its alternatives.

The most important *Economic Goals*, designed to be achieved by economic policy, are:

1. *Economic growth*—to produce more and better goods and services and to achieve a higher standard of living;
2. *Full employment*—people willing to work should be able to find jobs reasonably quickly. Widespread unemployment is demoralizing, and it represents economic waste;
3. *Economic efficiency*—to get as much as we reasonably can out of our productive efforts or to achieve maximum satisfaction of wants using the available productive resources;
4. *Price stability*—to avoid rapid increases (inflation) and decreases of prices (deflation);
5. *Economic freedom*—the right of people to choose their occupation, a high degree of freedom in their economic activities;
6. *Equitable distribution of income*—while some may live in affluence, no group of citizens should suffer stark poverty;
7. *Economic security*—freedom from the fear that an individual or a family, especially ones who are disabled, aged, or placed in other categories, could find themselves in a desperate financial situation, unable to earn minimal income; and
8. *Balance of trade*—to maintain a reasonable balance with the rest of the world in international trade and financial transactions.

Some of these goals are *complementary* and some other are *conflicting* and may entail tradeoffs; that is, to achieve one, we must sacrifice another (i.e., efforts to reduce income inequality may weaken incentives to work, invest, innovate, and take business risks). Finally, all goals cannot be achieved in a short period of time, and that's why they should be *prioritized*.

5. GRAPHS, FORMULAS, VARIABLES, SLOPE OF CURVE, POSITIVE AND NEGATIVE RELATIONSHIPS, CAUSE AND EFFECT

Economists are always using graphs, formulas, equations and other mathematical tools to illustrate key economic ideas, models, and principles. I am using them in this book to simplify economic categories and relationships and make them more concrete and applicable to real-world situations. A picture (a graph) is sometime more explicative than a thousand words. Let's start with a few definitions.

A graph is a two-dimensional illustration of the relationship between a set of numbers (data), usually two variables: a) the *independent variable* which changes first and is the cause of the changes (the price, for example) and b) the *dependent variable* which is the result of this change (quantity of goods bought). In mathematics, the independent variable is placed on the horizontal axis (X) and the dependent variable on the vertical axis (Y). Economists are inversing this order, putting the price and/or cost (independent) on the vertical axis and the quantity (dependent) on the horizontal. Although it conflicts with the mathematical approach, this is just matter of convenience. There are different types of graphs, such as scatter diagram, time-series, cross-section, and graphs with one and two variables. Sometimes relationships between more than two variables could be illustrated in a graph. The graph intersects the vertical axis at point called *Y-intercept* and the horizontal axis at *X-intercept*. The most important point to consider is how to interpret and use the graphs in visualizing economic models. To keep things simple, I will focus on some basic skills that you, my student, needs to better understand economics.

Table and Figure A.1 represent the relationship between annual income of a hypothetical person and his or her expenditure on entertainment. In this example, Income is a determinant factor—an independent variable, and is put on the horizontal axis-X while expenditures as dependent on the income variable are put on the vertical axis-Y (we are using here the mathematical approach). The graph is a straight line, and the relationship is *linear*. In our example, the relationship between annual income and expenditures is a *direct (positive) relationship* because both variables move in the same direction. When two variables are positively or directly related, the graph is an *upsloping line*. Take into consideration that we are examining the relationship between two interesting variables (income and expenditure), holding all other variables constant, the principal in economics called *ceteris paribus* as discussed earlier.

Annual Income	$15,000	$25,000	$35,000	$45,000	$55,000
Expenditures on Entertainment	$1,000	$1,200	$1,400	$1,600	$1,800

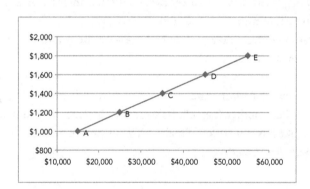

Let's consider another case scenario: two variables which are moving in the opposite direction (for example, the price of this book and the quantity of books sold). In this situation, there is an *inverse (negative) relationship* (table and figure A.2), and the respective graph is a downward-sloping straight line. This time we are following the long standing traditions of economists, putting the price on the vertical axis and the quantity on the horizontal.

It is important to know the directions of changes of variables but also the magnitude of changes, or how much one variable will change when another one is changing. This is measured by the *slope of a straight line* between two points, or the ratio of vertical change (rise or drop) to the horizontal change (run). The slope is positive when both variables are positively (directly) related and negative when variables are inversely related (price of a book and quantity sold). We can express this relationship algebraically: Slope = $\Delta Y/\Delta X$, where symbol Δ (Greek capitol letter "*delta*") means "change in." In the A.1 graph, the slope is positive, and movement from point A to point B is equal to:

$$Slope = \frac{\Delta Y}{\Delta X} = \frac{200}{10,000} = 0.002$$

Price/Book ($$)	$6	$12	$18	$24	$30
Books	25	20	15	10	5

Table A.2
Inverse
(Negative)
Relationship
Between
Variables

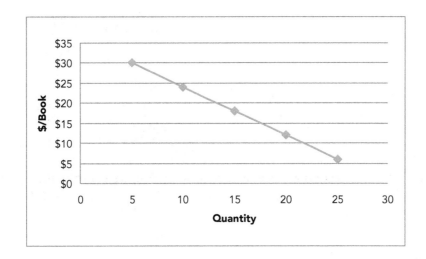

The graph visualizing two independent and unrelated variables represents an infinite slope of the line. For example, purchases of CDs and the price of coconuts are expressed graphically as an infinite line parallel to the vertical axis. In contrast, the relationship between the divorce rate and the consumption of bananas has a zero slope and is parallel to horizontal axis. In other words, consumption of bananas will remain the same, and it does not matter how the rate of divorce changes. In both cases, the two variables are completely unrelated.

It should be mentioned that the slope of a straight line is the same—constant at all points, but the relationship between two variables is not always linear. Actually, just a few economic relationships are linear. There is a nonlinear relationship between two variables when they change from one point to another, and the line is referred to as a *curve* (we will also refer to a straight line as a "curve," which is acceptable). In Table and Figure A.3, we have a hypothetical nonlinear relationship between hours of study (training) and a worker's productivity in the automobile industry. The slope of this nonlinear curve at any point is measured by the slope of the tangent line at this point using the same formula.

We also need to distinguish a *movement along the curve* and *shift of the curve* from one position to another (table and figure A.4). The rule is: a) a change in one variable shown on the graph—price of an ice cream cone on one of the two curves) causes a movement along the curve, determining a) the change in quantity bought and b) a change in one of the variables that is not shown on the graph (for example, changes in consumers' preferences from ice cream to frozen yogurt) shifts the curve upward or downward.

Table A.3 Learning Curve						
Hours of Study	10	20	30	40	50	60
Productivity (Produced Parts/Hour)	1	5	8	10	11	12

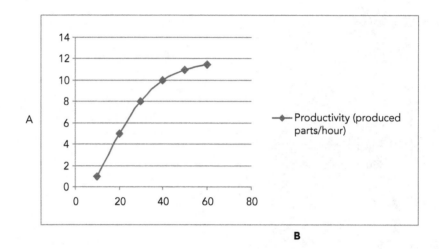

Figure A.3

Knowing the vertical intercept (a) and the slope of the curve (b), we can write the equation of a linear relationship:

Table A.4 Shift of the line					
Ice Cream Cones Purchased	10	20	30	40	50
Price/Cone 1	10	8	6	4	2
Price/Cone 2	7	5	3	1	

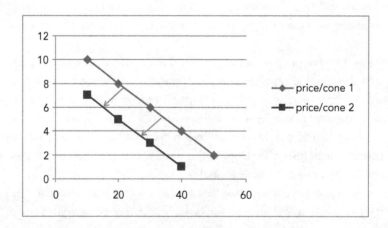

Figure A.4

$y = a + bx$, where y is a dependent variable, a, b, and x—independent variables. In our income-expenditure example, C (expenditure) is a dependent variable, Y (income)—independent variable, and the equation is: $C = a + bY$.

Percentage change formula is another important component of our economics theory, particularly in macroeconomics. For example, to calculate the percentage growth in real GDP, which is national output adjusted to inflation from one year to another, we need to use the following formula:

$$[(GDP2016 - GDP2015)/GDP2015] \times 100$$

Formulas for calculating the **area of a triangle** (Atr): ½ × Base × Height and for area of a rectangle (Ar): Base × Height.

After reading this section, you should be able to address the following questions:

1. What a graph is, how do you interpret it, and how do you construct one?
2. What is the difference between the positive (direct) and negative (inverse) relationship between two variables?
3. What is the slope of the curve, and how is it calculated for linear and nonlinear relationships?
4. What is the difference between movement along the curve and shift of the curve?
5. How do you represent an economic concept (category) in a formula, and how do you select the right formula for the problem you are solving?
6. What is the formula for a percentage change?

6. KEY TERMS

Three Fundamental Economic Problems
Scarcity
Factors of Production
Invention and Innovation
Production Possibilities Model
Rational Behavior and Rational Choice
Marginal Analysis, Marginal Benefit, and Marginal Cost
Opportunity Cost
Property Rights and Voluntary Exchange
Diminishing Return
Micro- and Macroeconomics
Ceteris Paribus
Laissez-Faire
Economic Policy and Economic Goals

7. PROBLEMS AND APPLICATIONS

1. Why do we confront the economic problem of scarcity?
   a. We are capable of producing more than we consume.
   b. There are not enough resources to satisfy everyone.
   c. Our desires can overcome the amount of goods available.
   d. The existence of costs must be considered.
   e. We are running out of nonrenewable resources.

2. Why do opportunity costs exist?
   a. All of our resources have an alternative use, and we cannot increase production of some goods without sacrificing resources designed for the production of other goods.
   b. The market fails to allocates resources wisely.
   c. The Law of Diminishing Returns explains that extra production obtained from an increase in a variable input will eventually decline.
   d. All our resources are abundant, but we have to choose among them anyway.

3. Identify which is *not* a factor of production?
   a. The $1,000.00 that you won in a lottery and intend to use to finance your studies
   b. The computer that the college gave to you.
   c. Your boss, the manager of Dominos.
   d. A vacant house in New Hampshire.

4. What is necessary to increase economic growth?
   a. An increase in your personal consumption.
   b. The reallocation of resources to defense production rather than investment and consumption.
   c. Encourage outsourcing of our businesses.
   d. Advances in technology and allocation of more resources to investment.

Figure 1.4 Production Possibilities Curve

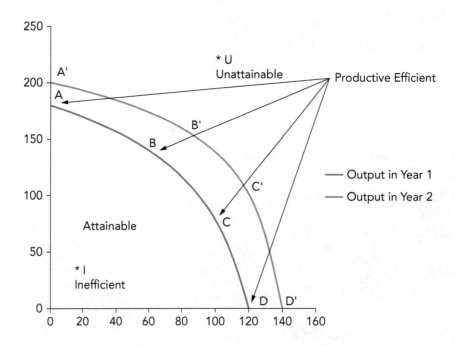

5. At what point can we produce a combination of goods and services that we are unable to produce with our existing resources if we use more advanced technology and international trade? (See Figure 1.4.)
   a. *I

b. C

c. *U

d. B'

6. What do we need to do to produce beyond the initial Production Possibilities Curve at a point B' on blue curve on a new Production Possibilities Curve (figure 1.4):
    a. We need to increase quantity and quality of our resources and better technology.
    b. We can't produce beyond the production possibilities.
    c. We need to withdraw from globalization and bring back to the country our outsourced businesses.
    d. We need more immigrant workers and additional foreign financial resources.

7. To solve the question of "HOW" to produce, we should:
    a. Use more factors of production, such as labor, land, and capital.
    b. Be productive, allocate efficiently, and choose the optimal method of producing.
    c. Restrict immigration and build a "wall" on the US-Mexico border.
    d. Choose to produce a combination of goods and services beyond our Production Possibilities curve.

8. In 1776, Scottish scholar Adam Smith published the pathbreaking book, *The Wealth of Nations*, in which he wrote: it is not "from the benevolence of the butcher, the brewer, or the baker that we expect our dinner, but from their regard to their own interest." There, Smith wrote that there is an "invisible hand" that causes the producer to promote the interests of society. Which of the following best describes the "invisible hand?"
    a. Government regulations and allocation of society's limited resources.
    b. The Internal Revenue Service's action to enforce the tax laws.
    c. When each producer is pursuing his or her own goal, he or she is promoting the interest of society more effectually than when he really intends to promote it.
    d. "No one need plan. No sovereign need rule. The market will answer all things."

8. REVIEW QUESTIONS

1. The three fundamental economic questions a society confronts are _____ goods and services should be produced? _____ these goods and services are produced? _____ they are produced.
2. The main factors of production are _____.
3. How you can assess the rationality of your choice among alternative uses of your limited resources?
4. Even Bill Gates and Warren Buffett may be facing scarcity. How are they and the other 1,200 world billionaires making their choices when they do so?
5. What is the Law of Diminishing Return and is it applicable to your economics studies?

CHAPTER 2.

HOW MARKETS WORK: DEMAND, SUPPLY, AND MARKET EQUILIBRIUM

The purpose of this chapter is to analyze what a competitive market is for a particular good or service and how it works through demand and supply, what are a demand curve and a supply curve, and how they interact, resulting in a market equilibrium and market prices.

1. COMPETITIVE MARKET: MARKET PARTICIPANTS, GOALS, INTERACTIONS, AND CIRCULAR FLOWS

In the US, there are more than 300 million individual consumers, 30 million businesses, and thousands of federal, state, and local government organizations and agencies. Each one of these subjects of the economy is involved in exchange transactions based on their skills, their experiences, and their own interests. The goals are: for an individual, to maximize his or her satisfaction, pleasure, or happiness; for a business firm, to maximize its profits (or to minimize losses); and for a government agency, to maximize security and general welfare. All of these participants in exchange transactions have to make choices facing the common-to-all-of-them problem of limited resources. Why do we have to participate in these transactions, and how does the market mechanism satisfies our needs? The answer is obvious from common sense: a) nobody is capable of producing everything he or she wants and b) even if we were able to produce everything, it would not be efficient to do it; it is much more reasonable to specialize on something concrete that we can do better than others and at lower (opportunity) cost. Adam Smith, in the first chapter, "Of the Division of Labour," of his book *The Wealth of Nations* provided a classical example of the benefits of specialization—a famous description of pin-making:

"A workman not educated to do this business … could scarce, perhaps, … make one pin in a day, and certainly not twenty. But in the way in which this business is now carried on, not only the whole work is a peculiar trade, but it is divided into a number of branches … One man draws out the wire, another straightens it, a third cuts it, a fourth points it, a fifth grinds it at the top for receiving the head … Ten persons, therefore, could make among them upwards of forty-eight thousand pins a day. Each person therefore, … might be considered as making four thousand and eight hundred pins in a day" (Adam Smith, *An Inquiry into the Nature and Causes of the Wealth of Nations,* New York, Random House, 1937, pp. 4–5.). The gains from specialization are obvious, but also obvious are the losses for some extreme specializations when a worker performs but only one single thing. Remember Charlie Chaplin's classic movie *Modern Times*? A worker accomplished during his whole lifetime just one operation: the turn of bolt 999 on the assembly line, becoming some kind of brainless robot and a socially alienated person.

The modern market economy is fundamentally about trade, acts of buying and selling. It is characterized by the use of a vast amount of capital—advanced technology, machinery, equipment, etc.—a term from which "capitalism" got its name, being based on private ownership of capital. Among other characteristics of a modern economy, I would mention the incredibly elaborate degree of specialization and intricate division of labor and, of course, an extensive use of money, which could lead to financial disasters if there were no a proper regulatory system and control. Anyway, there is no more *barter—when there is an exchange of one item for another without the exchange of money* (tax payment is avoided) in a modern economy, with some exceptions, some extreme cases.

Now we can start analysis of the essentials of market: Demand and Supply.

"A **market** is an institution or mechanism where buyers ("demanders") and sellers ("suppliers")" of particular goods, services, or resources get together (not necessarily face-to-face) (McConnell, Brue and Flynn p. 38). We can also define a market as an arrangement through which buyers and sellers interact for the purpose of exchanging (trading) goods and services. Some of these markets are local, others national or international, some of them are real (a physical place—a fish market, for example), and some are virtual (e-Bay). We will focus on highly competitive or perfect markets (in the real world, competition is nowhere near "perfect") with a large number of buyers and sellers of standardized products (a stock market or a market for foreign currencies, grain, oil, natural exchanges, etc.), without any one of them having the market power to produce or buy significant quantities of a product that could lead to domination on prices.

There are four main groups of market participants:

1. Consumers
2. Business Firms

3. Governments
4. Foreigners

All of these categories interact in two types of markets:

Factor (recourse) markets, where factors of production (resources) are bought and sold, and *product markets* where finished goods and services are bought and sold. The government acts as an intermediary, buying factors of production and providing some goods and services for consumers and business firms. The market transactions involve an exchange of dollars for goods (in product markets) and resources (in factor markets) (adapted from McConnell, Brue and Flynn).

The Circular Flow illustrates a few things:

1. A movement of resources (counterclockwise) through a factor market from their owners, Households, to their users, Firms, and return of these resources to Households in the form of goods and services through the product market;
2. A movement of money (clockwise) in the form of expenditures on goods and services from Households through product markets, in the form of revenues to Business firms, in the form of their cost for buying resources on factor market, and return of money to households in the form of their income for supplying resources to factor market;
3. There are two missing actors in this Circular Flow: Government, the role of which will be a subject of a special analysis and Foreigners who are performing the same functions as households and businesses, with some exceptions that will be studied separately;
4. In the real world, there are some movements of resources and money within the business sector (from a company that produces microchips to a company that produces electronics, for example) that are also a subject of special analysis and are not reflected in this model.

Figure 2.1
The Circular
Flow in a
Market System

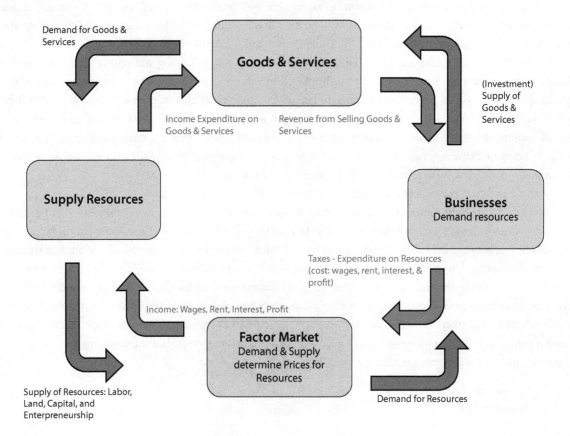

Demand for Goods & Services

Goods & Services

(Investment) Supply of Goods & Services

Income Expenditure on Goods & Services

Revenue from Selling Goods & Services

Supply Resources

Businesses
Demand resources

Taxes - Expenditure on Resources (cost: wages, rent, interest, & profit)

Income: Wages, Rent, Interest, Profit

Factor Market
Demand & Supply determine Prices for Resources

Supply of Resources: Labor, Land, Capital, and Enterpreneurship

Demand for Resources

2. LAW OF DEMAND: DEMAND, DEMAND SCHEDULE, AND DEMAND CURVE, INDIVIDUAL DEMAND VS. MARKET DEMAND

Any market transaction involves two parts: *Demand*—the willingness and ability of an individual or a group of consumers to buy specific quantities of a good at alternative prices in a given period of time—and *Supply*—the willingness and ability of an individual or a company to sell (produce) specific quantities of a good in a given period of time at different prices.

Let's start with the *Demand.* In a market-based economy, everyone has a great variety of options about what to buy and, of course, how to pay for the things he or she wants. Demand depends on many factors but first of all on prices and opportunity cost, which is when an individual decides what desired goods and services should be exchanged for what a consumer wants. We also have to make a distinction between desires, hopes, and demand that depend on the willingness and capacity to pay for chosen goods or services. We will operate with the notion of a *demand schedule*—which is a table showing in a given period of time what a person is willing and able to buy in goods and services—and a *demand curve*, which is a graphical illustration of a demand schedule. Each point on the curve shows a specific quantity that will be demanded at a given price. The amount of a good we buy depends on its price, first of all; it is commonly observed that the higher the price of merchandise, the less quantity of it consumers will be willing to buy and vice versa—the lower the price, the bigger the quantity consumers will be willing to buy.

We can now formulate one of the most important laws in economics, the *Law of Demand:* there is an inverse (negative) relationship between quantity demanded and the price. As the price of a good (or service) increases, quantity demanded of it decreases and vice versa—as the price decreases, the quantity of a good or service demanded increases. In other words, the demand curve is characterized by a downward slope. Why is the demand curve downward sloping, or what is the explanation of the inverse relationship between Price and Quantity demanded?

There are at least three factors (effects):

1. **Income factor:** Purchasing power of money income is increased when there is a lower price, and the consumer will buy more at that lower price. Common sense tells us: price is an obstacle that deters consumers from buying. Thus, lowering prices brings in more buyers, and each one is willing to buy more.

2. **Diminishing marginal utility factor:** For a specific period of time, a buyer will get less utility (satisfaction) from each successive unit of product consumed (example: with a second, third, or fourth burger consumed, a person's satisfaction could turn into the opposite—dissatisfaction and a stomach ache). So, consumption demand is subject to diminishing marginal utility, and an additional unit of a good will eventually be bought only if its price will be reduced.

3. **Substitution factor:** Why does my quantity demand tend to fall as price rises? First, I will try to substitute the good with a higher price with a similar one that has a lower price, and second, I find myself really poorer than I was before, and I have less real income. The reverse effect of this factor is: at a lower price, buyers have the incentive to substitute what is now a less expensive product for similar products that are now relatively more expensive.

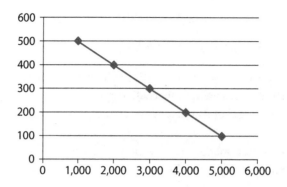

Figure 2.2
The Demand
Schedule and
the Demand
Curve for
Football Game
Tickets

3. DETERMINANTS OF DEMAND, SUBSTITUTES VS. COMPLEMENTS, NORMAL GOODS VS. INFERIOR GOODS

Consumers' demand is determined not only by prices but also by other factors—*determinants*—that include:

1. *Tastes and Preferences* that are strongly influenced by advertising;
2. *Consumer's income*: Products whose demand increases or decreases directly with an increase or decrease of money income are called **normal (superior) goods**, and **inferior goods** are those whose demand varies inversely with money income;
3. *The availability and price for related goods*: Demand for a good increases if the price for its substitute is increasing (price of one and demand for the other are moving in the same direction); **a substitute** is a good that could be consumed instead of another one; conversely, demand for a good decreases if the price for its complement is increasing (price of one and demand for another are moving in opposite directions); **a complement** is a good that is consumed with another one;
4. *Expectations of buyers for future changes in income, prices, tastes*: If prices for houses are expected to rise in six months, for example, potential buyers will buy them now; if prices for textbooks for courses that students plan to take next semester are expected to decline by 25–30%, the textbook will be bought next semester;
5. *Number of buyers*: The bigger the number of the buyers for a specific product, the bigger the demand for it and vice versa; and
6. *Accumulated savings* in the form of bank deposits, stocks, bonds, etc.: The more substantial are accumulated savings, the bigger might be the demand for certain goods (durables that last more than three years: houses, cars, refrigerators, etc.).

4. CHANGES IN DEMAND VS. CHANGES IN QUANTITY DEMANDED (SHIFTS OF THE CURVE VS. MOVEMENTS ALONG THE CURVE)

It is important to distinguish *shifts of the demand curve* to the right or to the left, which is *a change in demand* with *movements along the demand curve* downward or upward, which is *a change in quantity demanded.*

Shifts of the curve: If the underlying determinants of demand stay constant, the demand schedule and curve will stay the same. The demand schedule and curve remain unchanged only so long as the underlying determinants of demand remain constant. When any of them changes, the demand curve will shift to a new position. The shift of the demand curve to the right occurs when incomes go up or when we have a change in taste or expectations. If demand increases, the demand curve will shift rightward and vice versa. Similarly, the increase in the number of consumers (improvements in communications, opening of new markets as a result of trade agreements, etc.) results in a change in demand.

Changing prices for a good will result in *movements along a demand curve.*

Demand for tickets for a football game depends inversely on the price of tickets: the higher the price of the tickets, the fewer tickets will be demanded (movement along the curve). But changes in preferences (from football to a Beyoncé concert, for example) or changes in income, expectations, or any other of the above mentioned determinants will shift the curve from D1 to D2 (shift of the curve).

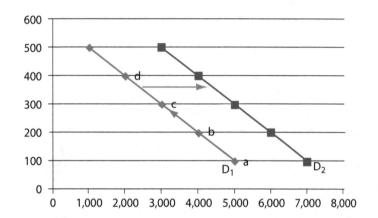

Figure 2.3 Change In Demand (Shift of the Curve) vs. Change in Quantity Demanded (Movement Along the Curve)

$ / Pizza	a) Mike's demand	+ b) Maria's demand	+ c) Joe's demand	= d) market demand
9	0	1	1	2
7	1	2	3	6
5	2	3	4	9
3	3	4	6	13

Figure 2.4 Market Demand Schedules and Curves for Pizzas (Per Week)

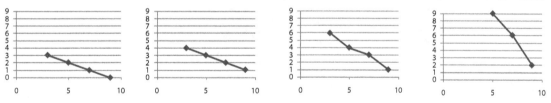

In Economics, we are not operating with individual demand but with the collective demand of all buyers in the market, called *Market Demand*. Market demand (in comparison with individual demand) is affected by the number of potential buyers and their respective tastes and incomes, as well as by availability of other goods—substitutes or complements—and expectations. In other words, market demand is the total quantity of a good or service consumers are willing and able to buy at alternative prices in a given time period, the sum of individual demands, or the combined demands of all market participants.

In conclusion, an increase (decrease) in demand may be generated by:

1. Changes in consumer tastes;
2. Changes in the number of buyers;

3. Changes in incomes (increased income leads to increased demand for a normal good; a decrease in income leads to an increase in demand for an inferior good and vice versa);
4. Changes in price of a substitute and of a complementary good; and
5. Changes in consumers' expectation for future prices or incomes.

5. LAW OF SUPPLY: SUPPLY, SUPPLY SCHEDULE, AND SUPPLY CURVE

Let's turn now to Supply. What are a "supply schedule" and a "supply curve"? What determines changes in supply and changes in quantity supplied? What is the difference between individual supply and market supply? If, for a consumer (demander), the price of a good is a barrier, for a producer (supplier), the price is an incentive. The higher the price of what he or she produces, the higher the total revenue (price multiplied by quantity produced and sold: TR = PxQ). So, the supply is another part of any market transaction and is expressed by a supply schedule and supply curve. The *supply schedule, or curve*, shows *the relationship between market prices and the amount of a good or a service producers are able and willing to supply at certain prices in a given period of time.* The market supply represents the total quantity of a good that sellers are willing and able to sell at alternative prices in a given period of time, other things being equal. According to common sense: the higher the price of a good, the more will be supplied and vice versa. *The Law of Supply* states: *there is a positive or direct relationship between price and quantity supplied: as prices rise, the quantity supplied rises; as prices fall, the quantity supplied falls.*

Price (Dollar)	Quantity Supplied
100	1,000
200	2,000
300	3,000
400	4,000
500	5,000

Figure 2.5 Supply Schedule and Supply Curve for Football Tickets. At a price of $100, 1,000 tickets for a game will be offered, but at $400, 4,000 tickets will be offered.

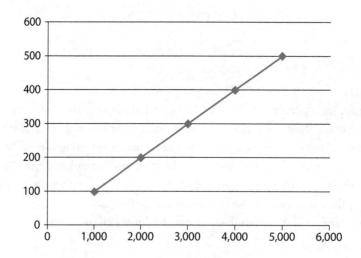

6. CHANGES IN SUPPLY VS. CHANGES IN QUANTITY SUPPLIED (SHIFTS OF THE CURVE VS. MOVEMENTS ALONG THE CURVE), INDIVIDUAL SUPPLY VS. MARKET SUPPLY

The main determinants (shifters) of supply are:

1. Changes in the prices of resources (inputs) necessary to produce a good—the *factor costs:* the higher resource prices are, the bigger the cost of producing a good and the smaller the profit from selling it (difference between the price and cost).
2. Changes in *technology* available to produce a good: A new technology could dramatically increase the productivity of workers and the volume of production and, at the same time, reduce its cost and, therefore, increase producer's profit. For example, Apple's philosophy is that the way to success is not through selling thousands of relatively expensive products but in selling millions of relatively inexpensive ones, such as the iPod.
3. *Taxes and subsidies*—government payments to companies to produce a product, sometimes called "taxes in reverse." The higher the sales or excise taxes imposed on a product, the higher its cost of production and the smaller the producer's profit.
4. Changes in *the prices of other goods,* substitutes, or complements in production: The higher the price of a substitute for a good, the less incentive a producer has to stay with the production of this good (supply of a good and the price of its substitute are moving in opposite directions) and the higher the price of a complement of a good, the bigger the incentive to produce it (supply of a good and the price of its complement are moving in the same direction).
5. Producer's *expectations* for changes in prices, technology, taxes, etc. Political turmoil in the Middle East or a natural disaster in the Gulf of Mexico (a hurricane) could disrupt the supply of oil and increase its price, which, in turn, will strongly influence a producer's decision about what and how to produce.
6. Changes in *the number of sellers*: An increase in the number of companies that are producing electronics—for example, smart phones—will increase the production and supply of such items to the market.

It is important to distinguish between a) *changes in supply*—shifts of a supply curve under the influence of any one of the above mentioned factors and b) *changes in quantity supplied*—movements along a given supply curve that result only from the changes in price.

An increase in the price of a product, for example, from $200 to $400, will increase its production from 2,000 to 4,000 units. The shift of the curve from S_1 to S_2 will occur only as a result of changes in any one nonprice determinant of supply.

Economics is focused not just on an individual producer's supply but on the **market supply**. Market supply is the sum of all individual producers' supply in the market, an expression of sellers' intentions, and of the ability and willingness to sell, not a statement of de facto sales. The market supply is reflected in the Market Supply Schedule and the Market Supply Curve.

A positive (direct) relationship between supply and price is determined by at least two factors: a) at higher prices, a producer is strongly motivated to increase production and sales of a good, with the inducement of a higher profit in the future and b) higher profits will attract new businesses to this industry, and the market supply inevitably will increase. As Adam Smith observed, "It is not from the benevolence of the butcher, the brewer, or the baker that we expect our dinner; but from their regard to their own interest. We address ourselves, not to their humanity but to their self-love, and never talk to them of our own necessities but of their advantage" (Adam Smith, *The Wealth of Nations*).

Figure 2.6
Changes in
Supply (Shift of
the Curve) vs.
Changes in
Quantity
Supplied
(Movement
Along the
Curve)

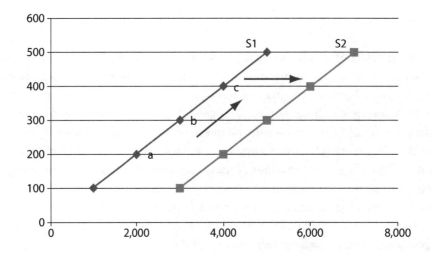

Figure 2.7
Market Supply
Schedule and
Curve for Pizzas
(Per Week)

$ / Pizza	a) Toni's supply	+ b) Anna's supply	+ c) Joe's supply	= d) Market supply
9	3	4	6	13
7	2	3	4	9
5	1	2	3	6
3	0	1	2	3

7. MARKET EQUILIBRIUM: TRADEOFF BETWEEN DEMAND AND SUPPLY, RATIONING FUNCTION OF PRICES

Which one—demand or supply—is the most important in determining price and equilibrium in a competitive market? This question was one of the most debatable in earlier economics theory. Alfred Marshall, a professor of Cambridge, who reigned over economics for a quarter of a century until his retirement in 1908 and who used graphs and diagrams extensively to illustrate economic theory (as he mentioned, some students never forgive him for that), compared demand and supply to a pair of scissor blades: "We might as reasonably dispute whether it is the upper or the under blade of a pair of scissors that cuts a piece of paper, as whether value is governed by utility [demand] or cost of production [supply]" (Alfred Marshall, *Principles of Economics*, 8th edition, New York, Macmillan, 1982, p. 348).

Price ($$)	Quantity Demanded	Quantity Supplied
100	5,000	1,000
200	4,000	2,000
300	3,000	3,000
400	2,000	4,000
500	1,000	5,000

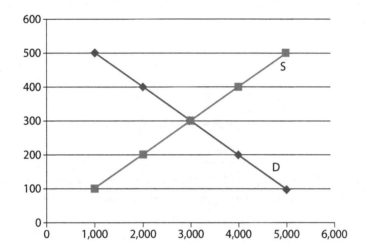

Figure 2.8
Market
Equilibrium for
Football Tickets

Let's bring together these two basic notions to see how market equilibrium and prices are determined. The *market equilibrium* is determined by both Demand and Supply, just as both scissors' blades are cutting a piece of paper. It is not determined by any single individual but by the collective behavior of buyers and sellers, each one acting in his or her own interest. So, the *equilibrium price* is determined by the quantity of a good or service that buyers are willing and able to buy and sellers are willing and able to sell in a given period of time, all other things remaining unchanged—*ceteris paribus.* This is a trade-off between the two sides of the market and will remain unchanged until demand or supply does not change. Quantity of a good sold at the equilibrium price is called *equilibrium quantity*. In our graph (figure 2.8), the equilibrium is at the intersection of the demand and supply curve and reflects the interaction of competitive forces of supply and demand. Who determines the equilibrium price and quantity? The government, the US Congress, the US president, or the local administration? The mechanism of trial and error reflects the interactions of competitive forces of market demand and market supply. The tendency of prices to move toward equilibrium, as happens in any auction, is called *market clearing* or *rationing functions of prices.*

At $300, both buyers and sellers will be satisfied, and the market is in equilibrium. But the problem is that markets do not represent just an "instant picture"; they are a dynamic mechanism in permanent motion, and the equilibrium will change each time a change occurs in a) demand, b) supply, or c) both of them.

Let's first examine two situations:

1. What happens when *prices are below the equilibrium* at, suppose, $100 for a ticket? In this situation, we have excess demand because consumers are willing to buy more (5,000 tickets) at this price than producers are willing to sell (1,000), or a *shortage.* It will not last for a long time if there is no intervention into the market. The market prices will increase, providing an incentive for

producers to increase their production (the quantity supplied—Qs—is moving upward on a supply curve). At the same time, higher prices will discourage buyers, which will reduce the quantity demanded (movement of the quantity demanded of a good—Qd—upward on the demand curve).

2. What happens when *prices are above the equilibrium* at, suppose, $500? The excess supply when producers are willing to sell more (5,000) than consumers are willing to buy (1,000) is a *surplus*. The market prices will decrease with reduction of demand (the quantity demanded—Qd—will move downward along the demand curve and, consequently, quantity supplied—Qs—will move downward along the supply curve). Only at the equilibrium price will no further adjustments be required. Business firms will discover equilibrium market prices by trial and error. However, no particular equilibrium price is permanent. The equilibrium price will change whenever the supply or demand curves shifts.

8. ANALYZING CHANGES IN PRICES: EFFECTS ON MARKET EQUILIBRIUM OF CHANGES IN BOTH DEMAND AND SUPPLY

Let's analyze the changes in equilibrium price—Pe—and in equilibrium quantity—Qe—in real market situations.

1. Changes in demand (D) while supply (S) remains constant (shifts of the D curve).
   a. Increase in demand, assuming that supply remains constant (figure 2.9a).

Price, Q	Q₁	Q₂	S (Constant)
$10	1	3	10
$8	2	4	8
$6	3	5	6
$4	4	6	4
$2	5	7	2

Figure 2.9a Change in Pe and Qe When the D Curve Shifts Right (S Curve Remains Constant)

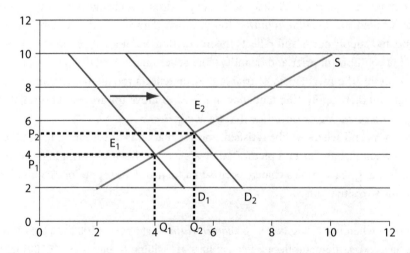

Increase in demand as a result of any nonprice determinants (increase in a consumer's income, increase in the price of a substitute or decrease in the price of a complement, increase in expectations and number of buyers, change in preferences, etc.) undoubtedly leads to increases in both equilibrium price and equilibrium quantity. We can express this by using symbols: $\uparrow$D (S const.): Pe$\uparrow$Qe$\uparrow$.

b. Decrease in demand, assuming constant supply (figure 2.9b).

Price, Q	Q_1	Q_2	S (Constant)
$10	3	1	10
$8	4	2	8
$6	5	3	6
$4	6	4	4
$2	7	5	2

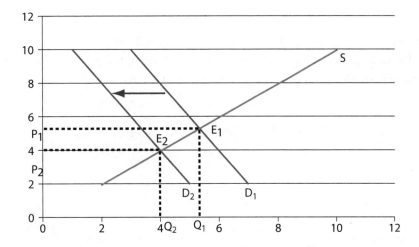

Figure 2.9b
Change in Pe
and Qe When
the D Curve
Shifts Left
(S Curve
Remains
Constant.

Decrease in demand under the influence of nonprice determinants (decrease in consumer's income, decrease in the price of a substitute or increase in the price of a complement, decrease in expectations and number of buyers, change in preferences) univocally leads to decreases in both equilibrium price and equilibrium quantity: $\downarrow$D (S const): Pe$\downarrow$ Qe$\downarrow$.

2. Changes in supply (S) while demand remains constant (shift of the S curve).
   a. Increase in supply, assuming constant demand (figure 2.10a).
   Increase in supply resulting from any nonprice determinants of supply (decrease in cost of inputs, advance in technology, increase in number of sellers, change in expectations, higher future prices, government subsidies, etc.) will end in a decrease in equilibrium price and an increase in equilibrium quantity: $\uparrow$S (D-const.): Pe$\downarrow$ Qe$\uparrow$.

Price, Q	Q (constant)	S_1	S_2
$10	3	8	10
$8	4	6	8
$6	5	4	6
$4	6	2	4
$2	7	0	2

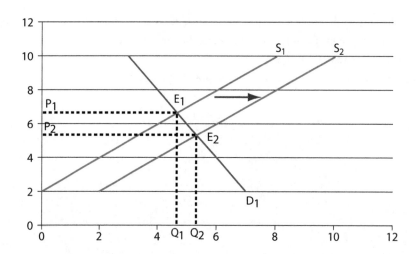

Figure 2.10a
Change in Pe &
Qe When the
S Curve Shifts
Right (D Curve
Remains
Constant)

b. Decrease in supply, assuming constant demand (figure 2.10b).

The same nonprice determinants of supply acting in the opposite direction lead to an increase in equilibrium price and decrease in equilibrium quantity: $\downarrow$S (**D const.**): $\uparrow$**PeQe**$\downarrow$.

Price, Q	Q (constant)	S_1	S_2
$10	3	10	8
$8	4	8	6
$6	5	6	4
$4	6	4	2
$2	7	2	0

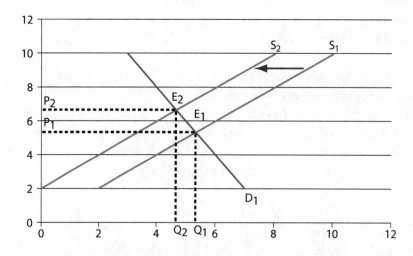

Figure 2.10b
Change in Pe &
Qe When S.
Curve Shifts Left
(D Curve
Remains
Constant)

3. Changes in both supply and demand (shift of both curves).

This is perhaps the most interesting case study; it reflects the market mechanism in action, with simultaneous changes in buyer and seller behavior.

a. Increase in both demand and supply (figure 2.11a).

Price, Q	D1	D2	S1	S2
$10	1	3	7	10
$8	2	4	5	8
$6	3	5	3	6
$4	4	6	1	4
$2	5	7	−1	2

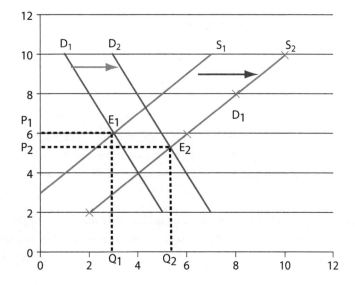

Figure 2.11a
Change in Pe &
Qe When Both
D & S Curves
Shift Right

These changes occur under the influence of nonprice determinants of demand and supply and depend on the magnitude of their changes: ↑D↑S: Qe↑Pe?.

The equilibrium price (Pe) will remain unchanged if demand and supply increase by the same magnitude. Equilibrium price (Pe) will increase if the increase in demand is larger than the increase in supply and vice versa—equilibrium price will decrease if increase in demand is less than increase in supply.

b. Decrease in both demand and supply (figure 2.11b) will result in decrease of the equilibrium quantity and unknown changes in equilibrium price: if the magnitude of decrease in demand and supply is the same, then equilibrium price remains unchanged; if the decrease in demand is bigger than the decrease in supply, then equilibrium price will fall and vice versa: if the decrease in supply is larger than the decrease in demand, then the equilibrium price will rise: ↓D↓ S: Qe↓ Pe?.

D_1	D_2	S_1	S_2
3	1	10	7
4	2	8	5
5	3	6	3
6	4	4	1
7	5	2	−1

Figure 2.11b
Change in Pe &
Qe When Both
D and S Curves
Shift Left

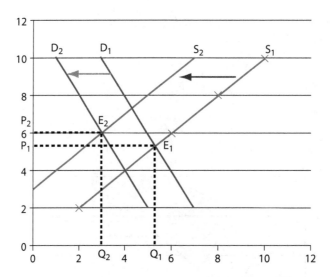

c. Increase in demand and decrease in supply (figure 2.11c). The simultaneous shift of the demand (rightward) and supply (leftward) curves in opposite directions result in an unambiguous increase in equilibrium price and an unknown effect on equilibrium quantity: $\uparrow$D$\downarrow$S: Pe$\uparrow$Qe?.

The quantity will not change if the size of changes in demand and supply is the same; with greater increase in demand than the decrease in supply, the equilibrium quantity will increase and vice versa—a smaller increase in demand and a larger increase in supply will result in a decrease in equilibrium quantity.

Price, Q	D_1	D_2	S_1	S_2
$10	1	3	10	8
$8	2	4	8	6
$6	3	5	6	4
$4	4	6	4	2
$2	5	7	2	0

Figure 2.11c
Change in Pe &
Qe When D
Increases and S
Decreases

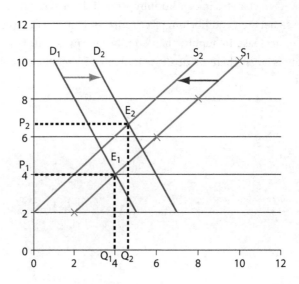

d. Decrease in demand and increase in supply (figure 2.11d) will result in decrease in equilibrium price with an ambiguous change in equilibrium quantity: ↓D↑S: Pe↓ Qe?.

It will remain unchanged if the size of changes in both demand and supply is the same; if the decrease in demand is larger than the increase in supply, then the equilibrium quantity will decrease and vice-versa—a smaller decrease in demand and a larger increase in supply lead to increase in equilibrium quantity.

Price, Q	D_1	D_2	S_1	S_2
$10	3	1	8	10
$8	4	2	6	8
$6	5	3	4	6
$4	6	4	2	4
$2	7	5	0	2

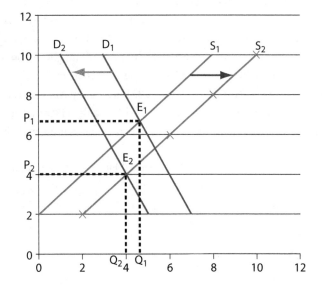

Figure 2.11d
Change in Pe &
Qe When D
Increases and
S Increases

9. DISEQUILIBRIUM PRICING: GOVERNMENT INTERVENTION INTO THE MARKET MECHANISM, PRICE FLOOR VS. PRICE CEILING

The market mechanism is far from perfect, and unregulated markets sometimes lead to too much pollution and too much inequality and poverty, providing strong arguments for government intervention to correct market failure, particularly through price control. Making a parallel for the notion of market efficiency, let's remember Winston Churchill's characteristic of democracy: it doesn't work very well, but it does work better than the alternatives that have been tried from time to time. Perhaps there is no more enduring form of government intervention than *price ceilings—the legal upper limit (maximum) imposed on the price of a good or a service*—which date back more than four thousand years. The intentions of the government (federal, state, or local) are noble: intervene in the price mechanism on behalf of poor people by imposing, for example, a limit on rents to make housing more affordable. Let me remind you again of that saying, the road to hell is paved with good intentions. Let's examine a few cases that will help us better understand how price ceilings work (or don't) and what the consequences are of such intervention.

In 1777, the legislature of the Commonwealth of Pennsylvania decided to enforce a limited price control (ceiling) on commodities needed by Washington's army. The goal was to reduce the expense of supplying the army and lighten the burden of the war on the population. But the result was that Washington's army nearly starved to death at Valley Forge (*The Wall Street Journal*, May 21, 1979). More than one hundred years and fifty years later, price ceilings were imposed during World War II on some raw materials (aluminum and steel) to prevent the earning of huge profits by those companies which had access to them. Here is one more example: rent control has been extensively used in New York City and some 200 other cities in the US to make apartments more affordable for low income families since two-thirds of these city's population lives in rental units. A median rent in New York City rent-regulated apartments was established at $330 in 1986, although for some similar apartments that were not the subject of regulation, the rent was 70% higher. As a result, sellers dramatically reduced the quantity and the quality of rental units supplied, which significantly increased shortages of rented apartments, with a large number of apartments abandoned by their owners because they lacked the resources to maintain them.

Due to such shortages, owners of apartments took advantage of their ability to choose renters on the basis of personal preferences, which was de-facto discrimination based on race, creed, or sex. They found other opportunities for "invisible" increases in rent: payments for trash removal services, repair services, etc. This rent ceiling policy also led to the emergence of black markets for illegal sales and purchases that flourished in spite of the law and defying it. In the time of the Roman Emperor Diocletian (245–313 AD), profiteering from the black market was punishable by death, but even this harsh punishment did not eliminate black market activities. A forgotten lesson of history proved to be a costly experience: the value of the government-mandated subsidy from landlords to tenants in New York City from 1943 to 1976 equaled, according to some estimates, twenty billion dollars (David Hyman, *Economics,* IRWIN, Boston, 1989, p. 83). Ironically, many of the rent control beneficiaries were middle and upper middle income people. The solution to this problem is provided by the market: permitting rents to increase and allocating available apartments to those consumers willing and able to pay the rent.

Rent/Month per Apartment	Q Demanded (Mill.)	Q Supplied (Mill.)
$1,500	1.3	2.6
$1,300	1.5	2.3
$1,100	1.7	2.1
$900	1.9	1.9
$700	2.2	1.6
$500	2.4	1.4
$300	2.6	1.3

Figure 2.12
The Effects of
Price Ceilings
on the Market
for Apartments

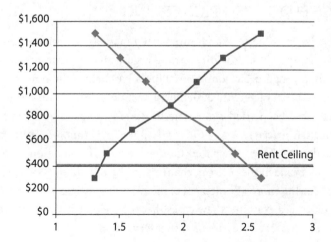

LET'S ILLUSTRATE THE EFFECTS OF RENT CONTROL GRAPHICALLY

Fixing a ceiling on rent (in our example, at $400) below the equilibrium price in a competitive market has at least four consequences:

1. Inefficient allocation of resources with increased demand and decreased supply, which causes shortages;
2. Wasted time and resources of those who want to rent an apartment but are not able to find one;
3. Infringement of the voluntary exchange principle in a competitive market leads to discrimination in selection of renters by owners of apartments based on race, creed, or sex; and
4. Emergence of illegal activities—black markets, lost tax revenues, and violations of the law.

Another example of inefficient price ceilings was President Richard Nixon's wage and price freeze in August 1971, which led to long lines of motorists for gasoline even before the Arab oil embargo of October 1973. The embargo convinced the government to reestablish price ceilings throughout the 1970s (in 1973, the government imposed a 55-cent price ceiling on gasoline), especially during President Jimmy Carter's administration (1977–1981); again it resulted in long lines at gas stations and various types of distribution based on ration stamps, coupons, emergence of a black market, and expanded bureaucracy and red tape. In 1981, President Ronald Reagan abolished price controls on gasoline—price controls that had discredited the government and violated market economy laws. Nevertheless, there were other attempts to use this policy, particularly in California in 2001 when price controls were imposed on the wholesale electricity market.

Another widespread practice of government intervention into the price mechanism occurs when the government imposes above-equilibrium prices, or a *price floor,* which is *a legal lower limit (minimum) imposed on the price of a good.* Again, government intentions are to protect producers, especially farmers, by allowing them to charge a price above the equilibrium so that they can be compensated for their cost of production and even ensure some profit. Government intervention in agriculture, referred to as the "farm program," for example, started during the Great Depression of the 1930s and affected all sectors of the economy and has continued to do ever since. The government guaranteed a minimum price above the equilibrium for farmers' products, such as milk and wheat, and agreed to purchase any surplus the farmers were unable to sell at this price. De facto, it was a subsidy for farmers, paid by consumers (taxpayers). The effects of a price floor for agricultural products are illustrated by the Figure 2.13.

Fixing the price floor (in our example at $4.0 per bushel) has at least four consequences:

1. Inefficient allocation of resources with an excess of supply over demand, which leads to surplus (2.7 billion bushels).
2. Inefficient high-cost producers can still receive profits even on low quality products as a result of government support of prices.
3. Taxpayers end up subsidizing farmers through prices used to purchase and stockpile the surplus.
4. To avoid unwanted surpluses, the government pays farmers not to produce (acreage allotments), or—an even worse situation—surplus products are deemed "out of condition" and must be thrown away or destroyed, which is clear waste.

$/bushel	Q demanded (bil. bushels/year)	Q supplied (bill./year)
$4.5	1.7	3.4
$4.0	2	2.9
$3.5	2.3	2.3
$3.0	2.6	1.8
$2.5	2.9	1.3

Figure 2.13
The Effects of a
Price Floor on
the Market for
Wheat

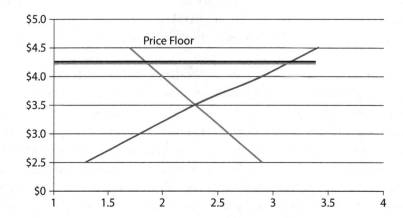

Price floors were imposed—with good intentions to help people, especially those with lower incomes—on such services like plane tickets (phased out in the 1970s) and on the hourly wage rate for workers, which is the subject of special analysis today. In both situations—price floors and price ceilings—society ends up with a wrong mix of output, inefficient allocation and use of limited resources, increased tax burden (in the case of a price floor), an altered distribution of income, and incentives for illegal activity in the black markets. In fact, *market failure* (markets fail to provide the efficient optimum output wanted by society) is replaced or is combined in a worst-case scenario by *government failure* to meet its goals and obligations. That's why the founder of modern economic theory, Adam Smith, advocated for the "*laissez-faire*" policy. This policy is motivated not only by the potential pitfalls and failures of government intervention but also by recognition of how well the price mechanism can work in competitive markets. However, it would be a mistake to conclude that government intervention in the economy via price controls is never justified; they may be useful, particularly during wars, natural disasters, or other exceptional situations.

IN CONCLUSION

In everyday business, the efficiency of market equilibrium as a result of free and loyal competition is a matter of fact. To allow market forces of demand and supply to reach such equilibrium in the interest of the society as a whole, at least a few criteria must be met:

1. Buyers and sellers should be well informed and aware of the cost and benefit of market transactions and make a rational choice, pursuing their own interests.
2. The markets should be perfectly competitive, with large amounts of buyers and sellers, with free entry and exit, and with efficient protection of property rights and voluntary exchanges.
3. Efficient government intervention should prevent situations when benefits go to someone other than those who contributed to them, or costs go to someone other than the producers who caused them by their activity.

SUMMARY

- *Market mechanism* functions through interactions and competition of large numbers of independent buyers and sellers;
- *Market prices* established at the equilibrium (intersection) of demand and supply signal what are the efficient resource allocation and socially desired output;
- *The government provides an alternative method for determining What, How, and For Whom to produce* and affects the economy through: a) spending, b) taxation, c) regulation, and d) public enterprises.
- A *price ceiling* is the maximum legal price a seller may charge for a product or a service; a price at or below the ceiling is legal; a price above is not and results in shortages as quantity demanded exceeds quantity supplied.
- A *price floor* is a minimum legal price fixed by the government (a price at or above the price floor is legal; a price below is not) and results in surpluses as quantity supplied exceeds quantity demanded.

10. KEY TERMS

Market, Factor Market, Product Market

Market Mechanism

Barter

Supply, Demand, Opportunity Cost

Demand Schedule, Demand Curve, Law of Demand

Shift in Demand

Market Demand, Market Supply

Law of Supply

Equilibrium Price, Market Shortage, Market Surplus

Price Ceiling, Price Floor

Government Failure

Laissez Faire

11. PROBLEMS AND APPLICATIONS

1. Why do people participate in market transactions?
   a. Factors of production are limited, and we need to choose among competing uses.
   b. Market specialization and efficient use of resources are saving our time and money and allow for better consumption options.
   c. Producers and consumers are pursuing different goals.
   d. We can produce everything that we want, and we do not need to participate in market transactions.

2. According to the Law of Demand, *ceteris paribus*, when the price of a good or service increases:
   a. Supply decreases.
   b. The quantity demanded will remain constant if we do not like the good.
   c. The quantity of demand increases.
   d. The quantity of demand decreases.

3. Which one best completes this statement: the quantity of a good that producers are willing and able to supply is determined by _____
   a. Movements along the supply curve resulting from changes in price.
   b. Changes in consumers' income.
   c. Consumers' tastes and preferences.
   d. The change in consumer demand for the good.

4. What determines the change in supply?
   a. A change in the price of a good.
   b. A change in the consumers' expectations, income, and preferences.
   c. Changes in resources price, new technology, and taxes.
   d. A change in number of buyers.

5. The market equilibrium price and equilibrium quantity are determined by:
   a. Consumers' intentions and expectations.
   b. Market demand and supply.
   c. The intervention of the government into market mechanism.
   d. The quantity of available resources and technology.

6. Suppose you are a manager of a food market and advertised a jar of peanut butter for $2.50, and you sold it immediately. How you can explain this situation?
   a. The peanut butter was priced at the equilibrium price.
   b. The peanut butter was priced above the equilibrium price.
   c. The peanut butter was priced correctly, but you misread consumers' tastes.
   d. The peanut butter was priced below equilibrium price.

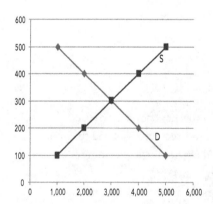

7. If the government wants to use a price ceiling to change the market outcome in the figure above, it should choose a price of:
   a. $200
   b. $300
   c. $400
   d. All of the above.

8. Kevin, a freshman at VSU, wants to maximize his grades to tuition ratio. To address this ratio, he needs to determine the factors which affect his income flows:
   a. Federal, state, and local government agencies.
   b. The ownership of factors of production (resources), how much they sell in the factor markets, and the prices received when sold.
   c. Financial institutions, such as banks, insurance companies, and credit unions.
   d. Market supply and market demand for education and jobs.

12. REVIEW QUESTIONS

1. In the Circular Flow model of the Factor Market, there is clockwise movement of _____ and counterclockwise movement of _____; it is the place where business firms sell _____ and buy _____; it is the place where households sell _____ and buy _____.
2. What are the origins and definitions of "capitalism," "barter," and "technology"?
3. Are you, as a rational consumer, confident that the market for a college education is competitive and an increase in college tuition is justified by supply and demand in this market and not by the greed of your college administration?
4. What is the difference between changes in Demand and Supply and changes in Quantity demanded and Quantity supplied?
5. Are Apple's iPhone and Samsung's Galaxy substitutes or complements? What will happen with the Demand for iPhones when the price for the Galaxy phone decreases significantly? Could the producers of the iPhone increase the price for their latest model without fear of losing market share?

CHAPTER 3.

CONSUMER AND PRODUCER BEHAVIOR: ELASTICITY OF DEMAND AND SUPPLY

1. CONSUMER BEHAVIOR (RESPONSIVENESS TO PRICE CHANGES): UTILITY THEORY, PRICE VS. QUANTITY

What are the main factors that influence consumer behavior? How do consumers decide what and how much to buy, being limited by their budget and guided by the goal of maximum satisfaction? What are the basic parameters of consumers' behavior?

We will address these questions in this chapter, focusing our analysis on an economic model of Consumer's Choice and Utility Theory.

First we need to introduce a few key notions (table and figure 3.1):

1. *Utility: The pleasure, enjoyment, or satisfaction people receive from consuming goods and services.* This concept has at least three characteristics: a) utility is subjective and its perception varies from person to person; b) it is difficult (if not impossible) to measure it; nevertheless, economists invented more than 200 years ago a term— *"utils"*—which attempts to measure utility in utils units, like meteorologists measure temperature in degrees (Fahrenheit or Celsius); and c) the term "utility" is different from "usefulness"; for example, a piece of art (paintings by Michelangelo) is of enormous utility, priceless for an educated person and useless for an uneducated one.

2. *Total Utility*: The amount of pleasure, enjoyment, or satisfaction people receive from the entire consumption of a good or service.

3. *Marginal Utility*: The amount of pleasure, enjoyment, or satisfaction from consuming an additional unit of a good or service; in other words, how total utility changes when we increase our consumption by one additional (extra or marginal) unit. The *Diminishing Marginal Utility* states that the marginal utility from any product tends to decline as more of this product is consumed in a given period of time. It should be mentioned that in spite of the increasingly smaller addition to satisfaction from consuming an additional unit of a good, total utility continues to rise, but at a slower rate, and the marginal utility still remains positive (at the point of intersection of the marginal utility curve when the horizontal axis, X, is equal to zero; below this point, it is negative). For example, we get satisfaction from consuming a piece of cake, and we may increase our satisfaction by consuming a second, third, and perhaps fourth piece in a given (short) period of time. Each successive piece of cake consumed brings less and less satisfaction until we will reach a point when another piece could cause discomfort, and its utility will be negative.

There are three phases of changes in Total and Marginal Utility:

1. Increasing total and marginal utility (eating the first piece of cake).
2. Increasing total utility at a decreasing rate and diminishing marginal utility (consuming the second to fifth pieces.
3. Decreasing total utility and negative marginal utility (consuming sixth, seventh, etc., pieces).

No of Pieces	Total Utility (utils)	Marginal Utility (utils)
0	0	0
1	10	10
2	13	3
3	15	2
4	16	1
5	16	0
6	15	-1
7	13	-2

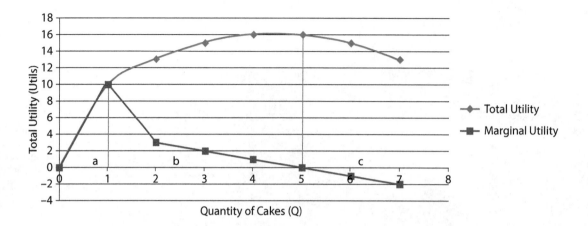

Figure 3.1
Total and
Marginal
Utilities from
Eating Cakes

How can a consumer make an optimal economic decision about what and how much to consume, taking into consideration that optimal decisions are made on the margin? To find the answer, we need to follow the principle of equal marginal utility per each dollar spent. First, marginal utility per dollar spent should be equal for all products that we consume. Economists call it the *utility maximizing rule*: we allocate our limited money income in such a way that a dollar spent on each product (sugar, salt, water, meat, fish, pizza, etc.) brings the same amount of marginal utility. Paul Samuelson, Nobel Prize laureate in Economics, identified it as the Law of Equal Marginal Utilities per dollar: "each good—such as sugar—is demanded up to the point where the marginal utility per dollar (or penny) spent on it is exactly the same as the marginal utility of a dollar (or penny) spent on any other good—such as salt" (Paul Samuelson, *Economics,* p. 435). This is a fundamental condition of consumer equilibrium and can be written in terms of the marginal utilities and prices of the different goods as follows:

MU Good 1/P1 = MU Good 2/P2 = MU Good 3/P3 = common MU/per $ of income

To illustrate this rule, suppose that the marginal utility (MU) of consuming an additional box of popcorn is 24 utils while its price is $6, so the marginal utility per dollar is 4 utils per dollar spent. The Marginal Utility of a new movie is 40 utils and the price of a ticket is $8, or 5 utils per dollar spent. Clearly, the rational choice is to go to the movie since we get more satisfaction per dollar spent—5 utils—than from a box of popcorn—4 utils. Recall that our goal as rational consumers is to get maximum satisfaction from each extra (or additional) dollar spent on good A, extra dollar spent on good B, or extra dollar spent on good C. Each dollar spent should yield the same amount of additional (marginal) utility.

Let's analyze a case related closer to your interest—succeeding on your examination. We will assume that you have a limited time (hours) to spend on your studies, and your goal is to maximize your GPA. How should you use your time? You need to spend an amount of time on economics, mathematics, or political science, which will result in maximum grade increase per hour spent for each of these disciplines. This is not only a law of economics but a rule of logic and common sense.

We can conclude that our behavior as ordinary rational consumers is based on the following parameters:

1. our income or budget, which is limited at a given moment in time;
2. maximization of our utility from each dollar spent;
3. tastes and preferences; and
4. prices for goods and services, bearing in mind that we are limited in our choices and cannot afford to buy everything we want.

One more remark in conclusion: we are always making decisions unconsciously or by habit. Sometimes we fail to avoid our own mistakes that we made in the past. In some circumstances, we make irrational choices from an economic point of view, which is the subject of a special discipline called **behavioral economics**. Economists R. Glenn Hubbard and Anthony O'Brien emphasized that consumers commonly make three mistakes in their decisions:

1. They consider monetary costs and ignore nonmonetary opportunity costs; this inconsistent behavior is a result of the so-called *endowment effect*: people are reluctant to sell a good even if they are offered a greater price than they would be willing to pay for it if they didn't own the good.
2. They fail to ignore sunk costs, which are previously incurred and irreversible (cannot be recovered) costs; these costs are irrelevant for any later decisions we make; this is always a good subject for psychologists' analyses.
3. They are overwhelmingly unrealistic about their future behavior; for example, many adults in the US are overweight, but, nevertheless, the majority of them postpone indefinitely the decision to reduce their consumption: they eat too much today hoping to eat less tomorrow, which is unlikely to happen in reality (R. Glenn Hubbard and Anthony Patrick O'Brien, *Essentials of Economics*, Second Edition, Prentice Hall, 2009, pp. 178–182).

A consumer, of course, is not supposed to be an academician and conform his or her decisions to the rules and principles of economics. Most of such decisions are taken in concordance with tastes and preferences. The most important things are to learn from our own experience and mistakes and not to repeat them in the future and to understand that the laws of the economy are objective and do not depend on anyone's will or mood. If a consumer's behavior is not compatible with these laws and principles, they will return and could hit painfully like a boomerang. To illustrate application of consumer behavior theory to the real world, we will refer to a classical example.

The diamond-water paradox. The great Scottish economist Adam Smith reflected on the idea that an essential resource (good) like water had a lower price than precious gemstones like diamonds. The abundance of water in comparison to diamonds resolved the paradox. Theory tells us that consumers should purchase any good until the ratio of its marginal utility to price is the same as that ratio for all other goods: a) the marginal utility of an extra unit of water may be low, as is its price, but the total utility derived from water is very large; b) the total utility of all water consumed is much larger than the total utility of all diamonds purchased; and c) society, however, prefers an additional diamond to an additional drop of water because of the abundant stock of water available. So, marginal utility (MU) of water (low): price of water (low) = MU of diamonds (high): price of diamonds (high). The *paradox is solved*: water has much more total utility than diamonds even though the price of diamonds greatly exceeds the price of water.

2. PRICE ELASTICITY OF DEMAND

A few years ago, I visited Iowa on the invitation of a good friend of mine, farmer Jim. I was impressed by the modern technology, combines, and equipment he used to grow and harvest corn and, of course, by his very good crops that year. He was not as enthused as I was. He explained to me that not only did he have a good crop but all of his neighbors did, as well. This meant that the market price for corn would be inevitably reduced and that would hurt more than benefit him and all the other farmers in Iowa and maybe all the farmers nationwide. The explanation of this apparently paradoxical situation resides in price elasticity of demand. My friend's revenue, which usually includes his profit, was highly dependent on changes in the price of corn, and the quantity he harvested was not very "sensitive" to these changes.

The Law of Demand tells us that the quantity demanded of the product we could buy increases when its price falls, but it does not tell us how much we will buy when the price decreases. We consumers are very responsive to the price change of some goods and services, for example, of airplane tickets, not so responsive to changes in prices for other goods, for example, the ticket price of public transportation, and totally unresponsive to changes in the prices of goods that we need for our everyday normal diet (salt, sugar, medicines, etc.).

This chapter is a continuation of the previous chapter detailing how the markets work with demand, supply, and equilibrium; the goal in this chapter is to introduce the concept of elasticity. What does price elasticity measure, and what is the difference between price elastic, price inelastic, and unit elastic? How does total revenue change with change in elasticity of demand, and what is the perfect price elasticity and the perfect price inelasticity? What are the practical applications of the concept?

To start, let's analyze how a consumer's dollar is spent (US Department of Labor, 2011, Consumer Expenditure Survey): 34 cents (C) are paid for housing (rent, utilities, etc.), 17C on food and clothing, 17C on transportation, 6C on health care, and almost 6C on entertainment. So, about 80% represents spending on our basic needs. During the last decade, our consumption of red meat, eggs, coffee, beer, and whiskey decreased while the consumption of chicken, asparagus, wine, and ice cream increased. We are drinking more water from springs and eating less of various brands of carbohydrates. What caused these changes in our consumption structure? The answer is the price elasticity of demand.

3. ELASTIC VS. INELASTIC DEMAND: MIDPOINT METHOD OF MEASUREMENT

The price elasticity of demand is a measure of the responsiveness or sensitivity of quantity demanded of a good to changes in its price. The terms elastic or inelastic define the degree of "responsiveness" of demand: if we are relatively responsive to price changes of a good or service by increasing the quantity bought, our demand is elastic. If we are relatively unresponsive to price changes and the quantity bought of a good remains unchanged, our demand is inelastic. In both cases, we behave according to the Law of Demand.

To measure the price elasticity of demand, we use a coefficient—Ed—that compares the percentage change in quantity demanded to the percentage change in price:

$$Ed = \%\Delta Qd : \%\Delta P$$

Two important remarks to be noted:
1. The elasticity coefficient is negative in mathematical terms since the price and quantity are moving in opposite directions, according to the Law of Demand. In economics terms, the minus sign is a nuisance, and economists drop it, operating with the absolute value of the coefficient of elasticity; so, the price elasticity of demand is equal to the absolute value of:

$$\frac{\text{Percentage change in quantity demanded}}{\text{Percentage change in price}}.$$

2. The price of a good could change in both directions, and the percentage change will be different. For example, the ticket price for a football game increased from $40 to $50, or according to the traditional method of computing, the percentage changed by 25%:

$$\left(\frac{\text{New price} - \text{Initial price}}{\text{Initial price}}\right) \times 100.$$

If the price changes in the opposite direction, from $50 to $40, then there is a 20% change. To avoid this confusion, we use average values of percentage change:

$$\left(\frac{\text{New price} - \text{Initial price}}{(\text{New price} + \text{Initial price}) \div 2}\right) \times 100.$$

The coefficient is 22.2% and does not depend on the direction of change. The same approach is also applied for computing the percentage change in quantity demanded:

$$\left(\frac{\text{New quantity} - \text{Initial quantity}}{(\text{New quantity} + \text{Initial quantity}) \div 2}\right) \times 100.$$

This most commonly used method is called the midpoint formula for price elasticity of demand:

$$Ed = [(Q_2 - Q_1)/(Q_1 + Q_2):2] : [(P_2 - P_1)/(P_1 + P_2):2]$$

Ed—coefficient of price elasticity of demand
Q_1—original quantity demanded
Q_2—new quantity demanded
P_1—original price
P_2—new price

The change in each variable is divided by the average of the beginning and ending values to obtain a more exact value of elasticity and to avoid ambiguities. The numerator: $(Q_2 - Q_1))/(Q_1 + Q_2):2$ indicates the percentage change in the quantity demanded, and the denominator: $(P_2 - P_1))/(P_1 + P_2):2$ shows the percentage change in price.

4. PRICE ELASTICITY AND TOTAL REVENUE

Why is price elasticity so important? Because it demonstrates how the total revenue (TR) of a producer is affected by the change in the price of a good or service Total quantity (Q) of sales of a product multiplied by its price (P): $TR = P \times Q$ will result in the total revenue of a producer

The method of determining the price elasticity of demand by analyzing the change in total revenue as result of change in price is called the *total revenue test.*

How can we determine the grade of elasticity of demand? What is the criterion that separates elastic from inelastic demand? Such a criterion in economics is shown in below (figure 3.2). Elasticity of demand ends up in one of *three alternative categories* with different shapes of the demand curve:

1. *Relatively Elastic: Ed > 1* (in absolute terms): When percentage change in quantity demanded exceeds percentage change in price and consumers are relatively responsive to price changes, the demand curve is relatively flat; a decrease in price raises quantity sold so much as to increase the total revenue and vice versa: an increase in price will decrease total revenue. Price and total revenue are moving in opposite directions (figure 3.2);

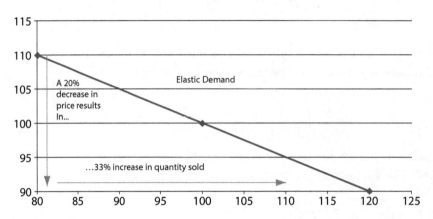

2. *Unit*   *elastic:*
Ed = 1 (in absolute terms): When the percentage change in quantity demanded equals the percentage change in price and consumers are relatively indifferent to change in price, total revenue remains unchanged (figure 3.3);

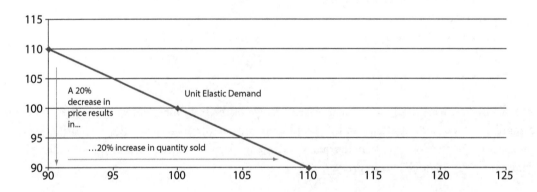

Relatively Inelastic: 0 < Ed < 1 (in absolute terms): When the percentage change in the quantity demanded is less than the percentage change in price, and consumers are relatively unresponsive to price changes, the demand curve is relatively steep. The cut in price evokes so small a percentage increase in Q as to make total revenue fall. The price and total revenue are moving in the same direction (figure 3.4).

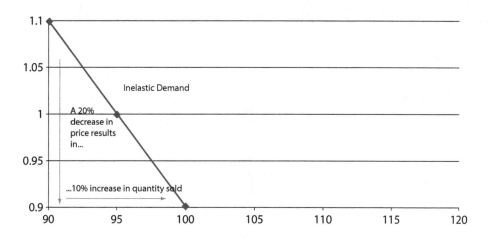

Figure 3.4
Price Elasticity
of Salt

There are also two limiting cases at the extremes of the scale of elasticity:

1. *Perfectly elastic demand: Ed = infinite*: When the quantity demanded changes by a large percentage in response to a tiny change in price, the demand curve is horizontal, parallel to the X axis (figure 3.5).

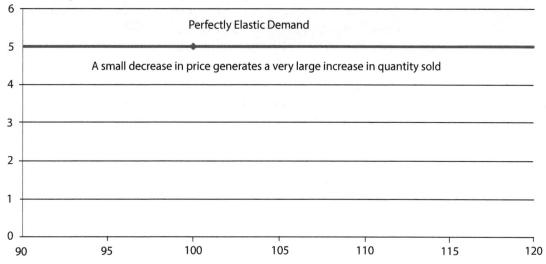

Figure 3.5
Price Elasticity
of Wheat

2. *Perfectly inelastic demand: Ed = 0*: When the quantity demanded remains the same so the percentage change is zero, regardless of changes in price, the demand curve is vertical, parallel to the Y axis (figure 3.6);

Figure 3.6
Price Elasticity
of Insulin

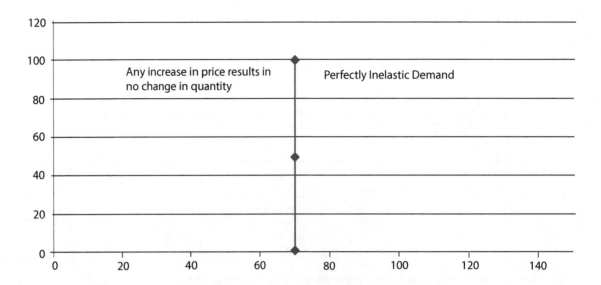

To summarize: if total revenue changes in the opposite direction from price, demand is elastic. If total revenue changes in the same direction as price changes, demand is inelastic. If total revenue does not change when price changes, demand is unitary elastic.

One important remark: the coefficient of elasticity ($\Delta Q/\Delta P$) should not be confused with the coefficient of the slope of the curve. For example, along the linear demand curve, the slope (measured by $\Delta P/\Delta Q$) is the same, and while they are all examples of elasticity, we also need to consider a change in prices along the curve (figure 3.7).

On the linear demand curve, the demand is elastic from A to D, and total revenue is increasing while the price is reduced from $70 to $35; it is unit elastic at point D and inelastic from D to G, with total revenue decreasing. In Figure 3.8, we illustrate how total revenue changes as a result of changes in the price elasticity of demand.

Price ($/ticket)	Qty Sold ('000)	Total Revenue
68	0	$0
60	1000	$60,000
45	3000	$135,000
30	5000	$150,000
15	7000	$105,000
0	9000	$0

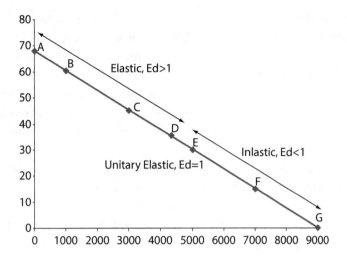

Figure 3.7
Elasticity and
Revenue Along
the Linear
Demand Curve

Figure 3.8
Total Revenue

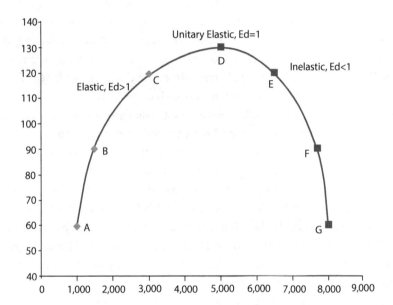

5. DETERMINANTS OF ELASTICITY OF DEMAND

What are the main determinants of price elasticity of demand for an item?

First, the most important factor is the **availability of close substitutes**: the more substitutes available, the more elastic the demand for a product. For example, there are practically no substitutes for insulin, and demand for it by diabetics is perfectly inelastic. The demand for tea or coffee is inelastic since there are not many substitutes for these items, but the demand for a particular brand of tea or coffee is much more elastic because there are many brands of them. Notice that the broader the definition of good (water or salt, for example), the fewer substitutes there are, if any, and vice versa—the narrower the definition for a good (herbal tea, cappuccino, etc.), the more elastic the demand.

Second, time: the longer the amount of time, the more elastic the demand is for a product because it is possible to find more substitutes over a longer period of time. A significant increase in the price of gasoline shifts the demand from gas guzzling automobiles to more fuel efficient cars: smaller, hybrids, electric. The "short-run" demand for gasoline is more inelastic (Ed = .2) than is the "long-run" demand (Ed = .7).

Third, when the demand for a good is more elastic, the bigger the **share of a consumer's income is spent** on it. For example, a 10% increase in the price of a house or of an automobile could substantially reduce the demand for them since they involve a bigger part of consumer's budget, but a 10% increase in the price of chewing gum or pencils will not, practically speaking, affect the demand for them;

Fourth, luxury vs. necessity: the demand for luxuries—items you can easily live without (a Mercedes or a BMW, a vacation in Hawaii, etc.)—is much more elastic than for necessities (food, medicines, etc.). Of course, whether a good is a luxury or a necessity varies from person to person: one person's necessity could be another person's luxury and vice versa.

Let's analyze a few cases of practical application of the price elasticity of demand. Most important is the prediction of changes in quantity demanded that we can compute by rearranging the formula of price elasticity of demand: $Ed = \%\Delta Qd: \%\Delta P$. From this formula, $\%\Delta Qd = Ed \times \%\Delta P$.

The price elasticity for higher education, for example, is 1.4. If a college decides to increase tuition, let's say, by 20%, then the percentage change in quantity demanded will be a decrease of 28% ($1.4 \times 20\%$). The demand for education is elastic, especially for students from low income families since it takes a big part of a family's budget. It is extremely important for a manager to have a good perception of the sensitivity of consumers' demand to price changes. Making a wrong decision—increasing instead of lowering the price—could be disastrous and cause a business to end up in bankruptcy. For a farmer, it is important to know how much the total revenue will change when the price changes since the elasticity coefficient for farmers' products is low: .20 or .25 (demand is inelastic). For example, a corn harvest of 100 million bushels with the price of $4 per bushel will bring total revenue of $400 million. In a particularly good year, the harvest might be 120 million bushels, which could depress the price to $3 per bushel; hence, total income will be $360 million. In a bad year, with the harvest of 80 million bushels and the price increased to $6 per bushel, revenue will be $480 million. Paradoxically, for farmers, a poor crop may be desirable and a bumper crop might not. To increase revenues, lawmakers could consider an increase in excise tax on a product with inelastic demand rather than for a good with highly elastic demand. A $1 tax increase for 100,000 units of a good with an elastic demand will result in $100,000 revenue for the budget. But if the tax is increased to $3 per unit, and as a result of the price increase, just 25,000 units are sold, then the total tax revenue will be $75,000. The government generally tends to increase taxes for products with inelastic demand (gasoline, liquors, tobacco, etc.), which will bring a guaranteed increase in budget revenues.

Along with the price, some other factors determine the demand for a particular good or service, such as a consumer's income and prices for a good's substitutes or complements.

In addition to price elasticity of demand, economists use two other important measures:

1. *Cross-price elasticity of demand:* shows how the demand for a good changes when the price of its substitute or complement changes:

$$CEd = \%\Delta Qd \text{ of good A}: \%\Delta P \text{ of good B}$$

The sign (plus or minus) is very important and cannot be ignored in these cases. If two goods are substitutes (Coca-Cola and Pepsi), then the demand for one and the price for another are changing in the same direction, and the coefficient is with a "plus" sign; if the price of Pepsi increases, the quantity demanded for Coca-Cola—its substitute—increases, as well. The plus sign shows the substitutability of the two goods. Conversely, if two goods are complements, like pizza and burgers, the cross-price elasticity is negative since the quantity demanded for one (pizza) is changing in the opposite direction of the price for another (burger). The "minus" sign shows the complementary nature of the two goods.

2. *Income elasticity of demand* measures the change in demand for a good as a consumer's income is changing:

$$IEd = \%\Delta Qd : \%\Delta I$$

Here, we again have two cases: if income elasticity of demand is positive (quantity demanded changes directly with the change in income), the two items are normal goods and vice versa, if the income elasticity is negative (Qd changes inversely with the I), then two items are inferior goods.

By applying the coefficient of income elasticity of demand, we can explain the expansion or contraction of some industries in the US. As income increased, industries producing income-elastic products expanded their outputs: IEd for automobiles = +3; housing = +1.5; books = +1.4; and restaurant meals = +1.4; all of them experienced strong growth of output in normal times. In contrast, industries that produced products with low income elasticity—agriculture, for example—have grown more slowly than the economy as a whole.

Examples of the application of the cross-elasticity coefficient: a) Businesses: before making the decision to lower the price of Sprite brand drinks, Coca-Cola will examine how sensitive Coca-Cola's sales are to a change in the price of Sprite and b) The government: regulators use the cross elasticity of demand in assessing a proposed merger between two large firms (ITT and T-Mobile, for example).

6. PRICE ELASTICITY OF SUPPLY

The concept of price elasticity also refers to producers' behavior by measuring their responsiveness to changes in price. The price elasticity of supply (Es) indicates the percentage change in quantity supplied in response to given percentage change in price:

$$Es = \%\Delta Qs / \%\Delta P$$

Note that the coefficient is a positive number since the quantity supplied and the price move in the same direction. This positive slope of the supply curve reflects the increase in marginal cost of production as the total output increases: the price of each consecutive unit produced is increasing to cover increasing cost of production, according to the Law of Increasing Opportunity Cost.

To avoid confusion related to directions of changes in price, economists use the same midpoint formula:

$$Es = [(Q_2 - Q_1)/(Q_1 + Q_2):2] : [(P_2 - P_1)/(P_1 + P_2):2]$$

Es—coefficient of price elasticity of supply
Q_1—original quantity supplied
Q_2—new quantity supplied
P_1—original price
P_2—new price

Three of the most common cases of price elasticity of supply are:

Figure 3.9
Elastic Supply
of iPods

1. *Relatively Elastic Supply: Es > 1;* percentage change in quantity supplied is larger than the percentage change in price (table and figure 3.9).

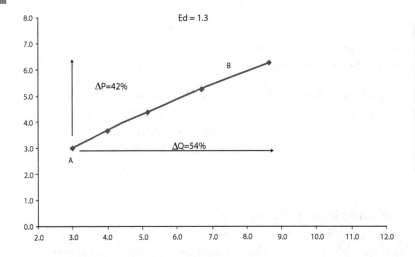

Price ($/unit)	Qty Sold ('000)
3.0	3.0
3.6	3.9
4.3	5.1
5.2	6.6
6.2	8.6
7.5	11.1

2. *Unit elastic supply: Es = 1;* percentage change in quantity supplied is exactly the same as percentage change in price (table and figure 3.10).

Figure 3.10
Unit Elastic
Supply (Bus
Tickets)

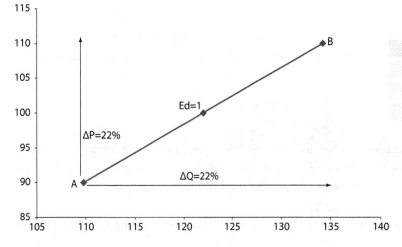

Price ($/unit)	Qty (Trips)
90	110
100	122
110	134

3. *Relatively Inelastic Supply: Es < 1;* percentage change in quantity supplied is less than percentage change in price (table and figure 3.11).

Price ($/unit)	Qty (Trips)
90	90
100	95
110	100

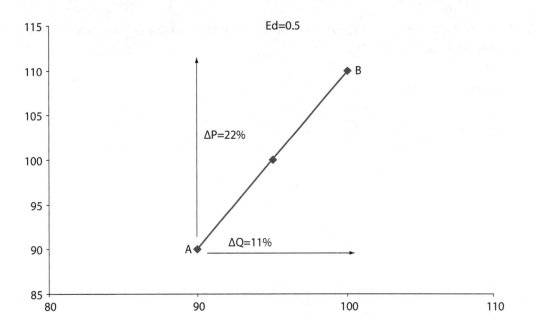

Figure 3.11
Relatively
Inelastic Supply
(Bus Tickets)

There are also two extreme cases:

1. **Perfectly inelastic supply:** Es = 0; change in price does not influence the quantity supplied (table and figure 3.12). An example of perfectly inelastic supply is land: "the trouble with land," in the words of Will Rogers, an American humorist, "is that they are not making it anymore."

Price ($/unit)	Qty (Trips)
90	10
100	10
110	10

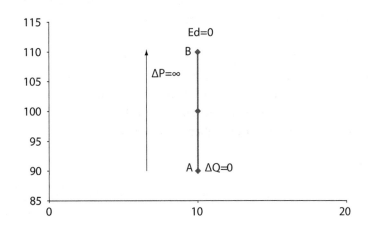

Figure 3.12
Perfectly
Inelastic Supply
(Antiques)

2. **Perfectly elastic supply: Es = infinite**: a small change in price results in a huge change in quantity supplied (table and figure 3.13).

Price ($/unit)	Qty (Trips)
90	10
100	10
110	10

Figure 3.13
Perfectly Elastic
Supply (Travel
Cruises)

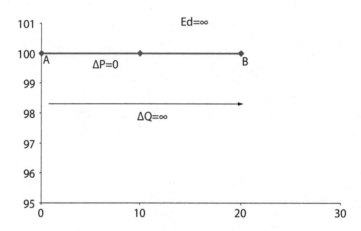

7. DETERMINANTS OF PRICE ELASTICITY OF SUPPLY, SHORT-RUN VS. LONG-RUN ELASTICITY OF SUPPLY

What determines price elasticity of supply? The price elasticity of supply depends, first of all, on how easily and quickly producers can shift resources between various uses: the easier and more rapidly the shift, the greater the price elasticity of supply. However, to shift resources takes time: the longer time a firm has to adjust to a price change, the greater the elasticity of supply. So, **the degree of flexibility** and, therefore, the time period differ from industry to industry. To address this question, let's recall the esteemed nineteenth–early twentieth century Cambridge economist Alfred Marshall's analysis of demand and supply with emphasis on the time component for market equilibrium. He made a distinction between three time periods:

1. *Momentary equilibrium* with fixed supply, called also the *market period*: The time immediately after a change in market price which is too short for producers to change their quantity supplied (figure 3.14a). The elasticity of supply is highly inelastic or almost perfectly inelastic (vertical). This is a case of a farmer who supplies a truckload of strawberries or tomatoes, but does not have enough time to increase the supply overnight and to respond to changes in prices.

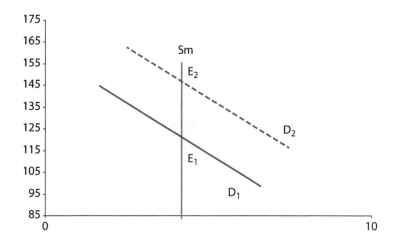

Figure 3.14a
Momentary
Equilibrium
(Market Period)

2. *Short-run equilibrium* (economists are usually referring to a period of a few weeks or months): A situation where at least one factor of production (input) is fixed, and a firm can increase its production using existing plants and equipment (figure 3.14b). The coefficient of elasticity of supply is more elastic than in the market period and is determined by the producer's ability to react to a change in price. The greater output resulting from overtime or more productive work is reflected in a more elastic supply, a smaller price adjustment, and a lower equilibrium price in the short-run than in the market period. Note that the short-run response to price changes is limited due to the Law of Diminishing Returns.

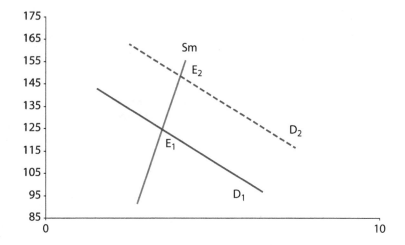

Figure 3.14b
Short-Run
Equilibrium

3. *Long-run equilibrium* (economists are referring to a several-years-long period): A situation with no fixed inputs, a period of time long enough for producers to adjust their size and production to changes in price (figure 3.14 c). Firms can expand their capacity and build new plants, new firms can enter into the industry, and old ones can leave it. As a result, the supply is more elastic than in the first two cases in response to a smaller price increase; there is a lower price equilibrium and larger output. It should be mentioned that the long-run price equilibrium is lower than the short-run equilibrium and much lower than the momentary price equilibrium while the equilibrium quantity is respectively higher.

Figure 3.14c
Long-Run
Equilibrium

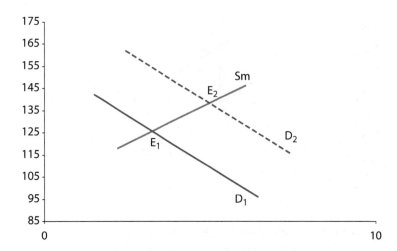

Along with the time period, there are some other factors that influence the elasticity of supply: change in technology (the supply of electronics shifts because more chips—core components—can be produced at lower cost); availability of inputs (the more resource inputs are available, the larger the elasticity of supply (for example for pizzas or burgers); and production possibilities, feasibility, and cost of storage capacities, etc. (table and figure 3.15).

Figure 3.15
Price Elasticity
of Supply for
Pizzas

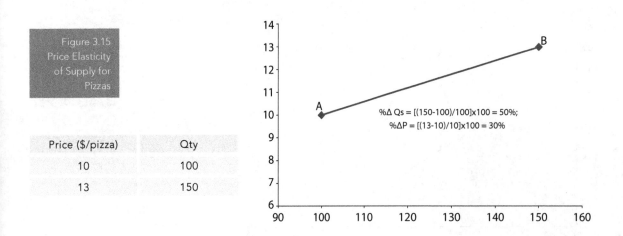

Price ($/pizza)	Qty
10	100
13	150

So, Es = %Δ Qs: %ΔP = 50/30 = 1.67. The supply of pizzas between these two points on the supply curve is elastic.

What are the practical applications of elasticities of demand and supply? How can we use elasticity's coefficients to predict changes in equilibrium price? To do this, we can use the *price-change formula*, which shows the percentage change in equilibrium price resulting from a change in demand or supply (Arthur O'Sullivan, Steven M. Shefrin, and Stephen J. Perez, *Survey of Economics: Principles, Applications, and Tools.* Prentice Hall, 2010, pp. 99–101). If consumers and producers are very sensitive to changes in price, even a small increase in price will eliminate the excess demand. An increase in demand, in other words, will cause a small increase in price if both demand and supply are elastic. To measure percentage change in equilibrium price, we can use a formula derived from the formula of the coefficient elasticity of demand (Ed = %ΔQd: %ΔP):

$$\%\Delta Pe = \%\Delta\ Qd/(Es + Ed)$$

What about the directions of the price changes? The percentage change in price is positive when the change in demand is positive (when demand increases, the demand curve shifts to the right) and negative when the change in demand is negative (when demand decreases, the demand curve shifts to the left). If both consumers and producers are very responsive to changes in price, a small decrease in price will eliminate the excess supply. An increase in supply, in other words, will cause a small decrease in price if both demand and supply are elastic.

To predict changes in price resulting from a change in supply, we just have to substitute supply for demand in the numerator of the price change formula derived from the formula of coefficient of supply (Es = $\%\Delta\ Qs$: $\%\Delta P$):

$$\%\Delta Pe = \%\Delta\ Qs/(Es + Ed)$$

8. CONCLUSION: WHY DIFFERENT CONSUMERS PAY DIFFERENT PRICES

1. Sellers can charge different prices for goods based on differences in consumers' price elasticity of demand.
2. The capacity to charge different prices depends on the grade of market power or on some ability to control the production of a good and, hence, its price (unlike the competitive model).
3. Customers are grouped by sellers in different categories according the elasticities of their demand (i.e., business travelers have more inelastic demand for air travel and can be charged more).

These are examples of price discrimination, which is the subject of another chapter (Chapter 6: Monopoly). An example of application of the coefficient of price elasticity of supply could be the prediction of price changes for antique commodities. An increased population and higher income has increased the demand for antiques and has greatly boosted the prices. In contrast with the inelastic supply for an antique is the elastic supply for modern "made-to-look-old" reproductions.

9. KEY TERMS

Utility, Total Utility, Marginal Utility
Utility Maximizing Rule
Behavioral Economics
Diamond-Water Paradox
Price Elasticity of Demand: Perfectly Elastic, Elastic, Unit Elastic, Inelastic, Perfectly Inelastic
Total Revenue Test
Cross-Price Elasticity of Demand
Income Elasticity of Demand
Price Elasticity of Supply: Perfectly Elastic, Elastic, Unit Elastic, Inelastic, Perfectly Inelastic
Alfred Marshall's Time Component of Market Equilibrium
Price-Change Formula
Price Discrimination

10. PROBLEMS AND APPLICATIONS

1. What is the definition of Utility?
   a. It is the same as usefulness.
   b. It means the pleasure or satisfaction from consuming a good.
   c. It changes in total utility when another unit of a good is consumed.
   d. None of the above.

2. Marginal utility refers to:
   a. Change in total satisfaction from consuming an additional unit of a good.
   b. Change in total utility when last unit of a good is consumed.
   c. Marginal benefit from consuming all amounts of good available.
   d. Diminishing opportunity cost of consuming an additional unit of a good.

3. The Law of Diminishing Marginal Utility states:
   a. Marginal utility from consuming an additional good always rises.
   b. Total utility from consuming one more unit of a good always falls.
   c. Marginal product of labor declines as more of a variable input is used with the same fixed input.
   d. Marginal utility of a good declines as more of it is consumed in a given time period.

4. The price elasticity of demand for education is defined as:
   a. Percentage change in price of tuition divided by the percentage change in quantity of education demanded.
   b. Unit change in price of tuition divided by the unit change in quantity of education demanded.
   c. Percentage change in quantity of education demanded divided by the percentage change in price of tuition.
   d. Unit change in quantity education demanded times the unit change in price of tuition.

5. Which of the graphs in the figure below represents a relatively inelastic response of supply to a price changes for railroad travel?
   a. Figure A
   b. Figure B
   c. Figure C
   d. figure D

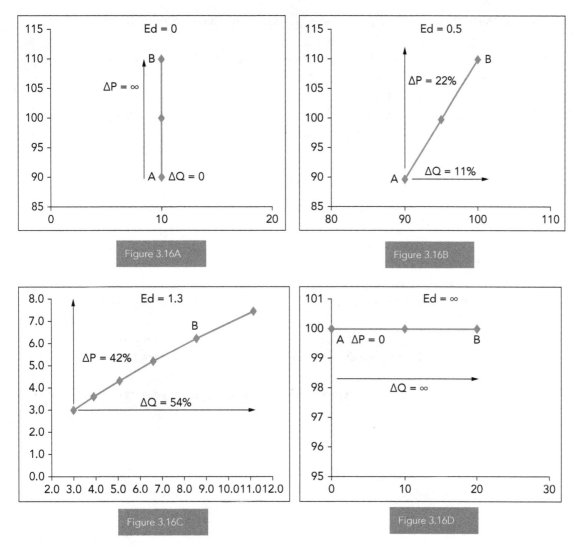

Figure 3.16A

Figure 3.16B

Figure 3.16C

Figure 3.16D

6. To compute the total revenue from an increase in rate of output we need to:
   a. Multiply the price of a product to the quantity sold.
   b. Compute the total profit a company earns from the sales.
   c. Deduct from total revenue the costs of production.
   d. Add the additional revenue earned from selling of one more unit.

7. The demand is more elastic with respect to price:
   a. When there is a shorter period of time to adjust to a price point change.
   b. When there are fewer substitutes and more complements.
   c. When the demand curve for a given price and quantity is steeper.
   d. Where there is a higher ratio of price to income.

8. The inelastic demand for necessities corresponds to the following situation:
   a. When consumer spending for necessities is sensitive to changes in income.
   b. When quantity demanded for necessities is not very responsive to changes in price
   c. When quantity demanded for necessities is very responsive to changes in price.

d. When total revenue from selling necessities increases in response to a price decrease.

9. According to Alfred Marshall's analysis of the market equilibrium, the long-run refers to:
   a. A time period in which at least one factor of production (input) is fixed.
   b. A time period immediately after a change in market price.
   c. A period of time long enough to adjust the size and production of product to changes in price.
   d. The time period required for a firm to recycle its inventory.

11. REVIEW QUESTIONS

1. Define utility and demand theory and using these definitions, explain why people stuff themselves at an all-you-can-eat buffet?
2. For more than 200 years, economists have tried to solve the diamond-water paradox: why is it that water—which is so vital to our survival—is so cheap while diamonds—which aren't a necessary resource—are so expensive? Explain.
3. Are consumers always rational in making their decisions? What are the determinants of rational behavior?
4. To compute the price elasticity of demand, you _____(divide/multiply) the percentage change in _____by the percentage change in _____and then take the value of the ratio.
5. On the linear curve, is the slope of the demand (supply) the same as the coefficient of elasticity of demand (supply)?

Essentials of Microeconomics

CHAPTER 4.

PRODUCTION, TECHNOLOGY, AND COST

1. TECHNOLOGY, BUSINESSES, COSTS, AND PROFITS

From previous chapters, we learned that the consumer is the King/Queen of the market, deciding which goods will be produced and which will not. But in reality, the market is a kingdom of dual regency: the producer is also a King/Queen. The producer is facing the same fundamental choices and challenges: Which goods should be produced? How many of each? What combination of inputs should be used in the production of these goods? If you, as a potential innovator, have been struck by a brilliant inspiration to produce a new good or service that would make you a millionaire (better—a billionaire, as in the famous song by Travie McCoy, featuring Bruno Mars) and tried to put your idea into reality, you'll discover soon that "there is no free lunch" and everything has a cost. Your way to the first million is full of stones, and your decision to produce something unique and totally new is influenced by production and cost considerations that determine the profitability of your business. To understand how production works in a real environment, we have to answer: What is the cost of production, and how does it change as a firm's output changes? What are the economic costs and economic profits, and how are they different from accountant's costs and accountant's profits? How does the Law of Diminishing Returns work in the short-run, and how does production cost change in the long-run? How do firms confront economies of scale and diseconomies of scale?

Every year, approximately 50,000 US businesses fail because they were unable to confront competition. Why does this happen? What are the limits of company's ability to produce, and what is the cost of production? At the same time, each year, some 50,000 other organizations are starting their journey in search of their best business opportunity.

From a technological standpoint, it is important to distinguish various forms of industries: *a plant*—a structure that uses *inputs* (labor, resources, machines, etc.) to produce *outputs* (goods and services); *a firm*—an organization that owns and operates a combination of plants; and *an industry*—a collection of firms that produce similar products. Firms may be *integrated horizontally*—its units perform practically the same functions (Wal-Mart, Coca-Cola), or *vertically*—its units perform different functions in different stages of production. Some firms are *conglomerates*—firms that produce various products in a few different industries. All of them are characterized by the processes that transform inputs into outputs—goods and services, called *technology*.

As there are different types of industries (a plant, a firm, an industry, and a multiplant firm) there are also various types of business organizations. The criterion that is used to classify them is the ownership:

1. A *Sole Proprietorship* is a business that is owned by one person and has less than $10,000 in assets. It is the most common type of business, representing 80% of business firms but only 6% of sales revenue. It dominates in agriculture, retail trade, and services. *Advantages* are that these businesses are easy to set up—where the proprietor is also his or her own boss. The proprietor's income (profit) comes from the business and he or she is incentivized to run the company efficiently. The *disadvantages* are that the owner (proprietor) is subject to unlimited liability and risks not only the firm's assets but his or her personal assets, as well; the financial resources for expansion are limited; the proprietor carries out all management functions.

2. *Partnerships* are owned by two or more individuals, each of whom receives a portion of any profits. It accounts for 10% of all business firms and for 4% of sales revenue. *Advantages* are almost the same as in the case of a sole proprietorship. For example, they are easier to specialize and have better access to monetary resources *Disadvantages:* financial resources can be limited or insufficient. There could be difficulties in sharing management responsibilities—the divided authority may lead to inefficient policies or action; still unlimited liabilities; still problems with continuity.

3. *Corporations* are owned by many individuals, each of whom owns shares (stock) of the corporation; a corporation has at least $4 million in assets and dominates market transactions (90% of all sales). For example, General Electric, Exxon-Mobil, Wal-Mart, and Verizon own more assets than 15 million

proprietorships. The corporation is the most efficient form of business organizations. It uses a unique method of finance—the selling of stocks and bonds. *Stocks* are shares of ownership of a corporation; *bonds* represent promises to repay a loan, usually at a set rate of interest. *Advantages:* as a legal entity, the corporation is independent of its owners and its officers, which permits long-run strategies and growth; it is easy to sell/buy stocks, and it has easier access to bank credit; a corporation has limited liability—its owners are not personally responsible (liable) for the debts or actions of the company; they risk only what they paid for stocks. Corporations must inform those with whom they do business of this limited liability. In the US, they do so by adding the designation "Inc." or "Incorporated" to their corporate title. The British have traditionally added "Ltd" or "Limited" to the title of their corporations although the official designation was changed to "Public Limited Company" or "PLC" in 1980. The French and Spanish use a more colorful warning: Corporations' titles are followed by the letters S.A.—for *Societe Anonyme* or *Sociedad Anonima* (anonymous society). The Russians use the abbreviation OOO, which means "society with limited responsibility." In addition to limited liability, the corporation offers the advantage of continuity. In law, the corporation is a fictitious "legal person." The corporation survives even if some of its stockholders want to get out of the business. They can just sell their shares to anyone willing to buy. *Disadvantages:* double taxation (dividends are taxed twice—as corporate profit and as stockholders' personal income); it can be expensive to obtain a corporate charter; financial scandals and mismanagement; eventual conflicts of interests between owner objectives and manager objectives. Sometimes corporations have difficulty with the *principal agent problem*. This is defined as differing interests between owners (principals) and managers (agents) which can lead to decisions being made without the owner's interests in mind. There are also cases of fraud and abuse as was the case with Enron and WorldCom. In some cases, there are illegal accounting practices which inflate company stock prices and, therefore, bring huge benefits executives.

4. *Hybrid structures* include a) the limited liability company (LLC) is an ordinary partnership for tax purposes (direct distribution of all profits to owners and investors) but resembles a corporation in matters of liability (shields the personal assets of owners from liability claims) and b) the S corporation (seventy-five or fewer shareholders, profits go directly to owners and, thus, avoids double taxation).

Let's analyze what determines the firm's capacity to produce goods and services, what the costs of production are, and how these costs influence a firm's profitability and its supply decisions. To do this, we need to introduce a few new concepts.

2. COST AND PROFIT: ECONOMIC VS. ACCOUNTING COST AND PROFIT

First, why do costs exist? Because resources are scarce, productive, and have alternative uses. We have to consider two types of costs:

1. A firm's *explicit costs* are the firm's actual cash payments, or money payments, to those who own and supply resources: labor, services, materials, fuel, transportation, etc. These costs are obvious and expressed, and they include the cost of the item being produced, the salary of workers, and payments for utilities.

2. A firm's *implicit costs* are the opportunity costs of using its self-owned, self-employed resources, or the cost of nonpurchased inputs. To the firm, these are the money payments that self-employed

resources could have earned in their best alternative way. These costs are present but not obvious. They include forgone interest, forgone rent, forgone wages, and forgone entrepreneurial income. For example, the implicit cost of your entrepreneurial talent is called a normal profit, or normal payment for your work. In other words, the principle of computation of economic cost is the principle of opportunity cost—what you sacrifice to get something you want. For an entrepreneur, this is the opportunity cost of his or her time and money.

Second, there are two approaches to the category "profit." An accountant refers to profit as the firm's total revenue minus its explicit costs, which is accounting costs. An economist refers to an economic profit, the total revenue minus economic costs, which includes both explicit and implicit costs.

Accounting profit = TR (total revenue) – total explicit cost.

Economic profit = TR (total revenue) – economic cost (explicit cost + implicit cost).

It is important to mention that an economic profit is not a cost. It is a return to the entrepreneur in excess of the normal profit, which is his or her compensation (wage) for the work and represents part of the cost (table 4.1).

1. Total Revenue		$175,000
2. Explicit Cost	$75,000	
Cost of Ingredients	$25,000	
Workers' Wages	$30,000	
Interest	$9,000	
Other payments	$11,000	
3. Accounting Profit (1-2)		$100,000
4. Implicit Cost	$50,000	
Forgone owner's wage	$35,000	
Forgone owner's interest	$4,000	
Forgone owner's rent	$6,000	
Economic depreciation	$5,000	
5. Economic Profit [1–(2 + 4)]		$25,000

Table 4.1 Economic Profit and Cost vs. Accounting Profit and Cost of a Firm

Third, to understand better what determines the firm's profitability, we have to examine the *period of production*, as well, which is divided into *short-run* and *long-run*. We are not referring to the calendar period of time but to conceptual periods when the decision is taken and the firm can vary the quantity of inputs.

The short-run is a time period where inputs cannot be changed and factors of production are fixed. For example, the size and technology of a plant. A variable input is one whose quantity can be changed (labor and raw materials, for example). A fixed input is one whose quantity cannot be changed over a short period of time. The short-run is too brief a time a period for a firm to alter its plant capacity (the size of a building, the amount of machinery and equipment, and other capital resources).

The long-run is a period of time long enough so that managers can change all factors of production, and there are sufficient time and conditions to vary all inputs used to produce a good. In other words, this is a time period long enough for a firm to change the quantity of employed recourses, including the size of a plant (fixed inputs). Respectively, we can distinguish between short-run adjustment and long-run adjustment.

3. PRODUCTION FUNCTION AND THE LAW OF DIMINISHING RETURNS

To produce any goods and services, a firm needs to use its limited resources or factors of production. The question is: What is the smallest amount of resources needed to produce a specific product, or what is the maximum amount of output that can be obtained from a given quantity of resources? The answer could be provided by examining the *production function (PF)*. The PF reflects *the maximum quantity of a good that can be produced from different combinations of factor inputs* or a statement of the relationship between a firm's limited resources and the output resulting from the use of these resources. In other words, a PF is a technological summary of our capacity to produce a particular good, and it tells us how much of this good can be produced with varying amounts of factors of production. Mathematically, the production function can be expressed as: $Q = f(X1, X2 \ldots Xn)$

Table 4.2
Short-Run
Production
Function

Labor	Total Output	Marginal Product
(Nr. of Workers)	(Bushels/Day)	(Bushels/Day)
0	0	0
1	9	9
2	21	12
3	34	13
4	43	9
5	50	7
6	55	5
7	53	–2

Q is output; X1, X2 … Xn—inputs used in production. If we are using only Labor—X and Capital—Y, we can restate this equation as: Q = f(X,Y), assuming a given state of technology and the maximum output from utilization of existing inputs. So, every point on the PF shows the most output that we can produce with existing inputs, which is efficient production. How can we increase efficiency and, particularly, productivity? There are several possibilities, two of which are: a) investing in labor by increasing education and training and b) spending on capital investment. This increases not only capital resources but also their quality. More capital investment usually results in improved technology, as well. Both human capital and nonhuman capital investments shift the production function upward. In each of these cases, the MPP of labor rises and marginal costs fall.

Let's focus on the labor-output relationship in the short-run period.

4. TOTAL, AVERAGE, AND MARGINAL PRODUCT

To increase its output in the short-run, a firm must increase the quantity of labor employed. There are three important relationships between the quantity of labor and the firm's output.

First: Total Product (TP). This is the total quantity of a particular good produced in a given period, and it is reflected by the total product curve. The total product curve shows the relationship between quantity of output (measured on the vertical axis) and quantity of variable input (labor, measured on the horizontal axis) for a given quantity of fixed input (figure 4.1).

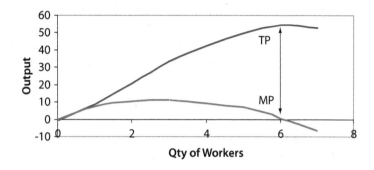

Second: Marginal Physical Product (MPP) or *Marginal Product (MP)* of labor. This is the increase in total product resulting from an increase by one unit of the quantity of labor employed, with all other inputs remaining the same. It represents *the change in total output divided by change in labor input quantity.* The MP curve shows the change in the quantity of total output (measured on the vertical axis) resulting from each additional input of labor (horizontal axis). The different marginal products produced by additional workers are explained by the structure of the production process (figure 4.2).

$$MP = \Delta Q : \Delta X \text{ (labor input)}$$

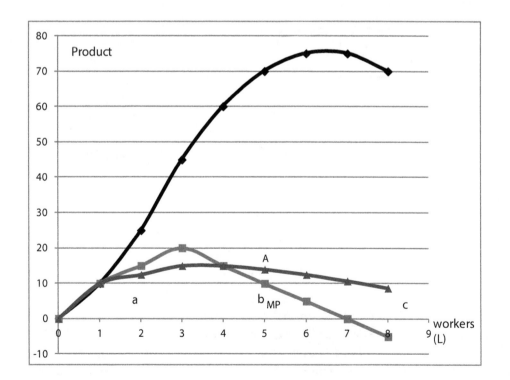

By comparing the TP and MP curves, we can observe the following:

- Three phases of TP and MP curves: a) increasing, b) decreasing, and c) negative marginal returns.
- When TP is increasing at an increasing rate, (a) marginal product is rising; when total product is increasing at a decreasing rate, (b) marginal product is falling; and when total product declines, (c) marginal product is negative. This is when quantity of total product (Q) is at its maximum, MP = 0.

Third: Average Product (AP), also called labor productivity, = *total product: units of labor.* The **average product** of labor is equal to the total product of labor divided by the quantity of labor.

$$AP = Q: X$$

The relationship between marginal and average product are of particular interest. Imagine the familiar relationship between your grade point average (GPA) each semester, which is "marginal GPA" for a particular semester, and your cumulative GPA, which is your "average GPA" (table and figure 4.3).

Table 4.3

		Semester	Semester GPA	Cumulative GPA
			(Marginal GPA)	(Average GPA)
1. Freshman Year	Fall Semester	1	1.75	1.75
	Spring Semester	2	2.25	2
2. Sophomore Year	Fall Semester	3	2.4	2.13
	Spring Semester	4	2.65	2.26
3. Junior Year	Fall Semester	5	3	2.41
	Spring Semester	6	3.3	2.56
4. Senior Year	Fall Semester	7	2.9	2.61
	Spring Semester	8	2.5	2.59

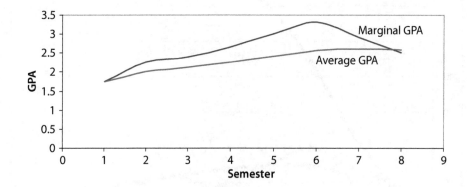

Figure 4.3
Average and
Marginal GPA

From these graphs, we can observe that when marginal product is greater than average product, average product rises, and when marginal product is less than average product, average product falls; MP = AP at AP's highest level.

In the short-run, the key principle is the **principle (or the Law) of Diminishing Marginal Returns** that states that the extra production obtained from an increase in variable input will eventually decline as more of the variable input is used together with the fixed inputs. Beyond some point, called the point of diminishing returns, output produced with one or more inputs will increase at a decreasing rate. The decline in the MPP is explained by the ratio of labor to other factors of production. The relative scarcity of other inputs (capital and land) constrains the marginal product of labor. The MPP can have a negative sense. Labor is the only factor that can be varied in the short-run. Each unit of labor has less capital and land to work with when more labor is hired.

The idea of diminishing returns was introduced by Thomas Malthus, an English pastor, in his *An Essay on the Principles of Population* (1798). According to Reverend Malthus, misery was a normal status of human-kind because the population grew in geometrical progression while production of food grew in arithmetical progression. As a result of the increasing difficulty to produce enough food even with more intensive cultivation, each successive farmer would add less to the total product than the last farmer, and, respectively, the marginal product of labor would decline. Was Reverend Malthus wrong? As Paul Krugman, Nobel Prize laureate in Economics, observed: the Malthusian theory works well as a description of fifty-seven out of the last fifty-nine centuries. Since the eighteenth century, technological progress has been so rapid that it has outpaced any problems caused by diminishing returns. But the concept of diminishing returns is still in force: marginal product declines when all other things—land, farming, technology, and other factors remain the same (Paul Krugman, Robin Wells, and Martha Olney, *Essential of Economics*. Worth Publishers, 2007, p. 165).

5. TOTAL, AVERAGE, AND MARGINAL COST

The Law of Diminishing Returns determines the manner in which the costs of the firm change as it changes its output in the short-run. As more units of a variable are added to a fixed resource, beyond some point (a manager could discover this point only by trial and error and experience), the marginal product from each additional unit of a variable resource will decline.

The production function shows how much output a firm could produce with its existing plant equipment but does not tell us how much the firm wants to produce. The most attractive level of output is the one that maximizes total profit which is the difference between total revenue and total costs. In the short-run, we have to distinguish between fixed, variable, and total costs (TC).

In the short-run, some costs don't increase at all when output is increased. These are *fixed costs (FC)*, which *do not vary with the quantity of output*. These costs are associated with the very existence of a plant and must be paid even if its output is nonexistent. They typically include rental payment, interests on the firm's debts, a portion of depreciation on equipment and buildings, insurance premiums, etc. In business, this cost is often referred to as "overhead cost."

The costs that *vary with the quantity of* output are the *variable costs (VC)*. How fast a TC changes depends only on variable costs. Previously, we learned that in this scenario, the variable cost of successive units of output decreases. They typically include payments for materials, fuel, power, transportation services, most labor, and similar variable resources.

The **Total Cost (TC)** is the sum of the value of all inputs used over any given period of time to produce goods, or the sum of fixed and variable costs. We can define the TC also as the market value of all resources used to produce a good or a service. At zero units of output, TC is equal to the firm's fixed cost.

$$TC = VC + FC$$

The distinction between the two costs is of significant importance in business. The only costs that can be controlled or altered in the short-run are variable costs. Fixed costs are beyond the manager's control; they must be paid regardless of output level.

As we already know, one of the key principles in economics is that optimal decisions are always made on margin: to produce, to sell, or to buy a few more or a few fewer goods. Accordingly, the most important factor in a short-run production decision is the *marginal cost (MC)*; that is, *the change in total cost resulting from producing one more unit of the good.* In other words, the marginal cost is the extra or additional cost of increasing production by one more unit. If the marginal cost of producing a unit exceeds the price at which is sold, it does not make sense to produce that last unit. So, *MC is a basic determinant of short-run supply (production) decisions.* The MC is an important indicator of the profitability of supplying more goods. MC may also dictate short-run pricing decisions and is equal to "rise"—increase in total cost—divided by "run"—increase in total product.

$$MC = \Delta TC/\Delta Q \text{ (change in total output)}$$

Marginal costs = the slope of the total cost curve. This will increase as an additional unit resulting from production requires more resources and, respectively, costs more than the previous unit. This cost can be controlled by the firm directly and immediately. A decision about what level of output to produce is typically a marginal decision—to produce one more or one fewer units.

Finally, one important note. It is very important to understand the difference between marginal and average relationships. Marginal product (MP) demonstrates the change in total output associated with each additional input. *Average product (AP) = the output per unit of factor input.* Marginal cost (MC) shows the change in total cost associated with producing another unit of output. *Average cost shows the per unit cost* of producing a certain level of output.

$$AC = TC/Q \text{ (total output)}$$

We have to distinguish three types of per unit or average cost:

1. *Average fixed cost (AFC),* calculated by dividing total fixed cost (TFC) by the quantity produced (Q): *AFC = TFC/Q.*

   Because TFC, by definition, is the same regardless of output, AFC must decline as output increases. Total fixed cost is spread over a larger and larger output as output rises.

2. *Average variable cost,* calculated by dividing total variable cost (TVC) by quantity produced (Q): *AVC = TVC/Q.*

   At low levels of output, production is relatively inefficient and costly, and average variable cost is relatively high. As output expands, greater specialization and better use of capital equipment yield more efficiency, and variable cost per unit declines.

3. *Average total cost (ATC)* is total cost divided by the quantity produced:

$$ATC = TC/Q = TFC/Q + TVC/Q = AFC + AVC$$

An example of production of pizzas in a Pizza Hut will help you to understand cost categories and the shape of the respective curves (table 4.4 and figure 4.4).

Table 4.4

Labor (Workers)	Output Q. of Pizzas	Fixed Cost (Ovens) $$	Variable Cost (Workers) $$	Total Cost $$	AFC $$	AVC $$	ATC $$	MC $$
0	0	600	0	600				
1	150	600	500	1,100	4	3.33	7.33	3.33
2	350	600	1,000	1,600	1.71	2.86	4.57	2.50
3	450	600	1,500	2,100	1.33	3.33	4.67	5.00
4	530	600	2,000	2,600	1.13	3.77	4.91	6.25
5	600	600	2,500	3,100	1	4.17	5.17	7.14

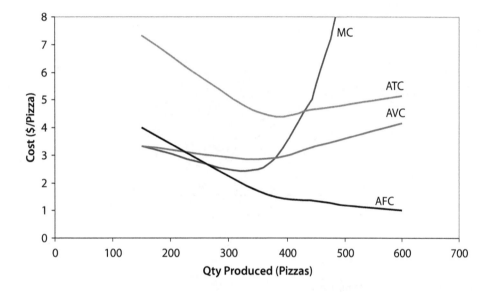

Figure 4.4
Cost Curves

Observe three important characteristics of these graphs:

1. An important feature of cost curves is their shape. An average cost starts high, will fall, and then rise which gives an ATC curve a U-shape as it is the shape of the AVC curve and of the MC curve. The MC curve intersects these two average cost curves at their minimum points.

2. As output increases, the AFC gets smaller and smaller. For small quantities of output, a one-unit increase in output reduces AFC by a large amount, the fixed cost being spread over just a few units of output. For small quantities of output, AVC decreases as output increases as a result of labor specialization. At very low levels of output, production is relatively inefficient and costly: the firm's fixed plant is understaffed, and average variable cost is relatively high. But as output expands, greater specialization and better use of the firm's capital equipment yield more efficiency—"spreading the overhead"—and variable cost per unit of output declines. When compared with marginal revenue (MR indicates the change in revenue from one more or one fewer unit of output), marginal cost allows a firm to determine if it is profitable to expand or contract its production.

3. As output increases, average variable cost also increases at a faster rate than the quantity of output increases. The difference between ATC and AVC decreases as output increases. So, an increasing output generates two opposing effects: a) spreading effect: the larger the output, the lower the

average fixed cost (this results in a downward sloping average fixed cost curve) and b) diminishing return effect: bigger output requires more variable input to produce and, respectively, generate a higher average variable cost. The marginal cost curve slopes up because of this diminishing return effect. This analysis presents a few more issues:

a. *Marginal and Average Product, Marginal and Average Cost Curves.* The shape of the cost curves is a mirror reflection of the marginal product curve. When MP is rising, marginal cost is falling. When marginal product is at its maximum, marginal cost is at its minimum; and when MP is falling, marginal cost is rising. The shape of the AVC curve is also determined by the shape of the AP curve. Over the range of output for which the AP curve is rising, the AVC curve is falling; and over the range of output for which the AP curve is falling, the AVC curve is rising (figure 4.5a).

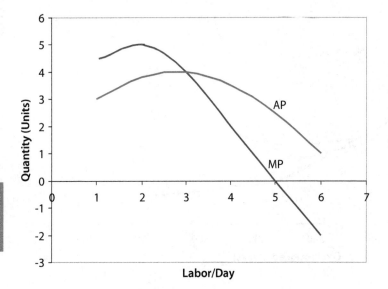

Labor	Marginal Product (MP) Qty/ Day	Average Product (AP) Qty/ Day
1	4.5	3
2	5	3.8
3	4	4
4	2	3.5
5	0	2.5
6	-2	1

Figure 4.5a
Average and
Marginal
Product

b. *Marginal and Average Cost Curves.* When the MC is less than the ATC (first segment of a downward sloping ATC curve), the average total cost is falling. Conversely, when the MC exceeds the ATC (second segment of the ATC curve), the average total cost is rising. At the intersection of the MC with ATC, the total cost curve is at its minimum point (figure 4.5b).

Cost $/ Unit	Output Qty/ Day	Marginal Cost $	Average Cost $
2	1	5	9
4	2	4	7
6	3	4.5	6
8	4	7	7
10	5	11	9

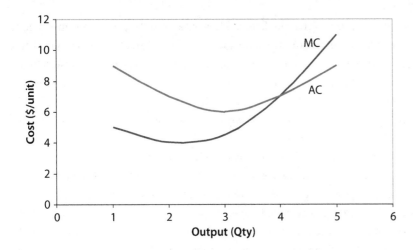

Figure 4.5b
Average and
Marginal Cost

d. *Shifts in the Cost Curves.* It is important to notice that changes in resource prices or technology will cause costs to change and cost curves to shift. If the price of variable inputs (labor) rose, AVC, ATC, and MC would rise, and those cost curves would shift upward. The AFC curve would remain in place because fixed costs have not changed. A change in price (decrease) of the fixed inputs shifts the AFC and ATC curves (downward) but leaves the AVC and MC curves unchanged.

e. A *Sunk Cost* is a cost that a firm or business has already paid or will pay in the future and will not be recouped. It should not have an effect on any current production decisions. In the short-run, the fixed cost has been paid and cannot be recovered. A sunken ship on the ocean floor is lost. This is why economists call these costs, a "sunk cost." These sunk costs should be disregarded.

Good advice for managers is to ignore any costs which are not associated with the decision. If the marginal benefit of the new decision is less than the marginal cost, a previous bad decision should not dictate steps moving forward. Here are two examples: a) if a business spends $100,000 on research and development of a product which turns out to be a flop and sells poorly, the loss cannot be recovered by losing still more money in continued production and is considered a sunk cost and b) when new menu items are introduced by McDonald's and are then abandoned because of their unprofitability, it is a typical example of unrecoverable loss—once again, the sunk cost.

6. SHORT-RUN VS. LONG-RUN COSTS: PRODUCTION DECISION VS. INVESTMENT DECISION

The *Short-Run Production decision* is affected by fixed costs. The decision that has to be made—how much output to produce with existing facilities—is the production decision, or the choice of how intensively to use available plant and equipment.

The most important factor in a short-run production decision is marginal cost. So MC is a basic criterion of short-run supply (production) decisions. The MC is an important indicator of the profitability of supplying more goods and may also determine short-run pricing decisions. If the marginal cost of producing exceeds the price at which is sold, it does not make sense to produce another unit and vice versa—as long as price exceeds MC, production should be expanded.

Figure 4.6
Short-Run and
Long-Run
Average Total
Cost Curves
(Source: Bade
and Parkin,
Foundations of
Economics, 5e.)

The *long-run* is a period of production during which the firm could vary all inputs used to produce a good and change the quantity of employed labor resources and the type and size of equipment and plant, etc. There are no fixed costs in the long-run, and the decision that a manager can make is an *investment decision*. Since there are no fixed costs, the Law of Diminishing Returns is not applicable in the long-run, total cost equals variable cost, and average total cost equals average variable cost. The long-run average total cost (LRATC) curve shows the lowest cost per unit at which a firm can produce any level of output after it chooses its desired number and size of plants.

Let's analyze what's happened with a firm's LRATC as a result of expansion operations that successively expand its capacities. Successively larger plants will lower average total cost, but, eventually, the building of a still larger plant may cause ATC to rise. The long-run firm's ATC curve is made up of segments of the short-run ATC curves for the various plant sizes. This curve is also called the firm's planning curve, and it is derived from the short-run average total cost curves. It shows the lowest average total cost at which any output level can be produced after the firm has had time to make all appropriate adjustments in its plant size. In Figure 4.6, the LRATC curve is represented by the darkened parts of the three short-run ATC curves.

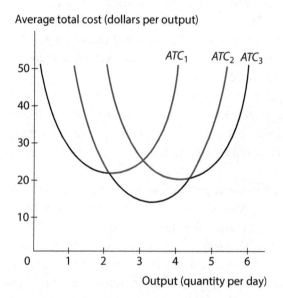

7. ECONOMIES OF SCALE AND DISECONOMIES OF SCALE

When a firm changes its size, its average total cost also changes: it might rise, fall, or remain the same. Accordingly, we can distinguish four different situations:

1. *Economies of scale,* or an *increasing return to scale,* which happens as increase in a firm's input generates an increase in output by a greater proportion. The main sources of economies of scale are:
   a. Labor specialization, which is more achievable with an increase of the size of a plant; this allows workers to work at fewer tasks and eliminates the loss of time.
   b. Management specialization, which is characteristic of larger firms. In contrast, small firms will combine the functions of marketing, personnel, and finance in one person, who often is also the firm's boss.

c. Efficient capital use, which, with effective use of robotics and assembly line equipment in mass production of automobiles, for example, results in considerable reduction of costs unaffordable for small firms.

d. Learning by doing, which can be combined with decline of the per unit cost of design, development, advertising (auto, computer, stereo system, etc.) as output increases.

2. *Constant return to scale* is a case when both a firm's inputs and its output are increasing by the same proportion.

3. *Diseconomies of scale:* A firm is experiencing a decreasing return to scale if output is increasing at a smaller rate than input increases. A firm which develops into a super large-scale producer becomes difficult to control and to coordinate its operations. The CEO of such a giant-sized firm cannot assemble, digest, and understand all the information essential to decision-making on a large scale. Authority must be delegated to many vice-presidents, second vice-presidents, and so on. Decision-making processes may be slowed down and inefficient and may not reflect changes in consumer tastes or technology. Workers may feel alienated from their employers and care little about working efficiently. With diseconomies of scale, an increase in all inputs, for example, by 20%, could lead to an increase in output of only 10%. As a result, the LRATC will increase, as well. Both economies of scale and diseconomies of scale occur in larger companies or corporations which are at first successful in lowering costs and realizing economies of scale. These companies can use smaller production units to decentralize decision-making and prevent diseconomies of scale.

8. INDUSTRY STRUCTURE AND MINIMUM EFFICIENT SCALE

Minimum efficient scale (MES) is the lowest level of output at which a firm can minimize long-run average costs:

1. In some companies or industries, MES can be attained with a small factory which produces apparel, food processing, furniture, wood products, snowboarding, or small appliances. This explains how relatively large and relatively small firms can coexist in some industries and be equally successful (the banking sector, for example) and even more efficient than big firms (retail trade, farming, clothing, shoe industry).

2. Some heavier industries can take advantage of economies of scale by using larger facilities. This helps the firms by spreading costs over an extending range of output. Some companies that do this produce automobiles, aluminum, steel, and other heavy industries.

3. In an extreme case, economies of scale might extend beyond the market size, resulting in what is defined as a natural monopoly—a relatively rare market situation in which average total cost is minimized when only one firm produces an entire volume of a particular good or service.

The LRATC is L-shaped. It is downward sloping at the firm's economies of scale, horizontal at the firm's constant returns to scale, and upward sloping at the firm's diseconomies of scale (table 4.6; figure 4.7).

Figure 4.7
Long-Run
Average Total
Cost Curve
(LRATC)

Output (Q)	Cost/unit ($)
10	50
30	25
50	25
70	25
80	25
100	50

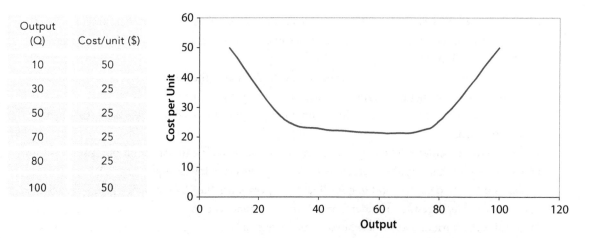

9. KEY TERMS

Technology; Business

Cost and Profit, Economic and Accounting Costs and Profits

Implicit and Explicit Costs

Production Function

Fixed and Variable Costs

Total, Average, Marginal Products

Total, Average, Marginal Costs

Sunk Cost

Short-Run and Long-Run Costs and Decisions

Economies of Scale, Diseconomies of Scale

Constant, Decreasing and Increasing Return to Scale, Minimum Efficient Scale

10. PROBLEMS AND APPLICATIONS

1. From this chapter, you learned that the production function reflects:
   a. A technological relationship between quantity of output and factor inputs,
   b. A technological summary of our capacity to produce a particular good.
   c. A technological relationship that expresses the productive efficiency of using limited resources.
   d. All of the above.
   e. None of the above.

2. The change in total output (in $$) resulting from one more unit of labor employed is:
   a. The opportunity cost of the good produced.
   b. The marginal physical product of labor
   c. The marginal revenue product of labor.
   d. The total quantity of good produced by labor employed.

3. A professor is explaining to students how to increase their income after graduation by being more efficient workers in any type of business. He tells them that they can do this by increasing their productivity which is measured by:
   a. Per unit costs of production.

b. Real output per unit of input, or per labor hours.

c. Changes in real wealth resulting from changes in price level.

d. The amount of capital and other factors of production used per worker.

4. The short-run is characterized by the following:

   a. All inputs are variable.

   b. The scale of operations can be changed by adding more fixed capital.

   c. The quantity of some factors of production cannot be changed.

   d. The strategic (investment) decision can be made.

5. A firm's economic profit is the:

   a. Sum of its revenue and costs of production.

   b. Difference between its total revenue and total explicit costs.

   c. Difference between its total revenue and total implicit costs.

   d. Price per unit times quantity produced minus sum of implicit and explicit cost.

6. To find the average total cost of a product, you should:

   a. Divide total cost by the quantity produced.

   b. Compute the change in total cost when the production is increase by one-unit of output.

   c. Divide the change in total output by the change in total cost.

   d. Multiply total output by total cost.

7. How is marginal cost calculated?

   a. Total cost divided by the total quantity produced.

   b. Increase in total cost resulting from one-unit increase in production.

   c. Cost of production remains constant while its rate changes.

   d. Market value of all inputs used to produce a good.

8. Which of the following represents economic cost?

   a. Explicit costs minus implicit costs.

   b. Dollar costs of production.

   c. Accounting cost minus explicit costs.

   d. The value of all resources used in production.

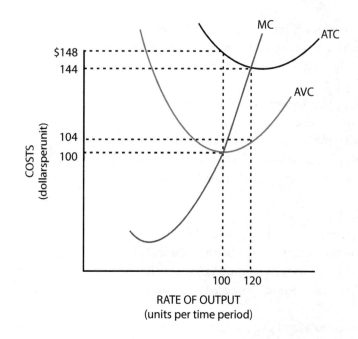

9. What is the change in total cost when the 400th unit of pizzas is produced in the above figure?
   a. $ 2.50
   b. $ 800.00
   c. $ 2.00
   d. $ 200.00

10. How do improvements in technology shift the production function?
    a. Upward shift because more resources are used in production.
    b. Downward because fewer inputs can now be used to produce any quantity of output.
    c. Downward because the marginal cost curves downward.
    d. Upward because the average total cost decreases, and the cost curves shift downward.

11. REVIEW QUESTIONS

1. How are Technology, Business, Cost, and Profit related?
2. Fill in the blanks with either "economic" or "accounting" to complete the following sentence: Because _____ cost usually exceeds _____ cost, _____ profit typically exceeds _____ profit.
3. Economically speaking, what are your explicit and implicit costs of being a University Student? Compute the amount for one year and four years.
4. Suppose you attend college 1,000 miles from your hometown and you have to decide whether to drive your car or fly back for Thanksgiving (You must get there either way!). Which costs—fixed, variable, or both would you take into account to make your decision? Explain your choice.

IMAGE CREDITS

CHAPTER 5

MARKET STRUCTURE: HOW "PERFECT" IS PERFECT COMPETITION?

1. PERFECT VS. IMPERFECT COMPETITION: FOUR MARKET MODELS

The goal of this chapter is to introduce you to the reality of competitive markets by examining:

1. the main components and types of market structures;
2. the perfectly competitive market and the competitive firm's production decision;
3. the determinants of supply behavior in a competitive market;
4. the competitive market's equilibrium and the entry to and exit from an industry; and
5. the main outcomes of a competitive market and the benefits of competition.

There are two segments of the market, perfect and imperfect, which incorporate four basic market models. At one extreme is perfect (pure) competition and at another, pure monopoly; in between are monopolistic competition and oligopoly. We can add here duopoly, as well—two firms that control the market. For economists, the category *competition* represents a state of affairs. The most important indicator of the degree of competition is the capacity of firms to control the price, called in economics the *market power*. It is determined by the number and relative size of firms in an industry, and it affects the behavior of producers and consumers and influences market outcomes.

2. MAIN CHARACTERISTICS OF PERFECT COMPETITION

A competitive market exists when the following conditions are present:

- There are very *large numbers of independently acting firms*—buyers and sellers—operating in national (local, regional) or international markets (stock markets, foreign exchange markets, farm markets, etc.), and no one has a market power.
- All market participants have *access to full and complete information* on the state of affairs in the market (prices, product quality, reliability, integrity, etc.).
- Sellers are offering a product viewed by buyers as *identical, or homogenous* (wheat, corn, fish, gold, etc.).
- Economic actors in this market are "*price takers,*" which means that no one can change the market price resulting from the interaction of market demand and market supply; they can only adjust to existing prices.
- Resources could be easily moved from industry to industry since *there are no legal, technological, financial, or other barriers to entry and exit* in these markets.

When all these conditions exist, we have a "perfectly competitive market" composed by the interaction of millions of "perfectly competitive firms." The essence of perfect competition can be expressed in a few words: optimal allocation of resources and zero economic profit in the long-run.

Pure competition is rare in the US economy, and there are just a few industries close to this type of market. But this basic model has been useful to economists for about a century for at least three reasons: 1) it helps analyze industries with characteristics similar to perfect competition, for example, markets for agricultural goods, fish products, foreign exchange, basic metals, and stock shares, etc.; 2) it provides a concrete context for application of revenue, profit, price, and cost concepts developed in previous chapters; and 3) it provides a norm or standard to compare and assess the efficiency of other forms of market structures in the real world.

The main objectives of our analysis of pure competition are: 1) examination of demand from the seller's point of view; 2) explanation of a competitive producer response to market price in the short-run; 3) analysis of the nature of long-run adjustment in a competitive industry; and 4) evaluation of the efficiency of competitive industries.

3. PROFIT MAXIMIZATION IN THE SHORT-RUN

Let's consider, first, how the competitive firm makes a production decision, keeping in mind that the firm's objective is maximization of economic profit, which, as we saw in the previous chapter, is the difference between total revenue (TR) and total cost (TC). Because a perfectly competitive firm has no control on price, it must choose only the rate of output that it should produce. This is the essence of its *production decision,* which is determined by the firm's interest in *maximizing its revenue* and, respectively, *economic profit.* What appears to be a price per unit for a buyer is also revenue per unit or average revenue of a seller.

To analyze how the firm makes its production decision, we have to distinguish: a) *the market demand* for a product, which is shown in the *downward sloping* market demand curve (figures 5.1a and b) and b) the individual *demand of a particular firm,* which is reflected in a *horizontal* individual demand curve (figure 5.1b). Changes in its output are so insignificant for the market that it does not influence the market equilibrium. So, the demand curve of the competitive firm is perfectly elastic. An entire industry (all firms producing a particular good) can affect price by changing industry output. But the individual firm cannot do that.

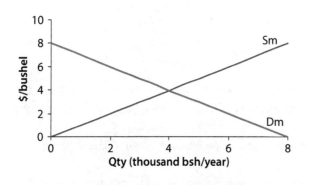

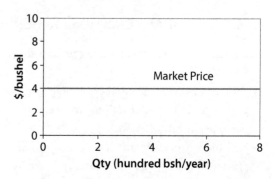

Figure 5.1a Market Demand and Supply for Corn

Figure 5.1b Demand for Individual Farmer

We need also to revisit the revenue and costs concepts:

1. Total Revenue is computed by multiplying the quantity sold by price per unit (P):

$$TR = P \times Q; \text{ Total Cost: } TC = \text{Total Fixed Cost} + \text{Total Variable Cost}$$

2. Marginal Revenue (MR) is the change in total revenue resulting from selling one more unit of a product:

$$MR = \Delta TR/\Delta Q; \text{ Marginal Cost: } MC = \Delta TC/\Delta Q$$

3. Average Revenue (AR) for a seller is the same as the price per unit for the buyer and is reflected in the average revenue schedule and demand curve:

$$AR = TR/Q; \text{ Average Total Cost: } ATC = TC/Q$$

Take into consideration that the main goal of a competitive firm is to *maximize* not the TR but *the total profit: TP = TR – TC.*

Another way to compute profit is to express it in terms of average total cost: TP = TR – TC = P × Q – TC.

We can rewrite the equation by dividing both sides by Q: TP/Q = (P × Q)/Q – TC/Q = P (price) – ATC; So TP = (P – ATC) × Q, which is the difference between price and average total cost multiplied by quantity sold.

How can a firm maximize its total profit in the short-run?

There are two approaches to determine at what level of output the firm can maximize profit (or minimize loss). We have to compare a) total revenue and total cost and b) marginal revenue and marginal cost. These approaches are applicable to all models of market structure. But, first, we need to address the following questions: a) should the firm produce? b) If so, how much? and c) what will the profit or loss be?

1. *Total revenue—total cost approach.* TR for each output level is found by multiplying output (total product) by price. TR (upward sloping supply curve) and TC are equal where the two curves intersect each other at two break-even points (table 5.1; figure 5.2).

    At the first point, A (at the lower intersection along the TR curve), TR does not cover the TC, and the firm is experiencing losses. The situation will be similar if the firm extends production beyond the second break-even point—B (at upper intersection). Only in the segment between two break-even points will the firm produce an economic profit. So, the firm achieves maximum profit where the vertical distance between the total revenue and total cost curves is the greatest. We can conclude that in the short-run, the firm:

    a. Should produce if TR exceeds TC; the outcome is profitable (between A and B).

    b. Should produce that output at which it maximizes its profit (the largest vertical difference between the two curves, point C).

    c. The profit or loss can be found by subtracting total cost from total revenue at each output level.

    d. Should close if its loss exceeds its fixed costs.

Qty	Price ($/unit)	Total Revenue (TR)	Marginal Revenue	Total Cost	Marginal Cost	Average Variable Cost	Average Total Cost	Total Profit	Table 5.1 Short-Run Profit Maximization
		Qty* Price	ΔTR/ΔQ	Fc+Vc	ΔTC/ΔQ	AVC	ATC = TC/Q	TR–TC	
0	$50	0		60		0	60	–60	
1	$50	50	50	110	50	50	110	–60	
2	$50	100	50	124	14	32	62	–24	
3	$50	150	50	140	16	27	47	10	
4	$50	200	50	152	12	23	38	48	
5	$50	250	50	160	8	20	32	90	
6	$50	300	50	175	15	19	29	125	
7	$50	350	50	193	18	19	28	157	

Table 5.1
Short-Run Profit
Maximization
(Continued)

Qty	Price ($/unit)	Total Revenue (TR)	Marginal Revenue	Total Cost	Marginal Cost	Average Variable Cost	Average Total Cost	Total Profit
		Qty* Price	ΔTR/ΔQ	Fc+Vc	ΔTC/ΔQ	AVC	ATC = TC/Q	TR–TC
8	$50	400	50	215	22	19	27	185
9	$50	450	50	240	25	20	27	210
10	$50	500	50	268	28	21	27	232
11	$50	550	50	300	32	22	27	250
12	$50	600	50	350	50	24	29	250
13	$50	650	50	460	110	31	35	190
14	$50	700	50	650	190	40	46	50
15	$50	750	50	860	210	53	57	–110

Figure 5.2
Total Revenue
and Total Cost

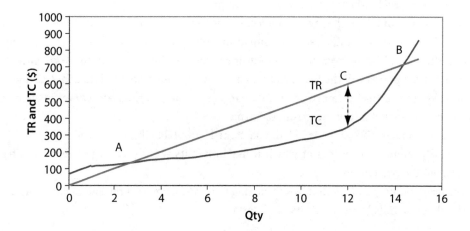

2. *Marginal-revenue—marginal cost approach.* The Marginal Principle analysis is an important analysis tool for a firm. It states: increase the level of an activity if marginal revenue (benefit) exceeds its marginal cost, but reduce the level if the marginal cost exceeds the marginal revenue. In the short-run, the firm will maximize profit or minimize loss by producing the output at which MR equals MC (as long as producing is preferable to shutting down). This profit maximizing guide is known as the MR = MC rule. This rule applies to all types of market structures, to any firm that intends to maximize its profit. For a perfectly competitive firm, which has no power to set the price, the rule can be restated as the P = MC = MR rule. Since the firm is a price taker, its marginal revenue is, de facto, the existing market price (table 5.1; figure 5.3).

Now we can formulate the conclusion for *short-run profits maximization*: *profits are maximized at the rate of output where price equals marginal cost* (P = MC). In other words, there are three concrete situations that affect the production decision of a competitive firm:

- *P > MC.* The additional revenue from selling another unit exceeds the additional cost of producing this unit, so the firm **should increase its output rate** to maximize its profit.
- P < MC. The additional cost of producing one more unit exceeds the additional revenue from producing one more unit, so *the firm should reduce its output rate* to minimize its losses.

- *P = MC.* The additional cost of producing another unit equals the additional revenue from producing this unit, so the firm's profit is maximized at this level, and *it should maintain its output rate.* In the figure, the firm maximizes its profit by producing *q*.

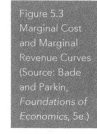

Price and costs (dollars per unit)

Quanitity (units per month)

Figure 5.3
Marginal Cost
and Marginal
Revenue Curves
(Source: Bade
and Parkin,
Foundations of
Economics, 5e.)

We can restate these criteria in terms of revenue and cost per unit of output, or average total cost: a firm is receiving profit if its average total cost of production is less than the market price and vice versa; a firm is unprofitable if the market price is less than its average total cost. So, if:

- P > ATC, the firm is operating with a profit;
- P < ATC, the firm is losing money; and
- P = ATC, the firms breaks even; this price at which economic profit is zero is called the break-even price.

Respectively, the firm's short-run equilibrium differs in good times (table 5.3, figure 5.4) and in bad times (table 5.3, figure 5.5). It is important to note that a producer never seeks to maximize per-unit profits. He or she is looking for maximization of total profits. Total profits are maximized only where p = MC.

Q	VC ($)	AVC ($)	TC ($)	MC ($)	ATC ($)	P₁	P₂	P₃
			VC + FC	ΔTC/ΔQ	TC/Q	MR₁	MR₂	MR₃
0	$0	$0	$15	$0	$15	$20	$18	$14
1	$14	$14	$30	$30	$30	$20	$18	$14
2	$16	$8	$32	$2	$16	$20	$18	$14
3	$27	$9	$43	$11	$14	$20	$18	$14
4	$40	$10	$56	$13	$14	$20	$18	$14
5	$55	$11	$71	$15	$14	$20	$18	$14
6	$78	$12	$94	$23	$16	$20	$18	$14
7	$105	$15	$121	$27	$17	$20	$18	$14
8	$144	$18	$160	$39	$20	$20	$18	$14

Table 5.2
Average Costs,
Profitability, and
Market Price
(revenue) for a
Firm Producing
T-Shirts

SHORT-RUN EQUILIBRIUM IN GOOD TIMES

Figure 5.4 illustrates a perfectly competitive firm that is earning an economic profit. The firm produces 4 units, has a price of $20 per unit, and earns an economic profit equal to the area of the darkened rectangle ($40).

Figure 5.4
Short-Run
Equilibrium in
Good Times

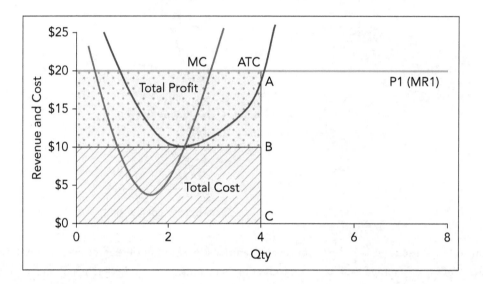

SHORT-RUN EQUILIBRIUM IN BAD TIMES

Figure 5.5 illustrates a perfectly competitive firm that is suffering an economic loss. The firm produces 4 units, has a price of $10 per unit, and incurs an economic loss equal to the area of the darkened rectangle ($20).

Figure 5.5
Short-Run
Equilibrium in
Bad Times

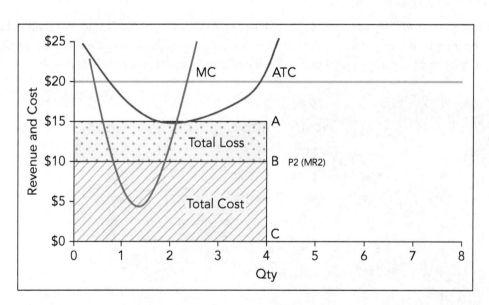

SHORT-RUN EQUILIBRIUM IN NORMAL TIMES

In normal times, the firm is operating at the point where average total cost equals price—$15 *break-even price*—and the firm is earning only normal profit, which is the management salary and part of the cost. Its economic profit is zero, according the formula: Total Profit = Price – ATC (Fig. 5.6).

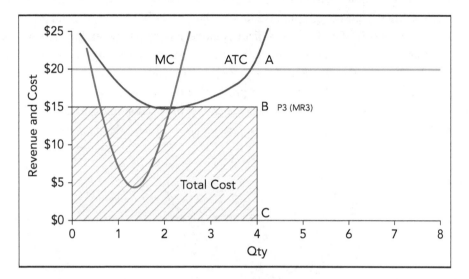

4. LOSS MINIMIZATION IN THE SHORT-RUN

The question is: How long should the firm continue to operate? To operate or shut down is a short-run decision. The answer is: until the benefits of operating (MR) will exceed or equal the cost of operating, or the firm's total variable cost. *The shut-down price* is the price at which the firm is indifferent between operating and shutting down. The firm could operate an unprofitable facility because it has already paid or agreed to pay fixed costs that are de facto sunk costs and should not influence the firm's production decision. The reason is simple: the firm will lose less money if it continues operating. The fixed costs should be paid in the short-run whether the firm is producing or not, but at least it can save variable costs by not producing in bad times (figure 5.5).

What are three features of this rule?

1. MR must be equal to or exceed minimum average-variable cost or the firm will shut down.
2. The rule doesn't just apply to companies with pure competition but also to those in any type of industry.
3. In purely competitive industries, the firm should produce that output where P = MC = MR. When a competitor would rather produce than shut down, it should produce at that point where price equals marginal cost (P = MC). This will ensure that the firm maximizes its profit or minimizes its loss.

5. SHORT-RUN SUPPLY CURVES

In Chapter 2, we defined *supply* as the ability and willingness to produce specific quantities of a good at alternative prices in a given period of time. This category is reflected in the supply schedule (table) and curve—the relationship between market prices and the amount of the goods that producers are willing to supply at alternative prices in a given period of time. We also defined *the Law of Supply*—there is a positive or direct relationship between price and quantity supplied: as prices rise, the quantity supplied rises; as prices falls, the quantity supplied falls.

What are the main determinants of a firm's supply? For perfectly competitive firms that are price takers, their only decision is how much output to produce at given prices. Their supply behavior is determined by the profit maximization rules where the most important decision is to ensure the balance of MC and price (MC = P). We can define the *short-run supply of an individual firm* as the relationship between the price of a product and the quantity of output supplied by a firm in the short-run. So, *the short-run supply curve for a competitive firm is its marginal cost curve above the shut-down price,* and this tells us how much output a firm will supply at different prices (Fig. 5.7a). Below the shut-down price, the firm's TR will not cover its total variable cost. The essential idea is: to maximize profits, a firm will expand its production until it reaches the output where its marginal cost has risen to the level of its marginal revenue, which is also the market price: MC = MR = P.

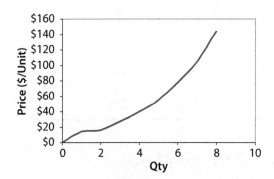

According to our assumption, the competitive firm is operating in a perfectly competitive market, and therefore, we need to review the sum of the supply (or marginal cost) curves of all firms operating in the market. This will give us the market supply curve. *The market (industry) supply* represents the total quantities of a good that sellers in the respective industry are willing and able to sell at alternative prices in a given period of time. *The short-run market supply curve* shows the relationship between price and the quantity of output supplied by all of an industry's firms in the short-run (figure 5.7b). As we know from Chapter 2, market supply is determined by:

- the price of resources—factor inputs;
- changes in technology available to produce a good;
- expectations (especially in changes in prices); and
- the number of sellers or the firm in the industry.

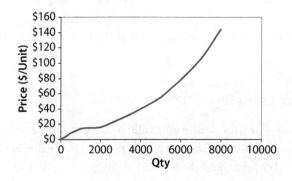

6. LONG-RUN SUPPLY CURVES: INCREASING-COST AND DECREASING-COST INDUSTRIES

Companies have the time to change their fixed factors of production in the long-run which can help decrease their costs or even to liquidate them. In this case, the market price will be reached at the point where competitive firms earn only a normal profit. This sounds a little bit strange, and it is quite difficult to find examples of this principle in action. It should be mentioned that for business decisions, the process of adjustment toward the equilibrium point is much more important than the equilibrium itself. To understand the conditions that motivate market entry and exit in the long-run, we need to consider the following arguments: a) the earlier the firms enter in the market, the better chances they have for an economic profit; b) to be successful, the firms already operating in the market should find opportunities to produce at the average total cost, below that of their competitors; and c) firms that are not capable of conforming to these requirements may try to compete on the basis of differentiation of their product. So, to reach a long-run market equilibrium, there are three necessary conditions:

1. quantity of supplied product equals the quantity demanded;
2. each firm maximizes its profit at a given market price in a given time; and
3. each firm in the market earns "0" economic profit (its total revenue is just enough to cover all its costs), and there is no incentive for other firms to come into the market.

The *long-run market supply curve* demonstrates the relationship between the market price and the quantity supplied by all firms in the long-run (figure 5.8). There are three types of industries with different shapes of the long-run supply curve:

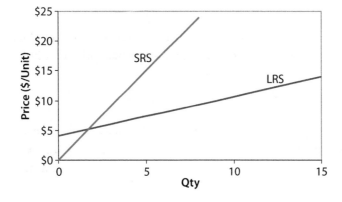

1. *Constant-cost industry*—an industry in which the typical firm's average costs remain the same as the industry expands (orange and apple industries). In such an industry, the long-run supply curve will be perfectly elastic (horizontal). Expansion or contraction does not affect resource prices or production costs; the entry or exit of companies into the market will affect quantity of output. The price will revert back to the equilibrium (figure 5.9); the condition is that the industry should be a small part of the respective input market, and its expansion does not have a big effect on this market to influence the prices.
2. *Increasing-cost industry*—an industry in which the average cost of production increases as the total output of the industry increases (sugar industry, rental housing); they have positively sloped

(upward-sloping) long-run supply curves (figure 5.10); there are two reasons for the increased average cost as the industry grows:

a. increasing input prices since the industry competes with other industries for a limited amount of various resources; and

b. involvement of fewer productive inputs; as the industry grows, firms may be forced to use less productive resources.

Figure 5.9
Long-Run
Supply Curve
in a Constant
Cost Industry

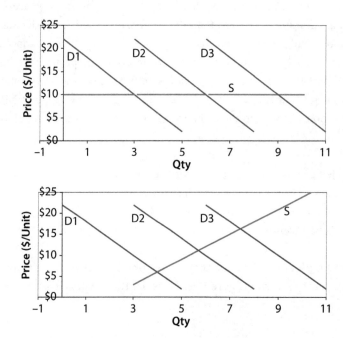

Figure 5.10
Long Run
Supply Curve in
an Increasing
Cost Industry

3. *Decreasing-cost industry*—an industry in which the average cost of production declines as the industry expands (computers, microchips); their long-run supply curve is downward sloping.

We can make two main conclusions here:

a. Entry of new firms expands the market supply and eliminates economic profits.

b. Exit reduces the market supply and eliminates losses. In such a way, the competition reflected in the entry and exit of firms eliminates economic profits or losses by adjusting the price to equal minimum long-term average total cost.

The industry is in **Long-Run Equilibrium** or "at rest" when there is no tendency for firms to enter or to exit. The firms will earn only normal profit that is part of their cost and will earn no economic profit. Let's consider two situations related to the short-run and long-run effects of changes in demand that affect the equilibrium (figure 5.11):

a. *Short-run effects* of an increase in demand. When demand increases, the market demand curve (D1) shifts to the right (D2). At a new quantity (Q2), the price exceeds the average total cost, and the typical firm is making profit. This is an incentive for new firms to enter the profitable market and to compete for customers' demand until the economic profit is driven to "0."

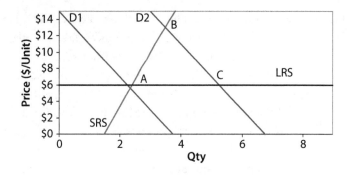

Figure 5.11
Price of a Bag
of Ice (A) Before
Hurricane
Katrina; (B)
Immediately
After; and (C) in
the Long Term

b. *Long-run effects* of an increase in demand. When demand increases in the short-run, firms will increase the quantity produced from their existing facilities, but this option is limited by the Law of Diminishing Returns. As we have already learned from previous chapters, in the long-run, there are no diminishing returns; new firms will enter the industry and build new factories, and that's why the long-run supply curve (S) is relatively flat in an increasing-cost industry.

To make the transition easier from short-run to long-run (for example, in the case of natural disasters like Hurricane Katrina, which created a situation of price gouging—higher prices for scarce goods), the government should leave prices to be regulated by the market and make it easier for entrepreneurs to enter the market. In the real world, it is not so easy for new firms to enter into profitable industries since these industries are protected by patents, brand loyalty, control of basic factors of production, price controls, and various other barriers.

7. HOW EFFICIENT AND FAIR IS PERFECT COMPETITION?

Perfect competition is probably the most efficient type of market structure for the following reasons:

First, the most efficient resource allocation in a market is the one which society values most highly, and the use of resources is the most efficient when the marginal benefit equals the marginal cost of producing a good or service.

In a perfectly competitive market equilibrium, the quantity demanded equals the quantity supplied. The demand curve is the same as the marginal benefit curve, and the supply curve is the same as the marginal cost curve, so at the competitive equilibrium, the marginal benefit equals the marginal cost, and there is no other allocation of resources that will generate greater benefits to society. Figure 5.12 shows that resources are efficiently used at the equilibrium quantity of 500 units.

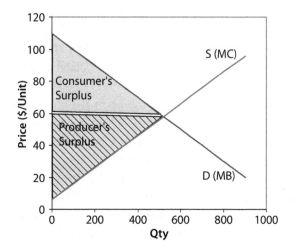

Figure 5.12
Efficiency of the
Perfectly
Competitive
Market

Second, fairness and equality of opportunity are achieved for the society as a whole in the long-run when any businesses are free to enter and exit the market, consumers and producers are maximizing their benefits, called in economics, consumer's and producer's surplus, and there is no deadweight loss—wasted resources—since marginal benefit (MB) equals marginal cost (MC). The consumer's surplus is the area between the MB (Demand) curve and the price, which is also marginal revenue (MR) for a perfectly competitive industry. The producer's surplus is the area between price (MR) and the marginal cost (MC) curve, which is also the supply curve.

Third, strong competition encourages technological progress and adoption of new cost-saving technology and equipment. It takes time for a new technology to spread throughout an industry, but those firms that adopt the new technology, lowering their costs and increasing their supply, have better chances of surviving in harsh competition. Conversely, firms that use old technology incur economic losses and are threatened by bankruptcy (about 50,000 annually) have lower chances of surviving.

The long-run equilibrium will have the same basic characteristics; it does not matter what kind of industry we have (constant-cost, increasing, or decreasing cost):

1. *Productive efficiency*—requires goods to be produced in the least costly way and occurs in situations where *P = minimum ATC*; at this point, firms are using the least-cost technology they need to survive;
2. *Allocative efficiency*—requires that resources be distributed among firms and industries to satisfy society's optimal combination of goods and services and occurs where *P = MC*; price is society's measure of relative worth of a product; and
3. In the long-run, a perfectly competitive market equilibrium is a multiple equation:

$$P \text{ (and MR)} = MC = \text{Minimum ATC}$$

8. VIRTUES AND IMPERFECTIONS OF PERFECT COMPETITION

In conclusion: the profit-motivated, perfectly competitive firms produce each good or service to the point where price (marginal benefit) and marginal cost are equal, and society's resources are being allocated efficiently. A distinctive advantage of competitive markets is their ability to restore efficiency when disrupted by changes in the economy by abrupt recessions, supply shocks, and natural disasters. Adam Smith's "invisible hand" is at work in a competitive market system. The competitive system not only maximizes profits for individual producers but, at the same time, creates a pattern of resource allocation that maximizes consumer satisfaction. These virtues could be summarized as follows:

1. High profits in a particular industry are a clear signal for entrepreneurs about consumers' wants. Low entry barriers and competition for profits result in capital mobility and production of more goods at better quality.
2. Maximum efficiency in the use of limited resources is the result of both productive efficiency (P = Minimum ATC—requires goods to be produced in the least costly way) and allocative efficiency (P = MC—requires resources to be apportioned among firms and industries to produce society's optimal combination of goods and services).
3. Although economic profits are driven to zero by market forces, the zero profit situation is rare. The pattern of a competitive market can be described as follows:
   a. High prices and profits are a consumer's signal for wanted goods and services.
   b. Economic profits attract new firms that increase production.

c. The market supply curve shifts to the right.

d. Prices moves down the market demand curve.

e. At a new equilibrium point, the average costs of production are at or near the minimum, and economic profits approach zero.

f. Producers are forced to reduce cost in order to maintain their profits which leads to product and technological innovation.

g. Competitive firms must continually improve technology, improve their product, and reduce costs to survive in competition.

4. Economic losses are also of social value—they signal to producers that they are not using society's scarce resources in the best way. The dog-eat-dog character of competitive markets often serves as the target of criticism, but society is aspiring to the best-possible mix of output produced in the most efficient way. The government should protect and maximize competition by dismantling entry barriers and allowing new entrants into an industry.

This perfect competition model has been useful to economists to test their theoretical findings and practical applications of economic concepts and notions for about a century. Of course, this model is not "perfect," and its use comes with some costs to our economic understanding. "The development of this model has obscured the institutional framework of a functioning economic system, has overlooked the dynamic of the market, and most importantly, has overlooked the entrepreneur and ignored the entrepreneurial adjustment process, which is at the center of market economies' vibrancy, economic growth, and prosperity" (*The Economic Way of Thinking*, p. 214).

9. KEY TERMS

Market Structure

Perfect and Imperfect Competition

Maximizing Total Revenue and Total Profit

Total Revenue-Total Cost

Marginal Revenue-Marginal Cost

Shut Down Price

Constant-Cost, Increasing-Cost and Decreasing-Cost Industries

Productive Efficiency

Allocative Efficiency

Consumer Surplus

Producer Surplus

10. PROBLEMS AND APPLICATIONS

1. A perfectly competitive firm is characterized by the following:

a. Is a price maker and has the market power.

b. Is considered a price taker and could not dominate the market price.

c. Is not large relative to the market but has brand loyalty.

d. Confronts a downward-sloping firm demand curve.

2. A competitive market is composed of interactions of large numbers of perfectly competitive firms and has:
   a. A downward-sloping demand curve.
   b. A horizontal demand curve.
   c. A selling price determined by a few leading firms in the market.
   d. All of the above.
   e. None of the above.

3. To maximize profit, a perfectly competitive firm should:
   a. Produce the rate of output that minimizes average total cost.
   b. Produce the rate of output where average product equals average total cost.
   c. Produce the level of output where price equals marginal cost.
   d. Charge the highest price possible for each unit produced.

4. To compute the profit per unit, we need to:
   a. Deduct average total cost from the price.
   b. Divide the average total revenue by average total cost.
   c. Subtract total cost from total revenue.
   d. Multiply total quantity produced by the price and divide by total cost.

5. In which situation is economic profit equal to zero?
   a. Price of a product is greater than its marginal costs.
   b. Price falls to minimum average total cost.
   c. Price of a good is higher than average variable cost.
   d. New firms enter an industry.

6. A competitive market will exist with the following conditions:
   a. There is a large number of firms, and each one has insignificant control over the price of its product.
   b. A small firms exit from the market leaving higher profits for large firms.
   c. In the long run, the firms receive only zero economic profit.
   d. Marginal revenue equals marginal cost, and never the price.

Figure 5.13

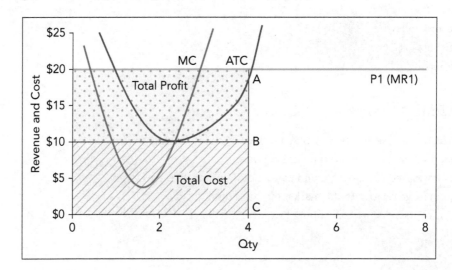

7. At the $15 in the long-run in the figure above:
    a. The firm will produce the quantity at which *MC* equals *MR but not P*.
    b. Total revenue equals average total cost.
    c. Firms will exit from the market since prospects for profit disappear.
    d. Firms will enter the market since there are still possibilities for profit.

8. In a perfectly competitive market, as firms exit:
    a. The market supply curve shifts to the right, and prices fall.
    b. Profits decrease for firms that are still operating in the market.
    c. Equilibrium output decreases for the market, and profit might appear with increased price.
    d. All of the above.
    e. None of the above

9. As a result of an increase in productivity in a perfectly competitive market:
    a. Average total cost and marginal cost curves shift downward.
    b. Average total cost and marginal cost curves shift upward.
    c. Quantity supplied decreases and the market price increases.
    d. The firm will supply less output.

10. Suppose you are a manager of a perfectly competitive appliance store that can sell 100 dishwashers per week at $500 each. In order to sell one more dishwasher, you should:
    a. Increase the price above $500.
    b. Decrease the price, and sell it for less than $500.
    c. Sell it for $500.
    d. Cannot sell an additional dishwasher at any price since the market is in equilibrium.

11. REVIEW QUESTIONS

1. List the main market models and their brief characteristics. Under which of these models (structures) below do the following businesses and industries most accurately fit? Explain and justify your classifications
    a. Key Food, a supermarket in your hometown
    b. Con Edison, an electric company
    c. the Town Bank, the commercial bank in which you have an account
    d. General Motors, the automobile industry
2. As you learned in this chapter, a perfectly competitive firm _____ (has/has no) power to alter the market price of its products; is a _____ (price maker/price taker); and confronts a _____ (horizontal/downward sloping) curve.
3. If perfect competition is relatively rare in real economy, then why it is important to study it?

CHAPTER 6.

MONOPOLY, PRICE DISCRIMINATION, AND ANTITRUST REGULATION

1. MONOPOLY STRUCTURE AND BEHAVIOR

The case of a perfect competition is very important, but it is only one case. The real world—in America, Europe, and Asia—contains significant mixtures of monopoly imperfections along with elements of competition and is, for the most part, classified in the realm of "imperfect competition": it is neither perfectly competitive nor perfectly monopolistic. In the words of Paul Samuelson, "'Imperfect competition' prevails in an industry or group of industries wherever the individual sellers are imperfect competitors, facing their own nonhorizontal demand curves and thereby having some measure of control over price" (Samuelson, 485).

The **monopoly**—the opposite extreme of perfect competition in the market structure—is a single firm that is the only seller of a particular good or service that does not have a close substitute in a market with blocked entry; the monopoly has market power and is **a price maker**. In the US, there are relatively few monopolies, and they are mostly local utility companies where the firm is the "only game in town": natural gas, electric, cable TV, etc. On the national level, there are the National Basketball Association, the National Football League, Intel, First Data Corporation, and a few others that could be considered "near monopolies" rather than pure or perfect monopolies. On an international level, the International Nickel Company of Canada dominates the nickel market supply (90%).

The word "*monopoly*" came from two Greek words: "*monos*"—"single" and "*polis*"—"to sell." The notion **monopoly** is extraordinarily ambiguous. For everyone and no one it is a sole seller, depending on how we define the commodity being sold. For example, McDonald's is the sole seller of "Big Macs," but is McDonald's a monopoly when there are a lot of fast-food substitutes such as Wendy's, Burger King, White Castle, Taco Bell, Pizza Hut, etc.?

2. HOW MONOPOLY ARISES

Let's try another approach. In the early nineteenth century, there was often no distinction made in the US between a monopoly and a corporation. Corporations had always been created by special governmental acts. The Crown and the British Parliament before the American Revolution, or the state and national legislatures afterward, issued special "patents" called "grants of monopoly" or corporate charters. They gave to one party a power that was withheld from others. In 1600, for example, Queen Elizabeth I chartered the East India Company and provided it with monopoly power over Britain's trade with India. The company was even given the right to coin money, to make peace and war with non-Christian powers and, of course, to make fabulous profits trading with Indian goods, such as cotton, silk, tea, and spices. The East India Company's special privilege of selling tea in the colonies, given to it in 1773, *volens-nolens* (like it or not), led to the "Boston Tea Party" and helped bring on the American Revolution. Another classical example is the De Beers diamond syndicate, a South African corporation created in 1880 by Cecil Rhodes, a British businessman, that consolidated all South African diamond producers into one company and, by 1889, controlled almost the entire world's production of diamonds. Through its Central Selling Organization (CSO), headquartered in London, it controlled 80% of all diamonds sold in the world. But "are diamonds forever"? The British East India Company was abolished in 1858, ending its monopoly on trade. De Beers closed its CSO in 2001 and proclaimed a new strategy of being "the diamond supplier of choice."

Thus, the word *monopoly* has contemporary relevance as well as historical significance. Let's examine what a monopoly is and why it is the only firm that is selling a particular good or service.

First, a monopoly is a single seller of a product that has no close substitutes and that could not be re-sold. In the real world there are few, if any, products that have no close substitutes. The US Postal Service, for example, monopolizes first-class mail, but it has a substitute, the fax machine, that, in its turn, has its own substitute—e-mail. How "close" substitutes are depends on the situation. If a firm could ignore the actions of other firms and all the other firms' prices, then it has a monopoly.

Second, a monopoly is a firm that is producing the entire volume of market supply and has the *market power*—the ability to alter the market price of a good or a service.

When Henry Ford designed the famous Model "T" in 1908 "for the common man"—a cheap, reliable, and as easy to drive "as the horse and buggy" car—he was the producer that dominated the market. He applied his market power when he abruptly increased the price of a car by $100 (12%) to finance a new assembly line factory at Highland Park. At that time, he could dictate the price, color, and other characteristics of the car Americans would buy. But it did not last for long. The most important thing is that a monopoly is an industry that obliterates the distinction between industry demand and the demand curve of the firm: the demand curve of a firm (monopoly) is identical to the market demand curve for a specific product.

Third, a monopoly does not face competition from other firms because it is protected by blocked entry to a respective industry. These barriers should be high enough to keep out competitors and may be provided for the following reasons:

1. The government grants a *patent* to a firm or an individual—an exclusive right for twenty years to produce a new product, or *copyrights,* to the author of a book, film, or music that will protect a creator and his or her heirs' exclusive right for seventy years after the author's death;
2. The government grants a *public franchise,* making a firm an exclusive legal provider of a product, for example, a sole provider of water, natural gas, or electricity.
3. *Control over an input or technique.* A famous historical example is Alcoa's control over bauxite ore supplies necessary to produce aluminum, which allowed it to monopolize the sale of aluminum from the late nineteenth century until the end of WWII. Another example is the control over large stadiums by professional sports leagues—a key resource for professional sports, such as Major League Baseball, the National Basketball Association, the National Football League, etc.
4. *Network externalities*—the usefulness of a product directly depends on the number of customers that use it—are viewed by economists as serious barriers to entry. For example, the Microsoft program Windows has a 95% share of the market for personal computers; eBay is the most attractive place for selling and buying collectibles, antiques, and other products.
5. *Economies of Scale,* where larger companies are more profitable because they can spread the fixed costs over a larger amount of product, reducing the average total cost and driving smaller companies out of business. This leads to a *natural monopoly* when one firm can supply the entire market volume at a lower cost than could two or more firms. Some examples are electricity transmission companies, cable TV, and water systems.

3. PROFIT MAXIMIZATION: MONOPOLY PRICE AND MONOPOLY PROFIT

To address this question—the most important characteristic that distinguishes monopoly from perfect competition—we have to revisit a few notions.

First, let's define a *monopoly:* a single firm that produces the entire volume of market supply of a good or service in an industry and has the ability to dictate its price—it has a market power. In contrast with competitive firms that have to reduce the costs of production and improve quality to survive in harsh competition, a monopolist sets its own rule by charging higher prices and receiving bigger profits. A monopoly is an industry that obliterates the distinction between industry demand and the demand curve of the firm; its demand curve is identical to the market demand curve for a specific product and is downward sloping (for a perfectly competitive firm, it is horizontal).

Second, the demand curve shows us the highest price consumers are willing to pay for a specific quantity of output. Note that there is only one price compatible with the profit-maximizing rate of output—point M on the demand curve—which tells how much consumers are able and willing to buy at a specific price ($8, point M in figure 6.1)

Unit Sold (Q)	Price ($)	Total Revenue	Marginal Revenue
		TR = PQ	MR = ΔTR/ΔQ
0	14	0	
1	12	12	12
2	10	20	8
3	8	24	4
4	6	24	0
5	4	20	−4
6	2	12	−8

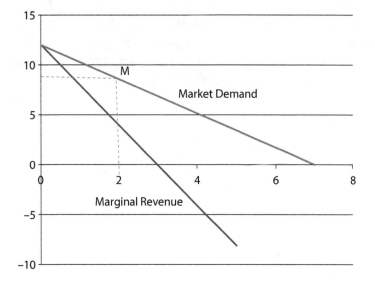

Figure 6.1
Demand Curve and Marginal Revenue Curve of a Monopoly

Third, how does the monopoly set the price for a product and maximizes its profit? We have to remember that in a perfectly competitive market, a firm maximizes its profit at the rate of output where price equals marginal cost: P = MC. The monopoly, in contrast, looks at the contribution to total revenue of an additional unit of output which is called *marginal revenue (MR)*. The *MR is the difference between the total revenues received before and after a one-unit increase in the rate of production or the change in total revenue that results from selling one more unit of output.* In the case of a monopoly, the demand curves—market and individual—are the same, and a monopolist can sell an additional unit of a product only if it reduces prices. For example, a firm (monopoly) could sell a unit of its product at $5,000, and its total revenue (TR) would be 1 × $5,000 = $5,000; to sell another unit it should reduce the price. The TR after price reduction would be: 2 × $4,000 = $8,000; the difference = $8,000 − $5,000 = $3,000 represents the MR of selling an additional unit. Since a monopolist firm must cut its price to sell more product, its MR is always less than price (P), and the marginal revenue curve always lies below the demand curve at every point, with the exception of the first.

But a monopolist in search of a profit maximizing rate of output is following the general **profit maximization rule**: MR (how much more revenue an additional unit brings in) = MC (what an additional unit costs to produce). In the case of a perfectly competitive firm, the profit maximization occurs where MC = MR = P.

A monopolist is looking for the rate of output at which marginal cost equals marginal revenue (figure 6.2).

The point of intersection of the MR and MC curves indicates the profit-maximizing rate of output. So, we have two opposing effects as described by Paul Krugman: a) a *price effect*—to sell another unit, the monopolist should reduce the price of all units (from $5,000 to $4,000 per unit) which decreases the total revenue (by $1,000) and b) a *quantity effect*—an additional unit sold increases the total revenue (from $5,000 to $8,000).

Fourth, let's look how at how a monopoly picks a quantity and price to maximize its profit.

1. It calculates profit per unit: P – ATC.
2. Total profit = profit per unit times quantity sold. A monopoly looking for a profit maximization output should increase the quantity produced as long as the MR exceeds the MC. In Figure 6.2, we have two cases: 1) P – ATC1, the profit maximizing rate of output (at the intersection of MR and MC curves, point A) is 4 units. The price charged by the monopoly per unit is shown on the demand curve—BSo, the profit per unit (segment A–B) is $16 and the total profit is $16 × 4 = $72 and 2) P – ATC2, which is the loss minimization case, = $5, and total losses: $5 × 4 = $20. The company is experiencing losses since the average total cost (ATC2) exceeds the price, all other things remaining the same. It is important to mention that a monopoly is not seeking to maximize the price or to maximize the profit per unit. Its goal is to maximize the total profit. However, there is no guarantee that, in the long-run, a monopoly will receive the profit even with the existence of barriers to entry in its respective industry. Weak demand and/or high costs could change the objective from profit maximization to loss minimization (as shown in figure 6.2b, case 2, with ATC2 higher than the market price).

Table 6.2 Profit Maximization for a Monopolist

Demand	Output	Price Per Unit	Total Revenue	Marginal Revenue	Marginal Cost	Average Total Cost 1	Average Total Cost 2	Profit	Losses
D	Q		TR	MR = ΔTR/ΔQ	MC	ATC1	ATC2	P = TR – ATC 1	L = TR – ATC2
76	0	75	0	0	0				
66	1	68	68	68	50	75	75	–7	–7
56	2	63	126	58	17	46	58	80	68
46	3	56	168	42	12	39	49	129	119
36	4	50	200	32	10	25	47	175	153
26	5	44	220	20	20	20	46	200	174
16	6	38	228	8	25	21	58	207	170
6	7	32	224	–4	33	21	69	203	155
	8	25	200	–24	40	23	80	177	120
	9	19	171	–29	50	30	92	141	79
	10	12	120	–51	60	40	101	80	19

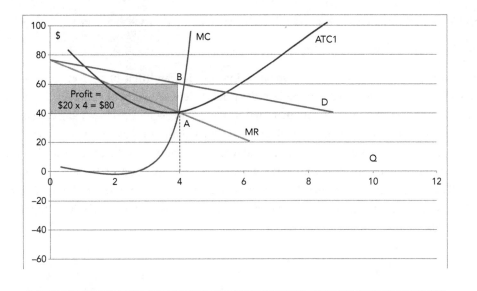

Figure 6.2a
Profit
Maximization

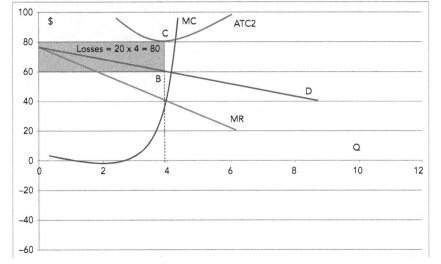

Figure 6.2b
Loss
Minimization

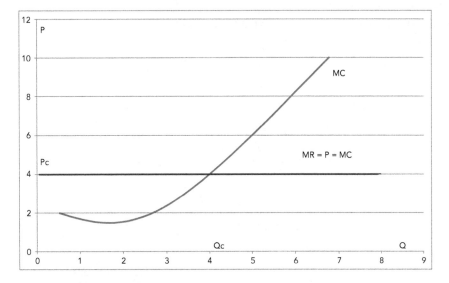

Figure 6.3a
Perfectly
Competitive
Firm: Profit
Maximization

4. ECONOMIC EFFECTS AND CONSEQUENCES OF MONOPOLY: MONOPOLY VS. COMPETITION

The difference between a monopoly's profit maximizing decision and that of perfect competitor's is shown in Figures 6.3 (a and b). For a perfect competitor, the price is determined by the market demand and market supply, and it is the horizontal curve where marginal revenue (MR) equals price (P) and equals marginal cost (MC). This is the only market structure for which this triple equation is applied. For a monopoly, the profit maximizing decision is on the intersection of MR and MC with quantity produced indicated on the horizontal axis (Q, the line drawn from the intersection MR and MC to the horizontal axis) and price charged—on the vertical axis (P, shown by the line drawn from demand curve above the intersection of MR and MC to the vertical axis). As you can see, a monopoly is always producing less output and charging a higher price than a perfect competitor.

Figure 6.3b
Monopoly:
Profit
Maximization

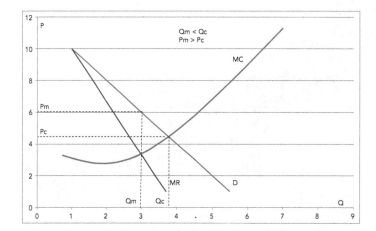

In previous chapters, we developed the idea of economic surplus (consumer's and producer's surpluses), which characterize the efficiency of a perfectly competitive market; the equilibrium results in maximization of surplus for both consumers and producers to the benefit of society as a whole. Let's see what happens to economic surplus in a monopoly market.

To address this question, we have to look, first at the **consumer surplus** (figure 6.4a):

Figure 6.4a
Consumer and
Producer
Surpluses
in a Perfect
Competition

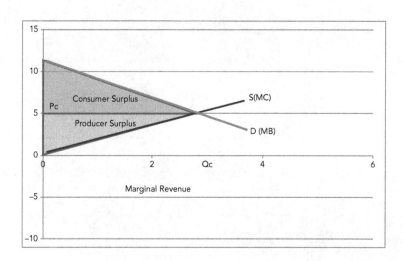

The consumer surplus is the difference between the maximum amount a consumer is willing to pay for a product (indicated by the points on the demand curve, which is also the marginal benefit curve) and the real price that he or she pays for it (shown by the points on the marginal revenue curve for a perfectly competitive industry). The producer's surplus is the area between the price (MR) and the marginal cost (MC) curve, which is also the supply curve. Knowing the price of a good or a service that everyone is paying, we can compute the total consumer surplus by adding up all consumers' individual surpluses. To examine what society will pay for monopoly behavior, let's consider the transition from a perfectly competitive market to a monopoly and explain how the consumer's surplus will change in this transition (figure 6.4b).

1. The switch to a monopoly will increase the price per unit of a product from Pc to Pm. In our example, triangle A is a consumer surplus that shrinks from a bigger initial triangle (ABC) in the case of a perfect competition.
2. This switch to a monopoly will lead to a decrease in quantity produced (from Qc to Qm) because of higher prices and less consumer demand at such prices.
3. The loss of consumers is the sum of rectangle B, which is a net gain of a monopoly, and triangle C, which, along with the triangle D, represents the so called *deadweight loss from a monopoly* and is not offset by a gain to anyone—a wasted resource and an *economic cost* for society as a whole.
4. The *social cost of monopoly* might exceed the deadweight loss it creates because of **rent seeking**, which is any attempt to capture consumer surplus, producer surplus, or economic profit. This can happen when an individual or a firm try to find the opportunity to buy a monopoly for a price less than the monopoly's economic profit. This also happens when an individual seeks to lobby the government to restrict competitors. The resources used up in rent seeking are a cost to society that adds to the monopoly's deadweight loss.

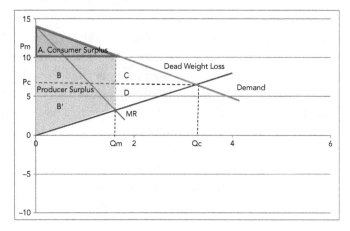

Figure 6.4b
Consumer and
Producer
Surpluses in a
Monopoly

The conclusion is that the monopolist produces less output and charges a higher price than a perfectly competitive market does. Obviously, monopoly is inefficient. The inefficiency may be caused by a government-sanctioned monopoly through various legal barriers to entry in an industry (licensees, franchises, and natural associations). In this case, we have to deal with a rent seeking that is a lobbyist's persuasion of legislators and other policymakers to grant a monopoly power and to erect barriers to entry. Firms in some industries spend up to one third of their revenues to get monopoly power.

Up to this moment, we analyzed a single-price monopolist's behavior that charges the same price for all consumers. To understand how the monopoly converts consumer surplus into its profit, let's have a look at the practice of price discrimination.

5. PRICE DISCRIMINATION

Price discrimination occurs when companies sell different units of a good or service at different price points. This practice converts consumer surplus into economic profit. To be able to price discriminate, at least three conditions should be present:

1. The firm must have some control over the price of a product it is producing—market power. Clearly, a perfectly competitive firm, which is a price taker and faces a horizontal market demand curve, cannot be engaged in price discrimination.
2. The firm should be able to identify and separate different types of consumers based on their sensitivity (responsiveness) to changes in prices, measured by the price elasticity of demand and their different degree of willingness to pay for a good.
3. The firm must sell a product that cannot be resold because resale will break down the price discrimination. In other words, it should be impossible or too costly for consumers to engage in *arbitrage*—a practice of earning profit by buying at a low price and reselling at a higher price.

There are three types of price discrimination:

First, discriminating among different categories of consumers. A firm selects and charges different customers' different prices for the same product. Groups with a higher average capacity to pay are charged a higher price, and groups with a lower average capacity to pay are charged a lower price. The most frequent case that most travelers encounter regularly involves airline tickets. Business travelers, who have a high average willingness to pay and often make last-minute reservations, are charged a higher price than students, who have a low average willingness to pay and often make reservations in advance. For example, business travelers can afford a $2,000 ticket from Los Angeles to Miami while a student will take a plane if the price does not exceed $500, and he or she is able to make the reservation in advance.

Second, discriminating between units of a good. A firm charges a higher price for the first unit purchased and a lower price for second, third, and other units purchased. An example is pizza delivery where the first large pizza costs $12, the second pizza is priced at $6 or three medium pizzas are priced at $10.

Third, perfect price discrimination. A firm is able to sell each unit of a good for the highest price anyone is willing to pay for it. The price of each unit is the same as the unit's marginal revenue, so the firm's (downward sloping) demand curve becomes the same as its marginal revenue curve. Output increases to the point where the demand (equals marginal revenue) curve intersects the marginal cost. In this case, a monopoly produces the efficient quantity of a good and the deadweight loss is eliminated. The firm's economic profit is the greatest, and consumer surplus equals zero because the firm captures the entire surplus. So, the greater the number of prices a monopoly charges, the bigger the quantity of consumer surplus extracted with a variety of prices, including the lowest possible price. In Figure 6.5, note a) price discrimination with different prices (per trips); b) sales to three categories of travelers; and c) perfect price discrimination.

The technique of price discrimination includes a variety of strategies: a) discounts on airplane tickets: lower prices for those who purchase well in advance or for travelers who spend a weekend between flights, and higher prices for last-minute purchases; b) discounts by grocery stores and restaurants (coupons): lower price for a larger volume or for senior citizens and higher prices for purchase of one unit or for regular buyers; c) manufacturers' rebates for appliances; and d) student discounts on movies, concerts, and sports events, etc. The price discriminating firm is increasing the efficiency of the market in comparison with a single price monopoly. It includes consumers with lower willingness to pay and increases total surplus extracted from consumers. At the same time, price discrimination could create serious equity problems—ambulance service, for example, being linked to the severity of an emergency and is likely to be prohibited.

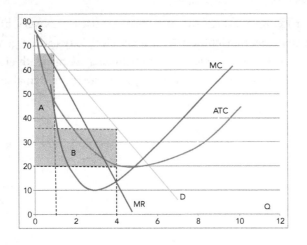

Figure 6.5a
Price
Discrimination
with Different
Prices (Per Trips)

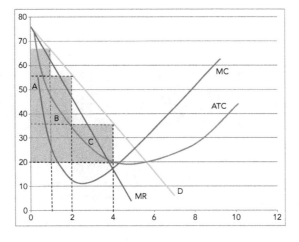

Figure 6.5b
Sales to Three
Categories of
Travelers

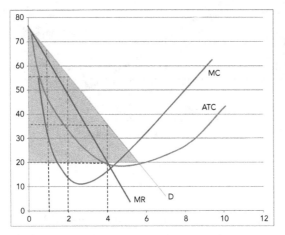

Figure 6.5c
Perfect Price
Discrimination

6. THE CASE OF NATURAL MONOPOLY

A natural monopoly is defined as a single large firm that due to economies of scale produces the entire market supply at a lower average total cost and more efficiently than any larger number of smaller firms. Natural monopolies occur in industries where fixed costs are extraordinarily high relative to variable cost, and marginal costs are exceptionally small. Local telephone, cable, and utility services are classic examples of natural monopolies. For example, a firm that produces electricity has very high fixed costs because of substantial investments in equipment, machinery to produce electricity (power generators), and in cable and wires to distribute it (transmission lines). Once these investments are made, the marginal cost of producing an additional kilowatt-hour is very small. A natural monopolist uses the marginal principle to pick a price and quantity (figure 6.6a).

Price	Quantity	Demand	MR	Average Total Cost
1	1		5.5	10
2	2	7.2	5	4
3	3	6.4	4.5	2.5
4	4	5.6	4	2
5	5	4.8	3.5	2.2
6	6	4	3	4
7	7	3.3	2.5	6
8	8	2.5	2	
10		1	1	

Figure 6.6a
Price, Cost
and Profit with
One Firm

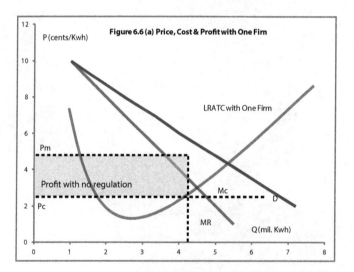

The firm produces at the point where long-run MC will equal MR. The difference between the price and long-run ATC is a monopoly profit per unit, and by multiplying it by the quantity produced, we can compute the total profit. The question is: What will happen if a second firm enters the market controlled by a natural monopolist? The new demand curve with two firms will switch to the left because they will share the market; the price will decrease to a level less than long-run ATC; and the profit will disappear (figure 6.6b). So, the second firm will not enter the market. With three, four, and more firms in this market, average cost will become even higher, and they could face only the prospect of economic losses. It should be mentioned that a natural monopoly in absence of regulation could charge almost any price it wants (the minimum price will be indicated on the demand curve by the intersection of the marginal cost and marginal revenue curves—Pm). That's why the government tries to prevent, eliminate, or regulate monopolies by enforcing antitrust policy.

Figure 6.6b
Price, Cost,
and Losses with
Two Firms

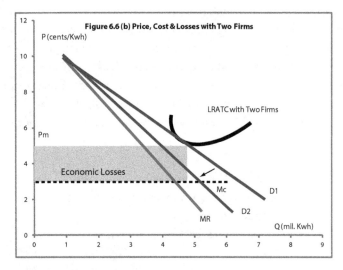

7. NATURAL MONOPOLY AND THE DILEMMA OF REGULATION

Fortunately, monopolies are not widespread in the economy. Technological progress erodes monopolies' power. For example, the US Postal Service's monopoly power was successfully limited by the invention of fax-machines, e-mail, and Skype. Cable Internet and television companies are challenged by satellite TV. Nevertheless, government policies have always been used to alter market structure and prevent abuse of market power. In the United States, this policy started to be used after the Civil War, in 1870s–80s, and is called *Antitrust Policy.* We will examine this issue in more detail in section 9 of this chapter, but in this chapter, the subject of our analysis will be the natural monopoly regulation dilemma. What kind of public policy should be chosen to prevent natural monopolies from charging the highest prices for their products?

There are two options: a) *Public Ownership:* Publicly owned companies, such as Amtrak, the US Postal Service, and utility companies, have some advantages—they can set prices based on the efficiency principle rather than profit maximization—and disadvantages—poor performance in reducing costs and providing high-quality products and b) *Price Regulation,* which has three approaches (figure 6.7):

Figure 6.7
Monopoly
Regulation:
What Price to
Choose?

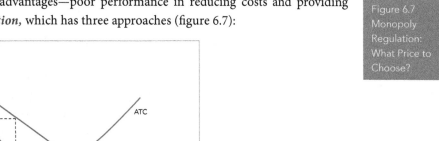

First, the socially optimum price—*marginal cost pricing rule,* which sets price equal to marginal cost, $P = MC$. In the figure, the firm sets a price of P_{mc} and produces Q_{mc}. The rule leads to efficient production since it maximizes the total surplus in the industry and corresponds to public interest. But the firm incurs an economic loss because $P < ATC$, and it is not going to stay in business for long;

Second, an *average cost pricing rule,* which sets price equal to average total cost, $P = ATC$. In the figure, the firm sets a price of P_{atc} and produces Q_{atc}. This could lead to inefficient production because there is a deadweight loss. But the firm earns a normal profit because $P = ATC$, which permits it to stay in business.

Let's consider this rule in more detail. The government picks the lowest price at which the market demand curve intersects the long-run average cost curve. Under this regulatory policy, the monopolist's production cost will not be affected because the government will adjust the regulated price to keep it equal to the average cost. Therefore, average cost policy will cause a movement along the demand curve in two steps:

1. Downward movement from the higher price and lower quantity of output of an unregulated monopoly to the lower price and bigger quantity of output of a regulated monopoly until it will not affect the monopolist's production cost.
2. Upward movement if the monopolist's cost of production is increased by the government regulation.

This is the explanation of the apparently paradoxical situation when a decrease in demand does not lead to a decrease in price. Any decrease in quantity of a good produced by a government-regulated monopoly will lead to a higher average cost of production. With average cost pricing, the higher the average cost, the higher the regulated price.

However, it is not easy to implement these rules because the regulator does not know the firm's real costs. So regulators often use two practical pricing rules:

- *Rate of return regulation* (fair-return price), which sets the price at a level to allow the regulated firm to earn a specified target percent return on its capital. The shortcomings: the managers of a regulated firm have an incentive to inflate its costs for their benefit.
- A *price-cap regulation,* which specifies the highest price the firm is permitted to set—a price ceiling. This gives managers an incentive to minimize costs and earn an economic profit. Usually, the price cap regulation requires *earnings sharing regulation*: profits above a target level must be shared with the customers.

8. COULD MONOPOLIES BENEFIT SOCIETY?

If monopolies are so bad, why do they still exist? Yes, monopolies charge higher prices and produce less. Yes, monopolies misallocate resources by choosing the rate of output to maximize their profit (MR = MC) and not the socially desired optimum (P = MC). Not all economists believe that monopolies are as bad as it appears as compared with perfect competition. Joseph Schumpeter, an Austrian economist, who served for many years as an economics professor at Harvard University, praised monopoly power as a generator of technological change, unleashing a "gale of creative destruction" by inventing new products that drive the older ones out of the market. John Kenneth Galbraith, a well-respected American economist, politician, and diplomat, believed that monopoly profit provides financial strength to invest and innovate which is crucially important for technological progress.

HOW COULD MONOPOLIES BENEFIT SOCIETY?

First, monopolies can invest in *research and development (R&D).* These monopolies are sheltered from the constant pressure of competition, from the "rat race" of technological change. They have sufficient resources for expansive R&D. Although monopolists can obtain a clear financial advantage from R&D, they have no clear incentive to pursue it. They often prefer to make substantial profits just by maintaining market power.

Let's consider the case of the patent as a measure to protect a monopoly's power and incentive for innovation. The potential challenger for a monopoly's business should take into consideration three factors before making a decision to enter in such an industry: 1) the cost of research and development; 2) the estimated annual profit from a monopoly granted by a patent; and 3) the time required to develop and produce its own product. Usually, there is a tradeoff between benefits and costs associated with this situation:

1. on the cost side, a monopolist is producing less output than a perfectly competitive market and at a higher price; and
2. on the benefit side, a patent or a license is an incentive for a firm that can lead to the development of new products.

Second, *entrepreneurial incentives.* There is no such person as an entrepreneur who does not aspire for a greater profit prize that could one day bring monopoly status.

Third, *economies of scale,* which represent reductions in minimum average costs that come about through increases in the size (scale) of plant and equipment. The paradox is that there is an inverse effect here: increasing the size (scale) of a plant may reduce operating efficiency and can generate diseconomies of scale, and production costs may be higher than for a competitive industry.

Fourth, *natural monopolies,* if well regulated, can supply an entire market at lower average total cost than two or more firms.

In today's real world, pure monopoly is as rare a phenomenon as is perfect competition. In between the monopoly (no competition) and perfect competition there are:

1. Fewer relatively large firms producing differentiated products in retail and service industries (books, clothing, etc.). This structure is called *monopolistic competition.* It is similar to pure competition except that it is characterized by differentiated products and nonprice competition (a strategy that distinguishes their products). We refer to this market as monopolistic because firms are able to exercise some market power through differentiation of their products,
2. *Oligopoly* is an industry in which only a few firms exist. Each of these firms is affected by the price output decisions of its rivals. An oligopolistic industry is dominated by a few large sellers that supply all or most of a particular product: IBM, Apple, Compaq, etc. IBM supplies 70% of business computers but only 10% of personal computers. Other examples include gasoline stations and fast-food outlets. Oligopoly also characterizes the production of automobiles, aircraft, large electrical generators, and steel; oil refining; and certain types of computer hardware and software. These firms are represented on the *Fortune 500* and the *Business Week Global 100;*
3. *Duopoly*—two firms supply a specific product and dominate the market. A classic example is Coca-Cola and Pepsi, which produce nearly 75% of soft drinks.

Altogether, these three models represent a segment of the market called imperfect competition.

9. ANTITRUST POLICY

Antitrust law provides a way in which the government may influence resource allocation in the marketplace and regulate or prohibit certain kinds of market behavior, such as monopoly and monopolistic practices. *A trust* is an arrangement under which the owners of several companies transfer their decision-making power to a small group of trustees, who make the decisions for all participant firms.

After the US Civil War, in 1870s–1880s, a few dominant firms, called trusts—business combinations that assign control to a single decision group ("trustees")—established their control over several industries: petroleum, meatpacking, railroads, sugar, lead, coal, whiskey, and tobacco. Farmers and small businesses were particularly vulnerable to such monopolistic price dictatorships and were among the first who opposed them. Later on, they were joint by consumers, labor unions, etc. The mechanism of monopoly behavior is quite simple in essence: in the perfect market environment, P = MC; in contrast, a monopolist maximizes profit when MR (not price) = MC; prices are artificially maintained at higher than the marginal costs level as a result of such under-allocation of resources; and society pays more for a particular good or service. To prevent such monopolistic behavior, the government, first, established public regulatory agencies and, second, enacted antimonopoly (antitrust) legislation design to inhibit or prevent the growth of monopoly.

There are three main laws that pursue this goal:

1. *The Sherman Act* was the first antitrust law and was passed in 1890. It was surprisingly brief and consisted of two main provisions: "*Section 1*. Every contract, combination in the form of a trust or otherwise, or conspiracy, in restraint of trade or commerce among the several states, or with foreign nations is declared to be illegal" and "*Section 2*. Every person who shall monopolize, or attempt to monopolize, or combine, or conspire with any person or persons, to monopolize any part of the trade or commerce among several states, or with foreign nations, shall be deemed guilty of a felony." The Sherman Act outlawed restraints of trade (collusive price fixing and dividing the market) as well as monopolization. Firms that violate this act are subject to fines up to $1 million, and consumers may recover damages. A firm's executives may be subject to imprisonment.

2. *The Clayton Act of 1914* has a principal goal of preventing the development of monopolies, and its four sections were designed to strengthen the Sherman Act: *Section 2* outlaws price discrimination when it is not justified by cost differences and reduces competition; *Section 3* prohibits tying contracts together (when a producer requires that a buyer purchase another of its products); *Section 7* prohibits the acquisition of stocks of competing corporations when it reduces competition; and *Section 8* prohibits the formation of interlocking directories (when the director of one firm is also a member of the board of a competing firm). The Clayton Act made illegal specific business practices if the practices "substantially lessen competition or create monopoly." Practices outlawed include price discrimination, tying arrangements, requirements contracts, exclusive dealing, territorial confinement, acquiring a competitor's shares or assets, or becoming a director of a competing firm.

3. *The Federal Trade Commission* was formed in 1914 to look for "unfair methods of competition and unfair or deceptive business practices." The FTC has the power to investigate unfair competition and enforce the antitrust laws.

There are a few subsequent acts: a) the *Robinson-Patman Act of 1936* which strengthens the price discrimination provisions of the Clayton Act and was the result of pressure by small independent grocery stores to make it difficult for large grocery chains to lower prices; b) The *Wheeler-Lea Act of 1938* gave the FTC the additional responsibilities of policing "deceptive practices in commerce"; c) The *Celler-Kefauver Act of 1950* amended the Clayton Act in *Section 7* by prohibiting a firm from merging with a competing firm by acquiring its stock. The Clayton Act now prohibits anticompetitive mergers; and d) *The Hart-Scott-Rodino Act (1976)* imposed a premerger notification requirement on large firms (where the acquiring firm has $100 million in assets and $10 million in annual sales).

There are two main schools of thought regarding the interpretation of antitrust laws: a) the main purpose of antitrust laws, according to the first school, is economic efficiency and lowering of costs and b) according to the second school, their main purpose is to protect smaller firms regardless of the effects on efficiency.

Three Antitrust Policy Debates: most economists agree that price fixing is illegal, but other practices generate debate:

1. *Resale price maintenance* occurs when a manufacturer agrees with a distributor on the price at which the product will be resold. Agreements between a manufacturer and distributors are illegal, but it is legal for a manufacturer to force a distributor to accept guidance.
2. *A tying arrangement* is an agreement to sell one product only if the buyer agrees to buy another, different product. A tying arrangement sometimes allows manufacturers to price discriminate.
3. *Predatory pricing* is setting a low price to drive competitors out of business with the intention of setting a monopoly price when the competition is gone. Economists are skeptical that predatory pricing occurs frequently because unless there is some barrier to entry, the predatory firm is unable to charge a monopoly price after the competition is eliminated.

There are two particularly interesting cases of government intervention to relate. The first case concerns AT&T, in which the government charged AT&T with violating the Sherman Act by engaging in anticompetitive practices to maintain its monopoly position. In 1982, AT&T agreed to be split into twenty-two independent regional companies. The second example is the case of Interstate Bakeries (the third largest wholesale baker) which tried to buy Continental Baker (the maker of Wonder Bread) in 1995, but the Department of Justice concluded that this merger would lead to higher prices on bread. Some other examples of government intervention into price fixing include:

a. GE/Westinghouse (1961)—the case resulted in a $2 million fine and imprisonment of thirty corporate executives for fixing the price for electrical generators.
b. Infant formula (1993)—the three major producers of this product (95% of the market) paid $200 million to wholesalers and retailers to settle lawsuits claiming that they had conspired to fix prices.
c. Airline pricing (1994)—the nation's major airlines used advanced price listing to fix ticket prices which cost consumers $1.8 billion.

10. KEY TERMS

Monopoly
Price Maker
Price Effect, Quantity Effect
Price Discrimination
Social Cost of Monopoly
Public Ownership
Price Regulation
Marginal Cost Pricing Rule, Average Cost Pricing Rule
Rate of Return Regulation, Price-Cap Regulation, Earning Sharing Regulation
Research and Development (R&D)
The Sherman Act, The Clayton Act

11. PROBLEMS AND APPLICATIONS

1. From this chapter, you learned that the demand curve facing the monopoly is:
    a. Flatter than in a competitive market.
    b. Always placed below *MR*.
    c. Used to determine the rate of output.
    d. The same as the market-demand curve.

2. What do a monopoly and a competitive market have in common?
    a. Maximize profit at the same production levels and at the same price.
    b. Earn the same economic profits, and incur the same economic losses.
    c. A goal of maximizing profit is the driving force of businesses.
    d. Achieve production and allocative efficiency at the profit-maximizing rate of output.

3. How we can identify the price charged by a monopolist?
    a. The price is indicated on the vertical axis where *MR* = *MC*.
    b. It is the price on the demand curve above the intersection where *MR* = *MC*.
    c. The price is compatible with the minimum of the average total cost curve.
    d. The price is on the average cost curve below the point where *MR* = *MC*.

4. What is the definition of a market structure in which a single firm can achieve economies of scale and produces the entire market supply at a lower average total cost?
    a. Perfectly competitive
    b. Monopolistic competition
    c. A contestable market
    d. A natural monopoly

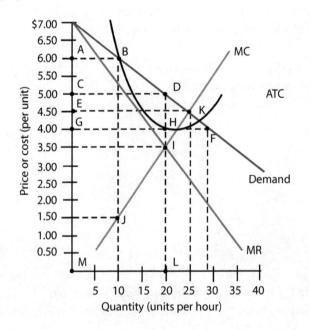

5. In the figure on page 114, a profit-maximizing monopolist will charge a price of:
   a. $4.0
   b. $5.0
   c. $6.0
   d. $8.0

6. Which of the following is true for a monopoly?
   a. It produces more output than a competitive firm.
   b. A monopoly charges a higher price than a competitive firm.
   c. A monopoly earns a zero economic profit in the long-run.
   d. A monopoly is producing a product that can be resold.

7. The marginal revenue curve of a monopolist is placed at a position:
   a. Lower than the demand curve and less than price since a monopolist is a price taker.
   b. Higher than the demand curve and above price because the firm is a price maker.
   c. The same as demand curve and always equal to price.
   d. Below the demand curve and less than price because to sell more output, the firm must reduce the price on all products sold.

8. Price discrimination is a practice when:
   a. Any firm in the market can discriminate by charging a higher price for its product
   b. Only firms that sell high-priced products can discriminate.
   c. A monopoly must sell a product that cannot be resold since the resale will break down the price discrimination.
   d. Price discrimination is always and everywhere illegal and cannot be practiced.

12. REVIEW QUESTIONS

1. Suppose you are the owner of the only coffee shop on a college campus, and you have an exclusive license to serve the college. Which of the following will offer you monopoly power: a) economies of scale; b) inelastic demand; c) government licenses; d) patents; Explain.

2. Suppose you are the manager of the only bookstore on the same college campus, what would be the price you charge for a particular new book (the publisher's recommendation is $100 per book)? How much would you pay students for this same book in used condition? How much would you charge when you resell it? Would you now be interested in encouraging the market for used books?

3. In 1908, Henry Ford, produced his famous Model "T" car, an inexpensive "motorcar for the multitudes." Soon after, he abruptly increased the price of a car by $100, or by 12%, to finance a new factory in Highland Park. He also decided to paint all his cars black, ignoring his executives' suggestions to attract more customers by diversifying the colors of cars. His statement became famous: "Give them any color they want so long as it's black," and he lost a significant share of the market. How would you explain Henry Ford's behavior?

4. Why is a monopolist's marginal revenue curve always_____ (greater/less) than price? To increase its revenue and sell more units of a good, a monopolist should _____ (increase/decrease) the price. To maximize the profit, a monopolist will produce a quantity indicated on the demand curve by the intersection of _____ (marginal revenue/marginal cost; marginal cost/price) curves.

5. An all-you-can-eat restaurant is charging you $10 for your meal and has 20 customers at this price. The slope of the demand curve is 0.20 per meal, and the marginal cost of providing a meal is $4. What price will correspond to the marginal pricing principle and maximize the restaurant's profit?

MONOPOLY, PRICE DISCRIMINATION, AND ANTITRUST REGULATION   115

CHAPTER 7

MONOPOLISTIC COMPETITION: QUALITY, PRICE, AND MARKETING

Let's start with a simple example: McDonald' slogan, "I'm lovin it." Everyone on a college campus recognizes it. And there is something to be said for its Big Mac. But to what kind of market structure should we attribute McDonald's? Is McDonald's a monopoly? Some may consider this fast-food giant a monopoly since "nobody does it like McDonalds's," which was another popular slogan not long ago. But wait a minute. Just across the street there are Wendy's, Burger King, Taco Bell, Pizza-Hut, and some Chinese, Mexican, Italian carryouts that offer a whole list of substitutes to Big Macs. So, McDonald's is not a monopoly? Is it a competitor? In fact, it is a monopolistic competitor—a market structure that combines elements of both of these extremes and probably coming closer to the Perfect Competition model than to a monopoly. The model of monopolistic competition was first elaborated on in the 1930s by two well-known economists: E. H. Chamberlin and Joan Robinson. In *Economics and Public Purpose*, John Kenneth Galbraith, an economist at Harvard, estimated that about 50% of private production comes from industries that are competitive or monopolistically competitive and another 50—from monopolies and oligopolies.

1. MONOPOLISTIC COMPETITION: MAIN CHARACTERISTICS AND BEHAVIOR

Perfect competition and pure monopoly are abstractions—models that explain how market forces influence price and quantities, how firms choose profit maximizing rates of output. In the real world, markets can be found somewhere between these two extremes, in the realm of imperfect competition with more than one competing seller, not with an individual seller who would have some degree of market power. Monopolistic competition is such a kind of hybrid market structure, with characteristics of both pure competition and monopoly, much closer to the first rather than to the second. It involves a small amount of monopoly and a large amount of competition. Competition is based on price, quality, location, service, and advertising. Oligopoly, in contrast, involves a large amount of monopoly power and a small amount of competition.

Monopolistic competition exists when many sellers compete to sell a slightly different product in a market with almost free entry and exit, and the demand curve facing an individual competitor is quite elastic; it is more elastic than the demand curve for a monopoly, but it is not perfectly elastic as in the case of a perfect competitor. It is characterized by:

1. A *relatively large number of sellers* that offer goods which are similar but not exactly the same. Each company acts independently and has a small percentage of the market. There are so many firms that collusion is practically impossible.

2. *Product differentiation* gives the individual company some slight monopoly that a purely competitive firm does not possess: a) products may be different due to physical attributes (qualitative), with each seller's product having unique qualities or characteristics that cause some buyers to prefer it to competing firms' products; b) services accompanying the sale represent an important aspect of product differentiation (personal computers differ in terms of speed, storage capacity, graphic displays, and included software); c) another type of differentiation could be attributed to location; d) yet another to brand names and packaging, trademarks, and celebrity connections; e) and product differentiation allows producers to have some control over the prices of their products. It is necessary to mention that the control of monopolistic competitors over price is quite limited.

3. With monopolistic competition, *firms can enter and exit their industries relatively easily.* This is similar to pure competition. Monopolistic competitors are usually small firms with low capital requirements and a few features of economies of scale, and they are particularly common in the service industry (restaurants, gas stations, grocery stores), but they also exist in some manufacturing industries (jewelry, leather goods, kitchen cabinets, etc.).

4. *Nonprice competition* is a particularly important characteristic of monopolistic competition and is related to a situation when firms compete by using advertising, packaging, product development,

quality, and services instead of (or in addition to) reducing the prices of their products. The role of advertising and product differentiation is to make price less of a factor in consumer purchases and make product differences a greater factor. There are some controversies about the social role of advertising. Proadvertising supporters believe that it a) helps consumers make better decisions by reducing search costs and providing them with information; b) helps producers to expand sales; c) stimulates research and new product development; d) provides financial support for the mass-media and communications industry; and e) promotes higher quality products and services, etc. On the other side, critics emphasize that a) most advertising is a waste of resources, leading to firms charging consumers a higher price; b) it creates frivolous wants and distorted tastes. In the words of the famous economist John Kenneth Galbraith, "it involves an exercise of imagination to suppose that the taste so expressed originates with the consumer" (John Kenneth Galbraith, "Economics as a System of Belief," *American Economic Review*, May 1970, p. 474; c) advertising often misinforms consumers and promotes lower-quality products; and d) much advertising is offensive and may lead to distorted news coverage, bombarding us through TV and radio programs with tasteless ads.

5. It is difficult to compare all these pros and cons, considering that advertising that involves "all losses" or "no losses at all" is too extreme. Why are consumers influenced by ads that sometimes do not provide any useful information about a product or service? Perhaps they are not as rational as economists typically assume. Consumer rationality is an important assumption but not an absolute truth. What do you think?

Let's consider the question of how prices and output determination take place under monopolistic competition and product differentiation.

2. PRICE AND PROFIT MAXIMIZING DECISIONS IN THE SHORT-RUN AND IN THE LONG-RUN

Monopolistic competition is, by far, the most common market structure in the United States and other advanced economies. To understand the price and output decisions for a monopolistically competitive firm, we need to analyze two types of equilibrium in this market: short-run equilibrium, which takes the number of firms in an industry as given, and long-run equilibrium, which, by contrast, is reached only after enough time has elapsed for firms to enter and exit from the industry. In the short-run, a monopolistic competitor's behavior resembles that of a monopoly; in the long-run, it is closer to a perfect competitor's behavior.

First, we have to examine the monopolistic competitor firm's demand curve, Dmc (figure 7.1).

Figure 7.1
Demand and
Marginal
Revenue Curves

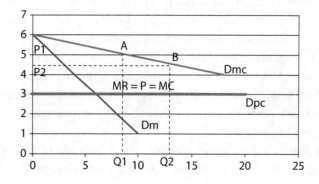

Cappuccino Sold/Hour	Price ($)	Total Revenue	Marginal Revenue	Total Cost	Marginal Cost	Average Total Cost	Profit
Q	P	TR = PxQ	MR = ΔTR/ΔQ	TC	MC = ΔTC/ΔQ	ATC = TC/Q	P = TR–TC
0	7	0		7	1		–7
1	6	6	6	8	1	9.5	–2
2	5	10	4	9	1	6.0	1
3	4	12	2	10	1	4.8	2
4	3	12	0	11	1	4.3	1
5	2	10	–2	12	1	3.9	–2
6	1	6	–4	13	1	3.7	–7

Table 7.1 Profit maximization in the short-run

The demand curve for a monopolistic competitor is mostly but not perfectly elastic. The seller has many rivals producing close substitutes; therefore, it is more elastic (flatter) than the monopoly's demand curve. The firm has some control over the price of product because it is differentiated from its rivals. The curve is less elastic (steeper) than in a pure competition (Dpc). To increase its revenue by selling an additional unit of a product (i.e., a cappuccino in Starbucks)—the output effect (from Q1 to Q2)—the firm should reduce its price (from P1 to P2)—the price effect. The marginal revenue curve, as in the case of a monopoly, always lies below the demand curve.

Second, a company will maximize profits in the short-run (or minimize losses) by producing at a point where marginal cost and marginal revenue are equal (MC = MR). In Figure 7.2, they intersect each other at point "A" (3.5 units), and the price charged is indicated by point "B"—$4.

The firm's total profit (TP) is computed by subtracting average total cost (ATC) from the price (P) times quantity produced (Q). TP = (P – ATC) × Q. In contrast with a perfectly competitive firm, which will produce at P = MC, for a monopolistic competitor, P > MR, which results from the marginal revenue curve being below the demand curve, and, therefore, P > MC.

Third, in the long-run, the firm will end up in **zero-profit equilibrium**, earning a normal profit only (figure 7.3b).

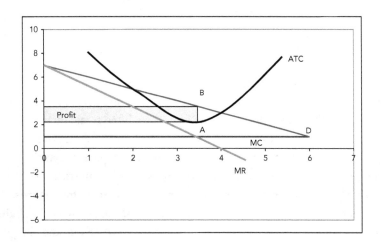

Figure 7.2a A Short-Run Profit

Figure 7.2b
A Short-Run
Loss

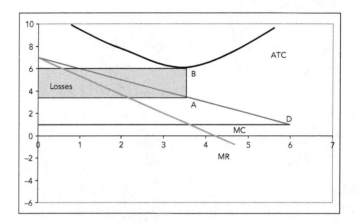

Figure 7.3a
Long-Run
Equilibrium for
a Monopolistic
Competitor

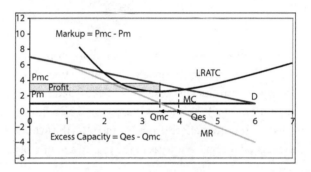

Figure 7.3b
Long-Run
Equilibrium
for a Perfect
Competitor

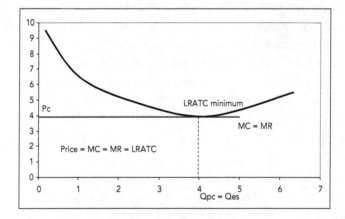

This situation is explained by the following factors:

1. If existing firms are making a profit, it is easier for firms to enter an industry.
2. Some firms will leave an industry (shut down) if they are making a loss in the short-run.
3. There are a few complicating factors: 1) some firms may differentiate their products so they cannot be easily replicated by rivals (brand names, location, etc.) and can make an economic profit in the long-run; 2) some restrictions to enter the market are purely financial, such as with new small businesses; and 3) producers may be content with below normal profits in the long-run. Some producers like to remain entrepreneurs despite the low economic returns.
4. To understand better how the price is formed in a monopolistic competition industry, let's have a look at the structure of the price. From Figure 7.4, you can see that the $70 you paid for pair

of sneakers includes $20 that was a shoe store's cost to its producer in China (or Malaysia or anywhere in Asia), a $35 retailer's cost, and an additional $15 cost of the retailer in your own town.

Manufacturer		Shoe Company		Retailer	
Materials	$9.00				
Labor	$2.75	Cost of shoe to company	$20.00	Cost of shoe to retailer	$35.50
Capital	$3.00	Sales, distribution, & administration	$5.00	Sales clerk's wages	$9.50
Profit	$1.75	Advertising	$4.00	Shop rent	$9.00
Shipping	$0.50	Research & development	$0.25	Retailer's other costs	$7.00
Import Duty	$3.00	Shoe company's profit	$6.25	Retailer's profit	$9.00
Total cost to company	$20.00	Retailer's cost	$35.50	Price paid by customer	$70.00

Figure 7.4
The Structure of
Shoe Prices

3. MONOPOLISTIC COMPETITION VS. PERFECT COMPETITION: EFFICIENCY, PRODUCT DEVELOPMENT, AND DIFFERENTIATION

Do the benefits of monopolistic competition exceed the costs? Is a monopolistic competitor efficient? What are the advantages and disadvantages of this market structure for individual consumers and for society as a whole? To answer these questions, we need to compare monopolistic competition with perfect competition as some kind of standard of efficiency.

First, in the long-run, both a monopolistic competitor and a perfect competitor earn zero economic profit. But in contrast with a perfect competitor, a monopolistic firm does not achieve an efficient use of resources. Let's recall that economic efficiency requires a triple equation: P = MC = minimum ATC. The first part of this equation, *P = MC*, yields *allocative efficiency*: the right amount—the social optimum—is produced. The second part, *P = minimum ATC*, means *productive efficiency*: production in the least costly way, with the price covering average total cost and normal profit. Neither productive nor allocative efficiency is achieved in the long-run by a monopolistic competitor.

Second, unlike firms in perfect competition, firms in monopolistic competition have *excess capacity*—they produce less than the quantity at which average total cost is at minimum, which is the *efficient scale* of production. In Figure. 7.3a, quantity produced by a monopolistic competitor is less than quantity at the efficient scale: Qmc < Qes.

Third, a monopolistic competitor charges a price greater than the marginal cost; the difference is called *markup*: Pmc > MC. A firm in perfect competition has no markup as Figure 7.3b shows.

Fourth, in comparison with a perfect competitor, the firms in monopolistic competition compete through product development, differentiation, and marketing. New product development allows a firm to gain a temporary competitive edge, and economic profit before competitors imitate the innovation. A firm decides upon the extent of innovation and product development by comparing the marginal cost of innovation or product development to its marginal revenue. The modalities of this competition include:

1. differentiation by size, color, shape, texture, taste, and other *physical characteristics*;
2. choosing a location that sets it apart from its competitors;
3. offering complementary services (home delivery, free technical assistance, etc.); and
4. creation of a distinctive image through advertising.

In conclusion, firms in monopolistic competition have higher costs than firms in perfect competition, but firms in monopolistic competition produce variety, which is valued by consumers. So, compared to the alternative of complete uniformity, monopolistic competition in the long-run provides advantages to individual consumers and society as a whole, first, by charging a lower price under the influence of competition among many firms and, second, by offering a greater variety of products. The disadvantage is a higher average cost of production (i.e., restaurants, clothing, CDs, music, etc.).

4. CLASSIFYING INDUSTRIES AND MEASURING MARKETS: HHI AND OTHER MARKET CONCENTRATION INDEXES

How can we measure an industry's degree of concentration in a market?

1. One measure of the extent of competition in an industry is the *concentration ratio*; for example, the *four-firm concentration ratios* which measure the percentage of an industry's output produced by its four largest firms while the eight-firm ratio measures the output of its eight largest firms. When the four largest firms in an industry control 40% or more of the market, that industry is considered oligopolistic. Every five years, the United States Census Bureau publishes *The Four-Firm Concentration Ratio*. But there are some shortcomings that characterize this index:
   a. Some markets are local rather than national, and a few firms may dominate within the regional market (the Four-Firm Concentration Ratio for ready mix concrete is only 7%, which means a highly competitive industry);
   b. It does not help very much to measure interindustry competition (competition between two products associated with different industries);
   c. It does not include sales in the US by foreign firms in spite of the fact that world trade has increased competition in some industries (i.e., the auto industry).
2. An alternative measure of degree of competition is *The Herfindahl-Hirschman Index,* which is the sum of squared percentage market shares of all firms in the industry. HHI $= (\%S_1)^2 + (\%S_2)^2 + (\%S_3)^2 +$, where $(\%S_1)$ is the percentage market share of firm 1 and so on. The formula for this index is:

$$HHI = \sum_{i=1}^{N} S_i^2,$$

where n is the number of firms in the industry, S—the *i* firm's firms market share. By squaring the percentage market share of all firms in the industry, the HH gives much greater weight to larger and more powerful firms than to smaller ones. For example, if the market shares of the four firms are, respectively, 50%, 25%, 15%, and 10%, then the HHI = 502 + 252 + 152 + 102 = 3,450. If there are four firms that are equally sharing the market, then HHI = 2,500. For a purely competitive industry, the index would approach zero, since its market share is insignificant. The larger the Herfindahl Index, the greater the market power within an industry. The maximum HHI is 1002 or 10,000, which indicates an industry with a complete monopoly power. According to the US Department of Justice Merger Guidelines, markets are considered "unconcentrated" if they have an HHI less than 1,500. If a merger in an industry will lead to an HHI that exceeds 2,500, this merger is likely to be challenged.

In Figure 7.5, there is the classification of firms in monopolistic competition, according to the Four Firms Concentration Ratio (the red bars show the percentage share of the largest four firms in the total industry's revenue and respective HHI).

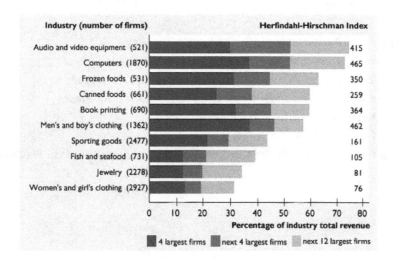

Figure 7.5 Percentage of Industry Total Revenue and HHI For 10 Industries in Monopolistic Competition (Adapted from United States Census Bureau; Bade & Parkin, p. 436.)

5. KEY TERMS

Monopolistic Competition
Product Differentiation, Nonprice Competition
Advertising, Quality, and Services
Profit Maximizing Decision, Short-Run, Long-Run
Zero-Profit Equilibrium
Excess Capacity
Markup
Efficient Scale of Production
Productive Efficiency
Allocative Efficiency
Four-Firm Concentration Ratio
Herfindal-Hirshman Index (HHI)

6. PROBLEMS AND APPLICATIONS

1. Based on what you studied in this chapter, what is characteristic for a monopolistic competition?
   a. Many relatively small firms supply, essentially, the same product but each has some brand loyalty.
   b. One big firm supplies the entire product to the competitive market.
   c. One firm supplies 40% of the product to the market and there are three other rival firms.

d. Two firms supply the entire volume of product to market.

2. Which one of the following represents examples of monopolistic competition?
   a. Shell, Exxon-Mobil, and BP gasoline stations in a nearby city
   b. Mc-Donald's, Burger King, Taco Bell, and other fast-food restaurants in your neighborhood
   c. Virginia State University (VSU), Virginia Commonwealth University (VCU), Virginia Tech (VT), and other colleges in Virginia.
   d. All of the above.
   e. None of the above.

3. How you can explain market power?
   a. All market structures have the power to dominate the market price.
   b. It is the ability of a firm(s) to determine the market price of a product
   c. It means that all firms in a market are price takers, not a price maker.
   d. It characterizes only existing monopoly behavior.

4. In the figure below, total profit for the monopolistically competitive firm is represented by the area:
   a. ABCF
   b. EBA
   c. EDG
   d. EBCF

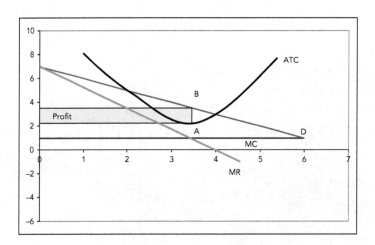

5. From this chapter, you learned that a contestable market is:
   a. One with high barriers to entry, like the car manufacturing market.
   b. A market in which there is potential for entry of new firms, for example, community colleges.
   c. A market that guarantees the lowest price for consumers, like a food market.
   d. One that requires a monopoly firm to behave like an oligopoly, i.e., a market for beverages.

6. Which of the following indicates the rate of output a monopolistically competitive firm would choose to maximize its profit?
   a. $P = MC$

b. MR = ATC

c. P = ATC

d. *MR = MC*

7. Explain why a firm in monopolistic competition can set the price for its product?

a. It could earn economic profit, which is its main goal.

b. Easy entry and exit to this market prevent monopolies from establishing their market power.

c. Advertisement and product differentiation.

d. Existence of many competitors in the market.

8. The monopolistic competition is identified by which of the following Four-Firm Concentration Ratios?

a. 100%

b. 0%

c. 25%

d. 60%

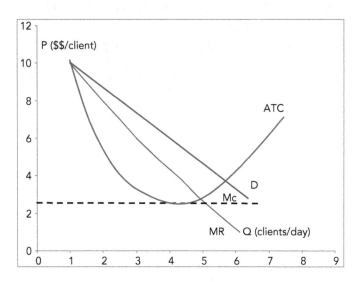

Figure 7.7

9. Ron owns a gym in Duluth, Iowa. The figure above shows the demand and cost curves for his firm that competes in a monopolistically competitive market. What is the price that Ron will charge per training (vertical axis is showing prices in tens of $$)?

a. $100

b. $50

c. $30

d. $25

7. REVIEW QUESTIONS

1. Suppose you are a financial consultant at Big Hibachi Grill, a monopolistic competitive restaurant in your neighborhood, and you are looking for the best price/output decision. To increase the revenue and, therefore, the profit, you want to sell an additional unit of a meal

at _____ (higher/lower) price, since the profit-maximizing decision is _____ (MC = MR/MC = P).

2. In Colonial Heights, Virginia, there are three firms that offer oil change service to motorists. For each one, there is a fixed cost of $200 per day and a marginal cost of $20 per oil change. Suppose each firm is maximizing profit by providing 10 oil changes per day. Find what the marginal revenue is for each firm $_____. So, this is a monopolistically competitive equilibrium if _____ equals $_____.

3. Could it be possible for the firms in a monopolistically competitive industry to establish a monopoly in the long-run by creating a single firm together? Illustrate your answer with real economic examples.

4. Why do monopolistic competitors frequently prefer nonprice competition to price competition? How do you explain the following statement: "Competition in quality and service for a monopolistic competitor may be just as effective as price competition in giving buyers more for their money"?

IMAGE CREDITS

CHAPTER 8

OLIGOPOLY AND GAME THEORY: STRATEGIC BEHAVIOR AND DECISION-MAKING

The great virtue of the market is competition, which is the key to efficiency. But in some markets, firms try to cooperate rather than compete. More than 200 years ago, Adam Smith recognized that "people of the same trade seldom meet together, even for merriment and diversion, but the conversation end in a conspiracy against the public, or in some contrivance to raise prices" (Adam Smith, *The Wealth of Nations*, New York, Modern Library, 1994). In October 1993, more than two hundred years after this famous economics book was published, in California's Marriot Hotel, executives of Archer Daniels Midland (ADM) met their Japanese competitor Ajinomoto to discuss how they could divide the market for *Lycine*, an additive in animal feed. These two companies were joined by a few other interested Asian and European firms. What they did not know is that the FBI caught these meetings on a hidden camera. This was a case of price-fixing, an illegal activity, which characterizes oligopoly behavior. (The term "oligopoly" has its origin in the Greek words "*oligi*"—"a few" and "*polein*"—"sellers."

1. OLIGOPOLY'S MAIN CHARACTERISTICS AND BEHAVIOR

The *Oligopoly* is a market structure in which a few sellers dominate the sales of a product and where entry of new sellers into the market is difficult or impossible. In contrast with monopolistic competition, an oligopoly involves a large amount of monopoly power and a small amount of competition. A monopoly represents the clearest type of market power. However, if we look at such giants of American business as Apple, Microsoft, GM, IBM, and GE, we find that most of them are not monopolists and are competing with national and foreign producers. They represent the oligopolies—the more significant actors in the US economy. The main characteristics of oligopolistic markets are:

First, like a monopolist, an oligopoly is a *price maker*, but unlike a monopolist, the oligopoly has to consider how its rivals will react to any changes in its price, output, product characteristics, etc. In short, there are two distinctive features in an oligopoly: a) *strategic behavior*—self-interested behavior that takes the reactions of others into account. The key strategies of an oligopoly include price, quality, location, service, and advertising; and b) *mutual interdependence*—each company should consider a rival's response to prices, output, and advertising.

Second, oligopolistic industries could produce different types of products. *Standardized products* are those like steel, zinc, copper, and cement. *Differentiated products* are things like automobiles, washing machines, etc. The latter differentiated oligopolies, are typically engaged in considerable nonprice competition supported by heavy advertising. For example, Coca-Cola and Pepsi control 75% of sales of soft drinks, and they realize that price competition is a no-win strategy. OPEC comprises twelve national producers of petroleum that meet every six months to limit supply and maintain high oil prices. Other examples are the "Big Three,"—Detroit's firms that dominate the national automobile market (GM, Ford, and Chrysler; the "Big Four"—Apple, Dell, Hewlett-Packard, and Acer that control more than 75% of the US market for laptops and desktop computers; or the "Big Six" in other industries.

Third, there are significant *barriers to entry* to an oligopolistic market: a) the economies of scale that give bigger firms a cost advantage over smaller ones are the largest source of oligopoly; economies of scale exist due to technological advances and considerable market share (aircraft, rubber, and copper industries); b) a large capital investment requirement (jet engines, automobiles, commercial aircraft, etc.); c) ownership (mining industries) and control of raw materials (electronics, chemical, office equipment, and pharmaceutical industries); pricing, advertising budgets, brand loyalty, etc.; d) government-imposed barriers, such as patents that give an exclusive right to a new product for twenty years, and occupational licensing—in the US there are about 500 occupational licensing laws, tariffs, and quotas on foreign competition.

Fourth, oligopolies emerged through a) *growth of dominant firms* in an industry (breakfast cereals, chewing gum) or b) *mergers* (steel, airlines, banking, and entertainment).

How can we measure an oligopolistic industry's degree of concentration in a market? By using the same Four-Firm Concentration Ratio (share in total industry's revenue) and HHI that were introduced in the previous chapter (figure 8.1).

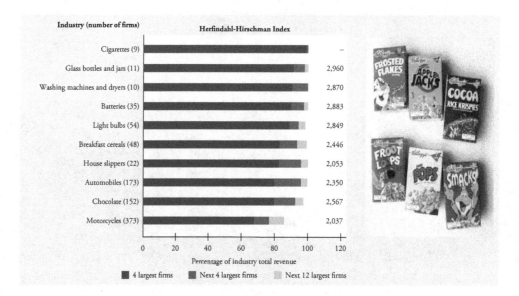

Figure 8.1
Percentage of
Industry Total
Revenue and
HHI for Ten
Industries in
Oligopoly
Markets
(Sources: United
States Census
Bureau; Bade
and Parkin,
p. 459.)

The HHI is used by the US Justice Department and the Federal Trade Commission to assess the market concentration and to enforce antitrust policy. For example, if the HHI is below 1,500, the market is considered highly competitive; if the HHI is between 1,500 and 2,500—somewhat competitive, and if the HHI goes above 2,500—it becomes an oligopoly market. Note that each merger results in a significant increase in HHI (by 50% and more).

2. GAME THEORY AND OLIGOPOLY'S BEHAVIOR

An oligopoly might behave like a monopoly when a few firms form a cartel agreement (illegal in the United States) to reach the monopoly outcome and maximize their profits. An oligopoly might also operate like a perfect competitor or as something similar to these two extremes.

First, oligopoly behavior is similar to strategy games like blackjack or checkers. Each player's actions are interdependent with other players' actions. A two firm model, or duopoly, which is the simplest version of an oligopoly, could be used to illustrate how each participant is playing a "game" in which the profit of each player depends on his or her own actions but also on those of his or her partner.

Second, we will use Game Theory—the study of how people make decisions in situations when attaining their goals depends on interaction with their partners/rivals. This theory was developed in the 1940s by the mathematician John von Neumann and the economist Oskar Morgenstern and includes three key components: Rules (what actions are allowable), Strategies (how to attain the objectives in a game), and Payoffs (interactions of players' strategies). But the most celebrated game theorist in the world is John Nash, a Nobel Prize laureate in Economics and professor at Princeton University who received his PhD in 1950 at the age of 21 for his twenty-seven-page dissertation on game theory. It was in this dissertation that he first proposed the concept that became known as the Nash equilibrium.

But his brilliant academic career was dramatically interrupted for the next twenty-five years by a severe form of schizophrenia. During these years, he was kept on the faculty list by Princeton University, which was a humane decision. He spent this time riding buses around Princeton, roaming the university campus, and covering blackboards in unused classrooms with indecipherable writings and formulas, becoming known as the "Phantom of Fine Hall." He gradually recovered in his late 70s, and in 1994 he was awarded the Nobel Prize for Economics, sharing it with John Harsanyi of the University of California at Berkeley and Reinhardt Selten of Rheinische Friedrich-Wilhelms University in Germany. Sylvia Nasar of the *New York Times* wrote a best-selling biography of Nash, *A Beautiful Mind,* which was made into movie starring Russell Crowe as John

Nash. The Nash equilibrium concept is applicable to a wide variety of situations: to study the nuclear arms race, terrorism, evolutionary biology, environment policy, art auctions, etc.

Third, the MR = MC rule is valuable for both perfect competition and monopoly, with one exception, a market where a manager's decision is limited by anticipation of the reaction of a rival to price and output decisions. This is the essence of game theory which deals with how individuals make decisions when they are aware that their actions affect each other's interests and when each individual takes this into account. The essence of game theory consists of the application of the logic of mathematics to arrive at the equilibrium. This theory is of special value because it helps to understand mutually interdependent behavior. There are a variety of such theories: a) a zero-sum game, where one player's gain is the other's loss and vice versa; b) a nonzero-sum game, where both players may gain or lose, depending on the actions of each other; c) a noncooperative game, which implies that opponents are not allowed to cooperate or share the information with each other; and d) a dominant strategy game, which means that there is one strategy that is best for a player no matter what the other player does. We will use game theory to analyze how the oligopoly makes price and output decisions to help us understand the mutual interdependent behavior of the players (companies) of the "game."

3. "PRISONERS' DILEMMA": JOHN NASH EQUILIBRIUM

"EACH PLAYER IS DOING THE BEST HE OR SHE CAN, GIVEN THE ACTION OF THE OTHER PLAYER"

One of the most well-known studies in game theory is the *"Prisoners' Dilemma,"* which is a *two-person, nonzero-sum, noncooperative game with a dominant strategy.* Since it is frequently used in economics, and it is important for understanding oligopoly behavior, we will consider one of its versions.

Two individuals, A and B, commit a serious crime together and have been caught by police. They know that there is insufficient evidence to convict them of this crime. Both of them also risk being charged and convicted for a less serious crime and could be sentenced to two years in jail for it. The two men are each interrogated for the more serious crime in separate cells, and they are not allowed to communicate with each other. Each prisoner is told that if he confesses and his partner denies, he will serve one year in jail, and his partner will serve fifteen years. If both deny, both will serve four years. The game's payoff matrix provides payoffs from each man's *strategy*, which is to confess or deny involvement in the serious crime.

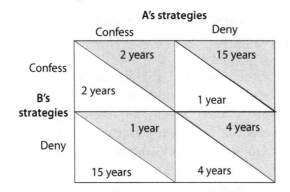

Figure 8.2 "Prisoners' Dilemma" (Source: Bade and Parkin, *Foundations of Economics*, 7e.)

How can we reach equilibrium in this game when these *strategies* are all the possible actions of each player? This kind of equilibrium, in which each player takes the action that is best for him or her, given the action of other players (and vice versa), is called a *Nash equilibrium*, which is also known as a noncooperative equilibrium. According to the Nash equilibrium, individual *A* takes the best possible action given the action of individual *B*, and individual *B* takes the best possible action given the action of individual *A*. The Nash equilibrium for the "Prisoners' Dilemma" is for both players to deny. This outcome is bad for them because both would be better off if each confesses. But they also know that denying is the option to make the best of a bad situation. So, following their dominant strategy—deny, both will be worse off than if each of them would confess. But this is the "Prisoners' Dilemma."

Oligopolistic companies often behave like the prisoners in this dilemma: should the oligopoly cut its price, gaining more sales, or should it keep the price stable, or raise the price, anticipating its rival reaction?

4. GAME THEORY AND THE PRICING BEHAVIOR OF OLIGOPOLIES

To understand oligopolistic pricing strategy, suppose two companies, such as Coca-Cola and Pepsi, are competing in a market of beverages in which price is the most important purchasing criteria for the consumers, and, of course, the companies' profit will depend on the price they will charge. Let's consider the four possible combinations of strategies for these two firms, the so called *payoff matrix*: a combination of high-price and low-price strategies (figure 8.3).

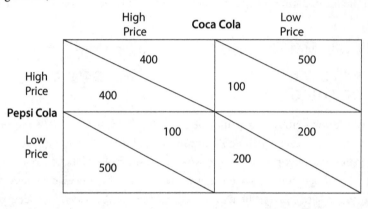

Figure 8.3
High-Price,
Low-Price
Strategies

The pricing strategies are classified as high-priced or low-priced, and the profits, in each case, will depend on the rivals' strategy. A dominant strategy for both firms is the low-price strategy although both prefer to be in the high-price situation (and win a profit of $400/$400). But the high-price/high-price situation is not stable, and each company will tend to change the situation: to charge a lower price, but to gain the bigger share of sales and to be compensated by larger profit as a result. That's why both companies choose the more secure situation of the low price ($200/$200), thereby guaranteeing that the other company will not gain an advantage by setting a lower price (which could be expected according to the Nash equilibrium). By understanding the rules under which companies operate, we can understand and explain things that otherwise are inexplicable, and we can predict the outcome.

There are also cases of repeated games when we bring *time* into our earlier pricing decision. In the real world, most of these such games are played repeatedly. For example, if one of two companies (Airbus) decides in the first round of the price game to "cheat" by increasing (decreasing) the price for its aircraft, in the second round, the rival company (Boeing) will have the opportunity "to penalize" the opponent for "bad behavior" by increasing(decreasing) its price to gain more market share and increase its profit. This strategy is called "*Tit-for-Tat.*". Alternatively, the competitors might learn how to cooperate tacitly, enjoying monopoly profit by adopting the monopoly strategy of output and price decision. At some point, cooperation may emerge between the two rivals, and they may choose to charge high prices for their products. This situation is likely to appear in stable industries. In another variation—*sequential games* and first mover advantage—decisions are made sequentially with the first mover having an advantage.

An oligopoly can lead also to *collusive behavior*—that is, cooperation with rivals. In our case, both firms could improve their positions if they both agreed to both adopt a high-price strategy. The most comprehensive form of collusion is the *Cartel*—a group of firms that come to an agreement on each member quotas for production and price charged. A Cartel cartel might be overt or implicit. The classical example of an international overt cartel is the Organization of Petroleum Exporting Countries (OPEC), comprising twelve oil-producing nations that control about 70% of the world's proven oil reserves, produce 41% of the world's oil, and supply 43% of all oil traded internationally. It had significant success in increasing the price of oil in the 70s and 80s: oil prices soared from $3 per barrel in 1972 to $39 per barrel in 1980 (to more than $100 in 2008 dollars' purchasing power). By 2008, prices skyrocketed to more than $145 per barrel, but in less than in one year of 2007-09 recession, they declined sharply —to $32 per barrel. In recent years, Iraq and Iran increased their oil production, the U.S. substantially raise the increased its oil affected extraction from shale formations and the oil production of Brazil and Canada increased, as well; as a result, the price of oil remained below $40 a barrel for quite a long time. OPEC members meet periodically to assign new quotas and to restrict the supply of oil to the level that permits OPEC to raise its price. In fact, they are participating in repeating games with a cooperative outcome.

Another type of cartel is implicit collusion, which can result from *price leadership strategy,* when one firm—a dominant firm—takes the lead in announcing (or not) the price change, and the other firms follow the leader. If collusion exists, there is much incentive on the part of one or both parties to cheat and secretly break the agreement. For example, in Figure 8.4, if this was a perfectly competitive market, the price in long-run would be a competitive price, Pc ($40 per barrel), and all firms would produce a competitive quantity, Qc (4.3 million barrels a day), making zero economic profit (at the point where MR1 = MC = LRATC = P1). But we assume that a cartel of two firms (oligopolies) has been established, and it agrees to increase the price to Pca ($70 per barrel) by restricting supply to Qca (3 mln. barrels per day).

This is an example of price fixing, an arrangement in which two or more firms conspire to fix prices. The total profit that they will share will be $60 mln (the area of the green rectangle). Recall that maximum profit is the dominant strategy; one of these two firms has a strong incentive to cheat and to increase its oil production to by another 3 mln barrels per day. Then, assuming that the price remains the same (Pca), this company will receive an additional profit of $60 mln (the area of yellow rectangle). Since this is the repeated and sequential game, another firm will increase its production in the next round, as well, and, if all firms in this market cheat and compete, then the initial long-run equilibrium with an initial price ($40 per barrel) will be reestablished.

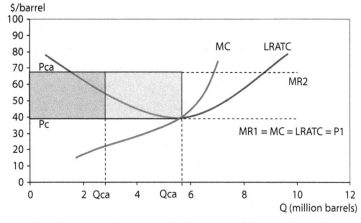

Figure 8.4
Incentives to
Cheat Under
a Cartel
Agreement

Cartel collusion is a costly affair generally due to: 1) the cost of forming it; 2) the cost of monitoring the actions of the cartel members; and 3) the potential cost of punishment by authorities.

Let's have a look at other cases of *price fixing* by cartels. One of the classic cases, at the beginning of the 60s, involved GE, Westinghouse, and some other companies that conspired on the price of a number of electrical products; the cartel ended in a Philadelphia court for seven of the companies' executives and resulted in approximately $2 million in fines. Price fixing was discovered, more recently, in a case that involved an agriculture business, ADM Company ($20 billion revenues in 2001), four Asian companies, and four European companies. ADM was fined $100 million and had to pay another $90 million in costs to settle lawsuits brought by customers and stockholders. In 1997, two of the largest auction houses, Sotheby's and Christie's, were found guilty of collusion over prices (together they control 90% of the art auction market). It cost Sotheby's a fine of $45 million and a $512 million class-action suit settlement between the two auction houses and 130,000 buyers and sellers. Both former chairmen were indicted.

It should be noted that cartels are illegal in the United States, and any such kind of collusion (overt or covert) is in violation of US antitrust laws.

It should also be noted that the US has a long and unique tradition of antitrust policy as was described in Chapter 6. One of the most interesting early antitrust actions was the breakup of Standard Oil more than one hundred years ago (1911). Many big oil companies—such as Exxon and Mobil, for example, have their roots in Standard Oil. The US Congress has adopted antitrust measures, such as the amnesty program, which allows price fixers a more lenient penalty if they inform the authorities about their coconspirators. The US Congress also significantly increased fines upon conviction. As a result—informing on your cartel partners became a dominant strategy of the time, and many oil executives from Britain, Canada, France, Germany, Italy, Mexico, South Korea, Switzerland, and the US ended their careers in jail when they were convicted in US courts.

5. OLIGOPOLY, ADVERTISING, AND EFFICIENCY

FIRST, OLIGOPOLY AND ADVERTISING

Product development and advertising under oligopoly represent, in general, an efficiency-enhancing activity, a type of nonprice competition that is more difficult to combat and match than lowering prices. At the same time, nonprice competition can produce more permanent gains in market share because it cannot be easily duplicated. Oligopolies also have considerable financial resources to support advertising and product development. Usually, these expenditures are undertaken under the strategy of "product development" or "research and development" (R&D). In 2011, American firms spent $103 billion on advertising inside the country and $498 billion outside to promote their products and services. Advertising prevails in both oligopoly and monopolistic competition markets and affects prices, competition, and efficiency both positively and negatively:

1. In a positive way, advertising reduces a buyer's search time and minimizes its costs; spreads information, especially though the Internet, about competing goods; diminishes monopoly power and increases economic efficiency; speeds up technological progress by facilitating the introduction of new products; increases output; and reduces long-run average total cost, facilitating the utilization of economies of scale, etc. Could Japanese carmakers strongly challenge "Big Three" Detroit carmakers without any advertising?
2. Too much advertising might be designed to manipulate rather than inform buyers; it leads to an increase of monopoly power or is self-canceling, resulting in economic inefficiency; it may also be a significant barrier to entry to industry. In some cases, heavy advertising may persuade consumers to pay higher prices for inferior but much-acclaimed products like the situation with premium motor oils. (According to *Consumer Reports*, they do not provide better engine performance and longevity as compared to cheaper brands.)

SECOND, OLIGOPOLY AND EFFICIENCY

To address this question, we need to find out how oligopolistic structures respond to the triple equation: P = MC = minimum ATC, which reflects the outcome of perfect competition.

1. Allocative and productive efficiency are not realized since oligopoly's price (Po) always exceeds marginal cost (P > MC), and oligopoly's output (Qo) is usually less than competitive output (Qc) at minimum average total cost (Q < ATC) (figure 8.5).

   Some economists believe that oligopoly is even less desired than pure monopoly because government regulates a monopoly's behavior and prevents its abuses. In the case of informal agreement (tacit collusion) among oligopolies, it is much more difficult to apply the same approach.

2. Economic inefficiency can be reduced since increased foreign competition has made many oligopolistic industries much more competitive, particularly, steel, automobiles, films, etc.

3. Oligopolies may limit prices below the profit maximizing level in the short-run just to deter entry of new firms. Keeping prices closer to MC and minimum ATC can benefit society.

4. Oligopolistic industries, having large economic profits, may foster technological advances through rapid product development and greater improvement of production technique that would not be possible if they were purely competitive firms.

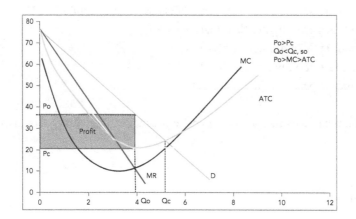

Figure 8.5
Profit
Maximization
Under
Oligopoly

6. KEY TERMS

Oligopoly
Price Maker
Strategic Behavior
Mutual Interdependence
Game Theory
Payoff Matrix
Nash Equilibrium
Prisoners' Dilemma
Price Fixing
Price Leadership Strategy
Tit-for-Tat Strategy
Sequential Games
Repeated Games
Collusive Behavior
Cartel

7. PROBLEMS AND APPLICATIONS

1. Suppose a book publisher's market is dominated by three firms. This type of market is called:
   a. Perfectly competitive
   b. Monopolistically competitive
   c. Monopoly
   d. Oligopoly

2. How do you define a group of firms coordinating their actions to restrict output, raise prices, and increase economic profit?
   a. Duopoly
   b. Monopolistic competition
   c. Cartel
   d. Oligopoly

3. For which of the following scenarios is marginal cost pricing applied?
   a. Offer goods at a price higher than marginal cost.
   b. Sale of goods at the highest possible price.
   c. Choose the rate of output at which $MR = MC$.
   d. Selling goods at prices at their marginal cost $(P = MC)$.

4. If two firms dominate a market and control price and output, then this type of market is identified as:
   a. Duopoly
   b. Oligopoly
   c. Monopoly
   d. Monopolistically competitive

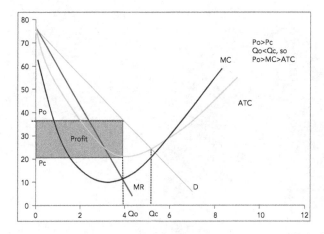

Figure 8.6

5. In the figure above, the price and output of an oligopoly will be:
   a. $10.00 and 4 units
   b. $37.00 and 4 units
   c. $25.00 and 5 units
   d. $37.00 and 2 units

6. In the situations when oligopolies act as a single-price monopoly, how will the firms maximize their profit? (Which of the following formulas is relevant?)

a. P = MC

b. P = MR

c. P < ATC

d. MR = MC

7. For two big airplane producers, Boeing and Airbus, a major dilemma for them might be:

a. If each firm separately tries to maximize its profit, it might end up with less profit for both of them.

b. Neither Boeing nor Airbus will respond to the changing behavior of the other.

c. Uncertainty following the reaction of each firm to the behavior of the other firm.

d. The harsh competition will drive their economic profit to zero.

8. All games that oligopolies play have the following features:

a. Prices, rules, and payoffs

b. Rules, markets, and prices

c. Rules, strategies, and payoffs

d. Equilibrium, prices, and quantities

9. A Nash equilibrium is defined as:

a. Earning zero economic profit in the long-run.

b. Each player taking the best possible action given the action of the other player.

c. Forming a cartel with strong penalties for cheaters.

d. Relying on other game players to realize the benefit of oligopoly.

8. REVIEW QUESTIONS

1. How do you characterize an oligopoly, and why do oligopolies exist? What are the main differences between oligopoly and monopolistic competition? List three or four oligopolies whose products you regularly buy.

2. How do barriers to entry impact the competition in an industry, and what are the most important barriers?

3. In Thomas K. McCraw's book *Creating Modern Capitalism* (Cambridge, 1997, pp. 61–62), the development of the cotton textile industry in England is described as follows: "The cotton textile industry was shaped by ruthless competition. Rapid growth in demand, law barriers to entry, frequent technological innovations, and a high rate of firm bankruptcy all combined to form an environment in which … oligopolistic competition became almost impossible." Based on this quote, what are the factors that make oligopolistic competition in this industry very difficult?

4. In economics, one of the most popular illustrations of oligopoly's pricing strategies is the "Prisoner's Dilemma" game. How would this dilemma apply to the pricing strategy of an oligopoly? Create a table showing the "Prisoners' Dilemma" game's choices for two companies (Coca-Cola and Pepsi, for example) when they are making decisions to advertise or not advertise in pursuit of their goal to increase their profits.

IMAGE CREDITS

8.1a: Copyright © 2015 by R.Bade & M.Parkin.

CHAPTER 9.

LABOR MARKET: INEQUALITY, POVERTY, AND INCOME DISTRIBUTION

The subject of this chapter is the behavior of the labor market. In the United States, this is a market of more than 150 million people. What are the main categories that describe this market, and, particularly, what are the wages and which factors determine their rates? Wage rates may be the most important price that you will encounter in your life. Wages and other forms of compensation account for 80% of the US national income (proprietor's income included). Labor is not just a commodity; labor involves people. There are major policy issues in labor markets which do not arise in the markets for other factors of production, such as capital or land.

In this chapter, we will examine: What are the main incentives for productive work? How do people decide how much time to spend working? What are the main determinants of hourly wages and annual salaries? Why are starting salaries of college graduates who major in engineering, economics, and accounting so much higher than for graduates majoring in the humanities or education? Why was the ex-chairman of the Walt Disney Company offered a ten-year contract for $500 million when the president of the United States receives a salary of $400,000? Why does an average college graduate in economics, for example, earn $50,000 a year while the average high school graduate earns $32,000? Collectively, wages and salaries—"compensation of employees"—make up more than two-thirds of the national income of the United States.

We will examine the determinants of demand and supply for labor and the price paid for it in different markets, the main types of labor markets, and how these markets affect wage rates and unemployment.

1. MARKET DEMAND FOR LABOR: SHORT-RUN VS. LONG-RUN

We need to introduce a few important categories and assumptions:

First, the term *"labor"* includes at least three categories of workers: a) blue- and white-collar workers. The term white-collar worker refers to a person who performs professional, managerial, or administrative work in contrast with a blue-collar worker, whose job requires mostly manual work; b) lawyers, economists, accountants, physicians, teachers, and other *professional people*; and c) plumbers, small shop retail sellers, barbers, and other *owners of small businesses*.

Second, wages are the price paid for the use of labor in the form of a) direct money payments (hourly pay, annual salaries, bonuses, commissions, and royalties) and b) benefits (paid vacations, health insurance, and pensions). The *wage rate* is the price paid per unit of labor services, for example, an hour of work. Labor earning is determined by multiplying the number of hours worked by the hourly wage rate. We must distinguish between the *nominal wage*—the amount of money ($$) received per hour, day, or year—and the *real wage*—the quantity of goods and services that we can obtain with nominal wages, or the "purchasing power" of nominal wages. Real wages depend on the price of goods and services which are needed and the nominal wage. For example, if the nominal wage increases by 10% and inflation is 5%, then the real wage rose by 5%.

Third, the labor market is different from other markets: machines have no rights but workers do. We will start our analysis with a *perfectly competitive labor market,* which is characterized by: a) mobility of workers, who can move from one job to another; b) many buyers of labor services (employers) and sellers (workers), none of whom have any market power to influence the wage rate; c) labor that is standardized; all workers are equally skillful and equally productive in the industry; and d) individual workers and firms who are "wage takers," having no market power to influence the "price" of labor (wage rate).

Now we can define the demand for labor. This is the quantity of labor during a given time period in which an employer is willing and able to hire at alternative wage rates. It is important to note that the demand for labor, as for any other factor of production, is a derived demand and results from the market demand for the goods and services that labor is producing. A firm demand for labor depends upon: a) the productivity of workers—output per labor hour and b) the market price of the product being produced.

What are the roles of productivity and product price in determining resource demand? Recall that the marginal physical product of labor (MPP), or additional output, results from hiring an additional unit of labor, or $MPP = \Delta Q / \Delta L$. The dollar value of the marginal product of labor, which is the marginal revenue product (MRP), equals the price of a unit of output multiplied by the marginal physical product of labor, or $MRP = P \times MPP$. According to the Law of Diminishing Returns, the marginal physical product (MPP) of labor eventually declines as the quantity of labor employed increases. As MPP diminishes, so does the value of the marginal revenue product. At the same time, MPP establishes an upper limit to the employer's willingness to pay. So the worker's contribution to output can be measured in either MPP or the dollar value of that product—MRP.

The general rule is: the greater the productivity of labor, the greater the demand for it. In the US and other industrially advanced countries, the demand for labor is large, and, respectively, the levels of wages are higher, primarily because of the higher productivity of labor. The level of wages is determined by the following factors:

1. Plentiful capital. In the US, there is about $120,000 of physical capital available on average per worker.
2. Abundant natural resources. The US is richly endowed with arable land, mineral resources, and sources of energy.
3. Advanced technology, improved through scientific studies and research.
4. Labor quality—health, education, and training are superior in the US.
5. Other factors in the United States include: a) the efficiency and flexibility of management; b) a business, social, and political environment that emphasizes production and productivity; c) the large size of the domestic market, which enables firms to be engaged in mass production; and d) the increased specialization of production.

The demand curve for labor—the higher the wage rate, the smaller the quantity of labor demanded. *The quantity of labor demanded depends on its price* (the wage rate), which is illustrated in the movement along the demand curve. The downward slope of the labor-demand curve reflects the changing productivity of workers.

It is also important to note that each (identical) worker is paid the same wage rate and each is worth no more than the MRP of the last worker hired. So, the *MRP curve is also a firm's short-run demand curve for labor*. It shows the relationship between the wage rate and the quantity of labor demanded in the short-run when at least one factor of production is fixed and cannot be changed (for example, the plant). The firm will pick the quantity of labor until the level where marginal revenue (the benefit from hiring an additional worker) equals the marginal cost of labor, which is the hourly wage rate. A firm uses its MRP curve to make a decision about how much labor it can hire at a specific wage. Figure 9.1 demonstrates that at the wage rate MC1 ($10/hour) two workers will be hired; at the wage rate MC2 ($8/hour), four workers; and at the wage rate MC3 (5/hour), six workers will be hired. All that the manager needs to do is to look at the point of intersection of MRP (demand curve) and MC (wage rate) curves.

The principles of marginal revenue product/marginal cost apply, for example, to a university football coach who earned more than $4.5 million in 2012. Why did he get paid ten times more than the university's president? Because his winning football team brought in 100,000 paying fans per game plus lots of media exposure. The university thought his MRP was justified.

The demand curve for labor in the long-run: reflects the inverse relationship between the wage rate and the quantity of labor demanded, taking into consideration that the number of firms in the industry is changing as are the firm's production facilities. The long-run demand curve for labor is negatively sloped—as the wage rate increases, the quantity of labor demanded decreases for two reasons: a) *the output effect*—an increase in the cost of labor increases the cost of a firm's production and reduces the quantity of output sold and, respectively, reduces the firm's demand for resources, including workers and b) *the input-substitution effect*—an increase in wages beyond a certain level (MRP) will cause a shift in the firm's demand from labor to other factors of production (machinery), which decreases demand for labor. We can conclude that demand for labor in the long-run is more elastic, and the demand curve is less steep than in the short-run, so the firm has more flexibility in its decisions.

Hourly Wage	Number of Workers	No. of Tennis Rackets	MPP	Price	MRP	MC 1	MC 2	MC 3
11	1	40	40	5	200	10	8	5
10	2	60	20	5	100	10	8	5
9	3	78	18	5	90	10	8	5
8	4	90	12	5	60	10	8	5
7	5	100	10	5	50	10	8	5
5	6	106	6	5	30	10	8	5
3	7					10	8	5
1	8					10	8	5
0						10	8	5

Table 9.1 Labor Demand for a Firm (Using the Marginal Principle)

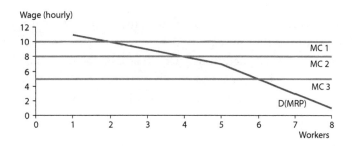

Figure 9.1 Labor Demand and Wages

WHAT CAUSES SHIFTS (CHANGES) IN THE DEMAND FOR LABOR?

Three factors can change the demand for labor and shift the labor demand curve:

1. *Change in price of the firm's products:* if the price of the firm's output changes, the demand for labor changes. An increase in the price of output increases the demand for labor and shifts the demand curve rightward and vice versa;
2. *Changes in prices of other factors of production:* if the prices of other factors of production change, in the long-run, the demand for labor changes. An increase in the price of a substitute factor leads the firm to increase the demand for labor.
3. *Changes in technology:* if a change in technology increases the productivity of one type of labor, the demand for this labor increases, and the demand curve shifts rightward.

2. MARKET SUPPLY FOR LABOR

In all type of economies, and especially in modern ones, labor is an important factor of production, and this market looks different from markets for goods and services.

Workers' willingness and ability to work a specified amount of time at alternative wage rates is demonstrated by the *market supply for labor.* In other words, the market supply for labor shows the relationship between the wage rate and the quantity of labor supplied. For example, when the first McDonald's restaurant was opened in Moscow, Russia, in 1989, 25,000 young Muscovites, mostly students who spoke two to three foreign languages, applied for 630 jobs for $2.50 per hour. The Moscow McDonald's at Pushkin Square is now the biggest in the world, with 900 seats, serving 15,000 diners a day.

The *market supply curve for labor* is positively sloped. As the wage increases, the quantity of labor supplied is likely to increase for three reasons even if not all individual labor supply curves are upward-sloping: a) hours per worker will increase for some workers; b) some workers will switch to this market from other fields; and c) some workers will migrate into this geographical area from other areas (figure 9.2).

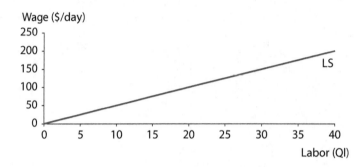

Working requires sacrifices in leisure time. So we have to consider the real *opportunity cost* associated with working, which includes free time for other activities which is given up in the process. Let's recall that opportunity costs are the most desired goods and services that are forgone to obtain something else. We face a real tradeoff when we decide to go to work or not.

It is important to note that for *the individual decision about how many hours to work*, supply of labor involves two effects:

a. *Substitution effect*: If we devote more time to working, we will have less time for leisure; as a result, the *opportunity cost of job time increases*, and we require correspondingly higher rates of pay;

b. *Income effect*: Our primary reason for working is the income a job provides. But as our income rises, the *marginal utility of income declines*. Back to our graph of labor supply—the upward slope of an individual's supply curve is a reflection of the increasing opportunity cost of labor and the decreasing marginal utility of income as a person works more hours.

As for motivations for working, money is the most important motivation, but it is not the only one. The wages offered for more work at some point lose some of their attractiveness, and this is the explanation for why an individual's supply curve bends backward (figure 9.3).

WHAT CAUSES SHIFTS (CHANGES) IN THE SUPPLY OF LABOR?

Three factors can change the supply of labor and shift the labor supply curve:

1. *Changes in adult population*: An increase in the adult population increases the supply of labor, and the supply of labor curve shifts rightward. In the US, the labor force grows by approximately 1% per year as a result of the relatively high birth rate (compared to other advanced economies) and immigration;

2. *Changes in preferences and social norms*: If more people decide they prefer working to spending time at leisure, the supply of labor increases, and the supply of the labor curve shifts rightward. A striking example is the increase in the number of employed women in the US since the 1960s.

3. *Changes in opportunities, wealth, time in school, and training*: For example, if people spend more time in school and training, the supply of low-skilled labor decreases and shifts leftward; the supply of high-skilled labor increases and shifts rightward.

Table 9.3

	Wage rate ($/hour)	Q Labor (hours/week)
a	60	30
b	50	35
c	40	39
d	30	40
e	20	38
f	10	30
g	5	0

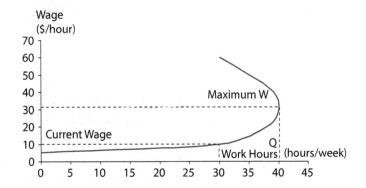

Figure 9.3
Individual
Supply Curve

3. LABOR MARKET EQUILIBRIUM: CHANGING OUTCOMES AND WAGE DIFFERENTIALS

As Figure 9.4a shows, equilibrium in the labor market determines the wage rate and quantity of employment. In the figure, the equilibrium wage rate is $100 per day and the equilibrium quantity of workers employed is 20.

The number of employers and the marginal revenue product of labor in each firm in an industry affects the market demand for labor. On the supply side, the market supply of labor depends on the quantity of available workers and each worker's willingness to work at alternative wage rates.

Figure 9.4a
Market
Equilibrium

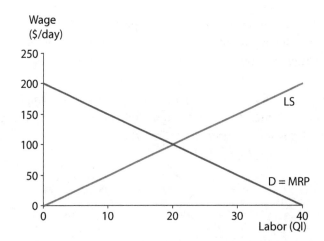

Figure 9.4b
Perfect
Competitor
Equilibrium

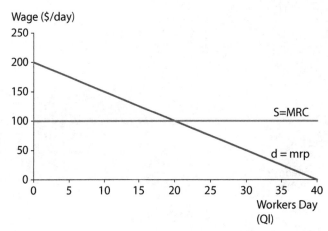

The *equilibrium wage* is the wage at which the quantity of labor supplied in a given period of time equals the quantity of labor demanded. The intersection of the market supply and demand curves establishes the equilibrium wage—the only wage at which the quantity of labor supplied equals the quantity of labor demanded—*equilibrium employment*. The intersection of labor supply and demand determines not just the prevailing wage rate but the level of employment, as well. For a firm in a perfectly competitive labor market, equilibrium wage is established by the intersection of market demand and market supply for labor (figure 9.4 b.).

In the real world, there are large disparities in average wages between those of different ethnic groups and between women and men. Occupation type is also another factor in wage rates.

WHY DO WAGES DIFFER?

Supply and demand for various occupations allow us to review wage differentials:

First, on the demand side, the strength of labor demand differs greatly among occupations. *The revenue contribution of workers to their employer depends on the workers' productivity* and the demand for their products. For top professional athletes, MRP is exceptionally high. If an occupation is in high demand, those workers will have higher wages, and where there is a reduced supply of workers, those workers will receive higher wages, too. The existence of *compensating differentials*—differences across occupations—shows that jobs differ in attractiveness, pleasure, and requirements. In order to persuade a worker to move, an employer should set the wage high enough to compensate the worker for: 1) the wage paid in the industry from which the worker is moving; 2) moving costs (financial and psychological); and 3) differences in the attractiveness of working in the old industry.

Second, on the supply side of the labor market, workers are not homogenous since the labor force is made up of many noncompeting groups of workers. There are strong *supply restrictions* based on: a) differences in people's talent, abilities, and skills; b) fewer workers have the required skills for a specific job; c) high training costs; d) undesirable and unpleasant job features; and e) artificial barriers to entry, etc.

Third, human capital acquired through education and training. An investment in human capital is an expenditure on education or training that improves skills and, therefore, productivity. Workers who have made greater investments in education achieve higher incomes in their careers. An average college graduate earns about twice as much as a high school graduate, and this disparity has only increased over time. College graduates obtain training and some skills so they can earn more based on productivity differences which, in economics, is called the *learning effect.* There is also a *signaling effect* with a college education. A college degree signals to an employer that the applicant has more skills and is a more productive worker.

Fourth, women typically earn less than their male counterparts, which is described as *gender discrimination.* There is also *racial discrimination.* Across all ethnicities: a) part of the gender gap is caused by differences in education, experience, and training, and, thus, some of the wage difference reflects a productivity difference; b) another explanation is occupational discrimination; women may choose only to enter certain occupations (perhaps due to past discrimination in other occupations), and, thus, the supply of workers in those areas is relatively high, and wages are consequently low; c) one reason why black workers tend to earn less than white workers is because of less education and training; and d) another reason is racial discrimination, which may be responsible for about half of the wage gap. Sometimes discrimination has been institutionalized by government policy. In the past, African Americans in the United States were prohibited from attending "whites-only" public schools and universities, and this, of course, had an impact on education, experience, and earnings.

Fifth, market imperfections: a) workers may lack information about alternative opportunities; b) workers may be reluctant to move to other locations; c) artificial restraint on mobility may be created by unions and professional organizations; and d) discrimination may crowd women and minorities into certain labor markets and out of others.

4. PUBLIC POLICY AND CHANGING OUTCOMES IN LABOR MARKETS

Can wages and employment rise together? The answer is yes; if productivity of labor rises, then wages can increase without sacrificing jobs. As we see in Figure 9.5, wage and employment decisions depend on productivity.

If productivity increases, the labor-demand curve shifts upward (from D1 to D2). In this case, the employer can pay higher wages (W2) or hire more workers (E2). Increased productivity is the most important factor for rising wages and living standards. This can lead to a situation where workers can earn higher wages without sacrificing jobs or lowering wages.

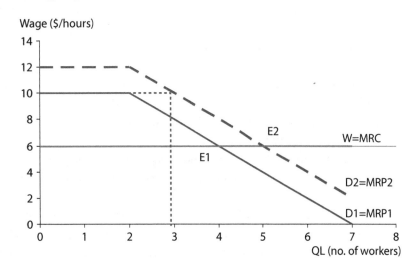

Figure 9.5 Increased Productivity and Wage Rates Wage ($$/Hours)

What are the main factors that influence market supply and demand for labor and level of wages?

1. *Changes in price of produced output.* We already know that marginal revenue product (MRP) represents the interaction of productivity and prices: if prices were to double for a specific product, workers that were producing this product would become twice as valuable, and this is an argument in favor of their wages increasing.
2. *Legal minimum wages.* The legal minimum wage was imposed by the Fair Standards Act of 1938, and the government decreed that no worker could be paid less than 25 cents per hour. Since that time, the federal minimum wage has increased to $7.25 per hour (2009)—after long and arduous congressional debates initiated by Democrats (the late Senator Edward Kennedy).

How does minimum wage, which is a *floor pricing practice,* affect the demand and supply for labor (figure 9.6)?

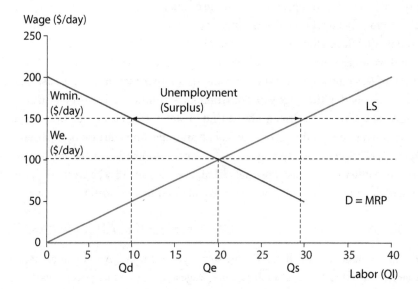

At the new equilibrium enforced by the government, when a Wm must be paid, it makes no sense for employers to hire more workers because MRP is not high enough to justify paying the legal minimum. As a result, some workers lose their jobs (Qe – Qd). At the same time, the higher minimum wage will attract more people into the market, and the supply of workers will switch from Qe to Qs. The outcome is a market surplus, with more job seekers than jobs (Qs – Qd), and this will lead to unemployment.

There are two approaches to minimum wage policy:

1. Negative, based on two major criticisms: 1) the minimum wage forces employers to pay a higher than equilibrium wage, and they will hire just a few workers and 2) the minimum wage is not an effective tool to fight poverty (teenagers from affluent families who are guaranteed this minimum do not need protection from poverty).
2. Positive: a) in a monopolistic market, the minimum wage increases wages with minimal effects on employment and b) increasing minimum wage may reduce labor turnover and training costs.

In *conclusion*: The government creates a market surplus of labor by enforcing a minimum wage (wage floor). This also reduces the quantity of labor demanded, and it increases the quantity of labor supplied. This leads to a tradeoff: some workers do better while others end up worse off (teenagers and inexperienced workers). Of course, this situation also depends on the degree of minimum wage increases (elasticity of labor demand) and on the state of the economy: if the economy is growing rapidly, the demand for labor will increase, too. The minimum wage has strong political support based on the evidence that many in the labor force benefit with a minimum wage. The minimum wage also gives some assurances that workers aren't taken advantage of my employers.

Some occupations are restricted by government licensing which results in fewer candidates for those positions. This is known as *occupational licensing* The licensing is a way to set requirements for entrance to such occupations as education, testing, experience, or residency. These restrictions can protect consumers from incompetent workers. Some of the criticisms of this practice are:

a. The link is weak between performance and licensing requirements.
b. Alternative measures of protecting consumers exist, such as providing information on the worker's past performance.
c. Entry restrictions raise prices.

5. MONOPSONY, UNION MODELS, AND BILATERAL MONOPOLY

We examined the purely competitive labor market, where each employer hires too small a quantity of workers to influence the wage rate, and, on the other side, where workers are not organized in a union, which could protect them and increase their wages.

Let's examine a different situation, a *monopsony*, after the Greek word which means "single buyer," just as "monopoly" means "single seller." In such a market a) there is only one buyer of labor; b) workers have no other employment alternatives; and c) the firm is a "wage maker." Since the monopsonist is the only "buyer" (employer) in this market, its marginal resource (labor) cost exceeds the wage rate (in Figure 9.7, the MRC curve lies above the labor cost curve, S).

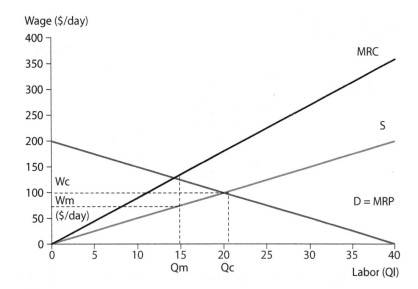

Figure 9.7
Monopsony
Labor Market

In comparison with a perfectly competitive labor market, a monopsonist would hire fewer workers (Qm < Qc) and pay less (Wm < Wc). The outcome is as inefficient as the case of a monopoly. In the US, there are not many examples of such markets. They include markets for professional athletes, public school teachers, and nurses. For example, the National Basketball Association, the National Football League, and Major League Baseball use "player drafts" for first-year players to bar teams from competing for players, at least for a few years, until some of them become "free agents."

An alternative model is a situation where workers sell their services collectively through unions which bargain with a relatively large number of employers. The union model represents an opposite model of imperfect competition in the labor market where the workers are organized and employers do not deal directly with individual workers but with their unions. Statistical studies indicate that US union members earn an average of 10% to 25% more than nonunion workers in comparable activities. At least half of these higher wages can be explained by the effect of union firms that are able to hire more productive workers.

Labor unions are usually created in capital intensive industries to take collective action for higher wages. The union negotiates with employers to get and maintain an above equilibrium wage, (Wu) as we can see in Figure 9.8a. In the case of success, a higher wage price will be fixed for the union's workers, and, at the same time, nonunionized workers will be excluded from this market. What happens to them? They will be forced to go into the nonunionized market and will shift the supply of labor in these industries to the right with a decrease in the wage rate (from We to Wn) (figure 9.8b).

Figure 9.8a
Unionized
Market

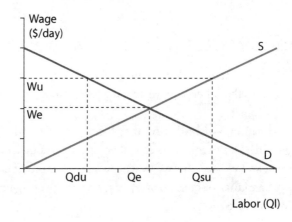

Figure 9.8b
Nonunionized
Market

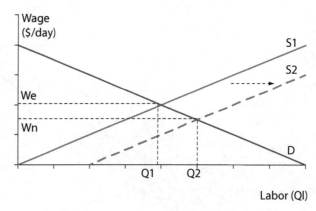

There are three union models:

1. *Demand-enhancement model*—to increase labor demand, the union might alter one or more of the determinants of demand by being engaged in political lobbying: a) to increase the demand for a product it is producing or b) to enhance the productivity of labor or alter the prices of other inputs. Examples are teachers' unions, which push for increased public spending on education, and aerospace industry unions, which lobby for increased military spending, etc.

2. *Exclusive or craft union model*—this type of union supports legislation that has a) restricted immigration; b) reduced child work; c) encouraged compulsory retirement; and d) enforced a shorter work week. In the case of craft unions, their members possess particular skills, for example, carpenters, plumbers, etc. These unions, by following restrictive membership policies, artificially restrict labor supply which results in higher wage rates and constitutes what is called *exclusive unionism.* They can accomplish such restrictions and higher wages through occupational licensing, for example, the American Medical Association, the National Education Association, the American Bar Association, etc. The licensing requirements often include a residency requirement, which inhibits the interstate movement of qualified workers. Some 600 occupations now require licenses in the United States.

3. *Inclusive or industrial union model*—instead of limiting membership, the model seeks to organize all available workers, such as automobile workers and steel workers. An industrial union that includes virtually all available workers in its membership can put firms under great pressure to agree to its wage demands.

Are unions successful in raising the wages of their members? Yes, of course. At least 15% of increases in wages is due to union activity. This success is sometimes caused by a so-called *unemployment effect*, by the decline by 20–30% in the number of workers employed. This effect can be annihilated in two ways:

1. Economic growth that increases the demand for labor and can offset the unemployment effect associated with an indicated wage increase; and
2. Elasticity of demand for labor: if the demand is inelastic, the wage increase will not have as much effect on employment as it would if the demand were elastic.

4. *The case of a bilateral monopoly model*: a monopsonist employer faces a unionized labor force; in other words, both the employer and employees have monopoly power: a union is a monopolistic "seller" of labor that can control supply and influence the wage rate, and a *monopsony* is the only "buyer" of labor that can affect wages by altering its employment. Examples are the steel, automobile, and construction equipment industries; professional sports; etc. In such a model:

1. The outcome is indeterminate and will depend on negotiations and bargaining power.
2. The outcome might be socially more desirable than the result of one-sided market power. The monopoly power of the union on one side of the market can offset the monopsony power of management on the other side. The resulting wage rate and level of employment may be closer to competitive levels than would be the case if monopoly existed on only one side of the market.

HOW CAN UNIONS INCREASE EFFICIENCY?

1. Unions can improve the morale of the work force and improve communication between workers and management which will lead to better decisions.
2. A union as a collective voice can improve working conditions rather than one employee leaving his or her job.
3. In the case when the labor market power is held by employers on one side of the market, a union on other side may be a counterbalance that increases efficiency.

PAYING EFFICIENCY WAGES

Employers can't really distinguish between good and bad (lazy) workers in the marketplace, so they offer a single wage. This may cause hard workers to leave the market; thus, an employer may make more profit by paying *efficiency wages*. These are higher wages offered to attract better workers.

As previously noted, Henry Ford, the founder of automobile industry who first introduced assembly-line production, dominated the industry in the 1920s. His attitude toward consumers' choices was unusual, to say the least. His famous Model "T" was only available in black. When one of his specialists told him that customers prefer different colors, not just black, his reaction was: "They can have any color of car they want—so long as it is black." He paid for his views with lost sales. He was challenged by Alfred P. Sloan, who had merged some smaller companies into what became General Motors. He gave consumers their choice of colors, with different types, price, and quality of his cars and GM became the dominant auto manufacturer for the rest of twentieth century. But Ford acted in a totally different way in the market for labor. He was the first to offer his workers $5 per day, up from $2.50. At that time, the typical market wage in manufacturing was $2–$3 per day. Ford raised the value of the job, and he created strong motivations for workers. Consequently, labor productivity rose just during that year (1914) by 51%, and $5 was an efficiency wage.

6. IN LIEU OF A CONCLUSION: WHAT'S A PRESIDENT WORTH? (CASE STUDY)

In order to better understand the practices of wage establishment, let's consider two concrete cases: The salary of the Walt Disney Company's CEO (Michael Eisner) and the salary of the President of the United States.

The Disney Company CEO became one of the richest rewarded employees in the history of the US, being offered in 1977 a ten-year contract for the astronomical figure of $500 million. This didn't include his annual salary—$750,000—and bonuses (up to $15 million annually). Of course, the performance of the company under his leadership was impressive: revenue increased from $1.5 billion in 1984 to $18.7 billion in 1996 (the stock value skyrocketed from $3 per share to $75.37) and the company became one of Wall Street's star performers. Nevertheless, critics consider such CEO pay unjustifiable:

4. The impressive increase in the stock price reflected not only the company's performance but also the general upswing in the market.
5. The revenues of the Walt Disney Company would be greater by $500 million in the absence of Michael Eisner.
6. Eisner might have been satisfied with just $300 or $400 million.

The question is: How do we measure the marginal revenue product of CEOs, in general?

How do we quantify his or her contribution to a company's performance? The same question confronted the US Congress when the annual salary of the American president was established. A president's salary of $400,000 per year is higher than the salary of 99.9% of all American workers. But it is insignificant in comparison with the salaries of CEOs who run big corporations ($38–$58 million per year) even though the president supervises a budget of $1.8 trillion, or eleven times bigger than that of GM, the nation's largest corporation; he is the boss of 4.2 million employees (civilian and military), which is six times larger than the number employed by Wal-Mart, the nation's largest employer. The President of the United States would have to work for 2,878 years to make the amount that the Walt Disney Company CEO made during just one year.

To find an explanation for this situation, we need to look at *the opportunity wage,* or the wage that public officials could earn in private industry. In the case of the President of the United States, the salary is not so much a reflection of his contribution to the total output of the country as a matter of custom. It is the reflection of the price voters believe is required for such a person.

Opportunity wages may help explain CEO salary but do not justify such high levels. In the opinion of their critics, it is necessary to revise the practice, in general, to involve independent experts and stockholder representatives rather than self-serving committees formed from executives of the same or similar huge companies.

7. KEY TERMS

Labor, Labor Market
Nominal and Real Wage
Demand for Labor, Marginal Revenue Product
Output Effect, Input Substitution Effect
Market Supply for Labor
Income Effect
Opportunity Cost of Working
Labor Market Equilibrium, Equilibrium Wage, Equilibrium Employment
Compensating Differentials
Learning Effect, Signaling Effect
Labor Productivity
Floor Pricing Practice
Legal Minimum Wage, Efficiency Wage, Opportunity Wage
Monopsony
Labor Unions Models, Demand-Enhancement, Exclusive (Craft), Inclusive (Industrial) Models
Bilateral Monopoly Model

8. PROBLEMS AND APPLICATIONS

1. Which of the following refers to labor supply?
   a. The number of people who want jobs and have respective qualifications.
   b. A wage that employers are willing to pay and workers are willing to accept.
   c. The quantities of labor supplied at alternative wage rates in a given period of time.
   d. The willingness and capacity of employers to hire workers.

2. How can we classify labor demand as derived demand?
   a. It depends on the incomes of individuals.
   b. The demand for the goods and services labor produces.
   c. It is dependent on the wage rate.
   d. It is affected by the number of people who are willing and capable to work.

3. The marginal revenue product of labor is the change in:
   a. Total revenue divided by the change in the quantity of labor.
   b. Total output divided by the change in the quantity of labor.
   c. The quantity of labor divided by the change in total revenue.
   d. Total revenue divided by the percentage change in the quantity of labor.

4. What conditions will cause additional workers to be hired?
   a. Labor supply curve is backward bending and depends on the opportunity cost of labor work.
   b. Wage rate exceeds the new worker's marginal revenue product and is attractive to new workers.
   c. The firm is making an economic profit and has enough resources to pay new workers.
   d. New workers' marginal revenue product is greater than or equal to their wage.

5. How is the equilibrium level of employment determined?
   a. The market demand for labor and the market supply of labor as in any other market.
   b. Government regulations.
   c. The intersection of MPP and MRP.
   d. It is determined by a monopsony, the most powerful employer in a market.

6. What would happen to wages if labor productivity is increasing?
   a. They will decrease, and the number of jobs will decrease by the same proportion.
   b. They can increase without a decrease in the number of jobs.
   c. They will decrease, but the number of jobs will remain the same.
   d. They can increase but only if the number of jobs is reduced.

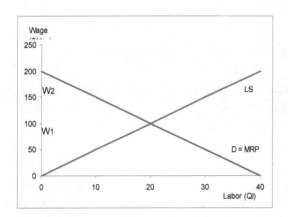

7. In the figure above, at a wage of W2, there is a:
   a. Surplus of labor equal to 30 workers.
   b. Shortage of labor equal to 20 workers.
   c. Surplus of labor equal to 20 workers.
   d. The market is in equilibrium.

8. Establishing the minimum wage above the equilibrium wage will result in:
   a. A surplus of labor since buyers move up the labor-demand curve.
   b. A shortage of jobs since sellers move down the labor-supply curve.
   c. A surplus of jobs because sellers move up the labor-supply curve.
   d. A shortage of labor because buyers move down the labor-demand curve.

9. When people are standing in line for jobs, and there are more applicants than jobs, then the labor market is characterized by a:
   a. Surplus of jobs from the point of view of the seller (workers).
   b. Surplus of labor from the point of view of an economist
   c. Shortage of labor from the point of view of a labor union.
   d. Shortage of jobs from the point of view of the buyer (employers).

10. What do labor unions do to the labor market?
    a. Attaining above-equilibrium wages for union members and pushing some workers into non-unionized markets.
    b. Increasing union employment and excluding some workers from the unionized market.
    c. Decreasing labor demand in a unionized market and increasing the labor supply in the non-unionized market.
    d. All of the above.
    e. None of the above.

9. REVIEW QUESTIONS

1. Suppose you are a manger of a small firm in a competitive craft market in Maryland. Which of the following factors will determine your firm's demand for labor: a) the market equilibrium wage rate; b) the price of a product your firm produces, and the wage rate you pay; c) the marginal product of labor and the market wage rate; or d) the price of the product the firm is producing, and the marginal product of labor.

2. The quantity of labor demanded in the market depends on two effects:
   a. The output effect: it implies that a decrease in the wage will _____ production cost, so the price of output will _____ and the quantity of output demanded will _____. As a result, the quantity of labor demanded will _____.
   b. The input-substitution effect: a decrease in the wage _____ (increases/decreases) the quantity of labor per unit of _____, so the quantity of labor demanded _____ (increases/decreases).

3. You open a car wash in your hometown that employs seven people. The employees are paid $10 per hour, and a standard wash sells for $5. If you are looking to maximize the profit, what should be the value of the marginal product of the last worker you hired? What is that worker's marginal product?

4. Assume that a perfectly competitive firm employs one worker. It produces 20 units of a good, and when it employs two workers, it produces 40 units of output. The firm sells its product for $10 per unit. What is the marginal revenue product connected with hiring the second worker?

5. How will the demand for labor be affected if: a) a new education program is launched by the company which will increase labor's marginal product and b) the firm completes a new plant with a larger workforce and new equipment.

CHAPTER 10.

HOW GOVERNMENT REACTS WHEN MARKETS FAIL

The market, through its verified mechanism of prices which result from the interaction of demand and supply, is the best system for achieving productive and allocative efficiency. We have already seen how Adam Smith's "invisible hand" works through the interaction of individuals in markets, each one acting in his or her own self-interest; it promotes society's interests in the best possible way: "It is not from the benevolence of the butcher, the brewer, or the baker that we expect our dinner, but from their regard to their own interest. We address ourselves, not to their humanity but to their self-love, and never talk to them of our own necessities but of their advantages ... [Man] led by an invisible hand to promote an end which was no part of this intention ... By pursuing his own interest he frequently promotes that of society more effectually than when he really intends to promote it ..." (Adam Smith, *An Inquiry into the Nature and Causes of the Wealth of Nations*, first published in 1776; New York, Random House, 1973, Book 4, Ch. 2). But what happens when the price mechanism fails to allocate the resources to produce society's optimum combination of goods and services (allocative efficiency) or to produce any particular good or service in the least costly way (productive efficiency)? When markets fail, people often use political means to force the government to step in and compensate for the shortcomings of markets.

The purpose of this chapter is to answer the following questions: Why do markets fail? What is the economic role of the government? How can the government intervene? What are the limits of such intervention? What is the nature of market failure? What are potential government inefficiencies?

1. MARKET FAILURE AND GOVERNMENT REACTION

At any moment in time, society is looking for the best possible (optimal) combination of goods and services that can be produced with existing resources, technology, and social values. This combination is usually provided by the market through its verified mechanism: prices and sales. But because the mix of output chosen by the market mechanism in pursuing the profit maximization target is sometimes different from society's optimum, we talk about market failure, or about the imperfections of the market mechanism. We can illustrate this situation by using a Production Possibilities model that shows what mix of output can be produced with our existing resources and technology (figure 10.1). To correct this failure, the government is required to intervene.

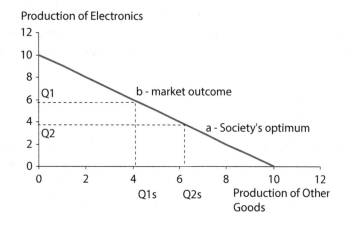

Figure 10.1
Market Failure

There are at least four main reasons for government involvement in a market economy:

First, government can provide a legal and institutional framework for market transactions, protecting against monopoly behavior and maintaining competition. The mechanism of monopoly behavior, as we analyzed it in

Chapter 6, is quite simple. It says, in essence, that if in the perfect market environment prices reflect the social optimum (P = MC), a monopolist, in contrast, maximizes profit by producing less and charging higher prices (MR = MC). Prices are artificially maintained higher than marginal costs, and, as a result of such under allocation of resources, society pays more for a particular good or service. To prevent such monopolistic behavior, the government should first establish public regulatory agencies and, second, enact antimonopoly (antitrust) legislation designed to inhibit or prevent the growth of monopoly. A special issue is the regulation of natural monopolies.

Second, government can reallocate resources because of market externalities and costs. We will examine in this chapter the spillover benefits related to public goods and the role of government in the provision of these goods. The benefits of producing or consuming a public good are not confined to the producer and/or consumer of the good. For this and other reasons, markets that produce public goods tend to be inefficient; that is, the quantities produced are usually too low. The government could attempt to correct this problem by paying a subsidy to producers equal to the external benefit of additional output. This chapter also explores the effects of spillover costs, or (negative) externalities. The economic approach to preventing spillover costs is to force producers to pay for the pollution they generate, for example.

Third, government can attempt to correct imperfect information, which is also a contributing factor in explaining why resources may not be allocated efficiently in a market system. As we will see, asymmetric information in a market may lead to a downward spiral of price and quantity. Adverse selection and the moral hazard problem are other components of the imperfect information scenario where both consumers and producers in the market may make less than optimal, fully informed decisions.

Fourth, government can attempt to stabilize the aggregate economy to maintain full employment and stable prices and can redistribute income and wealth through monetary, fiscal, and/or supply side policies. In light of the 2007–9 recession in the United States and other advanced markets, which was the worst recession since the Great Depression of the 30s, these functions of the government have become even more important, and we will analyze them in more detail in the macroeconomics section of the book.

Market failure reflects that the intersection of market supply and market demand curves do not always lead to the best (optimal) mix of output on the Production Possibilities Curve. In this case, the government, as a nonmarket force, should intervene and correct the market failure. There are four modalities of government intervention into the economy: a) public goods; b) externalities; c) market power; and d) equity.

2. PUBLIC GOODS VS. PRIVATE GOODS

The main characteristics of most of consumer goods are excludability and rivalry. *Rivalry* means that when you buy and consume a product, it is not available to another person. A doughnut or a hot dog purchased by John for his personal consumption is not available for Pete's, or anyone else's, consumption. *Excludability* means that you, as a producer (seller), can keep your product away from those consumers who are not able to pay for it. In contrast, a public good is characterized by nonrivalry and nonexcludability. In other words, the exclusiveness of private goods is not characteristic for public goods, such as national defense, environmental protection, or street lightening.

So, we can define a *Public Good* as a good or service which isn't limited to consumption by one person. Other people can also consume the public good. A *Private Good* is limited to one person's consumption and will not be consumed by others. It is important to note that the economic sense of public good is different from the popular perception of these goods. The distinction between these two types of goods is based on the nature of these goods and not for whom they are produced. The term "public good" refers only to those goods and services that are consumed jointly both by those who pay for them and by those who don't.

Public goods consumption involves the *free rider problem;* a free rider happens when someone gains benefits from another person's purchase or consumption of a good. The free rider does not purchase the good for him- or herself. One example is flood control: all farmers in the valley are interested in preventing a flood by building a dam, but none of them are willing to pay for it. The flip side of free riding is the chump problem—no one wants to be a chump who gives free rides to others. To overcome the free rider problem and provide public goods, many organizations, such as public radio and television and religious and charitable organizations, successfully encourage people to give voluntary contributions of private goods (books, CDs, magazine subscriptions, etc.) or matching cash contributions (when your $10 will be matched with your colleagues' cash contribution to support your favorite sports team). These organizations encourage people to give based on civic and moral responsibility, etc.

We can conclude that the main differences between public and private goods are technical considerations, the *technical capability to exclude nonpayers.* To the list of public goods, we could add the administration of justice, the regulation of commerce, and foreign relations.

How much of public goods should be provided? Because of nonrivalry and nonexcludability, private firms cannot profitably produce a public good if they will not be supported financially. So, if society wants this good, it would be the government that should produce it or finance its production through taxation. Otherwise, we will face the underproduction of this particular good. Hence, if public goods were marketed like private goods, everyone would wait for someone else to pay. As a result, the market tends to underproduce public goods and overproduce private goods. That's why government intervention is so important.

How do we determine demand and supply for public goods? The government usually estimates demand for public goods through voting or surveys. These may include hypothetical questions; for example, what price is too much to pay for a public good? One of the main reasons for the existence of the government is to provide to citizens the ability to tax themselves for the opportunity to have public goods, like national defense. To identify the collective *demand curve for a public good,* which is also called the *willingness to pay curve,* we have to vertically sum all individual demand curves. We add the prices that people are willing to pay for an additional unit of the public good at each possible quantity demanded. In fact, these curves are *marginal benefit curves.* Because of the Law of Diminishing Marginal Utility, each successive unit of any good yields less added benefit (Figs. 10.2a and b).

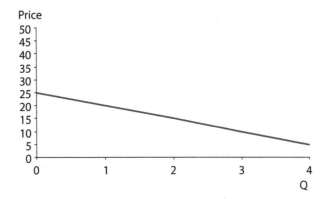

Figure 10.2a
John's
Individual
Demand (MB1)

Figure 10.2b
Pete's Individual
Demand (MB2).

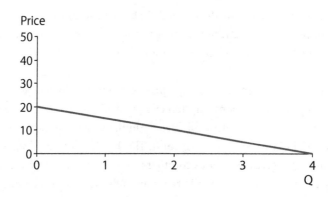

Figure 10.2c
Collective
Demand (MSB)

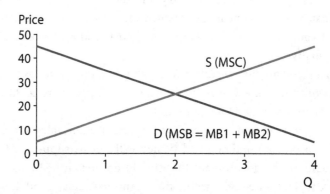

The *supply curve* is the same as a *marginal-cost curve* for a public or private good or service. Marginal cost rises as more of a good is produced, according to the Law of Increasing Opportunity Cost. But because of the Law of Diminishing Returns, the total quantity of a public good rises at a diminishing rate. In the short-run, the government adds more variable resources (labor) to the fixed resources. The intersection of the demand curve determines the optimal quantity of a public good and measures society's marginal benefit of each unit of this good (D = MSB). Society's marginal cost of each unit (S = MSC) is measured by the supply curve. The point of intersection equates the marginal benefit and marginal cost of allocating society's scarce resources (MSB = MSC) (figure 10.2c)

Cost-benefit analysis is used to identify whether or not to provide a particular public good and how much of it to provide. The analysis involves a comparison of marginal social costs and marginal social benefits. If the government intends to build a highway, for example, this will involve costs—the loss of satisfaction resulting from the accompanying decline in the production of private goods—and benefits—the extra satisfaction resulting from the output of more public goods. Should the resources be shifted from the private to the public sector in this case?

Back to our example: If there are a few projects of highway construction, we have to look, first, to total annual benefit, which must exceed total annual cost. Second, we must compare the additional, or marginal cost, and the additional, or marginal benefit, relating to each of these plans. The government should: a) increase an activity or output as long as the marginal benefit exceeds the marginal cost; b) stop the activity at, or as close as possible to, the point at which the marginal benefit equals the marginal cost; and c) not undertake a project for which marginal cost exceeds marginal benefit.

The *marginal-cost-marginal-benefit rule* provides us with the maximum net benefit (marginal benefit-marginal cost).

3. POSITIVE EXTERNALITIES VS. NEGATIVE EXTERNALITIES

The term *externalities* refers to all benefits or costs of a market activity born by a third party, that is, by someone other than the immediate producer or consumer; externalities can be positive or negative. Let's introduce a few key notions:

First, the *private benefit* is what the consumer receives when he or she consumes a good or service. The *social benefit* is the private benefit plus any *external benefit*, for example, resulting from your college education. The market is under producing goods that yield external benefits and overproducing those that generate external costs.

Second, let's consider the mechanism of *consumption decisions*, for example, the case of market demand and social demand for cars. The market demand reflects only private interest and private benefit. But when we are looking for collective well-being, we must distinguish the social demand for a product from the market demand whenever externalities exist (figure 10.3).

Social demand = market demand − externalities

In our case, the market demand overstates the social benefits because of the existing external costs of driving for society, such as congestion and pollution which, in this case, are negative externalities. Sometimes, externalities are positive. When external benefits exist, the social demand exceeds the market demand. Society wants more goods and services that generate external benefits, and that's why the government subsidies education, for example.

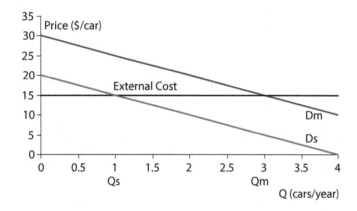

Figure 10.3
Social and
Market Demand

Third, externalities are also related to the *production process*. Let's analyze the mechanism of *production decisions* and profit maximization in the case of power plants that use coal to generate electricity and are, at the same time, a major source of pollution. Because production processes that control pollution may be more expensive than those that do not, the MC1 and ATC1 curves will shift upward, to MC2 and ATC2. This will reduce output and profits. A producer may have the incentive to use cheaper technology and to continue polluting (figure 10.4).

Eliminating the air and water pollution emanating from the electric plant will cost a lot of money, and who will benefit? The behavior of businesses is dictated by profit maximization and by comparison of revenues and costs, not by philanthropy, aesthetics, or concerns for the welfare of others. People tend to maximize their personal welfare, balancing private benefits against private costs. Whenever external costs exist, a private firm will not allocate its resources and operate its plant in such a way as to maximize social welfare.

Figure 10.4
Profit
Maximization
and Cost of
Pollution
Control

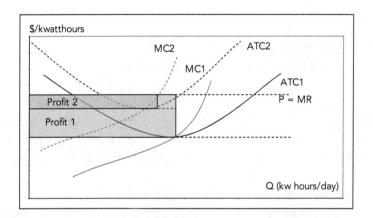

Figure 10.5
Social and
Private Cost

Fourth, social vs. private costs. Social costs are the total costs of all the resources that are used in a particular productions activity. *Private costs* are the resource costs that are incurred by the specific producer. The difference between the two costs represents the external costs.

External costs = social costs – private costs.

In Figure 10.5 we have the cost situation confronting the electric power plant. The social costs are higher than the private costs.

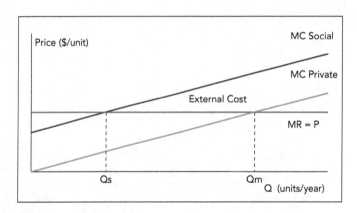

To maximize social welfare, we would equate social marginal costs with marginal revenue and produce the output Qs. The private profit maximizer equates private MC and MR and produces Qm. It makes more profits but also pollutes more.

4. HOW TO DEAL WITH EXTERNALITIES WITH OR WITHOUT GOVERNMENT INTERVENTION

There are *four main approaches to address the externalities* and solve the problem of misallocation of resources:

First, the Coase theorem, named after the Nobel Prize winning economist, Chicago University Professor Ronald Coase. In an article that he wrote in 1960, he emphasized that the ideal would be a situation where the private sector would address all types of externalities. In his opinion, private transaction is efficient if: a) property rights are clearly defined; b) the number of parties (people) involved is small; and c) transaction costs—the cost to make a deal—are negligible. Examples: transaction costs include the costs of communication, costs of making a legal agreement, costs of delays in bargaining, etc. The role of the government should be to encourage such bargaining rather than to get involved in direct restrictions or subsidies.

We can illustrate this approach with an example of the owner of a steel mill on a lake surrounded by forest who wants to clear-cut his land and expand his business, which could increase pollution, and the owner of a fishing farm on the lake: a) the owner of the farm has a strong economic incentive to negotiate with the owner of the steel mill, and he is willing to pay him to avoid the spillover cost and b) it doesn't matter which party is assigned the property rights. Both parties would have an economic incentive to eliminate the externality. Coase bargaining generates the efficient abatement (waste) level where the marginal benefit of abatement (an increase in fish harvest) equals the marginal cost of abatement (additional costs of abatement). If the steel mill owns the property rights to the lake, the fishing firm will pay the steel mill to abate pollution. If the fishing firm owns the lake, the steel mill will pay the fishing firm for permission to pollute (not to abate) the lake.

The limitations of the Coase theorem are linked with the fact that externalities affect many people, and bargaining may be too costly and inefficient.

Second, the assignment of liability through lawsuits. If one person's property damages another person, a private lawsuit may settle the dispute by assessing damage liability against the violator. The limitations are the cost and how many people can organize the lawsuit. "Clearly defined property rights and government liability laws help remedy some externality problems. They do [this] directly by forcing the perpetrator of the harmful externality to pay damages to those injured. They [also] do so indirectly by discouraging firms and individuals from generating spillover costs for fear of being sued" (McConnell, Brue and Flynn).

Third, the development of markets for externality rights. This policy was developed in regard to pollution abatement. The first program of marketable pollution permits was launched in 1976 by the US Environment Protection Agency (EPA) and then extended in 1985 to lead in gasoline and to the chemicals responsible for depletion of the ozone layer in 1988. The Clean Air Act of 1990 established a system of marketable pollution permits (known as allowances) for SO_2. In 2003, the EPA extended the market-based approach to the Clean Water Act, and in 2009 to the American Clean Energy and Security Act. This policy, called cap-and-trade, is one of the most effective ways to deal with pollution, and the United States has favored a global system of tradable emission permits for CO_2 similar to the system for controlling sulfur dioxide emission (SO_2) although some economists criticize the system as "licenses to pollute" (figure 10.6).

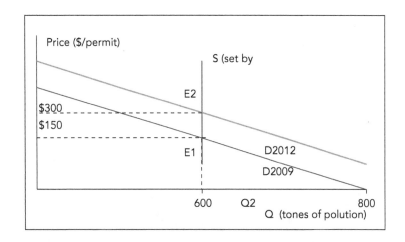

Figure 10.6
Market for
Pollution
Permits

Fourth, the direct application of government control or taxes to reduce negative externalities or spillover costs or to provide subsidies. The British economist Arthur Pigou, a professor at Cambridge University, was the first to propose a systematic analysis of externalities in his classical 1920 book, *The Economics of Welfare*. He introduced the notion of Marginal Social Cost (MSC) which accounts for the true cost to society of producing an additional unit of a product, which is the sum of the marginal private cost (MPC) plus the marginal external cost (MEC) caused by producing an additional unit of a good. To cover this cost, Pigou proposed that the government impose a tax on private producers. For example, to produce an additional unit of livestock, which generates an external cost for the society (pollution), will cost the farmer his or her marginal private cost plus the Pigouvian tax. By imposing such a tax, the government is internalizing the negative externality (figure 10.7).

To internalize an externality means that individuals are taking into account the externality when they make decisions.

Figure 10.7
Addressing
Negative
Externalities

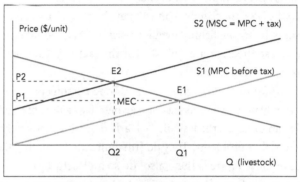

MSC = MPC + MEC
E1—equilibrium without tax, inefficient
E2—equilibrium with tax, efficient
P2—P1 = Piguvian Tax

An externality could be also positive and be related to an activity that generates external benefits for society as a whole for which the producer is not compensated. The most important source of external benefits is knowledge. To analyze its effects, we need to introduce a notion of *Marginal Social Benefit (MSB),* which is equal to the marginal private benefit (MPB) from producing an additional unit of a good plus the marginal external benefit (MEB) to society from this additional unit. How can the producer be encouraged to produce goods that yield external benefit? The government can provide a subsidy, known as a *Pigouvian subsidy* (figure 10.8).

Figure 10.8
Addressing
Positive
Externalities

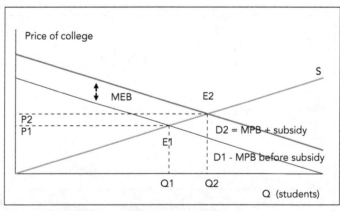

E1—equilibrium without subsidy, inefficient
E2—equilibrium with subsidy, efficient
P2—P1 = Piguvian subsidy

Economists prefer taxes that discourage negative externalities rather than policies that promote positive externalities. This is because it is a) much harder to identify and measure positive externalities that could lead to the benefits of knowledge and new technology than it is to identify negative externalities and b) producers receive a higher price—monetary gains—than they could otherwise, and this might degenerate into an inefficient allocation of resources under political pressure.

Examples are clean air and water legislation. The government can establish *emission charges* which are direct costs attached to the act of polluting. An emission charge increases private MC and reduces output. Another way to solve the solid waste disposal problem is to impose a deposit on all beverage containers. For example, the state of Oregon imposed a 5-cent deposit on beverage containers in 1972 and soon discovered that beverage container litter in Oregon declined by 81%.

In the case of *positive externalities* with large and diffuse spillover benefits, the government has at least three options to compensate for under allocation of resources: a) *subsidies to buyers*, for example, providing coupons for mothers to save up to 50% of the price of inoculations for their children; b) *subsidies to producers* which is a specific tax in reverse (taxes impose an extra cost on producers while subsidies reduce producers' cost); and c) *government provision*—providing a product as a public good (free vaccines to all children).

5. MARKET POWER AND ASYMMETRIC INFORMATION

As we learned, the market mechanism alone often fails to determine the socially desired, optimal mix of output. The response of the market to consumers' signals may be flawed. Let's analyze the factors that determine such a situation.

First, market power and restricted supply. We have already considered the notion of market power, which is the ability of a producer to alter (dictate) the market price for a good or a service. The most severe form of such power is the monopoly—a firm that can control the quantity of a good and dictate its prices to consumers. The mechanisms of such monopolist behavior are also well known: a) copyrights on books; b) patents (precluding others from making or selling a particular product); c) control of resources; d) restrictive production agreements; and e) efficiencies of massive production (economies of scale). Market power allows a single or a few producers to have discretionary power over the market response to price signals. They may use this power to enrich themselves as was the case with Microsoft a few years ago. This is a case of market failure. What should the reaction of the government be?

To prevent such monopolistic behavior, especially by natural monopolies, the government should: a) establish public regulatory agencies; b) enact antimonopoly (antitrust) legislation designed to inhibit or prevent the growth of monopolies, with clearly defined property rights and government liability laws (we addressed these issues in detail in Chapter 6); and c) develop and enforce clear merger guidelines to control the rise of market power through horizontal (between firms in the same industry) and vertical (between firms at different stages of production) mergers based on market definitions, measures of market concentration, and merger standards (see Chapter 7).

Second, we examined different types of market failure such as public goods, externalities, and market power. There is also *asymmetric information.* This is defined by parties to a market transaction who have unequal knowledge. Let's consider two cases: sellers and buyers.

1. *Sellers*: assume that in the milk market, there is no law-established system of weights or measurement. Every store could advertise a gallon of whole milk when in reality the container is filled with skim milk. In this example, grocery stores could sell gallons which were only filled half way. The government, of course, should intervene in such a market and establish a system of weights

and measures, employ inspectors to check the milk facilities to insure that their machinery is working correctly, etc. Licensing of surgeons and other highly skilled professionals also involves government-established standards that should be assured.

2. *Buyers* confront at least three challenges:
   a. The moral-hazard problem.
   b. The adverse-selection problem. This problem generates a downward spiral of price and quality of goods and services: the low-quality products on the market pull down the price consumers are willing to pay, which decreases the supply of high-quality products and the quality of goods in the market, in general, which, in turn, pulls down the price consumers are willing to pay, and so on.
   c. Workplace safety. Private methods of overcoming lack of information could be a solution to this problem. Here are a few methods:
      a. Warrantees
      b. Uniform standards
      c. Firms which specialize in providing information (travel guides, etc.)

6. EQUITY AND REDISTRIBUTION OF INCOME: TAXATION AND TRANSFERS

How should governments reallocate resources to support the production of public goods? How are externalities funded? How should the government redistribute income to address poverty and inequality since this is one of the most important issues of economic policy? To answer these questions, we need to analyze the principles, forms, and mechanisms of public sector financing. In comparison with other advanced nations, US government spending for all levels as a percentage of GDP is low, about 33% (in Sweden, France, and Italy it exceeds 50%). Americans pay less in taxes (as percentage of GDP—32%) than Swedes, French, Germans, Italians, Canadians, Spanish, and British. Nevertheless, income inequality in the United States is high, with about 13% of the population living below the poverty level and the gap between rich and poor increasing.

This is the explanation for why ***protecting labor and redistributing income*** through taxation, transfer payments, and intervention into the price mechanism represent some of the most essential functions of the government at each level: Federal, state, and local. *Taxes and Transfers* are a critical mechanism for redistribution of income. The art of taxation, according to Jean Baptist Colbert, finance minister to King Louis XIV of France, "consists of so plucking the goose as to obtain the largest amount of feathers while promoting the smallest amount of hissing." The largest **income transfer** program in the US is Social Security, which pays over $700 billion a year to 50 million older or disabled people. Income transfers are reserved exclusively for poor people: welfare benefits, food stamps, Medicaid, etc. Because of these transfers The poorest 20% of the low income population receive not only 1% of total income but 4%. As a result, the income-transfer system gives lower income households more output than the market itself provides.

Let's analyze the structure and size of government spending and revenues.

First, there are four types of *federal finance spending:* 1) Income security is the largest category by far—44%—and includes payments to the elderly and disadvantaged (Social Security, Medicare, unemployment compensation, etc.); 2) National defense represents the second largest category—20%; 3) Federal expenditures on education and health—21%—is the third largest expenditure; and 4) Interest on the public debt—6%. These expenditures are financed from four main sources of *tax revenue*:

1. *Personal Income Tax* (41% of total revenue) is levied on taxable income (exemptions constitute $3,700 for each household member, and deductions consist of business expenses, charitable

contributions, home mortgage interest payments, etc.). Personal income tax is a **progressive tax**: its average rate rises as income increases.

2. *Payroll taxes* (Social Security and Medicare contributions) are the second-largest source of revenues—40%. Payroll taxes are taxes based on wages and salaries and are used to finance two compulsory Federal programs for retired workers: Social Security and Medicare. Payroll taxes are regressive—they make up a lower percentage of income as income rises.

3. *Corporate income taxes* on corporate profits—the difference between a corporation's total revenue and its total expenses—are the third largest source of revenue—9%. This tax is proportional, or flat—it makes up the same percentage of income regardless of the size of income. For almost all corporations, the tax rate is 35%.

IRS figures based on income tax returns collected reveal that:
- The richest 1% paid 34% of all income tax collected.
- The richest 5% paid 53% of all income tax collected.
- The richest 10% paid 65% of all income tax collected.
- The lowest 50% paid less than 5% of the total income tax collected.

Clearly, the progressive nature of the federal tax system redistributes income away from richer households.

(**Source: Bade and Parkin,** *Foundations of Economics,* **5e.**)

---

4. *Excise taxes* on specific commodities (levied at the wholesale level) make up 4% of total revenue. The Federal Government collects excise taxes but does not levy a general sales tax which is a primary source of revenue for state governments.

Second, state and local governments have two major expenditures: providing goods and services and paying welfare benefits. State expenditures go to education—36%, public welfare—25%, health and hospitals—8%, highway maintenance and construction—8%, and public safety—5%. State revenues come primarily from sales and excise taxes (47%) and personal income taxes (36%). Seventy-two percent of *local finance* revenues come from property taxes; about 17% come from sales and excise taxes; about 44% of local expenditures go to education; 12% go to welfare, health, and hospitals; 11% go to public safety; and 8% go to housing, parks, streets, and highways. Altogether, local governments cover less than 50% of their expenditures; the remaining part is covered by grants from federal and state governments.

Third, in the United States, governments (Federal, state, and local) use two other ways to redistribute income along with taxes:

1. Income Maintenance Programs, such as:

   - *Social Security programs*: Old Age, Survivors, Disability, and Health Insurance (OASDHI) makes monthly cash payments to retired or disabled workers or their surviving spouses and children.
   - *Unemployment compensation*: Every state government has established an unemployment compensation program that taxes all employers in the state and gives unemployed workers in the state a periodic cash benefit for a specified period of time.
   - *Welfare programs*: Welfare programs provide incomes for people with incomes below a specified level who do not qualify for Social Security or unemployment programs. These programs

include the Supplementary Security Income (SSI) program, the Temporary Assistance for Needy Households (TANF) program, the Food Stamp program, and Medicaid.

2. *Provision of subsidized services*, provided by the government at prices below the cost of production. Examples include primary and secondary public education. The poorest 20% of households receive about 80% of their income from the government. Redistribution creates a net increase in income for the poorest 60% of all US households.

7. TRUST IN GOVERNMENT AND GOVERNMENT FAILURE

How well does the government perform when it replaces or regulates the market? James Buchanan won the Nobel Prize for Economics for his analysis of governments' decision-making in the process of allocating resources—the *public choice theory*. The essential principle of this theory is that politicians pursue their own self-interest to maximize their reelection chances rather than promote the best interests of society.

Sometimes, government intervention might worsen rather than improve market outcomes, failing to improve economic outcomes. This is *government failure*. It is possible for the mix of output or the income distribution to get worse after government intervention. That's why opinion polls often reveal little trust in the government. Usually, the confidence level is much higher in state and local governments than in the Federal Government. Government failure may have various forms:

1. *The special interest effect*—when a small number of people obtain a government program or policy that gives them large gains at the expense of a much greater number of people who individually suffer small losses. This effect is evident in the case of so-called pork-barrel politics, a means of securing government projects that yield benefits mainly to a single political district and its political representative. Politicians have a strong incentive to secure public goods ("pork") for their constituencies, and they engage in *logrolling* to remain elected: "You vote for my dairy price support bill, and I will vote for your tobacco price support bill."

2. *Rent-seeking behavior.* The appeal to government for special benefits at taxpayers' or someone else's expense is called rent-seeking. Corporations, trade associations, labor unions, and professional organizations employ vast resources to secure favorable government policies that result in rents—higher profits or income than would occur under competitive market conditions.

3. *Bureaucracy and inefficiency.* Some economists believe that public agencies are generally less efficient than private businesses. The market system creates incentives and pressures for internal efficiency that are absent from the public sector. The market system imposes a very obvious test of performance on private firms: the test of profit and loss. It is impossible to apply the same criteria to government institutions. What happens when a government official or an agency performs poorly? There is no competition like in a market, and taxpayers usually cannot exercise strong pressure like shareholders can in the case of a poorly performing company's manager. There is a lack of incentive to be efficient or creative. Conversely, bureaucrats may be extremely cautious and make all decisions by the book to secure their own or their agency's position.

8. KEY TERMS

Market Failure and Government Intervention in Economy
Public and Private Goods
Demand and Supply of Public Goods
Willingness to Pay Curve
Marginal Benefit and Marginal Cost Curves
Cost-Benefit Analysis
Marginal-Cost-Marginal-Benefit Rule
Social Demand, Social Cost
Private Cost
Externalities
The Coase Theorem
Market for Externality Rights
Piguvian Tax, Piguvian Subsidy
Asymmetric Information
Adverse-Selection Problem
Moral-Hazard Problem
Taxes, Personal Income Tax, Payroll Tax, Corporate Income Tax, Excise Tax
Income Transfer
Income Maintenance Programs
Public Choice Theory
Special Interest Effect
Rent-Seeking Behavior; Pork-Barrel Politics, Logrolling
Government Failure

9. PROBLEMS AND APPLICATIONS

1. What is a public good?
   a. Can be consumed by just one person, excluding others from consumption.
   b. Can be jointly consumed both by those who pay and by those who don't.
   c. Is produced or financed by the public sector instead of the private sector.
   d. Affects a third party and is different from popular perception.

2. Externalities are defined as:
   a. The difference between social and private costs or benefits of market activity born by a third party.
   b. The domestic economic impact of foreign events, such as oil shocks, wars, natural disasters.
   c. Effects of government actions on the private sector, including regulation.
   d. Outside costs that producers absorb when they are providing public goods.

3. Market power as a form of market failure is related to the following statement:
   a. It involves externalities, and it is imposed on a third party.
   b. Monopolies produce more output than is optimal and are selling it at lower price.
   c. Competition is restricted, output is reduced, and prices are higher.
   d. Administrative and other costs of compliance are high and borne by the immediate consumer.

4. The first legislation to prevent "conspiracies in restraint of trade" was which anti-trust law?
   a. Case decisions, such as those for AT&T and Microsoft
   b. The Clayton Act
   c. The Federal Trade Commission Act
   d. The Sherman Act

5. What are the three main ways in which the US government redistributes income?
   a. Income taxes, income maintenance programs, and subsidized services
   b. Private property rights, income taxes, and the minimum wage
   c. Income taxes, rent control, and food stamps
   d. Sales taxes, food stamps, and subsidized services

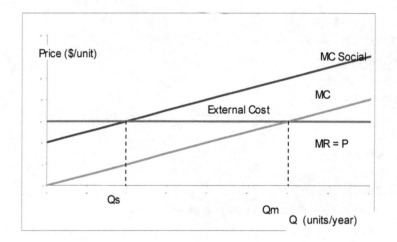

6. In the figure above, if pollution costs are internalized into private costs, the rate of output will be:
   a. Qm
   b. Between Qm and Qs
   c. Qs
   d. Greater than Qm

7. Price discrimination is prohibited by which of the following?
   a. The Sherman Act
   b. The Clayton Act
   c. The Full Employment and Balanced Growth Act
   d. The Federal Trade Commission Act

8. Transfer payments are not contributed directly to increase in GDP but are an efficient mechanism for correcting:
   a. Government failure to reduce inequality.
   b. Externalities caused by private producers.
   c. Market power of perfectly competitive firms.
   d. The inequitable distribution of goods and services.

9. Income taxes and income maintenance programs (Social Security, Medicaid, unemployment compensation, and welfare programs, such as food stamps) represent the:
   a. Main mechanism of enforcement of the rule of law and protection the property rights.
   b. Main sources of revenues and expenditures for the federal budget.
   c. The main tools that governments in the US use to redistribute income and reduce inequality.
   d. The major sources of inequality and poverty.

10. REVIEW QUESTIONS

1. What are two main differences between public goods and private goods? What is the significance of each one for public provision as opposed to private provision? Are free-rider problems related to private goods? Is US national defense a public or private good? What about GPS?
2. Fill in the following phrase with the appropriate definition using either a) rival; private; b) excludable; public; c) excludable; private; or d) nonexcludable, common resource:
3. A good is _____ if it is possible to prevent someone from enjoying its benefits and such a good might be a _____ good.
4. Let's consider the ways to protect your car from theft. You are assessing two options: a) the Club (a steering wheel lock) that makes it difficult for a car thief to take your car and b) a Lojack (a tracking device) that makes it easier for police to locate the car (and, hopefully, the car thief). Which kind of externality (positive/negative) do these two options convey on other car owners?
5. Ronald Coase, Nobel Prize laureate in Economics and professor at Chicago University, proposed an efficient way to address the externalities that you learned about in this chapter. In which of the following cases is the Coase theorem applicable? a) there is a significant externality between two parties; b) both parties understand the externality fully; c) transaction costs make negotiations difficult; d) the court system vigorously enforces all contracts.

Essentials of Macroeconomics

Do you know that your well-being is tied to the performance of the national economy? Your studies, job prospects, income, and the purchasing power of your hard-earned dollars all depend on the performance of the economy as a whole. The economy is a dynamic mechanism. *Macroeconomics is defined by the overall performance of the economy as measured by national production and income earned each year and by fluctuations in income, purchases, employment, and the level of prices.*

Rather than looking at the purchases of one household alone, as we did in microeconomics, in this section, we'll examine influences on total consumption by all households and purchases by business firms of tools, equipment, structures, and goods to hold in inventory. You will be introduced to the basic language of macroeconomics and national income accounting. Macroeconomic focuses on such major issues as long-run economic growth and fluctuations of economic activity, unemployment and inflation, and income and production. In macroeconomics, we develop techniques to measure the performance of the economy, to formulate policies to keep unemployment and inflation under control, and to ensure adequate growth of job opportunities and income. Macroeconomics affects our everyday life. In contrast with microeconomics, it examines the aggregate behavior of the economy, the whole picture, which is greater than the sum of its components. We will discover what the "Paradox of Thrift" is: when families and businesses, expecting hard times, reduce their spending and investment, which makes the situation even worse, further depressing the economy.

The government plays a much more important role in macroeconomics, developing the modern mechanism of fiscal policy—control of spending and taxation—and monetary policy—control over the interest rates and the quantity of money. Finally, macroeconomics operates with economic aggregates to evaluate the performance of the economy: aggregate output—the total product that the economy produces during a given period of time; aggregate price level—overall level of prices; aggregate income; and other indicators that analyze the data across markets for goods, services, and assets.

CHAPTER 11.

GDP AND ECONOMIC GROWTH: HOW TO MEASURE TOTAL PRODUCTION AND INCOME

1. NATIONAL ACCOUNTS AND GDP

Everything changed after just one event in American and world history—the Great Depression—the famous crash of the stock market in October 1929 that "unexpectedly" happened after the "Roaring Twenties"—a time of unprecedented growth and prosperity. Unemployment rose from 3.2% in 1929 to 25% in 1933, accompanied by a spectacular reduction in national output—real gross domestic product—27%; national output did not recover until a decade later. This was also a failure of classical economics, which has the famous "*laissez-faire*" at its core. The Great Depression led to a breakthrough in economic theory and economic measurement. De facto, the government started to track the economy's performance in 1930s. The publication in 1936 of *The General Theory of Employment, Interest and Money* by the British scholar John Maynard Keynes marked a new era in the development of economic theory, with Keynes's micro- and macroeconomic branches having an influence on economic, political, and social life comparable with the ideas of Adam Smith's *The Wealth of the Nations*.

Earlier in the 1930s, Simon Kuznets, an American economist of Russian origin, was commissioned by the US Department of Commerce to create a set of national income accounts. He published a small report in 1934: *National Income, 1929–32,* which earned him the title of "Father of GDP" and a Nobel Prize for Economics (1971). This innovation created the foundation of the national accounts used today by the United States and most other countries. Based on Kuznets's methodology, the Federal Government began issuing estimates of gross domestic product and gross national product in 1942. Every three months, the Bureau of Economic Analysis (BEA) of the US Department of Commerce issues new statistics on GDP and its components. This analysis is awaited by business managers, investors, economists, and policy makers. The data are compiled as part of the National Income and Product Accounts (NIPA), which is the official system in the United States. It helps us determine how well the economy is doing, to track its course in the long-run, to assess its potential for generating new jobs and income in the future, and to formulate policies to control inflation and unemployment. Without national accounts, economic theory would be guesswork.

In analyzing the performance of an entire economy, we focus on *aggregates* which are broad totals of economic variable such as production or unemployment.

The first notion that macroeconomics deals with is *Gross Domestic Product (GDP)*: in a given year, the total *market value of all final goods and services produced.* In other words, GDP is the measure of the monetary value of aggregate production. Because our economy today is diversified and physical quantities of computers, cars, homes, pizzas, etc., are dynamic and changing, the best that can be done to assess the performances of the economy is to measure the *dollar value of the nation's aggregate production of output. This is accomplished by multiplying the quantity (Q) of each individual type of product measured over the period by its market price.* The dollar values of all products are then added to obtain a sum that equals the market value of the economy's aggregate production.

To obtain **an accurate picture of GDP,** we have to include only the market value of **final goods** that are purchased for final use by consumers, and we have to exclude goods and services that are purchased for resale or for further processing—**intermediate goods.** We should exclude the value of intermediate goods from GDP to avoid multiple counting. In other words, we have to include only **a new value added** in a nation, which is the difference between the market value of all products and the market value of intermediate goods.

Let's consider an example: to make a pair of jeans available to the market, the cotton grown by the farmers should be sold to weavers. Assume that farmers are producing cotton without purchasing any materials from other firms:

1) Sales transactions	2) Intermediate purchases	3) Value added (1–2)
$1m Sale of cotton by farmers to weavers.	none	$1m
$2m Sale of cloth by weavers to manufacturer.	$1m of cotton	$1m
$4m Sale of blue jeans by manufacturer to consumers.	$2m of cloth	$2m.

Market value of all products – market value of intermediate products = Total value added

| $7m | $3m. | = $4m |

Purely financial transactions are excluded from GDP because they don't involve production of goods and services. This refers to a*) public transfer payments* which are payments for food stamps, social security, etc.; b*) private transfer payments* which are things like allowances paid to students or alimony payments; and c) The *sale of stocks and bonds* which represent the transfer of assets only. Changes in the value of existing assets are also excluded from GDP because they don't represent production of new goods and services. The value of used goods sold during the year is not part of GDP and is also excluded. Finally, goods and services not sold through markets, in most cases, are not reflected in GDP (cleaning your own apartment or cooking your own meal).

2. MEASURING GDP: INCOME VS. EXPENDITURE APPROACH (GDP AND OTHER MEASURES OF TOTAL PRODUCTION AND TOTAL INCOME)

How is GDP calculated? One way is to ask companies for the total value of their production of final goods and services. Another way is to add up aggregate spending (consumers, businesses, governments, and foreigners' spending) on final goods and services produced by the economy. A third way is to sum up the total income earned by households from firms in the economy—wages, profits, interest, and rent. Let's examine these approaches in more detail.

EXPENDITURE APPROACH: WHO PURCHASES GDP?

To calculate national product (GDP), the BEA divides its statistics of the final products into four categories: 1) personal consumption expenditures (C); 2) gross private domestic investment (Ig); 3) government expenditures for goods and services (G); and 4) net exports (NX).

Personal Consumption expenditure (C) is the expenditure by households on individual purchases of durable goods (lasting more than three years: cars, refrigerators, furniture, etc.), nondurable goods (bread, milk, gasoline, etc.), and services (by far the largest category: legal advice, medical treatment, education, etc.).

Investment (Ig)—the purchase of final products by business firms for use in production or as an addition to inventories (tools, instruments, machines, buildings, and other items). Gross private domestic investment includes: *a) business investment in plants and equipment* (construction of factories, warehouses, stores, etc.); *b) residential construction and construction of new factories, warehouses, and stores*; and *c) changes in business inventories*—final goods that have been produced but not yet sold (cars at a dealership, for example); these changes may be positive and negative. We have to distinguish *gross investment (Ig),* which includes investment in replacement capital and in added capital, and *net private domestic investment (In),* which includes only investment in added capital. The formula is: *net investment = gross investment – depreciation* (wear and tear of capital as it is used in production). For example, if the total investment in the third quarter was $1,689 billion, and $1,090 billion represents depreciation (64%), then, In = $599 billion.

It should be mentioned that when gross investment and depreciation are equal, a nation's production capacity is static; when gross domestic investment is less than depreciation, the economy's production capacity has declined and vice versa—when gross domestic investment exceeds depreciation, the productive capacity has expanded. Investment does not include purchases of paper assets (transactions with stocks and bonds) and resale of tangible assets (houses, cars, boats, etc.). Investments refer only to the creation of new capital assets that create jobs and income.

Question: Is the purchase of a home by an individual a part of investment or not?

Government expenditures on goods and services, G—government purchases of goods and services include expenditure on final products of business firms and all input costs, including labor costs, incurred by all levels of government. The two main components of G are *1) expenditures for goods and services* that government consumes in providing public services and *2) expenditures for social capital* (school, highways) with a long lifetime. At the same time, G does not include transfer payments—payments for which no goods or services are received in return and that do not represent production capacity of the nation (i.e., Social Security payments, unemployment compensation, veterans' benefits, welfare, and interest on government debt).

Question: Are wage payments to the police, postal workers, and the staff of the Internal Revenue Service included in government purchases or not?

Net exports of goods and services (NX) is the value of exports of goods and services minus the value of imports of goods and services. *Net exports (Xn) = exports (X) – imports (M).* Exports represent expenditures on US final products and services by citizens of foreign nations. Imports represent the value of goods and services produced in foreign nations and purchased by Americans. A country has a trade surplus if the value of exports exceeds the value of imports and vice versa—a country has a trade deficit when imports exceeds exports. Note that 1) expenditures on used goods are not part of current GDP since they were counted in the year when they were produced and 2) the purchases of stocks, bonds, and other financial assets are not included in GDP since these transactions represent just the transfer of ownership and not expenditures on goods and services.

All expenditures put together, or *aggregate expenditures*, are represented in the *GDP equation*: the sum of consumption expenditures, investment expenditures, government purchases, and net exports during 2011 (figure and table 11.1):

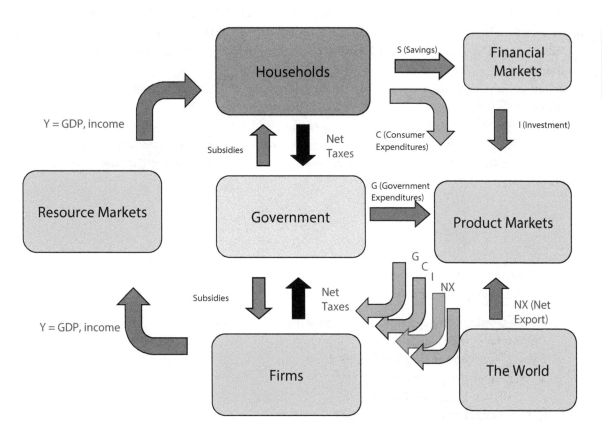

Figure 11.1
The Circular
Flow of Income
and Expenditure

Table 11.1
GDP:
Expenditure
Approach
($$ billion,
2013):

Personal Consumption Expenditure (C)	11.4
Business Investment (Ig)	2.6
Government Purchases (G)	3.1
Net Export (NX)	–0.5
Y (GDP)	16.7

GDP = C + Ig + G + (X – M) = $11.4 + $2.6 + $3.1 – $0.5 = $16.7 billion (2013)
(Source: US Department of Commerce, Bureau of Economic Analysis.)

INCOME APPROACH: WHO GETS THE INCOME?

The total income earned by US residents in the United States or abroad is called national income. Households receive 1) wages, identified in national accounts as *compensation of employees* and 2) interest, rent, and profit income, called *net operating surplus* in national accounts. Some parts of total income are not paid out to households by firms, but from an economic standpoint, this undistributed profit is income paid to households and then loaned back to firms.

To answer the question *"Who gets the income?"* and to measure national income, we need to make *a few adjustments*:

First, we add to GDP the net income earned by US firms and residents abroad and subtract any income earned in the US by foreign firms or residents. As a result, we will obtain the total income earned worldwide by US firms and residents which is called Gross National Product (GNP). For the US, the difference between these two notions is not very significant (1%), but for some other countries, it is more important, for example, Australia—4% and Kuwait—9%. So, if a US drug company is producing a pharmaceutical product in Ireland, it is counted as part of the US GNP but not GDP.

Second, we have to subtract depreciation (in the NIPA tables, it is referred to as the consumption of fixed capital) to obtain **Net National Product (NNP)**. "Net" means after depreciation.

Third, to calculate National Income (NI), we need to subtract indirect taxes from *NNP* (sales taxes or excise taxes). After making all these adjustments, we will obtain the national income, which is divided among five basic categories. This approach demonstrates how expenditures on final products are allocated to resource suppliers:

1. Compensation of employees:
   a. Wages, salaries
   b. Fringe benefits (employer-provided insurance and pension contributions)
   c. Payments on behalf of workers (Social Security, health and pensions plans). This is the largest component of national income (NI).

2. *Rents*—payments for supplying resources; the national accounts use the category net rent (gross rent income—depreciation of the rental property).
3. *Interest*—payments to suppliers of capital:
   a. Interest on savings deposit
   b. Certificates of deposit (CDs
   c. Corporate bonds

4. Proprietor's income—income of:
    a. Incorporated businesses
    b. Sole proprietorships
    c. Partnerships, and cooperatives

5. *Corporate profits*—after corporate income taxes are paid to the government, dividends are distributed to the shareholders, and the remaining part is undistributed corporate profits which is called retained earnings.

The sum of 1–5 is the national income earned by American-supplied resources (in the US or abroad).

Fourth, to determine the total payments that flow directly into households, or *personal income (PI)*, we must subtract from national income the income that is earned but not received and add the income that is received but not earned. In other words, we need to subtract from NI payroll taxes (Social Security contributions), corporate profit taxes, and undistributed corporate profits and add transfer payments.

Fifth, to find the amount of income that households have available to spend or save, called *personal disposable income (DI)*, we need to subtract from personal income the amount that households are *paying in taxes*: personal income taxes, personal property taxes, and inheritance taxes. Now, consumers are free to divide DI between consumption and savings: *DI = C + S.*

In summary, from the spending side, 72% of GDP consists of consumer expenditures; from the income side, 70% of national income is paid in wages and benefits. The difference between the expenditure approach and the income approach is called statistical discrepancy.

Expenditure Equals Income: total income, Y, equals total expenditure.

$$Y = C + I + G + (X - M)$$

So, the value of production equals income equals expenditure, or, in other words, GDP produced is equal to GDP earned and GDP consumed: $GDP = Y = C + I + G + (X - M)$.

3. REAL GDP VS. NOMINAL GDP

Dollar prices provide a satisfactory basis for calculating national product in any one year; they allow us to add apples and oranges, medical services and cars. But if we wish to evaluate the economy over a number of years, we face a major problem: the dollar is going down. The dollar measure of GDP increases for two different reasons: a) it is desirable to have an increase in the quantity of goods and services produced and b) the prices of those goods and services increases, as well, and this is undesirable. So, it is essential to separate the desirable and undesirable increases in prices. The way to do it is to deflate GDP when prices rise and to inflate GDP when prices fall. For these reasons, we use two notions:

1. Nominal GDP—the market value of all final goods and services produced in a given year expressed in the prices of the same year.
2. Real GDP—a GDP that has been deflated or inflated to reflect changes in the price level, or the value of final goods and services produced in a given year expressed in the prices of a base year.

How can we make this adjustment? There are *two alternative methods*:

First, we have to determine *the price index* (an index is a number which shows how an average of prices, or wages, etc., has changed over time)—*a measure of the price of a specified collection of goods and services, called a "market basket,"* in a given year as compared to the price of identical collections of goods and services in a reference year: *Real GDP = nominal GDP: price index.*

Second, we have to gather separate data on physical outputs and their prices. Then, we can multiply the units of physical output by the base year price to determine real GDP. By comparing real GDP and nominal GDP, we can measure the changes in prices for the economy. We do this by creating an index, called a *GDP deflator,* which measures how prices change over time. *GDP deflator = Nominal GDP: Real GDP × 100.*

At one time, the Department of Commerce used this method to calculate real GDP and measure changes in prices. But in 1996, the BEA switched to chain-weighted prices, and, today, it publishes statistics on real GDP in "chained (2000) dollars" using a *chain price index.* What does "chained" mean? Prices in each year are "chained" to prices from the previous year, and the distortion from changes in relative prices is minimized. We will not go into the details here, but the idea is to hold the purchasing power of a dollar the same from one year to the next. In the real economy, both prices and production increase each year, but the more prices increase relative to the increase in production, the more nominal GDP increases relative to real GDP and the higher the value of the GDP deflator. In practice, we can use the chain price index just as we did the GDP deflator—as a measure of price changes of GDP.

4. GDP AS A MEASURE OF WELFARE: SHORTCOMINGS AND LIMITATIONS

GDP can be a good measure of an economy's output but isn't without limitations.

First, GDP measures only the market value of output, and it ignores transactions that do not take place in organized markets: cleaning, cooking, free child care, repainting of one's own home, etc. Nonmarket transactions are not counted in GDP because it would be extremely difficult to a) collect data and assess the dollar value of services that consumers provide for themselves and b) decide which activities to include and which not to include. There is only one exception: the portion of farmers' output that farmers consume themselves is estimated and included in GDP.

Second, GDP ignores the underground economy where transactions are not reported to official authorities. It is often referred to as the informal sector and includes illegal business transactions by gamblers, smugglers, prostitutes, drug growers, and drug dealers but also such socially desired services as the work of a moonlighting plumber, whose only illegal act is tax evasion. Such "subterranean" or "irregular" activities occur not only in the US but also in France—*travauh au noir* ("work in the dark"), Italy—*lavorno nero,* Britain—*"fiddle,"* Russia—*"chornyi rynok"* ("black market"), and Germany—*schattenwirstchaft* ("shadow economy"). In the US, the value of underground transactions is estimated to be about 10% of the GDP; in other advanced economies, the underground economy's share of GDP is 15–20%, and in developing countries and economies of transition, between 30 and 40%.

Third, the value of leisure is not included in GDP. Between 1900 and 2012, the length of the typical workweek in the United States declined from fifty hours to about thirty-four because workers preferred to increase their time for family, recreation, and travel rather than work long hours.

Fourth, GDP does not value changes in the environment that arise through the production of output, which can represent social costs that reduce economic well-being. Ironically, when money is spent to clean up pollution and reduce congestion, those expenses are added to the GDP.

Fifth, GDP is not adjusted for health and life expectancy, political and economic freedom, criminality and social justice, poverty and inequality, or other social problems. To overcome such shortcomings, there are two approaches:

1. To downplay GDP as the measure of how the economy and society are performing *by using other important indicators of well-being in addition to real GDP:* life expectancy, infant mortality rates, availability of health care, education and literacy, the amount of leisure, the quality of the

environment, the degree of urban crowding. Each year, the United Nations produces the Human Development Report, which ranks countries by using the *Human Development Index (HDI)*, which is based on three factors: life expectancy at birth, knowledge measured by adult literacy and school enrollment, and standard of living, measured by GDP per capita in purchasing power parity of US dollars.

2. *A comprehensive Measure of Economic Welfare (MEW)*, created by two Yale University economists, William Nordhouse and James Tobin. They calculated that the average number of leisure hours had increased by 22% between 1929 and 1965 while the real per capita product rose by 90%. The question is what conclusion should be made from these facts? There are two answers: 1) production per person went up by 90%, and we had more leisure, too. So, economic welfare rose more than GDP and 2) production per person went up by 90%, but leisure increased by 22%. So, economic welfare rose by some average of 90% and 22%, or less than GDP. According to Nordhouse and Tobin's estimates of MEW, economic welfare did not drop even during the Great Depression because they included leisure as an element of welfare. Leisure after a good day's work may be bliss, but it is not so pleasant to be idle when you've lost your job.

A former chairman of the Presidential Council of Economic Advisors, Arthur Okun, emphasized that the calculation "of a summary measure of social welfare is a job for a philosopher king."

Question: What do you think about the HDI and MEW Indexes?

Conclusion: In late 1999, the US Department of Commerce announced the most important "achievement of the century." What could rival such great US accomplishments as providing electricity and interstate highways, landing a man on the moon, the Internet, and the New Economy? The Department of Commerce's Survey of Current Business (January 2000) selected the development of the *National Income and Product Account* as the greatest achievement of the twentieth century.

5. MEASURING ECONOMIC GROWTH

First, why do economies grow? To better understand this, let's consider how the typical American lived in 1783, a few years after the Declaration of Independence was written. The economic historian Stanley Lebergott described an average US home at that time. It had no central heat, one fireplace, no plumbing, no hot water, and toilets that were outdoor shacks surrounding a hole in the ground. A typical farmer took a bath once a week. Houses had no electricity or gas; a solitary candle provided light at night. There were no refrigerators, no toasters, or, for that matter, any appliances. For women, things were particularly hard. They were expected to bake more than half a ton of bread a year, kill chickens, and butcher hogs, as well as prepare all vegetables. Canned foods were not readily available until a century later.

Our living standards are dramatically different today because there has been a remarkable growth in GDP per person. Growth in GDP is, perhaps, the most critical aspect of a country's economic performance and the most important goal of economic policy because it is the basis of more material abundance and our ability to solve scarcity problems. Only on this basis, is it possible to address the problems of poverty and inequality; to protect the environment; and to increase the levels of consumption, investment, and production. There is no other way to raise the standard of living.

Before turning to policies and theories of economic growth, we have to consider an even more fundamental issue: Should we strive for a higher rate of growth? At first glance, it might seem obvious that growth is desirable. However, we should not simply assume that the faster the economy grows, the better. If our overriding goal is faster growth, we may sacrifice other important goals, such as current consumption, a cleaner environment, and leisure.

Second, we need to also focus on *the nature of growth*: a) in the short-run, economic growth is related to the mix of goods and services that could be produced with our existing resources and technology. On the Production Possibilities Curve (PPC) in Figure 10.2a, this is illustrated by movement from a point inside to a point on the curve, or to a full production capacity and b) in the long-run, economic growth is a result of expansion of our production possibilities and increased efficiency of existing resource utilization (figure 10.2b).

Third, how we can define economic growth? There are two definitions of economic growth:

1. The increase in real GDP over a period of time.
2. The increase in real GDP per capita over a period of time.

Figure 11.2a
Short-Run
Economic
Growth
(Increased
Capacity
Utilization)

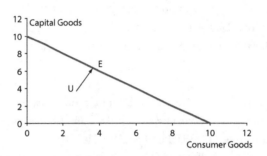

Figure 11.2b
Long-Run
Economic
Growth
(Expansion of
Capacity)

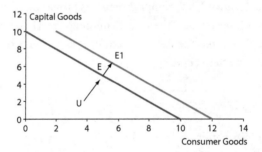

The second definition is superior because it takes into account the growth of population and is more accurate for comparison of living standards. Of course, the population issue is quite different for the advanced countries and the very poorest of less developed countries. But even in the most advanced countries, there are two conflicting effects on per capita growth of output. Obviously, there is a depressing effect—with more people and a larger labor force, there is less capital and fewer natural resources at the disposal of the typical worker (recall the Law of Diminishing Returns). On the other side, a larger population and a larger market may raise the standard of living by making economies of scale possible. So, the question is: Do we want a larger population if it holds down per capita output and income? Or would it be better to have about the same population with a much higher income per capita?

Fourth, how we can measure economic growth? The economic growth rate is the annual percentage change of real GDP.

The growth rate of real GDP equals:

Real GDP in current year − Real GDP in previous year × 100
(Real GDP in previous year)

The standard of living depends on *real GDP per person,* which is real GDP divided by the population. The growth rate of real GDP per person equals:

Growth rate of real GDP per person = Growth rate of real GDP – Growth rate of population

Fifth, there is a rule of thumb to better understand *the power of the growth rate.* Suppose we know the growth rate of real GDP, and we want to know how many years it will take until the level of GDP will double. The answer will be given by *the rule of 70,* which is derived by using the mathematics of logarithms and states that the number of years it takes for the level of any variable to double is approximately 70 divided by the annual percentage growth rate of the variable. So, years to double = 70/GDP growth rate (%). With only 1% growth, doubling the GDP would take 70 years; 2%—35 years, 5%—14 years, 10%—7 years. The Rule of 70 demonstrates the magic of economic growth.

6. BASIC SOURCES OF ECONOMIC GROWTH

What are the main sources of growth? There are two fundamental sources: 1) increasing inputs of resources—land, capital, labor, and entrepreneurial resources; increasing inputs contribute to about one third of US growth and 2) increasing productivity of labor, which contributes to about two thirds of economic growth.

The factors that influence real GDP growth can be divided into those that change aggregate hours and those that change labor productivity. Our standard of living improves only if growth occurs due to increases in labor productivity.

Why does productivity increase? Back in the late 20s of the last century, former Senator Paul Douglas, then a University of Chicago professor of economics, conducted significant research that showed how technological progress has been improving the productivity of American labor and capital: he found that a 1% increase in labor seems to increase output about three times as much as a 1% increase in capital. These findings were confirmed later on by Edward Denison of the Brookings Institution, a policy-oriented think tank in Washington that analyzed the main factors that contributed to the 2.5% annual increase in productivity over a period of twenty-five years (1948–1973). Of this increase, Denison attributed: a) 0.3% to changes in the quality of the labor force as measured by education; b) 0.4% to the increase in physical capital; c) 0.3% to reduced discrimination against minorities and lower barriers to international trade; d) 0.4% to economies of scale; and e) 1.1% to advances in knowledge and improvement of technology (almost half of the total increase). According to Denison, over a longer period of time—fifty-three years (1929–82), the output growth of 2.92% was due to capital growth (0.56%), labor growth (1.34%), and technological progress (1.02%). That means that one third of economic growth came directly from technological advances as shown in Figure 10.3 (Edward Denison, Trends in American Economic Growth 1929–1982, *Economic Journal,* March 1983, p. 56).

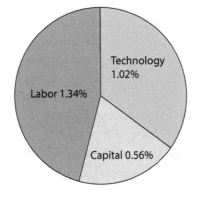

Figure 11.3 Contributions to Real GDP Growth

Technology 1.02%

Labor 1.34%

Capital 0.56%

Later on, Professor Robert Solow, a Nobel Prize laureate in Economics from the Massachusetts Institute of Technology, described a method for measuring technological progress based on contributions to economic growth from increases in capital, labor, and output called *growth accounting*. More recently, Nobel laureate Robert Lucas of the University of Chicago and Paul Romer of Stanford University developed a model of growth that contained technological progress as its essential feature. Their work was the foundation for what is known as *new growth theory*.

How do we measure Labor Productivity? Labor productivity is the quantity of real GDP produced by one hour of labor. Labor productivity = (Real GDP) ÷ (Aggregate hours). Rearranging this equation, we find that real GDP = (Aggregate hours) × (Labor productivity), so growth in real GDP can be divided into growth in aggregate hours and growth in labor productivity.

The most important factors that influence the growth of labor productivity are:

First, Technological Progress—the largest contributor, which accounts for about 35–40% of productivity growth. Technological progress had become a part of our everyday life, and it is based on three modern revolutions: a) software; b) new materials; and c) information and communication. Economic historians consider economic growth and increasing standards of living historically recent phenomena related to Scottish inventor James Watt's innovation of the steam engine in 1776, which began the Industrial Revolution. New technologies increase labor productivity and economic growth, and they are often embodied within new capital, such as more powerful computers, fuel-efficient aircraft, integrated microcircuits, wireless communications, etc.

Second, saving and investment in physical capital, which contributes roughly 30% to productivity growth. The quantity of capital—machines, equipment, and structures—available per worker, called *capital deepening*, increased tremendously over recent years to about $120,000 per worker in the United States. More saving and investment in physical capital increases labor productivity and economic growth.

Third, expansion of human capital—accumulated skills and knowledge from a) education and training and b) job experience adds an estimated 15% to productivity growth. Today, 90% of Americans complete high school and more than 60% go to college or university, compared with 41% and 8%, respectively, in 1960.

Fourth, economies of scale and improved resource allocation, together, contribute about another 15% of productivity growth. Economies of scale and increased firms' and markets' sizes over time lead to reduction of the per unit cost of production, and other competitive advantages, such as using computerization and robotics in assembly lines and other more productive equipment and manufacturing methods. Improved resource allocation contributed to the movement of workers from less-productivity to higher-productivity employment, from agriculture to manufacturing, and, most importantly, to the service sector (health care, computer science, software, etc.), which is the largest sector in today's economy, generating 70% of output. In next ten years, almost 100% of new jobs will be created in service industry.

What has been the rate of US growth during last 100 years? Real GDP per person grew at an annual rate of 2.0%, with almost no growth in the 1930s followed by the fastest growth in the 1940s and uneven rates in other decades. For example, economic growth during the first decade of twenty-first century was the slowest since the 1930s; this was caused by the recession of 2007–2009, the deepest recession since the Great Depression. US labor productivity growth has also slowed since the 1960s when it averaged 3.6 percent a year. In recent years, it has averaged 2.2 percent a year. But we have to remember that arithmetic numbers: a) do not measure quality improvements of products and services and understate the growth of economic well-being; b) do not measure increased leisure time (the standard workweek was reduced from fifty hours to thirty-four); and c) do not take into account adverse effects on environment and quality of life.

How does US economic growth look relative to other nations? Making comparisons of real GDP across countries is difficult. Not only do the countries have their own currencies but also patterns of consumption, traditions, and prices, which can differ sharply between countries. A team of economists led by Robert Summers and Alan Heston of the University of Pennsylvania has been developing methods for measuring real GDP across countries. They use data on prices of comparable goods and make adjustments for differences in relative prices and consumption patterns. These methods are now officially used by the World Bank and the IMF in making cross-country comparisons of real GDP. According to these estimates, the country with the highest level of income in 2008 was the tiny European country of Luxemburg, with $64,320 per capita. The US was in the top five with $46,970 (in 2010, it was $48,387).

7. KEY TERMS

National Income and Product Account
Gross Domestic Product (GDP)
Value Added, Final Goods
Expenditure and Income Approaches
Personal Consumption Expenditure (PCE)
Business Gross and Net Investment
Government Expenditure, Government and Private Transfers
Net Export
Compensation of Employees
Net Operating Surplus
Gross National Product (GNP); Net National Product (NNP)
Depreciation
National Income (NI); Personal Income (PI); Disposable Income (DI)
Nominal GDP; Real GDP; GDP Deflator; Price Index
Chain Price Index
Underground Economy
Human Development Index (HDI)
Comprehensive Measure of Economic Welfare (MEW)
Economic Growth
Growth Account
Capital Deepening

8. PROBLEMS AND APPLICATIONS

1. From this chapter, you learned that the GDP is best defined as the _____ in a given period of time:
   a. Market value of all final goods and services produced within a country.
   b. Number of physical goods and services produced within a country.
   c. Quantity of final and intermediate goods and services produced within a country.
   d. Market value of all goods and services consumed by citizens of a country.

2. Real GDP represents inflation adjusted GDP and is used most effectively to:
   a. Measure how much income households receive.
   b. Determine the value of final goods and services produced in a given year and expressed in the prices of a base year

c. Measure current monetary value of all goods and services in an economy.

d. Make international comparisons of the standard of living, and is the same as Purchasing Power Parity Index.

3. In comparison with the short-run, the process of long-run economic growth is:
   a. Not affected by the previous year's economic growth.
   b. Always occurring and is uninterrupted.
   c. Not significant for the overall economy.
   d. A cumulative, exponential process so that gains made in one year accumulate in future years.

4. There are three approaches to compute GDP: production, expenditure, and income. The GDP equation below represents the _____ approach and is:
   a. $Y = C + I - G + (X - M)$
   b. $Y = C - I + G + (X - M)$
   c. $Y = C - I - G - (X - M)$
   d. $Y = C + I + G + (X - M)$

5. Which of the following factors has made the greatest contribution to growth in labor productivity in the US?
   a. Economies of scale and improved resource allocation
   b. Expansion of human capital, accumulated skills and knowledge
   c. Technological progress
   d. Saving and investment in physical capital

6. Alicia will graduate next year from the VSU College of Engineering and Technology, and she is planning to do a research project on post crisis recovery of the US economy. She intends to apply her knowledge to identify and prioritize the economic goals of American society, starting with the most important goal, which is:
   a. To produce the optimal (best possible) mix of goods and services.
   b. To exploit its workers in order to produce more output and reduce inequality.
   c. To produce more military goods so that the US citizens and the entire world will be safe.
   d. To distribute an equal amount of goods and services to all citizens according to their needs.

7. Long-run economic growth can be illustrated in the figure below by:
   a. A movement from point U to point E.
   b. An outward shift of the production-possibilities curve from E to E1.
   c. An inward shift of the production-possibilities curve from E1 to E.
   d. A movement from point E to point U.

Item	Billions of dollars
Personal Consumption Expenditure	10.7
Business Investment	1.9
Government Purchases	3.0
Net Export	−0.6

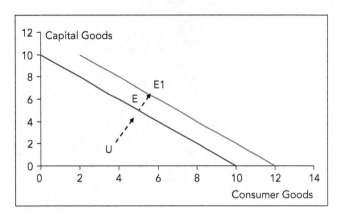

8. Based on the data above, what does GDP equal ($$ billion)?
   a. 16.2
   b. 10.7
   c. 15
   d. 15.6

9. $15,000 billion Nominal GDP measure the market value of goods and services produced in a given year using:
   a. Constant prices (base reference year)
   b. Future prices (forecast)
   c. No prices
   d. Prices of the same year (current)

9. REVIEW QUESTIONS

1. As you learned from this chapter, the GDP does not include all goods and services that the government is currently providing. What part of the following government expenditures are not included in GDP? a) National and antiterrorist defense; b) Transfer payments; c) Education and Public Health; d) Payment to police and IRS officers.

2. The manuscript of this book, *Economics, Society, Technology, and You,* was typed by the author of the book for free. Let's assume that the author hired a secretary to type the book. So, if the amount of output is the same, would GDP have been higher?

3. To what components of GDP (if any) would each of the following transactions refer? a) You buy a new pair of shoes; b) Subaru expands its factory; c) Your friend buys a new condo; d) Virginia repaves I-95; e) Your family buys a new car. Explain your choices.

4. Lucy, a stylist at the Best Hair Salon in Rhinebeck, New York, made $500 for haircuts on one day. Over this day, her equipment depreciated by $50. Of the remaining $450, she pays $50 to the government in sales taxes, takes home $250 in wages, and retains $100 to buy new equipment at the end of the month. Out of the $250 she takes home, Lucy pays $75 in personal income taxes. Based on this information, compute Lucy's contribution to the following income measures: a) GDP; b) NNP; c) NI; d) PI; e) DI.

5. You just read in the *Wall Street Journal* that GDP this year is higher by 2.4 percent, and the unemployment rate decreased to 4.7% lower than last year. Does this mean that you and your family are better off this year than last year?

CHAPTER 12.

BUSINESS CYCLE: UNEMPLOYMENT AND INFLATION

The business cycles, or economic fluctuations, are the focus of this chapter. Since World War II, the United States has experienced ten recessions. During these economic downturns, not only does real GDP decrease but other important economic indicators are also affected, such as unemployment, investment, and consumption spending. It is difficult to anticipate the precise timing and causes of an economic downturn and, thus, the precise impact it will have on the economy.

Economic fluctuations can occur for a variety of reasons, such as internal shocks or external shocks. We have seen the heavy hand of the business cycle in such noneconomic matters as marriages, births, divorces, suicides, crimes, and admissions to mental hospitals. Even political elections follow the business cycle: the Hoover depression of the 1930s helped elect Franklin Roosevelt just as the 1960 Eisenhower recession helped elect President Kennedy, or, more recently, the 1980s recessions brought Ronald Reagan in and Jimmy Carter out, and the 1990–91 recession advantaged Bill Clinton, who won the presidency, and disadvantaged George H. W. Bush, who lost it.

What are business cycles, and how can we prevent them? What are the damages of unemployment, and how does inflation affect society? The most important task of macroeconomics is to explain the business cycle, to identify the major factors that cause the expansion and contraction of the economy or that generate business cycle fluctuations.

We will focus on unemployment as a component of the labor force and use the labor-force participation ratio, the demographic profile of unemployment, to put into perspective the magnitude and extent of this problem. Then, we will look at the issues surrounding its measurement. Unemployment statistics don't tell the whole story about unemployment because there are discouraged workers who are not counted as unemployed as well as people who are counted as employed but are underemployed. Next, we will discuss the different types of unemployment: cyclical, frictional, and structural; the culmination of the discussion focuses on the natural rate of unemployment; and the meaning of full employment; and the costs of unemployment.

1. BUSINESS CYCLES ROLLER COASTER: MAIN CHARACTERISTICS AND TRENDS

Paul Samuelson, a famous American economist and Nobel Prize laureate in Economics, characterized economic development in this way: "Business conditions rarely stand still. Prosperity may be followed by a panic or a crash. Economic expansion gives way to recession. National income, employment, and production fall. Prices and profits decline and men are thrown out of work. Eventually the bottom is reached, and recovery begins. The recovery may be slow or fast. It may be incomplete, or it may be so strong as to lead to a new boom. The new prosperity may represent a long plateau of brisk demand, plentiful jobs, and increased living standards. Or it may represent a quick, inflationary flaring up of prices and speculation, to be followed by another disastrous slump." (P. Samuelson, p. 249). Such, in brief, is the so-called "business cycle," which has characterized the industrialized nations of the world for almost the last two centuries.

Let's have a closer look at the *business cycle* which is defined as *alternating periods of economic growth and contraction*. In other words, it describes the fluctuations in aggregate production as measured by the ups-and-downs of real GDP. Individual cycles vary substantially in duration and intensity. Business fluctuations are so irregular that it is surprising to call them "cycles." However, all of them have the same four phases. A typical business cycle chart resembles a roller coaster: it begins at a peak, drops to a bottom, climbs steeply, and then reaches another peak:

1. *Peak*—the date at which a recession begins—when the economy is near or at full employment and the price level is likely to rise. The peak is the highest level of real GDP in the cycle, and there are likely to be shortages of labor, parts, and materials in certain markets. The economy might be booming.
2. *Recession*—a period where total output, income, and trade decrease. It usually lasts six or more months. Production capacity is underutilized; the economy is functioning inside its Production Possibilities Curve.

3. *Trough or depression*—a period when the level of real GDP "bottoms out," when unemployment and idle production capacity are at their highest levels. A trough is the date at which a recession ends. The trough phase may be either short-lived or quite long. When the economy is in trough, there is an excessive amount of unemployment and idle productive capacity. What is the difference between a recession and a depression? The US President Harry S Truman once observed: "A recession is when your neighbor is out of work. A depression is when you're out of work." The term depression has a mostly historical connotation and is used to refer to the Great Depression of the 30s, which was a much more severe and long-lasting recession. The trough it is also a point at which things start looking up.

4. *Recovery, or expansion*—outputs rise, profits generally improve, and employment moves toward full employment, but the price levels also rise.

How far down does the economy have to go before a recession is identified, and who takes the responsibility for declaring it? Of course, no administration wants to be blamed for a recession. A private research group located in Cambridge, Massachusetts, and composed of professional economists, the *National Bureau of Economic Research (NBER)*, is the guardian of the keys and decides what a recession is and when it has happened. The NBER uses a broader definition: "A recession is a significant decline in activity spread across the economy, lasting more than a few months, visible in industrial production, employment, real income, and wholesale-retail trade." Typically, the NBER announces the economic recession well after the recession has begun. For example, it announced that a recession had begun in March 2001 eight months after the fact in November 2002. Ironically, that recession had already ended and that was only acknowledged eight months later in July 2003.

What are the factors that cause business cycles? Economists have suggested many theories to explain the causes of fluctuations in business cycles. We can mention at least five factors:

1. *Innovations*, such as the railroad, automobiles, synthetic fibers, computers, the Internet, and others, occur unexpectedly and irregularly and contribute to the variability of economic activity.

2. *Changes in productivity*: When productivity expands, the economy booms; when productivity falls, the economy recedes. Unexpected changes may result from resource availability or technological advances.

3. *Monetary phenomena*: When a nation's central bank creates too much money, an inflationary boom occurs; too little money triggers a decline in output and employment.

4. *Changes in the level of consumer spending*: When the level of total spending rises, an increase in production becomes profitable, and output, income, and employment will rise accordingly and vice versa—a decrease in spending and consumption leads to a decline in these indicators. Many economists consider this factor to be critical for economic fluctuations.

5. *Financial imbalances*: Abrupt increases and decreases in asset prices, financial bubbles, and rapid expanding or contracting of lending, followed by booms and busts in other sectors of the economy, may generate severe recessions, like the recession of 2007–09, called the Great Recession. It was generated by an explosive combination of excessive money, overvalued real estate, unsustainable mortgage debt, and lack of regulation in financial markets.

Those most affected by business cycles are firms and industries that produce *capital goods* (housing, commercial buildings, heavy equipment) and *consumer durables* (automobiles, personal computers, refrigerators). In contrast, industries that produce nondurable consumer goods and service industries are, to some extent, insulated from the most severe effects of a recession. In fact, recessions might even help some services to benefit, for instance, law firms specializing in bankruptcies.

HOW DO WE DESCRIBE THE FLUCTUATIONS AND TRENDS IN BUSINESS CYCLES IN US HISTORY?

The NBER has identified thirty-three complete cycles, starting from a trough in December 1854. Since then, expansions have lasted, on average, thirty-five months, and recessions have lasted, on average, eighteen months. It should be noted that during the years since World War II, the average recession has shortened to eleven months, and the average expansion has lengthened to fifty-nine months.

The most extreme recession was the *Great Depression of 1929–1933* in the United States. It was preceded by a period of prosperity when the stock market's value more than doubled (1921–1927). Then, October 29, 1929, or Black Tuesday, came. The stock market crashed. Millions of farmers lost their farms. Unemployment rose from 3% in 1929 to 9% in 1931 and to 25% in 1933. Rich men became paupers overnight; families lost their savings, homes, and even ended their lives. In 1933, President Roosevelt stated that one-third of the nation was ill clothed, ill housed, and ill fed. It was a catastrophe. The Great Depression deeply affected the thinking of economists, most of whom thought that recessions would quickly cure themselves without assistance from government authorities. This led to the birth of macroeconomics as a policy-oriented branch of economics designed to help formulate government programs to prevent severe recessions.

The Great Depression of the 30s was followed by *wartime prosperity (1940s) and the post-World War II expansions (1950s)*—a period of a prolonged and steady growth in real GDP when the economy worked at full capacity. After WWII, there were four remarkably mild and much shorter recessions in the 50s (1949, 1954, 1958, and 1961).

The booming sixties—a period of military expansion and the Vietnam conflict that was characterized by one of the fastest periods of economic growth in American history, was boosted by increased government purchases, substantial tax reductions enacted by President Kennedy, and rising inflation.

During the following period, *the curious seventies*, something strange happened to the US economy. In 1973, the Organization of Petroleum Exporting Countries (OPEC) instituted an embargo of oil shipments to the United States and other nations. It resulted in double-digit inflation and a severe recession. Real GDP fell substantially between 1973–75, and unemployment increased to 9% of the labor force.

One of the most challenging periods was *the troubled eighties,* when inflation remained a serious problem, running at 10% annual rates. The unemployment rate rose to 11% of the labor force, and the economy was plunged into the deepest recession since 1930s. President Ronald Reagan intended to radically change the situation and launched a policy designed to loosen the heavy hand of the government—"get the government off the backs of the people"—and invigorate private business. This policy, labeled *"Reagonomics,"* included reduction of domestic spending by the Federal Government, restraint of government regulation, reduction of the tax rates, and increased defense spending. The period between 1982–87 was a time of expansion of the economy, followed by the stock market crash of 1987.

The period of Bill Clinton's presidency (1992–2000)—*the expanding 90s*—remains the longest lasting period of uninterrupted economic growth and controlled inflation. It was one of the most successful periods in the postwar history of the US. After a recession that ran from July 1990 to March 1991, the US economy entered a record-breaking expansion that lasted 120 months, until March 2001, when the economy entered a recession. The period that began in 1991 and ended in 2007 was almost free from serious downturns in real GDP and other economic indicators; it was called the *Great Moderation,* in contrast with the Great Depression of the 30s. The trough was reached in the third quarter of 2001, after which the economy was in an expansion until 2007 when it entered into a deep recession, with a decline in output and a significant increase in the unemployment rate—above 10%. We will be examining the causes of the *Great Recession of 2007–2009* in greater detail through the rest of our macroeconomic analysis.

2. UNEMPLOYMENT: CHARACTERISTICS, TRENDS, AND FLUCTUATIONS

The Employment Act of 1946 declared it the responsibility of the US government to achieve a high level of employment by using all practical means consistent with free competitive enterprise. The US Congress amended this act by adopting the *Full Employment and Balanced Growth Act of 1978*, establishing more specific goals for unemployment and the level of prices. Each month, the US Bureau of Labor Statistics (BLS), in conjunction with the United States Census Bureau, conducts a nationwide random survey of about 60,000 households to identify through a series of questions who is employed and who is not, who is eligible and available to work and who is not. The BLS and the United States Census Bureau measure the population, the labor force, and the employment level by dividing the population into the following three groups (figure 12.1):

1. *The working-age population*—the total population, excluding people less then sixteen years old and people institutionalized (in mental hospitals or correctional institutions) or in the US Armed Forces. In August 2011, the working-age population was 239.9 million out of the total US population of 312 million.
2. *The labor force*, which includes 153.6 million people, or almost half of the population, and *people not in labor force*—86.3 million: adults who are potential workers—homemakers, full-time students, and retirees.
3. The labor force is divided into the *employed* (139.6 million) *and the unemployed* (14.0 million).

Figure 12.1
US Labor Force

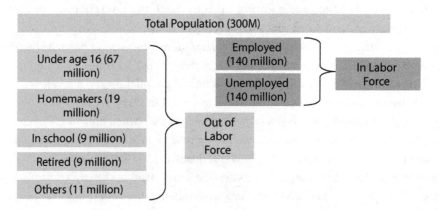

To be counted as unemployed, a person must be available for work and must be either: a) without work but has made specific efforts to find a job within the previous four weeks or b) waiting to be recalled back to a job from which he or she has been laid off.

Based on survey data, the BLS calculates the two main labor market indicators:

The *labor force participation* rate is the percentage of the working-age population who are members of the labor force. It equals:

$$\frac{(\text{Labor force})}{(\text{Working-age population})} \times 100.$$

In August 2011, it was 153.6 million: 239.9 million × 100 = 64.0%.

The amount of labor available to the economy is demonstrated with the labor force participation. It increased from 59% in the 1960s to 64% in 2011, with two notable trends: a) falling adult male participation (due to older men retiring and younger men remaining longer in school) and b) a remarkable increase in the female participation rate from 37% fifty years ago to about 60% today, which is explained by social attitudes (more women are pursuing college educations), technological changes in white-collar jobs (flexible work hours), and economic reasons (increased wages as an important source for the family budget), etc.

The *unemployment rate* represents the percentage of people in the workforce who aren't employed. It equals:

$$\frac{(\text{Number of people unemployed})}{(\text{Labor force})} \times 100.$$

In 2011, it was 14 million/153.6 million $\times$ 100 = 9.1%.

The rate of unemployment decreased from 25% during the Great Depression to 5.8% in the period from 1948 to 2011, reaching its highest level—above 10%—during the recessions of 1981–82 and 2007–09.

Two factors cause the official unemployment rate to understate actual unemployment:

1. *Discouraged workers,* who want a job but are not actively seeking employment. An unemployed individual who is not actively seeking employment is classified as "not in the labor force." Discouraged workers are people who have looked for work in the recent past but have not made specific efforts to find a job in the previous four weeks or gave up due to lack of opportunity.
2. *Part-time workers,* who work less than full-time (thirty-five hours per week). These include: a) those who took a part-time job for economic reasons—involuntary part-time—who are looking for a full-time position and b) those who work part-time for noneconomic reasons and are not looking for full-time jobs (health problems, family responsibility, education commitments, etc.). In 2011, almost 27 million people worked part-time as a result of personal choice. If this number were added to the number of unemployed, then the unemployment rate would almost double—16.2%.

3. UNEMPLOYMENT TYPES AND FULL EMPLOYMENT

An important fact that is not very well known is that job creation fluctuates (millions of jobs are created and removed) every year. Each month, The BLS announces the number of persons employed and unemployed, but we need to look at what is behind these figures. The change in the number of persons employed represents the difference between the total number of jobs created and the number of jobs eliminated. For example, in 2006, about 31 million jobs were created and 29 million were destroyed. This is a normal process for a vibrant market economy and results from technological advances, changes in consumer tastes and preferences, success or failure of businesses that are trying to adapt to new technological challenges, and changes in consumer behavior. These changes in the labor market are tracked by the Establishment Survey, also called the Payroll Survey, which the BLO conducts monthly along with the Household Survey.

The labor market is affected by flows of workers in and out of employment and in and out of the labor force (figure 12.2):

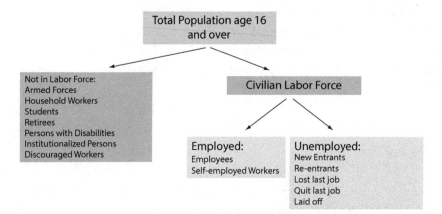

Job losers, *job leavers*, and *entrants* and *reentrants* are job market flows that lead to unemployment, rise in recessions, and falls in expansions. Job losers are the largest flow.

Hires, *recalls*, and *withdrawals* are job market flows that end unemployment. To better understand the changes in the labor market, economists break unemployment into its three most important categories:

First, frictional unemployment is the unemployment that arises from normal labor turnover and is, to some extent, unavoidable. The cause of this type of unemployment is the transition time to a new job; it is sometimes called *transitional* or *search unemployment*. Frictional unemployment consists of those searching for jobs or waiting to take jobs soon. At any period of time, some workers are "between jobs." Economists use the term *frictional unemployment* for workers who are searching for or waiting to take jobs in the near future. Frictional unemployment is inevitable and, to some extent desirable. It indicates that there is mobility as people change or seek jobs. The word "frictional" implies that the labor market does not operate perfectly, without friction, in matching workers and jobs.

Frictional unemployment is the unemployment that naturally occurs during the normal workings of an economy because people: a) change jobs; b) move across the country; and/or c) search for new job opportunities. Usually this is a short-term unemployment. For example, when you graduate from college, it might take a few months until you find a job suitable to your qualification and preferences. Frictional unemployment increases when more people enter the labor market or when unemployment benefits increase. *Seasonal unemployment* is also a frictional type of unemployment; it arises because of seasonal factors, such as weather, variations in tourism patterns, or calendar-related events, etc.

Second, structural unemployment occurs when technology or international competition changes the skills needed to perform certain jobs or changes the locations of jobs. Sometimes there is a mismatch between skills demanded by firms and skills provided by workers, especially when there are great technological changes in an industry. Structural unemployment generally lasts longer than frictional unemployment and occurs because the labor force does not respond immediately to the new structure of job opportunities.

The key distinction between frictional and structural unemployment is that frictionally unemployed workers have skills. Structurally unemployed workers find it hard to obtain new jobs without retraining, gaining additional education, or reallocating. Structural unemployment is due to changes in the structure of demand for labor. Examples of structural unemployment are: a) street sweepers being replaced by street-sweeping vehicles and b) technical or customer service support being transferred to foreign competition. These and other advances have led to a loss of jobs or a shift of jobs to other countries, also called *offshoring*.

Third, cyclical unemployment is the fluctuation of unemployment over the business cycle. This typically occurs during a recession phase of the business cycle and results in a decline in total spending. Cyclical unemployment is sometimes called deficient-demand unemployment. The 25% unemployment rate in the depths of the Great Depression in 1933 reflected mainly cyclical unemployment as did a significant part of the 9.7% unemployment rate in 1982 and the 9.6% rate in 2012.

How can we define the term *"full employment"*? Economists say that the economy is fully employed" when it experiences only frictional and structural employment. They describe the unemployment rate that is consistent with full employment as the full-employment rate of unemployment, or the *natural rate of unemployment (NRU)*. The NRU occurs when the number of job seekers equals the number of job vacancies, and the economy is said to be producing at its potential output. This is the real GDP produced when the economy is "fully employed." There are at least two controversies related to the NRU: 1) Many believe that there is nothing "natural" (good) in any type of unemployment, and from the perspective of an unemployed person, the lack of job is always "unnatural" (bad) and 2) What level of unemployment is consistent with the term "natural"? It is generally accepted among economists that the NRU varies over time; in the last thirty years, it has changed from 4% in the 1960s to 6% in the 1980s to 5% today. Some relevant factors are:

1. The proportion of younger workers in the labor force has declined as the baby-boom generation has aged, and the labor force now has a larger proportion of middle-aged workers, who traditionally have lower unemployment rates; this tendency could be reversed since "baby boomers" are starting to retire *en masse* because of age.
2. The structural changes in the labor force linked to technological advances, improved information from the Internet (i.e., the website Monster.com), and the growth of temporary help agencies have lowered the NRU by enabling workers to find job more quickly.
3. The work requirements under the new welfare laws and increases in minimum wage rates have moved many people from the ranks of the unemployed to the ranks of the employed. However, more generous benefits (food stamps, welfare, Social Security) make unemployment less painful and increase its duration.
4. Surprisingly, even the doubling of the rate of the US prison population since 1985 has removed relatively high-unemployment individuals from the labor force and, thus, lowered the overall unemployment rate.

One important clarification: the quantity of real GDP produced at full employment is called *potential GDP*. When the economy is at full employment, the unemployment rate equals the natural rate of unemployment and current (real) GDP equals potential GDP. When the unemployment rate is greater than the natural rate of unemployment, current GDP is less than potential GDP and vice versa: when the unemployment rate is less than the natural rate of unemployment, real GDP is greater than potential GDP.

4. COSTS OF UNEMPLOYMENT

The basic cost of unemployment is forgone output, or a GDP gap, which is the difference between current and potential GDP and measures the monetary losses of goods and services because the economy is operating below full employment level.

GDP gap = potential GDP − current GDP

The quantitative relationship between the unemployment rate and the real GDP gap was first estimated by economist Arthur Okun, who served as professor at Yale University and as chairman of President Johnson's Council of Economic Advisers. The law named after him—*Okun's Law*—indicates that for every percentage point by which actual unemployment is above (below) the natural rate, real GDP is 2% points below (above) potential GDP. For example, in 2009, the unemployment rate was 9.3%, or 4.3% above the 5.0% natural rate of unemployment. So the GDP gap was 4.3% × 2 = 8.6% of potential GDP of $13, 9 trillion, or $1.2 trillion of real output lost, according to Okun's Law.

The obvious cost of unemployment is the loss of income and the resulting financial difficulties for affected families. Unemployment insurance is not available to everybody and is, for a limited period, compensating for only a part of earnings. When the unemployment rate is high, people looking for work will find fewer job opportunities. The longer a person remains unemployed, the more his or her skills and good work habits depreciate. This will make it more difficult for him or her to find a job. Also, a person's social status is associated with the type of job that he or she holds. Losing his or her job can create psychological stresses for the individual. Overall, unemployment represents a true waste of society's resources.

There is a large variance in the unemployment rate between different categories of people, as follows:

1. Occupation—lower skilled occupations have higher unemployment rates than higher skilled occupations; lower skilled workers in manufacturing, construction, mining, and other industries are the first to be hard-hit by recessions and unemployment; in contrast, higher skilled workers are less likely to lose their jobs.

2. Age—teenagers, especially African American males, suffer much higher unemployment rates than adults, having less skills, experience, and education.

3. Race and ethnicity—the unemployment rate for blacks is roughly twice that for whites and higher than the rate for Hispanics; the main causes of these differences are rates of educational attainment, concentration in lower skilled professions, and discrimination in the labor market.

4. Gender—the unemployment rates for men and women are almost the same, but in the recession of 2007–09, the unemployment rate for men substantially exceeded that for women.

5. Education—less educated workers have higher unemployment rates and are more vulnerable to layoffs during recessions.

6. Duration—people unemployed for long periods—fifteen weeks or more—have a higher unemployment rate which is significantly higher during recessions.

There are also very high social and psychological costs of unemployment associated with a person's status and position. Unemployment and other economic problems have adverse effects on physical and mental health; shorten lifespans; and lead to increased alcohol consumption, drug trafficking, and criminality.

5. INFLATION VS. DEFLATION

Let's turn now to an aspect of macroeconomic instability that poses subtler threats than unemployment—inflation. You may often find news programs using this term, sometimes in combination with unemployment, to characterize the discomfort that inflation and unemployment jointly create for us. The sum of these two rates is called the *misery index*. Or you may hear another term, *stagflation*, which comes from the combination of the words inflation and stagnation. Is there any correlation or trade-off between the rate of unemployment and the rate of inflation? The New Zealand economist A. W. Phillips found that there is an inverse relationship in the short-run between these two categories and demonstrated it by using a curve that is named after him—the

Phillips Curve. How do these phenomena affect our everyday life? What is the cure for inflation, if any? Is deflation good or bad for us? What is hyperinflation? To address these issues, let's start with some important definitions.

First, inflation is a rise in the average level of prices for goods and services. It doesn't represent a change in any specific price. Even during periods of rapid inflation, some prices may be relatively constant while others are falling. For example, from 1973–1982, when the average annual rate of inflation was 8.8%, reaching a record high level in 1981—13.5%—the prices of video recorders, digital watches, and personal computers declined. An extremely rapid increase in the general level of prices by about 100% or more per year, as most economists agree, is called *hyperinflation*. Cases of hyperinflation were registered in Germany in 1922–23 and after World War II when prices increased twenty-five times during one month; in Russia after the USSR's collapse in 1991 when prices increased by 2000% a year; and, more recently, in Zimbabwe, with an unimaginable inflation rate in 2008 of 14.9 billion percent.

To determine who is hurt by inflation, it is necessary to understand the ideas of average and relative prices. This is an important distinction for the assessment of the redistribution of income—people buy different combinations of goods and services. Sometimes inflation is compared with a "tax" that is levied through changes in prices, changes in incomes, and changes in wealth.

Second, deflation is the opposite of inflation and means a decrease in the average level of prices of goods and services. The American economy experienced deflation during the Great Depression when prices fell 33% on average along with wages; briefly, after WWII; and in 2009, when the rate of inflation was negative. Sometimes, economists use another term—*disinflation*—to characterize the reduction in the rate of inflation as happened in the periods 1980–1983 and 1990–1992. Do not rush to make a conclusion that deflation is good for you because the average level of prices decreases. The biggest problem with deflation is that people cannot repay their debts. For example, if you owe $40,000 for your education, and you expect to cover it in a few years after graduation using part of your $30,000 average annual salary, then, because of deflation, your wage could fall to $20,000, and you might be forced to default on your loans as happened recently with millions of people during the recent recession.

Third, to evaluate the impact of inflation on your life, so-called *price effects,* let's have a look at how public college and university tuition increased during the last thirty-five years. In 1975, the average in-state tuition was $400 per year; it had increased twelve times by 2003 to $4,694; and eighteen times by 2010. For private universities, tuition increased just during last decade by more than eight times to $26,000. The *income effect* is also reflected in two distinctive notions: *nominal income,* the money you receive in a particular time period in current dollars, and *real income,* the purchasing power of that money (nominal income) measured by the quantity of goods and services your dollars (nominal income) will buy. If your nominal income remains unchanged, your real income has changed because the prices for goods and services that you buy changed. Inflation has an impact not only on your income, which is money flow earned by selling factors of production that you own, but also on your wealth—the value of your assets, including your bank accounts, stocks, bonds, home, etc. This is the so-called *wealth effect.* For example, if you paid $150,000 for a home purchased in 2002, and in 2012, its market value increased to $300,000, you would earn 100% by selling it, but this is the result of inflation. Conversely, for young couples, it might be unaffordable to buy a house at such prices.

6. CONSUMER PRICE INDEX AND COST OF LIVING

The *Consumer Price Index (CPI)* is compiled by the Bureau of Labor Statistics (BLS) and is sometimes referred to as the *Cost-of-Living Index.* This is the typical measure of inflation. Each month, hundreds of BLS employees visit 23,000 stores in thirty metropolitan areas (eighty-seven cities) and record prices of goods and services in a "market basket." The CPI reports the price of a "market basket" which contains 80,000 goods and services that are purchased by a typical urban consumer and arranged in eight large groups (figure 11.3).

An astonishing 88,000 families and individuals participate in this survey. The composition of this basket is based on spending patterns of urban consumers in a specific period. The BLS updates the composition of the basket every two years in order to reflect the most recent patterns of consumption. A major purpose of the CPI is to measure the *inflation rate*—changes in the cost of living and the value of money—by comparing the current value of the market basket with its value in a period called the *base reference period*. The current base reference period is 1982–1984, so the average CPI during that period was 100. For example, in April 2012, the CPI was 230.0. Thus, prices have increased 2.3 times from 1982–84 to 2012. The CPI equals the ratio of the cost of the market basket for this month to the cost of the same basket in the base period times 100:

$$\frac{\text{(Cost of CPI basket at current period prices)}}{\text{(Cost of the CPI basket at base period prices)}} \times 100.$$

The *inflation rate* is the percentage change in the price level from one year to the next. In the formula below, the inflation rate is determined by:

$$\left(\frac{\text{CPI in current year} - \text{CPI in previous year}}{\text{CPI in previous year}} \right) \times 100.$$

If we suppose that the CPI for 2012 is 140, and in 2011, it was 120, then the inflation rate equals 16.7%, according to this formula. The CPI Index could also be a negative figure, for example—2% as it was in 2009. In this case, the CPI reflected the deflation. Recall the mathematical approximation called the "**rule of 70**" which tells us how we can find the number of years it will take for some measures to double, given their annual percentage increase, by dividing that percentage increase into the number 70. So, the 3% annual rate of inflation will double the price level in about twenty-three years (= 70: 3). Inflation of 8% will double the price level in about nine years.

CPI Structure	Percent
Housing	41.5
Transportation	17.3
Food and Beverages	14.8
Medical Care	6.6
Education and Communication	6.4
Recreation	6.3
Apparel	3.6
Others	3.5

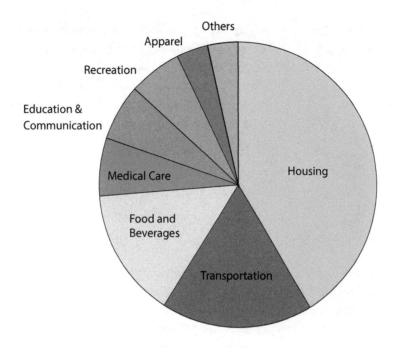

Figure 12.3
CPI Market
Basket

The CPI is not the perfect measure of inflation and is a subject of criticism of at least four biases that lead it to overstate the inflation rate:

1. *New products bias*: New goods are often more expensive than the goods they replace or vice versa. The prices for many goods, such as computers and cell phones, decrease immediately after they are introduced, and if the market basket is not updated frequently, these changes are not reflected in CPI.
2. *Increase in quality bias*: Sometimes price increases reflect quality improvements (safer cars, faster computers, improved health care) and should not be counted as part of inflation.
3. *Substitution bias*: Prices of the market basket products that consumers actually buy could rise less than the prices of goods included by BLS in the market basket. In other words, our market basket of products purchased does not always match the "typical" basket used by BLS.
4. *Outlet substitution bias*: When prices rise, people use discount stores, such as Sam's Club and Price Club, more frequently and convenience stores less frequently.

According to the report of the Congressional Advisory Commission (1996), chaired by Michael Boskin, an economics professor at Stanford, the CPI overstates inflation by 1.1%. This magnitude of bias for government outlays linked to CPI, for example for Social Security, equals to a trillion overpaid dollars over a decade. To reduce the bias, the BLS has decided to undertake consumer spending surveys more frequently.

To avoid bias in the CPI calculation of inflation, economists use several alternative measures of the price level and inflation rate:

First, the GDP Index, also called the *GDP deflator*, measures the percentage increase of prices of all goods and services—including consumption, capital, government, and export goods and services and not just consumption goods and services counted by CPI—to base year prices. This method also uses information about current quantities while CPI is based on information from the Past Consumer Expenditure Survey.

Second, the Personal Consumption Expenditure (PCE) Index represents the average of current prices of goods and services included in the consumption expenditure divided by base year prices. It has the same advantages as the GDP deflator and measures the cost of living.

Third, the Core Inflation Index measures the percentage of change in the PCE Price Index, with the exclusion of prices for food and energy which are highly volatile (variable) and can obscure the trends in prices. An economist (who shall remain anonymous) invented a joke referring to this index: "If you are not eating and driving, you are not affected by inflation."

7. DEMAND PULL VS. COST-PUSH INFLATION: COST OF INFLATION

Economists distinguish between two basic types of inflation, explaining it in the familiar terms of demand and supply:

1. *Demand-pull inflation.* The essence of this type of inflation is that spending increases faster than production: "too much money chasing too few goods." The excess demand bids up the prices of the limited output, producing demand-pull inflation. In other words, the price level is "pulled up" by the pressure from consumer spending (C, demand) as well as by spending from other key actors in the market: business investment (I), government spending (G), and net export (X-M). This type of inflation occurs when the economy is at or near full employment. The cause is over-issuance of money by the Central Bank.

2. *Cost-push inflation.* This type of inflation is linked to the supply side and is explained in terms of factors that raise per-unit production costs at each level of spending: costs are pushing the price level upward. Per-unit cost = total cost/units of output. The major source of cost-push inflation has been so-called supply shocks, specifically, abrupt increases in the costs of raw materials or energy inputs (rocketing prices of imported oil in 1973–74 and 1979–80). Cost-push inflation is automatically self-limiting: increased per unit cost will reduce supply which will result in a recession. In contrast, demand-pull inflation will continue as long as there is excess total spending.

The Costs of Inflation can be analyzed under two categories:

1. *Costs of Anticipated Inflation*: Menu costs, shoe-leather costs (people rash to spend their money to avoid its falling value—"take the shoes off"), confusion and uncertainty costs, and added financial and tax costs. The effects of anticipated inflation are less severe. Workers can protect themselves, for example, by including cost-of-living adjustment clauses in their labor contracts; lenders can charge an inflation premium (raising the interest rate to cover the effect of inflation). Inflation also affects borrowers and lenders which is reflected in the differences between two notions: the *nominal interest rate*—the percentage increase in money that the borrower pays the lender, and the *real interest rate*—the percentage increase in purchasing power that the borrower pays the lender. The real interest provides a better measure of the true cost of borrowing and true return from lending.

Real interest rate = nominal interest rate – Inflation premium

2. *Costs of Unanticipated Inflation*: Unexpected redistribution of income. Depending on how high the unanticipated inflation is, within the context of a contract (e.g., a loan contract), income is redistributed from one party to another—from borrower to lender or vice versa.

Who is affected by inflation? We analyzed the impact of inflation in the forms of price, income and wealth effects, and hyperinflation. Let's have a look at these effects from another angle, that of unanticipated inflation which also introduces huge uncertainty into the economy, disrupting the normal flow of business. Unanticipated inflation hurts three categories of people:

1. Fixed income groups—because their nominal income will not rise with prices (pensioners, public sector workers, and landlords).
2. Savers—because returns from interest rates may not cover the cost of inflation, and their savings will lose purchasing power.
3. Creditors (lenders)—because of inflation, the value of their dollars will be decreased by rising prices and the diminishing purchasing power of a dollar.

WHO IS HELPED BY INFLATION OR LEFT UNAFFECTED?

1. Flexible income receivers—individuals who derive their incomes solely from Social Security are largely unaffected by inflation because *these payments are indexed to the CPI*. Some union workers also get automatic *cost-of-living adjustment (COLAs)* in their pay when the CPI rises. Some flexible income receivers and all borrowers are even helped by unanticipated inflation. For example, property owners may be able to boost flexible rents more rapidly than the rate of inflation. Also, some business owners may benefit from inflation. If product prices rise faster than resource prices, business revenues will increase more rapidly than costs.
2. Unanticipated inflation benefits debtors (borrowers)—for example, Ron borrowed "dear" dollars five years ago, but because of inflation, he pays back the principal and interest now with "cheap" dollars whose purchasing power has been eroded by inflation. The inflation of the 1970s and 1980s benefited people who purchased homes with low, fixed-interest-rate mortgages, and inflation reduced the real burden of their mortgage indebtedness. The Federal Government, which had amassed a huge $10 trillion of public debt through 2000, also benefited from inflation because it permitted the Treasury to pay off its loans with dollars with less purchasing power than the dollars originally borrowed.

Some economists believe that full employment and economic growth depend on strong levels of total spending which, in turn, create more profits, demand for labor, and incentives for firms to expand. They believe that a little inflation may have positive effects because it makes it easier for firms to adjust real wages downward when the demands for their products fall. Anyway, it is much better to have an economy with strong spending, full employment, economic growth, and mild inflation than one with weak spending, unemployment, recession, and deflation.

The major goal of economic policy is *price stability*, the absence of significant changes in the average level of prices. According to the Full Employment and Balanced Growth Act of 1978, a rate of inflation under 3% was officially defined as the economic policy goal. Congress was guided by two considerations:

1. *Maintaining full employment*: the lowest rate of unemployment consistent with stable prices. "Zero" inflation raises the unemployment rate too high.

2. *Measurement capabilities:* CPI simply monitors the price of specific goods over time, but the goods themselves change over time, too, as we have already seen. Old products become better as a result of quality improvements—for example, TVs and cars. In 1958, the average price of a new car was $2,867; it is now $25,000, but the quality is incomparable: GPS, electronic ignition, emergency flashers, rear window defrosters, crash resistant bodies, air bags, antilock brakes, remote control mirrors, seat belts, and doubling of fuel mileage. Some goods even did not exist twenty-five to thirty years ago (computers and word processors), and the CPI did not include them.

8. KEY TERMS

Business Cycle
Peak, Recession/Depression, Trough, Expansion
National Bureau of Economic Research (NBER)
Great Depression
Working-Age Population
Labor Force
Labor Force Participation
Unemployment Rate
Frictional, Structural, Cyclical Unemployment
Full Employment
Phillips Curve
Okun's Law
Inflation, Deflation, Disinflation, Hyperinflation
Price Effect, Wealth Effect, Income Effect
Consumer Price Index (CPI, Cost-of-Living Index, Personal Consumption Expenditure (PCE)
Bureau of Labor Statistics (BLS)
Inflation Rate, Core Inflation Index
Demand-Pull Inflation, Cost-Push Inflation
Anticipated, Unanticipated Inflation
Price Stability

9. PROBLEMS AND APPLICATIONS

1. As a student in an economics class, you need to calculate the unemployment rate for your region, state and nation. Which one of the following will you use? You divide the number of:
   a. Unemployed by the size of the population and multiply by 100.
   b. Unemployed by the labor force and multiply by 100.
   c. Unemployed by the percentage of the employed population and multiply by 100.
   d. Employed by the labor force and multiply by 100.

2. What is best way to define the business cycle? It is:
   a. A measure of performance of the economy as a whole.
   b. A study of individual behavior in the economy.

c. Alternating periods of economic growth and contraction.

d. The market value of goods and services produced in the economy.

3. Andrew Mellon, secretary of the US Treasury, in assessing the prospects for the years ahead, declared in January 1930: "I see nothing ... in the present situation that is either menacing or warrants pessimism ... I have every confidence that there will be a revival of activity in the spring and that during the coming year the country will make steady progress." His vision, which dominated economic policy at that time, can be most appropriately defined as:

a. The Keynesian approach to the economy, which considers the market mechanism to be inherently unstable, requiring government intervention.

b. The classical optimistic view that flexible prices and flexible wages will provide the best economic adjustment without any government intervention.

c. The new growth theory—that our unlimited wants will lead us to ever greater productivity and perpetual economic growth.

d. The concept of what are the business cycles and how to prevent them

4. Which of the following best characterize the recession phase of a business cycle?

a. A period of decline in total output, income, employment, and trade that lasts six or more months.

b. When there are two consecutive quarters of negative economic growth, but the employment, output, and trade are still increasing.

c. The phase of the business cycle.

d. Moving of the economy from the trough to the peak. A period of time when unemployment increases.

5. Andy, a Texas A&M student in the honors program with a major in economics, graduated in 2016. He was selected by a pharmaceutical company for a job with a nominal annual salary of $60,000. Suppose that the rate of inflation is constant at 10 percent. To keep Andy's real salary constant, his nominal salary in 2013 should be:

a. $60,000

b. $54,000

c. $66,000

d. $100,000

	Year 1	Year 2
Population	300 million	310 million
Labor force	150 million	155 million
Number of employed	140 million	145 million

6. What is the unemployment rate in Year 1 in the table above?

a. 0.9%

b. 9.3%

c. 46.0%

d. 6.7%

7. Cherise is a Georgia Institute of Technology student and she received a scholarship to support her studies. She observed that the tuition now is much higher than her parents paid twenty-five years ago. She also discovered that the price for gasoline and for other goods and services increased even during her first semester. In this way, she learned that inflation means:
   a. All prices are rising on average but at different rates.
   b. All prices are rising at the same rate and in the same time.
   c. Prices in the average are increasing, but some particular prices may be falling.
   d. Real incomes are rising even if nominal income is decreasing.

8. To better understand the changes in the labor market, the economists break unemployment into the three most important categories. Which of the following types of unemployment is most directly related to real output growth?
   a. Structural unemployment
   b. Cyclical unemployment
   c. Seasonal unemployment
   d. Frictional unemployment

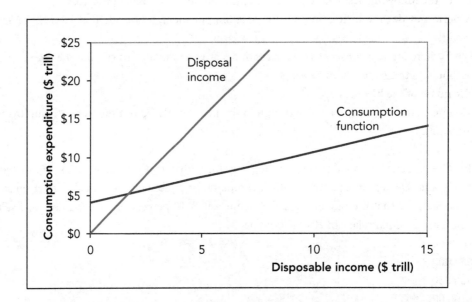

9. In the figure above, when disposable income equals $5 trillion:
   a. Consumers are dissaving because consumption expenditure is greater than disposable income.
   b. Consumers are saving because consumption expenditure is greater than disposable income.
   c. Consumers are dissaving because consumption expenditure is less than disposable income
   d. Consumers are saving because consumption expenditure is less than disposable income.

10. Economists say that the economy is fully employed when:
    a. Cyclical unemployment has been reduced to zero although there is still frictional and structural unemployment.
    b. The total unemployment rate has been reduced to zero which is compatible with "the natural rate of unemployment."

c. Cyclical and structural unemployment have been minimized, but cyclical unemployment still prevails.

d. Everyone who is willing and able to work has a job, and all types of unemployment are reduced to zero.

10. REVIEW QUESTIONS

1. Based on the Bureau of Labor Statistics data, between 2009 and 2015, by how much did: a) The US labor force increase? b) Total employment increase? c) The rate of unemployment increase? d) The labor force participation increase/decrease? Use the Bureau of Labor Statistics website: www.bls.gov.

2. Based on the following data: Civilian labor force = 100 million; Number of employed people = 82 million; Natural unemployment rate = 5%; and Frictional unemployment rate = 2%; compute a) the unemployment rate; b) the GDP gap, according to Okun's Law (the cyclical unemployment rate); c) the structural unemployment rate, based on the fact that NRU (UN) = Frictional unemployment rate (UF) + Structural unemployment rate (US).

3. Taking into account what you learned in this chapter, please comment on the following phrase: "The economy is operating at full employment." What is "natural" about a natural rate of unemployment, and how big was it in 2016? Use the National Bureau of Economic Research website: www.nber.gov.

4. Most economists consider that the immediate cause of a large majority of business cycles, and of changes in the level of output and employment, are due to the unexpected changes in: a) the level of the stock market and financial imbalances; b) the level of the trade deficit and changes in resource prices; c) the quantity of money in the economy (monetary phenomenon); and/or d) the level of total spending. Which of these represent the most important cause of the economy's fluctuations?

5. Let' focus on the new technology's impact on unemployment. When iPods and MP3 players were introduced, replacing CDs, what type of unemployment was created: a) Structural and Frictional; b) Structural and Cyclical; c) Frictional and Cyclical; or d) Discouraged and Cyclical.

CHAPTER 13.

AGGREGATE DEMAND AND AGGREGATE SUPPLY

The recession of 2007–09 brought the notions of *aggregate demand and aggregate supply* to the attention of newspapers, television, Internet websites, and not just professional economic and financial journals but also mainstream business magazines. What happened to aggregate demand? Why did economists and politicians fail to predict this deepest recession which had the highest record of unemployment in the last three decades? Did the Federal Government's stimulus package of $787 billion reduce unemployment and boost demand? How did political turmoil in the Middle East and increased oil prices affect aggregate supply? To answer these questions, we need to analyze the Aggregate Demand-Aggregate Supply model, one of the most important in macroeconomics, a virtual market for all final goods and services that make up real GDP.

The Aggregate Supply-Aggregate Demand model (AD-AS model) enables us to analyze changes in real GDP and the price level simultaneously. This model provides keen insights on inflation, recession, unemployment, and economic growth. Aggregate supply and aggregate demand curves are tools of analysis used for understanding key aspects of economic fluctuations both in the short-run and in the long-run. We look at those factors that explain the slope and cause the aggregate demand curve to shift, and illustrate the long-run and the short-run aggregate supply curves. We use these tools to show how wage and price adjustments bring the economy from a short-run equilibrium to a long-run full employment level of output. Let's start with analysis of how Classical and Keynesian theories address these issues.

1. AGGREGATE DEMAND-AGGREGATE SUPPLY MODEL: CLASSICAL VS. KEYNESIAN APPROACH

Historically, there have been two approaches to aggregate demand and supply. The first is the classical school of economics, which was mainstream economics from the 1770s to the Great Depression; the classical school's founding father, Adam Smith, believed in the *laissez-faire* ("leave it alone") theory that states that the economy has a self-regulating mechanism that will correct itself without any government interference. The second is the Keynesian approach, named after John Maynard Keynes, a Cambridge University economist, whose path breaking book *The General Theory of Employment, Interest and Money (1936)* had enormous influence on economic thinking and political decision-making as a way of explaining and combating the Great Depression.

Before the Great Depression of the 1930s, *classical economists* believed that the economy is self-adjusting to deviations from its long-term growth trend. In their opinion, if output occasionally declines and people lose their jobs, the internal forces of the market will quickly restore the equilibrium and prosperity. The core of the classical approach was *flexible prices and flexible wages*. Accordingly, if producers are not able to sell their output, they have two choices: 1) reduce the rate of output and throw some people out of the work or 2) reduce the price of their output, stimulating an increase in the quantity demanded. From the other side, workers, by offering their services at lower wages, will create the conditions for hiring more workers. Flexible wages will ensure that everyone who wanted a job will be able to find one. In the words of Jean-Baptiste Say, a nineteenth century French economist, "supply creates its own demand." If you are producing something, somebody will buy it. It is just necessary to find the "right price."

Classical economists put money at the center of aggregate demand. In their view, the willingness and ability of consumers to purchase goods and services depend on the quantity of money in their possession and on the purchasing power of that money. The *purchasing power of money* is the real quantity of goods and services that the dollar will buy. When the price level rises, the purchasing power of money falls and vice versa—a decrease in price level will increase the purchasing power of money. For example, when the price level doubles, the purchasing power of money falls to half its previous level.

In the classical economists' point of view, there is no necessity for government intervention into the self-adjusting market mechanism. Internal market forces—flexible prices and wages—can provide an automatic adjustment to external shocks. Andrew Mellon, the secretary of the US Treasury during the Great Depression, expressed this optimistic vision in January 1930, just a few months after the crash of the stock market: "I see nothing … in the present situation that is either menacing or warrants pessimism …" (David A. Shannon, *The Great Depression*. Englewood Cliffs, NJ:

Prentice Hall, 1960, p. 4). Nevertheless, the Great Depression occurred, and unemployment increased dramatically in spite of the fact that prices and wages fell.

The Great Depression of the 30s destroyed the credibility of the classical approach. British economist *John Maynard Keynes,* in his major work, *The General Theory,* attacked the classical view. He believed that the private economy is inherently unstable, and this requires government intervention. In his opinion, we cannot wait for a self-adjusting mechanism to protect jobs and income. Keynes put forward three major propositions:

1. *Unemployment in the market economy.* Keynes argued that a market economy might have no strong tendency to move to full employment; on the contrary, it rests in equilibrium with large-scale unemployment or in the unemployment equilibrium. In his opinion, the market economy is defective in two ways: a) it might lead to a persistent depression, such as the Great Depression of 30s and b) it might be quite unstable, so if we did achieve full employment, this might be short lived.
2. *The cause of unemployment.* According to Keynes, large-scale unemployment is the result of an insufficiency of aggregate demand—that is, too little spending for goods and services.
3. *The cure for unemployment.* Aggregate demand should be increased, and the best way to do this is by increasing government spending. The main message of *The General Theory* was that the government has the ability—and the responsibility—to manage aggregate demand and, thus, to ensure continuing prosperity. Cast aside was the classical view that market forces would solve the unemployment problem, and the government should strictly limit its interference in the economy. Keynes was impatient with classical economists who argued that in the long-run, market forces would reestablish full employment. "In long run we are all dead," he retorted. His book has had spectacular success, and it ranks with Adam Smith's *The Wealth of Nations* and Karl Marx's *Das Kapital* in groundbreaking achievement. With its appearance in 1936, the Keynesian revolution was under way.

2. AGGREGATE DEMAND: COMPONENTS AND DOWNWARD SLOPING AD CURVE

Aggregate Demand (AD), or collective demand, refers to various quantities of output that all market participants (households, businesses, governments, and foreigners) are willing and able to buy at alternative price levels in a given period of time. In other words, AD is the total demand for GDP as a function of price level. The quantity of real GDP demanded is the sum of consumption expenditure (C), investment (I), government expenditures (G), and net exports (X – M), or Y = C + I + G + (X – M).

To find out how much people will buy, we need to have a look at prices. The relationship between the price level and the amount of real GDP demanded is inverse or negative, according to the law of demand. The price level is the average level of prices in the economy as measured by a price index, such as the CPI or the GDP deflator. We are talking here about the average price level and about the aggregates measures, not about the price of any single good.

The aggregate demand curve plots the total demand for GDP as a function of the price level (see figure 13.1). The AD curve is downward sloping as is the demand curve for an individual product. Why does the AD curve have a downward slope?

In the case of a single product, the explanation lies in income and substitution effect. When the price for an individual product falls, the consumer's nominal income allows a larger purchase of a product (income effect),

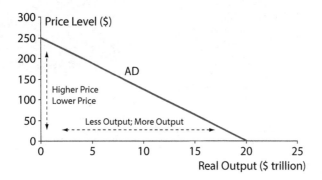

Figure 13.1
Aggregate
Demand

and the consumer wants to buy more of the product because it becomes relatively less expensive. The quantity of a good demanded falls when its price rises because people are switching their consumption to other goods and services that are cheaper (substitution effect). But this explanation doesn't work for aggregates when we are considering a simultaneous change in the prices of all final goods and services. The explanation for the downward sloping curve rests on *three effects of a price-level change:*

First, Wealth or Real-balances effect. This is produced by a change in the price level and can be defined as the increase in spending that occurs when the real value of money increases when the price level falls. A higher price level reduces the real value of purchasing power of the accumulated savings balances. So a higher price level means less consumption spending and vice versa. When consumers' real incomes and wealth increase because of the decline in the price level, consumers respond by buying more goods and services. They will save less of their income and will spend more, and this causes the AD curve to slope down. Aggregate demand is downward sloping because a change in the price level changes the purchasing power of money held by the public. So, the wealth effect could be also expressed as: $\uparrow P \Rightarrow \downarrow$ Real Wealth $\Rightarrow \downarrow$ Demand for Goods and Services.

Second, Interest-rate effect—a higher price level increases the demand for money. An increase in money demand will drive up the price paid for its use which is the interest rate. Higher interest rates curtail investment spending and interest-sensitive consumption spending. So, by increasing the demand for money and, consequently, the interest rate, a higher price level reduces the amount of real output demanded and vice versa—cheaper money stimulates more borrowing and loan-financed purchases.

Third, Foreign purchases (trade) effect—changes in export and import are the final reason why the AD curve is downward sloping. When American-made products become cheaper, US consumers will buy fewer imports and more domestic output and vice versa. The rise in the price level of American products reduces the quantity of US goods demanded as net exports.

3. AGGREGATE DEMAND CURVE: SHIFTS VS. MOVEMENTS ALONG THE CURVE

We analyzed the factor—price level—that caused movement along the AD curve and its three effects, explaining the downward slope of this curve. Now let's consider the factors that shift the AD curve to the right (increase) or to the left (decrease) (figures 13.2a and b).

1. Rightward shift of AD is determined by increase in consumer, business, or government spending; AD changes as a result of changes in expectations.
2. Leftward shift of AD is the result of the same factors' negative changes—for example, a fall in wealth caused by a stock market crash.

Figure 13.2a
Rightward Shift
in AD

Figure 13.2b
Leftward Shift in
AD

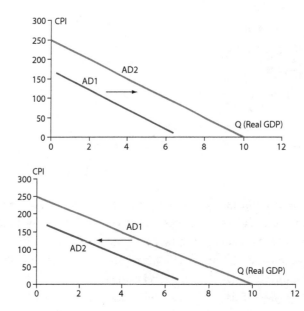

1. *Changes in consumer spending* caused by *changes in money supply*: $\uparrow$ M $\Rightarrow$ $\uparrow$ demand for goods and services. The increase in consumer spending, called the *wealth effect*, will shift the aggregate demand curve to the right (consumer wealth includes financial assets—stocks and bonds—and physical assets—houses and land). Note that in this case, the source of change in wealth is not a change in aggregate price level (which is an effect of movement along the AD curve) but is independent from change in price level. For example, a rise in real estate values or a rise in the stock market increases the real value of consumers' assets without any change in the aggregate price level and shifts the AD curve. Consumer spending depends also on consumers' expectations about the future: it increases when consumers become more optimistic and vice versa—it decreases when they become more pessimistic. That's why short-run economic forecasters are paying so much attention to the Consumer Confidence Index, which is calculated monthly by the Conference Board, and the Michigan Consumer Sentiment Index, which is calculated by the University of Michigan. Consumer spending is also influenced by household indebtedness and taxes (tax cuts shift the AD curve to the right; tax increases shift the AD curve to the left).

2. *Changes in business investment spending which is affected by changes in taxes*: $\uparrow$ taxes $\Rightarrow$ $\downarrow$ demand for goods and services. Investment spending, in turn, depends on the real interest rate (an increase in the interest rate will lower investment spending and reduce AD) and expected returns (expectations about future business conditions, technology, degree of excess capacity, and business taxes).

3. *Changes in government spending*: $\uparrow$ G $\Rightarrow$ $\uparrow$ demand for goods and services. The government exercises a powerful influence on aggregate demand through fiscal policy and monetary policy, which we will examine in the next chapter.

4. *Changes in net export spending*—a rise in net exports shifts the AD curve to the right. Net exports might change if: a) the national income abroad changes and b) exchange rates change: depreciation of the dollar in terms of the euro, for example, increases US exports and shifts the AD curve to the right and vice versa.

Foreign income and business confidence are two other relevant factors. When we analyze demand shifters, we must not include any changes in the demand for goods and services that result from change in the price level because these changes are already included in the curve.

4. AGGREGATE SUPPLY CURVE: SHORT-RUN VS. LONG-RUN

The **Aggregate Supply (AS)** is the total quantity of output producers are willing and able to supply at alternative price levels in a given time period. The AS curve shows the level of real domestic output that firms will produce at each price level. To understand how this concept works and how the economy comes to an equilibrium where aggregate supply and aggregate demand curves intersect each other, we need to distinguish the long-run—a period in which nominal wages (and other resource prices) match changes in the price level, and the short-run—a period in which nominal wages and other resource prices do not respond to price-level changes.

First, the *short-run AS* curve (SRAS) is upsloping and relatively flat: a rise in the price level increases real output; a fall in the price level reduces it; firms are assumed to supply all the output demanded with relatively small changes in prices. The short-run AS curve reflects the idea that prices do not change very much in this period and firms adjust production to meet the demand. So, over the short-run, the quantity of goods and services firms are willing to supply will increase as the price level increases. In the short-run, prices are *sticky*, and output is determined mostly by aggregate demand. The most common explanations for *stickiness of prices* in the short-run are: a) wages do not respond quickly to changes in demand or supply because of earlier signed contracts, especially those with cost of living adjustment terms in unionized markets; b) firms are often slower to cut wages than to increase them, which might affect the morale and productivity of workers; and c) changing prices, often on thousands of goods, would be costly for many firms—these are called *menu costs*. As illustrated in Figures 13.3a and b, the AS curve is upward sloping.

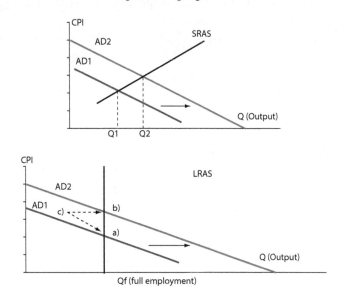

Figure 13.3a
Short Run
Aggregate
Supply (SRAS)

Figure 13.3b
Long Run
Aggregate
Supply (LRAS)

1. Full employment output, Qf, depends solely on the supply of factors, capital and labor, and the state of technology.
2. Full employment output is independent of the price level, and the long-run aggregate supply curve is vertical.

Interaction of LRAS and AD—their intersection determines the price level and the level of output. The position of the AD curve will be determined by the level of taxes, government spending, and the supply of money. The shift in AD curve will not change the level of output in the economy but only change the level of prices. In the long-run, output is determined solely by the supply of capital and the supply of labor. To summarize: Long-run aggregate supply ⇒ output; Aggregate demand ⇒ price level.

Why does the AS Curve slope upward? Three effects create the positive relationship between the price level and quantity of real GDP supplied:

1. *Business failure and startup*: When the price level increases relative to costs of resources, first of all, wages and profits increase; then, the number of firms in business increases; and, finally, the quantity of real GDP supplied increases and vice versa.
2. *Temporary shutdowns and restarts*: When the price level rises relative to costs, fewer firms will decide to shut down, so more firms operate, and the quantity of real GDP supplied increases and vice versa.
3. *Changes in output rate*: When the price level rises and the money wage rate doesn't change, the quantity of labor demanded increases and production increases.

Second, in the long-run, real GDP depends on labor, capital, technology, land, and entrepreneurial talent—on real factors of production. Wages and other input prices rise or fall to match changes in the price level. Changes in the price level do not change real profit, and there is no change in real output. In the long-run, wages and other input prices rise or fall to match changes in the price level.

The *long-run AS* (LRAS) curve is vertical at the economy's potential output (or full employment output). A vertical long-run supply curve reflects the idea that in the long-run, output is determined solely by the factors of production. The level of full employment output depends only on the supply factors and the state of technology and not on the level of prices in the economy.

Third, how does the economy move from the short-run to the long-run? The economy is almost always on the short-run aggregate supply curve. It can be on both curves at a point where the short-run curve intersects the long-run curve. At this point, the actual (current) output is equal to potential output. As Figure 13.4a illustrates, the initial SRAS is at a point on the left of LRAS (A1), which means that unemployment is high, production capacity is unused, and nominal wages haven't yet fully adjusted downward. This corresponds to a recessionary gap.

The shift of the SRAS curve (from position 1 to position 2) will return the economy to its full employment capacity in the long-run, with or without government assistance, as we will see in the next chapter. In Figure 13.4b, the situation is different: the economy is at a point on the SRAS to the right of potential output (A1), where production is booming, producers are receiving high profits, the nominal wages are rising, and the price level is increasing fast. This situation is called an inflationary gap. Eventually, the economy will move to the full employment (potential) output but with higher prices than in the first case. How this transition happens and how successfully the government manages it, we will see in the next chapters.

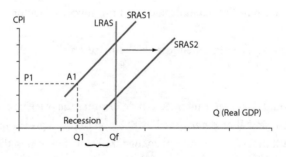

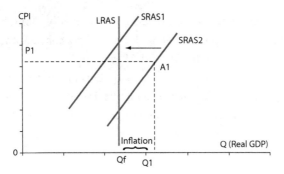

Figure 13.4b
Transition from
SRAS to LRAS
(Inflation)

5. CHANGES IN AGGREGATE SUPPLY

In our analysis of the market supply for an individual good, we pointed out the importance of the distinction between movements along the supply curve (caused by changes in price) and shifts of the supply curve (caused by nonprice factors). But there are movements and shifts of the aggregate supply curve, as well.

What are *the main determinants of AS* (AS shifters)? Changes in these determinants raise or lower per-unit production costs at each price level (per-unit production cost = total input cost/total output):

1. *Changes in input prices* (or resource prices) are a major ingredient of per-unit production costs and, therefore, a key determinant of AS. These resources can be domestic (wages and salaries represent about 75% of business costs) or imported (oil, tin, and copper). The increase in the labor supply (because of immigration) will shift the AS curve to the right; a decrease in the labor supply will shift it to the left. The same effect is caused by market power. (OPEC, which increased oil prices ten times in the 70s, increased per-unit costs and shifted the AS curve to the left.)

2. *Productivity*—a measure of the relationship between a nation's levels of real output and real input. Productivity = total output/total inputs. An increase in productivity enables the economy to obtain more output from limited resources and to reduce the per-unit production cost, thus, shifting the AS curve to the right.

3. *Changes in nominal wages*—a rise in nominal wages over time increases production costs and shifts the short-run aggregate supply curve to the left. A historic example is the surge in prices for oil during the 70s which, in combination with increased nominal wages (many wage contracts included cost-of-living allowances that automatically rose with increases in consumer prices), caused a double leftward shift of the SRAS.

4. *Legal-institutional environment*: a) changes in taxes and subsidies (higher business taxes—sales, excise, and payroll taxes increase per unit costs and reduce short-run AS and, thus, shift the AS curve to the left) and b) government regulation which is usually costly for businesses and tends to increase the per-unit cost, shifting the AS curve to the left.

6. DYNAMIC AD-AS MODEL: MACROECONOMIC EQUILIBRIUM
IN THE SHORT-RUN AND THE LONG-RUN

The Aggregate Supply and Aggregate Demand curves describe the economy's market activity. The intersection of the AS and AD curves establishes the economy's equilibrium price level and equilibrium real output. This is the only point at which the behavior of buyers and sellers are compatible. So, macroequilibrium is the unique combination of price level and output that is compatible with both buyers' and sellers' intentions. In contrast, at disequilibrium points, the intentions of buyers and sellers are incompatible, and the economy is experiencing recessions or expansions as a result of supply or demand shocks. Let's consider the short-run and long-run equilibriums and the consequences of shifts in the AD and AS curves.

The economy is always in some kind of short-run macroequilibrium with the short-run equilibrium aggregate price level (Pesr. in figure 13.5) and the short-run equilibrium output (Qesr). Let's see what happens when the economy's short-run AS and AD curves shift as a result of various shocks.

Figure 13.5
Short-Run
Macroeconomic
Equilibrium

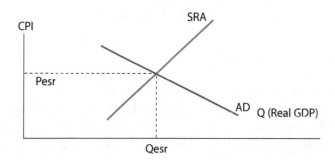

1. *Shifts in Short-Run Aggregate Supply* (SRAS) are generated by supply shocks that could be negative or positive.
2. *Decreases in AS* (figure 13.6a): in the case of *negative supply shocks* (disruption of oil supply with abrupt increase in prices), the SRAS curve shifts to the left because the production costs have increased, and the quantity that producers are willing to supply at any price level is reduced. So, the effects of this shift produces double damages: the economy is moving to a new equilibrium with higher prices and lower output. That is exactly what happened in the US and other advanced countries in the mid-1970s when the oil price skyrocketed as a result of the Middle East turmoil caused by the Arab-Israeli war. Higher energy prices caused a *cost-push inflation,* which was especially painful at that time, when oil expenditures formed about 10% of the US GDP. Today, the economy is much less vulnerable to such shocks since these expenditures have declined to only 3% of output, and the US is much less dependent on foreign oil sources and less vulnerable to cost-push inflation.

   The special case related to this situation is that of *stagflation* ("stagnation plus inflation") when falling aggregate supply and output are accompanied by rising prices and rising unemployment; stagflation, as it occurred in the 1970s in the United States, poses a serious dilemma for policy makers: what kind of fiscal policy should they choose, expansionary or restrictionary? We will analyze this situation in the next chapter.

Figure 13.6a
Negative
Supply Shock

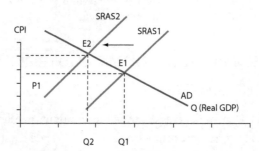

3. *Increases in AS* (figure 13.6 b): in the case of *positive supply shocks,* the economy's SRAS shifts to the right because production costs are reduced, quantity supplied increases, and prices go down—a double advantage. This was exactly the situation between 1995 and 2000 in the US when increasing use of the Internet and other information technologies led to a surge in productivity. The American economy benefited from a quite unique combination of full employment, strong economic growth, and low inflation. Some economists called it a "new era" in the American economy. But it lasted just one year until the next recession occurred in 2001. It should be mentioned that a distinctive feature of supply shocks (positive or negative) is that they generate movements of the aggregate price level and the aggregate real GDP (output) in opposite directions.

   a. *Negative supply shock* causes increases in price and decreases in output.
   b. *Positive supply shock* generates increases in output and decreases in price

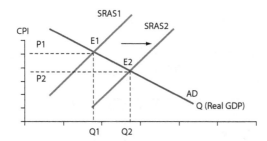

Figure 13.6b
Positive Supply
Shock

4. *Shifts in Aggregate Demand* result from demand shocks that could be either negative or positive, but in contrast to supply shocks, they cause the aggregate price level and aggregate output to move in the same direction as we will see.

5. *Decreases in AD* in the short-run—*negative demand shock*; a shift to the left of the AD curve causes a recession and cyclical unemployment (figure 13.7a), and the explanations are: a) Wage contracts are not flexible, and businesses can't afford to reduce prices; b) Employers are reluctant to cut wages; they seek to pay efficiency wages—wages that maximize work effort and productivity, minimizing cost; c) Minimum wage laws keep wages above that level; d) Menu costs are difficult to implement (estimating the duration of the shift in demand and repricing items held in inventory, printing and mailing new catalogs, and communicating the price to consumers); and e) Fear of price wars keeps prices from being reduced. Examples of negative shocks are the collapses in wealth and consumer and business confidence during the banking crises of 1930–31 and 2007–09.

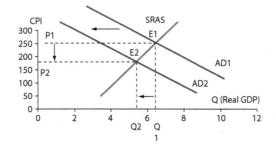

Figure 13.7a
Negative
Demand Shock

6. *Increases in AD—positive demand shock* cause *demand-pull inflation* (figure 13.7b)—AD "pulls up" the price level, and the explanations are: a) increases in AD increase real output and create upward pressure on prices, especially when the economy is operating at its full employment capacity and b) the multiplier effect weakens how much farther right the AD curve moves along the AS curve. A classic example of demand-pull inflation is that of the late 1960s when the escalation of the war in Vietnam led to a 55% increase in defense spending and shifted the economy's aggregate demand farther to the right, resulting in the worst inflation in two decades. Another example of demand-pull inflation occurred in the late 1980s when the aggregate demand curve shifted rightward and rising prices were at a level that created a positive (inflationary) GDP gap.

   a. *Negative demand shock* lowers the price and lowers the output.
   b. *Positive demand shock* increases the price and the output.

Figure 13.7b
Positive
Demand Shock

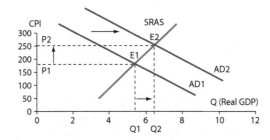

7. Recurrent Shifts of AS and AD—occur when AS and AD shift in different directions and create a difficult situation for policy makers. A leftward shift of the AD curve can cause a recession, while the falling rate of output and the rightward shift can cause a recovery, with the real GDP (and employment) increasing.

8. Long-Run Macroeconomic Equilibrium (fig 13.8) occurs when the short-run aggregate supply curve and the aggregate demand curve intersect each other at a point on the long-run supply curve. There are also two effects:

Figure 13.8
Long Run
Macroeconomic
Equilibrium

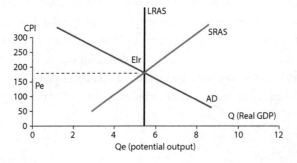

   a. *Effects of a Negative Demand Shock* (figure 13.9a): the AD1 curve shifts leftward (to AD2) with a reduction in price level (from P1 to P2) and a new equilibrium (E2) with reduced output and increased unemployment. At this point, the economy's current output is below potential GDP and is suffering a *recessionary gap* (Q2–Q1). But in the long-run, the economy has a self-correcting mechanism, and, eventually, the short-run aggregate supply (SRAS1) will shift rightward (to SRAS2) since nominal wages will fall in response to high unemployment (at Q2), and the economy will move to a new full employment equilibrium (E3) but at a lower price level (P3).

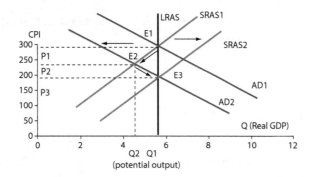

Figure 13.9a
Effects of a
Negative
Demand Shock

b. **Effects of a Positive Demand Shock** (figure 13.9b): AD1 shifts rightward to a new equilibrium point (E2) with higher prices (P2) and bigger output (Q2). At this new equilibrium point, the economy's current output is above the potential GDP and is suffering an *inflationary gap* (Q2–Q1). Since the economy is self-correcting in the long-run, the SRAS1 will eventually shift to SRAS2 at a new equilibrium point (E3) on the LRAS but with higher prices (P3).

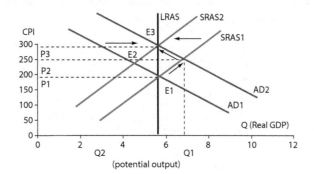

Figure 13.9b
Effects of a
Positive
Demand Shock

In conclusion, there are at least two potential problems with the macroequilibrium:

1. *Undesirable outcomes*: a) the quantity of output at the current equilibrium point may be more or less than required for the economy's full employment; b) the unemployment rate may be affected by cyclical unemployment since full employment is attained only at full production capacity GDP; and c) the current equilibrium price level might exceed society's optimum level, and we might end up with an undesired level of inflation.

2. *Unstable outcomes*: a) macroeconomic policy is less likely to be affected by supply shocks than by demand shocks as the US economy demonstrated after the WWII: out of ten officially recognized recessions, two of them (1973–75 and 1979–82) and one in a partial way (2007–09), resulted from supply shocks, and the rest were caused by demand shocks; however, these two recessions were much more painful and harder to deal with; b) although demand shocks affect aggregate output in the short-run and not in the long-run, they could produce damage similar to those caused by the supply shocks; and c) in the long-run, the economy has a self-correcting mechanism, but this does not mean that the government should do nothing and just wait until macroeconomic equilibrium is reached automatically by market forces.

A Tract on Monetary Reform is a short book on the economic problems of Europe after WWI by John M. Keynes (1923). He observed: "This long run is a misleading guide to current affairs. In the long run we are all dead. Economists set themselves too easy, too useless a task if in tempestuous seasons they can only tell us that when the storm is long past the sea is flat again."

7. HOW TO ADDRESS SHORT-RUN INSTABILITY: KEYNESIAN VS. CLASSICAL THEORIES

The goal of various theories of short-run instability is to find the macroeconomic equilibrium at full employment and price stability. This is almost the same as finding a needle in a haystack. The framework for comparing these various theories and practical approaches to the problems of macrostability provides the interpretations of the AS and AD curves and of their shifters (determinants). We can distinguish demand side and supply side theories and the mix of both of them.

1. *Demand side theories.* The most famous is the Keynesian theory which explains the downward sloping of the AD curve and, therefore, the contraction of the economy from insufficient spending. In Keynes's view, the only way to end the Great Depression was to start demanding more goods: "demand it and it will be supplied" (figure13.10a).

Figure 13.10a
Increase in AD

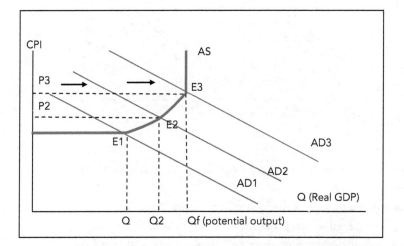

2. *Supply side theories.* This time, AD remains stationary, and the AS curve shifts. The decline in AS (figure 13.10b) (because of the rising costs, resource shortages, government taxes, and regulation) causes output and employment to decline, as well. To restore the equilibrium, the AS curve should move back to the initial equilibrium point.

Figure 13.10b
Decrease in AS

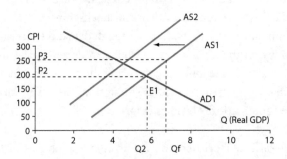

3. *Eclectic explanations*—both supply and demand can help achieve our policy goals or cause us to miss them (figure 13.10c).

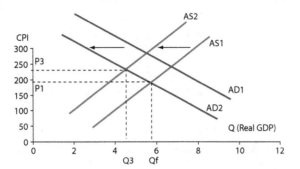

Figure 13.10c
AD-AS Shifts

Let's consider, in more detail, the Keynesian approach in comparison with the classical approach to macroeconomic issues of stability.

Keynes proposed that *AD* be analyzed by studying the demand for various components of national product: a) personal consumption expenditures; b) investment demand (demand for equipment, plants, houses, and additional inventories); c) government purchases of goods and services; and d) net exports. According to Keynes, even if a decline in investment demand may have been the principal cause of the depression, it was up to the government to provide a solution by increasing its spending—the component of AD directly under its control. The four components of AD highlighted by Keynesian theory correspond to the four components of GDP. Two major innovations in macroeconomics in the twentieth century—the development of national product accounts and the new Keynesian theory of employment—interacted with and reinforced each other during the 1930s and 1940s.

Keynesian theory suggests that the AD curve slopes downward to the right. So, the cure, according to Keynes, was to increase AD. Producers then would step up production. Output would increase, and the economy would move to the right along the horizontal range of the AS function to the point of full employment. Once the economy got to this point, Keynes had no major objection to the classical approach to the supply curve: the economy would move vertically upward (figure 13.11).

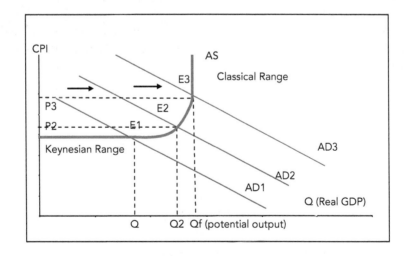

Figure 13.11
Keynesian and
Classical
Ranges

In short, the *Keynesian AS function* has two quite different ranges: First, it has a horizontal range when an inadequate demand results in high rates of unemployment. This range most interested Keynes and is frequently known as the *Keynesian range*. In this range, first, an increase in AD leads to an increase in national product, and, second, a vertical range would be reached when AD was high enough to ensure full employment. Further increases in AD would simply cause inflation. Because Keynes had no quarrel with the classical approach once full employment is reached, this vertical section is sometimes known as the *classical range.*

Keynes developed his theory in opposition to *classical macroeconomics*. The main points of the classical approach are (figure 13.12):

1. The AD curve slopes downward to the right. As prices fall, each dollar will buy more, and people, accordingly, will buy more.
2. The AS curve is vertical at the full employment output.
3. In the long-run, a shift in the AD curve causes a change in prices, not in output (in the long-run the economy moves back to the vertical range)
4. In the short-run—when wages and prices are sticky—a collapse in AD can cause a depression. Instead of moving from A to E, the economy moves from A to B
5. Although an economy at B will eventually move to E, a better solution is to increase the money stock and, thus, to increase the AD and to move the economy back to A.

Figure 13.12
Classical
Explanation of
the Great
Depression

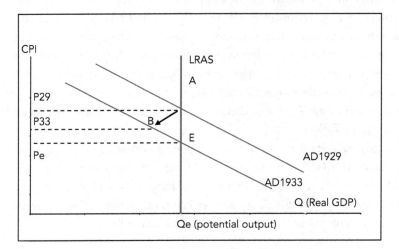

Other demand side theories emphasize the role of money in financing AD. If credit isn't available, consumers won't be able to buy as many cars, homes, and other products. Tight money will also curtail business investment.

8. AD-AS MODEL AND MACROECONOMIC POLICY

There are three policy options that the government can choose:

1. Do nothing.
2. Shift the AD curve (stimulate or restrain total spending).
3. Shift the AS curve (reduce the cost of production or stimulate more output at every price level).

All three approaches have been adopted. The classical "do nothing" approach was the main policy before the Great Depression. New, classical theories stressed not only the market's natural ability to self-adjust to long-run market outcomes but also the inability of the government to improve short-run market outcomes.

The Great Depression discredited the classical self-adjustment concept and served as a basis for the emerging Keynesian revolution, with recommendations to use budgetary tools to increase government spending. *Fiscal policy* is when macroeconomic outcomes are affected by the use of government tax and spending powers.

The macroeconomic equilibrium is also affected by the amount of money in circulation that is the subject of *monetary policy*—the use of money and credit controls (interest rates) to influence macroeconomic outcomes. Direct control over monetary policy is exercised by the Federal Reserve (Fed). Fiscal and Monetary policy refer to the demand side of the market; they are designed to change output or price levels through shifts in the AD curve.

Supply-side policies, in contrast, seek to shift the AS curve. The AS curve can be shifted using tax rates, (de)regulation, and other mechanisms. The Reagan administration used the tax cuts in 1981 to increase supply not just demand. A similar policy was used by Republicans to reduce the tax on capital gains (profits for the sale of property) from 20% to 15%, thus, encouraging investment. Government programs for employment and training were also launched to shift the AS curve as well as government regulation.

The choice of policy levers varied during various period of time.

1960s—fiscal policy dominated the economist's mind, but the failure to control inflation in the late 60s that occurred simultaneously with unemployment changed the focus from fiscal policy.

1970s—monetary policy became the major tool, and the Fed dominated the policy and targeted the reduction of inflation and the interest rates. But the reliance on monetary policy lasted only a short time until the economy slid into another recession.

1980s—supply side policies—the core of Ronald Reagan's economic policy—dominated economic policy. Tax cuts, deregulation of markets, and other policies were focused on reducing both inflation and unemployment.

When Ronald Reagan came to office, he intended to sharply change economic policy; this was labeled *"Reaganomics"* and included: a) increase of defense expenditures; b) restraint and reduction of domestic spending by the Federal Government; c) restraint of the growth of government regulation; and d) reduction of the tax rates from 1981 to 1984. Reagan's credo was: "get the government off the backs of the people." However, by the end of his first term in 1984, a) the deficit had increased instead of being reduced as was intended; b) economic expansion was much less vigorous than the administration hoped; and c) domestic spending was more difficult to cut than expected. During his second term, the size of the deficit dominated economic debates. It should be mentioned that two-thirds of total federal spending was made up of three large categories: a) interest on debt, which the government was contractually committed to pay; b) national defense; and c) Social Security, which President Reagan had pledged not to cut.

1990s—the George H. W. Bush administration promoted a *hands-off economic policy*, like classical economists, assuring the people that the economy would come around on its own, but it slid into depression. He proposed more active intervention only on the eve of the election of 1992, but it was too late. Bill Clinton promised to use tax cuts and to increase government spending to create more jobs. But after he was elected, he pushed a tax increase through Congress and focused on *monetary policy* as the decisive policy lever. After his reelection in 1996, his administration provided some tax cuts for consumers and cut the growth of government spending. This helped to restrain inflationary pressures and support the economy to approach full employment.

2000s.—The George W. Bush administration turned *fiscal policy* levers in the direction of stimulus for economic recovery. Three rounds of tax cuts were enacted by the Congress (2001, 2002, and 2003). The most debated issues in the 2004 election campaign become how to prevent the inflationary spiral caused by skyrocketing prices for gasoline and energy, how to reduce unemployment and create new jobs, and how to revive the economy, in general.

Current economic policy—Obamanomics. The Barack Obama administration renewed the emphasis on fiscal policy, facing the most serious recession since 1980s, with high unemployment (in 2009, it reached 10% of the labor force), rising oil prices (the price of a barrel of oil increased from below $30 in 2004 to above $140 in 2008), and the collapses of the housing market and speculative bubbles in the financial market. We will examine the Obama administration's response to these economic challenges in the next chapters.

9. KEY TERMS

Aggregate Demand (AD), Aggregate Supply (AS)
Classical School of Economics
Keynesian School of Economics
Flexible Prices and Flexible Wages
Purchasing Power of Money
Wealth (Real-Balances) Effect
Interest-Rate Effect
Foreign Purchases (Trade) Effect
Movements and Shifts of the AD, AS Curves
Short-Run and Long-Run AS Curves
Determinants of AD, AS
Positive/Negative Supply Shock
Positive/Negative Demand Shock
Short-Run, Long-Run Macroeconomic Equilibriums
Undesirable, Unstable Outcomes
Demand Side, Supply Side Theories
Keynesian Range of AS; Classical Range of AS
Fiscal Policy, Monetary Policy
Reaganomics
Hands-Off Economic Policy

10. PROBLEMS AND APPLICATIONS

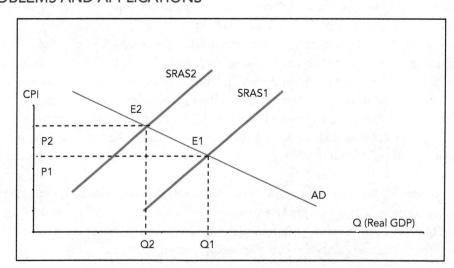

1. Cassandra is a high school student aspiring to be accepted by the University of California, Berkeley where she intends to take double majors in economics and information systems. She is addressing various economics issues to be better prepared for her university studies. For instance, Cassandra found that the macroeconomic equilibrium in the above figure changes under the impact of _____ (positive/negative) supply shock and new equilibrium occurs at price and quantity level:
   a. P1; Q1
   b. P2; Q2
   c. P1; Q2
   d. P2; Q1

2. In the AD/AS model, which are the most important policy tools that affect aggregate demand and aggregate supply?
   a. Government regulation, tax policy, and the quantity of money in the economy
   b. Population growth, spending behavior, and rational choices
   c. Wars, natural disasters, oil shocks and trade disruptions
   d. Jobs, prices, quality of goods and service, and economic growth

3. Opposing the classical economists, John Maynard Keynes, the most famous Cambridge University economist, emphasized in his book *The General Theory of Employment, Interest and Money*:
   a. *Laissez-faire* (live it alone) policy would automatically lead to macroequilibrium.
   b. Markets would naturally self-adjust under the influence of market forces of supply and demand.
   c. Wages and prices are flexible, and money is at the center of aggregate demand.
   d. The economy was inherently unstable and always rests in equilibrium with large scale unemployment.

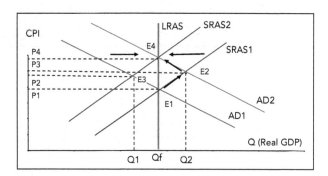

4. Analyzing the figure above, Lisa and Michael are University of Wisconsin econ major students. They came to the conclusion that the graph represents the effect of _____ (positive/ negative) _____ supply/demand) shocks with long-run macroeconomic equilibrium that can occur with a government contractionary fiscal policy at the price level of:
   a. P1
   b. P2
   c. P3
   d. P4

5. When the economy is at macroequilibrium E4 in the figure above and aggregate demand decreases from AD2 to AD1, then:
   a. Both the unemployment rate and price level will decrease, resulting in a recessionary gap.
   b. The unemployment rate will decrease and the price level will increase, resulting in an inflationary gap.
   c. Both the unemployment rate and price level will increase, resulting in a deflationary gap.
   d. The unemployment rate will increase, and the price level will decrease, resulting in a recessionary gap.

6. Using the figure below, if the economy is in equilibrium at a full employment output of Qf, then:
   a. Aggregate demand must be AD1.
   b. Aggregate supply could be either SRAS1 or SRAS2, depending on the level of aggregate demand.
   c. The equilibrium price level is P2.
   d. Aggregate demand is AD2, and aggregate supply is SRAS2.

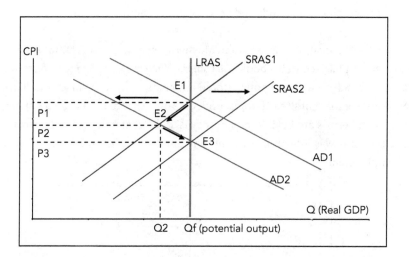

11. REVIEW QUESTIONS

1. Analyzing the theory that economic downturns result from an inadequate aggregate demand for goods and services, we can determine that it originated in the work of which of the following economists: a) Adam Smith; b) David Ricardo; c) Alfred Marshall; d) John Maynard Keynes.

2. President Barack Obama lowered taxes in 2009 and increased government spending, according to his administration stimulus package approved by the US Congress. *Ceteris paribus*, these actions shifted the aggregate demand curve to the _____, and prevented _____ (the increase/decrease) of unemployment. How efficient was this policy in the short-run and what are its consequences in the long-run?

3. During the Great Depression in the United States, prices decreased by 33 percent. This led to an increase in aggregate demand, causing the following three effects: the _____ effect, the _____, and the _____ effect.

4. What assumptions cause the immediate-short-run AS curve to be horizontal, and why is the long-run AS curve vertical? What determines the shape of the short-run AS curve, and why is this curve relatively flat to the left of full-employment GDP and relatively steep to the right?

5. The economy is always heated by some kind of natural or technology shocks. Describe and illustrate the short-run effects of each of the following shocks on the price level and on aggregate output:

   a. Severe weather destroys crops around the world and causes a _____ (demand/supply) shock.

   b. Tesla, an electric car manufacturer, and energy firms launch major programs of investment spending.

   c. The US Congress increases taxes and decreases government spending that causes a _____ (demand/supply) shock.

   d. The government sharply increases the minimum wage rates, raising the wages of many workers and causing a _____ demand/supply) shock.

CHAPTER 14.

FISCAL POLICY: HOW TO STABILIZE THE ECONOMY

1. FISCAL POLICY: NATURE AND ROLE IN US HISTORY

John Maynard Keynes wrote in his *General Theory of Employment, Interest, and Money* that we are not inevitably condemned to suffer the economic and social costs of high unemployment and the disruptive effects of inflation. We have to deal with the root causes of these problems. Unemployment is the result of too little aggregate demand (AD): people are thrown out of work when nobody buys the goods they can produce. Inflation is the result of too much aggregate demand: prices rise when too much demand is chasing the available supply of goods. The policy message of the Keynesian revolution was that the government is responsible for managing AD and regulating prosperity despite inflation. The government can affect this through changes in spending and taxes.

In the United States, the idea of the fiscal intervention of the government to stabilize the economy emerged out of the Great Depression of the 1930s although, at that time, politicians did not believe in modern fiscal policy because they feared large budget deficits. After WWII, the Federal Government passed the *Employment Act of 1946* which is the real landmark in American economic legislation. In fact, it allowed the government to take action through monetary and fiscal policy to "promote maximum employment, production, and purchasing power." The act established the *Council of Economic*

Advisors to assist the president and the *Joint Economic Committee of Congress (JEC)* to deal with economic problems of national interest.

It was not until the *Kennedy* presidency that fiscal policy came into an active role in economic policy. The economist Walter Heller was a strong advocate of active fiscal policy and was appointed chairman of the President's Council of Economic Advisors. The unemployment rate was 6.7% in 1960, and Heller, who believed the natural rate was 4%, convinced Kennedy to lower tax rates in order to increase output and stimulate the economy. At that time, tax rates were very high (the top rate was 91%), budget deficits were very small (less than 1% of GDP), and the deficit was supposed to disappear if GDP grew due to lower tax rates. Tax cuts were enacted in February 1964 after Lyndon Johnson became president following Kennedy's assassination. As a result of these tax cuts, consumption and GDP grew at a rapid rate, exceeding 4% per year.

One of the largest tax cuts, enacted by *President Ronald Reagan* in 1981, included a $250 billion cut off personal taxes and a $70 billion cut off business taxes over a three-year period. This helped the economy to overcome the 1981–82 recession. The intention was not to increase aggregate demand but to increase aggregate supply. Nevertheless, these tax cuts increased aggregate demand along with important effects on the supply of labor, savings, and economic growth, in general, helping the economy to recover after the severe recession of the early 1980s. By the mid-1980s, large government deficits began to emerge. As deficits grew very large, fiscal policy lost its importance.

President Bill Clinton, at the beginning of his administration in 1992, proposed a "stimulus package" to increase aggregate demand, but Congress did not support this initiative. This is explained by the fact that the economy was already moving toward full employment, and if too much fiscal stimulus is enacted, it will increase prices and generate inflation. Later on, Clinton successfully enacted a major tax increase that balanced the budget, and by 1998, the federal budget began to show surpluses for the first time in almost three decades. From 1998 through 2001, there were four years of budget surpluses.

President George W. Bush, in 2001, initiated an even bigger tax cut—$1.6 trillion over ten years. Congress ultimately passed a $1.35 trillion cut in taxes. After the September 11 terrorist attacks, the Bush Administration was less concerned with a balanced budget and authorized new spending programs to provide relief to victims and to stimulate the economy. In May 2003, President Bush signed another tax bill designed, in particular, to increase investment spending. A relatively large tax cut (1% of GDP) and rebates for 128 million households, some as large as $1,800, were enacted in early 2008 to stimulate the economy, which had entered into a recession.

In 2009, *President Barack Obama* signed into law a $787 billion stimulus package (more than 5% of GDP), which was the largest in the history of US fiscal policy. About two-thirds of this amount was designed to increase government spending for a large number of infrastructure, health care, and other projects, and one-third was devoted to tax cuts. According to White House advisers, with this stimulus package, unemployment would not rise above 8%, but, in fact, it reached about 10% by August 2009, and the budget deficit rose, as a result, to a staggering $1.4 trillion (9.9% of GDP), which, in turn, contributed to an increase in the size of the US public debt to $11.9 trillion, a record high for recent decades.

The principal purpose of this chapter is to explain how the government can use fiscal policies to manage AD. The Federal Government in the US plays a relatively smaller role in the economy than those of European countries or Canada, with the government spending about 36% of GDP and tax revenues constituting about 33% of GDP. The Swedish government spends nearly 60% of GDP, and French public spending is more than 50% of the economy. Fiscal policy and, especially, tax policy provide an excellent opportunity to establish ties between the theories and real-world applications. It should be mentioned that economists use the notion of fiscal policy to refer only to the actions of the Federal Government and not to those of state and local governments because they are not designed to influence the national economy as a whole. We can find current data from the Federal Reserve Bulletin, Economic Indicators, The Survey of Current Business, or the Economic Report of the President.

2. FISCAL POLICY AND AGGREGATE DEMAND: DISCRETIONARY VS. NONDISCRETIONARY FISCAL POLICY

The value of final goods and services produced (GDP) should equal total spending on those goods and services, which includes consumer spending (C), investment spending (I), government spending (G), and net export (X − M), or, in other words, the basic equation of national income is: GDP = C + I + G + X − M. Let's analyze each of these components of aggregate demand.

Consumption (C) represents the all-household expenditures of consumers on final goods and services, 70% of total spending in the US economy, and any changes in consumers' spending that have a serious impact on employment and prices. Usually, consumer behavior is evaluated through surveys of consumer confidence. The economic recessions of 2001 and 2007–09 were preceded by a sharp decline in household expectations about the future state of the economy. Recall that changes in consumer spending as one of the major determinants of the AD shift include a) consumer wealth; b) consumer expectations; c) household indebtedness; and d) taxes. Many factors determine the nation's levels of consumption, but the most significant is *disposable (after tax) income (DI)*, which could be spent or saved. Accordingly, savings (S) equals DI − C. So, C represents DI − S. Consumption is called also *personal consumption expenditures,* and it includes: a) durable goods; b) nondurable goods; and c) services. *The consumption function* shows how consumption expenditures depend on disposable income.

Investment (I) represents the expenditures on resources (new plant and equipment) in a given period of time plus changes in business inventories. The investment spending—the purchase of capital goods—is a second major determinant of AD. A decline in investment spending at each price level will shift the AD curve to the left; an increase will shift it to the right. Changes in investment spending are determined by a) interest rates and b) expected returns that include expectations about future business conditions, technology, degree of excess capacity (unused capital), and business taxes.

Government spending (G, purchases) is the third determinant of AD. An increase in government purchases will shift the AD curve to the right, and a reduction will shift it to the left. AD is directly affected only by goods and services that Federal, state, and local governments purchase—highways, schools, police, national defense, and all other services provided by the public sector. These represent almost 20% of AD, or about $2.5 trillion a year. Other types of government spending, such as income transfers, for example, Social Security payments ($700 billion a year), do not directly affect the AD.

Net exports (X – M, export – import). The factors that influence net exports are changes in the national income abroad (an increase may encourage foreigners to buy more US products and vice versa) and exchange rates. Depreciation of the dollar increases US net exports and shifts the demand curve to the right; appreciation will have an opposite effect. Currently, the trade deficit (imports exceeds imports) is approximately 4%.

The economy is in equilibrium when the combination of the price level and real output is compatible with both AD and AS. But not every equilibrium point is the one desired by society only that equilibrium point that establishes equilibrium price level and equilibrium real output. In reality, we can have a) *an insufficient demand*—when all components of AD generated an output incompatible with full employment and price stability, which may cause a recession, or b) an *excessive demand*, or the equilibrium point that exceeds the economy's full employment and can cause inflation.

Fiscal policy consists of the changes made by the Federal Government in its expenditures and tax policy to expand or contract the economy. The government may seek to increase real GDP and employment or to control the rate of inflation. Fiscal policy is designed by Congress to change the level of real output, employment, income, or the price level.

According to Keynes, it would be a miracle if GDP represented the exactly right aggregate demand that matched with full employment and price stability. This would involve too many actors: consumers, investors, government, and foreigners, each of whom are making separate decisions.

The use of government spending and taxes to adjust AD is **the essence of fiscal policy**. An active fiscal policy that we are examining is called *discretionary fiscal policy* when the changes in government spending and taxes are at the option of the Federal Government. For example, the tax cuts passed by Congress in 2008 and the stimulus package of 2009 are examples of a discretionary fiscal policy. Vice versa are the "passive" or "automatic" changes in some types of spending and taxes (unemployment insurance payments, changes in personal income taxes) that are triggered by the state of the economy and happen without any actions of the government characterized *a nondiscretionary policy*.

3. EXPANSIONARY FISCAL POLICY: HOW TO REMOVE THE ECONOMY FROM RECESSION

Why does the government want to influence aggregate demand? For two reasons: to close a recessionary gap, created when current aggregate output is below potential output, or an inflationary gap, which exists when current output exceeds potential output.

First, the *recessionary gap* is the difference between full employment output and the amount of output demanded at current price levels (figure 14.1).

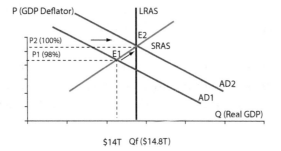

The fiscal policy applied during a recession period is called *Expansionary Fiscal Policy*. It has three main options: 1) increase government purchases of goods and service, such as the stimulus package of 2009; 2) reduce taxes as in 2001 and 2003; and 3) increase government transfers, such as benefits for the unemployed. An increase in government spending (by $0.8 trillion in Figure 14.1) will shift the AD curve to the right to the full employment output (to $14.8 trillion). Simultaneously, unemployment falls. If the federal budget is balanced before an expansionary fiscal policy is enacted, this will create a government *budget deficit—government spending in excess of tax revenues.*

An important fact should be mentioned: to cover the recessionary gap, the government will not necessarily increase its spending by the full amount—$0.8 trillion in our example, but it will spend much less, for example, $0.2 trillion (figure 14.2). What is the secret?

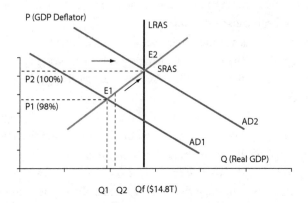

Figure 14.2
Effect of Fiscal
Multiplier
on AD

1. An increase in government spending (Q2 − Q1) by $0.2T leads …
2. To an increase in output by $0.8 trillion,
3. So, the spending multiplier is equal to 4.

Second, the Fiscal Multiplier effects. The most important fact is that the demand stimulus initiated by increased government spending has a multiplier effect, or is a multiple of the initial expenditure. Government spending leads to an increase in the income of market participants, who, in their turn will spend it. Each dollar of government spending has a multiplied impact on AD. *The multiplier* tells us *how much total spending will change in response to initial spending.* In other words, there is a direct relationship between changes in spending and changes in real GDP: more spending results in a bigger GDP and vice versa. So the multiplier (M) is the ratio of change in GDP to the initial change in spending.

M = Δ real GDP/initial change in spending. By rearranging this equation, we can find the change in real GDP; ΔGDP = multiplier × initial change in spending. If investment, for example, rises by $30 billion, and GDP rises by $120 billion, then the M = 4. Note three important points about the multiplier:

1. The *"initial change in spending"* usually is associated with investment spending, but changes in consumption, net export, and government spending have the same effect.
2. The "initial change in spending" associated with investment spending results from a change in the real interest rate and/or a shift of the investment demand curve.
3. The multiplier works in both directions: an increase in initial spending may create a multiple increase of GDP and a decrease, respectively, may create a multiple decrease in GDP.

The conclusion is: the fiscal stimulus to AD includes both the initial increase in government spending and all subsequent increases in consumer spending triggered by this initial spending.

Third, all new income created by initial government spending ($0.2 trillion) *will be either spent or saved*, and what is important to know is the percentage of income that will be spent and the percentage that will be saved. So, the spending multiplier begins with the Keynesian concept of *Marginal Propensity to Consume (MPC)*, which we introduced earlier and defined as the *proportion, or fraction, of any change in income consumed*. "Marginal" means "extra" or "a change in," expressed by the Greek symbol Δ—"delta." *MPC = Δ consumption/Δdisposable income*.

Similarly, the fraction of any change in income saved is the marginal propensity to save. MPS = Δsaving/Δdisposable income.

The sum of the MPC and MPS for any change in disposable income must be always equal to 1. Therefore, the fraction consumed plus the fraction saved must exhaust the whole change in income. MPC + MPS = 1.

The MPC and the Multiplier are directly related and, respectively, are inversely related: M = 1/1-MPC = 1/MPS.

Fourth, tax cuts, taxes and consumption, and taxes and investment represent another major issue of fiscal policy. *Tax reduction* is an alternative way for the government to shift the AD. The effect of a tax cut may be even stronger than that of increasing government spending because a part of a tax reduction increases savings (and indirectly investments) rather than consumption. Usually, the government uses both options: it increases spending and reduces taxes as both are important components of expansionary fiscal policy. The government could stimulate more consumer and business spending by reducing taxes. This can directly increase the disposable (after-tax) income (DI) of consumers and encourage spending. In turn, more spending shifts the AD curve to the right. A tax cut that increases DI stimulates consumer spending and starts the multiplier process. The effect is cumulative: the new consumer spending creates additional income for producers and workers, who will use this additional income to increase their own consumption.

Initial increase in consumption = MPC × tax cut
Cumulative change in spending = multiplier × initial change in consumption.

The conclusion is: a cumulative increase in AD is a multiple of the initial tax cut. In such a way, the multiplier makes both increased government spending and tax cuts very important fiscal policy levers. It is important to note that a tax cut must be larger than the proposed increase in government spending if it is to achieve the same amount of rightward shift in the AD curve. The explanation is: part of a tax reduction increases savings rather than consumption. To increase initial consumption by a specific amount, the government must reduce taxes by more than that amount.

A tax cut is a powerful stimulus for increasing *investment spending*. This is a strong injection into the circular flow and has a multiplier effect on total spending. Thus, tax cuts are an alternative to increased government spending for stimulating AD. This powerful economic leverage, as we saw, was widely used by US Presidents to stimulate the economy, starting with John F. Kennedy in 1963 and Ronald Reagan in 1981.

4. CONTRACTIONARY FISCAL POLICY: HOW TO FIGHT INFLATION

A restrictive or contractionary fiscal policy is used by the government to control inflation (figure 14.3).

1. Reduction of government spending by $0.2T leads to …
2. Decrease in AD by $0.8T,
3. So the multiplier is equal to –4.

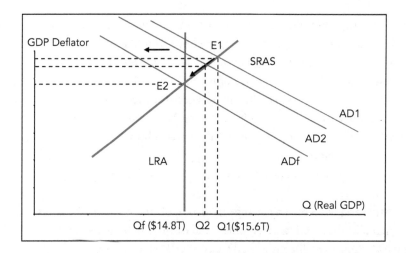

Figure 14.3
Contractionary
Fiscal Policy

The purpose of this policy is to reduce aggregate demand pressure, which causes demand-pull inflation. If the budget is balanced before the policy is enacted, it will create a *budget surplus—tax revenues in excess of government spending.* The government's options are opposite to those used to combat recession. It can: 1) reduce government purchases of goods and services; 2) increase taxes; or 3) reduce government transfers. Demand-pull inflation usually is experienced as a continual rightward shifting of the aggregate demand curve. Contractionary fiscal policy is designed to stop a further shift, to eliminate a continuing (inflationary) GDP gap, and to prevent further inflation. So, the threat of inflation will require reducing the excessive AD by using fiscal restraints or the same budget tools in reverse. Government cutbacks have a multiplied negative effect on AD: *Cumulative reduction in spending = multiplier × initial budget cut.*

Another way to eliminate the inflationary gap is to increase taxes, which will reduce consumer spending and business investment with the effect of a multiplier. Tax increases are used by the government to reduce consumer spending and to shift the AD curve to the left. In our example, to eliminate the inflationary gap of $0.8 trillion, the government might decrease spending by $0.2 trillion or increase taxes, which will have the same effect on consumer spending. President Clinton used this leverage in 1993 when a tax increase and a government spending slowdown amounted to roughly $40 billion, and this helped to keep inflation under control.

Which of these two tools is more efficient in combating inflation: decreased government spending or increased taxes? There are different opinions among economists:

1. Those who consider that there are too many unmet social, infrastructure, and other needs recommend an increase in government spending during recessions and an increase in taxes during demand-pull inflation;
2. Those who believe that the government becomes too large and inefficient advocate tax cuts during recessions and reduction in government spending during demand-pull inflation.

5. THE GOVERNMENT BUDGET AND COUNTER CYCLICAL FISCAL POLICY

The federal budget is an extremely large document that contains a detailed description of Federal Government spending and revenues and provides the general framework for fiscal policy. The US government doesn't maintain budgetary books for calendar years but for *fiscal years.* These *fiscal years* run from October 1 to September 30 of the next year and are named by the calendar year in which they end. The president proposes the budget to Congress every year by February 2, and Congress passes the budget (or not) in September. The president either signs it into law or vetoes the entire bill, returning it to Congress for further consideration. The government's budget is balanced when its tax revenues equal outlays—a very real situation in practice. In 2009, total federal spending was $3,520 billion, or 24.7% of GDP, and federal taxes amounted to 14.8% of GDP. The budget projections for the 2012 fiscal year provided $4,091 billion in outlays and $2,850 billion in tax revenues for a deficit of $1,241 billion.

First, total spending, or outlays, contains three large components:

1. *Discretionary spending*—about 35% of total federal spending, includes all government programs that Congress authorizes on an annual basis for the Defense Department, the Environment Protection Agency, the State Department, and other agencies;
2. *Entitlements and mandatory spending*—roughly 60% of spending, the single largest component of the federal budget, which Congress has authorized by prior law: Social Security (retirement pensions for retirees and benefits to disabled workers), Medicare (health care for individuals who have reached age sixty-five) and Medicaid (healthcare to the poor), unemployment, and other benefits, known as transfer payments;
3. *Net interest*—about 5% of total spending or 1.3% of GDP (2009), which the government pays on its debt held by the public (US Treasury bonds, bills, and savings bonds).

Second, there are four types (sources) of *revenues* for the federal budget:

1. *Personal Income Tax*—the single largest component (39% of total revenues in the 2012 budget), which is levied on taxable income. This is also a *progressive tax* whose rate rises as income increases. These tax rates are called *marginal tax rates,* or the rates at which the tax is paid on each additional unit of taxable income. *Average tax rate* is the total tax paid divided by total taxable income. Other taxes paid directly by individuals and families are estate and gift (sometimes known as the "death tax") taxes, excise taxes, and customs duties on goods imported to the US (cars, for example).
2. *Payroll taxes* (Social Security and Medicare contributions)—are the second source of revenues (36%). Payroll taxes are based on wages and salaries and are used to finance two compulsory federal programs for retired workers: Social Security and Medicare.
3. *Corporate income taxes* on corporate profits—the difference between a corporation's total revenues and its total expenses—are the third largest source (14, 7%) of the federal budget revenues. For almost all corporations the tax rate is 35%.
4. *Excise taxes* on specific commodities, which are levied at the wholesale level on the sale of gasoline, tires, firearms, alcohol and tobacco, make up 4% of federal revenues. The Federal Government collects excise taxes but does not levy a general sales tax, which is the primary source of revenue for state governments.

State and Local revenues come primarily from sales and excise taxes (47%) and personal income taxes (36%). State expenditures go to education, 36%; public welfare, 25%; health and hospitals, 8%; highway maintenance and construction, 8%; and public safety, 5%. Thirty-eight states augment their tax revenues with state-run lotteries; about 22% of their total revenue comes from the Federal Government.

Local finance: 72% of local revenue come from property taxes; about 17% come from sales and excise taxes. About 44% of local government expenditures go to education; 12% go to welfare, health, and hospitals; 11% go to public safety; and 8% go to housing, parks, streets, and highways. Altogether, local governments cover less than 50% of their expenditures; the remaining part is covered from grants from Federal and state governments.

Third, let's consider how the government uses its budget to manage AD. The complication is that the budget will often be unbalanced when the government is trying to prevent a recession (tax cuts and spending increases). *A budget deficit* exists when government expenditures exceed tax revenues: *Budget deficit = government spending > tax revenues.* To finance a deficit, the government has two methods:

1. Borrowing from the public (selling interest-bearing bonds) or private sector.
2. Money creation—the Central Bank supports deficit spending by creating new money; this is more expansionary than borrowing but more inflationary as well.

The accumulation of past deficits leads to increased US national debt, or *public debt*, which has increased by the huge amount of $4.1 trillion during the recent recession (since 2007); in 2012, the debt reached a record high level since WWII—$12.097 trillion (the structure of ownership of the public debt is illustrated in Figure 14.4). In 2004, the total public debt was "only" $4.3 trillion, or 37% of GDP. You can find out what the current size of the public debt is on the Department of the Treasury website: www.treasurydirect.gov/NP/BPDLogin?application=np.

Demand-pull inflation calls for fiscal action that will result in a *budget surplus*, which is an excess of government revenues over government expenditures in a given period of time:

Budget surplus = government spending < tax revenues

The movement from deficit to surplus refocused the political debates, as well, from "how to reduce the deficit" in the 1980s and 1990s to "how to use the surplus" in 1998–2001. This was the central issue of the presidential election debates in 2000.

Figure 14.4 Ownership of Public Debt, 2011

Debt Ownership Structure	Percent
US Government Agencies	36
Foreign Ownership	29
US Banks and Other Fin. Orgs	11
US Individuals	10
Federal Reserve Bank	7
State and Local Government	7

Fourth, counter-cyclical policy. To separate the effects of the business cycle from other factors, the government estimates what the budget balance would be in the absence of recessionary or inflationary gaps and computes a *cyclically adjusted budget balance.* In other words, the idea is to estimate what the budget balance would be if real GDP were equal to its potential output. Most economists believe that the government should only balance the budget on average, rather than annually, to allow the government to run deficits in bad years, offset by surpluses in good years. Otherwise, automatic stabilizers like taxes and transfers would be weakened. A balanced budget would be appropriate only if the resulting AD is consistent with full employment. An unbalanced budget, in Keynes's view, is perfectly appropriate if macroconditions call for a deficit (when the economy is booming, some fiscal restraints are preferable) or surplus (when the economy is ailing, and an injection of government spending and/or tax cuts will be appropriate).

6. AUTOMATIC (BUILT-IN) STABILIZERS

In the US economy, there are automatic, or built-in, stabilizers. Until now, we assumed that the amount of tax revenues collected by the government is the same at each level of GDP. But, in reality, *net tax revenues (tax revenues less transfers and subsidies) varies directly with GDP.* For example, personal income taxes have progressive rates and contribute to more than proportionate increases in tax revenues as GDP rises. The same is true for corporate income taxes, sales taxes, and excise taxes. Revenues from payroll taxes also rise with economic expansion and generate more jobs. In contrast, transfer payments, which are "negative taxes," behave in the opposite direction from tax revenues: compensation for unemployment, subsidies for farmers, and welfare payments all decrease during expansion and increase during economic recession.

An automatic built-in stabilizer is a mechanism that increases the government budget deficit (or reduces its budget surplus) during a recession period and increases the budget surplus (or reduces the budget deficit) during inflation. This mechanism does not require a direct intervention of decision-makers. Induced taxes and needs-tested spending are automatic stabilizers.

1. *Induced taxes* are taxes that vary with real GDP. In an expansion, induced taxes rise, helping to stabilize the economy, and in a recession, induced taxes fall, helping to stabilize the economy.
2. *Needs-tested spending* is spending on programs that entitle suitably qualified people and businesses to receive benefits that vary with need and with the state of the economy.

Induced taxes and needs-tested spending decrease the multiplier effects of changes in autonomous expenditure, and, in such a way, they moderate both expansions and recessions and make real GDP more stable.

Built-in stability depends on the responsiveness of tax revenues to changes in GDP. There are three types of tax systems: a) *progressive tax system*—the average tax rate rises with GDP (personal income taxes); b) *proportional tax system*—the average tax rate remains constant as GDP rises (corporate taxes); and c) *regressive tax system* (sales taxes, property taxes)—the average tax rate falls as GDP rises. The steepest tax line (T in figure 14.5) is for the progressive tax system. The most important conclusion is this: the more progressive the tax system, the greater the economy's built-in stability. One of the longest periods of economic expansion, during Bill Clinton's presidency, was due to the progressivity of the tax system: the marginal tax on personal income was increased from 31 to 39.6%, and the corporate tax rate was increased by 1 percentage point to 35%. This helped prevent demand-pull inflation. In general, 8–10% of the change in real GDP depends on built-in stabilizers. Take into consideration that the stabilizers can only

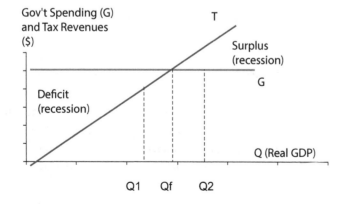

diminish but not eliminate business fluctuations. That's why discretionary fiscal policy may be needed. To summarize:

1. Government Spending (G) is independent from GDP.
2. Tax revenues (T) vary directly with GDP.
3. At full employment GDP (Qf), tax revenues equal government expenditures.
4. During recessions, deficits occur automatically with G > T and help moderate their impact.
5. During inflationary periods, surpluses occur automatically (T > G) and help offset the inflation effect.

7. THE LIMITS OF FISCAL POLICY TO STABILIZE THE ECONOMY

A fiscal policy is always a target of criticism, and there are certain problems and complications in applying fiscal policy:

First, recognition lag—it requires time to recognize the need for fiscal policy to be changed, to take appropriate steps in Congress, and to affect output, the rate of inflation, and employment by these actions. The government has to realize that a recessionary (or inflationary) gap exists: it takes time to collect and analyze the data, and, after all, recessions are recognized only months after they started. It is also difficult to predict the future course of the economy using such tools as the Index of Leading Indicators in spite of the fact that forecasting has improved tremendously in recent years. It usually takes four to six months with the economy in recession or inflation before some statistics are acknowledged and some signals are sent to decision-makers.

Second, administrative lag—once the problem has been recognized, it takes time to formulate the new target of fiscal policy and to take action. This delay is the most severe for fiscal policy since any change in taxes or in government spending has to be approved by both houses of Congress and signed by the president. For example, after the 9/11 terrorist attacks, the US Congress discussed the package of measures for five months before it passed a comprehensive economic stimulus law in March 2002. The Federal Reserve System (US Central Bank), in contrast, reacted immediately and started to lower interest rates just a week after the attacks.

Third, operational lag—the time elapsed between change in policy and its impact on the economy when the output, employment, and price level change. Because changes in taxes can be enacted relatively quickly in comparison with government spending that needs a long planning period, the government is always inclined to use tax changes as a discretionary fiscal policy rather than to increase spending. An example is the expansionary stimulus package proposed by President Clinton soon after his inauguration in 1993. By the time of debates and discussion in Congress, the economy started to grow rapidly, and these measures turned out to be unnecessary.

There are also some other complications related to political considerations:

1. *A political business cycle,* for example; election years have been characterized by more expansionary rather than contractionary fiscal policy since the electorate is much more inclined to support new programs of increased spending rather than new austerity measures.
2. *State and local government* may offset federal stabilization policies; sometimes state and local governments can make a recession worse with their procyclical actions; forty-nine out of fifty states (unlike the Federal Government) are facing constitutional and other requirements to balance their budgets every year, which is more destabilizing rather than stabilizing for the economy;

3. *A "Crowding out" effect* may occur with government deficit spending (it may increase interest rates or reduce private spending, which weakens the stimulus of fiscal policy). An expansionary fiscal policy may, by raising the level of interest rates in the economy, reduce (or crowd out) investment spending and weaken the effect of the policy on real GDP (figure 14.6). Without offsetting or complicating factors, the expansionary fiscal policy eliminates the negative GDP gap and restores full employment real GDP. The crowding out and other effects weaken expansionary fiscal policy and may turn it totally ineffective. Critics of the crowding out effect point out that the Fed can counteract it by increasing the supply of money.

   a. An Expansionary Fiscal Policy moved AD to the full employment equilibrium (Ef).
   b. But the AD decreases due to the crowding out effect.

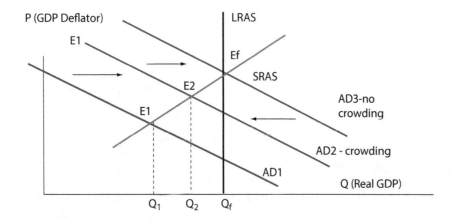

Figure 14.6
The Effects of
Crowding Out
on Expansionary
Fiscal Policy

The US Congress and the president use discretionary fiscal policy relatively infrequently, being aware of timing, political, and other problems. This is also an explanation for why the Fed plays a much more important role in "fine-tuning" the economy since monetary policy can be quickly changed to address the changing economic situation and is more flexible and less dependent on political factors.

Some economists believe that monetary policy is net superior as a stabilizing device than fiscal policy. But a majority of them believe that fiscal policy still remains an important part of the macroeconomic tool kit. In their view, fiscal policy can "push the economy" in a particular direction, especially during deep economic recessions, but cannot "fine-tune it" to a precise macroeconomic outcome. If monetary policy is working smoothly, the government should maintain a neutral fiscal policy with full employment and a budget deficit or surplus limited to 2% of potential GDP.

At the same time, a reasonable fiscal policy should provide necessary conditions for the growth of the AS curve. In this respect, a tax cut should enhance work effort and encourage investment and innovation. Government spending, in turn, should be centered on "public capital"—preplanned development projects such as highways, mass transit, ports, and airports. So, fiscal policy affects not only aggregate demand but aggregate supply, as well. Supply-side economists, whose intellectual roots reside in classical economics, believe that the government should orient its fiscal policy to increase aggregate supply and achieve stable long-term economic growth, full employment, and a lower price level. In their opinion, the stagflation of the 1970s was a consequence of government failure to adopt *supply side fiscal policy*, which became a popular concept with the election of Ronald Reagan in 1980.

8. KEY TERMS

Discretionary, Nondiscretionary Fiscal Policy

Expansionary Fiscal Policy

Contractionary Fiscal Policy

Fiscal Multiplier Effects

Government Budget Surplus, Deficit

Discretionary Spending

Entitlements and Mandatory Spending

Net Interest on Public Debt

Counter-Cyclical Policy

Cyclically Adjusted Budget Balance

Automatic (Built-In) Stabilizers

Induced Taxes

Needs-Tested Spending

Progressive, Regressive, Proportional Tax Systems

Recognition, Administrative, Operational Lags

"Crowding In" And "Crowding Out" Effects

Supply-Side Fiscal Policy

9. PROBLEMS AND APPLICATIONS

1. In 2007–2009, the US economy suffered one of the deepest recessions since WWII, with an unemployment rate above 10%, a decrease in the nation's total output, and a huge increase in public debt and trade deficit. Which of the following fiscal policy levers were used by the government to address economic hardships and accelerate economic recovery?

   a. Increase in government spending, decrease in taxes, and increase in transfer payments.

   b. Decrease in government spending, increase in taxes, and decrease in transfer payments.

   c. Government deregulation, decrease in investment spending, and loss of control over the quantity of money.

   d. Do-nothing policy, waiting until market forces removes the economy from recession.

2. On October 24, 1929, the stock market crashed. It happened "unexpectedly" after the "Roaring Twenties"—a time of unprecedented growth and prosperity. By the end of the year, tens of billions of dollars (wealth) had vanished. How this can be explained in terms of the AD-AS model?

   a. The output moves up along the aggregate demand curve.

   b. The output moves down along the aggregate demand curve.

   c. Aggregate demand and the aggregate supply shift to the left.

   d. Aggregate demand and aggregate supply shift to the right.

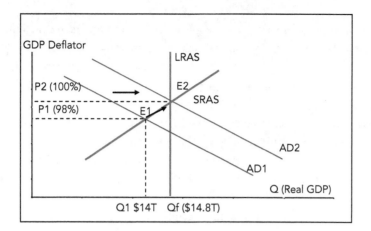

Figure 14.7

3. An economy is in a short-run equilibrium as illustrated in the figure above. What will be an appropriate fiscal policy to move the economy to full employment equilibrium (Qf)?
   a. Decrease government spending, reduce taxes, and decrease transfers.
   b. Decrease tax rates, increase government spending and transfers.
   c. Maintain the same level of government spending, tax rates, and transfer payments.
   d. Increase tax rates, increase government spending, and lower transfer payments.

4. Keynes believed that private economy is inherently unstable, and thus requires government intervention. He suggested that during a recession, policy makers should:
   a. Decrease taxes and/or decrease government spending.
   b. Increase taxes and/or increase government spending.
   c. Increase taxes and/or decrease government spending.
   d. Decrease taxes and/or increase government spending.

5. The GDP gap might be recessionary or inflationary; it is:
   a. The difference between current equilibrium output and full employment output.
   b. The current amount of output at the zero price level.
   c. The difference between imports and exports.
   d. Equal to the investment multiplier.

6. British economist John M. Keynes introduced in his book *General Theory of Employment, Interest and Money* (1936) two important concepts: Marginal Propensity to Consume (MPC) and Marginal Propensity to Save (MPS). The marginal propensity to consume is:
   a. That part of the average consumer income that goes to the purchase of final goods and services.
   b. The fraction of each additional dollar of disposable income that is consumed.
   c. The change in consumption divided by the change in saving.
   d. $1 + MPS$

7. Inflation, as you have already learned, is a rise in average level of prices and not a change in any specific price. It acts like a tax, and the explanation is:
   a. The government tends to benefit during periods of inflation since its debt is large.
   b. Everyone is affected because the purchasing power of money is diminishing.

c. It takes purchasing power from some people and gives it to others, redistributing the income.

d. Inflation benefits the rich and penalizes the poor, increasing poverty and inequality.

8. Suppose the multiplier is five and a change in government spending leads to a cumulative $500 million decrease in aggregate spending. This means:

a. Government spending decreased by $500 million, and aggregate demand shifts left.

b. Taxes increased by $500 million, and aggregate demand shifts right.

c. Taxes decreased by $100 million, and aggregate demand remains the same.

d. Government spending decreased by $100 million, and aggregate demand shifts left.

9. When economy is in expansion, federal tax receipts increase proportionally more than real GDP without the need for any government intervention. This policy is called:

a. Discretionary fiscal policy, and it is managed by law makers.

b. Automatic monetary policy and is directed by the Federal Reserve Bank.

c. Automatic fiscal policy, and it depends on the state of economy.

d. Discretionary monetary policy.

10. A budget deficit is compatible with recessionary times, according to John M. Keynes, and it occurs whenever:

a. The government is increasing spending and/or reducing taxes and uses fiscal policy to stabilize the economy.

b. Tax revenues exceed expenditures over the fiscal year.

c. Discretionary fiscal spending is used to combat inflation and achieve macroequilibrium.

d. The US Treasury engages in refinancing activities and cuts spending.

10. REVIEW QUESTIONS

1. The economy is in a recessionary gap, and both Daniel and Linda, economics grad students at Ohio State, advocate expansionary fiscal policy. Does it mean that both favor so-called big government?

2. Sue Taylor is sitting with a friend at a Dunkin' Donuts shop, and they are discussing the new tax bill adopted by the US Congress. Sue thinks that cutting tax rates at this time would be wrong. "Lower tax rates" she says, "will lead to a larger budget deficit, and the budget deficit is already big." Do lower tax rates mean a larger deficit? Why or why not? Are there any alternatives to this option?

3. The government is using an unconventional fiscal policy tool: it would issue time-dated debit cards to each person that had to be spent on goods and services produced only by US firms within the next three months or become worthless. In addition, suppose that the government was considering whether to issue $600 in time-dated debit cards to each household or give each household $600 in cash instead. Let's address the following questions: a) which plan do you think would lead to the greatest economic effect (stimulus)? b) Assume, you, as a household, have a large credit card debt which you wish to reduce. Which of the two plans would you prefer?

4. Explain how time lags in discretionary fiscal policy could thwart the efforts of Congress and the President to stabilize real GDP in the face of economic recession. Is it possible that these time lags could actually cause discretionary fiscal policy to destabilize the economy? Define fiscal policy time lags and briefly describe their effects.

5. During the last few years, the Federal Government has regularly borrowed funds to pay for at least 30 percent of government expenditures not covered by tax revenues. More than 60 percent of all federal expenditures now go for mandatory entitlement spending. How can the government finance most of its discretionary spending in a more efficient manner?

CHAPTER 15.

MONETARY SYSTEM AND MONETARY POLICY

The famous American writer O. Henry once observed: "You can't appreciate home till you left it, nor money till it's spent." Money is always a fascinating issue. If you believe that money is a product of modern development over the last few centuries, you're wrong.

Money as a commodity has been known and used at least since 9000 B.C. A great variety of commodities has served at one time or another as money: cattle, probably was one of the oldest forms, from which comes the Latin stem of "pecuniary," and also the words "capital" and "chattel." Some other commodities could be included in this list: tobacco, leather and hides, furs, olive oil, beer or spirits, slaves or wives, copper, iron, gold, silver, rings, diamonds, wampum beads or shells, huge rocks and landmarks, and cigarettes.

The first governor of Tennessee actually received a salary of 1,000 deerskins per year, and the Secretary of the Treasury received 450 otter skins per year. For nearly 2,000 years, until 1965, the people of the tiny South Pacific island of Yap, which is now a US trust territory, used different stone wheels, from 2.5 to 5 and even 12 feet across, to pay for their purchases, such as land, canoes, or permission to marry. Of course, there are some advantages of using massive stones for money: they are immune to black-market trading and pose a formidable obstacle to pickpockets. Interestingly, when US dollars were introduced to the people of Yap, their reaction was: "buying property with stones is much easier than buying it with US dollars … We don't know the value of the US dollar."

There is evidence that the primary motivation for inventing writing and the development of money in Mesopotamia (3100 B.C.) was for keeping accounts. The first coins were produced in the Greek city of Lidia from a naturally occurred mix of gold and silver—electrum.

In 390 B.C., when the Gauls attacked Rome, it was reported that geese began to cackle where the city's reserves of money were kept, which alerted soldiers. After this incident, the Romans built a shrine to Moneta, the goddess of warning. This shrine is where we get the word "money" from. In fact, in Spanish, the word for coins is *moneda*. There is only one letter difference in the spelling.

Do you know when and where the first paper bills were printed? In 1023 China formed a government agency to print money, and by 1107, it had begun to print money in three colors to thwart counterfeiters. In the US, the first national coin was issued in 1787, and it was a one-cent copper coin approved by Congress. On one side, it was decorated with a chain of thirteen links encircling the phrase "We are One." On the other side, it was a sundial, the noonday sun, and the Latin word "*fugo*," which means "time flies." The first paper money in the Americas was printed in 1690 by the colony of Massachusetts to pay soldiers returning from the unsuccessful fight with the French in Quebec. With the soldiers threatening to mutiny, the colony issued simple pieces of paper promising to pay soldiers.

In 1998, the US Treasury introduced a new $20-dollar bill, using modern technology to make the lives of counterfeiters more difficult. The portrait of Andrew Jackson is slightly off center. These bills are also printed with a special ink that looks green when viewed directly but changes to black when viewed from side to side. There is a famous saying: "As long as there has been paper money, there have been counterfeiters." By value, over 90% of all transactions in the United States today are made electronically. There may be many ingenious technological marvels, but the institution of money is an even greater marvel. Not accidently, popular wisdom says, "there are three great inventions over time: the wheel, fire and … money" (Glyn Davies, *History of Money from Ancient Times to the Present Day*. pp. 37, 41, 49, 61–63, 76, 458, 661).

So, what is money, and how it is created and used? What are the main functions of money, and what is the role of the banking system?

1. WHAT IS MONEY, AND WHAT ARE ITS MAIN FUNCTIONS?

To understand the role of money in the economy, let's imagine that there is no such an item as money. *Bartering* is where there is an exchange of goods without money. In this case, all of us will face a lot of inconveniences.

First, coincidence of wants. In order to get what we want, we need to find the person who has this item and is interested in exchanging it. Using a classical economic phrase: instead of there being a double coincidence of wants, there is likely to be a want of coincidence so that unless a hungry tailor happens to find an undraped farmer who has both food and a desire for a pair of paints, neither can make a trade.

Second, indivisibility of money. Initially, Cattle played the role of money but was hard to divide into small change; plus, while it was being hoarded, such "money" was likely to increase by reproduction, giving the lie to Aristotle's doctrine that "money is barren."

Third, preservation. Beer does not improve with age although wine may but not for very long time;

Fourth, mobility. It took twenty men to lift some stone wheels that were used as money by the people of Yap Island.

Fifth, relative scarcity of an item chosen to play the role of money. Sand, theoretically, could serve as money, but people can easily gather a bucketful to pay the bills. A Picasso painting could also be used as money, but there are only a few for circulation.

Only if we will find an item that solves these problems will that item be recognized as money and be able to play the proper role of money. Summarizing, here are the five criteria necessary to make a good substitute as a medium of exchange today:

1. *acceptable* (and usable) by most consumers;
2. *standardized* quality (all units are identically sized);
3. *durable* (the good can't deteriorate);
4. *valuable* and useful in transporting, with a transportable weight; and
5. *divisible* since different goods have different values.

An old saying goes, *"Money is what money does."* So, anything that is accepted as payment for goods and services that can be held for future purchases and that can serve as a yardstick for measuring the prices of goods and services is money. In other words, anything that performs the following functions is money:

1. *Medium of exchange:* money is an asset that is usable for buying and selling goods and services. Money allows society to avoid the complications of barter, and, at the same time, money enables society to gain the advantages of geographic and human specialization. In communist Romania of the 80s, Kent cigarettes were used as money for black market transactions. It had to be Kent; no other brand would do. The packs themselves were exchanged unopened for the goods. No one would even dream of smoking them because lighting a Kent would have been considered the same as burning a dollar bill.
2. *Standard of value or unit of account:* With money ($$) as an acceptable unit of account, the price of each item needs to be stated only in terms of this monetary unit. We do not need to state the price of cows in terms of corn, pencils, or apples. Money ($$) enables buyers and sellers to easily compare the prices of various goods, services, and resources to clearly define debt obligations, to determine taxes, and to calculate GDP. A new CD costs about five times as much as a Big Mac, but Amazon.com lists the price in dollars and not in Big Macs.
3. *Store of value:* Money is often the preferred store of value for short time periods—it is the most liquid (spendable) of all assets. With nonexistent inflation, holding money is a relatively risk free way to store wealth. Imagine an economy in which ice cream is used as a "store of value." It would turn into a sticky puddle before you could use it to buy something else.

Coins and paper currency are both known as currency although many payments are made by check. All three items act as media of exchange. *Fiat money* is any currency which holds value based on official status. In other words, fiat money is money accepted as a medium of exchange because of a government decree rather than because of its intrinsic value as a commodity. A dollar bill contains only about 4 cents worth of paper, printing inks, and other materials. A quarter contains maybe 10 cents worth of nickel and copper. Look at dollar bill closely: in the upper left corner on the front side you'll read: "This note is legal tender for all debts, public and private." Also, you will not find anywhere on the note any promise to redeem it for gold, silver, or anything else. In the US, individuals could exchange dollars for gold until 1933 when President Franklin Roosevelt banned private possession of gold; however, foreign governments could exchange dollars for gold until 1971.

2. MONEY SUPPLY DEFINITIONS, AND HOW MONEY IS MEASURED

In the United States and other modern economies, people can carry out economic transactions in a few different ways. We are using checking account (checks) or debit cards more often to buy goods and services or to pay our debts. These checking accounts perform the same market functions as cash, and they perfectly correspond to the definition of money—anything generally accepted as a medium of exchange. All checking accounts can be used directly and are collectively called *transactions accounts*. Their distinctive feature is that they permit direct payment to a third party without a trip to a bank. The payments can be in the form of a check, a debit card transfer, or an automatic payment transfer. In other words, the transactions accounts substitute for cash and represent a form of money.

There are many ways to perform a transaction since there are many definitions of money. The difference between the definitions is their *liquidity*—spendability—or how easily an asset can be traded for goods and services.

The narrowest definition of the US money supply—M1 (figure 15.1a)—consists of:

1. Currency, which is all coins and paper money in circulation held by the people and not by government and banks.
2. All checkable deposits in commercial banks and saving institutions.

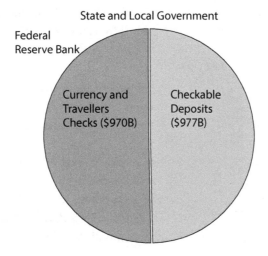

Figure 15.1a
Components of
Money Supply
M1 ($Bl)
(Source: Federal
Reserve System,
2010.)

3. Traveler's checks, which are issued by American Express, can be used directly in market transactions just like good old-fashioned cash although their total value is insignificant ($7 billion in 2008).

M1 = currency (coins + paper money) + checking deposits + traveler's checks

It should be noted that there are many types of checking account services, but all of them have a common feature: they permit direct payment to a third party (with a check), and these are referred to as transactions accounts. The balance in a transactions account substitutes for cash and is de facto a form of money. Before we focus on other, more sophisticated definitions of money, we have to make a few important clarifications:

1. *Currency held by the public in the form of coins and paper money is called "token" money*. This means that its intrinsic value (the value of the metal contained in the coins itself) is less than the face value of the coin. For example, the metal in a dime (penny, quarter, etc.) is worth less than 10 cents. All paper currency consists of Federal Reserve Notes issued by the Federal Reserve (the US Central Bank) with the authorization of Congress.

2. *Checkable deposits represent 50% of M1(June 2011)*. People prefer to pay with checks, which are safer than cash. Checks are a generally accepted medium of exchange, the way to transfer the ownership of deposits in banks and other financial institutions. The main source of checkable deposits for households and businesses are the *commercial banks*. They are the primary depository institutions. At the same time, the commercial banks are supplemented in this function by *saving or thrift institutions*. These institutions include savings and loan associations (S&Ls), credit unions, mutual savings banks, and other institutions. Checkable deposits are known as demand deposits, for example, NOW accounts—negotiable order of withdrawal—or ATS accounts—automatic transfer service.

3. Another popular medium of exchange is *credit cards* (about one third of all purchases), but they represent just a payment service and not a final form of payment, not money. What about *debit cards*? When you are using a debit card to make purchases, it is exactly the same as writing a check. So the debit card is not a source of money, it is just a tool to make payments from your checking account.

4. Currency and checkable deposits owned by the US Treasury (Federal Government) and by the Federal Reserve and other commercial banks and financial institutions *are not included in M1* because $1 counts for $2 when it is deposited in banks. In such a way, we avoid the problem of double counting.

A second and broader definition of money—M2—includes M1 (21% of M2) and several near-monies (figure 15.1b). Near monies represents highly liquid financial assets that do not function directly or fully as mediums of exchange. They can be converted into currency or checkable deposits:

1. *Savings deposits* (62% of M2), including money market deposit accounts (MMDA) which are interest-bearing accounts at a bank or thrift where a depositor can simply request that the funds be transferred from a savings account to a checkable account. Some savings accounts are not easily spendable, for example, certificates of deposit, which require a minimum balance and must be kept in the bank for a specified number of month or years.

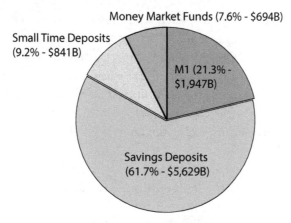

Money Market Funds (7.6% - $694B)

Small Time Deposits
(9.2% - $841B)

M1 (21.3% -
$1,947B)

Savings Deposits
(61.7% - $5,629B)

2. *Small (less than $100,000) time deposits* (9% of M2). Funds from time deposits become available at their maturity (six months for a certificate of deposit); in return for withdrawal limitations, the financial institution pays a higher interest rate on such deposits.
3. *Money market mutual funds* (MMMF, 7% of M2)—a mutual fund company uses the combined funds of individual shareholders to buy interest-bearing, short-term credit instruments (certificates of deposit and US government securities). In return, they offer interest on the money market account.

M2 = M1 + savings deposits (including MMDAs)
+ small (less than $100,000) time deposits + MMMFs

*A third definition of the money supply—M3—*includes *M2* and large ($100,000 or more) time deposits, usually owned by businesses as certificates of deposit and used for saving, not "money."

M3 = M2 + large ($100,000 or more) time deposits

Which definitions can we use? The most "usable" is *M1*, but *M2* is closely supervised by the Federal Reserve to determine monetary policy. All these definitions become important when the authorities attempt to control the money supply:

1. *M2* and *M3* are important because they can easily be changed into *M1* types of money and influence people's spending;
2. at the same time, the ease of shifting between *M1, M2,* and *M3* complicates the procedure of controlling the spendable money; and
3. *M3* and other broader definitions of money are so inclusive that some economists question their usefulness. The Fed is not using it any more to control the supply of money.

3. WHO CREATES MONEY? THE GOLDSMITH AND FRACTIONAL RESERVE SYSTEM

Who creates money? It seems that money creates money, or transactions account deposits come from transaction accounts balances. But who created the first transactions account balance?

The US, like a majority of other countries, has *a fractional reserve system*—only a fraction of the total money supply is held in reserve as currency. The history of this system began with the goldsmiths of the sixteenth century, who had safes for gold and other precious metals to keep them for consumers and merchants. For these deposits, they issued receipts. These receipts came to be used as paper money in place of gold. Goldsmiths realized that much of the stored gold was never redeemed, and they started to "loan" gold by issuing receipts to borrowers, who agreed to pay back the gold plus some interest. In this way, the "fractional reserve banking" system emerged. The gold in the vaults became only a fraction of the receipts held by borrowers and owners of gold.

The significance of the fractional reserve system consists of the following:

First, banks can create money by lending more than the original reserves on hand (today, gold is no longer used as reserves).

Second, lending policies must be prudent to prevent bank "panics" or "runs" by depositors worried about their funds. For these reasons, the United States created a deposit insurance system—the Federal Deposit Insurance Corporation (FDIC), which, along with the National Credit Union Administration (NCUA), insures individual deposits of up to $250,000 at commercial banks and thrift institutions.

A bank creates money by making loans. Transactions account balances are counted as part of the money supply and, more precisely, as the biggest part of the money supply. Banks create such balances by making loans.

When a bank lends "your money" to another client, there is a net increase in the value of transactions deposits but no increase in bank reserves. Bank reserves are only a fraction of total transactions deposits, and they represent the assets held by a bank to fulfill its deposit obligations.

The bank reserve ratio = bank reserves/total deposits

The question is, if a bank can create money, can the bank have a control over AD? There are two constraints. First, in reality, no single private bank has so much power. There are many banks and not just one monopoly bank. The second constraint is government regulation of money lending. The Federal Reserve System regulates bank lending and requires banks to maintain some minimum reserve ratio. This ratio directly limits the ability of banks to offer new loans.

Required reserves = required reserve ratio × total deposits

The minimum ratio of deposits that banks are required to keep as reserve is called *required reserve ratio (RR)*. This minimum threshold for a bank is imposed by the government and directly limits deposit-creation possibilities.

Excess reserves = total reserves – required reserves. So long as a bank has excess reserves, it can make additional loans. But the most important issue is how much excess reserves exist in the entire banking system not just in any specific bank.

To understand how commercial banks work, we have to start with a few elementary notions—first of all, the balance sheet of a commercial bank, a firm that is chartered by the Comptroller of the Currency or by a state agency to receive deposits and make loans. A balance sheet lists assets, liabilities, and net worth. *Assets* are what the bank owns, and *liabilities* are what the bank owes.

1. *Banks' assets* include: a) *Cash assets.* A bank's reserves are its currency in its vault plus the balance on its reserve account at a Federal Reserve Bank and b) *Securities and loans.* Banks buy

securities issued by the US government and large businesses. Banks also make loans to businesses and individuals.

2. *Banks' liabilities* include *deposits,* which are part of money. Banks take on liabilities, such as deposits, in order to obtain assets, such as loans, that generate higher returns than the interest paid on deposits. Banks are primarily in the business of making loans to corporations for purchases of capital equipment and to households to finance consumer durable goods.

A statement of the assets and claims on assets summarizes the financial situation of a bank at a certain point in time. These claims can be categorized into two categories: a) claims of nonowners against the bank's assets, or *liabilities* and b) claims of the owners of the bank against the bank's assets, or *net worth.* All balance sheets must balance; the value of assets must equal the value of claims. The equation is: *Assets = liabilities + net worth.*

Now we can answer the question, "Who creates money?" *A bank creates money by making a loan.* Transactions account balances are counted as part of money supply, more exactly, as the biggest part of the money supply. Banks create such balances by making loans.

4. THE MONEY MULTIPLIER AND THE MONEY MARKET

The excess reserves are necessary conditions and sources of bank lending authority. But the amount of excess reserves doesn't define the limit to further loans, and this is the most surprising fact about how a multibank system works.

Let's consider an example. Suppose the Federal Reserve establishes a minimum of required reserves in banks of 25% of deposited money. In this case, the 75% that represents excess reserves can be loaned to some other bank, and so on. In such a way, each loan made creates new excess reserves that will help fund the next loan. This situation is very similar to the income multiplier, which creates additional income every time income is spent. Recall that the multiplier is the ratio of change in GDP to the initial change in spending. In our case, we can refer to money (deposit) creation as the money-multiplier process where the money multiplier is the reciprocal of the required reserve ratio.

Money multiplier = 1: required reserve ratio = 1/RR, or in our example = 1/0.25 = 4

When a new deposit enters into the banking system, it creates both excess and required reserves. The required reserves can be identified with a leakage from the flow of money since these reserves cannot be used for new loans. The process of money creation can continue indefinitely until all reserves disappear (figure 15.2).

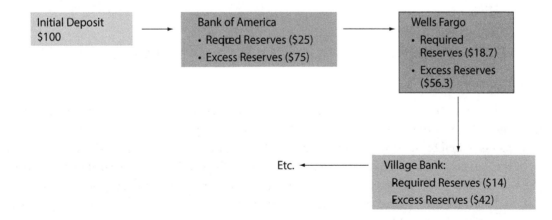

Figure 15.2
Money
Multiplier

WHAT ARE THE LIMITS OF DEPOSIT CREATION?

Potential deposit creation = Excess reserves of banking system × Money multiplier, or, in our case, $75 × 4 = $300. With its excess reserves of $75, the banking system can create loans of $300. So, we can summarize that 1) each bank may lend an amount equal to its excess reserves (no more) and 2) the entire banking system can increase the volume of loans by the amount of excess reserves multiplied by the money multiplier.

Thus, when the Federal Reserve changes the required reserve ratio, as it is permitted to do, it can have a powerful effect on the amount of loans that the banks can make and on the amount of checking deposits that they can create. The banking system, as a whole, does something that no single bank can do: it can create deposits equal to a multiple of the reserves that it acquires. There are *two complications:*

1. Banks may decide not to lend out the maximum but to hold some excess reserves, instead. This syndrome is reminiscent of the saying: "You can lead a horse to water, but you can't make him drink." During prosperous times, neither the Fed nor the banks are interested in holding their reserves immobilized—currency yields no interest. Banks have strong incentives to make loans and to increase their profits since they are the profit-oriented business organizations. The amount of excess reserves they hold generally is much less than 1% of total reserves. But the situation is different during a depression. For example, during the Great Depression, excess reserves skyrocketed, reaching 50% of total reserves by 1940.
2. As loans are made, and people get more checking deposit money, they may want to hold more currency, too, to withdraw cash from their deposits. If this happens, the reserves of banks are reduced, and the total amount of monetary expansion is reduced, as well.

We can conclude, therefore, that banks perform two essential functions to create additional money: a) they lend their funds (reserves) from savers to spenders and b) they make loans in excess of their total reserves. By performing these functions, banks change the money supply and the AD, as well. People are buying new cars, homes, business equipment, etc. Hence, increases in the money supply will increase AD and vice versa—decreases in the money supply will lead to decline in AD.

The banking system is the key link between consumer savings and the demand originating in other sectors of the economy. To understand it, it is enough to consider what would happen if all consumer savings were deposited in piggy banks: banks could not transfer money from savers to spenders, and they could not create the money needed to increase AD and to stimulate the economy, as a whole. In reality, banks are using a substantial portion of consumer savings as the bases for loans. The banks do not need to hold all of consumers' reserves to carry out their functions. They can increase or decrease loan activity in order to create the desired level of money supply.

5. THE FEDERAL RESERVE SYSTEM: HISTORY, ROLE, FUNCTIONS, AND STRUCTURE

The Federal Reserve (Fed) is the Central Bank of the US, the "bankers' bank." It's counterparts are the Bank of England in the UK, the European Central Bank (ECB), the Bank of Japan, and Sweden's Sveriges Rijksbank, the world's oldest central bank, which awards the Nobel Prize for Economics. The Central Bank controls the quantity of reserves held by the commercial banks and the amount of checking deposits that they can create.

In the United States, the very concept of a central bank was controversial. In the early nineteenth century, this role was, to some extent, played by the Second Bank of the US, but it came to an end at the hands of

Andrew Jackson, who attacked its political power: "The bank," said Jackson, "is trying to kill me, but I will kill it." And so he did. Decentralized, unregulated banking, the confusion of numerous private bank notes being used as a currency, and an unusually acute banking crisis in 1907 caused Congress to pass the Federal Reserve Act of 1913.

The legal status of the Fed is unusual and unique: it is not exactly part of the US government, but it is not really a private bank either (figure 15.3). The *Twelve Federal Reserve Regional Banks* act as central bankers for the private banks in their respective districts. Each of them is quasi-public: it is owned by member banks but controlled by the government's Federal Reserve Board, and any profits go to the US treasury. Unlike private firms, the Fed is not motivated by profit.

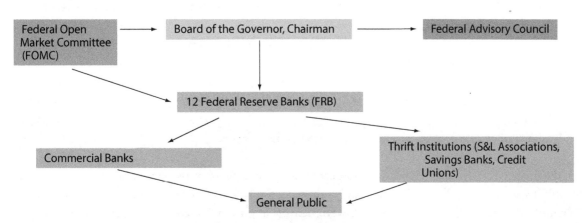

Figure 15.3 Federal Reserve System

The central authority of the US money and banking system is the *Board of Governors*, which designs the monetary policy to ensure the well-being of the economy as a whole. Its seven members are appointed for a period of fourteen years by the President of the United States and must be approved by the Senate; there are also a chairperson and vice-chairperson of the Board who also are selected by the president from the Board's members to serve for four-year terms. In the 1920s, the Board was dominated by the forceful Benjamin Strong, president of the New York Federal Reserve District Bank. William McChesney Martin headed the Board from 1951 to 1970; Arthur Burns (1970–1978 and Paul Volker (1979–1987) succeeded. In 1987, President Reagan appointed Alan Greenspan as chairman; he was reappointed by President George H. W. Bush, President Clinton (for two terms), and President George W. Bush in 2004. So, Alan Greenspan served as the Fed chairman for more than eighteen years, one of the longest chairmanships in US history. The former Fed chairman, Ben Bernanke, an economics professor from Princeton University, was appointed in January 2006 by President George W. Bush and reappointed by President Barak Obama in 2010. In 2014, President Obama appointed Janet Yellen, the first Fed chairwoman in the more than 100-year history of the Federal Reserve System. It is often argued that the Fed chair is the most powerful person in the US next to the president, but he or she has just one vote on the Board of Governors and the FOMC.

The *Federal Open Market Committee* (FOMC) and the Federal Advisory Council assist the Board of Governors in conducting monetary policy. The FOMC plays a very important role in directing the buying and selling of US government securities which are the most important instruments the Fed uses to control the money supply. It is composed of twelve individuals: seven members of the Board of Governors, the president of the New York FRB, and four remaining presidents of Federal Reserve Banks on a one-year rotating basis.

The Fed—the "bankers' bank"—performs the same functions that commercial banks and thrifts perform for the public: a) it accepts deposits and b) it makes loans to banks—normally only $150 million a day, but, in emergency situations, the Fed becomes a "lender of last resort" as it was on the day after 9/11 when the Fed lent $45 billion. There are also some specific functions performed only by the Fed's twelve districts banks:

1. *Issuing currency*—Federal Reserve Notes (paper currency; in the upper left of a dollar bill there is a sign of the bank that issued it: A1—Boston, B2—New York etc.). At the same time, Federal Reserve Banks provide currency for private banks and deliver it in armored trucks.
2. *Clearing checks* between private banks. This clearinghouse service (over thirty-five billion checks are written every year) saves a great amount of time and expense.
3. *Setting reserve requirements and holding reserves.* Private banks are required to hold some fraction of their deposits as reserves, and practically all of these reserves are held in accounts at the regional Fed; only a small amount is held in their vaults.
4. *Lending money to banks and thrifts.* The Fed lends money to banks and thrifts and charges them an interest rate called the discount rate.
5. *Acting as the fiscal agent for the Federal Government* (collecting taxes, selling bonds, etc.).
6. *Supervising banks*—assessment of their profitability, uncovering questionable practices or frauds.
7. *The Fed mainly controls the money supply and interest rates.*

The financial crisis of 2008 brought into play three more tools as extraordinary crisis measures, which we will discuss in more detail a little bit later. To protect the Fed from political influence and pressure, the Congress established it as an independent government agency. Even Congress cannot control the monetary policy of the Fed. The major task of the Fed is to manage the money supply (and, thus, the interest rates) in the best interest of the national economy. As studies have shown, countries with independent central banks (like the Fed) have lower rates of inflation, on average, than countries that have no central bank independence.

The Fed is on the top of the *monetary system pyramid*, which also includes:

1. about 7,250 *commercial banks* (down from 13,000 a few years ago); three-quarters of them are private banks authorized to operate within individual states, and one-quarter are private banks authorized by the Federal Government to operate nationally;
2. about 8,700 *thrift institutions*, such as *savings and loan associations* (S&Ls accept deposits and make personal, commercial, and home-purchase loans), *savings banks* (accept savings deposits and make consumer and home-purchase loans), *credit unions* (owned by a group, for example, a firm's employees; accept savings deposits and make consumer loans); and
3. *money market funds* (increase their funds by selling shares and use these funds to buy securities; US Treasury bills, for example).

6. THE MONEY MARKET MODEL: DEMAND AND SUPPLY FOR MONEY

To understand short-run fluctuations in output, we must understand what makes investment fluctuate. Investment spending responds to several factors, including interest rates. Monetary policy affects the economy in the short-run. By controlling the money supply, the Fed can control the level of interest rates, which is its main target. Changes in interest rates will, in turn, affect investment and output. In an open economy, the influence of the Fed is even stronger. Monetary policy also has different effects in the short-run than in the long-run. Understanding the distinction between the short-run and the long-run is critical to evaluating monetary policy. The secret is in monetary policy itself, which involves control over the quantity of money in our economy.

How does monetary policy work? Let's start with analysis of the *money market model*, which is the market where the amount of money supplied meets the amount of money demanded to determine the *nominal interest rate.*

First, there are two reasons why businesses and households tend to hold and demand money:

1. *Transactions demand (Dt)* for money (businesses, for example, need money to pay for labor, materials, power, and other inputs); its main determinant is the level of nominal GDP. Households and business firms will require more money for transactions if prices rise or if real output increases. Graphically, Figure 15.4a shows the quantity of money demanded for transactions against the interest rate—the transactions demand (Dt) is a vertical line and is positioned at $100 billion nominal GDP. This fact is based on the assumption that each dollar held for transactions purposes is spent three times per year and that nominal GDP is $300 billion. So, we (the public) need $100 billion to buy this GDP ($300: 3).

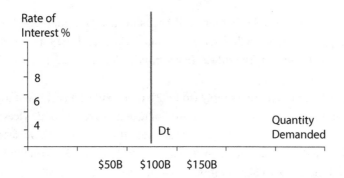

Figure 15.4a
Transaction
Demand for
Money

2. *Asset demand (Da)* is money kept as stored value for later use. It might be in many forms: corporate stocks, bonds, or money. The asset demand for money is determined, first of all, by its liquidity and lack of risk. It is especially convenient to hold it when the prices for goods and services and other financial assets are expected to decline. The biggest disadvantage is that when compared with bonds, money does not earn interest. When the interest rate is high, it is convenient to hold bonds and not "liquid money" and vice versa. So, the amount of money demanded as an asset varies inversely with the interest rate (figure 15.4b). So, *total demand for money (Dm)* is equal to the sum of quantities demanded for assets and transactions at each possible interest rate (figure 15.4c).

$$Dm = Dt + Da$$

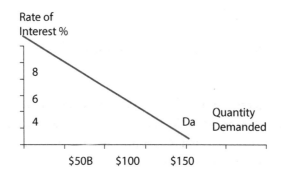

Figure 15.4b
Asset Demand

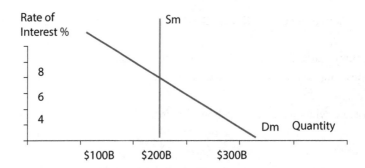

Figure 15.4c
Total Demand

Second, the money market demand and supply for money determines the interest rate. The demand for money is a downward sloping line, and the supply is a vertical line because the monetary authorities and financial institutions provide the economy with a specific stock of money (in our example, it is $200 billion). The intersection of these two curves determines interest rate (7%). Disequilibrium in this market is corrected by a change in bond prices and their inverse relationship with interest rates. There are two situations (figure 15.5):

1. If money supply decreases (to Sm1), there will be a shortage of money, and bonds will be sold. The increased supply for bonds will drive down their prices, and the interest rates will increase until the shortage is eliminated. The rule is: *lower bond prices are associated with higher interest rates.*

2. If there is an increase in the money supply (to Sm2), there will be a surplus of money, and bonds will be bought. In turn, an increased demand for bonds will drive up bond prices, causing interest rates to fall until the surplus is eliminated. Let's suppose that a bond with the face value of $1,000 yields $50 fixed annual interest. The interest yield on this bond is $50: $1000 = 5%. If the market price of this bond increases to $2,000, it will yield interest of $50: $2000 = 2.5%. So, the rule is: *higher bond prices are associated with lower interest rates.*

Figure 15.5
Money Market:
Supply and
Demand

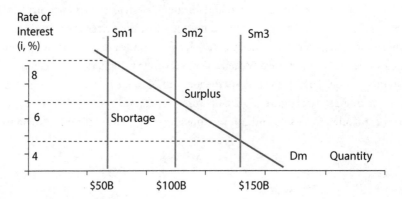

Third, last but not least, take into consideration that the Fed's influences on the interest rate differ in the long-run and the short-run:

1. *In the long-run*, savings supply and investment demand determine the real interest rate in global financial markets. In the long-run, the Fed influences the nominal interest rate by the effects of its policies on the inflation rate. But it does not directly control the nominal interest rate, and it has no control over the real interest rate.

2. *In the short-run*, the Fed can influence the nominal interest rate and the real interest rate, and this is the subject of our analysis.

Monetary authorities, by shifting the money supply, can affect interest rates, which, in turn, affect investment; consumption; aggregate demand; and, finally, output, employment, and prices. Let's see what the main monetary policy tools are that the Fed uses to control the money supply and, therefore, to alter the short-run interest rate. The interest that the Fed targets is the *federal funds rate*—the interest rate at which commercial banks can borrow and lend reserves in the federal funds market (the so-called market for overnight loans and reserves).

7. MONETARY POLICY TOOLS

The three main policy tools used by the Fed to control the money supply (M1) are: *Reserve requirements (ratio), Discount rates,* and *Open market operations* (purchases or sales of government bonds or short-term securities). Let's analyze these tools separately.

First, reserve requirements and reserve ratio; the Fed is using reserve requirements to influence the ability of commercial banks to lend. Recall that the ability of the banking system to make additional loans—create deposits—is determined by 1) the amount of excess reserves banks hold and 2) the money multiplier (Mm = 1/reserve requirement). So, the available lending capacity of a banking system = excess reserves × money multiplier.

A decrease in required reserves directly increases excess reserves and also increases the money multiplier. Raising the reserve ratio increases the amount of required reserves banks must keep. As a result, banks lose excess reserves and diminish their ability to create money by lending.

The second monetary tool is the discount rate which is the rate of interest charged by the Fed for lending reserves to private banks. Recall that the Central Bank is a "lender of last resort." Borrowing from the Federal Reserve Banks, the commercial banks increase their reserves and enhance their ability to extend credit. There are three sources of *last-minute reserves*: a) turning to other commercial banks for help, so called *interbank borrowing*, which is referred to as the *federal funds market*; b*) selling securities*; and c) going to the Fed and borrowing some reserves. This process is called *discounting.* "By raising or lowering the discount rate, the Fed changes the cost of money for banks and the incentive to borrow reserves" (McConnell, Brue and Flynn). When the Fed sets the discount rate above the federal funds rate, it is discouraging banks from turning to the Fed for emergency funds and vice versa.

Third, the most important mechanism for directly altering the reserves of the banking system is *open-market operations.* "Open" means open to all buyers and sellers. Open-market operations have an immediate and direct impact on the lending capacity of the banks.

The *FRB can buy or sell securities* (government bonds) and, thus, affect the money supply. Let's consider the effects of these operations:

1. *The Federal Reserve buys securities from Commercial banks*: the commercial banks give up part of their holdings of securities (the government bonds) to the FRB, and the FRB, by paying for those securities, increases the reserves of the commercial banks by the amount of the purchase. In this way the *FRB increases the reserves in the banking system and increases the lending capacity of the commercial banks.*

2. *The Federal Reserve purchases securities from the general public.* Two aspects of this transaction are important: a) as in the case of purchases of securities directly from commercial banks, the

purchases of securities from the public increase the lending ability of the commercial banking system and b) the supply of money is directly increased by the FRB's purchase of government bonds. This direct increase in the money supply has taken the form of an increased amount of checkable deposits in the economy. In both cases, the result is the same: *commercial banks' reserves are increased.*

3. *The Federal Reserve sells securities* to a) commercial banks: (i) the Fed gives up securities that the commercial banks acquire and (ii) the commercial banks pay for those securities by drawing checks against their reserves and b) the Federal Reserve sells securities to the public. When the Fed sells bonds to the commercial banks or to the public, the result is the same: *commercial banks' reserves are reduced.*

Why are commercial banks and individuals willing to sell and buy government securities? The price of bonds and their interest rates make these transactions attractive. By selling bonds, the Fed reduces bank reserves and banks' capacities to make loans. The reserves of the banking system are, thereby, diminished. Conversely, by buying bonds, the Fed increases bank reserves, and these reserves can be used to expand the money supply and to make loans.

8. STABILIZING THE ECONOMY AT ITS FULL EMPLOYMENT CAPACITY: EASY VS. TIGHT MONETARY POLICY (SHIFTING THE AD)

Let's consider real situations:

First, an economy that faces recession and unemployment. Since the current GDP is below the potential, unemployment is high, and output is in a negative zone (decreasing) during a recession, the Fed should increase collective demand (AD) to move the economy to its full employment capacity. To achieve this, it is necessary to increase the supply of money and the excess reserves of commercial banks. How can the Fed do this? There are three leverages:

1. *buy securities* in the open market and, thus, increase commercial banks' reserves;
2. *lower the reserve ratio,* and by changing the required reserves level, transfer them into excess reserves, and, in such a way, also increase the size of the money multiplier ($M = 1/required\ reserve\ ratio$); and
3. *lower the discount rate* and, thus, encourage commercial banks to borrow from the Fed.

All these actions of the Fed are called *easy,* or *expansionary, monetary policy.* As a result, the loans become less expensive and more available to commercial banks and other organizations, and the AD, as well as output and employment, will increase. This policy is applied during recessions or slow economic growth as in the case of expansionary fiscal policy.

Second, let's consider the situation when the economy is experiencing *rapidly increasing inflation,* and the Fed should reduce AD by limiting or contracting the supply of money. The Fed will apply a *tight money policy, or restrictive monetary policy,* and its goal is to reduce the supply of money, to reduce spending (AD), and to establish an effective control over inflation. How does the Fed do it? It uses the same three methods but this time in reverse:

1. *sell securities* and reduce the reserves of commercial banks;

2. *increase the reserve ratio,* which will automatically reduce the excess reserves of commercial banks and decrease the money multiplier. But this is rarely done because of the powerful impact of this action on banks' activity; and

3. *raise the discount rate,* which will discourage commercial banks from borrowing from FRB. Although it has a little impact on the money supply, the Fed may use it to "announce" a policy change.

The most important of the three instruments is the first one—*buying and selling securities* in the open market. Its impact is very prompt. The volume of trading in US government securities exceeds $1 trillion per day. The Fed alone owned $900 billion worth of government securities (2010). The advantage of this method consists of its flexibility, as well—government securities can be sold or purchased in small or big amounts and can affect the commercial banks' reserves immediately; they can even reduce them to zero. The Fed only occasionally uses changes in the *reserve ratio* since it could destabilize banks' lending and profit and, thus, disrupt the normal activity of the banking system. As of 2010, US banks were required to hold 3% in reserves against checkable deposits between $10.7 million and $55.2 million and 10% on all checkable deposits exceeding $55.2 million.

The Fed, more often, uses changes in *discount rate,* but this tool is less important because commercial banks borrow only 2–3% of their reserves from FRBs. The discount rate is largely symbolic because borrowing directly from the Fed is seen as an indication that a bank is in trouble. Changes in the discount rate are important as a signal about the Fed's future plans for the federal funds rate. This leverage is used as an announcement of future changes in the direction of monetary policy and has become a passive instrument of Fed policies.

9. HOW ARE MONETARY POLICY, REAL GDP, AND THE PRICE LEVEL RELATED?

To address this question, we need to find the link between *the money supply, the interest rate, investment spending, and aggregate demand.* Let's examine three study cases:

First, the money market—the supply and demand for money (figure 15.6a). The *demand curve for money* (*Dm*) is inversely related to the interest rate (*i*) but is directly related to GDP. There are three potential *money supply curves* (*Sm1, Sm2, and Sm3*); all of them are vertical and represent a fixed amount of money determined by the Fed. By shifting the money supply from Sm1 to Sm2 and Sm3, the Fed is "easing"—lowering the interest rate (from 8% to 6% and, respectively, 4%). The equilibrium interest rate is the rate at which the amount of money demanded equals amount of money supplied.

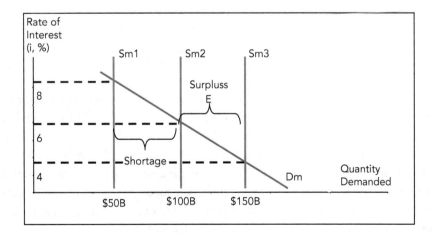

Figure 15.6a
Money Market

Second, businesses' investment is determined by the level of the interest rate. The investment demand curve is inversely related to the interest rate (figure 15.6b). Changes in interest rate affect, first of all, the investment component of total spending although these changes also affect consumer spending on durable goods purchased in credit. Changes in interest rate affect investment spending in another way—by changing the relative attractiveness of purchases of capital equipment vs. purchases of bonds. In purchasing capital goods, the interest rate represents the cost of borrowing the funds to make investments. In purchasing bonds, the interest rate represents the return on the financial investment.

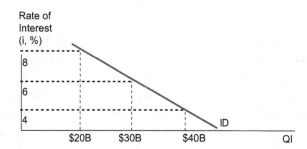

Third, equilibrium GDP—the impact of interest rates and corresponding levels of investment spending on AD consists of the following: the greater the investment spending, the farther to the right the AD curve lies (figure 15.6c). Thus, investment spending along with consumer spending, government spending, and net exports will cause the shift of AD and will determine the equilibrium level of output and prices.

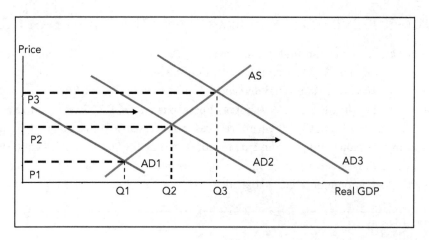

Fourth, problems and complications in managing monetary policy:

1. *Recognition and operational lags*—it takes time to recognize a problem and change the interest rate, and, after that, another three to six months will pass before this will have its full impact on investment, AD, real GDP, and prices.
2. *Changes in the velocity of money*—the number of times per year the average dollar is spent on goods and services. Velocity may counter changes in the money supply in some circumstances: it may increase the times that the Fed reduces the money supply to control inflation, and the result may not be the one targeted by the Fed. Conversely, velocity may decline at the same time the Fed takes measures to increase the money supply to combat recession.

3. *Estimating potential GDP and forecasting economic activity*—Monetary policy has an additional limitation since its effects are indirect and depend on how private sector actors (households and businesses) will react to a change in the interest rate.

Conclusion: Monetary policy or fiscal policy? Which one is considered to be more effective in stabilizing the economy? Monetary policy is considered to be more important because of its several advantages over fiscal policy: first, it is *quicker;* second, it is *more flexible;* and third, it is *more isolated and protected from political pressure*. It can be quickly altered since the Fed can buy and sell securities on the open market daily, and this affects the money supply and interest rates immediately. Recall that members of the Fed Board of Governors are appointed for fourteen-year terms and do not depend on a popular vote.

10. KEY TERMS

Money, "Token" Money, Fiat Money, Liquidity
Barter
Medium of Exchange
Standard of Value (Unit of Account)
Store of Value
Transactions Accounts
Checking, Savings Deposits
Money Market Mutual Funds
Credit, Debit Cards
Fractional Reserve System
Bank Reserve Ration
Banks Assets, Liabilities, and Net Worth
Money Multiplier
Federal Reserve System (FRS, or Fed)
Board of Governors
Federal Open Market Committee
Money Market Demand, Transactions and Asset Demand
Nominal and Real Interest
Monetary Policy Tools; Required Reserve Ration, Discount Rate, Open Market Operations
Selling, Buying Securities (Bonds)
Limitations of Monetary Policy
Recognition and Operational Lags
Velocity of Money
Estimating Potential GDP
Expansionary (Easy) and Contractionary (Tight) monetary policy

11. PROBLEMS AND APPLICATIONS

1. The central authority for US monetary policy decisions is:
    a. Twelve regional Federal Reserve banks and, first of all, New York FRB
    b. The Executive Branch of government and the Treasury Department
    c. The Federal Open Market Committee and the Federal Advisory Council
    d. The Board of Governors of the Federal Reserve

2. James just graduated from the University of North Carolina and was accepted by the local branch of Wachovia bank as a teller with a six-month probation period. Becoming a more effective specialist, he observed that the most important determinant of his clients' consumption and saving is:
   a. Level of bank credit and their credit score.
   b. Level of income, including their wages.
   c. Interest rate, Marginal Propensity to Consume and Save.
   d. Average price level.

3. One of the most important monetary policy tasks is to control the quantity of money in the US economy. In this respect, the money supply:
   a. Is controlled by the US Congress and the US Treasury.
   b. Includes savings deposits, small time deposits, and money market mutual funds.
   c. Includes coins and paper money and checking accounts.
   d. All of the above.
   e. None of the above

4. To control the money supply, the Federal Reserve Bank is using the reserve requirements ratio, discount rate, and open market operations, and the Fed is using the following monetary policy instrument:
   a. Discount rate as the "lender of last resort."
   b. Federal funds rate to regulate interbank borrowing.
   c. Monetary base and issuing money.
   d. Fixed or floatable exchange rate.

5. The money multiplier, which acts in similar way as investment multiplier:
   a. Is equal to the required reserve ratio times transactions deposits.
   b. Gets larger in the same proportion as the required reserve ratio increases.
   c. Has no limits in deposit (money) creation.
   d. Is the reciprocal of the required reserve ratio.

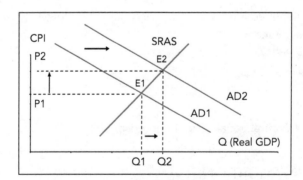

6. In the figure above, which of the following Fed actions will shift the aggregate demand curve from *AD1* to *AD2*?
   a. An increase in the discount rate that discourages borrowing funds from Fed.
   b. An increase in the reserve requirement, which will limit the excess reserves of commercial banks.
   c. The purchase of government bonds from the public or businesses in the open market by the Fed.
   d. Decrease in velocity of money.

7. An eclectic approach to the explanation of aggregate supply curve is based on following:
   a. Combines elements of both Monetarist and Keynesian assumptions about the shape of the aggregate supply curve and represents the intermediate range of the AS function (between horizontal and vertical sections of the AS).
   b. Is the supply side theory that is opposed to Monetarist and Keynesian explanations about the shape of the aggregate demand curve.
   c. Maintains a constant upward slope as the economy moves through the business cycle.
   d. Shows an increase of the AD along the Keynesian (horizontal) range of the AS until it will reach full employment and then becomes vertical.

8. The figure below shows the relationship between the demand and supply of money and the interest rates that it determines. Suppose the money market equilibrium occurs at Sm2 and D? In what position of the money supply curve will there be a shortage of money in the market, and will the Fed address it by buying/selling bonds?
   a. Sm3, and the Fed will sell bonds.
   b. Sm1, and the Fed will buy bonds.
   c. Sm1, and the Fed will sell bonds.
   d. Sm3, and the Fed will buy bonds.

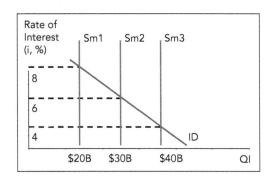

9. If the Fed sells more securities (bonds) to the commercial banks, then the money supply will:
   a. Decrease, and the AD curve will shift to the right.
   b. Increase, and the AD curve will shift to the right.
   c. Decrease, and the AD curve will shift to the left.
   d. Increase, and the AD curve will shift to the left.

12. REVIEW QUESTIONS

1. The Federal Reserve (Fed) is the central bank of the US, the "bankers' bank," and it has the Fed's "dual mandate," which means: a) zero unemployment and a stable price; b) a government budget surplus and low interest rates; c) a stable quantity of money and stable prices; d) low inflation and maximum employment.

2. "Money is what money does," the popular saying goes. So, what is money and how does money solve the problem of the double coincidence of wants: those of the buyer and those of the seller? Under what system would this occur? Is gold an example of commodity money? Explain.

3. The Fed is the only supplier of money and is doing so by issuing currency. What "backs" the money supply in the United States, and what determines the value (purchasing power) of money? Is the purchasing power of money related to the price level, and if so, how? In the US, who or what is responsible for maintaining the dollar's purchasing power?

4. Assume that Scott, a University of Arizona student majoring in economics, has $2,000 in his checking account at Town Bank and uses his checking account to withdraw $200 of cash from the bank's ATM machine. How does the M1 money supply change as a result of this single transaction?

5. The Fed is responsible for keeping the price level stable, unemployment at a low level, and a steady growth of output. What are the main functions of the Fed, and which of the following is NOT a function of Fed: a) setting reserve requirements for banks; b) advising Congress on fiscal policy; c) regulating the supply of money; d) serving as a lender of last resort.

SECTION 4

Essentials of International Economics

Can you imagine your life without international trade—without bananas from Honduras, chocolates from Nigerian cocoa beans, Colombian coffee, Indian tea, French wine, Japanese or German cars? Are you "leaving the world behind" when you backpack for an adventure in the Appalachian Mountains or the Alaskan wilderness? Most of your equipment seems to be imported—sleeping bags from China, rain gear from South Korea, knives from Switzerland, cameras from Japan, a Nokia cell phone from Finland. Even the car that you are driving might be a Toyota or a Range Rover or a Porsche Cayenne.

Do you know the true meaning of the word "Economics"? It comes from the Greek word, *economicus*, which means the affairs of the household, and, by extension, it also applies to neighborhoods, states, nations, and regions of the world.

In this section, we will examine US trade patterns and some key facts: What are the benefits and disadvantages of imports, exports, and changes in the value of the dollar? What are the motivations for and terms of trade? The concept of comparative advantage and specialization, or dividing production to minimize opportunity costs, shows why individuals gain through specialization and exchange. However, hardly a country in the world allows trade without restrictions. In this chapter, we study the rationale for various types of protectionist policies and look at various trade agreements between countries.

Then, we will turn our attention to the study of exchange rates. Exchange rates are determined by the desire of economic agents to purchase goods and assets in other countries. We will study the main determinants of supply and demand for a country's currency and analyze the impact of shifts in supply and demand on the level of the exchange rate. We will explain why a Big Mac is priced at 20,850 rupiah at the McDonald's in Jakarta (Indonesia), 3.5 euro in Paris (France), 70 baht in Bangkok (Thailand), 12 yuan in Beijing (China), 100 rubles in Moscow (Russia), and 30 ley in Chisinau (Moldova).

The chapter concludes with an overview of the global financial system today. We will look at the advantages and shortcomings of the fixed and flexible exchange rate systems that have prevailed over several decades. In closing, we will consider the process of financial liberalization taking place today throughout the world and point out that, in today's global economy, nations have become increasingly interdependent through both product and financial market linkages, creating efficiency but also vulnerabilities.

CHAPTER 16.

THE US AND THE GLOBAL ECONOMY: CHALLENGES OF MODERN TECHNOLOGY AND GLOBALIZATION

1. ECONOMIC SYSTEMS: MARKET VS. CENTRAL PLANNING, MIXED ECONOMIC SYSTEMS

An economic system represents a set of legal, institutional, and organizational arrangements based on ownership of factors of productions and mechanism of decision-making (motivation, coordination, and rewarding the economic activity). The economists are classifying economic systems into three broad categories: Market, Command (also called Central Planning) and Mixed Systems. Each of these systems makes its strategic choices through the political process. In the US, for example, Congress makes major strategic decisions. But this is not related to all situations. What, How, and For Whom to produce, as we have seen, are answered by the market through a verified price mechanism.

The Market System (capitalism) is based on private ownership and functions through market prices and sales. The Market through sales and prices provides information and incentives to producers about what mix of output the consumer wants. The system of market prices determines desired outputs and resource allocation, coordinates economic activity, and, however imperfectly it may function, through trial and error; it is not a chaotic and anarchic system. The economic decision-making is widely dispersed and is taken by each individual participant to the market, who is motivated by self-interest and assumes all risks for the consequences of his or her own activity.

We can define the market as an arrangement that allows buyers and sellers to exchange their products: buyer—money for a product; seller—a product for money. The main characteristics of the Market Systems are:

1. The right of private property which encourages investments, innovations, and stimulates economic growth.
2. Freedom of enterprise and choice that allows anyone to dispose of his or her property, choose his or her own profession, and buy goods and services that satisfy his or her wants.
3. Self-motivation and self-interest, which, in the end, promote social interest.
4. Competition of independently acting producers and consumers, who are free to enter or to leave the market.
5. Distribution of income based on ownership of factors of production (resources) and their price, etc.

Adam Smith's principle of the "invisible hand" stated: "every individual, in pursuing only his own selfish good, was led by an invisible hand, to achieve the best good for all, so that any interference with free competition by government was almost certain to be injurious." In a market system, everything has a price. Different kinds of human labor have prices, namely, wage rates. What is true for the markets and consumer goods is also true for markets of factors of production. In the end, we have a competitive equilibrium system of prices and production:

1. **What** will be produced is determined by the dollar votes of consumers;
2. **How** things are produced is determined by the competition of different producers; and
3. **For Whom** things are produced is determined by supply and demand in the markets for productive services: by wage rates, land rents, interest rates, and profits.

A dramatic example of the importance of a pricing system occurred in Germany after WWII, and is described in Samuelson's *Economics*:

In 1946-47 production and consumption dropped to a lowest level: money was worthless; factories closed down for lack of materials; trains could not run for lack of coal; coal could not be mined because miners were hungry; miners were hungry because peasants would not sell food for money and no industrial goods were available to give them in return. Prices were legally fixed, but little could be bought at such prices; a black market characterized by barter or fantastically high prices existed. Then in 1948 a "miracle" happened:

the currency reform set the price mechanism back into effective operation. Immediately production and consumption soared; again the What, How and for Whom problems were being resolved by markets and prices (Samuelson 1948).

"The Market is like evolution", stated Charles Wheelan in his *Naked Economics*, "it is an extraordinary powerful force that derives its strengths from rewarding the swift, the strong, and the smart" (p. 21). But, as President Kennedy observed, "Life is not fair" and neither is the market.

Market Failure: limitations of market mechanisms. At times, the market fails to produce an adequate amount of goods or services and also when it produces a mix of output inconsistent with society's most desired mix. The market mechanism might also fail to make full use of the economy's production possibilities. An eloquent example is the Great Depression of the 1930s and, more recently—the Great Recession of 2007–2009. The Market might select a wrong mechanism of how to produce that could result, for example, in *too much pollution*. In this case, we have to deal with *an externality*—a cost imposed by a producer or consumer on an innocent third party" (Bade and Parkin, 2014). The market might also fail to distribute income in the best possible way that will result in *too much poverty*. Sometimes, it creates the wants in the first place by advertising, or as John Galbraith observed: "It involves an exercise of imagination to suppose that the taste so expressed originates with [the] consumer."

Market failures are always a target of criticisms and an argument for more active implication of the government in the economy to correct market failure. This subject was considered in more detail in Chapter 10.

Government Failure: The government interventions became especially important at the beginning of twentieth century to prevent and smooth the consequences of fluctuations of an unregulated economy, especially those of the Great Depression, to protect property rights and enforce contracts. They are protected by two amendments to the US Constitution: the Fifth Amendment states that the Federal Government shall not deprive any person "of life, liberty, or property without due process of law," and the Fourteenth Amendment extends these guarantees to the state governments. Of course, the active implication of the government in the economy does not necessarily offer better answers and choices to the What, How, and For Whom questions. In many situations, the government fails to improve market outcomes and might not only worsen the mix of output but also even reduce the total amount of output (Bade and Parkin, 2014). According to one recent survey, only 11% of all Americans believe that government efforts to improve income distribution have succeeded. Forty-nine percent believe that the government has made the For Whom answer worse. This is a case of Government Failure.

Central Planning (i.e., socialism and communism) was established by force, first, in Czarist Russia after the revolution of 1917; it was conducted by the *Bolshevik* (communist) party. This big historical experiment led to creation of the Union of the Soviet Socialist Republics (USSR, or Soviet Union, called by Ronald Reagan the "evil empire") and administrative-command system (Central Planning) that was supposed to replace market mechanism. The major characteristics of the command system include:

a. The factors of production, including land and all natural resources, factories, financial institutions, etc., belong to the state or, according to communist ideology, to "all the people." In reality when property belongs to "all the people" and not to anyone personally, no one is responsible for its efficient use which in economics is called "tragedy of commons."

b. The authoritarian methods of coordination of economic activity by a special body, called in the Soviet Union *Gosplan* (Central Planning Board). It was an attempt to replace the market with an administrative mechanism of distribution of resources and establishment of prices according to the so-called *Piatiletki* (five-year development plans adopted by the congresses of the Communist Party of the Soviet Union (CPSU). Although communist propaganda presented those plans as "great performances" of the socialist economy, their implementation, sometimes even faster than their official terms (a popular slogan was "Five Year Plan to be implemented in four years"), led to huge disproportions and imbalances with an inefficient allocation of resources.

c. The distribution of well-being among the citizens was supposed to be equitable and egalitarian in correspondence with the slogan: "From each according to his or her capacities and to each according to his or her needs." In fact, there was not any connection between production and consumption or between labor productivity and rewards, and, as a result, consumers' wants were never satisfied, and their sovereignty was strictly limited. Not accidently, one of the most popular jokes in Soviet times among the workers was: "They pretend to pay us, and we pretend to work."

d. Freedom of enterprise, freedom of choice, incentives for technological innovation, and efficient use of resources were practically nonexistent in the former Soviet Union. The economy was strongly dominated by communist party politics and ideology, and democracy was replaced by some kind of surrogate called "democratic centralism," described in a popular saying: "When we are voting individually, we always say 'No,' but when we gathered altogether, we vote 'Yes.'"

e. Economic growth and productivity fell dramatically and had even become negative by the year of demise of the Soviet Union (1991). The desperate attempts of Mikhail Gorbachev, the last president of the Soviet Union, to modernize the system and restructure the economy (the policy known as *Perestroika*—reconstruction, in Russian), to reduce the role of Central Planning institutions, to democratize the society under the slogan of *Glasnost* (transparency, openness), and to solve interethnic conflicts had limited success and did not save the Soviet Union as a state in spite of strong internal approval, especially in the first years of a new economic policy (1985–1987) and with international support. Today, there are remnants of a command system in only a few countries, such as Cuba and North Korea and in China's official ideology and politics, but not in its economy, which is flourishing on market principles and foundations.

Mixed Economies: an economy that uses both market and nonmarket signals to allocate resources or a combination of government directives and market mechanisms to determine economic outcomes. The US economy and economies of industrialized countries, as well as economies of the former communist countries of the Soviet bloc in Central and Eastern Europe and central and southern Asia are mixed economies of various types and structures with strong market incentives and mechanisms and various degrees of government intervention.

2. THE US ECONOMY: PUBLIC VS. PRIVATE SECTORS

The United States is the leading economy in the world with one of the highest living standards based on efficient market mechanism and powerful social and cultural institutions, which in Douglas North's opinion as a Nobel Prize winning economist, represent "formal and informal rules that constraint human economic behavior." The United States is fourth largest country by territory after Russia, China, and Canada and covers about two billion acres, almost 50% of which represent forests, lakes, and national parks. Half of the land is used for agriculture, and just five percent is urban land, but urban land is growing fast while agricultural land is shrinking.

The US economy is composed by *four important components*:

1. *Businesses*—first of all, corporate business, which earned the US the title of "Corporate America," is responsible for about 80% of US production output and jobs.

2. *Households*—a group of people living together and making joint decisions—the most powerful economic institution, representing about two-thirds of total consumption expenditures in Gross Domestic Product (GDP), owning factors of production and determining governmental policy through a verified democratic mechanism.

3. *Government*—with limited participation in production and in spending (about 20% of total output) but with critically important roles as an "arbiter" between households and businesses, a guarantor of the "Rule of Law," and a provider of effective and loyal competition.

4. *Foreign sector*—represented by private and governments, investors, consumers. These key actors are playing an important role in America's economy, and we will analyze their interactions in the next chapter. Let's focus, first, on the role of the private sector in today's economy because as President Calvin Coolidge used to say, "*The business of America is business.*" To understand the business performances and challenges at the beginning of the twenty-first century, we need to examine the components of the US economy in more detail, making a distinction between technological and economic aspects and carefully analyzing their interactions.

From a technological standpoint, it is important to distinguish the various forms of industries: **a plant**—a structure that is using inputs (labor, resources, machines, etc.) to produce outputs (goods and services), a process called technology; **a firm**—an organization that owns and operates a combination of plants; and **an industry**—a collection of firms that are producing similar products. Firms may be integrated horizontally, those that are performing practically the same functions (i.e., Wal-Mart, Coca-Cola), or vertically (i.e., the "Big Three" United States automakers—General Motors, Ford, and Chrysler), those that are performing different functions in different stages of production. Some firms represent conglomerates, firms that are producing various products in a few different industries.

As there are different types of industries (a plant, a firm, an industry, and a multiplant firm) there are also various types of business organizations. From an economic standpoint, the key criterion that is used to classify them is the ownership:

1. *Sole proprietorship* is a business owned by one person with less than $10,000 in assets. It is the most common type of business, representing 80% of business firms but only 6% of sale's revenue. It dominates in agriculture, retail trade, and services. *Advantages:* easy to set up—a proprietor is his or her own boss; the profit is the proprietor's income, and there is a strong incentive to operate it efficiently. *Disadvantages:* the proprietor is subject to unlimited liability—risks not only the firm's assets but its personal assets, as well; the financial resources are limited; the proprietor carries out all management functions.

2. *Partnerships* are owned by two or more individuals, each of whom receives a portion of any profits. It accounts for 10% of all business firms and for 4% of sales revenue. *Advantages* are almost the same as in the case of sole proprietorship: easy to organize, greater specialization, better access to financial resources. *Disadvantages:* limited and insufficient financial resources; difficulties in sharing management responsibilities—the divided authority may lead to inefficient policies or actions; still unlimited liabilities; still problems with continuity.

3. *Corporations* are owned by many individuals, each of whom owns shares (stocks) of the corporation; a corporation has at least $4 million in assets; dominates the market transactions (90% of all sales). For example, General Electric, Exxon-Mobil, Wal-Mart, and Verizon own more assets than 15 million proprietorships. The corporation is the most efficient form of business organizations. It uses a unique method of finance—the selling of stocks and bonds. *Stocks* are

shares of ownership of a corporation; *bonds* represent promises to repay a loan, usually at a set rate of interest. *Advantages:* as a legal entity, the corporation is independent of its owners and its officers that permit long-run strategies and growth; easy to sell/buy stocks and easier access to bank credit; limited liability—their owners are not personally responsible (liable) for the debts or actions of the company; they risk only what they paid for the stocks. Corporations must inform those with whom they do business of this limited liability. In the US, they do so by adding the designation "Inc." or "Incorporated" to their corporate title. The British have traditionally added "Ltd" or "Limited" to the title of their corporations although the official designation was changed in 1980 to "Public Limited Company" or "PLC." The French and Spanish use a more colorful warning: Corporations' titles are followed by the letters S.A.—for *Societe Anonyme* or *Sociedad Anonima* (anonymous society). The Russians are using the abbreviation *OOO*, which means "society with limited responsibility." In addition to limited liability, the corporation offers the advantage of continuity. In law, the corporation is a fictitious "legal person." The corporation survives if some of stockholders want to get out of the business. They can just sell their shares to anyone willing to buy. *Disadvantages:* double taxation (dividends are taxed twice—as corporate profit and as stockholders' personal income); red tape and expense in obtaining a corporate charter; financial scandals and mismanagement; eventual conflicts of interests between owner objectives and manager objectives—*principal agent problem*; different interests of owners (principals) and managers (agents) often lead to the decisions not in the interest of owners and sometimes to fraud and abuse as in the Enron and WorldCom cases. The deceptive or illegal accounting practices are used to inflate company stock prices that bring huge benefits to their executives.

4. *Hybrid structures* include a) the limited liability company (LLC), which is an ordinary partnership for tax purposes (direct distribution of all profits to owners and investors) but resembles a corporation in matters of liability (shields the personal assets of owners from liability claims) and b) the S corporation (seventy-five or fewer shareholders; profit goes directly to owners and, thus, avoids double taxation).

Another key actor in American economy are Households. Their role resides in their power as owners of the most important factors of production: land, labor, capital, and entrepreneurship, which is the basic source of their income in form of wages, rent, interest, and profit. The households are the main suppliers of the labor force: 155 million people are working (or are available for work), providing about 280 billion hours of work annually (2013). Of course, quantity matters, but most important is the quality of the labor force and knowledge and skills accumulated through education, training, and work experience, which is called human capital. If before the World War II just one in 20 young Americans graduated from college, today one out of three are college graduates, over 85% are high school graduates. Improved quality of the labor force is the base for more productive work and a higher standard of living. America's inventors, innovators, entrepreneurs are generating an astonishing revolution in productivity, which is the foundation of economic power and growth and increased standard of living. According to statistical data, one American produces as much output per capita as six Chinese, out produces Japanese and Germans by about 30%, and European Union citizens by more than 40% (*Time*, March 14, 2011). That explains why the US has the world's leading economy.

The power of households resides in their control of business as suppliers of capital and as buyers of goods and services. The "dollar vote" of households determines what businesses will be produced and what will be sold. Finally, households' savings are the main source of capital investments and accumulated capital stock—more than $50 trillion in form of equipment, technology, factories, and buildings. The American economy is one of the most capital intense in the world, and this determines its role as an economic superpower.

Finally, it is impossible to understand how American economy works without analysis of the dual role of the government: "Arbiter" (referee) and "Economic Player" (actor). Since these issues are the subject of detailed analysis in the following chapters, we will limit our narrative to just a few observations.

Historically, at the beginning of the Industrial Era, the government was playing a relatively limited role, that of "night watchman" to the emerging and expanding property of a new capitalist class. The government is required to define and protect property rights today, as well, be it houses, cars, factories or ideas, inventions, songs, or artworks, called intellectual property. The government is protecting these rights by granting patents, royalties, licenses, etc. But the economic role of the government is much more important today than it was two to three hundred years ago since the modern economy is much more diverse, complex, and efficient.

As an "Arbiter," the government is required to enforce the Rule of Law, to provide rules and regulations, enforce contracts and antitrust legislation, protect consumers, workers, the environment, etc. A whole array of regulatory agencies are involved, such as EPA, FAA, FDA, FBI, IRS, INS, the US Patent Office, Federal Emergency Management Agency, NSA, and many others on the federal and state level. To better understand the importance of this principle on which the market system is based, let's refer to Hernando de Soto, the president of the Institute for Liberty and Democracy, headquartered in Peru: "Imagine a country where nobody can identify who owns what, addresses cannot be easily verified, people cannot be made to pay their debts, resources cannot conveniently be turned into money, ownership cannot be divided into shares, descriptions of assets are not standardized and cannot be easily compared, and the rules that governed property vary from neighborhood to neighborhood or even from street to street. You have just put yourself into the life of a developing country or former communist nation … What you are really leaving behind when you are traveling to these countries is the world of legally enforceable transactions on property rights" (Hernando de Soto. *The Mystery of Capital. Why Capitalism Triumphs in the West and Fails Everywhere Else*. Basic Books, 2000, pp. 15–16).

As an "Economic Player," the government is required to enhance the productive capacity of the nation, to promote economic development and improve the standard of living, and to reduce poverty and inequality. The government is providing so-called "public goods" (such as national defense, public education, building roads, and bridges), is redistributing wealth and ensuring the equitable distribution of income through taxation, Medicare, and Social Security. In short, the government is playing its role through various forms, mechanisms, of economic intervention, always facing a dilemma about which one to apply: "helping hand" or "grabbing hand.". By global standards, the United States Government has a relatively limited role and limited share in nation's property.

3. THE UNITED STATES OF AMERICA AND THE GLOBAL ECONOMY

What is the role of the US in the Global Economy? How are the US and the world economies interconnected in the process of recovering after the last major economic crisis 2007-08, called Great Recession? Is America's recent economic growth disappointing in comparison with other industrialized nations, or does it serve as a locomotive for the Global Economy? How does What, How and For Whom apply to the US and the Global Economy?

To address these issues, we need to introduce, first, some general information. The world population is more than 7.2 billion with about 330 million in the United States. According to the International Monetary Fund (IMF,) 189 economies are classified into three broad categories:

1. *Advanced economies*—Twenty-nine industrialized countries in North America (USA and Canada), western Europe (including Germany, France, Italy, United Kingdom, Spain) and Asia (Japan and newly industrialized Asian economies) add up to a population of about one billion people. Representing 15% of the world population, advanced economies' share in global production is

more than 50% due to more efficient and productive economies. The US is producing more than one-fifth of the global pie with less than 5% of the global population (figure 16.1). Industrialized economies are coordinating their decisions about global development in the framework of such institutions as the Organization of Economic Cooperation and Development (OECD), Group Seven of the most advanced nations (G-7), composed of the United States., Japan, Germany, France, United Kingdom, Italy, and Spain.

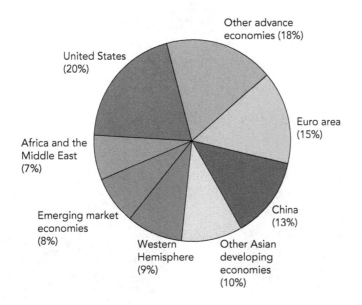

Figure 16.1 Global Production (Source: Bade and Parkin, *Foundations of Economics*, seventh edition, 2015.)

2. *Emerging markets*—twenty-eight countries in Europe and Asia, including the former Soviet Union and its Central and Eastern European satellites with approximately 500 million people (7.5%). There are some other classifications, for example, *BRIC* (an acronym composed of the first letter of the following countries: Brazil, Russia, India, and China) that comprise 42% of the global population with 28% share in global production, almost half of which is produced in China. The members of this organization have regular meetings to discuss various economic development issues, sometimes in opposition with advanced economies because BRIC is trying to counterbalance their influence. We will examine the roles of emerging markets in the world economy in more detail in section 4 of this chapter. Technology, Innovation and Information

3. *Developing economies*—One hundred thirty-two countries in Africa, Asia, the Middle East, Europe, and Central and South America, 5.5 billion people (77.5%). In spite of growing shares in the manufacturing sector, developing countries still remain the main producers and exporters of energy and natural resources (figure 16.2). The agricultural sector represents a large part of total production and provides employment for the majority of the working population of these countries although about 33 percent of the world's total agricultural output is produced by advanced economies.

The most important differences between these groups of countries reside in human capital accumulated though education, training and experience, and physical capital, with the much more sophisticated equipment, technologies, and infrastructure in advanced economies. Advanced economies are characterized by a rapidly increasing share of the service sector (about two-thirds of the US economy), the declining role of manufacturing, and an insignificant share of agriculture in the structure of production and employment (figure 16.3).

Figure 16.2
Global
Production of
Energy
Resources
(Source: Bade
and Parkin,
*Foundations of
Economics*, 7e.)

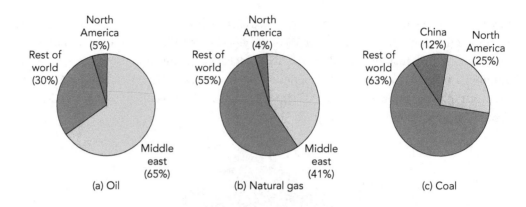

(a) Oil   (b) Natural gas   (c) Coal

Figure 16.3
Century of
Changes in the
US GDP
(Source: B.
Shiller,
*Essentials of
Economics*, 8e.)

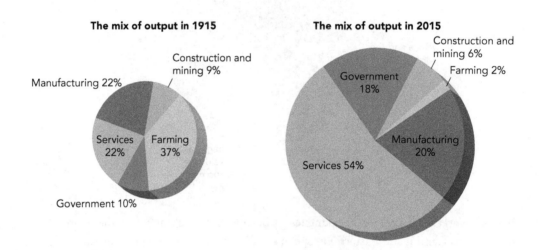

4. THE KNOWLEDGE ECONOMY: KEY TO COMPETITIVENESS AND ECONOMIC GROWTH

There is a direct correlation between knowledge, measured by the Knowledge Economy Index (KEI), and the level of development of the economy, its future growth rate. The larger the stock of accumulated knowledge, the higher the level of economic growth and development. Sustained long-term economic growth is a function of the quantity and quality of the factors of production, of their total productivity. In pursuit of long-term, self-sustainable growth and an increase in total factor productivity, the most important objectives, according to the World Bank Institute Special Report, are: a) creating a learning (knowledge) economy, with improving the quality of education, especially of higher education, as a priority; b) stimulating entrepreneurship and organizational efficiency; c) promoting competition and openness, particularly trade openness; d) building effective institutions and institutional infrastructure to implement long-term strategies; and e) managing urban systems to take advantage of agglomeration economies and positive spillover effects (WBI, *Pathways to Development*, 2011).

The Knowledge Economy Index (KEI, 2008) is a broad measure of preparedness of a country for the knowledge economy, summarized by a country's performances on twelve variables related to four knowledge economy pillars. The United States placed eighth in 2008, losing five positions from 1995 and, so, has lost ground in all four pillars. A higher KEI is associated with future higher rates of economic growth and development and vice versa. The US is in the top ten only on the innovation pillar (no. 7) and is no longer on the other three (WBI. *Measuring Knowledge in the World's Economies*, 2011).

The most impressive performers in this period (1995–2008) are, again, the BRIC countries: Russia climbed three positions, India climbed four, Brazil climbed eleven, and China climbed eighteen. These evolutions are closely related to the quality and effectiveness of education systems, which have been a priority for the last decade in the US, yet the results are still in doubt. In a set of standardized International Student Assessment tests, administered by the Organization for Economic Cooperation and Development (OECD) across more than sixty countries, the United States ranks close to the average in reading and science and well behind most countries in mathematics. Clearly, education should be boosted to restore the competitiveness and efficiency of the US economy and to ensure higher rates of growth.

The United States economy has some very strong comparative and competitive advantages that could make changes. How can we make the economy stronger and more competitive? The answer could be found in the budget proposal of the US administration for the 2013 fiscal year, starting October 1: $137 billion in spending proposals designed to spur economic growth by funding education and other programs that the White House describes as "mandatory."

5. AMERICAN ECONOMIC SUPREMACY: TECHNOLOGY, INNOVATION, INFORMATION, AND EDUCATION

More than 50 years ago, Gordon Moore, co-founder of Intel, a chipmaker, predicted that the computer's processing power doubles roughly every two years as smaller transistors are packed onto silicon wafers, increasing performance and reducing the cost. This rule of thumb is known as Moore's Law. The first commercial microprocessor chip, 4004, produced in 1971, contained 2,300 tiny transistors. Today's Intel Skylake processor contains about 1,75 billion transistors and has about 400,000 times more computing muscle. That stylish little slab in your pocket is 100,000 times more powerful that the computer behemoths of the 70s that occupied entire basements. If the transistors of 1971 were blown up to the height of a person, the modern Skylake devices would be the size of an ant. What is the future of computing? Are we coming to the end of Moore's Law? What are the areas of improvement for future computers? The answer to these questions is not only in technology but in economics, as well, and this is the area where these two disciplines are closely intertwined. Finally, the importance of Economics of Technology is related to the power and competitiveness of the US economy as the number one global power. *The Economist* magazine published a special report on the future of computing after Moore's Law with the title: "Double, double, toil and trouble" (*The Economist*, March 12, 2016).

Let's explore some of most important aspects of the role of technology, innovation, information, and education, the core components of the Knowledge Economy, for the current status and the future of American economic supremacy.

First, the most important technological transformations reshaping the world economy, providing new paradigms of development, and boosting economic growth in twenty-first century have their home in the United States, particularly:

1. Informational technology—the software revolution—with the Internet evolving into the "Cloud,"—a network of thousands of big-data centers that makes the supercomputer of 1990s look like an antique—led to the emergence of new markets with new services, products, and businesses that were unimaginable just a decade ago.

2. New material science—the smart manufacturing revolution—in combination with automation and information systems, 3D printing radically changed not only "what" but "how" our economy is producing and created new parameters "for" the quality of economic growth, representing the first tectonic structural shift since Henry Ford launched the system of "mass production."

3. Communication systems—the wireless revolution—opened new opportunities for billions of people to communicate, socialize, and trade—is transforming our economy into what is called "Borderless Economics." It's all about talent, the most important core resource that makes the US the richest and most powerful economy in the world (Guest, Robert. 2011. *Borderless Economics*. Palgrave Macmillan).

Second, the unique opportunities for entrepreneurship—a traditionally strong American characteristic, advantaged by favorable business cultures, mature venture capital industries, the integration of universities and industry, and an open immigration policy, placed the United States first in the 2009 Global Entrepreneurship Monitor Survey to provide such opportunities. (GEM is an academic consortium assessing entrepreneurial activity worldwide.) (Subramanian, Arvind. 2011. *Foreign Affairs*, September/October p. 72). These opportunities for inventors, innovators, entrepreneurs, and workers led to an astonishing revolution in productivity: one American produces as much, per capita, as six Chinese and out produces Japanese and Germans by nearly 30% and the citizens of the European Union by nearly 45% (Drehle D. 2011, *Time*, March 14, p.35.).

Third, American higher education, often criticized as inadequate to meet contemporary global challenges, is still the best system in the world and a strong generator of economic growth, supported by:

1. Higher public and private spending on education, research and development—sine qua non (an essential action) condition of future growth performances (close to 6% of GDP over the last quarter century)—than that of China, Brazil, India, Japan, Russia, and the EU.

2. Best universities, according to the classification of the Institute of Higher Education at Shanghai Jiao Tong University of the world's top 20 universities, all but three are American and of the top 10, more than half are American. They employed 70% of the world's Nobel Prize winners and produced more than a third of the world's output of articles on science and engineering (Joffe J. 2009, *Foreign Affairs*, September/October, p.30).

3. The key to America's higher education system's success lies in its organization: in its flexibility and diversity, in its competition for everything from students and professors to basketball stars, in forging links between academia and industry, and in the limited intervention of the government (there is no central plan for its universities). A unique combination of great research universities, pro-risk business culture, with innovation-seeking equity capital, and reliable business and contract law makes this massive technological shift unparalleled in the world and a profoundly positive environment for the American economy (Andreessen, 2011 *The Wall Street Journal*, August, 20.).

The world is changing and so is the American system of higher education. There is a lot of work to do to keep up, to address the wave of new criticism, and to manage the risk of erosion of its competitive principles. Among these challenges are the following: "The universities are no longer devoted to free inquiry as they ought to be"; "America's universities are pricing themselves out of the range of ordinary Americans" with astonishing increases in annual tuition costs; "The universities are becoming bastions of privilege rather than instruments of social mobility" (*The Economist*, 2005). But it should be also stressed that in good times or bad, Americans have always worried about falling behind, and this, most probably, could better explain why the US is still Number One, the leading economic power with good prospects for regaining its "Sputnik momentum."

6. KEY TERMS

Economic Systems: Market, Central Planning (Command-Administrative), Mixed
Market Failure, Government Failure
Sole Proprietorship, Partnership, Corporation, Hybrid Economic Structure
Households, Businesses, Governments, Foreign Sector
Advanced, Developing, Emerging and Transition Economies
Knowledge Economy
Knowledge Economy Index (KEI)
Software Revolution, Smart-Manufacturing Revolution, Wireless Revolution
Global Economy, Globalization
Economics of Technology

7. PROBLEMS AND APPLICATIONS

1. Why is the US economy one of the leading economies of the world?
   a. Its products make up about a quarter of total world output.
   b. It produces as much output as China.
   c. It is the second economic power of the world after the European Union.
   d. It produces 20% less than Japan but ten times more than Russia.

2. What is human capital, and how it is different from labor factor of production?
   a. It refers to the productive capabilities of labor, and it is accumulated through education, experience, and training.
   b. It cannot be increased without a large population.
   c. It requires a high ratio of capital, land, and other inputs to labor.
   d. It is the result of business investment and government spending.

3. The most important criteria to distinguish among corporations, partnerships, and proprietorships consists of:
   a. The number and technological characteristics of firms in each classification.
   b. Type of ownership characteristics.
   c. The size of the firms and industry as a whole.
   d. The size of profits, revenues, and sales.

4. Why are technological advances so important for economic growth and development?
   a. The allow production output to increase in quantity and move faster than manufacturing employment.
   b. They make it possible to grow more food with fewer workers and protect the environment.
   c. They contributes to increases in productivity of labor and efficiency of production
   d. All of the above.
   e. None of the above.

5. Which of the following characterizes a corporation?
   a. The owners are personally responsible for the actions of the company.
   b. It is typically owned by one or two individuals.
   c. It dominates market transactions and sales and is the largest by assets.
   d. It has unlimited liability.

8. REVIEW QUESTIONS

1. What is an economic system, and what are the basic criteria of classification of economic systems? Is the world, as a whole, still classified into First-, Second-, and Third-World economies?

2. What are the main characteristics of the market system? What are its advantages and limitations? Why does a market fail sometimes? Is the government always successful in correcting market failures?

3. The central planning system is characterized by _____ (public/private) ownership of factors of production, by _____ methods of coordination of economic activity, distribution of well-being among citizens according to the slogan _____, and, in reality, _____ (existent/nonexistent) freedom of enterprise, freedom of choice, and incentives for technological advance.

4. The US economy is _____ (market/administrative/mixed) with relatively _____ (big/moderate/small) government, and _____ (low/high) economic freedom and _____ (strong/weak) corporate sector.

5. The share of advanced countries in the global economy is _____, the share of the United States is _____, and the share of developing countries is _____. Is China's economy a market economy, central planning, or mixed economy?

IMAGE CREDITS

CHAPTER 17.

INTERNATIONAL TRADE AND FINANCE

1. WHY NATIONS TRADE: A GLANCE AT HISTORY'S LESSONS

More than eight decades ago, the US Congress tried to "leave the world behind" when it passed one of the most famous trade laws in American history—*The Tariff Act of 1930,* better known as *"Smoot-Hawley"* which amended "specific tariff schedules for over twenty thousand items, almost all of them increases." It established the highest general tariff rate structure that the US had ever experienced: duties actually collected reached an average of 20%, but for durables—one third of imports—they peaked at an unbelievable 60%! The US lawmakers, trying to protect national producers from foreign competition, forgot one of the classical principles of economics formulated almost two and a half centuries ago by Adam Smith. He emphasized that if a foreign country can supply us with a commodity cheaper than we can make it, better buy it from them with some part of the produce of our own industry, employed in a way in which we have some advantages (Adam Smith. *The Wealth of Nations,* p. 424). Markets exist because individuals can gain from specialization and exchange. Trade among countries is based on the same principles of trade between individuals. Specialization based on comparative advantage results in gains for all participants.

Let's also recall founding father Thomas Jefferson's wise advice: "Our interest will be to throw open the doors of commerce, and to knock off its shackles, giving freedom to all persons for the vent of whatever they may choose to bring into our ports, and asking the same in theirs."

What followed after Smoot-Hawley passed is well known. The law quickly occasioned, as one critic put it, "more controversy, more comment, and more vituperation in the national as well as in the international sphere than any other tariff measure in history. Country after country raised its tariff barriers in retaliation." World trade stagnated: for the United States, imports dropped from $4.40 billion in 1929 to $1.45 billion in 1933, and exports plunged even more: from $5.16 billion to $1.65 billion. The Great Depression—already well underway in 1930—deepened and become truly global. World War II followed less than a decade later. So, when nations are not involved in trade, they are trying to solve their disputes and animosities by force.

But barely four years after Smoot-Hawley, the American Congress enacted an entirely different sort of trade law. *The Reciprocal Trade Agreements Act of 1934* began a movement of tariffs in the opposite direction—downward—by authorizing the president to negotiate and implement pacts with other nations in which each agreed to cut tariffs on US exports by up to 50%, without further recourse to Congress. And the authority was renewed in 1937, 1940, and 1943. By 1945, the US had entered into thirty-two such bilateral trade agreements with twenty-seven countries, granting tariff concessions on 64% of all dutiable imports and reducing rates by an average by 44%. Under American leadership, the *General Agreement on Tariffs and Trade (GATT)* was negotiated and established (1947); it became, the prototype of the current World Trade Organization (WTO).

International trade enables nations to specialize their production, enhance their resource productivity, and acquire more goods and services. International trade expands the production possibilities frontier, raises the living standards of a country, and acts like an additional factor of production. To address the question *"why do nations trade?"* we have to consider three main arguments:

1. The endowments of economic resources are different for different nations since the distribution of natural, human, and capital resources among the nations is uneven.
2. Differences in technology, knowledge expertise level, and combinations of resources in different countries could make the production of various goods and services more efficient in one country than in another.
3. Products are differentiated as to quality and other nonprice attributes, and consumers may want foreign produced items rather than similar domestic products because their tastes and preferences are different. You may want to drive a Mercedes rather than a Cadillac or to buy a Sony Plasma TV, a Samsung DVD player or a bunch of roses imported from Colombia, etc.

Based on these arguments, we can explain why Japan is efficient in producing labor-intensive goods (digital cameras, video games, DVD players); why Australia is efficient in production of *land-intensive goods*, such as wheat, wool, and meat; and why Brazil is efficient in producing coffee; etc. Industrially advanced countries can inexpensively produce *capital-intensive good*, such as automobiles, agricultural equipment, machinery, and chemicals. The distribution of resources, technology, and products among nations is not forever fixed. One of the most convincing examples is South Korea, which half a century ago was one of the less developed countries in the world, an exporter of only agricultural products; now, it has joined the club of industrially advanced nations and is exporting large quantities of manufactured goods, including cars, TVs, refrigerators, etc.

2. INTERNATIONAL TRADE AND THE US ECONOMY

The United States is one of the leaders in the world in volume of trade (one-eighth of world exports) although exports of goods and services make up about 11% of the total US output (in the Netherlands—62%, Canada—41%, New Zealand—33%, and the United Kingdom—26%). During the last three decades, US exports have doubled as a percentage of GDP. In 1960, the United States exported 5% of total US production and imported 4%. Currently, China has the largest share of world exports, followed by Germany and the United States. The eight largest export nations account for almost half of the world's exports (China, Germany, US, Japan, the Netherlands, France, Italy, and Belgium).

Obviously, international trade affects our standard of living. In 2009, *US imports* (goods and services purchased from foreign sources) of over $2 trillion of products and services (travel, insurance, or entertainment) accounted for about 14% of US GDP. *US exports* (goods and services sold to foreign buyers) were over $1.5 trillion, including farm products (wheat, corn, soybeans), machinery (computers, aircraft, automobiles), raw materials (chemicals, iron ore, lumber), and services (tourism, insurance, and software). Many American industries are heavily dependent on exports (Boeing, Caterpillar Tractor, Eastman Kodak, Dow, Coca-Cola, and Pepsi, etc.).

Manufactured goods account for 54 percent of our exports and 66 percent of our imports. Services account for 30 percent of exports and 17 percent of imports. Trades of services include shipping, insurance, travel, and food while abroad. The value of exports minus the value of imports is called the *balance of trade*. In 2009, the United States imports of goods and services exceeded exports by $517 billion, causing a negative trade balance (trade deficit). But the US had a positive trade balance (surplus) on export of services, which exceeded imports by $138 billion. Canada is the largest US trading partner, followed by China, Mexico, and Japan (figure 17.1).

Like many other advanced countries, the US imports some of the same categories of goods and services that it exports (automobiles, computers, chemicals, semiconductors, telecommunication equipment). The question is *why does the US import many of the same products that it produces?*

The explanation is the same as what motivates individuals to specialize in production. Why, for example, don't you grow your own food or build your own home? Adam Smith, father and founder of economics, provided an answer in his famous *The Wealth of Nations* (1776): "It is the maxim of every prudent master of a family, never to attempt to make at home what it will cost him more to make than to buy. The tailor does not attempt to make his own shoes, but buys them of the shoemaker. The shoemaker does not attempt to make his own clothes, but employs a tailor. The farmer attempts to make neither the one nor the other, but employs those different artificers ..." (p. 424). Exactly the same is the situation with different nations. Specialization increases the production of output. The two countries that trade can together produce more total output than they could in the absence of trade.

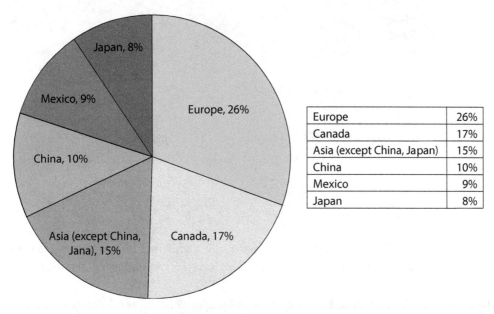

Figure 17.1
US Trading
Partners

Europe	26%
Canada	17%
Asia (except China, Japan)	15%
China	10%
Mexico	9%
Japan	8%

What kind of goods characterize US trade patterns: more capita-intensive goods or less capital-intensive goods? Many economists assume that US exports are more capital-intensive than imports because US workers are better equipped with capital and advanced technology than the workers of its trading partners' countries. But Vassily Leontief, an American economist of Russian origins and Nobel Prize laureate in Economics, made a surprising discovery in 1953: the goods that the United States imported were slightly more capital-intensive that those exported. This discovery was named after him—the *"Leontief paradox."* Today, US exports are less physical capital-intensive and more human capital-intensive, which is caused by a substantially higher share of highly educated workers in comparison with other countries. For example, one of the basic export industries in the US is aircraft production, which uses a large number of engineers and peoples with doctoral and professional degrees relative to manual workers.

3. MOTIVATIONS TO TRADE: COMPARATIVE VS. ABSOLUTE ADVANTAGE

To explain what motivates countries to trade, let's consider an example. Suppose the world economy is composed of only two nations, the US and Mexico, and that they are producing just two goods, wheat and avocados (figures 17.2a and b).

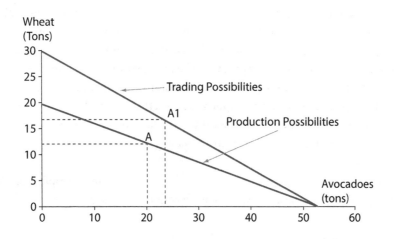

Figure 17.2a
US Trading
Possibilities

Figure 17.2b
Mexico Trading
Possibilities

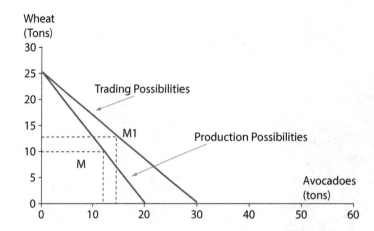

We have to analyze their Production Possibilities Curves (the alternative combinations of goods and services that could be produced in a given time period with available resources and technology), making three assumptions:

1. The curves are straight lines and not concave to the origin, which means that both countries have *constant costs*; to simplify the analysis, we will ignore the effects of increasing opportunity costs.
2. The PPC of these two countries reflect different combinations of resources and differing levels of technological advance and, therefore, *different cost of production*, which tells us how the opportunity costs of producing these two goods differ between the US and Mexico.
3. The US, a country of superlatives, richly endowed with human, capital and natural resources, has an *absolute advantage* in producing almost everything, including wheat and avocados; a country may have an *absolute advantage if it is producing some specific goods with fewer resources (per unit of output) than another country.* This advantage might exist because of its *much longer experience* in cultivating a farm product (grapes, for example) or just because it has *more talent, better education, better capital endowment, etc.*

What are the motives of these two countries to trade with these two goods? To understand this mechanism, we have to consider the *principle of comparative advantage* which says that total output will be greatest when each good is produced by the nation that has lowest domestic opportunity cost in producing that good. In other words, the *comparative advantage* is *the ability of a country to produce a specific good at a lower opportunity cost than its trading partners.*

In our example, the US has the lower opportunity cost for wheat, so the US has a comparative advantage in wheat and should specialize in its production. Similarly, Mexico has the lower opportunity cost for avocados, a comparative advantage in producing them, and should specialize in avocado production. Both countries would not be employing their resources economically if avocados, for example, can be produced by a higher-cost producer (US) rather than by a lower-cost producer (Mexico). World output and the potential gains from trade will be maximized when each country pursues its comparative advantage. It does so by exporting goods that entail low domestic opportunity costs and importing goods that involve higher domestic opportunity costs.

All we care about is the *opportunity cost*—what we have to give up in order to get more of a desired good. There are at least three sources of comparative advantage:

1. *Differences in climate and geographical conditions*; for example, tropical products, obviously, cannot be produced in Alaska or Scandinavian countries at the same cost as in Hawaii or tropical Africa;

2. *Differences in resource endowment*, which are explained in an influential model of international trade, the *Hecksher-Ohlin model*, developed by two Swedish economists in the first half of the twentieth century. The key notion of this model is *factor intensity* which describes differences between goods in terms of the ratio of capital to labor (oil refining is capital-intensive while clothing production is labor-intensive). According to this model, a country has a comparative advantage in a good when production is intensive in factors abundant in that country.

3. *Differences in technology*, based on superior techniques of production and accumulation of human capital through knowledge, education, and training.

4. TERMS OF TRADE: GAINS AND LOSSES FROM INTERNATIONAL TRADE

The Production Possibilities Curve (PPC), as we saw in earlier chapters, defines the limits to what a country can produce, and in the absence of trade, a country cannot consume more than it produces. The PPC also defines the *consumption possibilities*—the alternative combinations of goods and services that a country could consume in a given time period. Like a self-sufficient person, a country that doesn't trade can only consume the goods and services it produces.

First, international trade breaks the link between production possibilities and consumption possibilities. When nations specialize in production, not only does the mix of consumption change but the quantity of consumption increases, as well. Both countries end up consuming more output by trading than by being self-sufficient. With trade, a country's consumption possibilities exceed its production possibilities.

At what exchange ratio will the US and Mexico trade wheat and avocados? The United States must get a better "price" (more avocados) for its wheat in the world market than it can get domestically; otherwise, there is no gain from trade, and it will not occur.

1. Just as a Production Possibilities Curve shows the amounts of products a full employment economy can obtain by shifting resources from one to the other, a *trading possibilities line* shows the amounts of two products a nation can obtain by specializing in one product and trading it for the other. Specialization and trade create a new exchange ratio between wheat and avocados in our example, reflected in each nation's trading possibilities line. This exchange ratio is superior for both nations due to the unspecialized exchange ratio embodied in their PPC. Specialization, according to the principle of comparative advantage, results in a more efficient allocation of world resources, and larger outputs of both products are, therefore available to both nations. As a result of specialization and trade, both countries have more of both products. Let's recall that a nation can expand its PPC by:
   a. expanding the quantity and improving the quality of its resources; or
   b. realizing technological progress.

   Now we can add another factor:
   c. A nation can expand its PPC by understanding that the outcome of international specialization and trade is equivalent to having more and better resources or discovering improved production techniques.

Second, what are the terms of trade? Terms of trade are the rate at which goods are exchanged. First of all, we have to look at a country's domestic opportunity cost—a country will not trade unless the terms of trade are superior to domestic opportunity costs. We can assume that the terms of trade between any two countries lie somewhere between their respective opportunity costs in production. The terms of trade, like the price of any good, depend on the willingness of market participants to buy or sell at various prices.

The quantity of a good that a nation will export or import depends on differences between the equilibrium world price and the equilibrium domestic price. The *world price* is the price that equates the quantities supplied and demanded globally. The *domestic price* is the price that would prevail in a closed economy without international trade. In the absence of trade, the domestic prices in a closed economy may or may not equal the world equilibrium prices. Note that in the absence of trade (figure 17.3a), the equilibrium domestic price of a good (Pd) and the equilibrium quantity (Qd) are determined by the intersection of domestic demand and domestic supply curves, and consumer and producer's surpluses are maximized, assuming that there is perfect competition. A situation in which a country cannot trade with other countries is called *autarky*. When economies are engaged in trade, differences between world and domestic prices (Pw − Pd) form the basis for exports or imports (figure 17.3b).

Third, who are the winners and losers, and what are the net gains from trade?

1. Let's start with analyzing gains and losses from *imports* by examining their effect on consumer surplus, producer surplus, and total surplus. Winners see their surplus increase while losers see their surplus decrease. Figure 17.4 shows the market for T-shirts in the United States. The world price of a T-shirt ($5) is less than the US price ($13), so the United States imports 24 million T-shirts, and US producers reduce their production to 9 million, being unable to compete with cheaper foreign produced T-shirts. The consumers in this situation are clearly winners: consumer

Figure 17.3a
Consumer and
Producer
Surplus in
Absence of
Trade (Autarky)

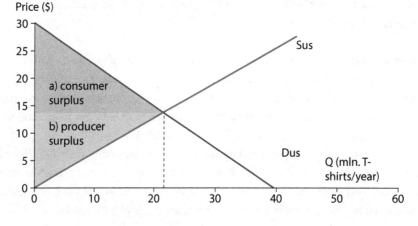

Figure 17.3b
Consumer and
Producer
Surplus with
Trade

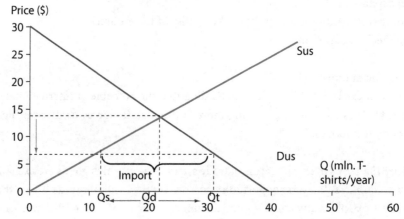

surplus increases and equals the sum of areas $A + B + C + D$. Of this amount, area B is lost by producers and gained by consumers. Areas C and D are newly gained surplus resulting from the trade. At the same time, the producer surplus decreases and equals area E. Without trade, the producer surplus would be the sum of areas $B + E$. It is important to note two points: a) opening up the market to imports increases the total economic surplus ($ABCDE$) by the amount of area $C + D$ and b) the consumers' gain exceeds the producers' losses. So, the United States is better off with trade although domestic producers lose as a result of international trade.

2. The gains and losses from **exports** are, likewise, calculated by examining their effect on consumer surplus, producer surplus, and total surplus. Figure 17.5 shows the market for airplanes in the United States. The world price of an airplane ($250 million) exceeds the US domestic price ($150 million), so the United States exports 200 airplanes.

Producer surplus increases and equals the sum of areas $C + B + D$. Of this amount, area B is lost by consumers and gained by producers. Area C is newly gained surplus resulting from the trade. Consumer surplus decreases and equals area A. Without trade, consumer surplus would be the sum of areas $A + B$. Note also two important points: a) the total economic surplus as a result of export increases by the amount of area C and b) the producer's gains are larger than consumers' losses. So, the United States is better off with trade although domestic consumers of a particular good are hurt by increased domestic prices.

	Autarky	With Import
Consumer Surplus	a	a + b + c + d
Producer Surplus	b + e	e
Econimic Surplus	a + b + e	a + b + c + d + e

Table 17.1

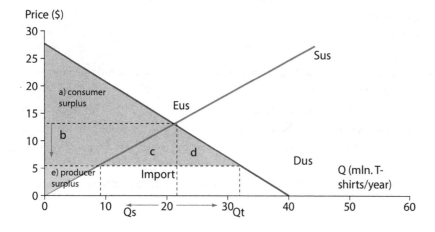

Figure 17.4
Effects of
Import on
Surpluses

	Autarky	With Import
Consumer Surplus	a + b	a
Producer Surplus	b + d	d + b + c
Economic Surplus	a + b + d	a + b + c + d

Table 17.2

Figure 17.5
Effects of
Export

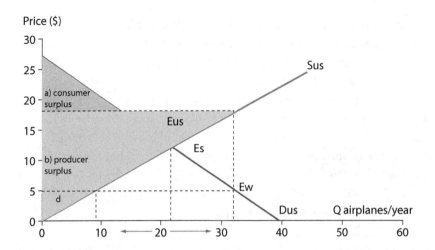

5. FREE TRADE AND BARRIERS TO TRADE: ECONOMIC EFFECTS

The case of free trade, trade without government restrictions, is backed by one compelling argument: through free trade, based on the principle of comparative advantage, the world economy can achieve a more efficient allocation of resources and a higher level of material well-being. David Ricardo, one of the most famous followers of Adam Smith, laid out the principle of comparative advantage in his book *Principles of Political Economy and Taxation* (1817). In his analysis of the principles of comparative advantage, he used as an illustration the production of wine and cloth in Portugal and England. Also, his legacy includes the theory of economic growth in which he posited that the economy ultimately would reach a "steady state" and cease to grow. A strong supporter of freedom of speech and an opponent of government corruption, Ricardo, nonetheless, enjoyed tremendous popularity and was frequently called on to speak at the British House of Commons. Since that time, most economists have advocated free trade, arguing that the government should not attempt to reduce or to increase the level of exports and imports that naturally results from the interaction of demand and supply in free markets.

The main benefits of free trade are:

1. It promotes competition and deters monopoly power, forcing domestic producers to be innovative, improve quality, and decrease costs.
2. International specialization increases the Production Possibilities Curve by raising the productivity of resources and the efficiency of production and contributing to economic growth; government barriers to trade act in the opposite direction—they reduce or eliminate gains from specialization.
3. Free trade links national interests and breaks down national animosities; trading partners tend to negotiate rather than to be engaged in wars.

Nevertheless, there is no free trade anymore except in the free trade zones. Despite economists' free trade arguments, governments extensively use *trade protection policies* under the motive of protection of domestic producers from foreign competitors in import-competing industries. Let's consider the main trade barriers and their effects on economic efficiency.

1. *Tariffs*—excise taxes on imports used as leverage for revenue purposes or as mechanisms to protect domestic producers from foreign competition (figure 17.6).

The tariff is one of most efficient restrictions on trade and is also called customs duties. In the eighteenth century, the British government imposed tariffs on the American colonies on tea, glass, wine, and lead. In 1773, a tariff on tea led to the Boston Tea Party and served as a spark for the American Revolution. At the beginning of twentieth century, the Germans introduced a new and higher tariff on "brown and dappled cows reared at a level of at least 300 meters above sea level and passing at least one month in every summer at an altitude of at least 800 meters." It was a selective tariff. The Germans wanted to lower the tariff on cattle imports from Denmark—the Danish cows never climbed that high—without extending the same break to Switzerland.

Loss in Consumer Surplus	Increase in Producer Surplus	Government Tariff	Dead Weight Loss	
a + b + c + d	a	c	b + d
Table 17.3 |

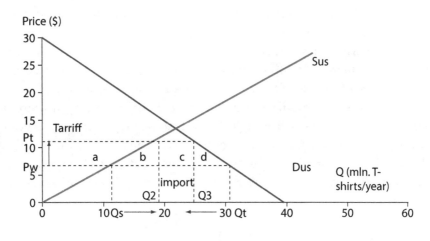

Q2 – Qs = increase in production by US Firms
Q3 – Qt = decrease in US consumption

Figure 17.6
Effects of a
Tariff on Ethanol
(Consumer and
Producer
Surplus)

a. Decline in consumption: US consumers are clearly injured by the tariff since they pay more for respective domestic substitutes. The losses in consumer surplus are reflected by areas: A + B + C + D;

b. Increased domestic production: domestic producers are clearly advantaged because they enjoy both a higher price and expanded sales. Increased producer's surplus is expressed by area A;

c. Decline in imports: Japanese producers of DVDs, for example, are hurt—the higher sales prices benefited the US government and not Japanese producers. In our example, these are areas B and D which represent deadweight losses;

d. The tariff revenue is a transfer of income from consumers to the government (area C) and does not represent any net change in the nation's economic well-being.

Tariffs are used as a means of import protection. In the US, tariffs are imposed on 9,000 different products that represent nearly 50% of all US imports. Although the average tariff is less than 5%, they vary widely from 2.5% on cars to 17.8% on cotton sweaters. A tariff on imported goods increases their prices and makes them less competitive with domestically produced similar goods. In the US, tariffs are applied for such goods as Scotch whiskey ($0.20), champagne ($0.76), baby food (34.6%), and imported stereos (4 to 6%).

There are also some *indirect effects*. Because of tariffs, Japanese producers receive fewer dollars, and, therefore they can buy fewer American export products. Tariffs, in this case, directly promoted inefficient domestic industries that do not have comparative advantages. They also indirectly cause the contraction of efficient industries that do have comparative advantages. So, resources are shifted in the wrong direction, and tariffs may reduce efficiency and the world's real output.

2. *Import quotas* are an alternative barrier to trade. A quota is a limit on the quantity of a good that may be imported in a given time period. Approximately 12% of American imports are subject to import quotas, such as sugar, meat, dairy products, textiles, cotton, peanuts, steel, cloth diapers, ice cream, etc. From 1959 to 1973, the US maintained a quota on imported petroleum. Low import quotas may be a more effective protective device than tariffs, which do not limit the amount of goods entering a country. At the same time, quotas are a much greater threat to competition than tariffs because quotas preclude additional imports at any price. The economic impact of quotas is similar to that of tariffs in terms of losses of consumer surplus and gains of producer surplus as Figure 17.7 shows, but it can be worse because no revenue is generated for the government. A tariff generates government revenue that can be used to cut other taxes or to finance public goods and services that benefit the US. In contrast, the higher price created by quotas results in additional revenue for foreign producers. According to some estimates, about 70% of the total cost of US import restrictions comes from transfers of quotas to foreigners. The most surprising is the fact that import licenses (mainly for sugar and clothing) are granted to foreign governments.

Figure 17.7
Effects of
Quotas on
Sugar Surpluses

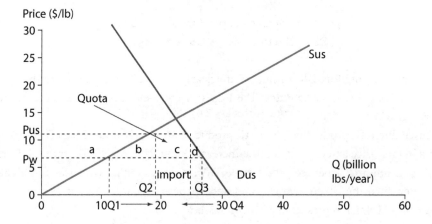

3. *Nontariff barriers (NTBs).* Tariffs and quotas are just the most visible barriers to trade. There are a lot of NTBs that are licensing requirements calling for adherence to unreasonable standards pertaining to product quality and safety or unnecessary bureaucratic red tape used to restrict imports. NTBs during last twenty years have increased along with the decline in tariffs. The US uses NTBs (product standards, licensing restrictions, restrictive procurement practices) to restrict 15% of imports; Japan restricts 30% of imports in this way. In 1999–2000, the EU banned imports of US beef because of the health hazards created by the use of hormones in US ranches.

The US responded by slapping 100% tariffs on dozens of EU products. The United Kingdom uses restrictions for issuance of licenses as a barrier for imports of coal.

4. *Voluntary export restrictions (VERs)*—agreements by foreign firms to "voluntarily" limit their exports to a particular country. In the 90s, Canadian producers of softwood lumber (fir, spruce, cedar, and pine) agreed to VERs on exports to the US under the threat of a permanently higher US tariff. Japan voluntarily limits its auto exports to the United States.

Protection raises the price of a product in three ways: 1) the price of the imported product goes up; 2) the higher price of imports causes some consumers to shift their purchases to higher-priced domestically produced goods; and 3) the prices of domestically produced goods rise as a result of the decline of import competition. The gains that US trade barriers create for protected industries and their workers come at the expense of much greater losses for the entire economy. The result is economic inefficiency.

6. THE POLITICAL ECONOMY OF PROTECTIONISM

Let's consider the *main arguments for protection* and how credible they are:

1. *The national security argument:* Some industries, especially those associated with national defense, should be protected to guarantee their operation in wartime and independent from other countries. But in a time of war, there is no industry that does not contribute to national defense. It is more efficient to achieve higher production in target industries through the use of subsidies rather than trade barriers. This is a veiled argument and is open to serious abuse since nearly every industry can claim that it makes direct or indirect contributions to national security.

2. *The infant industry argument:* Protection of a new industry to make it competitive in world markets. This argument is similar to the diversification argument for protection and may be used for temporarily shielding young domestic firms from international competition. But what are the criteria to determine which industries are the best to be protected? Protection, after all, may persist after industrial maturity is realized, and the economic cost maybe great, exceeding the benefits.

3. *The dumping argument:* Dumping is *the selling of excess goods in foreign markets at a price below cost.* But there are some shortcomings here: a) firms can use dumping to drive out domestic competitors and to obtain monopoly power and monopoly prices and b) dumping may serve as a form of price discrimination by charging different prices to different customers. To protect against such action, the US Federal Government can impose tariffs called "antidumping" duties on specific goods.

4. *Saves jobs*: The argument that trade protection saves jobs is flawed. International trade changes the type of jobs in an economy, but it does not decrease employment in the aggregate because jobs lost in one sector are offset by jobs created in other sectors. Let's consider the much speculated argument about *offshoring* (outsourcing), which is related to a shift of domestic firm production and jobs to other countries with cheap labor forces. Offshoring boomed in the Internet era (beginning in the 1990s) when the cost of telecommunication fell drastically, and it made it cheaper to move production to different countries. But this is also a flawed argument because differences in real wage rates generally reflect differences in productivity. So, when we think about competitiveness, we must consider both differences in wages and differences in productivity.

According to some recent studies: a) the job losses from outsourcing represent a normal phenomenon in a modern economy and are related to changes in technology and consumer tastes over time. Survey data suggest that roughly 2% of reported layoffs are caused by offshoring, which is not significant considering that, on average, 4.5 million workers quit or are fired each month and 4.6 million start a new job; b) the jobs lost to outsourcing are compensated for, at least partially, by new jobs created by *insourcing*, which is movement in the opposite direction from overseas to the US; and c) outsourcing is substantially decreasing the cost of production, and, respectively, the price for consumer, and is increasing the output and profitability for firms.

The political economy of protectionism includes some other arguments: a) *it brings diversity and stability* (the advanced economies are already diversified, but this argument may be relevant for smaller developing or emerging markets); b) *it penalizes lax environmental standards;* many low income countries have comparable environmental standards, and the best way to encourage improved environmental standards is to allow trade and the economic benefits (jobs, income) it brings to poorer countries; and c) *it protects national culture* (if governments truly believe in positive spillovers from domestic culture, it is more efficient to provide subsidies than to restrict foreign competition).

WHY IS INTERNATIONAL TRADE STILL RESTRICTED DESPITE ARGUMENTS AGAINST PROTECTION?

There are several key economic interests and benefits from protection:

1. *Tariff Revenues*: Tariffs provide a relatively inexpensive way for the government to collect revenues, and for some countries, especially small emerging markets, this represents one of the most significant source of budget revenues.
2. *Rent Seeking*: Rent seeking is lobbying and other political activity that seeks to capture the gains from trade. The costs imposed on consumers of tariffs and quotas are big numbers, but they are relatively small per person. For example, the sugar quota's total burden is more than $2.2 billion per year on consumers, but spread across 300 million Americans, it is only about $7.5 per person—too little to worry about. So, the benefits are concentrated on a smaller number of producers, and it is in their interests to promote protection by political lobbying.
3. *Compensating Losers*: When the gains from free trade exceed the losses, it is possible to compensate the losers so that everyone is in favor of free trade, for example, with unemployment compensation and job-retraining programs. However, it is hard to identify exactly who has lost a job as a result of free international trade and not for other reasons and to provide respective compensation for them. The conclusion is: by not trading, we do not increase our living standards at all.

7. TRADE AGREEMENTS AND FREE TRADE ZONES

In 1947, on the initiative of the United States, twenty-three of the world's largest trading nations signed the *General Agreement on Tariffs and Trade (GATT)*, which was based on three principles: 1) equal, non-discriminatory trade for member nations; 2) reduction of tariffs through multilateral negotiations; and 3) elimination of import quotas. At each of nine rounds of GATT negotiations, the tariff rates in developed countries were reduced from 40% in 1947 to 6.3% by 1986 and by the last, Uruguay round (1994), to 3.9%. At the Uruguay round, 117 nations signed the agreement to form the *World Trade Organization (WTO)*, which replaced GATT. They agreed to several trade liberalization measures: a) reductions in tariffs worldwide;

b) new rules to promote trade in services; c) reductions of agricultural subsidies that have distorted the global pattern of trade in agricultural goods; d) new protections for intellectual property (copyrights, patents, trademarks); and e) phasing out of quotas on textiles and apparel, replacing them with gradually declining tariffs. According to WTO estimates, the world output for 2005 was $6 trillion greater (8% higher) because of trade liberalization.

The WTO was created to resolve any dispute under the trade rules and to meet periodically to consider further trade liberalization. The WTO ruled in favor of the US in 2000 when the EU banned US beef imports, and it authorized the US to impose retaliatory tariffs. Later on, the WTO ruled in favor of the EU when the US raised the tariffs on steel in 2003, and the EU imposed retaliatory tariffs on $2.2 billion of US exports. The WTO is composed today of 153 nations (2010). De facto, the WTO has become the world's trade police force. It is empowered to cite nations that violate trade agreements and even to impose remedial actions when violations persist. The most recent round of negotiations started in 2001 in Doha, Qatar, but they collapsed in 2008, mostly because of China and India, rapidly growing economies with populations exceeding one billion people. China and India were interested in supporting their roaring manufacturing industries rather than promoting agricultural exports, which interested developing countries. The updated status of negotiations can be found at www.wto.org.

The *North American Free Trade Agreement (NAFTA)* took effect in 1994 and was implemented over nineteen years. It was designed to eliminate all tariffs and other trade barriers among Canada, Mexico, and the United States. In spite of predictions by some that NAFTA could become a "giant US job-sucking mechanism," the number of jobs in the United States between 1994, when NAFTA went into effect, and 2007 increased by more than 21 million, and each family of four's consumption increased by $400 per year. NAFTA may be extended to other interested nations in the Western Hemisphere.

The most dramatic example of creating regional free trade zones is the *European Union (EU),* which was designed to remove all trade barriers within Europe and create a "single market." Initially (1958), it was created by six European nations (Belgium, Germany, France, Italy, Luxemburg, and the Netherlands) as their "Common Market." By 2003, it comprised fifteen nations, and in 2004, the EU was expanded to include ten other countries, mostly Central and Eastern European former communist states. In 2007, the EU was joined by Bulgaria and Romania to form its present size of twenty-seven nations. The achievements of the European Union include: a) abolishment of tariffs and quotas for almost all products traded among the participants; b) establishment of a common system of tariffs and preferences for trade in products from outside the EU; c) liberalized movement of capital and labor; and, most significantly, d) creation of the Euro Zone (sixteen countries) in the early 2000s, which uses the common currency—the euro. The euro replaced the national currencies, such as German marks, French francs, Italian liras, Greek drachma, etc. (exclusions are the UK, Denmark, and Sweden, which chose not to join the euro, at least for now). It should be mentioned that the EU has achieved for Europe what the US constitutional prohibition on tariffs by individual states achieved for the United States: increased regional specialization, greater productivity and output, lower costs due to economies of scale, and economic growth. Of course, the EU did not eliminate all controversies and problems that its members are facing, particularly during the recent crisis, which threatens to start a movement in the opposite direction—disintegration—at least for those economies most affected by the crisis (Greece, Spain).

The document that formed the *Asian Pacific Economic Cooperation (APEC)* was signed in 1989 to reduce trade barriers among its nations, and, today, it has twenty-one nations.

Some critics believe that regional free trade accords and zones will make global agreements more difficult to achieve by creating new barriers, such as "Fortress North America," "Fortress Europe," "Fortress Asia," etc. Some others suggest that there is a link between increased trade and increased wage inequality. For example, if the US increases its exports of products requiring skilled labor, the demand for skilled labor and its wages will rise. And, if the US imports more goods requiring less skilled labor, the wages of unskilled workers in the US will fall.

8. INTERNATIONAL FINANCE: HOW DO WE FINANCE INTERNATIONAL TRADE?

A majority of financial transactions fall into two large categories: international trade and international asset transactions. The sum of all these transactions between residents of a country and residents of foreign countries is reflected in a country's *balance of payments*; in other words, a country's accounts record its international trading, borrowing, and lending (figure 17.8). The US Commerce Department's Bureau of Economic Analysis compiles a balance of payment statement each year. It includes three balance of payments accounts:

1. The *current account* includes payments for imports of goods and services from abroad, receipts for exports of goods and services sold abroad, net interest income paid abroad, and net transfers (such as foreign aid payments). The *current account balance* equals exports plus net interest income plus net transfers minus imports. In 2010, this account was $471 billion, which means that the US imported more goods and services that it exported, resulting in a negative trade balance.
2. The *capital and financial account* records payment flows for financial capital (real estate, corporate stocks, bonds, government securities, etc.): foreign investment in the United States minus US investment abroad. In 2010, this account equaled +$473 billion, which means that there was more foreign investment in the US than US investment abroad.
3. The *official settlements account* records the change in *US official reserves*, which are the government's holdings of foreign currency, certain reserves held with the International Monetary Fund (IMF), and stocks of gold. An increase in foreign reserves corresponds to a negative official settlements account balance. The sum of the balances always equals zero: *current account + capital account + official settlements account = 0.*

Table 17.5
The US Balance of Payments Accounts (2010, $$ billion)

Exports of goods and services	+1,838
Imports of goods and services	−2,338
Net interest	+165
Net transfers	−136
Current account balance	**−471**
Capital account	
Foreign investment in the U.S	+1,246
U.S. investment abroad	−1,005
Other net foreign investment in the U.S	+15
Statistical discrepancy	+217
Capital account balance	**+473**
Official settlements account	
Official settlements account balance	**−2**

(Source: Bureau of Economic Analysis [www.bea.gov].)

Facing current account deficits or surpluses, countries can be characterized as borrowers or lenders:

1. A country that is borrowing more from the rest of the world than it is lending to it is a *net borrower*; if a country has borrowed more from the rest of the world than it has loaned, it is called a *debtor nation*;
2. A country that is lending more to the rest of the world than it is borrowing from it is a *net lender*; if a country, during its entire history, has invested more in the rest of the world than other countries have invested in it, this country is called *creditor nation*. The United States became a net debtor in 1984 for the first time in about seven decades, changing its status from the largest creditor to the largest debtor nation. The concern is that the US international debt, which has been rising during recent years due to large trade deficits with China, Japan, Canada, and other countries, is artificially increasing the standard of living.

Let's recall that the formula of national accounts could be expressed in two equations:
$Y = C + I + G + X - M$ and $Y = C + S + NT$, where S means savings and NT means net taxes. Rearranging these equations: $(X - M) = (S - I) + (NT - G)$. This formula shows that *net exports*—the difference between exports and imports $(X - M)$—equal the sum of the *private sector balance*—saving minus investment $(S-T)$—and the *government sector balance*, which is net taxes minus government expenditure on goods and services. So, the level of net exports is determined by the private sector balance and the government sector balance.

9. FOREIGN EXCHANGE MARKETS AND FOREIGN EXCHANGE RATES

First, the exchange rate is the price of one country's currency expressed in terms of another country's currency. There are two types of exchange rate systems:

1. A *flexible or floating exchange rate system*. Demand and supply determine exchange rates and no government intervention occurs.
2. A *fixed exchange rate system*. The government determines exchange rates and makes any necessary adjustments in its economy to maintain those rates.

Exchange rates are a critical in global pricing of goods and services. For example, to determine the dollar price of an imported good (French wine), we have to multiply a) the foreign nation's price of a good (Euro) by b) the dollar-euro (or other currency) exchange rate.

Second, global prices of all imports and exports are changing with the changes in exchange rates. There are two cases:

1. *Currency ($$) appreciation*—an increase in the value of one currency relative to another; when the dollar price of pounds, for example, rises, the dollar has depreciated relative to the pound (and the pound has appreciated relative to dollar).
2. *Currency ($$) depreciation*—a decrease in the value of one currency relative to another.

If the value of a nation's currency declines, its exports become cheaper, and its imports become more expensive. In Brazil in 1999, when the currency (the real) depreciated by more than 70%, all foreign-made products became too expensive for Brazilians. But American tourists made Brazil a high point of their travels.

A foreign currency is a good like many others, and the exchange rate is a price for this good. The price of this good (foreign currency) depends on the supply and demand.

Third, international exchange rate systems (three main cases):

1. *The gold standard.* Between 1879 and 1934, the major nations adhered to a fixed rate system called the *gold standard.* This system collapsed in 1930s under the pressure of the Great Depression. Under this system each nation must:
   a. define its currency in terms of a quantity of gold;
   b. maintain a fixed relationship between its stock of gold and its money supply; and
   c. allow gold to be freely exported and imported.

2. *In 1944 in Bretton Woods* (New Hampshire), major nations held a conference and produced a commitment to a modified fixed exchange system called an *adjustable-peg system,* or, simply, the Bretton Woods system. This system was intended to maintain the advantages of the gold standard (fixed exchange rate) and avoid its disadvantages (painful domestic macroeconomic adjustment). The conference created the International Monetary Fund (IMF) to make the new exchange rate system feasible and workable. The system ended in 1971 with the demise of the thirty-seven-year-old policy of exchanging gold for dollars at $35 per ounce, and the US dollar finished its history of being as "good as gold" under the pressure of permanent deficit of the US balance of payment.

3. *The current international exchange system* (1971–present) is an almost flexible system called *managed floating exchange rates.* Exchange rates among major currencies are free to float to their equilibrium market levels, but nations occasionally use currency interventions in the foreign exchange market to stabilize or alter market exchange rates.

10. KEY TERMS

International Trade
Import, Export, Trade Balance
The Tariff Act of 1930 ("Smoot-Hawley")
The Reciprocal Trade Agreements Act of 1934
General Agreement on Tariffs and Trade (GATT)
"Leontief Paradox"
Comparative Advantage
Absolute Advantage
Hecksher-Ohlin Trade Model
Trading Possibilities Line
Terms of Trade
World Price, Domestic Price
Free Trade
Trade Protection Policy
Tariffs, Import Quotas, Nontariff Barriers (NTB), Voluntary Export Restrictions (VER)
National Security Argument
Infant Industry Argument
Dumping Argument, Anti-Dumping
Balance of Payment (BOP)

Current Account, Capital Account, Official Settlement Account
Exchange Rates: Flexible (Floating), Fixed
Currency Appreciation, Currency Depreciation
International Exchange Systems: The Gold Standard, Bretton Woods (Adjustable) Peg System, Current
(Managed Floating) Exchange System
Debtor, Creditor Nations
World Trade Organization (WTO)
European Union (EU)
Asian Pacific Economic Cooperation (APEC)
North American Trade Agreement (NAFTA)

11. PROBLEMS AND APPLICATIONS

1. A country has an absolute advantage in the production of certain goods. How do you define absolute advantage?
   a. The ability of a country to produce a specific good with fewer resources than other countries.
   b. The ability of a country to produce a specific good at a lower opportunity cost than its trading partners.
   c. Total market domination by one country of the production and sales of a certain good or service.
   d. The ability of a country to guarantee itself more favorable terms of trade at the expense of its trading partners.

2. Suppose, the world price of a good is below the domestic price in a country not involved in its trade. Then, this country:
   a. Will benefit from exporting that good.
   b. Has the comparative advantage in the production of that good.
   c. Will not engage in trade for that good.
   d. Will benefit from importing that good.

3. If the two countries are trading with each other, then the terms of trade between them should:
   a. Be in the favor of the country with the least comparative advantage.
   b. Be in the favor of the larger country.
   c. Be between their respective opportunity costs in production and factor intensity of production.
   d. Allow each country to develop its area of absolute and comparative advantages.

12. REVIEW QUESTIONS

1. How would the following transactions be categorized in the US balance of payment accounts? Would they be counted in the current account (as a payment to or from a foreigner) or in the financial account (as a sale of assets to or purchase of assets from a foreigner)? a) A Russian importer buys a case of California wine for $500; b) An American who works for a German company deposits his paycheck, drawn on a Berlin bank, into his New York bank; c) An American buys a bond from a Chinese company for $10,000; d) The American Red Cross sends $500,000 to sub-Saharan Africa to provide food for local residents.

2. The following example is a perfect study case for using notions of comparative advantage in a concrete situation. Suppose Nation A's opportunity cost of tables is five chairs while Nation B's opportunity cost of tables is only one chair. Which nation should produce tables, and which should produce chairs? What are the terms of trade between the two nations?

3. Explore current trade disputes on the World Trade website (http://www.wto.org). Pick one or two of these issues and search for additional information in *The Wall Street Journal, The Economist,* and other media, and try to analyze the nature of controversy.

4. Search on the website of the US Trade Representative (http://www.ustr.gov) to find the key trade issues for the US government in trade with China, Mexico, Saudi Arabia, and Israel.

5. The United States has, from time to time, restricted imports of steel from EU as the EU is restricting import of the United States' genetically modified food; for example, what arguments have the US and EU used to justify these restrictions (quotas, tariffs, etc.)? Who wins from these restrictions, and who loses?

CHAPTER 18.

TOWARD A NEW GROWTH ECONOMIC MODEL IN THE CONTEXT OF GLOBALIZATION

One of the most used words in today's public life is "hope," along with the word "change." The world economy is emerging from the 2007–2009 recession with some unusual characteristics: sluggish and uncertain recovery of the advanced economies, improved performances of the emerging economies, and a vigorous ascendance of the BRIC countries (an acronym for the first letters of Brazil, Russia, India, and China). They are at the core of the club of "growth economies" and are complemented by a few other economies (South Korea, Mexico, Turkey, Indonesia), each one contributing at least 1% to global output. But the most important impact of the recent crisis has been a redistribution of hope, an erosion of confidence in free markets and liberal capitalism and in the capacity of governments to reestablish the macroequilibrium with sustainable economic growth, low unemployment, and low prices, especially on oil and other energy recourses.

Restoring this confidence and regaining market credibility is crucially important to revising the existent model of economic growth, putting the emphasis on the knowledge economy and its major impact in the form of a) an information technology revolution and b) a pro-entrepreneurial revolution. We need to rethink economics itself, to redefine one of its most important concepts—economic growth—in the new context of globalization and human behavior. This concluding chapter is based on my articles and reports, which I have presented at various national and international conferences, on the financial crisis of 2007–09, a new paradigm of economic growth, and the role of emerging markets in post crisis recovery. I was inspired by the recently published books and articles on these subjects by Nobel Prize laureate in Economics Paul Krugman, who I have the privilege to know personally, Joseph Stiglitz, and Michel Spence, as well as by the well-known economists F. Myshkin, S. Mihm, N. Roubini, K. Rogoff, C. Reinhart, J. O'Neill, R. Frydman, M. Wolf, and others.

1. THE GREAT CRASH OF 2007–2009: CAUSES AND CONSEQUENCES

The end of 2007 and the beginning of 2008 were marked by a historical event: the world economy entered a major downturn in the face of the most dangerous shock in mature financial markets since 1930, with the United States lying in the center of the intensifying global financial storm. This extraordinary financial shock that started in August 2007, as the US subprime mortgage market collapsed, caused a significant slowdown of the world economy: an alarming drop in global growth in 2008, a decline in 2009—the first contraction since WWII—and a reemergence of economic growth in 2010–2012; but this growth was still well below its potential, according to International Monetary Fund estimations.

The recent global financial crisis was rapidly spreading throughout the world, having several symptoms besides dodgy lending: a tide of cheap money from emerging markets, outdated regulations, government distortions, and poor supervision. As *The Economist* stressed, "First there was disbelief and denial. Then fear. Now comes anger." To find solutions, it is important to focus on the causes rather than on the symptoms of the crisis that poisoned the faith in the free market, created an unprecedented situation, and required unprecedented, more systemic, and more global measures than before. It is necessary to look at the roots of the problems of the current financial system that have been accumulating during the last decades. Martin Wolf, the *Financial Times* columnist, in the recently published *Fixing Global Finance*—one of the most detailed and profound analyses of the global financial system's weaknesses—mentioned: "the failure of the past led to the so-called imbalances of the present" that are at the core of the current financial crisis. He described it as the outcome of a series of "obvious failures" to understand and appreciate:

1. the inherent risks of liberalized financial markets and market-oriented institutions' decisions;
2. the greater risks when finance crosses frontiers, especially for fragile emerging markets economies;
3. the inherent risks of borrowing in foreign currencies by debtor countries, and the importance of greater fiscal and monetary discipline;

4. exchange rate risks undertaken by both creditors and debtors in a world of liberalized capital movements;
5. what it means to live with exchange rate instability in today's multicurrency world; and
6. the importance of modernization of global institutions in time.

The 2007–2009 crisis is the deepest and most synchronized global recession since the Great Depression. Nouriel Roubini, professor at New York University's Stern Business School, characterized it as the "largest leveraged asset bubble and credit bubble in the history of humanity, [a] housing bubble, a mortgage bubble, an equity bubble, a private equity bubble, a hedge funds bubble, a bond bubble" that are "all now bursting at once in the biggest real sector and financial sector deleveraging since the Great Depression." This crisis has been provoked by a few major interrelated causes:

1. Excessive housing price appreciation elsewhere, with the collapsing of the housing market in the US, first of all.
2. Too low US savings rates, which were negative even a few years ago, with a recent upward tendency (5–10% of total income).
3. Too high savings rates in "excessive exporter" countries with a subsequent excessive export dependency on an unsustainable US consumer.
4. Unsustainable current-account imbalances (US, UK. and other advanced economies) and unsustainable current account surpluses (China, Germany, and Japan).

As the aggregate value of losses of banks' and other financial institutions' holdings reached $4.05 trillion in 2009 alone, just $1.1 trillion was available to help fix the problem. Cumulatively, during the three years of recession, Americans lost 33% of their largest and most valuable assets—equity in their homes (valued at $13 trillion at their peak in 2006 and $8.8 trillion in 2008)—22% of their total retirement assets—the second largest household asset (from $10.3 trillion to $8 trillion)—$1.2 trillion in savings and investments—and $1.3 trillion in pension assets. These losses together reached a staggering $8.3 trillion (it should be mentioned that the 2008 U.S. GDP was $14.2 trillion).

The most striking conclusion came from the 545-page report of the US Congress's Financial Crisis Inquiry Commission: the 2007–2009 financial crisis was an "avoidable" disaster caused by widespread failure in government regulation, corporate mismanagement, and heedless risk-taking by Wall Street.

2. POST-CRISIS RECOVERY: GENERATORS, RISKS, AND EFFECTS OF REBALANCING THE ECONOMY

The world economy's post crisis recovery (4.0% annual increase of global output) is a two-speed process, with a subdued 2.0% annual growth in advanced economies (the IMF expects the euro-zone economy to contract 0.3% in 2012 before growing by an anemic 0.9% in 2013, which could shave 2% from global economic output) and much more impressive rates for emerging and developing economies: 7% in 2011 and 6.0% in 2012 and 2013. The BRIC countries' growth prospects are even more optimistic, with 8.6% and 8.2%, respectively (IMF. *World Economic Outlook,* September, April 2011, April 2012).

The weak and unstable recovery of the US economy—1.7% growth in 2011, with forecasts of 2.1% for 2012 and 2.4% for 2013, is due to several reasons: severe deterioration of households' net worth during the three years of recession (by 25–30%); a persistent high unemployment rate (above 8.0%); and restrictive credit policies of banks that are still reluctant to lend.

First, generators of economic recovery. The challenges and potential of growth economies, emerging and developing markets that once were called "Third World," are obvious: a) eighty-five percent of the world population with the biggest potential and rapidly expanding consumer market; b) the largest explored reserves of oil, natural gas, and other energy and mineral resources; c) an impressive annual growth rate over the past few years with just a slowdown during the recession; and d) a "wall of money," more than $5 trillion in Central Bank reserves with much bigger rates of saving in comparison to advanced economies. These trends represent the most remarkable transformation at the beginning of the twenty-first century.

The US economy needs, today, perhaps more than ever, booming private investments and booming exports and its own "growth engine," which is the knowledge economy. To ensure strong and sustainable global economic growth, two rebalancing acts are necessary: internal rebalancing based on increasing private demand in advanced economies, which will lead to fiscal consolidation, and external rebalancing, requiring a rise in net exports in deficit economies, such as the United States, and a decrease in net export in surplus economies, especially those emerging in Asia (IMF. *WEO,* October 2010). To understand how these two difficult and intertwined rebalancing acts could be achieved, it is important to focus on a new paradigm of economic growth with an emphasis on the knowledge economy. The knowledge economy is at the core of a "*soft revolution*" and has four main pillars—an economic and institutional regime, education and skills, an information and communication infrastructure, and an innovation system (WBI. *Measuring Knowledge in the World's Economies*). The knowledge economy arises as the main driver of economic growth at the beginning of twenty-first century.

Second, risks of rebalancing the economy. Experts of the World Economic Forum (WEF) published the Global Risks–2011 Study on the eve of the G-20 meeting in Davos (G-20 is the abbreviation for the summits of the leaders of twenty of the most advanced nations), Switzerland (January 2011). The study indicated two major forces provoking global risks and generating external and internal imbalances: 1) economic disparities between countries and within states and 2) poor management on the global scale. These two major risks are complemented by three other types of risks: a) macroeconomic imbalances and volatility of exchange rates; b) the illegal economy, which amounted to $1.3 trillion by 2009; and c) depletion of natural resources, demand and prices for which, especially for food and energy, are expected to increase by 30–50% during the next few decades. These major risks are amplified by other types of risks, such as cyber security, demographic volatility, volatility of prices for resources, withdrawal from globalization, and the proliferation of weapons of mass distraction. The WEF experts believe that "Twentieth century systems are failing to manage twenty-first century risks; we need new networked systems to identify and address global risks before they become global crises."

The bigger the gap between the financial sector and the "real" economy, the riskier financial games and manipulations become, especially with the exotic financial instruments known as over-the-counter derivatives; the risks of a crash also become more inherent and, when a crash occurs, it is much more spectacular than whatever was came before.

The US government's financial and banking system policies represented the most powerful US administration policy reactions to the crisis, implemented through conventional and unconventional monetary policies, bank "stress tests," and bailouts of a few banks and financial institutions. The problem, as Frederic Mishkin, professor at Columbia University, emphasized, was in the modus operandi of the Fed during the crisis: "massive experimentation in an unprecedented situation: that is, it was employing a large number of measures to contain the crisis, not knowing exactly which ones would work."

Third, the effects of post crisis rebalancing policies. The paradoxical effects of the recent crisis are still dominating the agenda of the G-20, World Forums, and other international institutions, scholarly research, and debates. It is important to reassess the role and power of the developed and emerging markets, create a new post-Washingtonian Consensus, revise the economic development model, and, obviously, rethink economics itself. The most important consequences of this crisis, in the opinions of Nancy Birdsall and Francis Fukuyama, are:

1. The *"end of the foreign finance fetish."* It is the right time to learn that open capital markets combined with unregulated financial sectors are disasters in waiting.
2. A new respect among developing countries for the *political and social benefits of a sensible social policy* with increased social spending to reduce poverty and inequality. Since 1985, the share of national income of the top 1% has increased more in the US than in any other developed country—from 9 to 15 percent—but this has not contributed to increased economic growth and a "rising tide for all."
3. A necessity for *a new industrial policy*—a country's strategy to develop specific globally competitive industrial sectors, to encourage private investments in new industries and technologies, and to address coordination problems and other barriers with a more active role for the government.
4. A vital necessity to *reform public sectors* if countries are to promote industrial development and provide a social safety net.

The post crisis period will be recorded as the year that challenged (and eventually reshaped) the existing global financial system with its most critical issues: deep and prolonged asset market collapses, profound declines in output and employment, and the big jump in the real value of government debt—86%[1] on average.

Creating a twenty-first century regulatory system is the most pressing requirement and response to the crisis. As US President Barack Obama stressed, "it means using disclosure as a tool to inform consumers of their choices, rather than restricting those choices … We can make our economy stronger and more competitive, while meeting our fundamental responsibilities to one another."

3. EMERGING MARKETS' CHALLENGES

What is the role and contribution of the emerging markets in addressing the global financial system's problems? Will this crisis halt the rise of emerging economies? Will these economies follow the US and advanced countries into another global recession? Can these countries "decouple" and protect themselves from this global tendency? Or maybe the crisis is an opportunity for emerging economies, especially for those of BRIC (Brazil, Russia, India, and China), to make their decisive contributions to the stabilization of the world economy after the Great Recession? When Deng Xiaoping, the former Chinese leader, started China's economic reforms more than three decades ago (March 1978), Western economists argued that "only capitalism can save China"; now they claim that "only China can save capitalism." The emerging markets are hardly a homogenous group, but they are facing similar challenges and find themselves caught in the worldwide economic panic.

First, it is necessary to underline *what represents the emerging markets,* which are now the largest economic bloc[2]. The term was introduced in 1981 by Antoine van Agtmael, the author of *The Emerging Markets Century,* who was trying to launch a "Third World Equity Fund." He believed that "emerging markets" sounded more positive and invigorating than "third world," a term associated with poverty and stagnation. Later on, a

---

1   Carmen M. Reinhart and Kenneth S. Rogoff, The Aftermath of Financial Crises, December 19, 2008. www.economics.harvard.edu/faculty/rogoff/ff/files/Aftermath.pdf, p. 2.

2   The Washington-based Institute for International Finance classified as "emerging market economies" countries from four world regions: Asia/Pacific: China, India, Indonesia, Malaysia, the Philippines, South Korea, and Thailand; Latin America: Argentina, Brazil, Chile, Colombia, Ecuador, Mexico, Peru, Uruguay, and Venezuela; Europe: Bulgaria, the Czech Republic, Hungary, Poland, Romania, Russia, Slovakia, and Turkey; Africa:/Middle East: Algeria, Egypt, Morocco, South Africa, and Tunisia. To these economies should be added at least a dozen of other countries, such as Azerbaijan, Armenia, Georgia, Kazakhstan, Moldova, Ukraine, and other former Soviet Union states, as well as Albania, Croatia, Serbia, Slovenia, Vietnam, and some other ex-communist countries.

group of fast-growing economies of Southeast Asia (Singapore, Hong-Kong, Taiwan, and South Korea) were tagged the *"Asian Tigers"* until they ceased to roar, being halted by the financial crisis of 1997–98. In 2001, Jim O'Neal introduced the term *BRIC* for the economically largest emerging markets: Brazil, Russia, India, and China, decoupling from this group such countries as South Korea and Mexico as "fully emerged" already. To this league I would add some other performers, such as Nigeria, which has enjoyed, in recent years, one of the strongest performances of any emerging market, and some of the Gulf economies, including Saudi Arabia, the world's largest market by market capitalization.

Second, the emerging markets also comprise the former communist bloc countries of Central and Eastern Europe, including the three *"Baltic Tigers"* (Estonia, Latvia, and Lithuania), which experienced the worst policy dilemmas during the recent crisis with hefty current account deficits and fleeing capital; they slipped into recession after a decade of robust economic growth. It should be emphasized that the former communist countries faced the worst crisis since the collapse of the centrally planned economic system. The differences between ex-communist countries are often greater than those that distinguish them from the western European economies. Correspondingly, the risks of exposure to the crisis were different.

Assessed as the gap between the country's stock of exchange reserves and the external-financing needs (the sum of the current-account balance and the stock of short-term debt), the absolute risk of a crisis was greater for only sixteen of forty-five emerging market countries. All of them are in Central and Eastern Europe: a) starting with Latvia, a new European Union member and, not long ago, a performer—with the highest growth rate in Europe, following by Hungary, characterized by the EU's largest debt-to-GDP ratio; b) continuing with Ukraine, desperately struggling for its economic survival with a 50% devaluation of its currency, the *hryvna*, and a 30% decline in industrial output; and c) finishing with the poorest ex-communist economies of Tajikistan, Moldova, and Turkmenistan, which are highly dependent on remittances sent home by their workers abroad (10–40% of GDP).

If these countries were not very much affected by the recent financial meltdown, it is only because there was not much to melt. Their biggest threat and danger is the so-called contagion, or domino effect: failure in one country could spark a disaster in another, with much more grave repercussions and in far less manageable forms. Examples of contagion could be the collapse of currencies, the depositors' loss of confidence in the safety of their savings and attempts to convert them into hard currency, and finally, the disenchantment of the population in democratic values, in "the magic" of free markets; this could lead to the revival of nostalgic tendencies for strong authoritarian rule and "good czars." The cumulative effect of such a contagion is much stronger than it might appear, at first glance. "There's a domino effect," mentioned Kenneth S. Rogoff, a professor at Harvard. "International credit markets are linked, and so a snowballing credit crisis in Eastern Europe and the Baltic countries could cause New York municipal bonds to fall."

Third, what do emerging markets have in common with advanced economies when it comes to banking and financial crises? Carmen M. Reinhart (University of Maryland) and Kenneth S. Rogoff, in a series of brilliant historical comparative studies looking back to 1800, stressed that while each financial crisis is undoubtedly distinct, "they also share striking similarities, in the run-up of asset prices, in debt accumulation, in growth patterns, and in current account deficits …" Furthermore, the frequency or incidence, duration, and amplitude of crises across the two groups of countries do not differ much historically, even if comparisons are limited to the post-World War II period. "This result," as professors Reinhart and Rogoff concluded, "is surprising given that almost all macroeconomic and financial time series (income, consumption, government spending, interest rates, etc.) exhibit higher volatility in emerging markets"[3].

---

3   "Is the 2007 U.S. Sub-Prime Financial Crisis So Different? An International Historical Comparison," http://www.nber.org/w13761, January, 2008, p. 10; "Banking Crises: An Equal Opportunity Menace," http://www.nber.org/w14587, December, 2008, p. 3–4; "The Aftermath of Financial Crises," http://www.nber.org/w14656, January, 2009, p. 1.

The financial infernos that shocked emerging economies during the last two decades represented spontaneous phenomena mostly of local combustion: Latin America's "lost decade" in the 1980s; the Mexican "tequila crisis" of 1994–95; the Russian "transformational recession" of 1989–98 that ended with the spectacular currency crisis of August 1998 (the Russian ruble lost 75% of its value); the Asian financial crisis of 1997–98; Argentina's debt default of 2001; etc. One of the most comprehensive analyses of these crises was done by Paul Krugman, professor of economics and international affairs at Princeton University and a Nobel Prize-winning economist, in his new and updated edition of *The Return of Depression Economics*. Describing the "wrong lessons" learned from Latin American crises, particularly Mexico's "tequila crisis," he said: "We gave far too much credit to Washington, to the IMF and Treasury. The rescue wasn't really a well-considered plan that addressed the essence of the crisis: it was an emergency injection of cash to a beleaguered government ... And so nobody was prepared either for the emergence of a new tequila-style crisis in Asia a few years later ... We were even less prepared for the global crisis that erupted in 2007."[4]

Fourth, of course, the ***emerging markets are not immune to the current global financial shocks,*** and many of them were overheated. For example, by the beginning of October 2008, the US Dow had dropped 25% in three months while China's Shanghai exchange was down 30%, Brazil's BOVESPA was down 41%, and Russia's RTSI was down 61%. Emerging economies are being hit hard by weakening exports and collapses of private capital flows. Private capital flows into developing countries were projected to decline from $1 trillion in 2007 to about $530 billion in 2009, from about 7% of their GDP to less than 2%. This effect is amplified by what is called "*flight to quality*" as investors are withdrawing capital from risky emerging markets. The situation is aggravated by the rising threat of corporate defaults, particularly in those emerging economies heavily dependent on external financing. According to the IMF, banks, firms, and governments of the emerging markets, especially those of Central and Eastern Europe, have to roll over $1.8 trillion worth of borrowing in 2009, which, in the case of defaults, could seriously undermine investors' confidence.

Although the current global crisis was much different than previous crises of the emerging economies and, consequently, different "medicine" should be applied to treat the "illness," it is very important to learn the "right" lessons from those crises.

4. TOWARD A NEW PARADIGM OF GLOBAL GROWTH WITH NEW ENGINES?

The paradox of the twenty-first century, as the Global Risks–2011 Study emphasizes, is the fact that "the world is not only being integrated during the globalization process but is also becoming more disconnected as the majority of the fruits of globalization are enjoyed by the minority." The "decoupling" trends are illustrated by the increased disparities between the core of Europe and its periphery, between the real economy and its financial stresses, between emerging and advanced economies. Nevertheless, the global economy is still tightly interconnected and its rebalancing leads relentlessly to a new paradigm of growth, shifting the economic gravity to the emerging world.

First, The Economist's 2010 special report on the world economy, "How to grow?" pointed out three main reasons that explain "*stagnation of the West and the emergence of the rest*":

1. The sheer scale of the recent recession and the weakness of the following recovery with a high rate of unemployment and high degree of unused capacity expressed in persisting output gap as % of potential GDP;

---

4 Krugman, Paul, *The Return of Depression Economics and the Crisis of 2008.* W. W. Norton & Company, Inc., 2009, p. 54–55.

2. A slowing supply of workers caused by an aging population, especially in western Europe and Japan, and flat or slowing productivity growth due to a declining rate of capital investment and a sluggish pace of innovations.
3. The economic potential is damaged by hangover from the crisis and feebleness of recovery that may reduce rich countries' output by some 3%, and the situation may deteriorate further if their governments will not foster growth by supporting short-term demand and boosting long-term supply.

Second, a striking fact becomes obvious: *emerging economies have performed better after each of the last five advanced economies' recessions*: 1974–75, 1980–83, 1991–93, 2001, and 2007–09. They also become more correlated with advanced economies' growth rates, based on purchasing power parity. This surprising pattern of improved economic growth after each subsequent recession is also confirmed by the comparatively better performance of emerging economies after the current recession. The authors of the October 2010 *World Economy Outlook* pointed to three indicators:

1. *Growth differences* (the difference between the economy's average growth rate in the three years after the recession and its average growth rate three years before recession).
2. *Level differences* (output lost from the shock: the difference between the level of output three years after recession and the trend level on the seven years of output growth before recession).
3. *Relative growth* (the difference between the average growth rate during the three years after the recession for a concrete, emerging economy and the average growth rate of an advanced economy during 2007–09 (IMF, *WEO*, October 2010, pp. 13–15). It should be mentioned that strong growth from the productivity gains and continuing integration of emerging and developing economies into the global economy, as well as stabilization gains from a significantly improved macroeconomic policy framework are "the secrets" of the resilience of these countries to the global financial crisis and their much more robust post crisis development.

All these tendencies require *a redefinition of the economic growth paradigm* and *differentiation of the role of emerging markets in a post crisis recovery*, taking into consideration that 40% of recent global consumption and more than two thirds of global growth are accounted for by these markets.

Third, of this group of countries, eight were "graduated" recently by Goldman Sachs's experts *from "Emerging" to "Growth Markets,"* the threshold being at least 1% of the current global GDP (Mexico; Korea; Turkey; and Indonesia, with good prospects for Nigeria, and the Philippines and, in the more distant future, Egypt, and, eventually, Iran). The BRIC countries are expected to make an outsized contribution to the increase in global GDP between 2011 and 2020—twice that of the G-7. Adding all four BRIC countries together, their real GDP growth will bring its collective size to one that is larger than the US economy. Michael Spence, a Nobel Prize laureate in Economics, emphasized in his recent book *Next Convergence*: "The huge asymmetries between advanced and developing countries have not disappeared, but they are declining, and the pattern for the first time in 250 years is convergence rather than divergence."

Fourth, to understand the prospects and the limits of a strong growth momentum, which is the basis of a new global growth paradigm, especially important is an analysis of the *growth in productivity*—an increase in output from a given quantity of inputs. This is a key factor of economic growth that determines long-run prospects and the new role of emerging and developing markets, including those of BRIC countries, in the world economy.

The Goldman Sachs economists analyzed productivity growth in these countries by using the *Growth Environment Score (GES) model* to show a process *of catch-up* to the developed economies. This index is based on thirteen variables critically necessary for sustainable economic growth and productivity; it is a proxy of the economic, political, and social conditions required for the convergence in the productivity growth rate of the developed economies. The higher the GES, the higher the growth rate of productivity and the better and faster the convergence. The experts expect BRICs' productivity to outperform both developed markets and other emerging markets. Over the past decade, the average productivity growth in these countries was 3.0% per year, being particularly impressive in Russia (6.7%) and China (3.5%). This reflects the BRICs' recent performance in the following five components of GES:

1. *Human capital* (increased life expectancy, secondary school enrollment, etc.).
2. *Technology* (rapid increase in the number of Internet users—66.6 per 100, computers—20 per 100, and phones—6.3 per 100 since 2000) (*The Economist,* 2010, April 17).
3. *Political conditions* (productivity growth has been encouraged by privatization, trade liberalization and financial openness, removal of economic rigidities in Russia, etc.).
4. *Macroeconomic conditions* (an impressive increase in investment in China—40% and India—35%).
5. *Macroeconomic stability* (great strides in Brazil, China, and Russia in the reduction of high inflation, the large government deficit, and reliance on foreign borrowing).

Fifth, the BRICs and Emerging Markets, in general, are benefiting from the breakthrough innovations that are becoming major factors in their fast growth. According to the UN World Investment Report, there are more than 21,500 multinational companies based in the EMs, many of them leaders in their respective industries: China's *BYD* in batteries, India's *Arcelor Mittal* in steel, Brazil's *Embrayer,* etc. The number of companies from the BRICs in the *Financial Times* 500 list quadrupled during the last three years (from fifteen to sixty-two). There are already some areas where the EMs are ahead of the advanced markets, such as mobile money (using mobile phones to make payments); using computer programs to recognize handwriting; designing products; organizing processes to reach billions of consumers; reinventing systems of production and distribution; and proposing totally new business models. The four main factors of the disruptive power of innovations in emerging markets, according to *The Economist's* special report, are:

1. *much more liquid and transparent markets* for corporate control and senior managerial talent than existed two decades ago;
2. the *sheer size of the emerging markets,* with the world's recognized export-oriented leaders in practically every industry;
3. the big impact of the volume of the market; and
4. the biggest Western companies are increasingly looking for the *potential of emerging markets* not only as sources of cheap labor forces for assembling and manufacturing but also *as sources of innovations and growth.* At the same time, it is important not to overestimate this potential and nourish illusions that the world economy could be "saved" from recession by the "Rise of the Rest."

5. EX-COMMUNIST EUROPEAN EMERGING MARKETS: POLITICS VS. ECONOMICS

The global financial crisis has had a very negative impact on the emerging markets of the former communist countries of Central and Eastern Europe/Southeastern Europe (CEESE) that represent the "Achilles heel" of a united Europe, or putting it in more familiar terms, "Europe's version of the subprime market." The abrupt change of fortune occurred after the surprisingly rapid growth of these countries after the fall of the Berlin Wall. As a result of the economic boom of the last decade and the rapidly increasing prices for oil and other energy resources, Russia, for example, became the eighth-largest world economy in terms of nominal GDP; its GDP rose from $82 billion in 1992 to a whopping $1,778 billion by 2008, according to IMF estimations, although it ranks only No. 74 when it comes to per capita income. But the surprise winner in this race was the CEESE region, whose GDP rose from $535 billion in 1992 to $4,687 billion by 2008, twice as fast as Russia's[5].

The emerging economies vary enormously in their domestic financial development, but for all of them, politics matters as much as economics to market outcomes, as Ian Bremer of Eurasia Group observed. The financial crisis has political ramifications everywhere, but they are particularly pronounced in the former Soviet republics that formed the *Commonwealth of Independent States (CIS)* after the collapse of the USSR in 1991. Real GDP in this region expanded by 8.5% in 2007and contracted by over 5% in 2009, with the biggest rate of contraction among all regions of the global economy. The IMF attributed this large reversal of economic fortune to three major shocks: a) financial turbulence, which greatly limited access to external funding; b) slumping demand from advanced economies; and c) a related abrupt fall in commodity prices, specifically for energy resources[6]. The economic, social, and political crises in this region both closely bind and amplify each other. This is just as true in such large countries as Russia, Ukraine, and Kazakhstan, where big business and the state are closely intertwined, as it is in tiny Moldova, where the 2009 (April) parliamentary elections, which were considered by the opposition to have been falsified by authorities, erupted into massive anticommunist protests, a so called "twitter revolution" of young people desperately struggling for "some changes in our country ... any kind of changes."

Let's analyze the effects of crisis and recovery in this region in more detail.

First, the initial reaction to the crisis in most ex-Soviet countries was: "*it is not our crisis;* it is Washington's problem." "We did not have a crisis of liquidity; we did not have a mortgage crisis. We escaped it. Russia is a safe haven," stated Vladimir Putin, the then Russian prime minister, now president of the Russian Federation. At that time—fall 2008—the Russian political and economic elites were engaged in discussions on prospects for Russia to become the number five or number six economic power in the world economy by 2020, as observed by professor V. Mau, president of the Russian Academy of Economy. The reaction of Moldovan officials was similar when they declared in October 2008 that "there is no financial or economic crisis in Moldova and there are no factors that might provoke it." In spite of such overoptimistic statements, the financial storm did not bypass these countries or other former Soviet republics and Central and Eastern European ex-communist countries.

Second, the facts proved the opposite: Russia's stock markets, for instance, have plunged more dramatically than most others. For example, a government-controlled giant, *Gazprom*, which not long ago had a value of $359 billion, has fallen to slightly more than $100 billion. During just one year of the current crisis, there was a sharp decline in the value of the ruble—the national currency—by one third, and Russia lost fifty-five of its eighty-seven billionaires, according to *Forbes* magazine. Overall, Russia's market capitalization has lost about $1 trillion since its peak in May 2008. This wealth simply vaporized. The damage had been largely limited to the Russian elite, to the no more than 1.5% of the population that had investments in stocks. Russia has not yet developed a broad investor class. Meanwhile, the Kremlin sent an order to all broadcasters banning the words "collapse" and "crisis." The word "fall" should be substituted with "decline." Reporters were encouraged to reflect on the global financial crisis everywhere but Russia and criticize the US as "the epicenter where the

---

5   www.businessneweurope.eu, January 29, 2009.
6   IMF World Economic Outlook. April 2009, p.84.

crisis is nested," but they were advised not to publish "provocative reports that can cause panic" at home. As the crisis gained momentum, the foreign currency reserves rapidly drained, and large masses of people were painfully affected by unemployment, which soared to 12%, double the level of 2008; the Russian authorities have become much more realistic, launching a massive anti-crisis program amounted a "world record"—12% of GDP.

This was Russia's most serious test and threat in almost two decades; it could have ended the social contract between the Kremlin and the people after an eight-year consumer boom fueled by high oil prices. Mikhail Gorbachev, the ex-Soviet leader and my former boss, for whom I worked in the troubled times of *perestroika and glasnost*[7], warned that Russia faced "unprecedentedly difficult and dangerous circumstances" and could be "heading into a black hole." Paradoxically, the crisis in the short-term may help Russia reintegrate into the international community after Russia's invasion of Georgia, a small ex-Soviet republic, in August 2008, and improve Russian-American relations, but in the long-run, the fate of its economy depends heavily on the price of oil; Russia's explored reserves make Russia one of the best-positioned oil suppliers in the world.

The global crisis has significantly affected other CIS emerging markets—Moldova, for example. Its negative impact has been multiplied by the political crisis provoked by an unacceptable reaction to the anti-communist youth protests of April 7–8, 2009, including brutal repressions. These events made headlines in the world press, marking perhaps the first time Moldovia had made the news on such a scale since it became independent in 1991.

The economic and political crisis in Moldova has been aggravated, according to local and international experts, by poor quality of governance, significant deterioration of the business environment (the country ranks 158 out of 176 economies in the Doing Business Dealing with Construction Permit indicator), and worsened and widespread corruption (the Transparency International Corruption Index placed Moldova at 109th place, thirty positions down from 2006). All these factors seriously undermined the country's prospects for recovery and its European integration aspirations.

Third, the real problem for the governments of ex-communist Central and Eastern European countries (sometimes referred to as "New Europe") in facing the current crisis *is weak governance*, based on the unique combination of special interest lobbying, populist statements, bad economics, and sheer incompetence of authorities. The crisis in this region was the worst possible mix of the East Asian crisis of 1997 and of the Latin American crisis of 2001 although there are some differences, as well.

1. These countries are much more at risk than Asian economies from the global deleveraging process; their impressive growth before the crisis was fueled mostly by borrowing from abroad. This resulted in their disproportionate dependence on foreign currency loans. According to the Institute of International Finance, the volume of capital flowing into emerging European economies is expected to fall by more than eight times: from $254 billion in 2008 to just $30 billion in 2009, with the increasing prospects of widespread defaults.

2. A distinctive feature of Eastern Europe is that the liquidity boom in emerging Eastern Europe is linked almost solely to the private sector, whose foreign currency debt rose dramatically to 126% of foreign exchange reserves while the public sector's net external debt fell during the last few years. This heavy borrowing led to: a) increased debt in foreign currencies (Swiss francs, euros, and even yen) that represented 30%–40% of household debt in Poland and Romania, 50% in Hungary, and over 70% in the Baltic States; b) huge imbalances in Eastern European currents accounts; and c) massive amounts of foreign debt, which subsequently led to a credit crunch.

---

7 "Mikhail Gorbachev: "The Decay of Socialism and the Renaissance of Eastern Europe (from the perspective of an insider)," by Ceslav Ciobanu. *East European Politics and Societies*, Vol. 18, No. 1, 2004.

3. The economies of these countries, particularly of the smaller and worst-performing countries in Eastern Europe, are overweight in financial stocks and underweight in energy and technology names. For example, financial stocks represent 67% of Romania's stock index, 39% of Poland's, and 37% of Bulgaria's compared with 20% of Brazil's. At the same time, energy and technology stocks make up 27% of Brazil's index, 21% of China's, and 0% of Bulgaria's index.

It is important to mention that the societies of these countries are much more resilient to the challenges of the current recession than one might expect, having had the experience of living through communism, dictatorships, and 300% inflation. As an expert pointed out: "People in this region are ten times better equipped to cope with a crisis than spoiled investment bankers in New York."

Fourth, along with the main causes of the crisis, rooted in fundamental, systemic problems of the world economy, there were *some specific, apparently paradoxical Russian circumstances.* The Russian economy was characterized by a favorable macroeconomic environment, double surpluses (budget and balance of payment), a significant increase of foreign currency, and gold reserves. This makes the situation quite different in Russia's economy in comparison to the crisis of 1998, and Russia's response to the current crisis was much more efficient:

1. The biggest part of the external debt before the crisis of 2007–09 was not in short-term securities, which affected the market immediately in 1998, but in credit debt.
2. The volume of Foreign Currency Reserves reached about $590 billion, the world's third largest reserves; was incomparably higher than in 1998 (about $10 billion in 1998); and the establishment of the State Stabilization Fund served as a strong bumper to crisis.
3. The main characteristic of the recent crisis was also different—the crisis was an institutional one because the major part of the debt was not public but corporate debt, and the private sector, in theory, is responsible for solving its own problems.

Russia definitely coped better than many other countries with the crisis, reemerging to its precrisis level much faster than other economies. Not accidently, Mr. Alexei Kudrin, Russia's finance minister and deputy prime minister, was named "the best finance minister of the year" by the IMF at its 2009 meeting in Washington, DC.

Fifth, nevertheless, there are still *important issues that need to be addressed*: a) gradual liberalization of the flows of capital, labor, and commodities; b) reduction of the excessive interference from the state in the economy, particularly through stakes in major companies and corporations; c) poor quality of the state-run regulatory agencies and insufficiently clear regulation, with persisting administrative barriers that lower competition; and d) accession to the World Trade Organization, still blocked for different reasons, mostly political. It is also important for Russia to solve these problems if Russian authorities want to reestablish the trust of foreign investors and the credibility of their policies and to enforce the rule of law and the protection of property, which were and still are the most vulnerable parts of Russia's business environment.

Russia today, according to the UNCTAD report, is on the list of top five most attractive countries for Foreign Direct Investments (FDI) behind China, India, Brazil, and the US. Paradoxically, the sum of FDI declined drastically over the last few years: from $130 billion in 2007 and 2008 to $38 billion in 2009 and to just $5.4 billion in the first half of 2010, which is equal to its monthly investment in China. This happened in spite of several purely Russian benefits with advantages for investors in comparison with other developing markets: a) clearly undervalued Russian securities (they are traded well below the price/earnings ratio norm—at ratio 7×, while India's, Brazil's. and China's are well above: 21×, 15×, and 14× respectively; b) a stable macroeconomic situation; and c) a low ratio of debt to GDP—under 10%, which is well below other G-8 and G-20 countries.

Sixth, US-Russian economic relationships have great potential, which is still grossly underutilized. Russia is the world's eighth largest economy but only number twenty-five among America's trading partners. In 2009, US-Russian bilateral trade was only $25.3 billion, or about one-twentieth of US-Chinese trade. Only 4% of FDI in Russia came from the United States. There are a few encouraging signs of the reevaluation of bilateral economic relationships, such as PepsiCo's decision to invest $1 billion in Russia, the $2 billion contract between Boeing and Russian Aeroflot signed during US Vice-President Joe Biden's visit to Moscow (2010), an initiative on cooperation in energy efficiency, and the resubmission to the US Congress of a bilateral civil nuclear energy deal. The legislation recently passed by the *Russian Duma* (Parliament) on the *Skolkovo Project,* which is supposed to become a Russian version of California's Silicon Valley, is creating good opportunities for U.S.-Russian cooperation in energy efficiency and conservation, nuclear technology, space technology, medical technology, and strategic computing.

6. CONCLUSIONS: LEARNING THE RIGHT LESSONS

First, the main lesson from the current recession isn't about market failure or the downside of open borders for capital. It's about the *importance of sound economic policy.* In this respect, the role of the government should be reconsidered for rescuing the financial system and for insuring its sustainability, integrity, and transparency. "Economies need a balance between the role of markets and the role of government—with important contributions by nonmarket and nongovernmental institutions," as Joseph Stiglitz, Nobel Prize laureate in Economics, wrote in his recent book *Free Fall.*

Second, learning the right lessons of this and past crises is important for all advanced economies, and especially for the US, taking into account its unique role in the world economy and responsibility for solutions to the global financial turmoil. This credit crunch provided at least four important lessons, including:

1. The top management's reward and remuneration has been excessive.
2. The risk management models based on Basel II have proven to be inadequate.
3. The financial supervisors in the US and Europe have not been involved thoroughly enough.
4. The US framework of financial supervision has proven to be largely fragmented and totally ineffective.

Third, the global financial crisis marked a historic momentum: *the beginning of restructuring of the global financial system* by addressing its most vulnerable aspects and existing imbalances and weaknesses and launching a new paradigm for global economic growth. There is no doubt about the decisive role of a new global alliance between advanced economies and growth and emerging markets in addressing the consequences of the 2007–2009 financial crisis. It is the right time to propose a new paradigm for financial markets?

Fourth, it is equally important to *learn from past errors and not to repeat the mistakes of the past.* The US has a history of bad legislative acts and government programs. However noble the intent, many of them often wound up delivering less at a slower pace and higher cost than projected, with potentially damaging unintended consequences, in the words of Michael J. Boskin, an economics professor at Stanford University. For example, the famous Tariff Act of 1930, better known as "Smoot-Hawley," which was designed to protect US producers from foreign competition, de facto aggravated the situation and deepened the Great Depression already under way. More recently, the Sarbanes-Oxley Act of 2002, enacted in response to the high-profile Enron and WorldCom financial scandals to protect shareholders and the general public from accounting errors and fraudulent practices in enterprise, led to similar consequences regarding the inflow of foreign capital to the US. "Sarbanes-Oxley" is one of those Congressional classics, passed amid the post-Enron panic, that has done much harm at great cost. Its biggest beneficiaries have been the same accounting firms the law sought to punish and which have, nonetheless, been able to charge far more money for their services," as a *Wall Street Journal* editorial pointed out.

Another example is the Russian plan to reform "the obsolescent unipolar world economic order" and replace it "by a system based on the interaction of several major centers," "to reduce inconsistencies between the supra-national nature of instruments and institutes of financial markets and the national character of regulators' activities," and "to examine possibilities for creating a supra-national reserve currency," etc. The plan was unveiled on the eve of the G-20 meeting in London. The proposal for rearrangement of the global financial system according to the "five principles in eight specific areas" proposed by Russia was designed to strike at the positions of the United States and the European Union in the global economy. This fits well into Moscow's crusade against a unipolar world order, this time in the financial sphere. Even Russian experts do not think much of these initiatives and do not expect the US or the European Union to quit their roles as economic leaders or that the new financial framework and a new supra-national world currency will be created on the "ashes" of the still functioning system.

Problem Solutions

Chapter 1: Basic Principles, Models, and Economic Systems
1. C
2. A
3. A
4. D
5. C
6. A
7. B
8. C

Chapter 2: How Markets Work: Demand, Supply, and Market Equilibrium
1. B
2. D
3. A
4. C
5. B
6. D
7. A
8. B

Chapter 3: Consumer and Producer Behavior: Elasticity of Demand and Supply
1. B
2. A
3. D
4. C
5. B
6. A
7. D
8. B
9. C

Chapter 4: Production, Technology, and Cost
1. A
2. C
3. B
4. C
5. D
6. A
7. B
8. D
9. A
10. D

Chapter 5: Market Structure: How "Perfect" is Perfect Competition?

1. B
2. A
3. C
4. A
5. B
6. C
7. D
8. C
9. A
10. C

Chapter 6: Monopoly, Price Discrimination, and Antitrust Regulation

1. D
2. C
3. B
4. D
5. B
6. B
7. D
8. C

Chapter 7: Monopolistic Competition: Quality, Price, and Marketing

1. A
2. D
3. B
4. A
5. B
6. D
7. C
8. C
9. B

Chapter 8: Oligopoly and Game Theory: Strategic Behavior and Decision-Making

1. D
2. C
3. C
4. A
5. B
6. D
7. A
8. C
9. B

Chapter 9: Labor Market: Inequality, Poverty, and Income Distribution

1. C
2. B
3. A
4. D
5. A
6. B
7. C
8. A
9. B
10. D

Chapter 10: How Government Reacts when Markets Fail

1. B
2. A
3. C
4. B
5. A
6. C
7. A
8. D
9. C

Chapter 11: GDP and Economic Growth: How to Measure Total Production and Income

1. A
2. B
3. D
4. D
5. C
6. A
7. B
8. C
9. D

Chapter 12: Business Cycle: Unemployment and Inflation

1. B
2. C
3. B
4. A
5. C
6. D
7. C
8. B
9. A
10. A

Chapter 13: Aggregate Demand and Aggregate Supply

1. B
2. A
3. D
4. D
5. A
6. B

Chapter 14: Fiscal Policy: How to Stabilize the Economy

1. A
2. C
3. B
4. D
5. A
6. B
7. C
8. D
9. C
10. A

Chapter 15: Monetary System and Monetary Policy

1. D
2. B
3. D
4. B
5. D
6. C
7. A
8. C
9. B

Chapter 16: The US and the Global Economy: Challenges of Modern Technology and Globalization

1. A
2. A
3. B
4. D
5. C

Chapter 17. International Trade and Finance

1. A
2. D
3. C
4. C
5. B
6. D
7. A
8. C
9. A

GLOSSARY

CHAPTER 1: WHAT IS ECONOMICS ABOUT: PRINCIPLES, MODELS, AND AN ECONOMIC WAY OF LIFE

Ceteris Paribus: The other-things-equal assumption (Latin).

Diminishing Return: As one input increases while the other inputs are held fixed, output increases but at a decreasing rate.

Economic Goals: Courses of action based on economic principles and intended to resolve specific economic problems.

Economic Policy: Designed to be achieved by economic policy.

Factors of Production (Economic Resources): Basic inputs necessary to produce goods and services.

Invention: The development of new commodities or a new process to produce them.

Innovation: A process of practical application of an invention.

Laissez-Faire: "Leave it alone" (French).

Macroeconomics: A branch of economics focused on performance of the nation's economy as a whole.

Microeconomics: Aa branch of economics focused on choices made by individual participants in the economy: individuals, households, businesses, and government organizations.

Marginal: "A change in," "extra," or "additional."

Marginal Benefit: The extra benefit resulting from an additional increase in an activity.

Marginal Cost: The extra cost resulting from an additional increase in an activity.

Opportunity Cost: What can be sacrificed to get what you want.

Property Rights: Assigned to individuals in the form of legal ownership.

Production Possibilities Model: Various combinations of goods and services that could be produced with available resources and technology in a given period of time.

Rational Behavior: Rational self-interest motivated be the scope of maximization of utility from an action.

Rational Choice: Compares costs and benefits; it is made on margin, responding to incentives.

Scarcity: Lack of enough resources to satisfy all desired wants.

Three Fundamental Economic Problems: What to produce, how, and for whom.

Voluntary Exchange: "… is common to all men, and to be found in no other … animals" (Adam Smith).

CHAPTER 2: HOW MARKETS WORK: DEMAND, SUPPLY, AND MARKET EQUILIBRIUM

Barter: Direct exchange of one good for another good without the use of money.

Demand: The willingness and ability of an individual (or group of consumers) to buy a specific quantity of goods and services at alternative prices in a given period of time.

Demand Curve: Graphical illustration of demand schedule.

Demand Schedule: A table showing the quantities of a good or service a person is willing and able to buy at alternative prices in a given period of time.

Equilibrium Price: Is determined by the quantity of a good or service that buyers are willing and able to buy, and sellers are willing and able to sell in a given period of time.

Equilibrium Quantity: Quantity of a good sold at equilibrium price.

Factor Market: Markets where factors of production (resources) are bought and sold.

Law of Demand: An inverse (negative) relationship between quantity of goods and services demanded and the price.

Law of Supply: A direct (positive) relationship between quantity of goods and services supplied and the price.

Market: Institution, mechanism, or place where buyers ("demanders") and sellers ("suppliers") of particular goods and services or resources get together.

Market Demand: Collective demand of all buyers in the market.

Market Supply: A sum of all individual producers' supply in the market; an expression of sellers' intentions and not a statement of de facto sales.

Market Shortage: Excess demand over supply at certain price level.

Market Surplus: Excess supply over demand at certain price level.

Movement Along the Demand/Supply Curve: Changes in quantities of goods and services demanded/supplied as a result of changes in their prices.

Price Ceiling: The legally fixed upper limit of the price.

Price Floor: The legally fixed lower limit of the price.

Product Market: Markets where finished goods and services are bought and sold.

Shift in Demand/Supply: Shift of the demand/supply curve (to the right—increased, or to the left—decreased) as a result of nonprice determinants (tastes, income, availability of substitutes and complements, expectations, number of buyers/sellers in the market, technology, factor cost, etc.).

Supply: The willingness and ability of a producer (group of producers) to supply specific quantity of goods and services at alternative prices in a given period of time.

CHAPTER 3: CONSUMER AND PRODUCER BEHAVIOR: ELASTICITY OF DEMAND AND SUPPLY

Alfred Marshal's Time Component of Market Equilibrium: Analysis of demand and supply with emphasis on the time component for market equilibrium.

Behavioral Economics: Applications of concepts of anthropology, sociology, psychology, and other social sciences to the study of economic behavior.

Cross-Price Elasticity of Demand/Supply: How the demand/supply for a good changes as consumer's/producer's income is changing.

Diamond-Water Paradox: Why the price of a diamond is so high despite its uselessness for human survival while the price of water is so low despite its crucial importance for human survival.

Elasticity of Demand: Responsiveness (sensitivity) of quantity demanded by consumers of a good/service to changes in its price.

Elasticity of Supply: Responsiveness (sensitivity) of quantity supplied by producers of a good/service to changes in its price.

Income Elasticity of Demand: Change in demand for a good as a consumer's income changes.

Perfectly Elastic, Elastic, Unit Elastic Inelastic, Perfectly Inelastic Demand/Supply: Degree of responsiveness of consumers/producers to changes in prices.

Price-Change Formula: Percentage change in equilibrium price resulting from a change in demand or supply.

Price Discrimination: Practice of charging different prices for a good/service to different consumers according their ability to pay.

Total Revenue Test: Method of determining the price elasticity of demand by analyzing the change in total revenue as a result of change in price.

Total Utility: The amount of pleasure (satisfaction) people receive from entire consumption of a good/service.

Marginal Utility: How total utility changes when we increase the consumption by one additional (extra or marginal) unit.

Utility Maximizing Rule: Allocation of limited money income in such a way that a dollar spent on each product brings the same amount of marginal utility.

Law of Diminishing Marginal Utility: The marginal utility from any product consumed tend to decline as of this product is consumed in a given period of time.

CHAPTER 4: PRODUCTION, TECHNOLOGY, AND COST

Average Product (AP, Labor Productivity): Total product of labor divided by the quantity of labor or total output per unit of input.

Average Total Cost (ATC): Total cost divided by quantity produced or per unit cost.

Economies of Scale (Increasing Return to Scale): Increase in a firm's input generates an increase in output by greater proportion.

Constant Return to Scale: Both firm's input and output are increasing by the same proportion.

Diseconomies of Scale (Decreasing Return to Scale): Output is increasing at a smaller rate than input increases.

Minimum Efficient Scale (MES): The lowest level or output at which a firm can minimize long-run average cost.

Efficiency: Producing maximum output with given resources or producing in the least costly way.

Marginal Cost (MC): The change in total cost resulting from producing one more unit of a product or change in total cost divided by change in total output.

Marginal Product (MP): Change in total product resulting from an increase by one unit of quantity of labor employed or change in total output divided by change in quantity of labor.

Total Cost (TC): The sum of the value of all inputs used to produce goods or the sum of fixed and variable costs.

Fixed Cost (FC) or "Overhead Cost": Costs associated with existence and functioning of a plant that do not vary with the change in quantity of output.

Variable Cost (VC): Costs that vary with the change in variable resources (labor, materials, fuel, transportation, etc.).

Explicit Costs: Cash payments for resources owned by a company or individual other than the immediate producer or "out of pocket money.

Implicit Costs: The opportunity costs of using self-owned, self-employed resources.

Sunk Cost: Previously incurred cost that cannot be recouped, i.e., "Don't cry over spilt milk."

Production Function (PF): Maximum quantity of a good that can be produced from available combination of inputs.

Total Revenue (TR): Price times quantity produced.

Total Profit (TP): Difference between total revenue and total cost.

Accounting Profit: Difference between total revenue and total explicit cost.

Economic Profit: Difference between total revenue and economic cost (implicit + explicit).

CHAPTER 5: MARKET STRUCTURE: HOW "PERFECT" IS PERFECT COMPETITION?

Competition: State of affairs.

Perfectly Competitive Market: Interaction of millions of "perfectly competitive firms" that do not have market power.

Market Power: Capacity of firm(s) to dictate the price.

Market Structure: Combination of various firms in an industry.

Constant-Cost Industry: An industry in which the typical firm's average costs remain the same as the industry expands.

Increasing-Cost Industry: An industry in which the average cost of production increases as the total output of industry increases.

Decreasing-Cost Industry: An industry in which the average cost of production declines as the industry expands.

Consumer's Surplus: The area between Demand curve (which is also a Marginal Benefit curve) and the price (which is also Marginal Revenue for a competitive industry).

Producer's Surplus: The area between price (Marginal Revenue) and Supply curve (which is **also a Marginal Cost curve).**

Profit Maximization Criteria: Maximizing the difference between total revenue and total cost.

Marginal—Marginal Cost Rule: Maximizing profit by increasing the level of an activity if marginal revenue exceeds (equals) marginal cost.

Allocative Efficiency: Producing the optimum amount of output wanted by society.

Productive Efficiency: Maximum output from existing input.

Shut Down Price: The price at which the firm is indifferent between operating and shutting down.

CHAPTER 6: MONOPOLY, PRICE DISCRIMINATION, AND ANTITRUST REGULATION

Monopoly: A single seller (from Greek word *monopolion*: *mono*—one, and *polein*—to sell).

Natural Monopoly: A single firm that produces the entire market supply at lower average cost and more efficiently than any larger number of smaller firms.

Patent: An exclusive right for an innovation, granted by the government.

Public Franchise: An exclusive right granted by the government as the legal provider of a product.

Price Maker: Capacity to dictate the price in the market.

Price Effect: To sell another unit, the monopolist should reduce the price of all units.

Quantity Effect: An additional unit sold that increases total revenue.

Price Discrimination: Selling different units of a good or service at different prices to different customers.

Perfect Price Discrimination: Selling each unit of a good for the highest price anyone is willing to pay for it.

Rent Seeking: Any attempt to capture consumer surplus, producer surplus, or economic profit.

Social Cost of Monopoly: A wasted resource and economic cost for society as a whole.

Public Ownership: Publicly owned companies.

Price Regulation: Government intervention into the price mechanism.

Marginal Cost Pricing Rule: Setting the price equal to marginal cost (P = MC).

Average Cost Pricing Rule: Setting the price equal to average total cost (P = ATC).

Rate of Return Regulation: Setting the price at a level that allows the firm to earn specified return on capital.

Price-Cap Regulation: Setting the highest price the firm is permitted to—a price ceiling.

Earning Sharing Regulation: Profit above a target regualtion must be shared with customers.

Antitrust Policy: A way in which the government may influence resource allocation in the marketplace and regulate or prohibit certain kinds of market behavior.

Trust: An arrangement under which the owners of several companies transfer their decision-making power to a small group of trustees.

Resale Price Maintenance: A manufacturer agrees with a distributor on the price at which the product will be resold.

Tying Arrangement: An agreement to sell one product only if the buyer agrees to buy another different product from the same manufacturer.

Predatory Pricing: Setting the price at low level to drive competitors out of business.

CHAPTER 7: MONOPOLISTIC COMPETITION: QUALITY, PRICE, AND MARKETING

Efficient Scale of Production: Quantity produced at which average total cost is at minimum.

Excess Capacity: A firm's production at level, which is less than efficient scale.

Equilibrium: a) short-run, which takes the number of firms in an industry as given or b) long-run, which is reached only after enough time has elapsed for firms to enter and exit from the industry.

Four-Firm Concentration Ratio: Measure of degree of competition, the percentage of an industry's output produced by its four largest firms.

Herfindahl-Hirschman Index (HHI): Measure of degree of competition, the sum of squared percentage market shares of all firms in the industry, an average of the 50 largest firms in the market.

Markup: The difference between the price charged by monopolistic competitor and the marginal **cost**.

Monopolistic Competition: Competition base on price, quality, location, service, and advertising.

Zero-Profit Equilibrium: Long-run production level at which a firm will earn only normal profit.

CHAPTER 8: OLIGOPOLY AND GAME THEORY: STRATEGIC BEHAVIOR AND DECISION-MAKING

Cartel: A group of firms that come to an agreement on each member's quotas for production and price charged; the most comprehensive form of collusion; illegal in the US.

Collusive Behavior: Cooperation with rival competitors to maximize firms' profits.

Game Theory: The study of how people make decisions in situations when attaining their goals depends on interaction with their partners/rivals; a) **a zero-sum game**—when one player's gain is the other's loss and vice versa; b) **a non-zero-sum game**—both players may gain or lose, depending on the actions of each other; c) **a non-cooperative game**—opponents are not allowed to share information with each other; d) **a dominant strategy game**—there is one strategy that is the best for a player no matter what the other player does; e) **repeated games**—the time is brought into earlier pricing decisions; and f) **sequential games and first move advantage**—decisions are made sequentially with the first mover having an advantage.

Mutual Interdependence: Each firm must consider its rival's reaction in response to its decisions about price, output, and advertising.

Nash Equilibrium (Noncooperative Equilibrium): Individual (firm) A takes the best possible action given the action of individual (firm) B, and individual B takes the best possible action given the action of individual A.

Oligopoly: A market structure in which a few sellers dominate the sales of a product and where entry of new sellers is difficult or impossible; the term oligopoly has its origin in the Greek words *oligi*—a few, and *polein*—sellers.

Payoff Matrix: A matrix showing the interactions of players' strategies.

Price Fixing: An arrangement in which companies or individuals conspire to fix prices.

Price Leadership Strategy: A situation in which one firm—a dominant firm—takes the lead in announcing (or not announcing) the price change, and the other firms follow the leader.

Price Maker: Unlike the monopoly, the oligopoly has to consider how its rivals will react to any changes in its price, output, product characteristics, etc.

"Prisoners" Dilemma: A two-person, non-zero sum, noncooperative game with a dominant strategy.

Strategic Behavior: Self-interested behavior that takes the reactions of others into account.

CHAPTER 9: LABOR MARKET: INEQUALITY, POVERTY, AND INCOME DISTRIBUTION

Bilateral Monopoly Model: A monopsonist employer faces a unionized labor force; both the employer and employees have monopoly power.

Compensating Differentials: Differences in wage rates across occupations for jobs that differ in attractiveness, pleasure, and requirements.

Demand for Labor: The quantities of labor employers are willing and able to hire at alternative wage rates in a given time period.

Efficiency Wage: A higher wage rate offered by employer to attract hardworking and skillful workers and increase the productivity of labor.

Equilibrium Employment: The quantity of labor employed as a result of the intersection of the labor demand and labor supply curve at equilibrium wage rate.

Equilibrium Wage: The wage at which the quantity of labor supplied in a given period of time equals the quantity of labor demanded.

Floor Pricing Practice: Minimum wage is a practice when price for labor is legally fixed and no employer can pay less than this level.

Income Effect: As our income rises, the marginal utility of income declines.

Input Substitution Effect: An increase in wages beyond a certain level that will cause the shift in the firm's demand from labor to other factors of production (machinery).

Labor: Physical and mental capacity of workers used in production of goods and services.

Labor Market Equilibrium: Equilibrium in labor market resulting from supply and demand for labor, which determines the wage rate and quantity of employment.

Labor Productivity: Output per input (labor hours of work).

Labor Unions: Are usually created in capital intensive industries to take collective action for higher wages; the labor union's main models are: Demand-Enhancement, Exclusive (Craft), and Inclusive (Industrial) models.

Learning Effect: The premium that college graduates earn based on productivity differences.

Legal Minimum Wage: The minimum wage imposed by the government (the Fair Standards Act of 1938).

Marginal Physical Product (MPP): Additional output resulting from hiring an additional unit of **labor**.

Marginal Revenue Product (MRP): The dollar value of the marginal product of labor.

Monopsony: "Single buyer" from the Greek words *mon*—one, *opsonia*—purchase of victuals.

Occupational Licensing: The number of workers in some occupations restricted by government licensing, which sets requirements (education, testing, experience, or residency) for employees.

Opportunity Cost of Working: Time for leisure.

Opportunity Wage: The wage that public officials could earn in private industry.

Output Effect: An increase in the cost of labor that increases the cost of a firm's production and reduces the quantity of output sold.

Substitution Effect: The more time devoted to working, the bigger the opportunity cost of job time, and the worker requires higher pay.

Supply for Labor: The workers' willingness and ability to work specific amounts of time at alternative wage rates in a given time period.

Signaling Effect: A college degree signals to a prospective employer the skills of a more educated and more productive worker.

Wage: a) nominal—the amount of money received by a worker per hour, day, month, or year and b) **real**—the quantity of goods and services that can be bought by nominal wage; the purchasing power of nominal wage.

CHAPTER 10: HOW GOVERNMENT REACTS WHEN MARKETS FAIL

Asymmetric Information: An unequal knowledge possessed by parties to a market transaction.

Adverse-Selection Problem: A situation when information known by the first party to a contract or agreement is not known by the second, and, as a result, the second party incurs major costs.

Benefits: a) private—benefit received by the consumer of a good or service and b) **social**—benefit enjoyed by society as whole; private plus external benefits.

The Coase Theorem: Private transaction is efficient if: a) property rights are clearly defined; b) the number of parties (people) involved is small; and c) transaction costs—the cost to make a deal—are negligible.

Cost: a) private—the resource costs that are incurred by the specific producer; b) **social**—the total costs of all the resources that are used in a particular production activity; and c) **external**—the difference between social and private costs.

Cost-Benefit Analysis: Involves a comparison of marginal social costs and marginal social benefits.

Externalities: Benefits or costs of a market activity born by a third party, someone other than the immediate producer or consumer.

Free-Rider Problem: A free rider is someone who reaps direct benefits from someone else's purchase (consumption) of a good but does not pay for it.

Government Failure: Sometimes government intervention might worsen rather than improve market outcomes; failing to improve economic outcomes.

Income Transfer (Social Security): Income reserved exclusively for low-income wage earners: welfare benefits, food stamps, Medicaid, etc.

Marginal-Cost-Marginal-Benefit Rule: Explains which plan provides the maximum excess of total benefits over total costs, or the plan that provides society with the maximum net benefit, which is marginal benefit minus marginal cost.

Marginal Social Benefit (MSB): The sum of the marginal private cost (MPC) plus the marginal external cost (MEC) caused by producing an additional unit of a good.

Marginal Social Cost (MSC): The sum of the marginal private cost (MPC) plus the marginal external cost (MEC) caused by producing an additional unit of a good.

Moral-Hazard Problem: The tendency of one party to a contract to alter his or her behavior after the contract is signed in ways that could be costly to the other party.

Pigovian Tax: Named after the British economist Arthur Pigou; by imposing such a tax, the government is internalizing the negative externality, which means that individuals are taking into account the externality when they make decisions.

Pigovian Subsidy: To encourage the producer to produce goods that yield external benefit, the government provides a subsidy.

Public Choice Theory: Politicians pursue their own self-interest to maximize their reelection chances rather than promoting the best interests of society.

Public Good: Not excludable and not rival; a good or a service whose consumption by one person does not exclude consumption by others.

Pork-Barrel Politics: A means to secure public goods ("pork"); government projects that yield benefits mainly to a single political district and its political representative.

Private Good: Rival and excludable; a good or a service whose consumption by one person does not exclude consumption by others.

Rent-Seeking Behavior: The appeal to government for special benefits at taxpayers' or someone else's expense.

Taxes and Transfers: Critically important mechanism for redistribution of income.

Taxes: a) personal income tax—the tax levied on taxable income; b) **payroll tax**—taxes based on wages and salaries and used to finance two compulsory federal programs for retired workers (Social Security and Medicare); c) **corporate income tax**—difference between a corporation's total revenue and its total expenses; and d) **excise tax**—taxes levied on specific commodities, such as tobacco, liquor, and gasoline.

CHAPTER 11: GDP AND ECONOMIC GROWTH: HOW TO MEASURE TOTAL PRODUCTION AND INCOME

Business investment (I): a) **gross**—includes investment in replacement capital and in added capital and b) **net**—includes only investment in added capital.

Chain Price Index: Statistics on real GDP are published in "chained" dollars; prices in each year are "chained" to prices from the previous year, and the distortion from changes in relative prices is minimized.

Depreciation: "Wear and tear" of capital as it is used in production; the difference between gross and net investments.

Disposable Income (DI): After-tax income.

Personal Consumption Expenditure (PCE): The expenditure by households on individual purchases of durable goods and nongoods and services;

Government Expenditure (G): Government purchases of goods and services include expenditure on final products of business firms and all input costs, including labor costs, incurred by all levels of government.

Gross Domestic Product (GDP): The market value of all final goods and services (purchased for final use by consumers) produced in a given year; monetary value of aggregate production.

Growth Account: A method for measuring technological progress based on contributions to economic growth from increases in capital, labor, and output developed by Robert Solow, a Nobel Laureate in economics and professor of economic at the Massachusetts Institute of Technology.

GDP Calculation: a) production approach—total value of firms' production of final goods and services; b) **expenditure approach**—aggregate spending on final goods and services (how income is spent); and c)

income approach—how income is earned in the forms of compensation of employees (wages) and net operating surplus (interest, rent, and profit).

GDP Equation (Y): The sum of consumption expenditures (C), investment expenditures (I), government purchases G), and net exports (X-M).

GDP: a) **nominal**—the market value of all final goods and services produced in a given year expressed in the prices of the same year; b) **real**—the GDP that has been "deflated" or "inflated" to reflect changes in the price level or in the value of final goods and services produced in a given year in the prices of a base year; and c) **GDP deflator**—measures how prices change over time and is equal to a fraction of Nominal GDP and Real GDP multiplied by 100 percent.

Gross National Product (GNP): GDP plus the net income earned by US firms and residents abroad minus any income earned by foreign firms and residents in the US.

Human Development Index (HDI): A method developed by the United Nations based on three factors: life expectancy at birth; knowledge, measured by adult literacy and school enrollment; and standard of living, measured by GDP per capita in purchasing power parity of US dollars.

National Income (NI): The total income earned by US residents in the United States or abroad.

National Income and Product Account (NIPA): The official system of GDP calculation in the United States.

Personal Income (PI): Subtract from the national income the income that is earned but not received, and add the income that is received but not earned, or subtract from NI payroll taxes (Social Security contributions), corporate profit taxes, and undistributed corporate profits and add transfer payments.

Price Index: A measure of the price of a specified collection of goods and services; called a "market basket."

Net Export (NE, Trade Balance): The value of exports of goods and services minus the value of imports of goods and services.

Value Added: The difference between the market value of all products and the market value of intermediate goods.

CHAPTER 12: BUSINESS CYCLE: UNEMPLOYMENT AND INFLATION

Business Cycle: Alternating periods of economic growth and contraction; the fluctuations in aggregate production measured by the ups and downs of real GDP.

Business Cycle, the Four Phases: a) **peak**—the date at which a recession begins when the economy is near or at full employment, and the price level is likely to rise; b) **recession**—a period of decline in total output, income, employment, and trade; usually lasts six or more months; c) **trough**—a period when the level of real GDP "bottoms out"; when unemployment and idle production capacity are at their highest levels; the date at which a recession ends; and d) **expansion**—output rises, profits generally improve, and employment moves toward full employment, but the price level also rises.

Discouraged Worker: An unemployed individual who is not actively seeking employment and is classified as "not in labor force."

Full Employment: The economy is "fully employed" when it experiences only frictional and structural employment.

Great Depression: The most extreme recession in the United States that began on October 29, 1929, "Black Tuesday," when the stock market crashed.

Labor Force: People both employed and unemployed.

Labor Force Participation: The percentage of the working-age population who are members of the labor force

Misery Index: The sum of inflation and unemployment rates.

National Bureau of Economic Research (NBER): A private research group located in Cambridge, Massachusetts, composed of professional economists, that decides what a recession is and when it has happened.

Natural Rate of Unemployment (NRU): Occurs when the number of job seekers equals the number of job vacancies, and the economy is said to be producing its potential output.

Okun's Law: Indicates that for every percentage point by which actual unemployment is above (below) the natural rate, real GDP is 2% points below (above) potential GDP.

Part-Time Worker: A worker who work less than full-time (thirty-five hours per week).

Phillips Curve: An inverse relationship in the short-run between rates of unemployment and corresponding rates of inflation within an economy; named after New Zealand economist A. Phillips, who demonstrated it by using a curve.

Stagflation: Combination of stagnation in production and inflation.

Unemployed: A person who is available for work and must be either: a) without work but has made specific efforts to find a job within the previous four weeks and b) waiting to be recalled back to a job from which he or she has been laid off.

Unemployment Rate: The percentage of the people in the labor force who are unemployed.

Unemployment Types: a) **frictional (transitional or search) unemployment**—consists of those searching for jobs or waiting to take jobs soon or workers who are "between jobs; b) **structural (compositional)**—arises when changes in technology or international competition change the skills needed to perform jobs or change the locations of jobs; and c) **cyclical**—is caused by a decline in total spending; is likely to occur in the recession phase of the business cycle.

Working-Age Population: The total population, excluding people less then sixteen years old and people who are institutionalized.

Consumer Price Index (CPI, Cost-of-Living Index): The price of a "market basket" of goods and services purchased by a typical urban consumer.

Core Inflation Index: The percentage change in the PCE price index, with the exclusion of prices for food and energy.

Cost of Inflation: Menu costs, shoe-leather costs (people anxious to spend their money to avoid its falling value—"take the shoes off"), confusion and uncertainty costs, and added financial and tax costs.

Deflation: A decrease in the average level of prices of goods and services.

Disinflation: The reduction in the rate of inflation.

Hyperinflation: An extremely rapid increase in the general level of prices by about 100% or more per year.

Inflation: A rise in the average level of prices, not a change in any specific price.

Inflation Rate: The percentage change in the price level from one year to the next.

Inflation Types: a) **demand-pull inflation**—spending is increasing faster than production; "too much money is chasing too few goods" and b) **cost-push inflation**—rise in per unit cost of production at each level of spending; costs "are pushing" the prices up.

Interest Rates: a) **nominal**—percentage increase in money that the borrower pays the lender and b) **real**—the percentage increase in purchasing power that the borrower pays the lender.

Personal Consumption Expenditure (PCE): The average of current prices of goods and services included in the consumption expenditure divided by base year prices.

Price Stability: The absence of significant changes in the average level of prices.

CHAPTER 13: AGGREGATE DEMAND AND AGGREGATE SUPPLY

Aggregate Demand (AD): Various quantities of output that all market participants (households, businesses, governments, and foreigners) are willing and able to buy at alternative price levels in a given period of time; the total demand for GDP as a function of price level.

Aggregate Demand Determinants (Shifters): a) changes in consumer spending caused by changes in money supply; b) changes in business investment spending, which is affected by changes in taxes; c) changes in government spending; and d) changes in net export spending.

Aggregate Supply (AS): The total quantity of output producers are willing and able to supply at alternative price levels in a given time period; the level of real domestic output that firms will produce at each price level.

Aggregate Supply Determinants (Shifters): a) change in input prices; b) productivity; c) changes in nominal wages; and d) legal-institutional environment.

Classical School of Economics: The economy is self-adjusting to deviations from its long-term growth trend; at the core of the classical approach are flexible prices and flexible wages.

Classical Range of Aggregate Supply Function: A vertical range would be reached when AD was high enough to ensure full employment.

Fiscal Policy: The use of government tax and spending powers to alter macroeconomic outcomes.

Keynesian Range of Aggregate Supply Function: A horizontal range of AS when an inadequate demand results in high rates of unemployment.

Keynesian School of Economics: Named after the British economist John Maynard Keynes, who believed that the private economy is inherently unstable, and this requires government intervention.

Long-Run AS Curve (LRAS): Is vertical at the economy's potential output (or full employment output); in the long-run; output is determined solely by the factors of production.

Macroeconomic Equilibrium: a) **short-run**—the unique combination of price level and output that is compatible with both buyers' and sellers' intentions and b) **long-run**—occurs when the short-run aggregate supply curve and the aggregate demand curve intersect each other at a point on the vertical long-run supply curve.

Monetary Policy: The use of money and credit controls (interest rates) to influence macroeconomic outcomes which is exercised by the Federal Reserve (Fed).

Movements AD, AS Curves: Are determined solely by the changes in price level.

Negative Demand Shock: Shift to the left of the AD curve causes a recession and cyclical unemployment.

Negative Supply Shock: Disruption of oil supply with abrupt increase in prices shifts the **Short-Run Aggregate Supply Curve** (SRAS) curve to the left and the economy to a new equilibrium with double damages: higher prices and lower output.

Positive Demand Shock: A shift to the left of the AD curve causes a recession and cyclical unemployment.

Positive Supply Shock: The **Short-Run Aggregate Supply Curve** (SRAS) shifts to the right because production costs are reduced, quantity supplied increases, and prices go down—a double advantage.

Purchasing Power of Money: The real quantity of goods and services that the dollar will buy.

Short-Run Aggregate Supply Curve (SRAS): Is up sloping; relatively flat prices do not change very much in this period; firms adjust production to meet the demand.

Three Effects of a Price-Level Change: a) **wealth (real-balances) effect**—the increase in spending that occurs when the real value of money increases when the price level falls; b) **interest-rate effect**—a higher price level reduces the amount of real output demanded and vice versa—cheaper money stimulates more borrowing and loan-financed purchases; and c) **foreign purchases (trade) effect**—when American-made products become cheaper, US consumers will buy fewer imports and more domestic output and vice versa.

CHAPTER 14: FISCAL POLICY: HOW TO STABILIZE THE ECONOMY

Automatic (Built In) Stabilizers: A mechanism that increases the government budget deficit (or reduces its budget surplus) during a recession period and increases the budget surplus (or reduces the budget deficit) during inflation; it does not require a direct intervention of decision makers.

"Crowding In" Effects: Occur with government budget surplus—government is investing the excess money into the economy, "crowding in" private sector finances.

"Crowding Out" Effects: Occur with government budget deficit spending—to cover it, the government is borrowing from the general public and the private sector.

Cyclically Adjusted Budget Balance (Counter-Cyclical Fiscal Policy): The budget balance that would be in the absence of recessionary or inflationary gaps.

Discretionary Spending: Spending on all government programs; the single largest component of the federal budget that the US Congress authorizes on an annual basis.

Entitlements and Mandatory Spending: The single largest component of the federal budget that the US Congress authorizes by prior laws.

Fiscal Policy: The use of government spending and taxes to adjust Aggregate Demand (AD); a) **discretionary**—the changes in government spending and taxes are at the option of the federal government and b) **nondiscretionary**—changes in some types of spending and taxes (unemployment insurance payments, changes in personal income taxes) that are triggered by the state of the economy and occur without any actions of the government.

Fiscal Policy Types: a) **expansionary**—increased government spending and decreased taxes; a policy applied during a recession period and b) **contractionary**—decreased government spending and increased taxes; a policy applied during inflation.

Fiscal Multiplier: The ratio of change in GDP to the initial change in spending or to initial reduction in taxes.

Government Budget: a) **deficit**—government spending in excess of tax revenues and b) **surplus**—tax revenues in excess of government spending.

Fiscal Policy Lags: a) **recognition**—it requires time to recognize the need for fiscal policy to be changed; b) **administrative**—once the problem has been recognized, it takes time to formulate the new target of fiscal policy and to take action; and c) **operational**—the time elapsed between change in policy and its impact on the economy when the output, employment, and price level change.

Net Interest on Public Debt: The amount which the government pays on its debt held by the public (US Treasury bonds, bills, and savings bonds).

Marginal Propensity to Consume (MPC): Is the proportion, or fraction, of any change in income consumed.

Marginal Propensity to Save (MPS): The fraction of any change in income saved.

Induced Taxes: Taxes that vary with real GDP. In an expansion, induced taxes rise, and in a recession, induced taxes fall, helping to stabilize the economy.

Needs-Tested Spending: Spending on programs that entitle suitably qualified people and businesses to receive benefits that vary with needs and with the state of the economy.

Public Debt: The accumulation of past federal budget deficits that leads to increased US national debt.

Supply-Side Fiscal Policy: Tax cuts, deregulation of the markets, and other policies for investors and business-men designed to trickle-down to the rest of the economy.

Three Types of Tax Systems: a) **progressive**—the average tax rate rises with GDP (personal income taxes); b) **proportional**—the average tax rate remains constant as GDP rises (corporate taxes); and c) **regressive**—the average tax rate falls as GDP rises

CHAPTER 15: MONETARY SYSTEM AND MONETARY POLICY

Bank Reserves and Reserve Ratio: The assets held by a bank to fulfill its deposit obligations; these reserves are only a fraction of total transactions deposits.

Bank's Assets: a) **cash assets** and b) **securities and loans**.

Bank's Liabilities: Deposits, which are part of money.

Bank's Net Worth: Assets minus liabilities.

Barter: Direct exchange of one good for another without the use of money.

Board of Governors: Designs the monetary policy to ensure the well-being of the economy as a whole.

Credit/Debit Cards: Represent just a payment service and not a final form of payment or money.

Demand for Money: a) **asset demand (Ad)**—money kept as stored value for later use in forms of corporate stocks, bonds, or cash and b) **transactions (Td)**—for money (businesses, for example, need money to pay for labor, materials, power, and other inputs); its main determinant is the level of nominal GDP.

Deposits: a) **checking**—perform the same market function as cash and are collectively called transactions accounts; b) **savings**—which are interest-bearing accounts at a bank or thrift, including money market deposit accounts (MMDA); c) **small time deposits**—less than $100,000 deposits that become available upon their maturity; and d) **money market mutual funds**—use the combined funds of individual shareholders to buy interest-bearing short-term credit instruments (certificates of deposit and US government securities).

Federal Funds Rate: The interest rate at which commercial banks can borrow and lend reserves in the federal funds market.

Federal Reserve System (FRS or Fed): Is the central bank of the US, the "bankers' bank."

Federal Open Market Committee (FOMC): With the Federal Advisory Council, assists the Board of Governors to conduct monetary policy.

Fiat Money: Money that derives its value entirely from its official status as a means of exchange.

Fractional Reserve System: Only a fraction of the total money supply is held in reserve as currency.

Functions of Money: a) **medium of exchange**—money is an asset that is usable for buying and selling goods and services; b) **standard of value (unit of account)**—with money ($) as an acceptable unit of account, the price of each item needs to be stated only in terms of this monetary unit; and c) **store of value**—a means of holding purchasing power over time.

Liquidity: Spendability.

Money Market: The demand and supply of money.

Money Multiplier: The reciprocal of the required reserve ratio.

Monetary Policy Tools: a) **required reserve ratio**—minimum threshold for a bank imposed by the government that directly limits deposit creation possibilities; b) **discount rate**—the rate of interest charged by the Fed for lending reserves to private banks; and c) **open market operations**—the most important mechanism for directly altering the reserves of the banking system; "open" means open to all buyers and sellers.

Monetary Policy Types: a) **expansionary (easy) policy**—increases the aggregate demand during recession by buying securities (bonds), lowering the reserve ratio, and lowering the discount rate; b) **contractionary (tight) monetary policy**—decreases the aggregate demand during inflation by selling securities, raising the reserve ratio and increasing the discount rate.

Token Money: Currency held by the public in the form of coins and paper money.

Velocity of Money: The number of times per year the average dollar is spent on goods and services.

CHAPTER 16: THE US AND THE GLOBAL ECONOMY: CHALLENGES OF MODERN TECHNOLOGY AND GLOBALIZATION

Advanced Economies: Twenty-nine industrialized countries of North America (USA and Canada) and Western Europe.

Bonds: Promises to repay a loan, usually at a set rate of interest.

BRICS Economies: An acronym composed from the first letter of the following countries: Brazil, Russia, India, China, and South Africa.

Business Organization Types: a) **sole proprietorship** is a business owned by one person with unlimited liability; b) **partnerships** are owned by two or more individuals, each of whom receives a portion of any profits; and c) **corporations** are owned by many individuals, each of whom owns shares (stocks) of the corporation, which is characterized by limited liability.

Central Planning (Command-Administrative) System: a) The factors of production, including land and all natural resources, factories, financial institutions etc., belong to the state; b) The authoritarian methods of coordination of economic activity are run by a special body, such as Gosplan (Central Planning Board) in the former Soviet Union; and c) The distribution of well-being among the citizens is supposed to be equitable and egalitarian.

Developing Economies: One hundred and thirty-two countries in Africa, Asia, the Middle East, Europe, and Central and South America.

Dual Role of the Government: "Arbiter" (referee) and "Economic Player" (actor).

Economic Systems: A set of legal, institutional, and organizational arrangements based on ownership of factors of productions and mechanism of decision making (motivation, coordination, and rewarding the economic activity).

Emerging Markets: Twenty-eight countries in Europe and Asia, including the former Soviet Union and its Central- and Eastern-European satellites.

Government Failure: Failure of the government to improve market outcomes which might reduce the total amount of output.

Human Capital: Knowledge and skills accumulated through education, training, and work experience.

Industry's Types (Technology Standpoint): a) **a plant**—a structure that is using inputs to produce outputs; b) **a firm**—an organization that owns and operates a combination of plants; and c) **an industry**—a collection of firms that are producing similar products.

Knowledge Economy Index (KEI): A broad measure of preparedness of a country for the knowledge economy summarized by a country's performances on twelve variables related to four knowledge economy pillars: a) **economic and institutional regime**; b) **education and skills**; c) **information and communication infrastructure**; and d) **innovation system**.

Market Failure: The market fails to produce goods and services that its society wants.

Market System (Capitalism): It is based on private ownership and functions through market prices and sales; it determines desired outputs and resource allocation, coordinates economic activity, and widely disperses economic decision making, which is taken by each individual participant in the market, who is motivated by self-interest.

Mixed System: An economy that uses both market and nonmarket signals to allocate resources or a combination of government directives and market mechanisms to determine economic **outcomes.**

Principal-Agent Problem: Eventual conflicts of interests between owner objectives and manager objectives.

Technology Revolutions: a) **the informational technology**—software revolution; b) **the new material science**—smart manufacturing revolution; and c) **the communication systems**—wireless revolution.

CHAPTER 17: INTERNATIONAL TRADE AND FINANCE

Absolute Advantage: A country may have an absolute advantage if it is producing some specific goods with fewer resources (per unit of output) than another country.

Asian Pacific Economic Cooperation (APEC): Was signed in 1989 to reduce trade barriers among its nations, and today it has a membership of 21 nations.

Autarky: A situation in which a country cannot trade with other countries.

Balance of Payment (BOP): A country's accounts record its international trading, borrowing, and lending. Composed by three balances: a) **current account**—equals exports plus net interest income plus net transfers minus imports; b) **capital account**—records payment flows for financial capital (real estate, corporate stocks, bonds, government securities, etc.); foreign investment in the United States minus US investment abroad; and c) **official settlement account**—the government's holdings of foreign currency, certain reserves held with the International Monetary Fund (IMF), and stocks of gold.

Comparative Advantage: The ability of a country to produce a specific good at a lower opportunity cost than its trading partners; total output will be greatest when each good is produced by the nation that has lowest domestic opportunity cost in producing that good.

Currency: a) **appreciation**—an increase in the value of one currency relative to another currency and b) **depreciation**—a decrease in the value of one currency relative to another.

Domestic Price: The price that would prevail in a closed economy without international trade.

Dumping Argument: Selling of excess goods in foreign markets at a price below cost.

European Union (EU): Designed to remove all trade barriers within Europe and create a "single market"; includes 27 European countries.

Exchange Rates: The price of one country's currency expressed in the price of another country's currency.

Exchange Rates Types: a) **flexible (floating)**—demand and supply determine exchange rates and no government intervention occurs and b) **fixed**—the government determines exchange rates and makes any necessary adjustments in its economy to maintain those rates.

International Exchange Systems: a) **the gold standard**; b) **Breton Woods (adjustable) peg system**; and c) **current (managed floating) exchange system**.

Factor Intensity: Describes differences between goods in terms of the ratio of capital to labor.

Free Trade: Trade without government restrictions.

General Agreement on Tariffs and Trade (GATT): GATT was created in 1947 based on three principles: a) **equal, nondiscriminatory trade for member nations**; b) **reduction of tariffs through multilateral negotiations**; and c) **elimination of import quotas**.

Import Quotas: A limit on the quantity of a good that may be imported in a given time period.

Infant Industry Argument: Protection of a new industry to make it competitive in world markets.

International Trade: a) **import**—goods and services purchased from foreign sources; b) **export**—goods and services sold to foreign buyers; and c) **trade balance**—the value of exports minus the value of imports.

Hecksher-Ohlin Trade Model: A country has a comparative advantage in a good when production is intensive in factors abundant in that country; this model is named after two Swedish economists.

"Leontief Paradox": Some goods that the United States imported were slightly more capital-intensive that those exported; named after the author Wassily Leontief, an American economist.

National Security Argument: Some industries need be protected to be able to operate in wartime and remain independent from other countries.

Non-Tariff Barriers (NTB): Licensing requirements calling for adherence to unreasonable standards pertaining to product quality and safety or unnecessary bureaucratic red tape used to restrict imports.

North American Trade Agreement (NAFTA): Established in 1994 to eliminate all tariffs and other trade barriers between Canada, Mexico, and the United States.

Offshoring (Outsourcing): Related to a shift of a domestic firm's production and jobs to other countries with cheap labor forces.

Tariffs: Excise taxes on imports used as leverage for revenue purposes or as mechanisms to protect domestic producers from foreign competition.

Terms of Trade: The rate (prices) at which goods and services are exchanged.

The Tariff Act of 1930 ("Smoot-Hawley"): Amended "specific tariff schedules for over twenty thousand items, almost all of them increases."

The Reciprocal Trade Agreements Act of 1934: Reduced the tariffs and authorized the US president to negotiate and implement pacts with other nations in which each agreed to cut tariffs on US exports by up to 50%, without further recourse to Congress.

Trading Possibilities Line: The amounts of two products a nation can obtain by specializing in one product and trading it for the other.

Trade Protection Policy: Is promoted under the motive of protection of domestic producers from foreign competitors in import-competing industries.

Voluntary Export Restrictions (VER): Agreements by foreign firms to "voluntarily" limit their exports to a particular country.

World Price: The price that equates the quantities supplied and demanded globally.

World Trade Organization (WTO [replaced GATT in 1994]): Agreement to several trade liberalization measures: a) **reductions in tariffs worldwide**; b) **new rules to promote trade in services**; c) **reductions of agricultural subsidies** that have distorted the global pattern of trade in agricultural goods; d) **new protections for intellectual property** (copyrights, patents, trademarks); and e) **phasing out of quotas on textiles and apparel**.

Printed in the USA
CPSIA information can be obtained
at www.ICGtesting.com
LVHW082223250823
756330LV00019B/116

9 781634 8783

Adventures in Ray Tracing

Alfonso Hermida

Publisher: David P. Ewing

Director of Publishing: Michael Miller

Managing Editor: Corinne Walls

Marketing Manager: Ray Robinson

Dedication

To my wife, Linda, and my parents Alfonso and Betsy.

About the Author

Alfonso Hermida

Alfonso Hermida has a B.S. and an M.S. in mechanical engineering from the University of Puerto Rico, and an M.S. in mechanical engineering/space systems from The George Washington University in Washington, D.C. He currently works with NASA/Goddard Space Flight Center in Maryland as an aerospace engineer. He is also an adjunct professor of the Mathematics Department at Capitol College in Laurel, Maryland, where he teaches ordinary differential equations, CAD, and thermodynamics. He has worked as a software consultant and in his free time enjoys writing his own software programs. His main interests include structural analysis, dynamics, computer graphics, and animation.

iii

Credits

Publishing Manager
Joseph B. Wikert

Product Development Specialist
Bryan Gambrel

Production Editors
Phil Kitchel
Lori Cates

Copy Editor
Linda Seifert

Technical Editor
Dan Richardson

Cover Designer
Dan Armstrong

Cover Illustration
Mike Miller, Headspin Studios

Book Designer
Amy Peppler-Adams

Illustrator
Katherine Hanley

Production Team
Angela Bannan
Danielle Bird
Charlotte Clapp
Teresa Forrester
Joelynn Gifford
Bob LaRoche
Tim Montgomery
Caroline Roop
Dennis Sheehan
Tina Trettin
Sue VandeWalle
Mary Beth Wakefield
Donna Winter
Lillian Yates

Indexer
Johnna VanHoose

Composed in Stone Serif and MCPdigital by Prentice Hall Computer Publishing

Acknowledgments

I have to thank a lot of people who were responsible in one way or another for this book:

- Joe Wikert, for giving me the opportunity; the Que team, for cleaning up my typing, especially Phil Kitchel and Lori Cates; and Kathy Hanley, for her great work with my sketches. Thanks also to my technical editor, Dan Richardson, who was very enthusiastic about cleaning up after me.

- Alexander Enzmann, for doing such a great job writing Polyray.

- Bob Berry, the author of CompuShow, for letting us use his program.

- A special thanks to Dan Farmer, for telling me about CompuServe's GraphDev forum and for his feedback on POVCAD. He was kind enough to upload POVCAD to CompuServe.

  Finally, I want to take the opportunity to mention several people who have helped with POVCAD:

- Albert Waltner, Peter Jack, and Curtis Olson, for the initial Beta testing and all the helpful comments.

- Phil Long, Jerry Thomaston, Amanda Osborne, and James P. Hawkins, who continue to Beta test.

- David Standring, for Beta testing version 2.0b and checking the book manuscripts.

Trademarks

All terms mentioned in this book that are known to be trademarks or service marks have been appropriately capitalized. Que cannot attest to the accuracy of this information. Use of a term in this book should not be regarded as affecting the validity of any trademark or service mark.

Overview

Table of Contents

Introduction

Welcome to the exciting world of ray tracing! A little while ago, when personal computers starting coming out, computer image generation was only a dream. Computer graphics programs were usually power-hungry applications requiring lots of memory and speed. Now there are the 386 and 486 machines, and it's been worth the wait (at the time of this writing, Pentium chip-based computers are starting to come out—they promise to take ray tracing to a new level). Computer image generation is everywhere, from advertising and movies to games and art. The incredible growth in the popularity of computer-generated art has developed into a quest for the ultimate goal: a perfect photo-realistic image.

As you become familiar with the subject, you'll be able to develop your own images, and you might even take it as a personal challenge to improve their quality as much as possible.

This book helps you develop your own images and animation by presenting the Polyray ray tracer, developed by Alexander Enzmann. Polyray is loaded with features, which this book presents while teaching you the basics of ray tracing, 3-D modeling, and animation. You'll have the chance to use the included sample files and modify them to suit your own taste. Eventually, you'll be able to start from scratch and convert your own thoughts into computer images.

If you have already taken a quick glance over the book, you must be interested in the topic, and if after looking through it you can't figure out what's going on, then this book is for you. If you are already familiar with the topic, this book can help you increase your knowledge.

In any case, it's all about having fun and learning something useful at the same time.

Who Should Read This Book?

This book is for everyone interested in computer graphics, but it is specifically for

- Anyone who wants to learn how to create photo-realistic computer images. This group includes people who have never been exposed to the subject as well as people who have read about it but want to take a hands-on approach.

- Anyone who wants to learn what ray tracing is and what the basic concepts are. This group includes people who wish to increase their knowledge of computer graphics techniques, or who want to incorporate it as an additional tool in their work.

- Anyone who knows about ray tracing and is looking for new ideas for their own projects.

- Anyone interested in understanding the basics of 3-D modeling and how it relates to computer image generation.

- Anyone interested in learning how to create animations using ray tracing and 3-D modeling tools.

What This Book Is About

Adventures in Ray Tracing has many goals, but it is specifically intended to

- Help you learn how to create photo-realistic images in your computer by means of ray tracing (and the use of Polyray, the ray tracing program included with the book).

- Show you why a 3-D modeler is an important visualization tool for computer image generation, and show you how to use the one included with the book (POVCAD—both DOS and Windows versions are included).

- Show you how to combine the first two purposes to create your own animation sequences or movies.

This book takes you through all the necessary steps, starting with the basics of ray tracing: creating simple images and using the built-in objects available. Then you take a look at more complex objects and learn how to literally "cut and paste" pieces of objects together to form new objects. You are then introduced to POVCAD, the 3-D modeler included with the book, and shown how to generate scenes for the ray-tracing program. Finally, you develop animations using all the techniques you acquire working through the book.

By the end of the book, you'll have a good working knowledge of ray tracing, 3-D modeling, and animation.

Included Software

Bundled with this book you'll find three interesting programs:

1. POLYRAY 1.6a (PLY386.ZIP and PLYEXE.ZIP)

    This is the main tool you'll be using to create those awesome computer graphics images. The book explains Polyray's features, and the disk includes the author's documentation files and additional sample files. A must-have for those of you who like to modify code!

2. POVCAD 2.0b (PVCWIN.ZIP and PVCDOS.ZIP)

    This is a 3-D modeler that generates Polyray-compatible data. With POVCAD, you're able to visually create a scene that will eventually be converted into a photo-realistic image. Included on the disk are both

DOS and Windows versions. The Windows version is more advanced than the DOS version, and is presented in greater detail.

3. COMPUSHOW 8.61a (CSHOW.ZIP)

This is an excellent utility program you can use as an image file viewer.

Needless to say, all the examples done in the book are on the disk.

Shareware Information

All the programs included with the disk are copyrighted by their authors and are distributed based on the shareware concept. If you wish to continue using these programs, you should register them. All of them require very modest fees, ranging from $15 to $35. For details, check the documentation available for each program.

Equipment Requirements

POLYRAY

There are two versions distributed with the disk (for use on computers with or without co-processors). At a minimum, both require a 386 microprocessor and 2 Megabytes of RAM. A VGA graphics card is also required (Super VGA is recommended).

POVCAD

The Windows version requires Windows 3.1. A co-processor is highly recommended. The DOS version requires a VGA graphics card and a mouse.

COMPUSHOW

Requires a graphics card.

Software Installation

Check the READ.ME file included in the disk for the latest information on how to install the programs.

Introduction to Ray Tracing

In this chapter, you learn what ray tracing is and what components make up a ray tracing model. First, you learn how to define a 3-D scene and how to "look" at it by positioning an observer. Next, you place 3-D objects in the scene. Finally, you learn how to add photo-realism to the final image.

What Is Ray Tracing?

Ray tracing is a technique by which you can create photo-realistic images. This technique simulates the interaction between objects and light. Photo-realistic images are created by modeling the optical properties of light.

Ray tracing theory is based heavily on modeling light, 3-D objects, surface

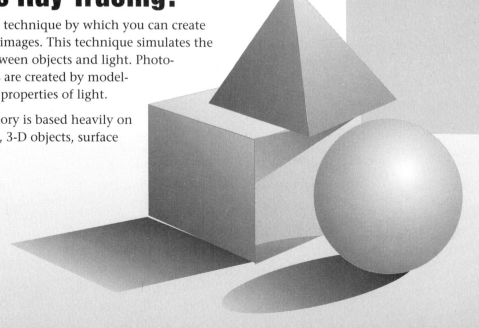

finishes, textures, and colors mathematically. Most ray tracing programs make most of the math clear to the user by using their own specialized and simplified language. Everything from light-object interaction to ripples on a surface is explained mathematically. Some of these mathematical expressions are not perfect, but they are good enough to simulate the "real thing."

In a ray tracing scene, you position objects as you want them to appear in the final image. The surface and color characteristics of each object are defined. Finally, light sources are located in specific places to create highlights and shadows, and an observer is positioned. This observer is your point of view. Next, the ray tracing program creates a mathematical model of the objects, the light, and the observer, then it computes the color for each pixel on-screen based on what the observer should be seeing (see fig. 1.1).

Figure 1.1

A representation of a ray tracing scene.

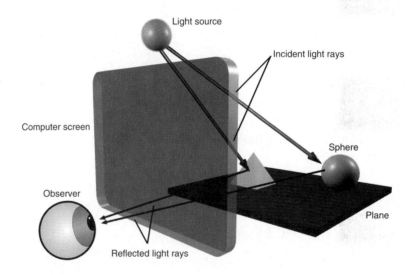

For example, in figure 1.1, one of the light rays intersects a sphere, is reflected by the sphere, and finally crosses the computer screen. The color of the pixel where the light ray hit is affected by the color of the sphere and the light source. In more complicated scenes where some of the objects are highly reflective (mirror-like) or transparent, the final color is a combination of the colors of any surrounding objects. A complex scene can be described like this: Imagine a room with only one open window and an infinite amount of walls. All of the walls have been recently painted with different colors and the paint is still wet. You can imagine that the light is a

highly elastic ball that was thrown inside the room. The ball keeps bouncing off the walls and hitting other walls until it goes through the window. Every time the ball bounces, it gets some paint from the wall. The color of the ball will be a combination of the colors of the walls it touched.

Here are two examples of ray-traced images. Figure 1.2 displays the top of a desk. The desk has a wood finish. On top of it is a yellow sphere that appears to be metallic, a lamp that has a very polished finish, and a frame with a picture in it. The picture is a photo of one of NASA's space shuttles. Can you determine where the light source is located? (Hint: Check the shadows.)

Figure 1.2

A ray-traced desk scene.

The second image (fig. 1.3) shows a box with a face. The surface finish is similar to that of the lamp in figure 1.2. The box is placed on top of a brown, flat plane. How many objects are there in this scene? You might be tempted to say three; however, the face alone consists of 807 triangles!

In the next section, you start with the basic concepts of ray tracing and work your way up.

Figure 1.3

Ray-traced box with a face scene. (3-D model created with the HyperSpace 3-D digitizer from Mira Imaging, Inc.)

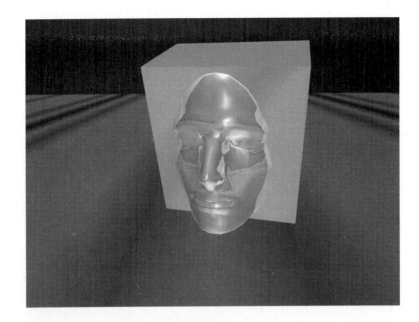

General Concepts

Before you create your first ray-traced image, you have to become familiar with some basic concepts. Later, this knowledge will help you control the creation of a photo-realistic scene. This section starts by describing how a 3-D world is defined mathematically and how to position objects in it.

3-D Coordinate Systems

A 3-D coordinate system is used to describe the location of an object in space. A 3-D coordinate system consists of three axes labeled x, y, and z, which are 90 degrees relative to one another. Two common orientation conventions used in coordinate systems are the *right-handed* and the *left-handed* conventions, as shown in figure 1.4. Note that the z axis is different in both coordinate systems. The direction of the rotations about a given axis also are different.

Figure 1.4

Coordinate system conventions.

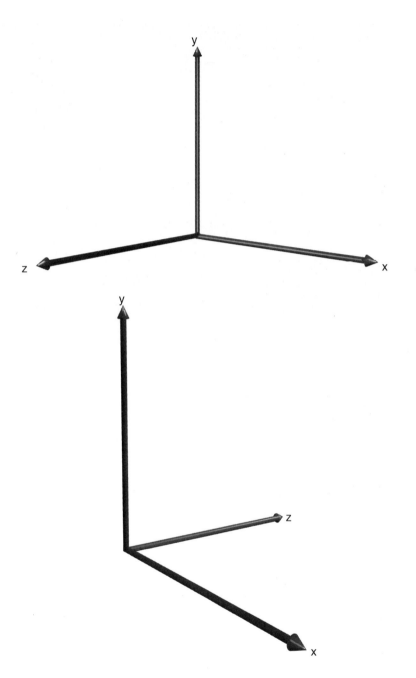

Throughout the book, the left-handed coordinate system is used. You'll see the reason for this choice when you run the ray tracing program. The following section reviews how to locate points and apply rotations using the left-handed coordinate system.

Defining a Point

The location of a point in a 3-D coordinate system can be expressed by three values: the X, Y, and Z coordinates. The origin of the coordinate system is the point where all axes intersect one another. The coordinates of the origin are <0 0 0>, where the symbol <X Y Z> denotes coordinates of a point. This means that a point located at <a b c> has displaced *a* units along the x axis, *b* units along y, and *c* units along z, starting from the origin. A point defined as <1 0 0> would be located at the 1 unit in the x axis. Figure 1.5 shows a unit cube that describes the coordinate locations of different points.

A point, due to its simplicity, requires only three values or coordinates to be located in space; however, a 3-D object such as a box requires six: three coordinates <X Y Z> and three *rotations* <Rx Ry Rz>. First, you should know how to define a rotation.

Defining Rotations

To understand how rotations can be used to define the position of a 3-D object, look at the convention used in left-handed coordinate systems. The expression *left-handed* comes from the fact that you can use your left hand to express the direction of a rotation about an axis. By aligning the thumb of your left hand in the positive direction of an axis, the fingers of your left hand curl in the positive direction of the rotation about that axis. Figure 1.6 shows the concept. Observe how the thumb points in the positive direction of the X axis. The fingers are curled, following the positive sense of the rotation.

You can use another method to present the same concept. If you imagine standing very far away in the same direction of a given axis and looking at the origin, a positive rotation will always be in a clockwise direction. For example, if an object is at the origin and aligned with the positive y axis, a positive 90-degree rotation about x would position the object in the positive z axis. A negative rotation of 90 degrees from its new position would align it again with the y axis. Figure 1.7 shows this idea.

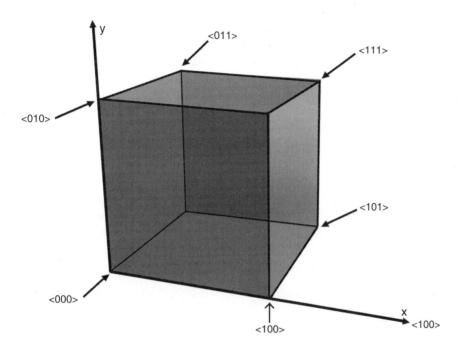

Figure 1.5

Point locations on a box.

Defining the Location of an Object

Now that you are familiar with the left-handed convention and how to define a rotation, the next step is to define the position of a 3-D object. As mentioned earlier, three coordinates and three rotations are required to describe the object's position. Why? Take a flower vase as an example. We want to locate the vase on top of a table where the origin of a coordinate system is. We decide to locate it at the origin <0 0 0>. Now a question arises: when we mentioned the position <0 0 0>, did we describe the orientation of the vase? Is it standing up? Lying down? If we compare both cases, the flower vase is rotated by 90 degrees (see fig. 1.8).

In both cases, the center of the vase is located at <0 0 0>; however, the orientation is different. To describe its position absolutely, you have to use coordinates and rotations rather than just coordinates (which is the method for describing points).

After an object or set of objects is positioned, an observer can "walk" through the scene and position himself in different locations to look at it. By moving around, different parts of the scene are exposed and what appeared to be hidden is now visible. This brings us to the viewpoint concept.

11

Figure 1.6

Using the left-hand rule.

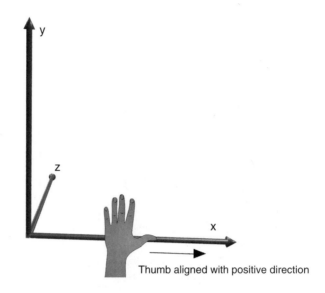

Thumb aligned with positive direction

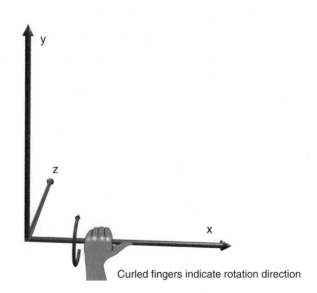

Curled fingers indicate rotation direction

Figure 1.7

Positive rotation as viewed by an observer.

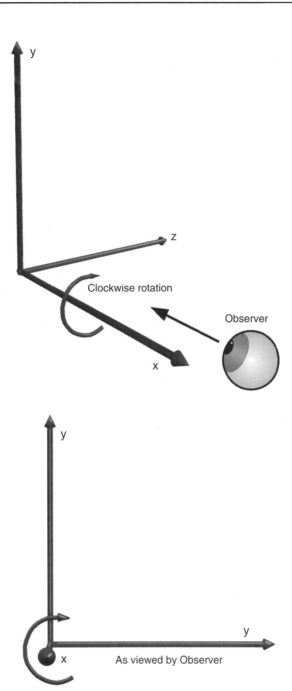

Viewpoint

A *viewpoint* defines the location of an observer, and the direction and point at which the observer is looking. A standard format usually includes information such as the location of the observer, the direction of the view, and where are the "up" and "right" directions relative to the observer (see fig. 1.9). Two observers can be looking at the same place—each in a different position—and their "up" and "right" directions will be different. The combination of direction and the point being looked at act as a field of view in the same way real cameras work. Varying these two creates a zooming effect on the final scene.

Figures 1.10, 1.11, and 1.12 present a scene viewed from three viewpoints: front, side, and top, respectively. The red and yellow spheres are used as an orientation aid.

What the observer sees is relative to the location of the "eye" and also dependent on the amount of light that reaches the object or objects being looked at. Therefore, light sources are an important part of ray tracing.

Light Sources

Light sources make ray tracing "happen." Two common types of light sources are the *point source* and the *spotlight*. The point source can be compared to a normal light bulb that radiates light in all directions. The spotlight is directional and can be controlled. Light sources are described by their location and the color they produce. A spotlight has parameters that describe how its intensity varies from the center to the edge of the cone.

You can create interesting effects with the liberal use of light sources. (It is fair to warn you, however, that ray tracer computation time increases with the number of light sources.) An example of an interesting effect is the use of arrays of low-intensity light sources to create the effect of soft shadows. Another example is locating a light source at the center of an object to create the effect of the object itself being the light source.

Shadows are a very important part of ray tracing, and are usually a planned result of using light sources. There are times when you will be more interested in the creation of shadows than in the creation of highlights on an object. Light sources are studied in more detail in Chapter 2, in which we explore the Polyray ray tracing program.

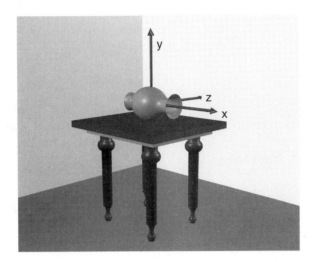

Figure 1.8

*Objects located
at the origin.*

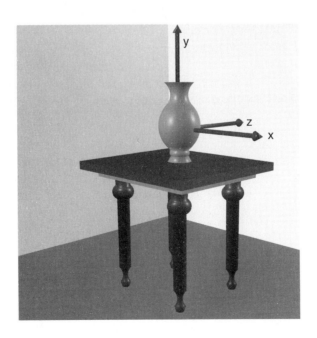

Figure 1.9

Defining an observer.

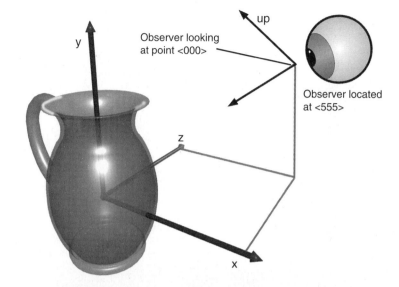

Figure 1.10

Front view of a face scene. (3-D model created with the HyperSpace 3-D digitizer from Mira Imaging, Inc.)

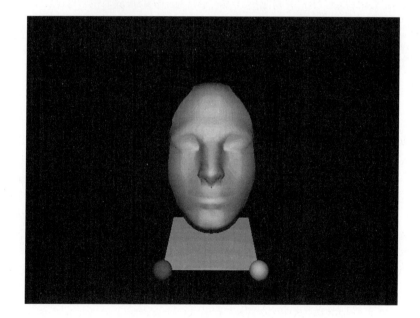

Figure 1.11

Side view of a face scene. (3-D model created with the HyperSpace 3-D digitizer from Mira Imaging, Inc.)

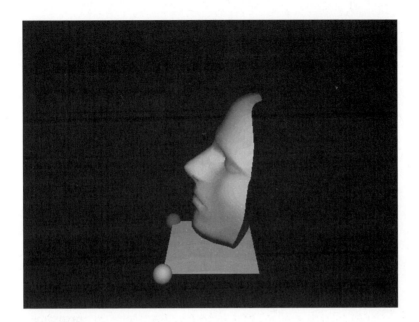

3-D Geometry

As mentioned earlier, ray tracing relies heavily on mathematically defined models. The objects a ray tracer uses are no exception. If you look around you, you can see that everyday objects can be modeled as a combination of simpler objects. For example, a table can be modeled as a long, thin, rectangular box with four cylinders as the legs.

Ray tracers usually have a standard set of 3-D objects defined and optimized for speed (see fig. 1.13). They also have other objects that have been defined in equation form. These equations have parameters that can be modified to generate different results. By varying the coefficients, a ray tracer can generate ellipsoids, hyperboloids, elliptic cones, and other objects. These objects tend to require longer computation time than other predefined objects such as the sphere.

There are other kinds of objects that cannot be generated by equations, and they require special techniques. Examples of such objects are lathe surfaces, extrusions, and rare undulating surfaces such as those used to create stylish and aerodynamic features in expensive sports cars.

Figure 1.12

Front view of
a face scene.
(3-D model
created with the
HyperSpace
3-D digitizer
from Mira
Imaging, Inc.)

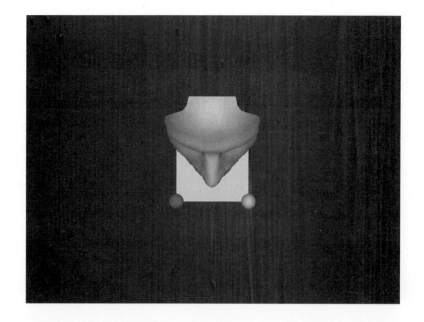

Figure 1.13

Examples of
standard ray
tracer objects.

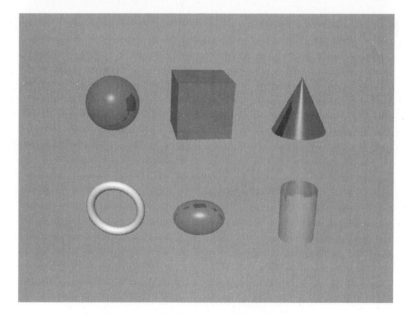

Lathe Surfaces

Lathe surfaces are constructed by rotating a contour curve about an axis. These objects are also called *solids of revolution*. The surface is approximated by a collection of *slabs* or flat patches. The object appears as a faceted solid. The surface can be smoothed out by increasing the number of patches; however, this has the negative effect of increasing the time it takes to generate the image. Figure 1.14 shows the construction of a contour line and the final object.

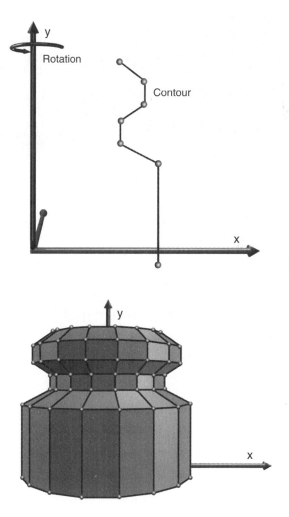

Figure 1.14

Constructing a lathe surface.

Sweep/Extruded Surfaces

Whereas a lathe surface is constructed by rotating a contour line about a given axis, an extruded surface, also known as a sweep surface, is created by translating the given contour curve along an axis. The new copied contour is then connected to the original one and patches are created. Figure 1.15 shows the creation of an extruded surface. Again, by increasing the amount of patches on the surface, you increase the smoothness.

Smooth Surfaces

In order to create objects with smooth surfaces, a special kind of patch, called a Bézier patch, can be used. Defining this patch is cumbersome; computer programs are usually used to create the Bézier patch. Bézier patches require that an array of 4 X 4 control points be defined. These control points are weighted, and they "pull" the patch in different directions. The final form of the patch is thus molded through the position of the control points. Figure 1.16 shows an example of control points and their corresponding Bézier patch.

Ray tracing programs usually require that you input the 16 control points in order to define the patch. The ray tracer then can generate the surface based on this information. Each of the 16 points is a 3-D point. In other words, you have to type 48 values.

Programs are available (such as POVCAD, which is included with this book) that enable you to manipulate Bézier patches. These programs usually create simple objects such as cylinders and ellipsoids by using Bézier patches. The user can then select any of the control points and "pull" the point in any direction, thus modifying the final form of the patch.

The ability of these patches to create complex undulating surfaces cannot be overlooked. You have the opportunity to experiment with Bézier patches in Chapter 3.

Figure 1.15

Constructing an extruded surface.

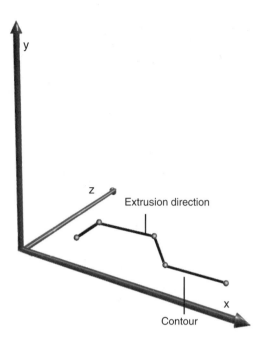

y

z

Extrusion direction

x

Contour

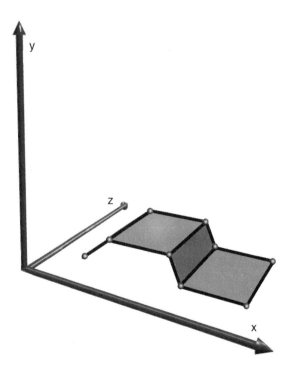

y

z

x

Figure 1.16

Example of a control point array and the final Bézier patch.

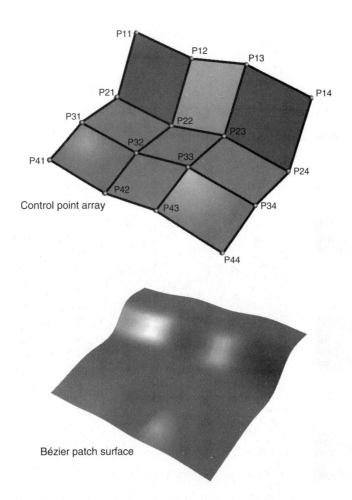

Control point array

Bézier patch surface

Building Complex Objects

Modeling a complex object such as a gear requires more than just using simply defined objects. A gear can be constructed as a disc from which prism-like objects have been cut out (the teeth) and a cylinder has been subtracted from the center (the hole). These operations of subtracting objects from other objects—and others where objects are added—are called *constructive solid geometry*.

Constructive Solid Geometry

Constructive solid geometry, or CSG, is used to create objects that are too complicated to be defined mathematically but that are based on adding or subtracting combinations of simpler objects. You can use the + and – signs to represent addition and subtraction operations, respectively.

Figure 1.17 shows a subtraction operation between a box and a cylinder. Observe that the operation is (box – cylinder) and *not* (cylinder – box). The result is a box with a hole in it. The subtraction operation gives a different result depending on the order of the objects.

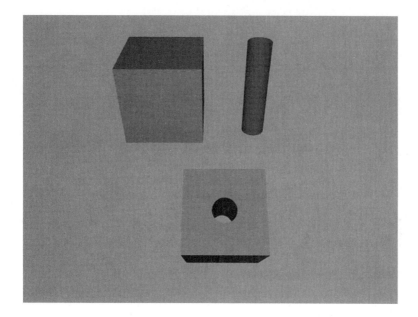

Figure 1.17

A difference operation—the cylinder is subtracted from the box.

An example of a union operation is given in figure 1.18, in which another box is used. The box is placed at the origin, whereas the cylinder is placed at one of the box's corners. The result is a box with a corner that forms a cylinder.

There is yet another operation that has not been mentioned. It is called *intersection*, and can be represented by the * symbol. This operation keeps what is common between all the objects involved. The rest is discarded.

We have been using the symbols +, –, and * to describe these operations. These operations are called *Boolean operations*. Although some programs use the mentioned convention, others simply use explicit keywords to describe them: union (+), difference (-), and intersection (*). The operations are the same. Figure 1.19 illustrates each operation.

Figure 1.18

An example of a union operation

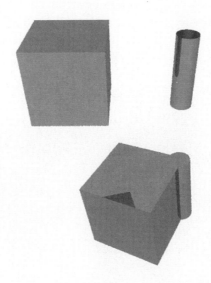

Boolean Operations

Some ray tracers use keywords for Boolean operations (CSG) to construct complex geometry. The usage is fairly straightforward; the following is the format:

```
Boolean operation name { first object  second object .... nth object}
```

The following are explicit examples:

```
union { box cylinder  }
difference { box cylinder}
intersection { sphere cylinder }
```

24

Figure 1.19

An example of an intersection operation.

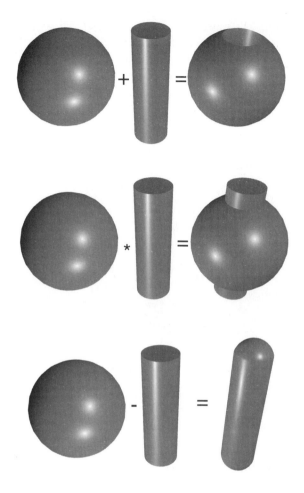

Boolean (CSG) operations also can be nested to create more complex definitions, as in the following:

```
union {
        sphere
        difference {
            box
            cylinder
        }
}
```

In mathematical form, this operation looks like this:

sphere + (box – cylinder)

Because this type of definition increases the amount of typing required, another important feature that you will use later is the ability to attach names to groups of operations and then use that name to simplify the creation process. This "attaching" of names to groups of objects and operations is similar to some macro capabilities found in most PC applications. The following is an example:

```
union {
      ellipsoid
      difference {
            box
            cylinder
      }
}
```

To simplify this operation, attach a name to the difference operation, as follows:

```
MyObject = difference {
                box
                cylinder
            }
```

Now that a name has been given, rewrite the example:

```
union {
      ellipsoid
      MyObject
}
```

This expression is identical to the one given previously. Throughout the book, we use the symbols +, –, and * rather than the keywords to describe Boolean operations.

Adding Photo-Realism

There are various mechanisms by which you can increase the realism of a ray-traced scene. The color of a surface can be modified by varying the red, green, and blue contents. The surface can be made transparent or opaque. You can give a surface mirrorlike qualities by modifying the reflection and roughness values, or you can make it metallic by changing the brilliance value.

Most ray tracers include different types of texture models, such as wood, agate, marble, and checkered. You can use these as-is, or modify them to create the effect that you are looking for. Their effects can be increased or decreased. For example, in wood textures, you can use a scaling factor to change the number of rings in the object.

Perturbation techniques are used to add randomness to textures and are used to create such great effects as waves, ripples, or bumps on surfaces. The surface is not really rippled; however, the intensity of the light at each point is calculated as if it were, resulting in a wavy surface. You can easily modify the size and frequency of the effects of these types of textures.

Mapping textures are used to "paste" an image on a surface. For example, you might want to map an image of a clown on a sphere, or map the image of your favorite soda on a cylinder when you create a kitchen scene.

Another technique to improve image quality is called *antialiasing.* Antialiasing is used to smooth out an image by reducing the "jagged" look (see fig. 1.20). If you have used computer drawing programs, you have been aware that straight lines do not look perfectly smooth; they have rough edges or "jaggies." Antialiasing is used to eliminate the jaggies. This is accomplished by filtering the image data as it is generated or by studying a given pixel or point on the screen in more detail (*over sampling*). Needless to say, these techniques enhance your image at the expense of computer time (see fig. 1.21).

Figure 1.20

An image without antialiasing.

There are many other interesting features and more in the ray tracing program included with this book. In the next chapter, you get your first look at Polyray, an excellent ray tracer that will help you get started with photo-realistic image creation.

Figure 1.21

An image with antialiasing.

Summary

In this chapter, you learned what ray tracing is and the basic concepts necessary to develop a scene file. You studied what a left-handed coordinate system is and how to define points and 3-D objects in it. You became acquainted with different standard 3-D objects. You were presented with the concept behind Boolean operations or constructive solid geometry and its importance in building more complex objects.

The importance of texture used to create realism was described. Also described were the different effects that can be created, such as metallic and marble finishes, waves, and bumps. In the next chapter, you have the chance to develop your first ray-traced image.

Your First Ray-Traced Image

Chapter 1 introduced you to basic ray tracing concepts. This chapter gives you the opportunity to create your first scene file and ray trace it. You also are guided through the development of a simple scene file. After you create the file, you will "dissect" it and study its parts. Finally, you ray trace the scene file.

The Polyray Ray Tracer

Polyray is an excellent ray tracer that enables you to create image files by using its database of standard primitives such as the ones mentioned in Chapter 1 (spheres, cones, boxes, and so on). It also enables you to create your own objects by using mathematical functions—such as z = f(x,y). All of the features that were presented in the previous chapter and more are available. As you progress in the book, you will become familiar with Polyray's features.

Polyray was developed by Alexander Enzmann, using as a starting point the source code from another ray tracer called MTV, written by Mark VandeWettering. The MTV ray tracer is in the public domain. Although the code for MTV is freely available, Polyray is a shareware program.

Using Polyray

Let's start getting acquainted with Polyray by learning how to run the program from the DOS prompt and understanding which command-line parameters are available.

Running POLYRAY.EXE

To start Polyray, move into the directory containing Polyray, and simply execute the following command at the DOS prompt:

```
C:\ POLY>polyray [Press Enter]
```

This example works if you installed the program on drive C: under a directory named POLY.

If you typed the previous command you might have already figured out that Polyray requires a set of command-line parameters to execute. The parameters indicate which file to use and other pertinent information. Read the next section and Table 2.1 for more information on the command-line parameters

NOTE: Polyray requires an IBM PC or compatible computer with at least a 386, a VGA graphics card, and 2M of RAM. You can run it from DOS or a DOS window inside Windows.

There are two versions available for those with or without coprocessor. Refer to the Introduction for more details.

Command-Line Parameters

The following is a list of the command-line parameters Polyray accepts. It is not practical to type them every time you want to ray trace a scene file, so I suggest you create a batch file to execute Polyray. Normally, to run Polyray you should use the following format for the command:

```
polyray.exe filename.ext [rest of command-line parameters]
```

in which filename.ext is the name of the scene file. Table 2.1 describes in detail the rest of the command-line parameters. Don't worry about memorizing all the Polyray options; you can refer to this table when you need help.

Table 2.1. Command-line parameters.

Parameter	Action
Antialiasing Parameters	
-a	Performs a simple antialiasing method of averaging the neighboring pixel colors. Degradation of the image will occur due to the averaging process.
-A	Performs an adaptive antialiasing method. It is dependent on the threshold value (parameter -T) and the number of samples per pixel (parameter -S). This method samples a pixel and its neighbors. If the color difference is greater than the threshold value, additional samples are made to find the best color.
-J	Performs a random (jittered) method. The number of samples per pixel is constant. The average of all the samples determines the color.
-T n	Sets the threshold value to force over sampling. Over-sampling is active if the difference in colors is greater than n. **Example:** -T 0.1
-S n	Sets the number of samples per pixel (n) for the adaptive (parameter -A) method.

continues

Table 2.1. Continued.

Parameter	Action

File Output Operations

-b n	Saves the image data after calculating n pixels. **Example:** -b 1280
-B	Saves the image data after calculating every line. Use this parameter if you are concerned with saving as much data as possible in case something goes wrong.

File Output Operations

-o f	Specify the output file name f. If the parameter is not used, OUT.TGA is assumed. **Example:** -o table.tga
-p n	Set the number n of bits per pixel on the output image file. Acceptable values are 8, 16, 24, and 32. **Example:** -p 24
-u	Use uncompressed TARGA format on the output file.

Image Quality and Size

- r m	Select method m to generate the image (the lower the number, the better the quality).

Value	Method
0	ray trace
1	scan convert (requires substantial amounts of memory)
2	wireframe (to screen only)

-d p	Dither objects with probability p (the number must be between 0 and 1). Use this parameter to reduce image generation time. Quality is also reduced.

Example: -d 0.5

-D p

Dither p percent of rays used (the number must be between 0 and 1).

Use this parameter to reduce image generation time. Quality is also reduced.

-P n

Use palette number n.

Value	Colors
0	gray
1	666
2	884

-q n

Select shading options.

Flag	Option
1	shadows
2	reflectivity
4	refraction
8	highlighting on both sides of a surface
16	check if object casts shadows
32	primary (eyes) rays will be checked

To use, simply add the number of the features you want, for example, *shadows + reflectivity = 1 + 2 = 3*. The parameter usage would be -q 3.

Render Flag	Default
-r 0	-q 63 (all ON)
-r 1	-q 8
-r 2	N/A

-x

Set image x resolution.

Example: -x 640

-y

Set image y resolution.

Example: -y 480

33

continues

Table 2.1. Continued.

Parameter	Action
Miscellaneous	
-Q	Abort run by pressing any key.
-R	Resume an interrupted trace.
-t n	Display tracing information.

Miscellaneous		
	Value	**Status**
	0	none
	1	totals at the end of trace
	2	line
	3	pixel (slows program down)
-v	Ray trace image from bottom to top.	
-V m	Screen preview status.	
	Value	**Mode**
	0	none
	1	VGA
-W	Wait for a keypress to clear the screen.	
-z n	Start ray tracing at line n. This feature is good for checking partial images.	

A good approach to using command-line parameters is to create a series of batch files. Each batch file would have a different set of parameter combinations. You could use one of them to create a quick rough draft of the image and use another to create a final high-quality image.

Creating a Scene File

Creating a scene file is easy. In the following section, you start by using the text editor of your choice to create your first scene file. This section also helps you become familiar with Polyray's syntax.

Using a Text Editor

To create a scene file, use your favorite text editor, for example the EDIT editor included with MS-DOS 5.0 and 6.0. The text editor must be capable of saving the file in straight ASCII format. When you begin typing the scene file presented in one of the next sections, remember to use the Tab key to create multiple indentation levels in the file. This makes the file more readable.

Syntax Considerations

Polyray is case-sensitive, and you must type all keywords correctly for Polyray to parse the command. You don't need any programming skills to use Polyray; however, if you have programmed in C, it shouldn't take you long to get used to Polyray's syntax, because it has a C-language "feel." As an example, the braces—{ and }—are used extensively to denote the beginning and end of a definition. In the C language, the same brackets are used for roughly the same purpose.

A Detailed Look at a Scene File

Listing 2.1 shows an example of a Polyray scene file. You should run your text editor at this point and type the complete listing. This will help you become familiar with some of Polyray's keywords and format style. After typing the listing, read the following section, in which you'll "dissect" the scene file and study it in detail.

Save the file as DEMO.PI (this and all other listings are available in the companion disk).

NOTE: All of the images in this book are set up for 100×100 resolution to minimize the rendering time. If you want to see more detailed, higher-resolution images on a 640×480 display, just change the resolution statement to

```
resolution     640,480
```

and the aspect statement to

```
aspect         1.33
```

Remember, however, that these higher-resolution images take much longer to render.

Listing 2.1. A first look at Polyray.

```
//DEMO.PI

include "colors.inc"
include "texture.inc"

viewpoint {
 from       <0.2, 1.0, -1.7>
 at         <0.0, 0.0, 0.0>
 up         <0.0, 1.0, 0.0>
 resolution    100,100
 aspect        1.0
 }

// LIGHT_SOURCE
    light <0, 5, -10>

// PLANE (Polygon)
object {
    polygon 4, <-100,0,100>, <-100,0,-100>, <100,0,-100>, <100,0,100>
    translate <0, -1, 0>
    texture { checker matte_white, matte_black }
}

// BOX
object {
    box <-1, -1, -1>, <1, 1, 1>
    scale <0.5, 0.5, 0.5>
    shiny_green
}

// CONE
object {
    cone <0.0, -1, 0.0>, 0.5, <0.0, 0.0, 0.0>, 0.0
    translate <1.6, 0.48, 0>
    shiny_blue
}

// SPHERE
object {
    sphere < -0.96, 0, -1.12>, 0.25
    shiny_red
}
```

Header Section

Listing 2.2 contains the header section. In the first line, the symbol // is used to indicate a comment. Polyray ignores this line, but you will use it to identify the file. If you need more than one line of comments, simply add two slash marks at the beginning of each line you want to make a comment, as in the following:

```
// This is the first line
// This is another commented line
```

```
//DEMO.PI

include "colors.inc"
include "texture.inc"
```

The two lines following the comment are very important. The `include` statement indicates that there is some information—in this case, color and texture information—that was defined in external files. In this case, the color definitions can be read from the file `colors.inc`, whereas texture definitions can be read from the file named `texture.inc`. You can have as many external files as necessary. This feature enables you to include as many files as needed which may have colors, textures, objects, or groups of objects. This eliminates the need for retyping the definitions each time you have to use them. You should take some time and become familiar with the `colors.inc` and `texture.inc` files.

As we progress with the examples, you will need to save objects to a file for repeated access.

Viewpoint Definition Section

As mentioned in the first chapter, the `viewpoint` definition indicates the position of the observer and at which point the observer is looking. In this case (see Listing 2.3), the observer is positioned at X=0.2, Y=1.0, and Z=–1.7. Recall that we are using a left-handed coordinate system; therefore, the z axis points into the computer screen, whereas the x axis points to the right and the y axis points up. The observer is also looking at the origin <0.0, 0.0, 0.0 > (`at`). To orient the observer, the up direction is defined using the statement `up < 0.0, 1.0, 0.0 >`.

Listing 2.3. The viewpoint definition section of DEMO.PI.

```
viewpoint {
  from      <0.2, 1.0, -1.7>
  at        <0.0, 0.0, 0.0>
  up        <0.0, 1.0, 0.0>
  resolution    100,100
  aspect        1.0
  }
```

The resolution statement is used to define the size of the final image: 100 × 100 pixels. The aspect ratio is the ratio of the width to the height: 100 / 100 = 1.0 (assuming the pixels are square). If an image size of 640 × 480 is used, the aspect ratio is 640 / 480 = 1.33. After the image is generated, the sphere will appear deformed. This is due to its closeness to the screen. A normal check for correct aspect ratio is, for example, that a sphere must appear to be round, unless you want to create a different effect. You might have to modify the aspect ratio value if you are using a non-square pixel video mode.

Light Source Definition

At least one light source has to be included in a scene file or your final image will be dark. To include a light source, use a definition similar to that in Listing 2.4. The only required parameters are the X, Y, and Z coordinate positions of the light source. If no color is attached to the definition, white light is assumed.

Listing 2.4. The light source definition of DEMO.PI.

```
// LIGHT_SOURCE
   light <0, 5, -10>
```

There are other types of light sources; however, this is the simplest example that can be presented. In the next chapter, you experiment with different light sources.

Object Definition

Listing 2.1 has four objects: a plane or polygon, a box, a cone, and a sphere. The following paragraphs describe each individually.

Plane

Polygons are used as planes to create a floor effect in a scene. You can construct a plane with a collection of four 3-D points to define the corners of the floor, as in Listing 2.5. The idea is to separate these four points as much as possible to create the illusion of an infinite floor.

Listing 2.5. Plane definition.

```
// PLANE (Polygon)
object {
    polygon 4, <-100,0,100>, <-100,0,-100>, <100,0,-100>, <100,0,100>
    translate <0, -1, 0>
    texture { checker matte_white, matte_black }
}
```

To lower the floor by one unit, the statement <0, -1, 0> is used to displace the points in the y axis. This is similar to the definition

```
polygon 4, <-100,-1,100>, <-100,-1,-100>, <100,-1,-100>, <100,-1,100>
```

Translating a plane down by a certain amount (as in Y = –1) creates the illusion that the objects on top of the plane are floating. Figure 4.16 in Chapter 4 shows three spheres and a plane which simulates water. Two of the spheres appear to be floating on top of the water, and the center sphere is in it.

Finally, the plane will have a checkered pattern consisting of matte_white and matte_black tiles as defined by texture { checker matte_white, matte_black }. More on this later (Chapter 4 deals entirely with light, colors, and textures).

Box

The box object is initially a unit box with two opposing diagonal corners at <–1, –1, –1> (lower corner) and <1, 1, 1> (upper corner). To scale it down by half, you can use the scale <0.5, 0.5, 0.5> statement. This is similar to the definition box <-0.5, -0.5, -0.5>, <0.5, 0.5, 0.5> (see Listing 2.6).

At this point there is no benefit to using the box definition by itself or with the scaling operation, but it gives you the idea that objects can be manipulated by means of other operations.

Listing 2.6. Box definition.

```
// BOX
object {
    box <-1, -1, -1>, <1, 1, 1>
    scale <0.5, 0.5, 0.5>
    shiny_green
}
```

The surface of the box will have a shiny_green finish. Surface finishes are described later in this chapter in the "Textures" section.

Cone

Cones are described by the location of the center of the base and apex points. Also, the base and apex radii are required. In Listing 2.7, the base of the cone is located at <0.0, –1, 0.0> with a radius of 0.5 units, whereas the apex is located at <0.0, 0.0, 0.0> with a radius of 0.0. If the radius of the apex is different from zero, you will be defining a truncated cone (see fig. 2.1). To locate the cone in the final position, use the translate <1.6, 0.48, 0> statement.

Figure 2.1

Normal and truncated cones.

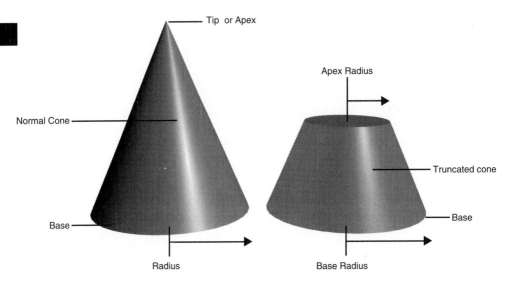

The final line, shiny_blue, attaches a surface color/finish to the cone.

Listing 2.7. Cone definition.

```
// CONE
object {
    cone <0.0, -1, 0.0>, 0.5, <0.0, 0.0, 0.0>, 0.0
    translate <1.6, 0.48, 0>
    shiny_blue
}
```

Sphere

The last object is the sphere. The sphere requires the location of its center point and its radius. In Listing 2.8, the center point is located at <–0.96, 0, –1.12> with a radius of 0.25.

The sphere has a `shiny_red` finish.

Listing 2.8. Sphere definition.

```
// SPHERE
object {
    sphere < -0.96, 0, -1.12>, 0.25
    shiny_red
}
```

Textures

In the scene file, notice that the plane object uses a texture keyword, whereas the other objects use just one word (for example, `shiny_green`). The reason behind this is that the words `shiny_red`, `shiny_green`, and `shiny_blue` have already been defined externally and were included in this scene by means of the `include "colors.inc"` statement. In other words, the `shiny_xxxx` words are basically just the name of a longer definition that was replaced with a short name.

To give a better example, let's replace the statement

```
texture { checker matte_white, matte_black }
```

with a short name such as `CheckerWB`. You can do this with the keyword `define`, which you use in the following manner:

```
define   CheckerWB     texture { checker matte_white, matte_black }
```

Now all you need to do to call `texture { checker matte_white, matte_black }` is use the defined word CheckerWB, as in Listing 2.9.

Listing 2.9. Replacing a texture definition with a short name.

```
define   CheckerWB     texture { checker matte_white, matte_black }

// PLANE (Polygon)
object {
    polygon 4, <-100,0,100>, <-100,0,-100>, <100,0,-100>, <100,0,100>
    translate <0, -1, 0>
    CheckerWB      // this is the same as Listing 2.5
}
```

41

Textures usually require the declaration of various parameters, which makes the texture statement long. Therefore, it's a good idea to use the define keyword as much as possible to simplify the scene file, by replacing long definitions with a short name. You can either bundle them all in another file and include them in the header section or attach the definitions on the top of the scene file. You can use the define keyword to attach short names to anything. You explore this feature more in Chapter 3.

Ray Tracing a Scene File

If you typed Listing 2.1, you are almost ready to start ray tracing. The following sections explain how to simplify the process.

Creating a Batch File

As I mentioned in the "Command-Line Parameters" section, it is a good idea to create batch files to handle all the necessary command-line parameters. Using a text editor, create a batch file which contains the following line and name it DRAFT.BAT:

```
polyray %1.pi -r 0 -V 1 -t 0 -W -o %2.tga
```

Save the file in the same directory where Polyray resides. You'll use the DRAFT.BAT file to create a good-quality image without the time-consuming antialiasing methods. This means that some of the object edges might look rough. If you want a faster output, replace the -r 0 parameter with either -r 1 or -r 2. This reduces time, but it also lessens the final quality of the image.

Now, create a second batch file containing the following line and name it FINAL.BAT:

```
polyray %1.pi -r 0 -V 1 -t 0 -A -T 0.2 -S 25 -p 24 -W -o %2.tga
```

This file sets up Polyray to do antialiasing and saves the output with 24 bits per pixel. Use this batch file to create a high-quality final image. Needless to say, this method is very time-consuming, and you should use it after you have previewed the image using the DRAFT.BAT batch file.

Ray Tracing Your First Scene

Start by making the directory where Polyray resides the current directory. Type the following,

```
DRAFT  DEMO TEST1
```

at the DOS prompt and press the Enter or Return key. The input file is DEMO.PI and the output file will be TEST1.TGA. As the ray tracer generates the image line by line, you should be able to see a rough preview of the image. Because you are using the DRAFT.BAT file, the final image will be good, but not the best quality. This image is just a rough preview of the true output, so don't be disappointed.

A note about resolution: Most images in the book use the command "resolution 100,100" and "aspect 1.0". This is done to generate a quick image. You can modify these two statements in order to increase the size of the image and the aspect ration. Needless to say, the larger the image, the longer it takes to generate it; the smaller the image, the less quality you will see.

After the image is completed, press any key to go to DOS.

The next step is to run the final high-quality image by typing FINAL DEMO TEST2 at the DOS prompt and pressing Enter. This image might take a little longer to generate than the previous image.

Both images will be of the same resolution, but the one generated with FINAL.BAT will be smoother and will offer more details (it also tends to be larger in size).

The next step is to use an image file viewer program to check the results of the ray tracer.

Viewing a Ray-Traced Image

After running the ray tracer, you have two image files: test1.tga and test2.tga. Both are compressed Targa files. Use your favorite image-file viewer, or the CompuShow viewer included on the bundled disk, and take a look at both files. Beware that some viewers do a poor job of showing image files. Also, the graphics card you have on your computer might have some effect on the colors that you see. It is highly recommended that you have a Super VGA card. Figures 2.2 and 2.3 display the output of files test1.tga and test2.tga respectively.

Both figures 2.2 and 2.3 show the same image, but with a subtle difference. Check for ragged lines on each, and look at the finer details.

Figure 2.2

The output of test1.tga at 640 X 480 (aspect = 1.33).

Figure 2.3

The output of test2.tga at 640 X 480 (aspect 1.33).

Summary

In this chapter, you were introduced to Polyray, an excellent ray tracer which helps you create photo-realistic images. Next, you saw the command-line parameters that you can use with Polyray. You use some of the parameters to enhance the quality of the final image by using antialiasing techniques and by increasing the number of bits per pixel. Use others parameters are used to control file output operations or miscellaneous features such as waiting for a key response at the end of the trace.

You also saw a sample scene file that was divided into five main sections: header, viewpoint, light source, object, and textures.

After reviewing the sample scene file, you received instructions on how to create batch files to simplify the ray tracing process. You created two images —in draft and final form—and received information on how to view them.

In the next chapter, you learn the Polyray ray-tracing program and learn how to create photo-realistic images in more detail. You will begin by creating simple objects, adding other objects to make complex objects, and finally, applying more of the characteristics of 3-D modelling by adding textured surfaces to the objects.

Using Polyray

The Polyray ray tracer is rich in features. In this chapter, we will expand on most of the concepts presented in Chapter 1. You have the opportunity to ray trace the available objects and experiment with different surfaces and strange objects, such as blobs. The chapter takes a detailed look at each object and includes sample scenes.

Background

The following four sections present the basic concepts discussed in Chapter 1 as they apply to Polyray. I suggest you take a moment to review them in preparation for the rest of this chapter.

3-D Coordinate System

Polyray uses a left-handed coordinate system. Recall that the x axis points to the right, the y axis points upward, and the z axis points into the screen (refer to fig. 1.1). The coordinate system does not have any specific units. You can express the object dimensions in inches, feet, miles, or any other type of units. The important point to remember is to be consistent.

Vectors

Vectors are written as <X, Y, Z>, where X, Y, and Z are the x, y, and z coordinate values, respectively. Notice that the values are separated by commas. They are used to represent 3-D points such as the center of a sphere. Also, they can be used to represent a direction—as the vector <0, 1, 0> represents a direction along the positive y axis and the vector <–1, 0, 0> represents a direction along the negative x axis.

Transformations

Polyray supports many types of transformations. The most commonly used ones are translation, rotation, and scaling. These operations are used extensively throughout this book.

Translate

The translate operation moves the position of an object from the current position to a new position as determined by a vector. The syntax is

```
translate <X, Y, Z>
```

where x, y, and z are the amounts of translation to be applied to an object. The following is an example:

```
object {
    sphere <1.0, 1.5, -3.0>, 0.25
    translate <5.0, 6.0, 7.0>
    shiny_red
}
```

In this example, the sphere is located originally at <1.0, 1.5, –3.0>. After you apply the translate operation, the final position of the sphere is

```
X =  1.0 + 5.0 = 6.0
Y =  1.5 + 6.0 = 7.5
Z = -3.0 + 7.0 = 4.0
```

In other words, you can replace the previous example with the following:

```
object {
    sphere <6.0, 7.5, 4.0>, 0.25
    shiny_red
}
```

and you would get the same results.

Rotate

Use rotate <rx, ry, rz> to revolve an object about each axis. The object is rotated rx degrees about x, then ry degrees about y, and finally rz degrees about z. The rotations are in the same order they were described. Recall that the rotations follow the "left-hand rule" explained in Chapter 1 (refer to fig. 1.3 and fig. 1.4). The following is an example:

```
object {
    cone <0.0, -1.0, 0.0>, 0.5, <0.0, 0.0, 0.0>, 0.0
    rotate <90.0, 90.0, 0.0>
    shiny_red
}
```

Let's study the operations by steps. The first transformation is to rotate the cone by 90 degrees about x. Initially, the base of the cone is located at <0.0, –1.0, 0.0> and the apex is at <0.0, 0.0, 0.0>. After rotating 90 degrees about x, the base point is at <0.0, 0.0, –1.0> and the apex is still at <0.0, 0.0, 0.0>. In other words, the cone is aligned with the z axis.

Next, the rotation of 90 degrees about y is performed. The base is at <–1.0, 0.0, 0.0> and the apex is at <0.0, 0.0, 0.0>. In this case, the cone is now aligned with the x axis. Because the angle of rotation rz is 0, no rotation is applied about the z axis. Observe that the apex location never changed. This is due to the fact that the apex point is located at the origin, which is the center of rotation. You can think of a car wheel as a similar case. The center of the wheel remains at the center of the axle, whereas any other point on the wheel rotates to a new position every time the wheel turns.

Scale

Scaling is a straightforward operation that simply involves size incrementing or decrementing. The operation scale <sx, sy, sz> scales the object on each axis proportional to sx, sy, and sz. Any number greater than 1 increases the size, and numbers between 0 and 1 shrink the object. To keep the object the same size on any of the axes, use a value of 1. Using 0 gives you an error.

Viewpoint

In Chapter 1, you learned about the importance of positioning an observer, commonly called the "viewpoint" of the scene. In Chapter 2, we looked at an example of a scene file and the format used by Polyray to define such an observer. Polyray uses 13 parameters to define the viewpoint. Most of them are normally not used unless you want to experiment with effects such as changing the field of view or dissolving an image. The viewpoint format is shown in Listing 3.1.

Listing 3.1. Viewpoint definition.

```
viewpoint {
    from < xo, yo, zo>
    at <xa, ya, za>
    up <xup, yup, zup>
    resolution xres, yres
    aspect     ar
    angle fov
    max_trace_depth n
    hither d
    yon d
    dither_rays value
    dither_objects value
    aperture a
    focal_distance d
}
```

The description of each parameter is presented in Table 3.1.

Table 3.1. Viewpoint parameters.

Parameter	Meaning
Commonly Used Parameters	
from	Observer is located at <xo, yo, zo>; default vector is <0, 0, –1>.
at	Observer is looking at point <xa, ya, za>; default vector is <0, 0, 0>.
up	The "up" direction relative to the observer; default vector is <0, 1, 0>.
	Examples:
	<0, 1, 0> = along y axis.
	<1, 0, 0> = along x axis.
	<1, 1, 0> = along a direction 45 degrees from the x axis.

resolution	Final image size; this size is independent of the screen resolution; default values 512, 512. **Example:** resolution 640, 480 means xres = 640, yres = 480
aspect	If the screen pixels are square, then ar = xres/yres; default value = 1. **Example:** ar = 640/480 = 1.33
angle	Indicates the field of view in degrees, from top to bottom of the image; default = 45 degrees.
max_trace_depth	Scenes with high values of reflection or transparency require more calculations; the number "n" determines the maximum number of levels deep of recursion that Polyray will compute; default = 5. **Example:** max_trace_depth 3

Special-purpose Parameters

hither	Sets a lower limit on intersections; anything closer to the viewpoint than "d" is ignored, default = 1e–3.
yon	Sets an upper limit on intersections; anything farther from the viewpoint than "d" is ignored, default = 1e5.
dither_rays	Polyray generates an internal random number; If this number is greater than value, the current light ray is skipped; value is between 0 and 1.
dither_objects	Same as dither_rays, but the current object is skipped.
aperture	Used to produce depth of field blurred images; must be greater than 0 to produce blur; Values between 0.1 and 0.6 are suggested.
focal_distance	Distance from observer to the point being focused at; the value d defaults to the distance between from and at. This value is only relevant if aperture is greater than zero.

Table 3.1 divides the viewpoint parameters into two groups: commonly used and special purpose. Normally, the commonly used parameters appear in the scenes. Most of these parameters have default values; however, you'll need to modify them to suit your needs. A common viewpoint definition is presented in Listing 3.2. The variables xa, ya, za, xo, yo, and zo must be replaced with values.

Listing 3.2. Standard viewpoint definition.

```
viewpoint {
    from <xo, yo, zo>
    at <xa, ya, za>
    up <0, 1, 0>
    resolution 640, 480
    aspect 1.33
}
```

The examples discussed in this book use a resolution of (100, 100) and an aspect ratio of 1. This is done so that you can preview the final images quickly. The images displayed throughout the book are the same ones as the listing examples but the resolution was changed to (640, 480) with an aspect ratio of 1.33 to increase the quality. Some of the images took as long as four hours to complete because the Jitter antialiasing method was used to enhance the quality.

All the samples have their own viewpoint definition, which you can modify to view other areas of the image.

Naming Definitions

Polyray uses the special keyword define to attach token names to standard definitions. The syntax for define is

```
define NAME expression
define NAME transform {.....}
define NAME object {.....}
define NAME texture {.....}
define NAME surface {.....}
```

where NAME is the name of the object or expression that is being defined on the right side of the define statement.

For example, to attach a name to a sphere, use the following:

```
define MySphere object {
            sphere <0,0,0>, 1
        }
```

You can use the following to position the sphere elsewhere and attach a color to it:

```
object {
    MySphere
    translate <1, 3.4, 5.2>
    shiny_red
}
```

As you can see, the entire expression is not substituted but the object that's being defined is:

```
object {
    sphere <0,0,0>, 1
    translate <1, 3.4, 5.2>
    shiny_red
    }
```

Throughout this book, you'll see examples of the use of the define keyword.

Creating Objects

Polyray has a wide variety of objects which are referred to as *primitives*, such as the sphere, cone, cylinder, and others. In Chapter 1, you read about modeling common everyday objects by starting with simpler primitives. In the following sections, each object is described in detail with examples of their use. Due to their complexity, some objects—for example, Bézier patches, lathe objects, and extruded objects—require external programs or utilities to create them. The disk that comes with this book includes a modeler called POVCAD, which can help you easily create lathe and extruded surfaces. In fact, most of the scenes included in this book were initially created in POVCAD and then exported to Polyray. Chapter 7, "Using a 3-D Modeler," describes POVCAD in more detail.

Creating Simple Objects

Polyray primitives are divided into three groups: simple objects, modeling surfaces, and miscellaneous objects. Simple objects are usually defined with a few constants and location vectors, for example, the sphere. The sphere needs a vector for the location of the center and a radius. Modeling surfaces are either functions of the type f = (x,y,z), collections of triangles that make an object, or Bézier patches that require 16 points to define the whole surface. Finally, miscellaneous objects are those that cannot be categorized in any of the previous two groups but still are interesting and useful, for example, one of them can be used to create landscapes. The following sections describe some simple objects.

Box

The box object can be declared by two corner points. The syntax is

```
box <xl, yl, zl>, <xu, yu, zu>
```

in which xl, yl, zl are the coordinates of the front lower left corner, and xu, yu, zu are the coordinates of the back upper right corner

Listing 3.3 shows an example of using the box primitive, and figure 3.1 displays the final image.

Listing 3.3. Using the box primitive (BOXES.PI).

```
//BOXES.PI

include "colors.inc"
include "texture.inc"

viewpoint {
 from      <-0.5, 2.0, -5.0>
 at        <0.0, 0.0, 0.0>
 up        <0.0, 1.0, 0.0>
 resolution    100,100

 aspect        1.0
}

// LIGHT_SOURCE
    light <0.0,  0.0, -3.0>
// LIGHT_SOURCE
    light <0.5,  3.0, -3.0>
// LIGHT_SOURCE
    light <1.0,  0.0, -5.0>

// BOX
object {
    box <-1, -1, -1>, <1, 1, 1>
    reflective_yellow
}

// BOX
```

```
object {
    box <-1, -1, -1>, <1, 1, 1>
    translate <-1.65, -2.1, 0>
    white_marble
}

// BOX
object {
    box <-1, -1, -1>, <1, 1, 1>
    scale <2, 1, 3>
    translate <2.4, -2.1, 0>
    dented_red
}
```

Observe how only one type of box was defined, box <-1, -1, -1>, <1, 1, 1>. Using this box is practical because it's easy to size just by applying a scaling factor. The box is normally called a *unit box*. In other words, the first two boxes are unit boxes and the third one was scaled to <2, 1, 3> in the x, y, and z axes, respectively. The third box could have been written as box <-2, -1, -3>, <2, 1, 3>.

Sometimes it's much easier to define a standard object such as the unit box and then scale it appropriately than it is to modify all the parameters, which is an error-prone operation. For example, use the define keyword to create a unit box object and modify the last box in Listing 3.4.

Listing 3.4. Using the define keyword to create a unit box.

```
define UnitBox   object {
                     box <-1, -1, -1>, <1, 1, 1>
                     }

object {
    UnitBox
    scale <2, 1, 3>
    translate <2.4, -2.1, 0>
    dented_red
}
```

The power of the define keyword becomes more apparent when you deal with complex scene files.

Figure 3.1

*Box example
(BOXES.PI).*

Plane

If you recall Listing 2.1, we used a polygon definition to create a floor.
Listing 3.5 shows the section of Listing 2.1 in which the plane was defined.

Listing 3.5. Plane definition extracted from Listing 2.1.

```
// PLANE (Polygon)
object {
    polygon 4, <-100,0,100>, <-100,0,-100>, <100,0,-100>, <100,0,100>
    translate <0, -1, 0>
    texture { checker matte_white, matte_black }
}
```

To create the effect of an infinite plane, the coordinates of the polygon were
much higher numbers than the rest of the objects. It is useful to have a
plane object to create floors or walls in your scene. Because Polyray does not
have a plane object, we will create three, each one perpendicular to an axis.

The first step is to create an infinite plane. You can do this by using a
definition such as

```
polygon 4,     <-10000,0,10000>, <-10000,0,-10000>,
               <10000,0,-10000>, <10000,0,10000>
```

This ensures that the polygon is always larger than the other objects.

Another way of doing this is to use a `define` statement such as

```
define UnitPlane object { polygon 4, <-1,0,1>, <-1,0,-1>,
}                                      <1,0,-1>, <1,0,1>
define InfinitePlane object { UnitPlane scale <10000, 1, 10000> }
```

In this example, the plane called `InfinitePlane` is extremely large in the x and z axes. It's a personal choice to use the previous method or

```
polygon 4,     <-10000,0,10000>, <-10000,0,-10000>,
                    <10000,0,-10000>, <10000,0,10000>
```

The next step is to define the planes depending on their orientation:

```
define Plane_XZ object {
                    polygon 4, <-10000,0,10000>,
                                    <-10000,0,-10000>,
                                    <10000,0,-10000>,
                                    <10000,0,10000>
            }

define Plane_XY  object {
                    polygon 4, <-10000,10000,0>,
                                    <10000,10000,0>,
                                    <10000,-10000,0>,
                                    <-10000,-10000,0>
                    }

define Plane_XZ  object {
                    polygon 4, <-10000,0,10000>,
                                    <-10000,0,-10000>,
                                    <10000,0,-10000>,
                                    <10000,0,10000>
                    }
```

Listing 3.6 presents a scene in which three planes, a cone, and a sphere are used. The planes have mirror finishes, and the cone and the sphere are made of stone. The planes are located in a fashion similar to a room with two walls but no ceiling. The cone and the sphere are in the center of the room. The scene looks extremely "busy" due to the many reflections.

Listing 3.6. Defining and using planes (PLANES.PI).

```
//PLANES.PI

include "colors.inc"
include "texture.inc"
include "stones.inc"

define Plane_YZ  object {
                polygon 4, <0,-10000,10000>, <0,10000,10000>,
                    <0,10000,-10000>, <0,-10000,-10000>
                }
define Plane_XY  object {
```

continues

Listing 3.6. Continued.

```
                   polygon 4, <-10000,10000,0>, <10000,10000,0>,
                   <10000,-10000,0>, <-10000,-10000,0>
                   }

define Plane_XZ  object {
                   polygon 4, <-10000,0,10000>,  <-10000,0,-10000>,
                   <10000,0,-10000>, <10000,0,10000>
                   }

viewpoint {
 from       <0.0, 1.0, -4.0>
 at         <0.0, -0.25, 0.0>
 up         <0.0, 1.0, 0.0>
 angle          45
 resolution     100,100
 aspect         1.0
}

// LIGHT_SOURCE
   light <5.0, 5.0, -5.0>

// PLANE (Polygon)
object {
// normal in X direction
    Plane_YZ
    translate <-0.6, 0, 0>
    mirror
}

// PLANE (Polygon)
object {
// normal in Z direction
    Plane_XY
    translate <0, 0, 0.6>
    mirror
}

// PLANE (Polygon)
object {
// normal in Y direction
    Plane_XZ
    translate <0, -0.6, 0>
    mirror
}

// SPHERE
object {
    sphere < 0, 0, 0>, 0.25
    Stone5
}

// CONE
object {
    cone <0.0, -0.5, 0.0>, 0.2, <0.0, 0.0, 0.0>, 0.0
    translate <0.8, 0.4, -0.8>
    Stone6
}
```

Observe that in the header section, a new include file named `stones.inc` was used. This file has the definition for the `stone5` and `stone6` textures used on the last two objects. The file `stones.inc` has approximately 23 different stone textures.

After the header section, three "infinite" planes were used, all of which have mirror finishes. Figure 3.2 shows the many reflections produced as a result of the mirrored finishes.

Figure 3.2

Using planes as mirrors (PLANES.PI).

Sphere

Spheres are the most common ray-traced object. Why? Because a sphere is the fastest ray-traceable object. A good application for spheres is to test various textures and colors. You can create an array of spheres, each with a different color or finish. You can then use the final image for comparison purposes. Various sphere examples have been presented in previous chapters. The syntax is as follows:

```
sphere <xc, yc, zc>, radius
```

where xc, yc, and zc define the center point of the sphere. Listing 3.7 shows a sphere example that generates the images shown in figure 3.3.

Listing 3.7. Using spheres (SPHERES1.PI).

```
//SPHERES1.PI

include "colors.inc"
include "texture.inc"
include "stones.inc"

viewpoint {
  from      <0.0, 0.0, -2.0>
  at        <0.0, 0.0, 0.0>
  up        <0.0, 1.0, 0.0>
  resolution   100,100
  aspect       1.0
}

// LIGHT_SOURCE
    light <0, 5, -5>

// LIGHT_SOURCE
    light <0, 10, 0>

// LIGHT_SOURCE
    light <5, 5, 10>


// SPHERE
object {
    sphere < 1.6, 0, 0>, 0.5
    Stone1
}

// SPHERE
object {
    sphere < 1.38564, 0.8, 0>, 0.5
    Stone2
}

// SPHERE
object {
    sphere < 0.8, 1.38564, 0>, 0.5
    Stone3
}

// SPHERE
object {
    sphere < -0, 1.6, 0>, 0.5
    Stone4
}

// SPHERE
object {
    sphere < -0.8, 1.38564, 0>, 0.5
    Stone5
```

```
}

// SPHERE
object {
    sphere < -1.38564, 0.8, 0>, 0.5
    Stone6
}

// SPHERE
object {
    sphere < -1.6, -0, 0>, 0.5
    Stone7
}

// SPHERE
object {
    sphere < -1.38564, -0.8, 0>, 0.5
    Stone8
}

// SPHERE
object {
    sphere < -0.8, -1.38564, 0>, 0.5
    Stone9
}

// SPHERE
object {
    sphere < 0, -1.6, 0>, 0.5
    Stone10
}

// SPHERE
object {
    sphere < 0.8, -1.38564, 0>, 0.5
    Stone11
}

// SPHERE
object {
    sphere < 1.38564, -0.8, 0>, 0.5
    Stone12
}

// SPHERE
object {
    sphere < 0, 0, 0>, 0.8
    Stone13
}
```

Figure 3.3

*Using spheres
(SPHERES1.PI).*

In the scene file spheres1.pi, 12 spheres are positioned in a circle, each rotated about the z axis 30 degrees apart from the one before it. The equations to calculate each position are

X = 1.6 COS (angle) where angle = 0, 30, 60,…,330 degrees

Y = 1.6 SIN (angle)

Z = 0.0

I didn't do the calculations myself—I used POVCAD to generate the spheres automatically! In Chapter 7, the section "Creating Multiple Copies of Objects" (Tutorial #3) explains how to create objects similar to these (see also figs. 7.9 and 7.10).

The last sphere is larger than the rest, and it is located at the origin. Observe that I used 13 types of stone textures to differentiate the spheres. This scene would require you to compute the X and Y positions of all the spheres (assuming you didn't have POVCAD). Listing 3.8 shows an easier way.

Listing 3.8. Simplifying Listing 3.7 (SPHERES2.PI).

```
//SPHERES2.PI

include "colors.inc"
include "texture.inc"
include "stones.inc"
```

```
define FirstSphere object {
                    sphere < 1.6, 0, 0>, 0.5
                }

viewpoint {
 from       <0.0, 0.0, -2.0>
 at         <0.0, 0.0, 0.0>
 up         <0.0, 1.0, 0.0>
 resolution     100,100
 aspect         1.0
}

// LIGHT_SOURCE
    light <0, 5, -5>

// LIGHT_SOURCE
    light <0, 10, 0>

// LIGHT_SOURCE
    light <5, 5, 10>


// SPHERE
object {
    FirstSphere
    Stone1
}

// SPHERE
object {
    FirstSphere
    rotate <0, 0, 30>
    Stone2
}

// SPHERE
object {
    FirstSphere
    rotate <0, 0, 60>
    Stone3
}

// SPHERE
object {
    FirstSphere
    rotate <0, 0, 90>
    Stone4
}

// SPHERE
object {
    FirstSphere
    rotate <0, 0, 120>
    Stone5
}

// SPHERE
```

63

continues

Listing 3.8. Continued.

```
object {
    FirstSphere
    rotate <0, 0, 150>
    Stone6
}

// SPHERE
object {
    FirstSphere
    rotate <0, 0, 180>
    Stone7
}

// SPHERE
object {
    FirstSphere
    rotate <0, 0, 210>
    Stone8
}

// SPHERE
object {
    FirstSphere
    rotate <0, 0, 240>
    Stone9
}

// SPHERE
object {
    FirstSphere
    rotate <0, 0, 270>
    Stone10
}

// SPHERE
object {
    FirstSphere
    rotate <0, 0, 300>
    Stone11
}

// SPHERE
object {
    FirstSphere
    rotate <0, 0, 330>
    Stone12
}

// SPHERE
object {
    sphere < 0, 0, 0>, 0.8
    Stone13
}
```

Although this file is as long as the SPHERES1.PI file, it saves you from having to calculate the positions.

Both listings produce identical results in terms of the location of the spheres. The textures might vary due to rounding errors. The difference between SPHERE1.PI and SPHERE2.PI resides in the use of the rotate statement to move the original sphere to its new position. The statement rotate <0, 0, D>—where D varies from 0 to 330—is extremely useful, and you should keep it in mind for cases like this. The trick is to locate the initial sphere in a position outside the origin. Recall that if the object is at the origin, any rotation applied to it does not translate it.

After locating the sphere outside the origin, the rotate statement is applied, which has the same effect as a child spinning a rope with a stone tied to it. The hand of the child is the origin and the length of the rope is the original displacement of the sphere. The spin is the increase in rotation angle, from 0 to 330 degrees. Observe that the original sphere is being rotated at every step, creating a new sphere. Sometimes this is referred to as *orbital rotation* due to its resemblance to a satellite orbiting the Earth.

Disc

The disc object behaves as two different objects. It can be either a circular plate (thin coin) or a washer (coin with a hole in the middle). The syntax is as follows

circular plate   `disc <xc, yc, zc>, <nx, ny, nz>, r`

washer   `disc <xc, yc, zc>, <nx, ny, nz>, ir, or`

in which `r` is the radius of the circular plate, `ir` is the inner radius of the washer, `or` is the outer radius of the washer, `<xc, yc, zc>` is the center of the object, and `<nx, ny, nz>` defines the normal vector of the disc. Think of the normal as a line that goes from `<xc, yc, zc>` to `<nx, ny, nz>` and is always perpendicular to the disc. You can imagine the disc as a wheel and the normal is an axle that goes through its center. The axle is always perpendicular to the wheel.

Example 1:

```
disc <0,0,0>, <0,1,0>, 0.5
```

This is a circular plate located at the origin, with the normal pointing along the y axis. The disc is in the xz plane.

Example 2:

```
disc <0,0,0>, <1,1,0>, 0.5
```

This is a disc, again at the origin, with the normal at 45 degrees relative to the x and y axis. If you look into the z axis, you see the disc slanted at 45 degrees.

An easier way to handle discs is to use `define` statements and create known positions that could be easily rotated to a new position (see Listing 3.9).

Listing 3.9. Defining standard disc positions.

```
define Disc_XZ object {disc <0,0,0>, <0,1,0>, 1}

define Disc_XY object {disc <0,0,0>, <0,0,1>, 1}

define Disc_YZ object {disc <0,0,0>, <1,0,0>, 1}
```

Listing 3.9 helps you simplify the use of discs. Remember to use the `scale` command to set the correct sizes, and the `rotate` and `translate` commands to move and rotate the disc.

The washer definition is more difficult to simplify than the disc because the values `ir` and `or` are required. Listing 3.10 shows an example of discs. Figure 3.4 shows the output.

Listing 3.10. Using discs (DISCS.PI).

```
//DISCS.PI

include "colors.inc"
include "texture.inc"

define Plane_XZ  object {
                     polygon 4, <-10000,0,10000>, <-10000,0,-10000>,
                     <10000,0,-10000>, <10000,0,10000>
                }

define CheckerWB texture {checker matte_white, matte_black}
viewpoint {
 from      <0.0, 1.2, -5.0>
 at        <0.0, 0.0, 0.0>
 up        <0.0, 1.0, 0.0>
 resolution      100,100
 aspect          1.0
}

// LIGHT_SOURCE
    light <0, 0, -5>
```

```
// LIGHT_SOURCE
    light <1, 1, -5>


// PLANE (Checkered Floor)
object {
    Plane_XZ
    CheckerWB
    scale <2, 1, 1>    // make tiles larger!
    translate <0, -3, 0>
}

// SPHERE
object {
    sphere <0, 1, -1>, 0.7
    shiny_red
}

// WASHERS(Rings)
object {
    disc < 0, 0, 0>, <0, 1, 0>, 0.7, 0.9
    reflective_yellow
}

object {
    disc < 0, -0.2, 0>, <0, 1, 0>, 1.2, 1.5
    reflective_yellow

}

object {
    disc < 0, -0.4, 0>, <0, 1, 0>, 1.7, 1.9
    reflective_yellow
}

object {
    disc < 0, -0.6, 0>, <0, 1, 0>, 2.2, 2.4
    reflective_yellow
}

object {
    disc < 0, -0.8, 0>, <0, 1, 0>, 2.7, 2.9
    reflective_yellow
}

object {
    disc < 0, -1.0, 0>, <0, 1, 0>, 3.2, 3.4
    reflective_yellow
}

//DISC
object {
    disc <0, -5, 10>, <0, 0, 1>, 10.0
    rotate<-35, 0, 0>
    mirror
}
```

Figure 3.4

*Creating discs
and rings
(DISCS.PI).*

The scene DISCS.PI has some interesting features. Washers are positioned on top of each other along the Y axis, separated by a certain distance. There is a sphere on top of the rings. Observe how the sphere is reflected on the rings. At the back of the rings and sphere, a disc is placed to act as a mirror. It is slanted to reflect both the rings and the checkered floor. Note that the Plane_XZ and the CheckerWB definitions were included in the header section.

Parabola

Parabolas require an apex point (the tip of the curve), a base point, and the radius at the base point. The syntax is

```
parabola <xa, ya, za>, <xb, yb, zb>, r
```

in which xa, ya, and za are the coordinates of the apex, xb, yb, and zb are the coordinates of the base, and r is the radius of the base.

It is easier to define a parabola by aligning it with an axis and then rotating it to its required position. Listing 3.11 shows a quick example of parabolas (see fig. 3.5 for the output). Two parabolas are defined. One of them is rotated 180 degrees so that their bases meet.

Listing 3.11. Using parabolas (PARABOLA.PI).

```
//PARABOLA.PI

include "colors.inc"
include "texture.inc"

viewpoint {
 from      <0, 0, -5.0>
 at        <0.0, 0.0, 0.0>
 up        <0.0, 1.0, 0.0>
 resolution    100,100
 aspect        1.0
}

// LIGHT_SOURCE
    light <1, 6, -6>

// LIGHT_SOURCE
    light <0, -7, -6>

// PARABOLA
object {
       parabola <0, 5, 0>, <0, 0, 0>, 3
       white_marble
}


// PARABOLA
object {
       parabola <0, 5, 0>, <0, 0, 0>, 3
       rotate <0, 0, 180>
       sapphire_agate
}
```

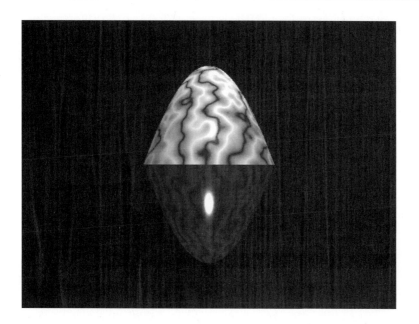

Figure 3.5

*Two parabolas
(PARABOLA.PI).*

Parabolas are not closed (capped). If you need to close a parabola, use a disc object of the same size and orientation as the parabola's base.

Cone

Cones have four parameters: two points (base and apex) and two radii. The syntax is

```
cone <xb, yb, zb>, rb, <xa, ya, za>, ra
```

If one of the two radii, ra or rb, is equal to zero, the corresponding point becomes the apex of the cone. As with parabolas, cones are not closed. Refer to Listing 3.6 (PLANES.PI) for an example of using cones.

Cylinder

Cylinders require two endpoints and a radius:

```
cylinder <xo, yo, zo>, <x1, y1, z1>, r
```

Listing 3.12 shows an example of cylinders (see fig. 3.6 for the output).

Listing 3.12. Using cylinders (CYLINDER.PI).

```
//CYLINDER.PI

include "colors.inc"
include "texture.inc"

viewpoint {
 from      <0.1, 0.0, -0.7>
 at        <0.0, 0.0, 0.0>
 up        <0.0, 1.0, 0.0>
 resolution     100,100
 aspect         1.0
}

// LIGHT_SOURCE
   light <0, 5, -5>

// LIGHT_SOURCE
   light <10,1,0>

// CYLINDER
object {
    cylinder <0.0, -0.5, 0.0>, <0.0, 0.5, 0.0>, 0.2
    rotate <0, 0, 90>
    reflective_yellow
}
```

```
// SPHERE
object {
    sphere < 0.5, 0, 0>, 0.2
    reflective_yellow
}

// SPHERE
object {
    sphere < -0.5, 0, 0>, 0.2
    reflective_yellow
}

// CYLINDER
object {
    cylinder <0.0, -0.5, 0.0>, <0.0, 0.5, 0.0>, 0.2
    reflective_yellow
}

// SPHERE
object {
    sphere < 0, 0.5, 0>, 0.2
    reflective_yellow
}

// SPHERE
object {
    sphere < 0, -0.5, 0>, 0.2
    reflective_yellow
}
```

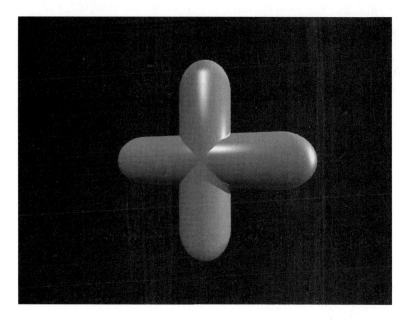

Figure 3.6

Using cylinders and spheres (CYLINDER.PI).

To cap a cylinder, use the following code:

```
define Cylinder_Y object {
            object { cylinder <0, -1, 0>, <0, 1, 0>, 1}
                + object { disc <0, -1, 0>, <0, 1, 0>, 1 }
                + object { disc <0,  1, 0>, <0, 1, 0>, 1 }
        }
```

Recall that the + sign refers to the Boolean operation union. Chapter 5, "Constructive Solid Geometry," explains Boolean operations in more detail.

Ellipsoid

Polyray doesn't have an ellipsoid object. You can, however, create one by scaling a sphere as in the following:

```
object {
    sphere < 0, 0, 0,>, 2
    scale <5, 2, 2>
    shiny_red
}
```

This creates an ellipsoid with the major axis along x.

Torus

A torus is a donut-shaped object with a major radius (the distance between the center of the torus and the center of the donut ring) and a minor radius (the radius of the ring). A torus also requires a normal vector, in the same fashion as disc objects (see fig 3.7). The syntax for a torus is

```
torus   rmaj, rmin, <xc, yc, zc>, <nx, ny, nz>
```

in which xc, yc, and zc are the coordinates of the center of the torus; nx, ny, nz is the normal vector; rmaj is the major radius; and rmin is the minor radius.

Listing 3.13 shows multiple torus objects rotated in the same fashion as in Listing 3.8 (see fig. 3.8 for the output).

Figure 3.7

Torus Definition.

Listing 3.13. Torus example (TORUS.PI).

```
//TORUS.PI

include "colors.inc"
include "texture.inc"
include "stones.inc"

viewpoint {
 from      <1.0, 2.0, -5.0>
 at        <0.0, 0.0, 0.0>
 up        <0.0, 1.0, 0.0>
 angle 45
 hither 1
 resolution    100,100
 aspect        1.0
}

// LIGHT_SOURCE
    light White, <3, 3, -6>
// LIGHT_SOURCE
    light <-3, 3, -6>

// TORUS
object {
    torus  0.8, 0.1, < 0.0, 0.0, 0.0>, <0.0, 1.0, 0.0>
    rotate <90, 0, 0>
    Stone5
}
```

continues

73

Listing 3.13. Continued.

```
// TORUS
object {
    torus  0.8, 0.1, < 0.0, 0.0, 0.0>, <0.0, 1.0, 0.0>
    translate <1.2437, 0.004338, 0>
    Stone5
}

// TORUS
object {
    torus  0.8, 0.1, < 0.0, 0.0, 0.0>, <0.0, 1.0, 0.0>
    rotate <0, 0, 30>
    translate <1.07491, 0.625606, 0>
    Stone5
}

// TORUS
object {
    torus  0.8, 0.1, < 0.0, 0.0, 0.0>, <0.0, 1.0, 0.0>
    rotate <0, 0, 60>
    translate <0.618092, 1.07924, 0>
    Stone5
}

// TORUS
object {
    torus  0.8, 0.1, < 0.0, 0.0, 0.0>, <0.0, 1.0, 0.0>
    rotate <0, 0, 90>
    translate <-0.004338, 1.2437, 0>
    Stone5
}

// TORUS
object {
    torus  0.8, 0.1, < 0.0, 0.0, 0.0>, <0.0, 1.0, 0.0>
    rotate <0, 0, 120>
    translate <-0.625606, 1.07491, 0>
    Stone5
}

// TORUS
object {
    torus  0.8, 0.1, < 0.0, 0.0, 0.0>, <0.0, 1.0, 0.0>
    rotate <0, 0, 150>
    translate <-1.07924, 0.618092, 0>
    Stone5
}

// TORUS
object {
    torus  0.8, 0.1, < 0.0, 0.0, 0.0>, <0.0, 1.0, 0.0>
    rotate <0, 0, 180>
    translate <-1.2437, -0.004338, 0>
    Stone5
}

// TORUS
object {
    torus  0.8, 0.1, < 0.0, 0.0, 0.0>, <0.0, 1.0, 0.0>
```

```
        rotate <0, 0, 210>
        translate <-1.07491, -0.625606, 0>
        Stone5
}

// TORUS
object {
        torus  0.8, 0.1, < 0.0, 0.0, 0.0>, <0.0, 1.0, 0.0>
        rotate <0, 0, 240>
        translate <-0.618092, -1.07924, 0>
        Stone5
}

// TORUS
object {
        torus  0.8, 0.1, < 0.0, 0.0, 0.0>, <0.0, 1.0, 0.0>
        rotate <0, 0, 270>
        translate <0.004338, -1.2437, 0>
        Stone5
}

// TORUS
object {
        torus  0.8, 0.1, < 0.0, 0.0, 0.0>, <0.0, 1.0, 0.0>
        rotate <0, 0, 300>
        translate <0.625606, -1.07491, 0>
        Stone5
}

// TORUS
object {
        torus  0.8, 0.1, < 0.0, 0.0, 0.0>, <0.0, 1.0, 0.0>
        rotate <0, 0, 330>
        translate <1.07924, -0.618092, 0>
        Stone5
}
```

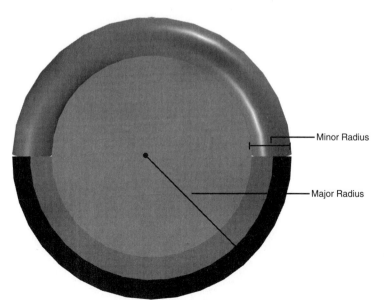

Figure 3.8

Torus example: rings on a ring (TORUS.PI).

Minor Radius

Major Radius

Modeling Surfaces

Not all everyday objects can be modeled with those primitives presented in the previous chapter. In some cases, surfaces composed of triangular patches or polygons must be used to replicate a complicated object. In the following sections, you study techniques used to create and model surfaces.

Smooth Triangles

Smooth triangles or triangular patches are defined by three vertices and three normal vectors (one for each vertex). The normal vector is used to tell Polyray the orientation of the curvature at that vertex. This information is then used to compute the shades that will make the object look smooth instead of looking as if it was composed of flat triangles. Figure 3.9 shows an example of a flat triangle and a smooth one.

Figure 3.9

Flat and smooth triangles.

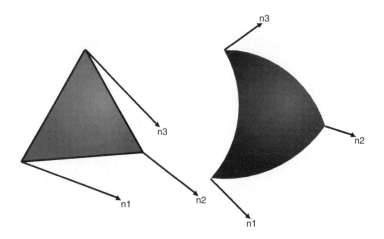

As shown in figure 3.9, flat triangles have all three normals pointing in the same direction. Therefore, the intensity of the color throughout the triangle is constant. On the other hand, the normals of a smooth triangle are pointing in various directions, so Polyray is able to interpolate between them, calculate what the curvature is, and determine what shading variation to apply. Polyray's syntax for smooth triangles is

```
patch <x1, y1, z1>, <n1x, n1y, n1z>,
      <x2, y2, z2>, <n2x, n2y, n2z>,
      <x3, y3, z3>, <n3x, n3y, n3z>
```

in which x1, y1, and z1 are the coordinates of vertex #1, and <n1x, n1y, n1z> is the normal vector of vertex #1, x2, y2, and z2 are the coordinates of vertex #2, and <n2x, n2y, n2z> is the normal vector of vertex #2 and finally x3, y3, and z3 are the coordinates of vertex #3, and <n3x, n3y, n3z> is the normal vector of vertex #3.

In the next section, you explore how smooth triangles are created.

Generating Smooth Triangles

Generating smooth triangle data by hand is extremely difficult, to say the least. It is not uncommon to see objects composed of thousands of triangles! Imagine typing all those values and their normals. There are utilities available that will help you create such objects. POVCAD (the 3-D modeler included with this book) can create them easily with just a few commands. Figures 3.10 and 3.11 show the two steps necessary to generate an object similar to a flower vase.

The first step is to create an outline of the object (see fig. 3.10). This outline consists of points interconnected with straight lines. You can do this by clicking the mouse in the places where the points are to be created.

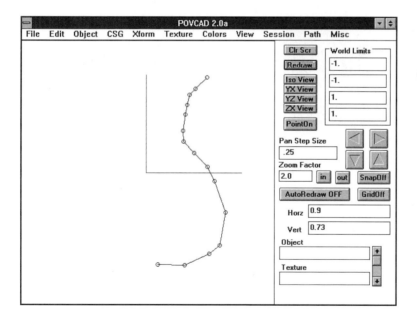

Figure 3.10

A vase outline created in POVCAD.

The next step is to select Sweep from the Object menu. The Sweep command in POVCAD is similar to the lathe object in Polyray. The contour is then rotated the necessary number of degrees. The result is an object that looks like a flower vase composed of flat triangles (see fig. 3.11).

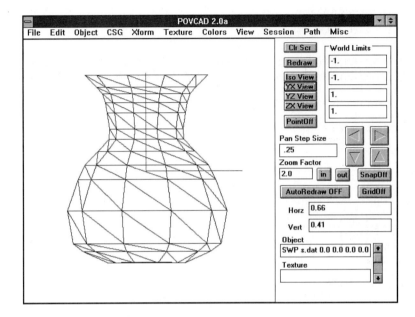

Figure 3.11

A complete vase created with the Sweep command.

Most utilities (including POVCAD) save triangular data in RAW data format. This format consists of an ASCII file with one line per triangle. If the object is composed of 100 triangles, the file will have 100 lines. There are 9 values (3 vertices × 3 coordinates) on each line. One line inside a RAW data file can look like this

```
0 0 0 1.5 0 0 0.7 1.2 0
```

The triangle's vertices are <0, 0, 0>; <1.5, 0, 0>; and <0.7, 1.2, 0>.

Because the data file already has the information that defines the flat triangles, you need a utility to calculate the normals and generate the smooth triangle information. The next section shows a programming example in QBasic (QBasic is the BASIC interpreter bundled with Microsoft's MS-DOS 5.0 and 6.0. The example should also be compatible with Quick Basic 4.5.)

Programming Example

In the previous section, you read that a computer program can be very helpful in creating smooth triangle information. This section presents two examples written in QBasic. The first program, FLAT.BAS, reads a RAW data file and creates an object composed of polygons. The data file that we are using is called RAW.DAT. It was created with POVCAD's Sweep command.

Listing 3.14. RAW data to polygon converter (FLAT.BAS).

```
' PROGRAM: FLAT.BAS
' by Alfonso Hermida 6/23/93
'
' This program reads a RAW data file <triangle data, 1 triangle per
' line> and outputs data as flat triangles for the Polyray ray
' tracer.
'
' This program is compatible with QBasic and Quick Basic 4.5.


TYPE POINT3D
   x AS SINGLE
   y AS SINGLE
   z AS SINGLE
END TYPE

   DIM ain AS STRING
   DIM aout AS STRING
   DIM i AS INTEGER
   DIM p1 AS POINT3D
   DIM p2 AS POINT3D
   DIM p3 AS POINT3D

   CLS
   PRINT "FLAT TRIANGLE GENERATOR by Alfonso Hermida"
   PRINT
   INPUT "Enter Name Of RAW Data File [RAW.DAT]", ain$
   IF ain$ = "" THEN ain$ = "RAW.DAT"

   INPUT "Enter Name Of Output File [FLAT.OUT]", aout$
   IF aout$ = "" THEN aout$ = "FLAT.OUT"


   OPEN ain$ FOR INPUT AS #1
   OPEN aout$ FOR OUTPUT AS #3

   PRINT #3, "//Flat Triangles Created With FLAT.BAS"
   PRINT #3, "//"; DATE$; " "; TIME$
   PRINT #3, ""
   PRINT #3, "define FlatTriangleTexture YOUR/TEXTURE/GOES/HERE!"
   PRINT #3, " "
   PRINT #3, ""
   PRINT #3, "object {"
```

continues

Listing 3.14. Continued.

```
i = 0
DO WHILE NOT EOF(1)

  INPUT #1, p1.x, p1.y, p1.z
  INPUT #1, p2.x, p2.y, p2.z
  INPUT #1, p3.x, p3.y, p3.z

  i = i + 1
  IF i > 1 THEN PRINT #3, "+";
  PRINT #3, "   object {"
  PRINT #3, "       polygon 3, "
  PRINT #3, "                     <";
  PRINT #3, USING "#####.###"; p1.x;
  PRINT #3, ",";
  PRINT #3, USING "#####.###"; p1.y;
  PRINT #3, ",";
  PRINT #3, USING "#####.###"; p1.z;
  PRINT #3, ">,"
  PRINT #3, "                     <";
  PRINT #3, USING "#####.###"; p2.x;
  PRINT #3, ",";
  PRINT #3, USING "#####.###"; p2.y;
  PRINT #3, ",";
  PRINT #3, USING "#####.###"; p2.z;
  PRINT #3, ">,"
  PRINT #3, "                     <";
  PRINT #3, USING "#####.###"; p3.x;
  PRINT #3, ",";
  PRINT #3, USING "#####.###"; p3.y;
  PRINT #3, ",";
  PRINT #3, USING "#####.###"; p3.z;
  PRINT #3, ">"
  PRINT #3, "    }"

LOOP
PRINT #3, "    FlatTriangleTexture"
PRINT #3, "}"
CLOSE #3
CLOSE #1
PRINT
PRINT "Done!"
```

The program opens a RAW data file (in this case, the default name is
RAW.DAT) and saves each vertex in the variables p1, p2, and p3. The three
points are then written to a file to comply with Polyray's polygon format.
At the top of the file is the following statement:

```
define FlatTriangleTexture YOUR/TEXTURE/GOES/HERE!
```

Replace the expression YOUR/TEXTURE/GOES/HERE! with the corresponding
texture (finish) or color. For example:

```
define FlatTriangleTexture marble_finish
```

In the preceding line, the expression was replaced with `marble_finish`. This texture is used for all the polygons generated in that file. The token name `FlatTriangleTexture` appears at the end of the output file.

Generating flat triangles is easy if the RAW data file is available. The next program, named SMOOTH.BAS (see Listing 3.15), reads the same RAW data file and creates smooth triangles or patches. To calculate the normals of the smooth object, the program does the following:

1. Calculate the normal of each vertex and save that information. Because the triangles are initially flat, all the normals of a given triangle must be equal.

2. Check which vertices are shared between triangles. If a vertex is shared by other triangles, add all the normals and calculate an average normal for the given vertex.

3. Repeat step 2 until all vertices are checked.

4. Output the data.

The normal of a triangle (or plane) is calculated in the subroutine named `NormalVector`. I will not get into the details of how to calculate a normal; however, you might want to review this process in a calculus book. The subroutine is very short and easily understood.

Listing 3.15. Smooth triangle generator (SMOOTH.BAS).

```
' PROGRAM: SMOOTH.BAS
' by Alfonso Hermida 6/23/93
'
' This program reads a RAW data file <triangle data, 1 triangle
' per line> and outputs data as smooth triangles for the Polyray
' ray tracer.
'
' NOTE: The array sizes of
'
' DIM Vertex(3300) AS POINT3D
' DIM Normal(3300) AS POINT3D
' must be big enough to hold all your input data.
' If you can't run the program, experiment by decreasing the size.

' This program is compatible with QBasic and Quick Basic 4.5.

DECLARE SUB NormalVector (pc AS ANY, p1 AS ANY, p2 AS ANY, pn AS ANY)

TYPE POINT3D
    x AS SINGLE
    y AS SINGLE
    z AS SINGLE
```

continues

81

Listing 3.15. Continued.

```
END TYPE

    DIM a AS STRING
    DIM TOL AS SINGLE
    DIM i, j, k, RST, total, count AS INTEGER
    DIM p1 AS POINT3D
    DIM p2 AS POINT3D
    DIM p3 AS POINT3D
    DIM pnt AS POINT3D
    DIM pn AS POINT3D
    DIM pnormal AS POINT3D
    DIM Vertex(3300) AS POINT3D    'Change this number if necessary
    DIM Normal(3300) AS POINT3D    'Change this number if necessary
    DIM Magnitude AS SINGLE

    TOL = .0005#
    CLS
    PRINT "SMOOTH TRIANGLE GENERATOR by Alfonso Hermida"
    PRINT
    INPUT "Enter Name Of RAW Data File [RAW.DAT]", a$
    IF a$ = "" THEN a$ = "RAW.DAT"

    OPEN a$ FOR INPUT AS #1
    count = 1
    DO WHILE NOT EOF(1)

        INPUT #1, Vertex(count).x
        INPUT #1, Vertex(count).y
        INPUT #1, Vertex(count).z
        INPUT #1, Vertex(count + 1).x
        INPUT #1, Vertex(count + 1).y
        INPUT #1, Vertex(count + 1).z
        INPUT #1, Vertex(count + 2).x
        INPUT #1, Vertex(count + 2).y
        INPUT #1, Vertex(count + 2).z
        p1 = Vertex(count)
        p2 = Vertex(count + 1)
        p3 = Vertex(count + 2)

        'Calculate the triangle normal
        CALL NormalVector(p1, p2, p3, pnormal)

        'Copy the normal to each vertex
        Normal(count) = pnormal
        Normal(count + 1) = pnormal
        Normal(count + 2) = pnormal

        'Increment vertex counter
        count = count + 3

    LOOP
    count = count - 1
    CLOSE #1


    PRINT "Results:"
```

```
PRINT "Points    = "; count
PRINT "Triangles = "; count / 3
PRINT

INPUT "Enter Name Of Output File [SMOOTH.OUT]", a$
IF a$ = "" THEN a$ = "SMOOTH.OUT"
PRINT "Please wait..."

OPEN a$ FOR OUTPUT AS #3
PRINT #3, "//Smooth Triangles Created With SMOOTH.BAS"
PRINT #3, "//"; DATE$; " "; TIME$
PRINT #3, ""
PRINT #3, "define SmoothTriangleTexture YOUR/TEXTURE/GOES/HERE!"
PRINT #3, " "
PRINT #3, ""
PRINT #3, "object {"
RST = 0
FOR i = 1 TO count
 LOCATE 10, 1
 PRINT i
  p1 = Vertex(i)
  total = 0
  RST = RST + 1
  IF RST = 1 THEN
      IF i > 1 THEN PRINT #3, "+";
      PRINT #3, "   object { patch"
  END IF
  pn.x = 0
  pn.y = 0
  pn.z = 0
  total = 0
  FOR k = 1 TO count
    ' Check And Add All Normals Of A Given Vertex
    IF (ABS(p1.x - Vertex(k).x) < TOL AND
    ➥ABS(p1.y - Vertex(k).y) < TOL AND
    ➥ABS(p1.z - Vertex(k).z) < TOL) THEN
    pn.x = pn.x + Normal(k).x
    pn.y = pn.y + Normal(k).y
    pn.z = pn.z + Normal(k).z
    total = total + 1
    END IF
  NEXT

  ' Compute Normal Average
  pn.x = pn.x / total
  pn.y = pn.y / total
  pn.z = pn.z / total

  ' Find The Magnitude Of The Normal
  Magnitude = (pn.x ^ 2 + pn.y ^ 2 + pn.z ^ 2) ^ (.5)

  ' Make the Normal A Unit Vector
  pn.x = pn.x / Magnitude
  pn.y = pn.y / Magnitude
  pn.z = pn.z / Magnitude

  PRINT #3, "              <";
  PRINT #3, USING "#####.###"; p1.x;
```

83

continues

Listing 3.15. Continued.

```
        PRINT #3, ",";
        PRINT #3, USING "#####.###"; p1.y;
        PRINT #3, ",";
        PRINT #3, USING "#####.###"; p1.z;
        PRINT #3, ">, < ";
        PRINT #3, USING "#####.###"; pn.x;
        PRINT #3, ", ";
        PRINT #3, USING "#####.###"; pn.y;
        PRINT #3, ", ";
        PRINT #3, USING "#####.###"; pn.z;
        PRINT #3, " >";
        IF RST < 3 THEN PRINT #3, ","
        IF RST = 3 THEN
            PRINT #3, ""
            PRINT #3, "    }"
            RST = 0
        END IF
    NEXT
    PRINT #3, "    SmoothTriangleTexture"
    PRINT #3, "}"
    CLOSE #3
    PRINT ""
    PRINT "Done!"

SUB NormalVector (pc AS POINT3D, p1 AS POINT3D,
    ➥p2 AS POINT3D, pn AS POINT3D)
DIM V1 AS POINT3D
DIM V2 AS POINT3D

    V1.x = (p1.x - pc.x)
    V1.y = (p1.y - pc.y)
    V1.z = (p1.z - pc.z)

    V2.x = (p2.x - pc.x)
    V2.y = (p2.y - pc.y)
    V2.z = (p2.z - pc.z)

    ' calc normal vector N = Ai+Bj+Ck
    pn.x = V1.y * V2.z - V1.z * V2.y
    pn.y = -(V1.x * V2.z - V1.z * V2.x)
    pn.z = V1.x * V2.y - V1.y * V2.x

END SUB
```

Figures 3.12 and 3.13 show the ray-traced images of the output generated by FLAT.BAS and SMOOTH.BAS, respectively.

Figure 3.12

The output from data generated by FLAT.BAS.

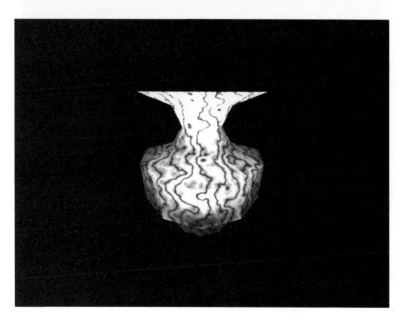

Figure 3.13

The output from data generated by SMOOTH.BAS.

Polygons

Polygons are collections of points that are interconnected to create a flat surface. Recall how in previous examples we used polygons to create a floor. The syntax is

```
polygon n,
     < vertex1.x,  vertex1.y,  vertex1.z>,
     < vertex2.x,  vertex2.y,  vertex2.z>,
     < vertex3.x,  vertex3.y,  vertex3.z>,
          .... etc. ...
     < vertexn.x,  vertexn.y,  vertexn.z>
```

where n is the number of vertices.

Check previous examples, for example PLANES.PI, for the use of polygons.

Lathe

Lathe objects are a collection of points that define the contour of a symmetric object. The contour is then revolved about an axis creating a *solid of revolution*. There are two types of lathe objects. Type 1 connects the points with line segments, whereas type 2 uses a smooth curve (spline). The contour can be rotated about any axis by defining a direction vector. To rotate about the y axis, use <0, 1, 0>. To rotate about the x or z axis, use <1, 0, 0> or <0, 0, 1>, respectively.

The syntax is

```
object {
    lathe  type , axis,  n ,
          <p1.x, p1.y, p1.z>,
          <p2.x, p2.y, p2.z>,
.............etc..........
          <pn.x, pn.y, pn.z>
}
```

in which

type	Either 1 (faceted finish) or 2 (smooth finish).
axis	Axis of rotation, i.e. <0, 1, 0> is about the y axis.
n	Number of points that define the curve.
<pi.x, pi.y, pi.z>	The ith point's coordinates.

The program LATHE.BAS is included on the disk and works in the same way as FLAT.BAS (see Listing 3.16). It opens a data file and creates another file that follows Polyray's format, in this case for lathe objects.

Listing 3.16. Program LATHE.BAS.

```
' PROGRAM: LATHE.BAS
' by Alfonso Hermida 6/23/93
'
' This program reads a list of 3D points that defines a contour
' and outputs data as a LATHE object for the Polyray ray tracer.
'
' This program is compatible with QBasic and Quick Basic 4.5.


TYPE POINT3D
  x AS SINGLE
  y AS SINGLE
  z AS SINGLE
END TYPE

  DIM ain AS STRING
  DIM aout AS STRING
  DIM LatheType AS INTEGER
  DIM Total AS INTEGER
  DIM Direction AS STRING
  DIM i AS INTEGER
  DIM p1 AS POINT3D

  CLS
  PRINT "LATHE OBJECT GENERATOR by Alfonso Hermida"
  PRINT
  INPUT "Enter Name Of RAW Data File [POINTS.DAT]", ain$
  IF ain$ = "" THEN ain$ = "POINTS.DAT"

  INPUT "Enter Name Of Output File [LATHE.OUT]", aout$
  IF aout$ = "" THEN aout$ = "LATHE.OUT"

  INPUT "Select A Type: (1) Line Segments (2) Smooth (Spline)  [2]"; LatheType
  IF LatheType = 0 THEN LatheType = 2

  INPUT "Enter Direction Of Axis Of Rotation [<0, 1, 0>]"; Direction$
  IF Direction$ = "" THEN Direction$ = "<0, 1, 0>"

  'Check Total Number Of Points
  i = 0
  OPEN ain$ FOR INPUT AS #1
  DO WHILE NOT EOF(1)
    INPUT #1, p1.x, p1.y, p1.z
    i = i + 1
  LOOP
  CLOSE #1
  Total = i

  OPEN ain$ FOR INPUT AS #1
```

continues

Listing 3.16. Continued.

```
OPEN aout$ FOR OUTPUT AS #3

PRINT #3, "//Lathe Object Created With LATHE.BAS"
PRINT #3, "//"; DATE$; " "; TIME$
PRINT #3, ""
PRINT #3, "define LatheTexture YOUR/TEXTURE/GOES/HERE!"
PRINT #3, ""
PRINT #3, ""
PRINT #3, "object {"
PRINT #3, "    lathe "; LatheType; ", "; Direction$; ", "; Total; ","

i = 0
DO WHILE NOT EOF(1)

   INPUT #1, p1.x, p1.y, p1.z

   i = i + 1
   PRINT #3, "           <";
   PRINT #3, USING "#####.###"; p1.x;
   PRINT #3, ",";
   PRINT #3, USING "#####.###"; p1.y;
   PRINT #3, ",";
   PRINT #3, USING "#####.###"; p1.z;
   PRINT #3, ">";
   IF i < Total THEN
      PRINT #3, ","
   ELSE
      PRINT #3, ""
   END IF
LOOP
PRINT #3, "    LatheTexture"
PRINT #3, "}"
CLOSE #3
CLOSE #1
PRINT
PRINT "Done!"
```

The data file used was PAWN.DAT, which has the following format:

```
PAWN.DAT

0              5.44      0
0.672269       5.15401   0
0.87395        4.52928   0
0.638655       3.97397   0
0.336134       3.86985   0
0.806723       3.80043   0
1.10924        3.59219   0
1.14286        3.27983   0
0.705882       3.10629   0
0.336134       3.10629   0
0.470588       2.44685   0
0.638655       1.96095   0
0.941176       1.54447   0
1.31092        1.09328   0
```

```
2.01681        0.67679      0
2.38655        0.295011     0
2.38655       -0.225597     0
2.01681       -0.537961     0
2.52101       -0.607375     0
2.92437       -0.885033     0
2.85714       -1.30152      0
2.31933       -1.44035      0
1.64706       -1.54447      0
0             -1.6          0
```

The format is simple: there is one 3-D point per line to define the contour of a chess piece. The program LATHE.BAS read this data and creates an output similar to Listing 3.17.

Listing 3.17. The output from LATHE.BAS (LATHE.PI).

```
// LATHE.PI

include "colors.inc"
include "texture.inc"

viewpoint {
  from      <0.0, 4.0, -9.0>
  at        <0.0, 1.0, 0.0>
  up        <0.0, 1.0, 0.0>
  angle 80
  resolution      100,100
  aspect          1.00
}

background White

// LIGHT_SOURCE
    light White, <0, 1, -6>
// LIGHT_SOURCE
    light <-3, 3, -6>
    light < 3, 3, -6>


//Lathe Object Created With LATHE.BAS
//06-24-1993 10:38:17

define LatheTexture shiny_red

define FlatPawn
object {
    lathe  1 , <0, 1, 0>,  24 ,
        <    0.000,    5.440,    0.000>,
        <    0.672,    5.154,    0.000>,
        <    0.874,    4.529,    0.000>,
        <    0.639,    3.974,    0.000>,
        <    0.336,    3.870,    0.000>,
        <    0.807,    3.800,    0.000>,
        <    1.109,    3.592,    0.000>,
```

continues

Listing 3.17. Continued.

```
            <    1.143,    3.280,    0.000>,
            <    0.706,    3.106,    0.000>,
            <    0.336,    3.106,    0.000>,
            <    0.471,    2.447,    0.000>,
            <    0.639,    1.961,    0.000>,
            <    0.941,    1.544,    0.000>,
            <    1.311,    1.093,    0.000>,
            <    2.017,    0.677,    0.000>,
            <    2.387,    0.295,    0.000>,
            <    2.387,   -0.226,    0.000>,
            <    2.017,   -0.538,    0.000>,
            <    2.521,   -0.607,    0.000>,
            <    2.924,   -0.885,    0.000>,
            <    2.857,   -1.302,    0.000>,
            <    2.319,   -1.440,    0.000>,
            <    1.647,   -1.544,    0.000>,
            <    0.000,   -1.600,    0.000>
        LatheTexture
}

define SmoothPawn
object {
    lathe  2 , <0, 1, 0>,  24 ,
            <    0.000,    5.440,    0.000>,
            <    0.672,    5.154,    0.000>,
            <    0.874,    4.529,    0.000>,
            <    0.639,    3.974,    0.000>,
            <    0.336,    3.870,    0.000>,
            <    0.807,    3.800,    0.000>,
            <    1.109,    3.592,    0.000>,
            <    1.143,    3.280,    0.000>,
            <    0.706,    3.106,    0.000>,
            <    0.336,    3.106,    0.000>,
            <    0.471,    2.447,    0.000>,
            <    0.639,    1.961,    0.000>,
            <    0.941,    1.544,    0.000>,
            <    1.311,    1.093,    0.000>,
            <    2.017,    0.677,    0.000>,
            <    2.387,    0.295,    0.000>,
            <    2.387,   -0.226,    0.000>,
            <    2.017,   -0.538,    0.000>,
            <    2.521,   -0.607,    0.000>,
            <    2.924,   -0.885,    0.000>,
            <    2.857,   -1.302,    0.000>,
            <    2.319,   -1.440,    0.000>,
            <    1.647,   -1.544,    0.000>,
            <    0.000,   -1.600,    0.000>
        LatheTexture
}

object {
  FlatPawn
  translate <-4, 0, 0>
}

object {
  SmoothPawn
  translate <4, 0, 0>
}
```

In LATHE.PI, two lathe objects were created with the same data points. Each uses a different type of lathe finish. The first one uses type 1, whereas the second uses type 2. Figure 3.14 shows both objects.

Figure 3.14

Chess pawns created with the lathe command (LATHE.PI).

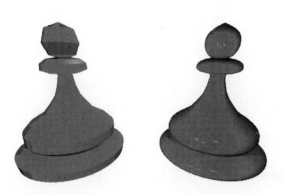

Sweep/Extruded

Sweep surfaces are similar in syntax to lathe surfaces with some minor differences. You must replace the word lathe with the word sweep. Also, the direction vector defines a translation rather than a rotation axis.

The syntax is

```
object {
    sweep  type , axis,  n ,
          <p1.x, p1.y, p1.z>,
          <p2.x, p2.y, p2.z>,
..............etc...........
          <pn.x, pn.y, pn.z>
}
```

in which

type	Either 1 (faceted finish) or 2 (smooth finish).
axis	Axis of translation, i.e. <0, 1, 0> is along the Y axis.
n	Number of points that define the curve.
<pi.x, pi.y, pi.z>	The ith point's coordinates.

91

The magnitude of the translation vector is very important, because it determines the total displacement (extrusion) of the curve along the vector. To calculate the magnitude of a vector, use the following formula:

$$\text{given } <a, b, c>, \qquad \text{magnitude} = \sqrt{a^2 + b^2 + c^2}$$

As a small experiment, we use the same contour data from PAWN.DAT to create a sweep object. Listing 3.18 is a modification of Listing 3.16.

Listing 3.18. Creating a sweep surface (SWEEP.PI).

```
// SWEEP.PI

include "colors.inc"
include "texture.inc"

viewpoint {
  from      <0.0, 3.0, -9.0>
  at        <1.0, 1.0, 0.0>
  up        <0.0, 1.0, 0.0>
  angle 80
  resolution    100,100
  aspect        1.00
}

background White

// LIGHT_SOURCE
    light White, <0, 1, -6>
// LIGHT_SOURCE
    light <-3, 3, -6>
    light < 3, 3, -6>


define SweepTexture shiny_red

define FlatPawn
object {
    sweep  1 , <0, 0, 3>,   24 ,
        <    0.000,    5.440,    0.000>,
        <    0.672,    5.154,    0.000>,
        <    0.874,    4.529,    0.000>,
        <    0.639,    3.974,    0.000>,
        <    0.336,    3.870,    0.000>,
        <    0.807,    3.800,    0.000>,
        <    1.109,    3.592,    0.000>,
        <    1.143,    3.280,    0.000>,
        <    0.706,    3.106,    0.000>,
        <    0.336,    3.106,    0.000>,
        <    0.471,    2.447,    0.000>,
        <    0.639,    1.961,    0.000>,
        <    0.941,    1.544,    0.000>,
```

```
          <     1.311,    1.093,    0.000>,
          <     2.017,    0.677,    0.000>,
          <     2.387,    0.295,    0.000>,
          <     2.387,   -0.226,    0.000>,
          <     2.017,   -0.538,    0.000>,
          <     2.521,   -0.607,    0.000>,
          <     2.924,   -0.885,    0.000>,
          <     2.857,   -1.302,    0.000>,
          <     2.319,   -1.440,    0.000>,
          <     1.647,   -1.544,    0.000>,
          <     0.000,   -1.600,    0.000>
     SweepTexture
}

define SmoothPawn
object {
    sweep  2 , <0, 0, 3>,  24 ,
          <     0.000,    5.440,    0.000>,
          <     0.672,    5.154,    0.000>,
          <     0.874,    4.529,    0.000>,
          <     0.639,    3.974,    0.000>,
          <     0.336,    3.870,    0.000>,
          <     0.807,    3.800,    0.000>,
          <     1.109,    3.592,    0.000>,
          <     1.143,    3.280,    0.000>,
          <     0.706,    3.106,    0.000>,
          <     0.336,    3.106,    0.000>,
          <     0.471,    2.447,    0.000>,
          <     0.639,    1.961,    0.000>,
          <     0.941,    1.544,    0.000>,
          <     1.311,    1.093,    0.000>,
          <     2.017,    0.677,    0.000>,
          <     2.387,    0.295,    0.000>,
          <     2.387,   -0.226,    0.000>,
          <     2.017,   -0.538,    0.000>,
          <     2.521,   -0.607,    0.000>,
          <     2.924,   -0.885,    0.000>,
          <     2.857,   -1.302,    0.000>,
          <     2.319,   -1.440,    0.000>,
          <     1.647,   -1.544,    0.000>,
          <     0.000,   -1.600,    0.000>
     SweepTexture
}

object {
  FlatPawn
  rotate <0, 55, 0>
  translate <-3, 0, 0>
}

object {
  SmoothPawn
  rotate <0, 70, 0>
  translate <3, 0, 0>
}
```

Again, two objects are created (see fig 3.15). One of the objects uses type 1 (faceted), and the other uses type 2 (smooth).

Figure 3.15

Extruded chess pawn curves (SWEEP.PI).

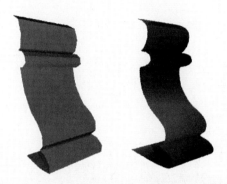

You can easily modify the program LATHE.BAS to create sweep objects. This programming exercise is left to the reader.

Bézier Patches

Bézier patches consist of 16 control points arranged in a 4 × 4 matrix or array. By displacing these control points, the patch can be molded. The syntax is

```
bezier s, f, u, v,
      <x0, y0, z0>,
      <x1, y1, z1>,
      .........,
      <x15, y15, z15>,
```

in which

s is the subdivision control and refers to how the data is stored:

$s = 1$ uses less memory but takes longer to generate

$s = 2$ uses more memory but takes less time

94

f	Sets the flatness value. Lowering this number increases the amount of subdivisions as determined by u and v. The suggested value of f is 0.05.
u,v	Number of subdivisions to be performed on the local x and y axis of the patch. Increasing this number forces the surface to be smoother at the expense of memory and computation time. Suggested values: u = 3, v = 3.

Listing 3.19 shows an example of two surfaces created with Bézier patches. The SheetBezier object was created by deforming a flat Bézier patch, and the CylinderBezier object was created by deforming four Bézier patches initially arranged as a cylinder. The ends of the cylinder were stretched outward (see fig. 3.16).

Observe the interesting effect of applying a checkered finish to the SheetBezier surface. One of the tiles is made of stone and the other is just the color matte_black. Another interesting feature is that the CylinderBezier surface is four Bézier patches combined into one by using Boolean operations (+).

Listing 3.19. Bézier patches (BEZIER.PI).

```
// BEZIER.PI

include "colors.inc"
include "texture.inc"
include "stones.inc"

viewpoint {
  from        <-5.0, 5.0, -30.0>
  at          <0.0, 0.0, 0.0>
  up          <0.0, 1.0, 0.0>
  angle 85
  resolution      100,100
  aspect          1.0
}

background White

// LIGHT_SOURCE
    light White, <0, 1, -6>
    light <0,-6,-6>
// LIGHT_SOURCE
    light <-20, 5, 0>
    light < 3, 3, -6>

define SheetBezier object {
            bezier  2, 0.05,  3,  3,
    <-7.441097,      0.175513,      8.736674>,
```

95

continues

Listing 3.19. Continued.

```
            <0.775496,   -1.090713,    4.650486>,
            <2.999994,   -0.058649,    4.433383>,
            <9.859163,   -2.451552,   -1.003611>,
           <-2.348895,   -0.067749,    2.807758>,
           <-0.332253,    0.867879,    2.610940>,
            <2.060343,    2.696604,    8.953340>,
            <4.012816,    2.883789,    2.186876>,
           <-3.204923,    1.445780,    1.231671>,
           <-0.367755,    1.198388,   -4.274309>,
            <1.036218,    3.413472,    0.817750>,
            <3.156788,    4.397318,    0.610789>,
           <-8.325093,    6.300124,    4.751141>,
           <-2.203973,    4.177238,   -0.835203>,
            <0.000567,    5.244590,   -1.089052>,
            <4.265499,    6.530803,   -2.477069>
                  }

define b21    object {
                  bezier  2,  0.05,  3,  3,
          <-13.157171,    3.747712,  -13.266072>,
          <-15.994769,   -2.360541,  -13.257848>,
           <-9.888506,   -9.988533,  -12.331910>,
           <-6.020190,  -10.754260,  -12.339270>,
          <-10.325383,    1.543393,   -0.767010>,
          <-10.806159,   -1.222832,   -0.967095>,
           <-8.392786,   -4.410553,   -1.158496>,
           <-5.681259,   -4.927205,   -1.098878>,
          <-10.599442,    1.220823,    1.557361>,
          <-10.882533,   -1.412619,    1.840276>,
           <-8.590908,   -4.663777,    1.682831>,
           <-5.818507,   -5.148710,    1.725471>,
          <-14.989909,    2.110008,    5.359019>,
          <-15.732432,   -1.233681,    3.958136>,
          <-16.821856,   -5.317152,    3.020572>,
           <-7.121402,   -8.133587,    3.127131>
                  }

define  b22    object {
                  bezier  2,  0.05,  3,  3,
           <-6.020190,  -10.754260,  -12.339270>,
           <-2.151873,  -11.519988,  -12.346631>,
            <0.620599,   -6.774581,  -12.403907>,
            <3.010568,   -2.939457,  -12.403823>,
           <-5.681259,   -4.927205,   -1.098878>,
           <-2.969733,   -5.443857,   -1.039260>,
            <0.283443,   -3.162564,   -0.796536>,
            <0.764219,   -0.396339,   -0.596452>,
           <-5.818507,   -5.148710,    1.725471>,
           <-3.046107,   -5.633643,    1.768111>,
            <0.207069,   -3.352351,    2.010834>,
            <0.687845,   -0.586125,    2.210919>,
           <-7.121402,   -8.133587,    3.127131>,
            <2.579052,  -10.950022,    3.233690>,
            <4.089041,   -5.230404,    3.897720>,
            <6.646496,    0.560038,    6.933765>
                  }
```

```
define  b23     object {
                bezier  2, 0.05,  3,  3,
        <3.010568,    -2.939457,    -12.403823>,
        <5.400538,     0.895668,    -12.403738>,
        <4.485245,     4.545848,    -12.846294>,
        <0.519430,     8.286380,    -12.888933>,
        <0.764219,    -0.396339,     -0.596452>,
        <1.244994,     2.369887,     -0.396368>,
        <-1.046631,    5.621045,     -0.238923>,
        <-3.819031,    6.105978,     -0.281563>,
        <0.687845,    -0.586125,      2.210919>,
        <1.168620,     2.180100,      2.411003>,
        <-1.123004,    5.431259,      2.568448>,
        <-3.895405,    5.916192,      2.525808>,
        <6.646496,     0.560038,      6.933765>,
        <9.203951,     6.350481,      9.969809>,
        <-0.198922,    8.480721,      5.740788>,
        <-6.165601,   10.466374,      6.160175>
                }

define  b24     object {
                bezier  2, 0.05,  3,  3,
        <0.519430,     8.286380,    -12.888933>,
        <-3.446385,   12.026911,    -12.931573>,
        <-10.319574,   9.855964,    -13.274297>,
        <-13.157171,   3.747712,    -13.266072>,
        <-3.819031,    6.105978,     -0.281563>,
        <-6.591431,    6.590911,     -0.324202>,
        <-9.844608,    4.309619,     -0.566926>,
        <-10.325383,   1.543393,     -0.767010>,
        <-3.895405,    5.916192,      2.525808>,
        <-6.667805,    6.401125,      2.483169>,
        <-10.316352,   3.854265,      1.274445>,
        <-10.599442,   1.220823,      1.557361>,
        <-6.165601,   10.466374,      6.160175>,
        <-12.132281,   6.579563>,
        <-14.247386,   5.453698,      6.759902>,
        <-14.989909,   2.110008,      5.359019>
                }


define CylinderBezier object {
  b21 + b22 + b23 + b24
}


object {
    SheetBezier
    scale <2,2,2>
    translate <-14,0,0>
    texture { checker Stone13, matte_black}
}

object {
    CylinderBezier
    rotate<-90,-45,0>
    translate < 15,0,0>
    Stone6
}
```

Figure 3.16

Flat and cylindrical Bézier patches (BEZIER.PI).

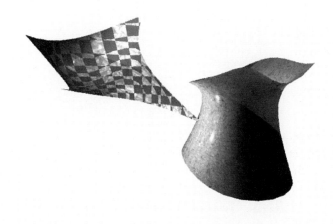

Bézier patches can become very complex to handle and normally require an external program to create and manipulate them (POVCAD, included with the book can handle Bézier patches).

Miscellaneous Objects

The following sections present a group of interesting objects and surface-generation techniques. In them, you work with blobs (objects that interact through attraction and repulsion) and with height fields to create landscapes. Finally, surface definition through the use of mathematical functions is discussed.

Blobs

Blobs are objects that can interact with other objects through potential fields (similar to a force field surrounding the object). They can attract and repel each other. In the process, they can be deformed or appear to merge with one another. There are three types of objects you can use in a blob: planes, cylinders, and spheres. The syntax is

```
blob threshold:
     component #1,
     component #2,
     ... etc ...
```

in which `threshold` is the minimum potential field value to be considered when computing the interaction between components and `component` is one of the following:

```
sphere <x, y, z> , strength, radius

cylinder <x0, y0, z0>, <x1, y1, z1>, strength, radius

plane <nx, ny, nz>, d, strength, distance
```

In all of the preceding component lines, `<x, y, z>` is the center of the blob sphere, `<x0, y0, z0>` and `<x1, y1, z1>` are the endpoints of the cylinder, `radius` is the radius of the sphere of the cylinder, `strength` is the strength of the potential field around the center of the component, `<nx, ny, nz>` is the normal vector of the plane, and `d` is the offset distance from the plane to origin along the normal.

The attractive or repulsive properties of a given component are based on the sign of the strength value. If the strength value is positive, objects attract. If the value is negative, they repel. There is no interaction between blobs, only between components of a blob.

Plane components are infinite. To limit their size, use the `bounding_box` `< corner1>, < corner2>` statement. This box clips any part of the object that exceeds the `bounding_box` limits.

Listing 3.20 shows three blob objects with different behaviors. The first object (see fig. 3.17) is a dumbbell created with two attracting spheres. The object in the center is a plane being deformed by a sphere. Observe the effect of the `bounding_box` statement. I suggest you comment it out and ray trace it to see what happens. The final object is a cylinder and a sphere attracting each other. Observe how the cylinder deforms and merges with the sphere. Blob cylinders have hemispherical caps at the ends.

Listing 3.20. Using blobs (BLOB.PI).

```
// BLOB.PI

include "colors.inc"

define RedFinish   texture {
      surface {
         color red
         ambient 0.2
```

99

continues

Listing 3.20. Continued.

```
                diffuse 0.8
                specular white, 1
                microfacet Phong 5
                }
            }

viewpoint {
    from  <0, 10, -10>
    up    <0, 1, 0>
    at    <0, 1, 0>
    angle 35
    resolution 160, 160
    aspect 1.0
    }
// LIGHT_SOURCE
light < 10, 30, -20>

background midnightblue


object {
    object {
      blob 0.5:
      plane <0,1,0>, 0, 2, 5,
      sphere <0,3,0>, -4, 2
      RedFinish
    }
    bounding_box <-3,1,-1>, <3,3,3>   // <- bounding box
    scale <0.5,0.5,0.5>
}

object {
 object {
      blob 0.5:
      sphere <-2, 1.5, 0>, 1, 3,
      sphere < 2, 1.5, 0>, 1, 3
      reflective_yellow
 }
 scale <0.4, 0.4, 0.4>
 translate <0, 3.7, 0>
}


object {
 object {
      blob 0.5:
      sphere <0, 0, 0>, 1, 3,
      cylinder < -2, 2, 0>, <2, 2, 0>, 1, 1.5
      reflective_yellow
 }
 scale <0.6, 0.6, 0.6>
 translate <0, -3.5, 0>
}
```

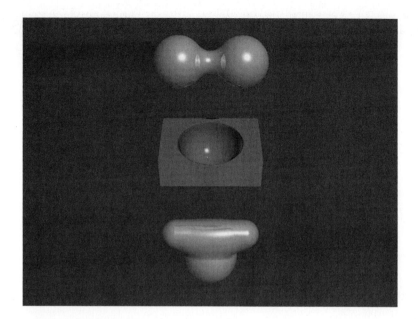

Figure 3.17

*Three examples
of blobs
(BLOB.PI).*

Height Fields

Height fields are commonly used to produce interesting and realistic land-scapes. Landscapes are created by reading an image file. This file can be of any image as long as it is in Targa uncompressed format (8-, 16-, or 24-bit). The best images to use are those of plasma images like the ones created with Fractint. (See the introduction of this book for bulletin board phone numbers from which you can download Fractint and ray tracing utilities.)

The image file is read and the colors are converted into height values. Initially, the height field object is scaled to $1 \times 1 \times 1$ units, with the bottom left corner located at the origin. The syntax, which follows, is extremely simple for such a powerful feature.

```
height_field "filename"
```

or

```
smooth_height_field "filename"
```

If you use the `smooth_height_field` option, the final ray-traced image is smoother at the expense of more memory. Listing 3.21 shows a height field generated with a plasma image. Figure 3.18 shows the original plasma image, and figure 3.19 shows the plasma image converted into a height field. A stone texture was attached to it.

Listing 3.21. Using height fields (HEIGHT.PI).

```
// HEIGHT.PI

include "colors.inc"
include "texture.inc"
include "stones.inc"

define Plane_XZ   object {
    polygon 4,  <-10000,0,10000>, <-10000,0,-10000>,
                <10000,0,-10000>, <10000,0,10000>
                  }


viewpoint {
    from < 0, 10, -70>
    at <0,-10,0>
    up <0,1,0>
    angle 45
    resolution 100, 100
    aspect 1.0

    }

light <-45, 25, -4>
light <0, 25, 0>

object {
    Plane_XZ
    rotate <90,0,0>
    translate <0,0,10000>
    texture { surface {color White} }
}

object {
    height_field "plasma.tga"
    translate <-0.5, 0,-0.5>
    scale <100, 0.05, 100>
    rotate <0, -15, 0>
    Stone6
    }

object {
    Plane_XZ
    translate <0,-6.7, 0>
    texture { surface {color Blue} }
}
```

In addition to the height field, there are two planes being used. The first plane used in the image creates a white sky in the background. The second plane is used to create the effect of an ocean. You can experiment by modifying the height of the ocean in the y axis to hide or show the height field more.

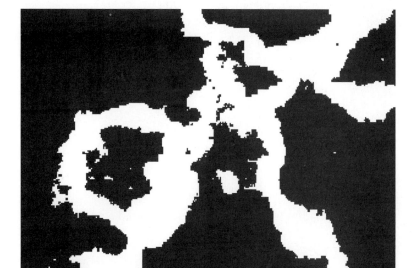

Figure 3.18

A plasma image (PLASMA.TGA).

Figure 3.19

A plasma image as a height field (HEIGHT.PI).

Functions

Another method of creating surfaces is through the definition of mathematical functions. The syntax for this method is

```
function mathematical function
```

in which `"mathematical function"` can be any relationship between the variables x, y, z and other functions such as `cos()`, `sin()`, `tan()`, `exp()`, and others. To elevate an expression to a power, use the ^ sign (for example, `3^2` means *three squared*). The following is an example of a function:

```
define a 2.0
define b 3.0
object {
        // this is an elliptical cylinder
        function (x^2)/a^2 + (y^2)/b^2 - 1
        shiny_red
        bounding_box <-5,-5,-5>, <5, 5, 5>
}
```

Due to numerical inaccuracies, the final image can have dark spots. Check Polyray's documentation for techniques of how to reduce this problem.

Summary

In this chapter, you covered most of the same concepts presented in Chapter 1 and how they applied to Polyray. You reviewed Polyray's left-handed coordinate system and how to rotate, translate, and scale objects in it. You studied viewpoint definition and parameters.

You also saw an array of Polyray primitives such as boxes, planes, spheres, discs, ellipsoids, and the torus. The task of modeling surfaces by using small utility programs was discussed and examples of programs that create flat and smooth triangles were studied. Other surfaces such as polygons, lathe, sweep, and Bézier were created and the degree of difficulty when developing them was discussed. Finally, you were exposed to some strange but interesting objects such as blobs, whose components interact with each other and height fields, commonly used to create landscapes. Surface generation by the use of mathematical functions was discussed briefly; however, it requires some math knowledge of functions and methods to reduce numerical inaccuracies.

In the next chapter, you start studying what makes one surface look like a mirror and another look dented. The study of light, colors, and textures is next.

Light, Colors, and Textures

In this chapter, you study three key elements to photo-realistic image creation. First, the chapter covers different types of light sources, ranging from the standard positional type to spot lights. Next, you learn how to apply colors to surfaces and the background of a scene, and even how to create haze on an image. Finally, you study the topic of textures in detail. Textures have a wide variety of parameters that enable you to create different types of finishes on your objects. By understanding the relationship between the parameters, you gain control over the final image look.

Light Sources

Light sources not only help you see the objects that compose a scene, but they also let you create shadows and the "mood" of the scene. There are three types of light sources available: positional, directional, and spot light. The simplest and most commonly used light source is the positional light source.

Positional Light Sources

Positional light sources can be compared to a light bulb. To use one in your scene, you need to define the location <x,y,z> in space and color. The syntax is

```
light color, <x, y, z>
```

or

```
light <x,y,z>
```

in which *color* is either a color vector of the type <Red, Green, Blue> or a token word such as white or yellow. The values for Red, Green, and Blue normally vary from 0 to 1.

In the second format, light <x,y,z>, because no color is specified, white light is assumed. It is useful to know the token names for the available colors. The next section contains a list of the available color names. All the examples you have seen so far in this book have used positional light sources.

Directional Light Sources

Directional light sources work slightly differently than positional light sources. These lights do not produce shadows. Directional light is handy in scenes in which there are too many objects or the objects are too near one another. If the shadows of these objects have a negative effect on the scene, directional light sources are recommended. Also, directional light sources are suggested in space scenes when you don't want any of the objects to cast shadows on planets. You can combine positional and directional light in the same scene. Figures 4.1 and 4.2 compare the same scene ray-traced with positional and directional light, respectively. Observe that figure 4.1 has shadows of the objects on the floor, whereas in figure 4.2 all the objects can be seen clearly.

Listing 4.1. Using positional light sources (LIGHT.PI).

```
//LIGHT.PI

include "texture.inc"
include "colors.inc"

define Plane_XZ  object {
            polygon 4, <-10000,0,10000>, <-10000,0,-10000>,
                       <10000,0,-10000>, <10000,0,10000>
            }

viewpoint {
   from <0,0,-10>
   at <0,0,0>
   up <0,1,0>
   angle 45
   resolution 100, 100
   aspect 1.0
   }

background <0, 0, 0>

light <-10,6,-20>
light < 10,6,-20>

object {
   sphere <0, 0, 0>, 2
   shiny_red
   }

object {
   sphere <3, 0, 3>, 2
   shiny_yellow
   }

object {
   sphere <-3, 0, 3>, 2
   shiny_green
   }

object {
   Plane_XZ
   texture { surface {color White}}
   translate <0,-3,0>
}
```

Figure 4.1

Spheres illuminated with positional light sources (LIGHT.PI).

Listing 4.2. Using directional light sources (DIRECTLT.PI).

```
//DIRECTLT.PI
include "texture.inc"
include "colors.inc"

define Plane_XZ  object {
            polygon 4, <-10000,0,10000>, <-10000,0,-10000>,
                       <10000,0,-10000>, <10000,0,10000>
                }

viewpoint {
   from <0,0,-10>
   at <0,0,0>
   up <0,1,0>
   angle 45
   resolution 100, 100
   aspect 1.0
   }

background <0, 0, 0>

directional_light <-10,6, -20>
directional_light < 10,6, -20>

object {
   sphere <0, 0, 0>, 2
   shiny_red
   }
```

```
object {
   sphere <3, 0, 3>, 2
   shiny_yellow
   }

object {
   sphere <-3, 0, 3>, 2
   shiny_green
   }

object {
   Plane_XZ
   texture { surface {color White}}
   translate <0,-3,0>
   }
```

Figure 4.2

Spheres illuminated with directional light sources (DIRECTLT.PI).

Spot Light Sources

Spot lights are basically cones of light that you can use to create some interesting effects. The walls of the cone of light are invisible; only the base, or "hot spot," is visible. The syntax is

```
spot_light color, <location>, <point at>, Tightness, Ang, Fall-off
```

or

```
spot_light color, <location>, <point at>
```

In which the placeholders stand for the following: *color* indicates the color of the spot light. Use <R,G,B> vector or a token name. *<location>* is replaced with the location of the apex of the cone of light. *<point at>* indicates the location at which the spotlight is aiming. *Tightness* determines the shape of the spot (the smaller the number, the larger the spot). A good value to start with for *Tightness* is 3 (change as necessary; it requires some experimentation). *Ang* specifies the angle in degrees, where the spot is in full effect. *Fall-off* indicates an angle larger than *Ang* where the spot light turns off.

Listing 4.3 shows an example of using spot lights.

Listing 4.3. Using spot lights (SPOTLITE.PI).

```
//SPOTLITE.PI

include "colors.inc"
include "texture.inc"

define LampColor reflective_grey

viewpoint {
  from        <0.0, 0.9, -2.8>
  at          <-0.6, 0.2, 0.0>
  up          <0.0, 1.0, 0.0>
  angle           45
  resolution      100,100
  aspect          1.0
}

spot_light White , <-0.28,0.67, 0>, <-1.5, 0, 0>, 3, 45, 50
light <0, 100, -100>

background Grey

// PLANE (Polygon)
object {
// normal in Y direction
   polygon 4, <-1,0,1>, <-1,0,-1>, <1,0,-1>, <1,0,1>
   scale <3,1,3>
   texture {
       checker matte_white, matte_black
       scale <0.1, 1, 0.1>
   }
}

// LAMP BASE
object {
// SPHERE
object {
   sphere < 0, -0.1, 0>, 0.3
   LampColor
```

```
}
-
// BOX
object {
    box <-1, -1, -1>, <1, 1, 1>
    scale <0.5, 0.5, 0.5>
    translate <0, -0.5, 0>
}
    LampColor
}


// LAMP "NECK"
object  {
// TORUS
object {
    torus  0.4, 0.05, < 0.0, 0.0, 0.0>, <0.0, 1.0, 0.0>
    rotate <90, 0, 0>
    translate <-0.375, 0.3, 0>
}
*
// BOX
object {
    box <-1, -1, -1>, <1, 1, 1>
    scale <0.4, 0.4, 0.4>
    translate <0.125, 0.575, 0>

}
 LampColor
}

// OBJECT ON FLOOR
object {
    sphere <-1.3,0.1, 0>, 0.1
    shiny_red
}

// LAMP "HEAD" DONE USING POVCAD AND LATHE.BAS
object {
    object {
    lathe  2 , <0, 1, 0>, 9 ,
        <    0.000,    0.575,    0.000>,
        <    0.075,    0.550,    0.000>,
        <    0.143,    0.488,    0.000>,
        <    0.155,    0.410,    0.000>,
        <    0.185,    0.332,    0.000>,
        <    0.223,    0.284,    0.000>,
        <    0.311,    0.215,    0.000>,
        <    0.374,    0.119,    0.000>,
        <    0.408,    0.011,    0.000>
    LampColor
    }
    rotate <0, 0, -65>
    translate <-0.6, 0.675, 0>
}
```

The spot light is located inside the lamp, where the bulb would be in a real lamp. The point aimed at is near the sphere (see fig. 4.3).

Figure 4.3

Using a spot light to model a lamp (SPOTLITE.PI).

Figure 4.3 has some interesting features that we should discuss further:

- The lamp's color is defined by means of the token name `LampColor`. This enables you to modify the color of the lamp without having to edit each individual component.

- A spot light and a positional light source are used in the same scene. The positional light source is used to aid the spot light and create a slightly lit scene.

- In the definition of the plane, the size of the checkered tiles was modified by scaling inside the texture definition:

```
texture { checker matte_white, matte_black
        scale <0.1, 1, 0.1>
}
```

This is done to force the tiles to be smaller without affecting the size of the plane.

- The base and neck of the lamp were created using Boolean operations. The base is a sphere that had a box subtracted from it to create a hemisphere. The neck is created by intersecting a torus and a box. In other words, whatever part of the torus is inside the box will remain. The rest is discarded.

- The lamp head was created in POVCAD by drawing the contour. The data was saved and the program LATHE.BAS was used. Observe that a type 2 (smooth) lathe object is used to give better quality.

Colors

Colors in Polyray can be defined in two ways:

- By using a vector of the form <R, G, B>, in which R, G, and B stand for the red, green, and blue components of the color. For example, <0,0,0> is black, and <1,1,1> is white.

- By using the defined token name of the color. Instead of using the color <0,0,0>, it is better to use the token name black. The file COLORS.DOC included in Polyray has a list of the token names of all the colors and their respective <R,G,B> values.

> **NOTE:** The predefined colors (like the ones included in COLOR.DOC) can be either uppercase or lowercase: both Black and black are OK. If you create your own colors using the define statement, those colors *are* case-sensitive—if you create define MYCOLOR <0.5, 0.2,0.45>, then you have to use the name MYCOLOR exactly as you defined it.

There are a number of named colors acceptable to Polyray. These were present in MTV and are carried through to Polyray. The colors (case is important) and their RGB values are shown in Table 4.1.

Table 4.1. Colors defined in Polyray (COLORS.DOC).

Name	Red	Green	Blue
Aquamarine	0.439216	0.858824	0.576471
Black	0	0	0
Blue	0	0	1
BlueViolet	0.623529	0.372549	0.623529
Brown	0.647059	0.164706	0.164706
CadetBlue	0.372549	0.623529	0.623529
Coral	1	0.498039	0
CornflowerBlue	0.258824	0.258824	0.435294
Cyan	0	1	1
DarkGreen	0.184314	0.309804	0.184314
DarkOliveGreen	0.309804	0.309804	0.184314
DarkOrchid	0.6	0.196078	0.8
DarkSlateBlue	0.419608	0.137255	0.556863
DarkSlateGray	0.184314	0.309804	0.309804
DarkSlateGrey	0.184314	0.309804	0.309804
DarkTurquoise	0.439216	0.576471	0.858824
DimGray	0.329412	0.329412	0.329412
DimGrey	0.329412	0.329412	0.329412
Firebrick	0.556863	0.137255	0.137255
ForestGreen	0.137255	0.556863	0.137255
Gold	0.8	0.498039	0.196078
Goldenrod	0.858824	0.858824	0.439216
Gray	0.752941	0.752941	0.752941
Green	0	1	0
GreenYellow	0.576471	0.858824	0.439216
Grey	0.752941	0.752941	0.752941
IndianRed	0.309804	0.184314	0.184314

Name	Red	Green	Blue
Khaki	0.623529	0.623529	0.372549
LightBlue	0.74902	0.847059	0.847059
LightGray	0.658824	0.658824	0.658824
LightGrey	0.658824	0.658824	0.658824
LightSteelBlue	0.560784	0.560784	0.737255
LimeGreen	0.196078	0.8	0.196078
Magenta	1	0	1
Maroon	0.556863	0.137255	0.419608
MediumAquamarine	0.196078	0.8	0.6
MediumBlue	0.196078	0.196078	0.8
MediumForestGreen	0.419608	0.556863	0.137255
MediumGoldenrod	0.917647	0.917647	0.678431
MediumOrchid	0.576471	0.439216	0.858824
MediumSeaGreen	0.258824	0.435294	0.258824
MediumSlateBlue	0.498039	0	1
MediumSpringGreen	0.498039	1	0
MediumTurquoise	0.439216	0.858824	0.858824
MediumVioletRed	0.858824	0.439216	0.576471
MidnightBlue	0.184314	0.184314	0.309804
Navy	0.137255	0.137255	0.556863
NavyBlue	0.137255	0.137255	0.556863
Orange	0.8	0.196078	0.196078
OrangeRed	1	0	0.498039
Orchid	0.858824	0.439216	0.858824
PaleGreen	0.560784	0.737255	0.560784
Pink	0.737255	0.560784	0.560784
Plum	0.917647	0.678431	0.917647

continues

Table 4.1. Continued.

Name	Red	Green	Blue
Red	1	0	0
Salmon	0.435294	0.258824	0.258824
SeaGreen	0.137255	0.556863	0.419608
Sienna	0.556863	0.419608	0.137255
SkyBlue	0.196078	0.6	0.8
SlateBlue	0	0.498039	1
SpringGreen	0	1	0.498039
SteelBlue	0.137255	0.419608	0.556863
Tan	0.858824	0.576471	0.439216
Thistle	0.847059	0.74902	0.847059
Turquoise	0.678431	0.917647	0.917647
Violet	0.309804	0.184314	0.309804
VioletRed	0.8	0.196078	0.6
Wheat	0.847059	0.847059	0.74902
White	0.988235	0.988235	0.988235
Yellow	1	1	0
YellowGreen	0.6	0.8	0.196078

You can use colors on objects, on the background, and when you're creating a haze effect.

Surface

Using colors on an object's surface is straightforward. To attach a color to the surface, use the following syntax:

```
texture { surface { color MyColor } }
```

An example of a red sphere is

```
object {
     sphere <0,0,0>, 2
     texture { surface { color Red } }
}
```

where `Red` is a color found in Listing 4.3. The keyword `texture` was used to define the color of the surface. This keyword and its components are explained in the "Textures" section later in this chapter. There are two different methods you can use to specify the color of an object inside a texture definition:

Method 1:

```
object {
   sphere <0,0,0>, 2
   texture { surface { color Red } }
}
```

Method 2:

```
define MyColorRed texture { surface { color Red } }

     object {
          sphere <0,0,0>, 2
          MyColorRed
     }
```

Method 1 is the long format, where all the details of the texture definition are written inside of the object. Method 2 uses the a `define` statement to attach a token name to the texture definition as a whole. Method 2 is recommended.

Background

When Polyray finds out that a light ray doesn't intersect any of the objects in a scene, the pixel on-screen is set to black as the default. You can change the color of the background by using the keyword `background` as in the following:

```
background color
```

in which `color` is either an <R,G,B> vector or a token name.

You can also use an image file as a background. The syntax for this operation is background planar_imagemap (image("`file.tga`"),P) in which the Targa image file `file.tga` is projected to the background and scaled to fit in the background frame. Listing 4.4 shows the use of a `planar_imagemap` as a background (see fig. 4.4 for the output).

Listing 4.4. Using an image file as a background (BACK.PI).

```
//BACK.PI

include "texture.inc"
include "colors.inc"

viewpoint {
    from <0,0,-10>
    at <0,0,0>
    up <0,1,0>
    angle 45
    resolution 100, 100
    aspect 1.0
    }

background planar_imagemap(image("plasma.tga"),P)

light <-10,6, -20>
light < 10,6, -20>

object {
    sphere <0, 0, 0>, 2
    shiny_red
    }

object {
    sphere <3, 0, 3>, 2
    shiny_blue
    }

object {
    sphere <-3, 0, 3>, 2
    shiny_green
    }
```

Listing 4.4 uses the same plasma image that created the height fields in Chapter 3. Figure 4.4 was ray traced without antialiasing.

Global Haze

Polyray creates a haze effect by using a color that becomes thicker the farther the light has to travel. The syntax for haze is

```
haze thickness, start, color
```

in which *thickness* is the amount of nontransparency of the haze. The value is between 0 and 1, with 0 being nontransparent and 1 being fully transparent. The parameter *start* determines at what distance the haze effect starts. The parameter *color* can be a token name or a color vector.

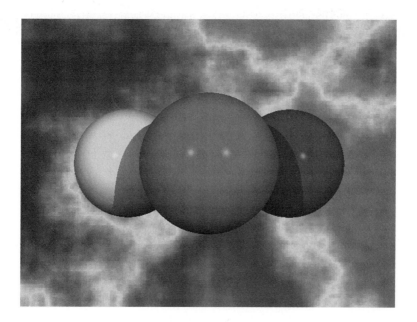

Figure 4.4

Using an image as a background (BACK.PI).

Listing 4.5 is a modification of HEIGHT.PI (see Listing 3.2). The statements

```
background Gray
```

and

```
haze 0.95, 50, Gray
```

were added. Usually, haze is the same color as the background.

Listing 4.5. A landscape with the haze effect (HAZE.PI).

```
// HAZE.PI

include "colors.inc"
include "texture.inc"
include "stones.inc"

define Plane_XZ  object {
          polygon 4, <-10000,0,10000>, <-10000,0,-10000>,
                      <10000,0,-10000>, <10000,0,10000>
          }

viewpoint {
   from < 0, 10, -70>
   at <0,-10,0>
   up <0,1,0>
   angle 45
   resolution 100, 100
   }
```

119

continues

Listing 4.5. Continued.

```
light <-45, 25, -4>
light <0, 25, 0>

background Gray
haze 0.95, 50, Gray

object {
   height_field "plasma.tga"
   translate <-0.5, 0,-0.5>
   scale <100, 0.05, 100>
   rotate <0, -15, 0>
   Stone6
   }

object {
   Plane_XZ
   translate <0,-6.7, 0>
   texture { surface {color Blue} }
}
```

Figure 4.5 shows the landscape immersed in haze.

Figure 4.5

*Adding a haze
effect to a
landscape
(HAZE.PI).*

Textures

This section familiarizes you with Polyray's texture format. The format is flexible and has a variety of parameters that you can modify. If you feel comfortable using the standard colors or some of the previously used textures, it's time to go into more detail on how to create your own textures or modify the existing ones. Textures are challenging, and the rewards for understanding how to manipulate them are great.

Texture Surface Parameters

Polyray supports what is commonly called a *standard shading model*. A standard shading model describes how a surface handles incident light in terms of reflection, refraction, and diffusivity. Examples of standard surface textures look roughly like this:

Reflective Red Surface

```
texture {
    surface {
        color red
        ambient 0.1
        diffuse 0.5
        specular white, 0.5
        microfacet Phong 7
        reflection white, 0.5
    }
}
```

Blue Glass Surface

```
texture {
    surface {
        color blue
        ambient 0.1
        diffuse 0
        specular white, 0.2
        reflection white, 0.1
        transmission white, 1, 1.5
    }
}
```

The next section explains the various parameters in detail.

Color

The keyword `color` is followed by an <R,G,B> vector or a token color name. This is the color of the surface. If this statement is included inside of the texture definition, it is not required to declare the color on the other parameters.

Ambient Light

Ambient light hits the object's surface from all directions. As a result, the object becomes visible. The syntax for creating ambient light is

```
ambient color, scale
```

or

```
ambient scale
```

In the first example, `color` is the color of the surface. You may want to use the second format if you already declared the color using the keyword `color`. For example,

```
color red
ambient 0.1
```

has the same effect as

```
ambient red, 0.1
```

You can use other colors to create different effects. The parameter `scale` determines the amount of contribution of the color to the scene. A value of 0 will show no color at all and a scale value of 1 will use the full color effect.

Diffuse Light

Diffuse light is light that has been absorbed by the surface and spread out equally in all directions (see fig. 4.6). The syntax for creating the diffuse light effect is

```
diffuse color, scale
```

or

```
diffuse scale
```

The `scale` parameter determines the amount of contribution of diffuse light to the scene. A value of 0 does not diffuse light, whereas a scale value of 1 diffuses all the incident light.

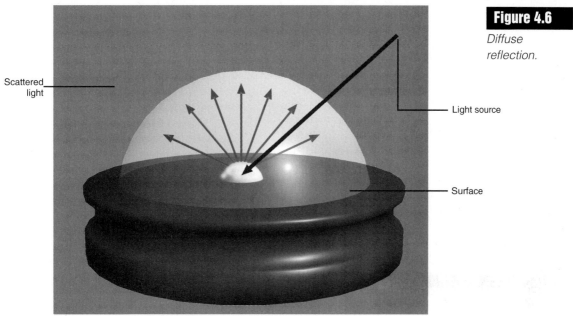

Figure 4.6

Diffuse reflection.

Scattered light

Light source

Surface

Specular Highlights

On a perfect mirror surface, the incident angle of the light is equal to the reflection angle (see fig. 4.7a). On a rough surface (see fig. 4.7b), the reflected light is concentrated on an area. What the observer sees is called a *specular highlight*. The light scatters or spreads out due to the roughness of the surface. The syntax for a specular highlight is

    specular color, scale

or

    specular scale

The `color` parameter refers to the color of the highlight, which can be different from the color of the surface. The `scale` parameter determines the intensity of the specular highlight, the value being between 0 and 1.

Figure 4.7

The effect of surface roughness on reflected light.

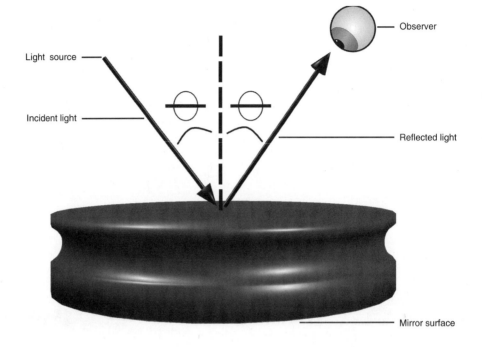

Observer

Light source

Incident light

Reflected light

Mirror surface

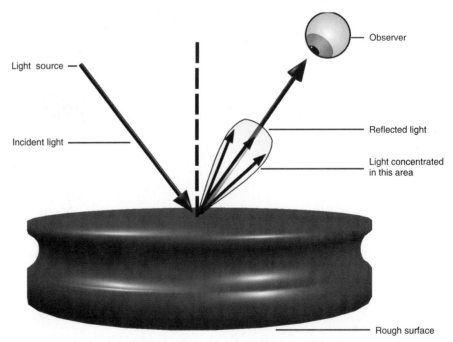

Observer

Light source

Incident light

Reflected light

Light concentrated in this area

Rough surface

Later in this chapter, the section "Microfacet Distribution" discusses how to experiment with different surface roughness models.

Reflected Light

Reflected light bounces off surfaces at an angle. The syntax for reflected light is

```
reflection color, scale
```

or

```
reflection scale
```

If you use the first format, the color becomes a filter. Normally, the second format is used because it reflects all colors. The `scale` value determines the contribution of the reflected light to the final color of the surface. The values are between 0 and 1.

As an example of different scale values for some surfaces, metallic surfaces have a scale of 0.25, reflective surfaces are 0.5, and mirrors 1.0.

Transmitted Light

On transparent materials, light goes through the surface and bends. (The same effect occurs when you put a spoon in a glass filled with water. The spoon's image bends.) The *index of refraction*, or IOR, determines how much the light will bend. Table 4.2 shows various IOR values for different materials.

Table 4.2. Index of refraction values for various materials.	
Material	**IOR**
Diamond	2.42[2]
Ice	1.31[2]
Quartz	1.46[2]
Water	1.33[1,2]
Air	1.0003[1]
Crown Glass	1.52[1,2]
Rock Salt	1.54[2]

References:
1. "Physics, Part 2" by D. Halliday and R. Resnick, 3rd Ed. 1978, John Wiley and Sons.
2. "Fundamentals of Waves, Optics, and Modern Physics" by H. D. Young, 2nd Ed., 1976, McGraw-Hill Book Co.

The syntax for transmitted light is

```
transmission color, scale, ior
```

or

```
transmission scale, ior
```

The `scale` parameter indicates how much light will be transmitted throught the surface. An non-transparent surface uses a value of 0, whereas a fully transparent surface uses 1. The parameter `ior` is the index of refraction (see Table 4.2 for examples).

Microfacet Distribution

As mentioned earlier, the size of the specular highlight is dependent on the roughness of the surface. Figure 4.8 shows the variation in the diffuse and specular reflections as a function of the surface roughness.

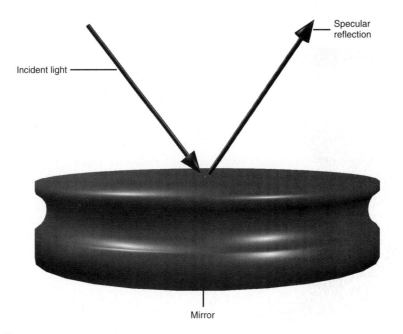

Figure 4.8

Diffuse and specular reflections for different roughness values.

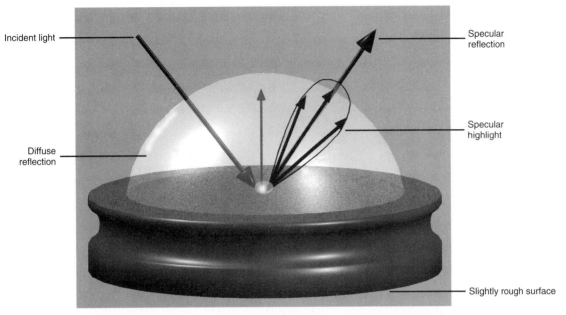

Incident light

Diffuse
reflection

Specular
reflection

Specular
highlight

Slightly rough surface

Incident light

Diffuse
reflection

Extremely rough surface

A widely used approach to modeling surface roughness is called the *microfacet model.* In this model, the surface of the object is assumed to consist of very small mirror surfaces that are oriented in all directions. A small roughness value indicates that all the mirrors are basically aligned with the object's surface, whereas a large value indicates that the mirrors are aligned randomly in all directions (see fig. 4.9).

Figure 4.9

The microfacet model.

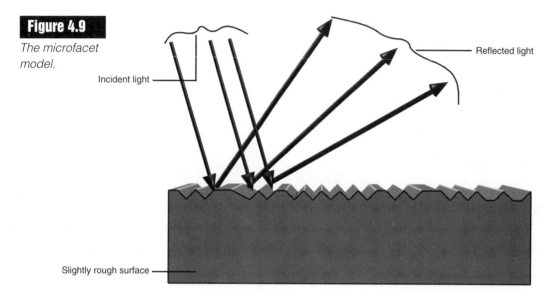

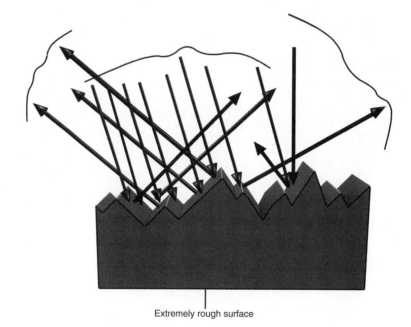

There are different models available, and each assumes a certain alignment distribution. The choice of a particular model affects the size and shape of the specular highlight. (For more details, read *Advanced Animation and Rendering Techniques*, by A. Watt and M. Watt, 1992, ACM Press, pp. 52-62.)

The syntax Polyray uses to select a microfacet model is

```
microfacet name angle
```

or

```
microfacet angle
```

in which *name* is one of the different models available: Blinn, Cook, Gaussian, Phong (the default), and Reitz. The *angle* parameter is the fall-off angle at which the highlight decreases to 50 percent of its intensity (*angle* must be between 0 and 45 degrees). The greater the value, the rougher the surface.

In the next section, you can compare the different effects that occur when the texture parameters are changed.

Examples

In this section, you can experiment by changing the values of different parameters in the standard shading model. Figure 4.10 is a collection of the images generated by modifying the parameters. In each row, only one parameter is modified.

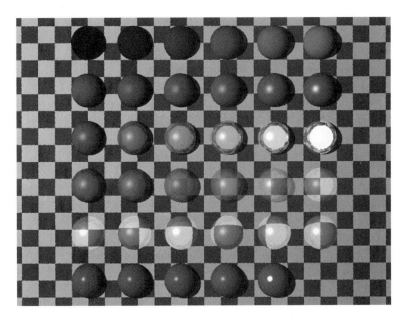

Figure 4.10

Effects of changing parameters in textures.

You can start with a dull, red surface,

```
texture {
    surface {
        color red
        ambient 0.1
        diffuse N
    }
}
```

in which *N* is changed from 0 to 1 in increments of 0.2 (see fig. 4.10, top row).

The sphere changes from almost black to red without highlights (refer to fig. 4.8). The next variation is on the specular highlights. Take the previous definition and add `specular` to it:

```
texture {
    surface {
        color red
        ambient 0.1
        diffuse 0.7
        specular white, N
    }
}
```

in which *N* varies from 0 to 1 in increments of 0.2 (see fig. 4.10, second row).

Because no microfacet model was selected, the default Phong is used. The color white is used to create a white highlight.

The third row of figure 4.10 shows reflection effects. Again, use the previous definition

```
texture {
    surface {
        color red
        ambient 0.1
        diffuse 0.7
        specular white, 0.5
        reflection white, N
    }
}
```

in which *N* varies from 0 to 1 in increments of 0.2 (see fig. 4.10, third row).

The color white on the reflection indicates that all colors are reflected. Observe how the spheres that are near the last ones on the third row are reflected. Because the sphere is facing the light source, the surface turns into a very light color.

The fourth row of figure 4.10 experiments with the use of the `transmission` parameter. By changing the scale, the spheres become more transparent.

The texture definition used is

```
texture {
    surface {
        color red
        ambient 0.1
        diffuse 0.7
        specular white, 0.5
        reflection white, 0.1
        transmission white, N, 1
    }
}
```

in which *N* varies from 0 to 1 in increments of 0.2 (see fig. 4.10, fourth row).

In this example, the transmission scale is changed and the `ior` remains fixed at 1.0 (`ior` of air). As the objects become more transparent, you can see the undeformed background. If you do the opposite—that is, fix the scale and vary the `ior` value—the result is that of the fifth row. The `ior` value was changed from 1.0 to 3.5 in increments of 0.5. As the `ior` increases, the background is bent more.

Finally, the sixth row in figure 4.10 shows the different microfacet models arranged as Phong, Blinn, Gaussian, Reitz, and Cook. The fall-off angle used was 5 degrees.

This completes a look at the standard shading model. In the next section, you study other types of textures and techniques.

Texture Types

Besides the standard model, Polyray supports procedural, functional, and layered textures. Procedural textures are based on mapping a 2-D pattern to a given surface. A cone with a checkered surface gives the impression that the pattern was projected on the cone's surface. Procedural textures have the mathematical representation of the patterns hard-coded in the program. Functional textures, on the other hand, require that users specify a mathematical expression to evaluate the colors. Therefore, procedural textures are faster to produce than functional textures. Layered textures are used to stack different textures, one on top of the other. You read about these textures later in this chapter.

Checker

The checker texture has been presented in a wide variety of examples throughout this book. It consists of two tiles, each with a different texture. This pattern is repeated throughout the entire surface. The syntax is

```
texture {
    checker texture#1, texture#2
    [transformations]
}
```

in which *texture#1* and *texture#2* are texture declarations or token words representing textures. The *transformations* parameter consists of optional scaling, rotation, and translation operations that are performed on the texture itself. To apply colors to the tiles, you can use the definition presented in the "Colors" section of this chapter.

```
define BlueColor
    texture { surface {color Blue } }

define GreenColor
    texture {surface {color Green} }

texture {
    checker BlueColor, GreenColor
}
```

In some cases, you may want to either rotate the pattern or scale the tiles to create a specific effect, for example, to scale the tiles by half, use the following:

```
texture {
    checker BlueColor, GreenColor
    scale <0.5, 1.0, 0.5>
}
```

The tiles are scaled by half in the x and z directions.

Hexagon

The hexagon texture is similar to the checker texture in the sense that it repeats a pattern throughout the surface. The tiles are hexagonal and in groups of three. The syntax is

```
texture {
    hexagon texture#1, texture#2, texture#3
}
```

in which *texture#1*, *texture#2*, and *texture#3* are texture declarations or token words representing textures.

132

Listing 4.6 shows a sphere inside another sphere. The inner sphere is a solid red color and the outer sphere has a hexagonal texture. The texture names for the three tiles used are Diamond, Mirror, and Air. The Air texture is really not air, but it's a way of creating an empty space by creating a glass that has an ior of 1.0 (ior of air) and doesn't bend the images. The floor is composed of hexagons also, with one of the tiles being made out of stone. Figure 4.11 shows the ray-traced image.

Figure 4.11

Hexagon textures (HEX.PI).

Many things are happening in figure 4.11. First, the Diamond and Air textures have different ior values. The Diamond texture bends the light rays and deforms the background. Observe that when you look through the Diamond tile, the sphere seems to be smaller than when you look through the Air tile. The Mirror tile reflects whatever hits the surface at that point. Listing 4.6 presents the scene file used to create figure 4.11.

Listing 4.6. Using the hexagon texture (HEX.PI).

```
// HEX.PI

include "texture.inc"
include "colors.inc"
include "stones.inc"

define Plane_XZ  object {
          polygon 4, <-10000,0,10000>, <-10000,0,-10000>,
                     <10000,0,-10000>, <10000,0,10000>
        }

define Air
texture {
   surface {
      color white
      ambient 0
      diffuse 0
      specular 0
      reflection white, 0
      transmission white, 1, 1
      }
}


define Diamond
texture {
   surface {
      color white
      ambient 0.1
      diffuse 0.1
      specular 0.8
      reflection white, 0.1
      transmission white, 1, 2.42
      microfacet Phong 0.5
      }
}


// Set up the camera
viewpoint {
   from <0,0,-10>
   at <0,-1.3,0>
   up <0,1,0>
   angle 45
   resolution 200,200
   aspect 1.0
   }

background <0, 0, 0>
light <0,1, -20>
light <0, 10, 0>

object {
   sphere <0, 0, 0>, 2
   texture { hexagon Mirror, Diamond, Air
          rotate <-90, 0, 0>
          scale <0.25, 0.25, 0.25>
```

```
    }
}

object {
    sphere <0,0,0>,0.5
    shiny_red
}

object {
    Plane_XZ
    texture { hexagon matte_white, Stone5, matte_black
            scale <1.5,1, 1.5>
    }
    translate <0,-5,0>
}
```

Noise Surface

Noise surface is a general type of texture. You can control the surface of an object in the same manner as the standard shading model. In addition, you can modify the appearance of the surface by introducing noise, bump, dents, and ripples. To increase the randomness of the effects, you can use a turbulence scale value.

The syntax for noise surface is

```
texture {
   noise surface {
// Standard shading model values
      color color

ambient scale
      diffuse scale
      specular color, scale
      transmission color, scale, ior
      reflection scale
      microfacet name angle
      color_map(map_entries)

// Solid texturing functions
      position_fn index
      position_scale scale
      turbulence scale
      octaves scale
      lookup_fn index

// Surface bump/dent/ripple modifiers
      normal index
      bump_scale scale
      frequency number
      phase scale
   }
}
```

135

The first part of the `noise` surface format is identical with that of the standard model, except for the new `color_map` feature. The next sections explain the parameters in detail.

color_map

When a light ray intersects an object, the ray tracer computes an index value. This value is generated by the 3-D texturing function defined by the surface. The number is compared against an internal color lookup table and a color is selected. If you decide to change Polyray's color lookup table (also known as a *color map*), you can do so by creating your own. The syntax for a color map is

```
color_map(
    [start_value, end_value, start_color, end_color]
        ...etc...
)
```

or

```
color_map(
    [start_value, end_value, start_color,start_alpha,
                    ➥end_color, end_alpha]
        ...etc...
)
```

in which *start_value* and *end_value* are numbers that indicate the range of values calculated by Polyray. The values are between 0 and 1. For example:

```
[0, 0.5, Gray, White]
```

If the ray tracer calculates an index value between 0 and 1, it will interpolate between `Gray` and `White` to find the correct color. If the value is 0, use `Gray`. If the value is equal to 1, use `White`.

start_color and *end_color* are related to the start and end values of that segment.

start_alpha and *end_alpha* stand for the amount of transparency in a given color. If alpha is 0, the material is opaque. A value of 1 indicates a transparent color.

For example, Listing 4.7 uses the same noise surface definition for each texture but the color maps are different. The color maps used are for white marbles:

```
color_map(
    [0.0, 0.8, <1, 1, 1>, <0.6, 0.6, 0.6>]
    [0.8, 1.0, <0.6, 0.6, 0.6>, <0.1, 0.1, 0.1>])
```

for red marbles:

```
color_map(
   [0.0, 0.8, <1, 0.8, 0.8>, <1, 0.4, 0.4>]
   [0.8, 1.0, <1, 0.4, 0.4>, <1, 0.1, 0.1>])
```

and for Jade marbles:

```
color_map(
   [0.0, 0.8, <0.1, 0.6, 0.1>, <0, 0.3, 0>]
   [0.8, 1.0, <0.1, 0.5, 0.1>, <0, 0.3, 0>])
```

and for alpha yellow marbles:

```
color_map(
[0.0, 0.2, yellow, 0, yellow, 0]
[0.2, 0.5, yellow, 0, black, 0.2]
[0.6, 1.0, black, 0.2, black, 1])
```

To learn what colors compose a given color map, compare the <R,G,B> values to the colors in Table 4.1. For example, the color <1,1,1> is white, <0.6,0.6,0.6> is a gray tone, near LightGrey, and <0.1,0.1,0.1> is almost black. These three colors help create the white marble texture. If Polyray calculates a value of 0.4, then the color that is halfway between <1,1,1> and <0.6,0.6,0.6> is used.

For the red marble map, observe that the value of red in all the colors is 1 and the rest of the components vary. Thus, most of the tones are based on red, the first of which is near white. For the Jade texture, all tones are based on green. Finally, the alpha yellow marble uses alpha values for some of the colors. If the color index is between 0 and 0.2, the surface color is yellow. Between 0.2 and 0.5, the colors vary from yellow (opaque, because alpha is 0) to black (partially transparent because alpha is 0.2). Between 0.6 and 1.0, the color is black and the alpha value goes from 0.2 to 1 (fully transparent). Because a color different than white was used for the transparent areas on the texture, the surface will act as a filter (similar to colored glass). In other words, whatever colors go through the transparent areas will be combined with the color of the surface at that point. To eliminate this feature, the statement transmission white, 1,1 was added to the texture. The color white indicates that all colors will be able to go through the transparent areas of the texture (no filtering will be performed).

Some of the objects used in Listing 4.7 are Bézier patches. The cone with its apex bent to one of the sides uses the white marble texture. The flat patch uses the red marble texture and the cylinder object uses the Jade. The Bézier patches were created with POVCAD using the Bézier features (see fig. 4.12).

Listing 4.7. Using color maps (COLORMAP.PI).

```
// COLORMAP.PI

include "texture.inc"

define white_marble
texture {
    noise surface {
        color white
        position_fn position_objectx
        lookup_fn    lookup_sawtooth
        octaves 3
        turbulence 3
        ambient 0.3
        diffuse 0.8
        specular 0.3
        microfacet Reitz 5
        color_map(
        [0.0, 0.8, <1, 1, 1>, <0.6, 0.6, 0.6>]
        [0.8, 1.0, <0.6, 0.6, 0.6>, <0.1, 0.1, 0.1>])
        }
}

define red_marble
texture {
    noise surface {
        color white
        position_fn position_objectx
        lookup_fn    lookup_sawtooth
        octaves 3
        turbulence 3
        ambient 0.3
        diffuse 0.8
        specular 0.3
        microfacet Reitz 5
        color_map(
        [0.0, 0.8, <1, 0.8, 0.8>, <1, 0.4, 0.4>]
        [0.8, 1.0, <1, 0.4, 0.4>, <1, 0.1, 0.1>])
        }
}

define Jade
texture {
    noise surface {
        color white
        position_fn position_objectx
        lookup_fn    lookup_sawtooth
        octaves 3
        turbulence 5
        ambient 0.3
        diffuse 0.8
        specular 0.3
        microfacet Reitz 5
        color_map(
        [0.0, 0.8, <0.1, 0.6, 0.1>, <0, 0.3, 0>]
        [0.8, 1.0, <0.1, 0.5, 0.1>, <0, 0.3, 0>])
        }
```

```
}

define alpha_yellow_marble
texture {
    noise surface {
        color white
        position_fn position_objectx
        lookup_fn   lookup_sawtooth
        octaves 3
        turbulence 3
        ambient 0.3
        diffuse 0.8
        specular 0.3
        microfacet Reitz 5
        transmission white, 1,1
        color_map(
        [0.0, 0.2, yellow, 0,   yellow, 0]
        [0.2, 0.5, yellow, 0,    black, 0.2]
        [0.6, 1.0, black, 0.2, black, 1]
        )
        }
}

viewpoint {
 from      <-1, 5, -15 >
 at        <2.0, -0.5, 0.0 >
 up        <0.0, 1.0, 0.0 >
 angle     45
 resolution 200,200
 aspect    1.0
}

// LIGHT_SOURCE
directional_light < 0 , 5 , -15  >


object{
// BEZIER PATCH CONE
object{
    bezier 2, 0.05, 3, 3,
     <0.183045,2.457585,0.0>, <-0.915,1.755,0.0>,
     <-0.3885,0.702,0.0>, <1.10442,0.0936,-0.013455>,
     <0.183045,2.457585,0.0>, <-1.2075,1.755,0.506025>,
     <-0.94425,0.702,0.962325>, <-0.76875,0.053235,2.644785>,
     <0.183045,2.457585,0.0>, <-1.7925,1.755,0.506025>,
     <-2.05575,0.702,0.962325>, <-2.23125,0.053235,2.644785>,
     <0.183045,2.457585,0.0>, <-2.085,1.755,0.0>,
     <-2.6115,0.702,0.0>, <-3.26319,-1.44261,0.0>
  white_marble
}
+
// BEZIER PATCH CONE
object{
    bezier 2, 0.05, 3, 3,
     <0.183045,2.457585,0.0>, <-0.915,1.755,0.0>,
     <-0.3885,0.702,0.0>, <1.10442,0.0936,-0.013455>,
     <0.183045,2.457585,0.0>, <-1.2075,1.755,-0.506025>,
     <-0.94425,0.702,-0.962325>, <-0.76875,0.013455,-2.63133>,
```

139

continues

Listing 4.7. Continued.

```
          <0.183045,2.457585,0.0>, <-1.7925,1.755,-0.506025>,
          <-2.05575,0.702,-0.962325>, <-2.23125,0.013455,-2.63133>,
          <0.183045,2.457585,0.0>, <-2.085,1.755,0.0>,
          <-2.6115,0.702,0.0>, <-3.26319,-1.44261,0.0>
   white_marble
 }
 }

// BEZIER PATCH   FLAT
object{
     bezier 2, 0.05, 3, 3,
       <-3.8536,-3.1144,1.0>, <-2.356,-3.26,1.0>,
       <-0.5296,-3.8632,1.0>, <2.9768,-5.5984,1.0>,
       <-1.0,-2.0,1.7>, <-0.3,-2.0,1.7>,
       <0.3,-2.0,1.7>,  <1.0,-2.0,1.7>,
       <-1.0,-2.0,2.3>, <-0.3,-2.0,2.3>,
       <0.3,-2.0,2.3>, <1.0,-2.0,2.3>,
       <-1.9728,-0.0088,3.0>, <0.9496,0.776,3.0>,
       <2.7576,1.324,3.0>, <3.7808,0.2832,3.0>
   scale<2,1,2>
   translate<2.5, -1.5, 0>
   red_marble

 }

object{
// BEZIER PATCH   CYLINDER
object{
     bezier 2, 0.05, 3, 3,
       <2.0,0.0,0.0>, <-0.0864,-2.8496,-1.0>,
       <2.9816,-3.0688,-1.0>, <6.5432,-2.5568,0.0>,
       <2.0,0.5,0.0>, <2.0,0.5,-1.0>,
       <4.0,0.5,-1.0>, <4.0,0.5,0.0>,
       <2.0,1.0,0.0>, <2.0,1.0,-1.0>,
       <4.0,1.0,-1.0>, <4.0,1.0,0.0>,
       <1.3016,2.1008,0.0>, <-0.6344,0.7488,-1.0>,
       <4.0,1.5,-1.0>, <5.612,1.936,0.0>
   Jade
 }
 +
// BEZIER PATCH   CYLINDER
object{
     bezier 2, 0.05, 3, 3,
       <6.5432,-2.5568,0.0>, <4.0,0.0,1.0>,
       <2.0,0.0,1.0>, <2.0,0.0,0.0>,
       <4.0,0.5,0.0>, <4.0,0.5,1.0>,
       <2.0,0.5,1.0>, <2.0,0.5,0.0>,
       <4.0,1.0,0.0>, <4.0,1.0,1.0>,
       <2.0,1.0,1.0>, <2.0,1.0,0.0>,
       <5.612,1.936,0.0>, <6.3056,3.324,1.0>,
       <2.324,3.5616,1.0>, <1.3016,2.1008,0.0>
   Jade
```

```
    }
    +
object {
    polygon 4, <-1,1,0>, <1,1,0>, <1,-1,0>, <-1,-1,0>
    scale <2, 2, 2>
    translate<0,0,-8>
    alpha_yellow_marble
    }
    translate<2, 0, 0>
    }
```

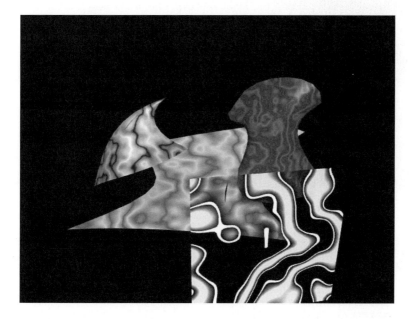

Figure 4.12

Applying the same textures with different color maps— white marble, red marble, jade, and alpha yellow marble (COLORMAP.PI).

There is an excellent utility called CMAPPER that composes different color maps visually (check the Introduction for bulletin boards that carry CMAPPER).

The next sections present other parameters used by the Noise Surface texture definition—solid texturing functions. They are used to modify and add noise to the texture patterns.

position_fn

When a light ray intersects an object, Polyray computes the location of that intersection point. When the intersection point is defined in terms of a coordinate system that is attached to the object, it is called a *local* coordinate system. If the point is defined in terms of the coordinate system that

you normally use to locate geometry, it is called the *global* system. You can use the location of the intersection point to modify the color. The keyword `position_fn` lets you select how to use that point to affect the color calculation. The available values for `position_fn` are

Index	Method
0	Default. None.
1	Use the X value in the local coordinate system (object x).
2	Use the X value in the global coordinate system (world x).
3	Use the distance from the Z axis (cylindrical).
4	Use the distance from the origin (spherical).
5	Use the distance of the point around the Y axis. The coordinate system goes from 0 to 1 counterclockwise (radial).

The file TEXTURE.INC defines the following token names, which can be used in place of the index values:

```
define position_plain        0
define position_objectx      1
define position_worldx       2
define position_cylindrical  3
define position_spherical    4
define position_radial       5
```

Examples of this function are given later.

position_scale

If you select a parameter for `position_fn` other than 0, you can use a scale factor to increase or decrease the effect. The keyword `position_scale` affects the contribution of `position_fn`. As a result, the contribution is equal to `position_fn * position_scale`.

turbulence

Turbulence is the amount of distortion that can be introduced into the calculations. The distortion is produced by a noise function. The `turbulence` value can be looked at as a scaling factor for the noise function; in other words,

```
noise contribution = turbulence * noise3D
```

in which `noise3D` is Polyray's internal noise function generator.

octaves

`octaves` is the number of times that the `noise` function is called. By increasing the number of octaves, the amount of detail in the texture increases. The `noise3D` function is dependent on the `octaves` value.

```
noise contribution = turbulence * noise3D(octaves)
```

lookup_fn

The final value of the color depends on the contribution of `position_fn`, `position_scale`, `turbulence`, and `octaves`. The value that results from these is modified in turn by a procedure that uses different kinds of functions: `sawtooth`, `sine`, and `cosine`. The keyword to define the function used is `lookup_fn`, in which the values are as follows:

Index	Function
0	No modification (plain)
1	sawtooth
2	cosine
3	sine

The file TEXTURE.INC has defined token words that can be used in place of the lookup functions:

```
define lookup_plain    0
define lookup_sawtooth 1
define lookup_cos      2
define lookup_sin      3
```

All the lookup functions return a number between 0 and 1.

Figure 4.13 shows an array of spheres with a white marble texture. For each row, the `position_fn` value is constant and the `lookup_fn` function is changed.

143

The arrangement is

```
Row (position_fn)    Column(lookup_fn)
               plain     sawtooth  cos  sin
plain
objectx
worldx
cylindrical
spherical
radial
```

Observe that with `lookup_fn` 0 the spheres have a color (the first color in the map) and no pattern.

Figure 4.13

Variation in position and lookup functions.

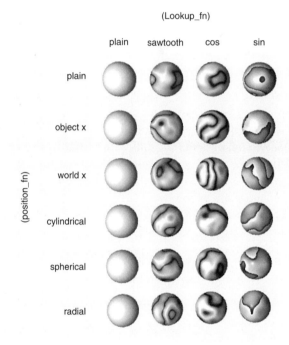

Figure 4.14 shows the same image, this time showing the relationship between `turbulence` and `octaves`. `turbulence` varies from 1 to 4 in increments of 1 (left to right) and the `octaves` vary from 1 to 11 in increments of 2 (top to bottom). For this figure, `position_fn` = 1, `lookup_fn` = 1 and `position_scale` = 2.

turbulence

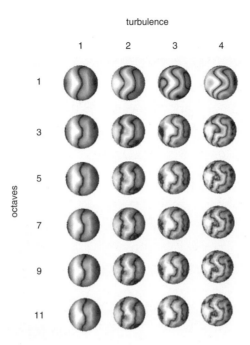

Figure 4.14

The relationship between octaves and turbulence— turbulence varies from left to right; octaves vary from top to bottom.

normal

The keyword `normal` is used to specify if a virtual surface deformation is done on the object. The deformation is called virtual because the surface will not be deformed, but the calculations the ray tracer does will assume that it is. There are three types of deformation methods: `bumps`, `ripples`, and `dents`. The usage for `normal` is

    normal type

in which *type* stands for the type of deformation. Possible values for *type* are

Value	Type
0	Plain (no deformation)
1	bumps
2	ripples
3	dents

bump_scale

The scaling factor for `normal` is the `bump_scale`. This value increases the effect of the deformation on the surface. The usage is

```
bump_scale scale
```

in which `scale` is the scaling factor. The scaling factor varies from 0 (no bumps) to any positive number.

frequency

Use the `frequency` keyword to increase or decrease the repetitiveness of ripple patterns. For example, if ripples are used, increasing the `frequency` increases the number of ripples in a given area. The usage is

```
frequency n
```

in which `n` is the repetition factor.

phase

`phase` acts as a displacement function to offset the ripples. The syntax is

```
phase n
```

in which `n` is the amount of displacement.

Surface Normal Modifier Examples

Following are a few examples of the use of surface normal modifiers. Listing 4.8 shows an attempt to create the moon (see fig. 4.15). If you look closely, the `noise surface` declaration is similar to that of the white marble texture. The `turbulence` value was lowered to produce a subtle effect. To deform the surface lightly, I used the following parameters:

```
normal dented_normal
bump_scale 0.2
frequency 10
```

I used these parameters in an attempt to simulate the deformed surface of the moon. Feel free to experiment with the texture and improve the look.

Listing 4.8. Moon with surface deformation and turbulence (MOON.PI).

```
// MOON.PI

include "texture.inc"
include "colors.inc"
```

```
// Types of Normal Deformation
//plain_normal   0
//bump_normal    1
//ripple_normal  2
//dented_normal  3

define Moon
texture {
    noise surface {
        color white
        position_fn position_spherical
        position_scale 1.0
        lookup_fn    lookup_sawtooth
        octaves 3
        turbulence 0.53
        ambient 0.4
        diffuse 0.8
        specular 0.2
        microfacet Reitz 5
        normal   dented_normal
        bump_scale 0.2
        frequency 10
        color_map(
        [0.0, 0.8, <1, 1, 1>, <0.6, 0.6, 0.6>]
        [0.8, 1.0, <0.6, 0.6, 0.6>, <0.1, 0.1, 0.1>])
        }
}


// Set up the camera
viewpoint {
    from <0,0,-15>
    at <0.5,0,0>
    up <0,1,0>
    angle 45
    resolution 200,200
    aspect 1.0
    }

background <0, 0, 0>
light <-10, 3, -20>

object {
    sphere <0, 0, 0>, 5
    Moon
}
```

The next example uses ripples to create a water-like surface. Three spheres are also in the scene, and you can see their reflections in the water (see Listing 4.9 and the output in fig. 4.16).

Figure 4.15

Using a lightly dented surface to model the moon (MOON.PI).

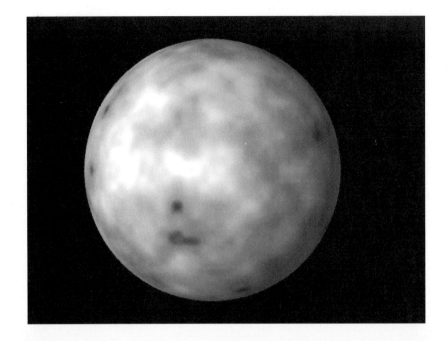

Listing 4.9. Modeling an ocean.

```
// WATER.PI

include "texture.inc"
include "colors.inc"

define Plane_XZ  object {
           polygon 4, <-10000,0,10000>, <-10000,0,-10000>,
                       <10000,0,-10000>, <10000,0,10000>
           }

define Water
texture {
   noise surface {
      color <0.4, 0.4, 1.0>
      normal ripple_normal
      frequency 100
      bump_scale 1
      ambient 0.3
      diffuse 0.3
      specular white, 0.7
      reflection 0.9
      microfacet Reitz 10
      }
      scale<10, 1, 10>
   }
```

```
// Set up the camera
viewpoint {
   from <0,5,-15>
   at <0,0,0>
   up <0,1,0>
   angle 45
   resolution 200,200
   aspect 1.0
   }
background White
directional_light <0, 3, -10>

object {
   sphere <0, 1.5, 0>, 2
   shiny_red
}
object {
   sphere <-4.5, 3, 1>, 1
   shiny_green
}
object {
   sphere <4.5, 4, 2>, 1
   shiny_yellow
}


object {
   Plane_XZ
   Water
}
```

Figure 4.16

*Modeling
ripples in water
(WATER.PI).*

149

The statements used in the scene to create the ripples are

```
normal ripple_normal
frequency 100
bump_scale 1
```

A `scale <10,1,10>` statement is used to separate the ripples in the surface. Another interesting effect is to add transparency to the water and define an ior. To create the effect of depth, you can put a second plane with a darker blue tone under the water plane.

The final example uses dents. In Listing 4.10, two of the objects have dented textures. The back plane is a dented mirror, which shows irregular reflections. The red sphere in the middle of the scene is also dented, and it is used to show contrast with the other two spheres, which are smooth (see fig. 4.17).

Listing 4.10. Mirror and red sphere with dented surface (DENTS.PI).

```
// DENTS.PI

include "texture.inc"
include "colors.inc"

define Plane_XZ   object {
          polygon 4, <-10000,0,10000>, <-10000,0,-10000>,
                      <10000,0,-10000>, <10000,0,10000>
        }

define dented_mirror
texture {
   noise surface {
      normal dented_normal
      frequency 10
      bump_scale 2
      ambient white, 0.1
      diffuse white, 0.2
      specular 0
      reflection  white, 1
      microfacet Reitz 10
      }
   scale <5, 5, 1>
   }

define dents
texture {
   noise surface {
      color <1, 0, 0>
      normal dented_normal
```

```
            frequency 2
            bump_scale 3
            ambient white, 0.2
            diffuse white, 0.5
            specular 0.7
            microfacet Reitz 10
            }
        scale <0.2, 0.2, 0.2>
        }

// Set up the camera
viewpoint {
    from <0,5,-15>
    at <0,2,0>
    up <0,1,0>
    angle 45
    resolution 200,200
    aspect 1.0

    }

background <1, 1, 1>
light <0, 3, -10>
light <0, 3, 4>

object {
    sphere <0,0,0>, 1.5
    dents
}
object {
    sphere <-3,0,0>, 1.5
    shiny_green
}
object {
    sphere <3,0,0>, 1.5
    shiny_yellow
}

object {
    Plane_XZ
    texture { checker matte_white, matte_black }
}

object {
    Plane_XZ
    rotate <90, 0, 0>
    translate<0,0, 8>
    dented_mirror
}
```

Figure 4.17

A dented mirror and sphere (DENTS.PI).

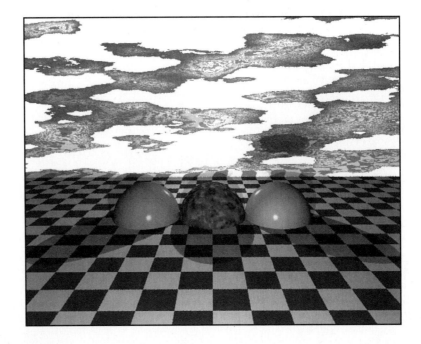

Layered

Polyray can stack different types of textures on top of each other. The resulting texture is called a *layered* texture. The syntax for constructing layered textures is

```
texture {
     layered
         texture#1,
         texture#2,
         .....etc.....
         texture#N
}
```

in which *texture#1* is the top layer and *texture#N* is the bottom layer.

For layered textures to work correctly, the textures must be transparent either through transmission or by including alpha values in the color maps. The idea is to make the top layers transparent and the final layer opaque. The result is a combination of the textures to make the final color. Listing 4.11 presents an example that is a combination of transparent yellow marble and checker textures. The transparent yellow marble texture is located on the top layer, and the checker texture is last. The checker pattern will be visible through the transparent areas on the top layer. Figure 4.18 presents a plane and a sphere with the created texture.

Listing 4.11. Layered texture with transparent yellow marble and checkers.

```
// LAYERED.PI

include "texture.inc"
include "colors.inc"

background white

define alpha_yellow_marble
texture {
   noise surface {
      color white
      position_fn position_objectx
      lookup_fn   lookup_sawtooth
      octaves 3
      turbulence 3
      ambient 0.3
      diffuse 0.8
      specular 0.3
      microfacet Reitz 5
      transmission white, 1,1
      color_map(
      [0.0, 0.2, yellow, 0,    yellow, 0]
      [0.2, 0.5, yellow, 0,    black, 0.2]
      [0.6, 1.0, black, 0.2, black, 1]
      )
      }
}

define Yellow_Marble_Checker
   texture {
      layered
      alpha_yellow_marble,
      texture {checker matte_white, matte_black
          scale <0.2, 0.2, 0.2>
      }
   }

viewpoint {
 from       <-2, 3, -7 >
 at         <0.0, -0.2, 0.0 >
 up         <0.0, 1.0, 0.0 >
 angle      45
 resolution 100,100
 aspect     1.0
}

// LIGHT_SOURCE
directional_light < 0 ,  5 , -7  >


object {
   polygon 4, <-1,1,1>, <1,1,1>, <1,-1,1>, <-1,-1,1>
   scale <2, 2, 2>
   Yellow_Marble_Checker
}
object {
   sphere <0,0,-3>, 1
   Yellow_Marble_Checker
}
```

153

Figure 4.18

Using layered textures (LAYERED.PI).

Functional

Functional textures are evaluated at run time; they are not hard-coded in the ray tracer program. You can use a mathematical expression to determine the color or to deflect the normal of the surface (Chapter 6, "Additional Features," goes into more detail about mathematical expressions). You shouldn't be concerned with the mathematics of color definition or normal deflection because Polyray has a set of defined functions ready for you to use. The lookup functions, which are listed next, are really token names for mathematical expressions. The expressions are given in the COLORS.INC file. The following are the defined token names for the functions:

```
agate_fn       marble_fn        granite_fn     wood_fn
odd_wood1      noisy_wood_fn    bozo_fn        leopard_fn
onion_fn       noisy_onion_fn   checker_fn     checker3_fn
radial_fn
```

After reading Chapter 6, you will be able to create your own functions.

The syntax for a functional texture is

```
texture {
    special surface {
        parameter declaration
    }
}
```

in which the `parameter declaration` is similar to the noise surface.

The primary difference between noise surface texture and functional texture is that you can use any function to look up the colors in the color map. On the other hand, the noise surface texture has a limited set of lookup functions, and those are built into the program.

Listing 4.12 uses two color lookup functions: `bozo_fn` and `granite_fn` (see fig. 4.19 for the output). These functions return a value between 0 and 1. In order to find the correct color, a color map must be defined. The lookup function and the color map are used as follows

```
define BlueSkyMap
       color_map(
       [0.0, 0.5, <0.25,0.25,0.5>, <0.25,0.25,0.5>]
       [0.5 , 0.6, <0.25,0.25,0.5>, <0.7,0.7,0.7>]
       [0.6,  1.0, <0.7,0.7,0.7>, <0.3,0.3,0.3>])

define Sky
texture {
   special surface {
      color BlueSkyMap[bozo_fn]
      .....etc.....
      }
    .....etc.....
   }
```

As you can see, the color map is defined like any other color map. When we get to the `Sky texture` definition, the statement `color BlueSkyMap[bozo_fn]` declares that the lookup function `bozo_fn` is used to generate an index value that will be used to select a color from the `BlueSkyMap` color map. The same method is used with the `PinkGranite` definition.

Initially, the `bozo_fn` function returns a number between 0 and 1. That value is then compared against the `BlueSkyMap` color map and a color is chosen. Finally, the result of that operation is given to the keyword `color` as an <R,G,B> vector.

Another interesting method is to declare the `color` as

```
color <expression#1, expression#2, expression#3>
```

in which *expression#1*, *expression#2*, and *expression#3* are mathematical expressions. Each is responsible for calculating one of the color's components. For example, the expression

```
color <agate_fn , marble_fn, granite_fn>
```

indicates that the contribution of the color red will be given by `agate_fn`, the green component by `marble_fn`, and the blue component by `granite_fn`.

Listing 4.12. Using functional textures (SPECIAL.PI).

```
// SPECIAL.PI   Functional Textures

include "texture.inc"
include "colors.inc"

define Quartz   <0.85, 0.85, 0.95>
define Feldspar <0.82, 0.57, 0.46>

define Plane_XZ  object {
            polygon 4, <-10000,0,10000>, <-10000,0,-10000>,
                       <10000,0,-10000>, <10000,0,10000>
        }

define PinkGraniteMap
      color_map(
      [0,    0.4 , Black ,    Black]
      [0.4,  0.45, Quartz,    Feldspar]
      [0.45, 0.5 , Quartz,    Gray]
      [0.5 , 0.55, Gray,      Feldspar]
      [0.55, 0.8,  Feldspar, Feldspar]
      [0.8,  1.0,  Feldspar, Orange])

define BlueSkyMap
      color_map(
      [0.0, 0.5, <0.25,0.25,0.5>, <0.25,0.25,0.5>]
      [0.5 , 0.6, <0.25,0.25,0.5>, <0.7,0.7,0.7>]
      [0.6,  1.0, <0.7,0.7,0.7>, <0.3,0.3,0.3>])


define Granite
texture {
   special surface {
       color PinkGraniteMap[granite_fn]
       ambient 0.3
       diffuse 0.8
       specular 0.3
       reflection  white, 0.3
       microfacet Reitz 10
       }
   }

define Sky
texture {
   special surface {
       color BlueSkyMap[bozo_fn]
       ambient 0.3
       diffuse 0.8
       specular 0.3
```

```
            turbulence 100
            octaves 3
            microfacet Reitz 10
            }
            scale <15, 1, 1>
            translate<0, 0, 5>
    }
// Set up the camera
viewpoint {
    from <0,5,-15>
    at <0,2,0>
    up <0,1,0>
    angle 45
    resolution 200,200
    aspect 1.0

    }

directional_light <0, 3, -10>
directional_light <0, 3, 4>

object {
    sphere <0,1.5,0>, 1.5
    Granite
}
object {
    sphere <-3.5,1.5,0>, 1.5
    Granite
}
object {
    sphere <3.5,1.5,0>, 1.5
    Granite
}

object {
    Plane_XZ
    texture { checker matte_white, matte_black }
}

object {
    Plane_XZ
    rotate <90, 0, 0>
    translate<0,0, 10>
    Sky
}
```

Figure 4.19

Functional textures Granite and Bozo (SPECIAL.PI).

Image Mapping Textures

Functional textures support the use of images as image maps. The image can be projected to a surface in four ways: planar, cylindrical, spherical, and environment. The syntaxes for the four types of projection are

```
planar_imagemap(myimage,coordinate[,repeat])
cylindrical_imagemap(myimage,coordinate[,repeat])
spherical_imagemap(myimage,coordinate)
environment_map(coordinate,environment("myfile1.tga","myfile2.tga",
                                       "myfile3.tga","myfile4.tga",
                                       "myfile5.tga","myfile6.tga"))
```

where *myimage* is defined as

```
define  myimage image("myfile.tga")
```

in which *coordinate* is a vector <x,y,z> used to select a color. The value of x is multiplied by the number of columns and z is multiplied by the number of rows. The color found at the new position in the image is used. The suggested vector is P. P is a reserved symbol for the position of the intersection between the light ray and the surface to be colored. In the environment map, the vector reflect(I,N) is suggested. The vector I defines the direction of the light ray that intersected the object, and N is the normal of the surface at the intersection point. The function reflect(I,N) then rotates the direction of I so that it is aligned with N. Polyray has various internal variables defined at run time; the variable P is a vector that represents the current intersection point between a light ray and the object. The vector P is normally used as the coordinate parameter, for example:

158

```
define myimage image("clown.tga")
planar_imagemap(myimage,P)
```

Chapter 6," Additional Features," explains Polyray's runtime variable P and others.

repeat stands for a value that indicates that the image pattern is repeated in the same object. The image can be 8-, 16-, 24- or 32-bit uncompressed, RLE compressed, or color-mapped Targa.

In planar projections, the image is mapped in x between 0 and 1 and in z between 0 and 1. In other words, the image is perpendicular to the y axis, and resting on the xz plane, with the lower left corner at the origin. The cylindrical mapping takes place on a cylinder with one end at the origin and the other end at <0,1,0>. If the pattern is repeated, the copies are added along the y axis. The spherical projection uses a sphere at the origin. The top edge of the image will be located in the north pole and the bottom edge at the south. Finally, the environment projection maps six images around the surface (top, bottom, left, right, front, and back). On all projections, any part of the object that is not covered by the image is given the color of the pixel (0,0).

Listing 4.13 uses all four properties with the same image file that was used to create the height fields (PLASMA.TGA). See figure 4.20 for the output of Listing 4.13.

Listing 4.13. Image mapping (MAPS.PI).

```
// MAPS.PI

include "texture.inc"
include "colors.inc"

define Plane_XZ  object {
        polygon 4, <0,0,0>, <1,0,0>, <1,0,1>, <0,0,1>
     }

define myimage image("plasma.tga")
define CImage
  texture {
     special surface {
      color cylindrical_imagemap(myimage,P)
      ambient 0.9
      diffuse 0.1
     }
   }

define SImage
  texture {
```

continues

Listing 4.13. Continued.

```
      special surface {
       color spherical_imagemap(myimage,P)
       ambient 0.9
       diffuse 0.1
      }
     }

define PImage
  texture {
     special surface {
      color planar_imagemap(myimage,P)
      ambient 0.9
      diffuse 0.1
     }
    }

define EImage
  texture {
     special surface {
      color environment_map(reflect(I, N),
                            environment("plasma.tga","plasma.tga",
                                        "plasma.tga","plasma.tga",
                                        "plasma.tga","plasma.tga"))
      ambient 0.9
      diffuse 0.1
     }
    }


// Set up the camera
viewpoint {
   from <0,5,-10>
   at <0,4,0>
   up <0,1,0>
   angle 45
   resolution 200,200
   aspect 1.0

   }

background <1, 1, 1>
light <0, 3, -10>

object {
   sphere <0,2,0>, 1.5
   SImage
}

object {
   sphere <0,6,0>, 1.5
   EImage
}
```

```
object {
  cylinder <0, 0, 0>, <0, 1, 0>, 1
  CImage
  scale <1,3,1>
  rotate <-20, 10, 0>
  translate <3.5, 2, 2>
}

object {
  Plane_XZ
  PImage
  scale <5,5,5>
  rotate <90, -30, 0>
  translate<-10,3, 15>
}
```

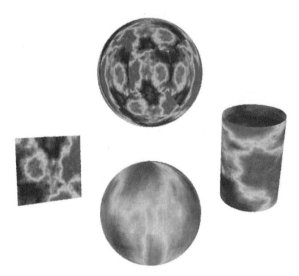

Figure 4.20

Mapping an image file to several surfaces: sphere, cylinder, and plane (MAPS.PI).

Scaling and translation are very important when you're using image maps. For example, the cylinder is initially the same size and in the same location as the mapping procedure requires. To scale it appropriately, you need to apply the transformation after the texture declaration, as in the following:

```
object {
  cylinder <0, 0, 0>, <0, 1, 0>, 1
  CImage
  scale <1,3,1>
  rotate <-20, 10, 0>
  translate <3.5, 2, 2>
}
```

If the object isn't created in the place and size required by the mapping function, the object might not receive the mapping image at all.

This concludes the texture discussion. In Chapter 5, we cover some miscellaneous features, and you look at Polyray's mathematical computation capabilities. If you're not a math-oriented person, you may want to skip the last section of Chapter 5, "Constructive Solid Geometry."

Summary

In this chapter, you learned the different types of light sources: the positional, the directional, and the spot light. Each light source helps you create a different effect: positional light produces shadows, directionals produce only light and no shadows, and spot lights create a "hot spot" on the image.

Next, you saw a list of all the colors available in Polyray and different techniques for attaching colors to surfaces and image backgrounds. You also took a detailed look at all of the different texturing models: standard shading model, procedural textures, functional, and layered.

The standard model was used to create everything from opaque surfaces to transparent surfaces and mirrors. Procedural textures are ready-to-use patterns that were mapped into surfaces such as the checker, the hexagon, and the noise surface. The noise surface texture was handy in creating marble, ripples in water, and dents and bumps in surfaces. You can use the layered texture to stack different types of textures. The next texture studied was the functional texture, with which you can define a lookup function that tells Polyray what color to use, working in conjunction with color maps.

Finally, you learned how to map images to different surfaces by means of image maps. The four kinds of image maps are planar, cylindrical, spherical, and environment.

In the next chapter, you take a look at constructive solid geometry and how Polyray handles those operations.

Constructive Solid Geometry

Chapter 1 presented the concept of creating complex objects with simple primitives such as the cylinder, the sphere, and the box, in conjunction with Boolean operations. In this chapter, you take a practical approach at using Boolean operations such as union (+), difference (-), and intersection (*). In addition, you learn the clipping (&) operation, the inverse (~) of an object, and how to define artificial boundaries through the use of a bounding box.

Boolean Operations

Polyray supports a variety of Boolean operations. Although some of the operations affect the final form of a given geometric object, other operations group objects or limit the extension of an object by clipping any part that is outside a defined boundary. Grouping objects is an extremely powerful feature you can use to manipulate a group of objects as a whole instead of having to apply transformations to each object. For example, a car consists of a group of objects: the tires (tori) and the chassis (box). By grouping them together, you can translate the *set* of objects (the car) without having to translate each tire and each section of the chassis.

Union

Unions in Polyray are represented by the symbol +. When a union operation is performed on a set of shapes or objects, the resulting set itself becomes a single object consisting of all the individual shapes. The new object can be manipulated by means of transformations or other Boolean operations. For example, assume you have a set of four spheres on the xy plane and wish to rotate them as a group, around the y axis by 15 degrees. You can do this in two ways:

Method #1

```
// sphere #1
object {
    sphere <1,1,0> ,2
    rotate <0,15,0>
    shiny_red
}
// sphere #2
object {
    sphere <-1,1,0> ,2
    rotate <0,15,0>
    shiny_red
}
// sphere #3
object {
    sphere <-1,-1,0> ,2
    rotate <0,15,0>
    shiny_red
}
// sphere #4
object {
    sphere <1,-1,0> ,2
    rotate <0,15,0>
    shiny_red
}
```

Method #2

```
object {
     object {sphere <1,1,0>, 2}
+ object {sphere <-1,1,0>, 2}
+ object {sphere <-1,-1,0>, 2}
+ object {sphere <1,-1,0>, 2}
        rotate <0,15,0>
        shiny_red
}
```

As you can see, you greatly reduced the amount of typing by using the union (+) operator. Only one rotation and one texture statement were needed for the entire group. You can still apply transformations to individual objects as before; you can replace the statement

```
object { sphere <1,1,0>,2}
```

with

```
object {sphere <0,0,0>,2
translate <1,1,0>
}
```

giving the same result. Sometimes you have to control a group of objects as a whole, even though each object in the corresponding group has a different texture. Take the following set of spheres, for example:

```
object {
     object { sphere <0,1,0>,2
            shiny_red
     }
+    object { sphere <0,-1,0>,2
            shiny_green
     }
     translate <1,1,5>
}
```

A union operation groups the two spheres together so they can be translated with just one statement. In some ray tracers, when objects with different textures are grouped together, they are called "composite" objects.

Listing 5.1 presents examples of union and composite objects, and figure 5.1 displays the final image.

Listing 5.1. Union and composite objects (UNION.PI).

```
//UNION.PI
include "colors.inc"
include "texture.inc"
```

continues

Listing 5.1. Continued.

```
viewpoint {
 from      <0.2, 4.0, -5.0 >
 at        <0.0, -1.0, 0.0 >
 up        <0.0, 1.0, 0.0 >
 angle     45
 resolution 100,100
 aspect    1.0
}
// LIGHT_SOURCE
 light < 10 ,  10 , -10  >
// LIGHT_SOURCE
 light <-10 ,  10 , -10  >

define TwoSpheres
object {
  object { sphere <  0.5, 0, 0>, 0.47  }
+ object { sphere < -0.5, 0, 0>, 0.47  }
}
define GraySpheresUnion
object {
  object {
    TwoSpheres
  }
+  object {
    TwoSpheres
    rotate<0, 0, 90>
  }
+ object {
    TwoSpheres
    rotate<0, 90, 0>
  }
  reflective_gray
}
define GraySpheresComposite
object {
  object {
    TwoSpheres
    matte_red
  }
+  object {
    TwoSpheres
    rotate<0, 0, 90>
    matte_green
  }
+ object {
    TwoSpheres
    rotate<0, 90, 0>
    matte_yellow
  }
}
object {
  GraySpheresUnion
  translate<-1.5, 0, 0>
}
object {
  GraySpheresComposite
```

```
      translate<1.5, 0, 0>
   }
object {
   object {
      cone <0.0, -1.3, 0.0>, 0.8, <0.0, 0.0, 0.0>, 0.0
      translate<-0.2, -1.5, 0>
      reflective_red
   }

+  object {
      cone <0.0, -1.3, 0.0>, 0.8, <0.0, 0.0, 0.0>, 0.0
      translate<0.2, -1.5, 0>
      reflective_gray
   }
}
```

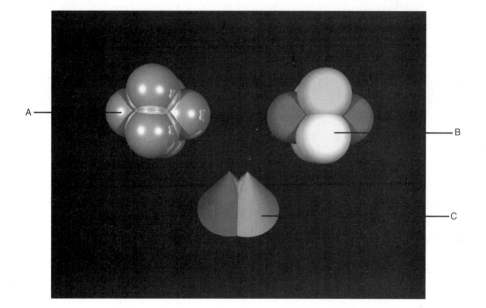

A —
B —
C —

Figure 5.1

Using unions and composite objects (UNION.PI).

In the UNION.PI scene, initially two spheres are grouped together and called TwoSpheres. This new object (A) becomes the base object you will use to create a more complex object. The object GraySpheresUnion is composed of three copies of the TwoSpheres primitive. The second and third objects (B and C) are rotated about Z and Y by 90 degrees, respectively. The color used is reflective_gray. Using the same primitive, the GraySpheresComposite object is created by attaching individual textures to each shape and the appropriate transformation. The statements

```
object {
    GraySpheresUnion
    translate<-1.5, 0, 0>
}
object {
    GraySpheresComposite
    translate<1.5, 0, 0>
}
```

are used to locate the objects in their final position. Finally, two cones are created as a composite and located underneath `GraySpheresComposite` and `GraySpheresUnion`. Observe that even though the cones are intersecting each other, their individual colors show the limits of each one.

Difference

The difference (-) operation is used to subtract one object from another and is commonly used to create holes in shapes. In figure 1.11, a cylinder was used to create a hole in a cube by using the difference operation. One interesting result of using differences can be seen if the colors of the objects are different (as it happens in fig. 1.11). The surface where both objects are in contact takes the color of the object being subtracted, thus giving the appearance of a "missing" section. Again, in figure 1.11, the cube has a reflective gray color while the cylinder has a reflective red surface. After applying the difference, the volume of the cube that was inside the cylinder disappears and the surface in contact with the cylinder becomes reflective red. This method relates to the previous section where some of the objects had only one texture while another group had individual textures for each object.

It is important to note that when a difference operation is performed on more than two objects, the first object becomes the primary, and the rest are invisible and only used to define what will be subtracted from the primary one. Listing 5.2 uses a cube to represent the primary object. Two torus objects will be subtracted from the cube. In addition, a second example in the same image also is presented. A sphere is used as the primary object from which two more tori will be subtracted. Figures 5.2 and 5.3 present the objects without and with the difference operations, respectively. To generate figure 5.2, change the difference operators (-) with union operators (+).

Listing 5.2. Two difference operations (DIFFR.PI).

```
//DIFFR.PI
include "colors.inc"
include "texture.inc"
viewpoint {
 from      <1, 1.0, -7.0 >
 at        <1.2, 0.0, 0.0 >
 up        <0.0, 1.0, 0.0 >
 angle     45
 resolution 100,100
 aspect    1.0
}
// LIGHT_SOURCE
  light < 10 ,  10 , -10  >
// LIGHT_SOURCE
  light <-10 ,  10 , -10  >

object {
// BOX
    object {
          box <-1, -2, -1>, <1, 2, 1>
    }
// TORUS
-   object {
       torus  1.5, 0.6, < 0.0, 0.0, 0.0>, <0.0, 1.0, 0.0>
       translate <0, 1, 0>
    }
// TORUS
-   object {
       torus  1.5, 0.6, < 0.0, 0.0, 0.0>, <0.0, 1.0, 0.0>
    }
    rotate<0, 15, 0>
    reflective_red
    translate<-0.5, 0.1, 0>

object {
   object {
      sphere <0, 0, 0>, 1.2
      matte_green
  }
-   object {
      torus  1.1, 0.3, < 0.0, 0.0, 0.0>, <0.0, 1.0, 0.0>
      matte_blue
    }
-   object {
      torus  1.1, 0.3, < 0.0, 0.0, 0.0>, <0.0, 1.0, 0.0>
      rotate<0, 0 ,90>
      matte_red
    }

   rotate<15, 0, 0>
   translate <3, 0, 0>
}
```

Figure 5.2

*Listing 5.2
without the
difference
operations.*

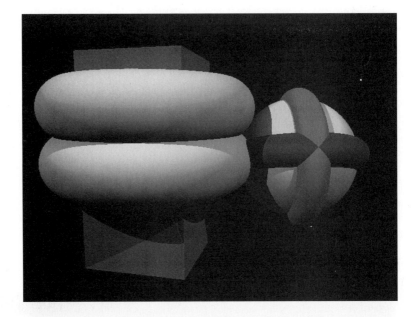

Figure 5.3

*Listing 5.2 with
the difference
operations
(DIFFR.PI).*

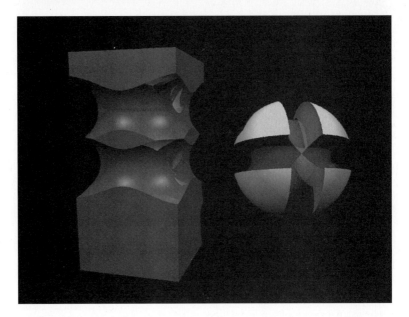

Observe in figure 5.3 how the sphere's surfaces that were in contact with the tori have taken their respective colors. This feature accentuates the grooves on the sphere.

Intersection

Intersections (*) are easy to use but sometimes difficult to visualize. An intersection operation creates an object that consists of all the surface sections of each object which are inside one another, or overlapping. In Listing 4.3, an intersection was used to create the neck of the lamp. The code used was

```
// LAMP "NECK"
object  {
// TORUS
object {
    torus  0.4, 0.05, < 0.0, 0.0, 0.0>, <0.0, 1.0, 0.0>
    rotate <90, 0, 0>
    translate <-0.375, 0.3, 0>
}
*
// BOX
object {
    box <-1, -1, -1>, <1, 1, 1>
    scale <0.4, 0.4, 0.4>
    translate <0.125, 0.575, 0>

}
  LampColor
}
```

As you can see, the order of the objects is not important. The box was used as an artificial boundary. Any part of the torus that was outside of the box was cut. The next section covers the clipping operation, which you can use for the same purpose.

Listing 5.3 presents an intersection operation.

Listing 5.3. Intersection operation (INTERS.PI).

```
//INTERS.PI
include "colors.inc"
include "texture.inc"
define ColoredGlass
    surface {
        ambient 0.3
        diffuse 0
        specular 0.2
        reflection white, 0.1
        transmission white, 0.7, 1
        }
define RedGlass texture {ColoredGlass {color red}}

viewpoint {
  from      <1, 1.0, -7.0 >
  at        <0.0, -1.5, 0.0 >
```

continues

171

Listing 5.3. Continued.

```
up          <0.0, 1.0, 0.0 >
angle       45
resolution 100,100
aspect      1.0
}
// LIGHT_SOURCE
  light < 10 ,  10 , -10  >
// LIGHT_SOURCE
  light <-10 ,  10 , -10  >

object {
// BOX
    object {
        box <-1, -1, -1>, <1, 1, 1>
        rotate<-15, 0, 0>
        RedGlass
    }
+   object {
        sphere <1, 0, 0>, 1
        shiny_yellow
    }
    rotate<0, 15, 0>
}
object {
// BOX
    object {
        box <-1, -1, -1>, <1, 1, 1>
        rotate<-15, 0, 0>
    }
*   object {
        sphere <1, 0, 0>, 1
    }
    translate<0, -3, 0>
    rotate<0, 15, 0>
    shiny_yellow
}
```

There are two parts in Listing 5.3. The first part displays the box as a transparent red object and the sphere as yellow. Looking at both objects, you can see that the only part of the sphere that is inside the box is the left hemisphere. And only the part of the box that is inside the left hemisphere will remain after the intersection operation.

The second part of Listing 5.3 is the final intersection operation. The box has no texture, so it will only be used as an artificial boundary. The only part of the box that will be visible is the surface that covers the open area in the hemisphere.

Figure 5.4

Example of intersection operation between a box and a sphere (INTERS.PI).

Clipping

Clipping an object can be accomplished by using the & operator. Any part of the primary object that goes beyond the clipping boundary (the clipping object) will not be seen. Let's use figure 5.4 as an example. If we had used a clipping operation instead of a difference, we would have the same results, except that the left hemisphere would appear hollow instead of solid. Listing 5.4 uses the same objects presented in Listing 5.3 (the box and the sphere) to demonstrate a clipping operation.

Listing 5.4. Clipping objects (CLIP.PI).

```
//CLIP.PI
include "colors.inc"
include "texture.inc"
define ColoredGlass
    surface {
        ambient 0.3
        diffuse 0
        specular 0.2
        reflection white, 0.1
        transmission white, 0.7, 1
        }
define RedGlass texture {ColoredGlass {color red}}

viewpoint {
  from      <1, 1.3, -7.0 >
```

continues

173

Listing 5.4. Continued.

```
    at        <0.0, -1.5, 0.0 >
    up        <0.0, 1.0, 0.0 >
    angle     45
    resolution 100,100
    aspect    1.0
}
// LIGHT_SOURCE
directional_light < 10 ,  10 , -10  >
// LIGHT_SOURCE
directional_light <-10 ,  10 , -10  >
background gray
object {
// BOX
    object {
        box <-1, -1, -1>, <1, 1, 1>
        RedGlass
    }
+   object {
        sphere <0, 0, 0>, 1.2
        shiny_yellow
    }
    rotate<0, 20, 0>
}
object {
    object {
        sphere <0, 0, 0>, 1.2
    }
&   object {
        box <-1, -1, -1>, <1, 1, 1>
    }
    translate<0, -3, 0>
    rotate<0, 20, 0>
    shiny_yellow
}
```

Listing 5.4 follows the same approach used in the previous section. The box (the clipping object) is transparent, permitting the view of what is inside and what is outside the boundary. The sphere is the primary object, and since it is larger than the box, parts of it will be clipped. In figure 5.5 (the lower section), the sphere is clipped, appearing to be hollow. The clip operation does not close the surface.

Figure 5.5

Clipping a sphere with a box (CLIP.PI).

Bounding Box

A bounding box defines the limits on an object or group of objects in order to speed up the ray tracing operations. Bounding boxes were covered briefly in Chapter 3, in the "Blob" section and later in the "Functions" section. This is a section of the code used in the scene BLOB.PI in Chapter 3:

```
object {
    object {
      blob 0.5:
      plane <0,1,0>, 0, 2, 5,
      sphere <0,3,0>, -4, 2
      RedFinish
    }
    bounding_box <-3,1,-1>, <3,3,3>
    scale <0.5,0.5,0.5>
}
```

In this section, we used a bounding box to limit the plane surface. A plane is an infinite flat surface. Since planes have no boundaries, one was created using the statement bounding_box <-3,1,-1>, <3,3,3>. This statement forces the ray tracer to check the plane only if the current light ray intersects (passes through) a box with the limits <-3,1,-1> and <3,3,3>. This feature speeds the ray tracing calculations since it is faster to check the bounding box than to check the blob object for its visibility.

175

Interestingly enough, bounding boxes can be used to clip an object (even though it is NOT recommended). Listing 5.5 uses a box and a sphere. The box is located inside the sphere and is roughly half as big as the sphere. The box is only used to represent the bounding box; a true box is not used in the operation. Using bounding boxes as a clipping operation is risky and prone to errors. If you need to clip an object use the appropriate operation. This example is given only to present the similarities between bounding box and clipping. Figure 5.6 shows the output of Listing 5.5.

Listing 5.5. Using bounding boxes to clip objects (BOUNDED.PI).

```
//BOUNDED.PI
include "colors.inc"
include "texture.inc"
define ColoredGlass
    surface {
        ambient 0.3
        diffuse 0
        specular 0.2
        reflection white, 0.1
        transmission white, 0.7, 1
        }
define YellowGlass texture {ColoredGlass {color yellow}}
viewpoint {
  from      <1, 1.3, -7.0 >
  at        <0.0, -1.5, 0.0 >
  up        <0.0, 1.0, 0.0 >
  angle     45
  resolution 100,100
  aspect    1.0
}
// LIGHT_SOURCE
directional_light < 10 ,  10 , -10  >
// LIGHT_SOURCE
directional_light <-10 ,  10 , -10  >
background gray
object {
    object {
        box <-0.5, -0.5, -0.5>, <0.5, 0.5, 0.5>
        texture { surface {color red}}
    }
+   object {
        sphere <0, 0, 0>, 1.2
        YellowGlass
    }
    rotate<0, 20, 0>
}
object {
    object {
        sphere <0, 0, 0>, 1.2
    }
```

```
        bounding_box <-0.5, -0.5, -0.5>, <0.5, 0.5, 0.5>
        translate<0, -3, 0>
        rotate<0, 20, 0>
        shiny_yellow
    }
```

Figure 5.6

Clipping objects with bounding boxes (BOUNDED.PI).

The section that clips the sphere is

```
object {
    object {
        sphere <0, 0, 0>, 1.2
    }
    bounding_box <-0.5, -0.5, -0.5>, <0.5, 0.5, 0.5>
    translate<0, -3, 0>
    rotate<0, 20, 0>
    shiny_yellow
}
```

The bounding box object tells the ray tracer not to look beyond the limits `<-0.5, -0.5, -0.5>`, and `<0.5, 0.5, 0.5>`, even though the sphere is larger than this range.

Bounding boxes are used to speed up ray tracing calculation in objects such as a collection of polygons. If you have an object consisting of 1,000 polygons, each time the ray tracer has to evaluate the polygons it will take a long time looking at each polygon. If a bounding box is used to define the limits, the ray tracer will only check one box. If it doesn't see the box, it doesn't need to check the polygons. Compare that to checking 1,000 polygons!

177

Inverse

The inverse (~) operation specifies what part of an object (the inside or outside) is important. If a given object is located inside another object, by attaching the inverse symbol (~) to the first object, the ray tracer assumes that the object is outside the second one. Listing 5.6 compares the difference operation between a box and a sphere and between another box and the inverse of that sphere. In both cases, the center of the sphere is located inside of the box, but in the second example, the sphere has an inverse (~) symbol.

Since the sphere is larger than the box, a difference operation of SPHERE - BOX results in only those parts of the sphere which are outside of the box remaining. In the inverse sphere, only the sections of the surface that are inside of the box remain. Figure 5.7 shows a comparison between a difference operation with and without the inverse.

Listing 5.6. Using the inverse operation (INVERSE.PI).

```
//INVERSE.PI
include "colors.inc"
include "texture.inc"
define ColoredGlass
    surface {
        ambient 0.3
        diffuse 0
        specular 0.2
        reflection white, 0.1
        transmission white, 0.7, 1
        }
define RedGlass texture {ColoredGlass {color red}}

viewpoint {
  from      <1, 1.3, -8.0 >
  at        <0.0, -1.5, 0.0 >
  up        <0.0, 1.0, 0.0 >
  angle     45
  resolution 100,100
  aspect    1.0
}
// LIGHT_SOURCE
directional_light < 10 , 10 , -10 >
// LIGHT_SOURCE
directional_light <-10 , 10 , -10 >
background gray
object {
// BOX
    object {
        box <-1, -1, -1>, <1, 1, 1>
        RedGlass
    }
+   object {
```

```
            sphere <0, 0, 0>, 1.2
            shiny_yellow
        }
        rotate<0, 20, 0>
}
object {
    object {
        sphere <0, 0, 0>, 1.2
    }
-   object {
        box <-1, -1, -1>, <1, 1, 1>
    }
    translate<-2, -3, 0>
    rotate<0, 20, 0>
    shiny_yellow
}
object {
    object {
        sphere <0, 0, 0>, 1.2
    }
-   ~object {
        box <-1, -1, -1>, <1, 1, 1>
    }
    translate<2, -3, 0>
    rotate<0, 35, 0>
    shiny_yellow
}
```

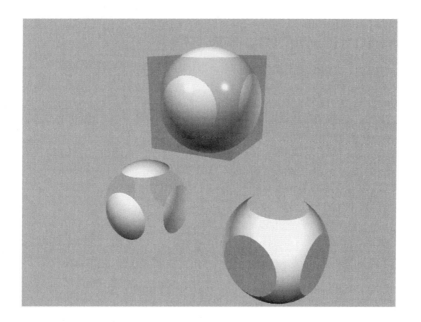

Figure 5.7

Comparison
between a
difference
operation with
and without the
inverse
(INVERSE.PI).

The section of code that applies the difference to the inverse of the box is

```
object {
    object {
        sphere <0, 0, 0>, 1.2
    }
    ~object {
        box <-1, -1, -1>, <1, 1, 1>
    }
    translate<2, -3, 0>
    rotate<0, 35, 0>
    shiny_yellow
}
```

Place the ~ symbol in front of the object to invert.

Summary

In this chapter, you took a more detailed look at Boolean operations and how they are applied in Polyray. The union (+), difference (-), and intersection (*) operations are the most commonly used, and the syntax is similar. When you apply difference operations, the order of the objects is important. The first object becomes the primary object, and any additional objects will be used to subtract from the primary. The union and intersection operations do not have that requirement. Composite objects are unions in which each shape or object has its own texture.

You also were introduced to a new set of operations: clipping (&), bounding box, and inverse (~). Clipping is very similar to intersection, except that clipping does not close any open surfaces (for example, a hemisphere appears to be hollow), and it is faster than intersections. Use bounding boxes to speed up ray tracing calculations, since they define the limits of an object or groups of objects. You should not use them as a clipping operation. The ray tracer simply tests the limits of the bounding box first; then, if necessary, it tests the objects inside it. This feature can save considerable time when you are ray tracing a large number of objects which are grouped together. Finally, use the inverse operation to define which part of an object (inside or outside) is important. If an object is located inside of another, applying an inverse to it causes it to be outside, and vice versa.

In the next chapter, you take a look at some additional features which can help you speed up the development process of images. In addition, you see how you can use mathematical expressions to increase Polyray's versatility.

Additional Features

So far, you have been able to create some interesting images in Polyray with only a fraction of its capabilities. You created high-quality images, using all of the available surface features: reflection, refraction, and highlights, to name a few. Occasionally, you might want to turn on or off some of those features to create a certain effect on your image, or to speed up the process. To turn on or off such features as reflection, refraction, or shadowing locally, you would have to go to each object and select them individually. In this chapter, you learn how to control some of those features globally, applying settings to a whole scene. You also learn ways of controlling the quality of the image generated, so that in the development phase, when you don't have to see high-quality images, you can sacrifice quality in order to get a faster preview. Finally, you take a look at Polyray's powerful math support.

Shading Flags

In Table 2.1 (which also is located on your tear-out card in the back of the book), one of the command-line parameters accepted by Polyray is -q. This parameter controls the quality of the shading. By reducing the amount of shading features, you can increase the speed of the ray tracer and have a quick turn-around of the final image, and do some interesting special effects.

Table 6.1 shows the options controlled by the -q parameter.

Table 6.1. Shading options controlled with command-line parameter -q.	
Value	**Option**
1	shadows
2	reflection
4	refraction
8	highlights (both sides of a surface)
16	check if object casts shadows
32	check primary light rays (rays that go from observer to object)

You can turn on or off any option by including or excluding it when defining the parameter. For example, assume you have an image that contains many reflective objects. Light bounces everywhere, causing the ray tracer to dedicate more time to checking the reflections. In order to speed up the image, you can turn off that option:

1	shadows generation
4	refraction
8	highlights both sides of a surface
16	shadows checking (determines if object casts shadows)
+32	primary rays (rays from the observer to the object)
61	parameter value

If DEMO.PI is the scene file, the command-line parameter is:

POLYRAY DEMO.PI -q 61 [press the Enter key]

As you can see, the only option missing is the second one (reflection). You can change any number of options this way.

If you wish to control those same options on specific objects, Polyray has defined the `shading_flag` keyword, which also uses the -q parameter values.

Polyray also has defined some handy keywords that represent the values of the different options. These definitions are available in Listing 6.1, the TEXTURES.INC file: .

Listing 6.1. Defined shading flag keywords (taken from TEXTURES.INC).

```
// Names of the various shading flags
define shadow_check            1
define reflect_check           2
define transmit_check          4
define two_sided_surface       8
define cast_shadows            16
define primary_rays            32

// Default shading flags during ray tracing—everything gets checked.
define all_shading_flags             shadow_check
                                   + reflect_check
                                   + transmit_check
                                   + cast_shadows
                                   + two_sided_surface
                                   + primary_rays

// Shading flags for surfaces that shouldn't have their backsides illuminated
define one_sided_surface   all_shading_flags - two_sided_surface
```

Since Polyray understands mathematical expressions, the keyword `all_shading_flags` is defined by adding all of the possible options (each option represents a value).

If you use this method of defining shading flags for each object in CSG operations, you must apply the flags to each object in the definition.

Rendering Method

Ray tracing produces the highest quality output. Polyray supports two other rendering methods: scan conversion and wireframe. You can select which rendering method by using the -r command (see Table 2.1). Both methods are described here briefly.

Scan Conversion

Scan conversion handles all objects as a collection of polygons. You can improve the quality of the surfaces by increasing the number of polygons used to create the object. You can improve the smoothness of the surface by using two keywords: u_steps and v_steps. These keywords define the number of subdivisions to be performed on a given object. The u_steps keyword refers to the dimension you measure from left to right. The v_steps keyword refers to the dimension you measure from top to bottom. Note the following example:

```
object {
    sphere <0, 0, 0>, 2
    shiny_red
    u_steps 10
    v_steps 30
}
```

The sphere in this scene is divided from the north pole to the south pole into 30 segments, while the equator (from left to right) will be subdivided 10 times. Increasing the number of subdivisions increases the smoothness of the surface.

Scan conversion can be faster than ray tracing depending on the amount of u_steps and v_steps, but there is a catch—it requires substantial amounts of memory. You may find that with your current computer setup, you may be able to ray-trace scenes, but not scan-convert them due to the memory requirements.

Finally, when scan-converting a scene, use the command-line parameter -r1. Use the -q parameter also to explicitly turn on or off shading options, since scan conversion by default does not support shadows, reflectivity, or transparency.

Wireframe

Wireframe representation is a variation of scan conversion. Only the edges of the polygons are visible, giving the appearance that the objects are made with wires. One of the benefits of wireframe representation is that it generates the image the fastest. On the other hand, wireframe rendering does not support Boolean operations.

To select wireframe rendering, use the -r2 command-line option to select wireframe representation and -W to pause the screen. Figure 6.1 displays the scene file INVERSE.PI in wireframe representation. Note that none of the Boolean operations are shown in the image.

Mathematical Expressions

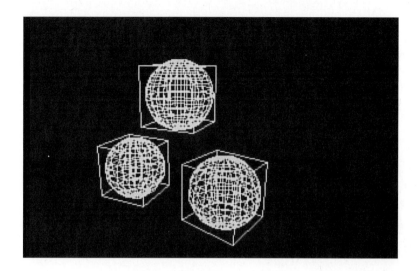

Figure 6.1

*Wireframe
representation
of scene
INVERSE.PI.*

One of Polyray's most powerful features is the capability to understand mathematical expressions. There are four valid types of expressions: floating point, vectors, arrays, and conditional.

Floating Point Expressions

Floating point expressions, or "fexper," can consist of integer numbers (1, 5, –3) real numbers (0.05, 25.93, 100.04) alone or combined with functions that return real or integer numbers. Table 6.2 presents a list of available functions in Polyray that return a number. The available mathematical relations are:

(fexper)	Parenthesized expression
fexper 1 ^ fexper 2	fexper1 to the power of fexper2
fexper * fexper	Multiplication
fexper / fexper	Division
fexper + fexper	Addition
fexper – fexper	Subtraction
–fexper	Minus sign

185

Table 6.2. Functions that return integer and floating point numbers.

Notes:

1. All trigonometric functions require the argument in radians

2. fexper is a floating point expression

3. vexper is a vector expression, for example: <23.6, 2*10.3, 0.0>

acos(fexper)	Arccosine
asin(fexper)	Arcsin
atan(fexper)	Arctangent
ceil(fexper)	Ceiling function, finds smallest integer not less than fexper
cos(fexper)	Cosine
cosh(fexper)	Hyperbolic cosine
degrees(fexper)	Converts radians to degrees
exp(fexper)	Standard exponential function
fabs(fexper)	Absolute value
floor(fexper)	Floor function, finds largest integer not greater than fexper
fmod(fexper, fexper)	Modulus function for floating point values
ln(fexper)	Natural logarithm
log(fexper)	Logarithm base 10
noise(vexper,fexper)	Correlated noise function based on a location vector <x,y,z>. fexper is the number of times the output will be fed back as a new input to generate a new pseudo-random number between 0 and 1.
pow(fexper1,fexper2)	Exponentiation (same as fexper1 ^ fexper2)
radians(fexper)	Converts degrees to radians

sawtooth(fexper)	Sawtooth function, range between 0 and 1
sin(fexper)	Sine
sinh(fexper)	Hyperbolic sine
sqrt(fexper)	Square root
tan(fexper)	Tangent
tanh(fexper)	Hyperbolic tangent
visible(vexper,vexper)	Returns 1 if second point is visible from the first
vexper[i]	Extract component i from a vector or an array
vexper . vexper	Dot product of two vectors
lfexperl	Absolute value (same as fabs)
lvexperl	Length or magnitude of a vector

Floating point expressions can be used anywhere a real number is required. Assume you want to create a sphere with the center located at the origin <0, 0, 0> and the surface touching the point <1, 1, 3>. To find the radius, you can calculate the distance between <0, 0, 0> and the point <1, 1, 3>:

vector from origin to point = point – origin

$$= < 1–0, 1–0, 3–0 >$$

$$= <1, 1, 3>$$

the distance or magnitude of the vector is

$$\sqrt{x^2 + y^2 + z^2} \ \text{ or } \ \sqrt{1^2 + 1^2 + 3^2}$$

The magnitude of a vector can be written in Polyray as l<1, 1, 3>l. First, transfer these calculations to Polyray:

```
define origin < 0, 0, 0>
define m <1, 1, 3>
define radius ¦ m - origin ¦
object {
    sphere origin, radius
    shiny_green
}
```

In this case, you didn't need a calculator to find out any numbers; Polyray takes care of the calculations. By changing the location vectors origin and m, you can redefine new spheres.

Try another example. Assume you are interested in creating a group of spheres that will model a sine function. The sine function will be used as the y value:

```
define p1 <0,   sin(0), 0>
define p2 <5,   sin(radians(5)), 0>
// radians(5) = convert 5 degrees to radians
define p3 <10, sin(radians(10)), 0>
define p4 <15, sin(radians(15)), 0>
define p5 <20, sin(radians(20)), 0>
define p6 <25, sin(radians(25)), 0>
...ect...
object {
     sphere p1, 0.2
      ...ect...
}
object {
     sphere p2, 0.2
      ...ect...
}
object {
     sphere p3, 0.2
      ...ect...
}
.... ect ...
```

This previous example can be accomplished using arrays (presented later in this chapter).

Vectors

As you can see in the previous example, floating point expressions can be used inside vectors. You are already familiar with various vectors such as colors <R, G, B>, and the ones used in the viewpoint definition:

```
viewpoint {
     from <x, y, z>
     at <x, y, z>
     up <x, y, z>
     ...ect...
}
```

The keywords `from`, `at`, and `up` all use vectors to define locations and directions. Each of the values of a vector is called a *component* and can consist of any floating point expression.

The operations you can perform between vectors and floating point expressions are

vexper + vexper	Addition
vexper – vexper	Subtraction
vexper * vexper	Cross product
vexper * fexper	Scaling of a vector by a scalar
fexper * vexper	Scaling of a vector by a scalar
vexper / fexper	Inverse scaling of a vector by a scalar

Table 6.3 presents a list of functions that return vectors.

Table 6.3. Functions that return vectors.

brownian(vexper)	Makes a random displacement of a vector
color_wheel (x, y, z)	RGB color wheel using x and z, the color returned is based on <x, z> using the chart below. Intermediate colors are generated by interpolation.

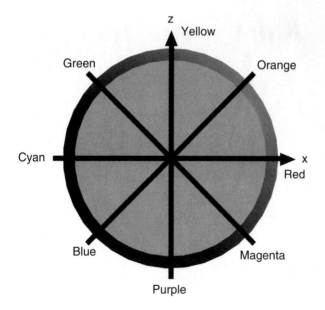

continues

Table 6.3. Continued.

rotate(vexper,vexper)	Rotate the point given in the first argument by the angles given in the second argument. (Angles in degrees.)
rotate(vexper,vexper,fexper)	Rotate the point in the first argument around the axis given in the second argument, by the angle in the third argument. (Angle in degrees.)
reflect(vexper,vexper)	Reflect the first vector about the second vector (second vector is rotated about the first by 180 degrees).
dnoise(vexper,fexper)	Returns a pseudo-random vector where each component is between 0 and 1. The value fexper determines the number of times the output will be fed back to generate a new random vector.

In addition to the functions presented in Table 6.3, Polyray has a set of vectors that are defined at run time (not in the scene file but as Polyray analyzes the data internally). Some of the vectors are defined in terms of object coordinates; others describe world coordinates. Object coordinates are measured from a coordinate system that is attached to the object internally by Polyray, and world coordinates are measured from the global coordinate system (the one you use to define the location of objects). The defined vectors are:

I	The direction of the ray that struck the object.
P	The point of intersection in object coordinates. (You can also use x = P[0], y = P[1], or z = P[2] to represent single components of P.)
x, y, z	Single components of P.
N	The normal vector at the point of intersection in world coordinates.
W	The point of intersection in world coordinates.

Listings 6.2 and 6.3 present an example of using the defined vectors in Polyray.

Listing 6.2. Using the color wheel function (WHEEL1.PI).

```
//WHEEL1.PI
define WheelTexture
texture {
    special surface {
        color color_wheel(x, y, z)
        normal N
        ambient 0.2
        diffuse 0.8
        specular white, 0.2
        microfacet Reitz 10
        }
}
include "colors.inc"
include "texture.inc"
viewpoint {
  from      <1, 1.3, -7.0 >
  at        <0.0, -1.5, 0.0 >
  up        <0.0, 1.0, 0.0 >
  angle      45
  resolution 100,100
  aspect     1.0
}
// LIGHT_SOURCE
directional_light < 10 ,  10 , -10  >
// LIGHT_SOURCE
directional_light <-10 ,  10 , -10  >
background grey
    object {
        box <-1, -1, -1>, <1, 1, 1>
        WheelTexture
        rotate <-10, 0, 0>
    }
    object {
        sphere <0, -3, 0>, 1.2
        WheelTexture
        rotate <-10, 180, 0>
    }
```

In Listing 6.2, the color_wheel function I use, to calculate the color value based on the current point intersected by the light ray. The coordinates x, y, and z are the components of P. In addition, the normal is N, which is the normal of the surface at the point where light intersects it. Figure 6.2 shows the resulting color wheel applied to a cube and a sphere. The top of the cube displays the color wheel variation. The procedure can be summarized by saying that initially a light ray intersects an object at the location P (or x, y, z). In order for Polyray to calculate the color of the surface, it substitutes the x, y, and z values into color_wheel, returning a color vector.

Figure 6.2

Using the color wheel function (WHEEL1.PI).

In order to cause turbulence, there are two approaches: create a disturbance in the color function or deform the surface by modifying the normal. Listing 6.3 uses both approaches. Figure 6.3 shows the result.

Listing 6.3. Creating turbulence in Listing 6.2 (WHEEL2.PI).

```
//WHEEL2.PI
define WheelTexture
texture {
    special surface {
        color color_wheel(x, y, z) + 2*(dnoise(3*P,3) - <0.5, 0.5, 0.5>)
        normal N + 10*(dnoise(P,3) - <0.5, 0.5, 0.5>)
        ambient 0.2
        diffuse 0.8
        specular white, 0.2
        microfacet Reitz 10
        }
}
include "colors.inc"
include "texture.inc"
viewpoint {
 from      <1, 1.3, -7.0 >
 at        <0.0, -1.5, 0.0 >
 up        <0.0, 1.0, 0.0 >
 angle     45
 resolution 100,100
 aspect    1.0
}
// LIGHT_SOURCE
```

```
directional_light < 10 ,  10 , -10 >
// LIGHT_SOURCE
directional_light <-10 ,  10 , -10 >
background grey
    object {
        box <-1, -1, -1>, <1, 1, 1>
        WheelTexture
        rotate<-10, 0, 0>
    }
    object {
        sphere <0, -3, 0>, 1.2
        WheelTexture
        rotate<-10, 180, 0>
    }
```

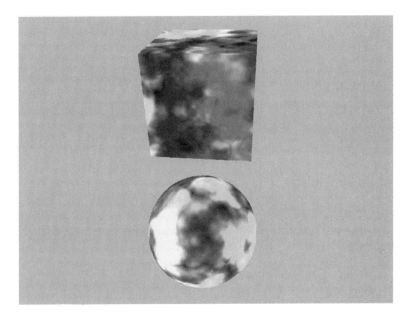

Figure 6.3

Creating turbulence by modifying surface colors and normals (WHEEL2.PI).

In Listing 6.3 the color is affected by adding a noise function:

```
color color_wheel(x, y, z) + 2*(dnoise(3*P,3) - <0.5, 0.5, 0.5>)
```

The `dnoise(3*P,3)` function takes the ray intersection point and scales it by a factor of 3. The second 3 is the amount of times that the random-generated vector is fed back to the `dnoise` function to increase its randomness (this number is usually referred to as *octaves*). Since the resulting vector will have components in the range of 0 to 1, the vector `<0.5, 0.5, 0.5>` is used to reduce the total effect. Finally, the resulting vector is scaled by 2 and added to the color vector generated by `color_wheel(x,y,z)`.

The normal of a surface can be modified by adding a disturbance to the original normal (N), the same way we did with the surface color:

```
normal N + 10*(dnoise(P,3) - <0.5, 0.5, 0.5>)
```

Again, a disturbance is added to the normal N. This will have the effect of changing the orientation of the surface; for example, if a flat surface is used, the changes in the normal vectors will make the surface appear bent.

Arrays

Polyray can group sets of expressions (fexper, vexper) into lists called arrays. The syntax for an array is

```
define ArrayName [ exper#1, exper#2, exper#3,...,exper#N]
```

where exper#1, exper#2, exper#3, ..., exper#N can be floating point expressions or vectors. Arrays can have more than one dimension; in other words, an array can have elements which are arrays themselves.

The next example uses three arrays to hold red, green, and blue color values and a fourth array to save vector positions. To select specific elements of any array, the array name is followed by the index (number) of the array element enclosed in square brackets (the first element starts with the index 0). Listing 6.4 is a section of a scene that presents this method.

Listing 6.4. Using arrays (section of a scene file).

```
define R [0, 0.5, 0.7, 0.9]
define G [0.1, 0.15, 0.6, 0.65]
define B [0.05, 0.4, 0.45, 0.77]
define  POS [<0, 0, 0>, <1, 0, 0>, <0, 1, 0>, <0, 0, 1>]
object {
     sphere POS[0],2
     texture{ surface {color <R[2], G[2], B[3]> }}
}
object {
     sphere POS[1],2
     texture{ surface {color <R[1], G[2], B[0]> }}
}
```

The first sphere is located at <0, 0, 0> and has the surface color <0.7, 0.6, 0.77>. The second sphere is located at <1, 0, 0> and the color is <0.5, 0.6, 0.05>.

If you recall the example where we were positioning spheres to model a sine function, we can replace the code using arrays:

```
define Loc  [  <0,    sin(0), 0>,
              <5,    sin(radians(5)), 0> ,
              <10, sin(radians(10)), 0>,
              <15, sin(radians(15)), 0>,
              <20, sin(radians(20)), 0>,
              <25, sin(radians(25)), 0> ]
object {
     sphere Loc[0], 0.2
       ...ect...
}
object {
     sphere Loc[1], 0.2
       ...ect...
}
object {
     sphere Loc[2], 0.2
       ...ect...
}
```

In Chapter 8, you'll take a look at how arrays can be used in animation.

Conditional Expressions

Conditional expressions have two values depending on the status of a certain expression. If the expression is True, one value is given; if it's False, the other is returned. The syntax for a conditional expression is

```
(cexper ? true_value : false_value)
```

where cexper has one of the following forms:

Conditional Expression	Returns True If
!cexper	NOT(cexper)
cexper && cexper	cexper AND cexper
cexper || cexper	cexper OR cexper
fexper < fexper	fexper LESS THAN fexper
fexper <= fexper	fexper LESS THAN OR EQUAL TO fexper
fexper > fexper	fexper GREATER THAN fexper
fexpcr >= fexper	fexper GREATER THAN OR EQUAL TO fexper
fexper == fexper	fexper IS IDENTICAL TO fexper
vexper == vexper	vexper IS IDENTICAL TO vexper

and true_value or false_value can be a floating point expression or a vector expression.

Listing 6.5 presents two examples of conditional expressions. The first expression defined as "ĸ"

```
define K (x >= -1 && x <= 1 && y >= -1 && y <= 1 ?  white: red)
```

determines the color of the surface. The condition can be described as "IF x is between the values of –1 and 1 AND y is also between the values of –1 and 1, THEN the color of the surface will be white, ELSE the color will be red."

The expression defined as "T"

```
define T (x >= -1 && x <= 1 && y >= -1 && y <= 1 ?     1 : 0)
```

can be described as "IF x is between the values of –1 and 1 AND y is also between –1 and 1 THEN return a value of 1, ELSE a zero is returned."

Recall that x, y, and z are the components of the point P defined by Polyray, and they refer to the point where the current light ray intersects the surface of the object. The coordinate system is "local" (attached to the object).

Finally, the texture definition for the outer sphere,

```
texture {
  special surface {
      color K
      ambient 0.3
      diffuse 0.1
      specular 0.1
      reflection white, 0.3
      transmission T ,1
  }
}
```

uses both ĸ and T. Observe that T is used to determine if a given area of the surface is transparent or not. Another important point is that in order to use the run-time variables I, N, P, x, y, z, and w inside of a texture, you must use the "special surface" texture definition and not "surface" (refer to Chapter 4, sections "Texture Surface Parameters" and "Functional"). Recall that at run time the "special surface" definition can evaluate expressions that make reference to the variables I, N, P, x, y, z, and w.

Now that you have seen the major components of the scene, here is the rationale behind it. Your goal is to create an object that has a "window" to let you see whatever is inside of it. You can accomplish this with Boolean operators, but we are looking for an alternate method. First, the window has two distinct features: it's transparent and colorless. Second, the window has limits, which we chose as x between the values of –1 and 1 and y between the values of –1 and 1. The z value is not important since the window will be located in the front (where light rays hit first).

To take care of the transparency requirement, the expression T changes to 1 (fully transparent) when the light ray hits the window, and to 0 when it is outside of it. The color is approached the same way—it is white when the light is inside the window and red when touching the rest of the sphere. To test the effectiveness of this approach, create a blue sphere inside the outer one. If the window is transparent, you'll be able to see it; if the window doesn't act as a filter, the inner sphere will be blue. Figure 6.4 displays the final image. A checkered plane was positioned on the back to see if a second window is created in the back of the sphere. (it isn't.)

There are better ways to simplify the K and T expressions. An alternate approach could be

```
define Status (x >= -1 && x <= 1 && y >= -1 && y <= 1 ?  1: 0)
define K (Status == 1? white: red)
define T  Status
```

Try experimenting with other methods.

Listing 6.5. Using conditional expressions (COND.PI).

```
//COND.PI
include "colors.inc"
include "texture.inc"
define Plane_YZ   object {
              polygon 4, <0,-10000,10000>, <0,10000,10000>,
                         <0,10000,-10000>, <0,-10000,-10000>
              }
define K (x >= -1 && x <= 1 && y >= -1 && y <= 1 ?  white: red)
define T (x >= -1 && x <= 1 && y >= -1 && y <= 1 ?    1 : 0)
viewpoint {
 from      <1, 1, -7.0 >
 at        <0.0, 0.0, 0.0 >
 up        <0.0, 1.0, 0.0 >
 angle     45
 resolution 100,100
 aspect    1.0
}
// LIGHT_SOURCE
light < 5 ,  5 , -10  >
// LIGHT_SOURCE
light <-5 ,  5 , -10  >

object {
   sphere <0, 0, 0>, 2
   texture {
    special surface {
      color K
      ambient 0.3
      diffuse 0.1
      specular 0.1
      reflection white, 0.3
```

continues

197

Listing 6.5. Continued.

```
transmission T ,1
      }
    }
}
object {
   sphere <0, 0, 0> , 1
   shiny_blue
}
object {
  Plane_YZ
  rotate <0, 90, 0>
  translate <0, 0, 10>
  texture {checker matte_white, matte_black}
}
```

Figure 6.4

Creating a window on a sphere with conditional expressions (COND.PI).

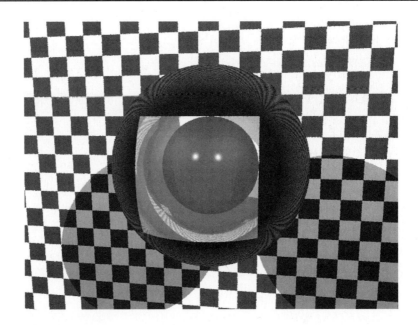

Summary

In this chapter, you saw different ways of speeding up the rendering process, either by reducing the quality of the image or by using alternate rendering methods. To reduce the quality of the image for faster viewing, you can disable some of Polyray's shading features using the -q command-line parameter or the keyword `shading_flag` inside of the scene file. Another way to speed up the image-creation process is to select scan conversion or wireframe representation. Both are fast methods, but scan conversion

requires a large amount of memory, and wireframe representation can only be used to preview the geometry. Wireframe representation does not support Boolean operations.

In addition, you took a detailed look at Polyray's powerful math support. Polyray can understand a wide variety of floating point and vector functions which you can use throughout the scene. Another interesting feature is the use of the run-time variables I, N, P, x, y, z, and W, which give information concerning the direction of the light ray, and the location where it intersected a given object. You can use these to modify the color and characteristics of the surface.

Arrays are collections of vectors or expressions you can organize in list form. You can select individual elements of an array by using the array name followed by the element index enclosed in square brackets . Finally, you studied conditional expressions, which are expressions that return two values or vectors depending on the relationship between two expressions.

In the next chapter, you'll be introduced to 3-D modeling as a tool for creating scenes visually. You'll have the chance to use POVCAD, a wireframe-based 3-D modeler that can help you create different scenes by positioning objects visually. You'll take a look at POVCAD's major features and have the opportunity to create scenes for the Polyray ray tracer.

Using a 3-D Modeler (POVCAD)

Included with this book is POVCAD, a wireframe-based modeler which will be used as a front-end for Polyray. POVCAD is a 3-D modeler you can use for prototyping your own scene files. By visually positioning the objects on-screen, you can get a better idea of how the final scene will look. After the scene is complete, POVCAD generates Polyray code which can be used with little or no modification. A modeler should not be a substitute for understanding how to use the ray tracer in the first place—which is the main reason why this chapter appears near the end of the book. Now that you've seen the creation of scene files by hand, you can create better compositions and modify them efficiently.

The chapter is a collection of tutorials. Each scene you'll see created will have the name TUTOR#.PI; # will be replaced with the corresponding tutorial number. It is beneficial to study how the modeler creates each scene file.

Introduction

I wrote POVCAD some time ago because of my own need to be able to visualize how objects were located in a scene file. Ray tracing the image every time you move an object puts stress on the user as well as the computer! Use a modeler as a tool to help you go beyond the worries of correct syntax, typing, and remembering the format of a function, and get on with developing a more interesting scene. Here is a list of objects you can create with POVCAD:

- plane
- cylinder
- cone
- sphere
- ellipsoid
- torus
- box
- height field
- Raw data files
- Sweep (solid of revolution, also known as Lathe)
- Extrude
- Bézier patches
- Polygon Decomposition (tessellation) of curves

- light sources
- viewpoint definition

This is by no means a complete list. Polyray has more features than those supported by POVCAD. As time progresses I'll be adding other features to POVCAD. You'll become familiar with POVCAD's features as you develop your own scene files.

Note to DOS and Windows users: POVCAD is available in both versions. Usually the Windows version is ahead of the DOS version in terms of features. This chapter presents the features included in the Windows version of POVCAD. Some of these features might not be in the corresponding DOS version, but they should be added in future releases.

Running POVCAD

The program is usually distributed with the name POVCAD.EXE or possibly POVCAD?.EXE where ? is replaced by a number. I'm assuming you have installed the program following the instructions in the READ.ME file that comes with the disk.

To run the DOS version, simply make the directory where POVCAD resides the current directory and type

  POVCAD [press the Enter key]

To run the Windows version from file manager, click the POVCAD.EXE file; to run it from the desktop, select **R**un from the **F**ile menu. Type the path and name of the executable file, and press Enter. If you're running the Windows version, after running POVCAD, select Polyray as your ray tracer and you should get a screen similar to figure 7.1.

Figure 7.1

*Initial POVCAD
screen
(Windows
version).*

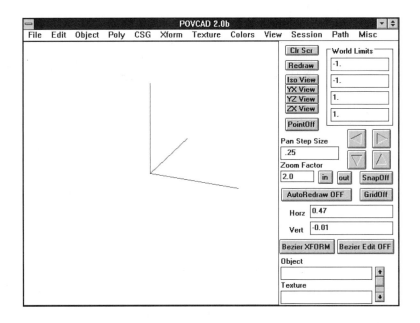

Figure 7.2 shows a section of figure 7.1 describing the name of the icons
used for quick access to some of POVCAD's commands.

Figure 7.2

*Icon section in
POVCAD.*

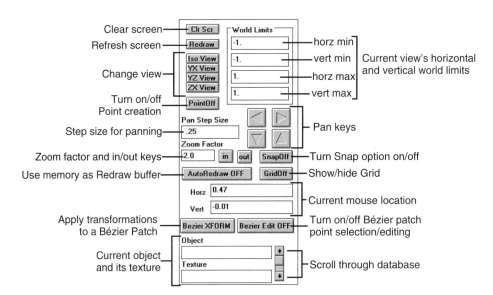

Table 7.1 describes each icon in more detail:

Table 7.1. The POVCAD icons.

Icon	Description
Clr Scr	Clears the drawing area, leaving only the 3-D axis.
Redraw	Redraws the complete scene and 3-D axis, if grid is ON it will be refreshed too.
Iso View	Scene is presented in a perspective point of view.
YX View	Scene is presented with y as the vertical axis and x as the horizontal axis.
YZ View	Scene is presented with y as the vertical axis and z as the horizontal axis.
ZX View	Scene is presented with z as the vertical axis and x as the horizontal axis.

World Limits	Displays the limits of the horizontal and vertical axis. The order of the numbers from top to bottom is:
	
	    horizontal minimum
	
	    vertical minimum
	
	    horizontal maximum
	
	    vertical maximum
	
	To change these numbers, from the View menu select the World command.

PointOff	Turn ON/OFF point creation routine. If status is ON, then any point clicked on the drawing area is saved and a curve is created.
Left, Right, Down, Up	Displaces the scene in the appropriate direction (Pan). The increment of this displacement can be modified by changing the number inside the Pan Step Size text box.
in, out	Zoomin and Zoomout keys. The zoom factor can be modified by changing the number inside the Zoom Factor text box.

continues

Table 7.1. Continued.

Icon	Description
SnapOff	Turn snap funtion ON/OFF. If status is ON any point created will be moved to the nearest grid point.
AutoRedraw OFF	Selects between saving the drawing area to a buffer in memory (redraw is needed less) or continuous redraw. Enabling AutoRedraw (ON) will consume more memory. Normally is disabled.
GridOff	Show or hide grid.
Horz, Vert	Current mouse location.
Bézier XFORM	Apply transformations to a selected Bézier Patch.
Bézier Edit OFF	Enable/disable editing of current selected Bézier Patch.
Object	Displays current selected or created object.
Texture	Displays current selected or created object's texture. ScrollBar (located to the right of Object and Texture) scrolls through database of created objects. To view the complete list select the Session command.

The top menu selections are:

File	File operations.
Edit	Select objects or points to be deleted.
Object	Select from the different primitives (sphere, cone, sweep, and so on).
Poly	Create flat plates with holes.
CSG	Boolean operations menu.
XForm	Applies transformations to objects and curves.
Texture	Select from a list of predefined textures.
Colors	Select from a list of predefined colors.
View	Changes world limits, views (Iso, YX, and so on), grid spacing.

Icon	Description
Session	Displays a complete list of all the objects in the database.
Path	Saves points created with the mouse, applies curve smoothing and other data file operations.
Misc	Create light sources, define the viewpoint of the scene, select setting for Bézier patch displaying.

The best way to learn how to use POVCAD is by creating your first scene. In the next section, you create a few spheres and attach textures to them. In addition, you locate a few light sources and define the viewpoint. Finally, you see a Polyray scene file created and studied.

Creating a Scene File (Tutorial #1)

In this section you go through the process of creating a quick scene, which is basically the same for any scene you develop. These are the steps to create TUTOR1.PI:

1. From the Object menu select the Sphere command.

2. Enter the following values as they are requested (press Enter after each answer):

Radius	0.3
x	0.0
y	0.0
z	0.0

3. Click the YX button to change the view. Now y is the vertical axis and x is the horizontal axis.

4. Click the center of the sphere. This selects the object.

5. Move the mouse to the location Horz = 0.53 and Vert = –0.53 (check the Horz and Vert mouse position boxes).

6. When the Copy/Move window appears, select Copy with the right mouse button.

At this point, a copy of the original sphere should have been created and located at the position where you pressed the right mouse button. If you made a mistake, select Delete All from the File menu and start again at step 1.

Continue with the following steps:

7. Select the sphere located at the origin by clicking the left mouse button at the center of the sphere.

8. Move the mouse to the location Horz = –0.53 and Vert = –0.53.

9. Press the right mouse button; when the Copy/Move window appears, select Copy.

Another copy of the sphere has been placed at the location where the right mouse button was pressed. Click the Iso View button to change the view. Figure 7.3 shows the image that should appear on your screen.

Figure 7.3

Three spheres created in POVCAD.

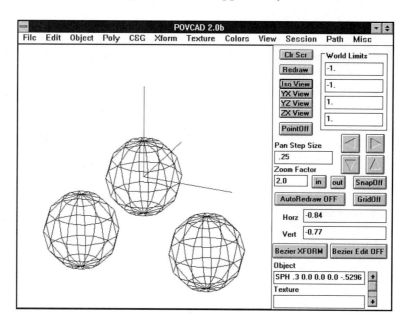

The next steps attach textures to the spheres. If you define a texture for the first sphere and copy it, all the copied spheres will have the same texture. This is why you perform these steps after creating all the objects.

1. Select the center sphere by clicking the left mouse button on the center of the object.

2. After clicking on the Texture command, click the down arrow to display a list of textures.

3. Select the reflective_grey texture.

4. Repeat the previous steps for the other two spheres, defining white_marble for the right sphere and sapphire_agate for the left sphere.

At this point, all three spheres should have textures associated with them. The next step is to create and position light sources. To create a light source, select the Light command from the Misc menu. Enter the following coordinates: X = 5, Y = 5, and Z = –5. Repeat the same process and create a second light source with the following coordinates: X = –5, Y = 5, and Z = –5. In order to view the light sources, you have to zoom out of the scene. To do this, click three times on the out button. The light sources appear as small coordinate systems. Observe that the world definition has changed from (–1, –1, 1, 1) to (–8, –8, 8, 8). Click three times on the in button to return to the original world definition.

The final step in the creation of a scene is the definition of a viewpoint. To create one, select the Viewpoint command from the Misc menu. Figure 7.4 shows what the Viewpoint definition windows looks like. Enter the appropriate numbers in your definition so it looks identical to figure 7.4. After entering the appropriate values, click the radio button titled "include viewpoint." This flags POVCAD to include the current viewpoint definition in the Polyray scene file. To exit the window, click OK.

Viewpoint			
viewpoint {			
from <	0.0	1.0	-5.0 >
at <	0.0	0.0	0.0 >
up <	0.0	1.0	0.0 >
angle	45		
hither	1.0e-3		
resolution	100	100	
aspect	1.0		
yon	1.0e5		⊙ include viewpoint
* dither_rays			
* dither_objects			OK
max_trace_depth	5		
aperture	0		
* focal_distance			
}			* leave empty to discard

Figure 7.4

Viewpoint screen.

As with any document file or program you are creating, it is important to regularly save the file. To save the current scene, select Save As from the File menu. Type the name "TUTOR1" and press Enter. Notice that the extension was not included, since POVCAD appends the .CAD extension automatically.

The scene has been completed. You can exit POVCAD at any time and return later to continue editing TUTOR1.CAD, but in order to create a Polyray-compatible file, you have to take one additional step. Select the Export command from the File menu. You see two choices, since POVCAD supports both Polyray and the Persistence of Vision (POV) ray tracers. Select Polyray and rename POVCAD.PI as TUTOR1.PI. Press Enter to generate the final Polyray file.

Taking a Closer Look at the TUTOR1.CAD Scene

If you exited POVCAD, return to it and load the TUTOR1.CAD scene by selecting Open from the File menu and clicking on the TUTOR1.CAD file.

POVCAD can display a list of all the objects that compose a given scene. To see this list, click the Session command. Figure 7.5 presents the Session List.

Figure 7.5

POVCAD's Session List for TUTOR1.CAD.

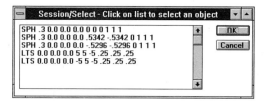

POVCAD uses the following format to represent spheres:

SPH Radius Rx Ry Rz Tx Ty Tz Sx Sy Sz

where

SPH	code for sphere
Radius	radius of the sphere
Rx, Ry, Rz	rotations in x, y, and z
Tx, Ty, Tz	translations in x, y, and z (defines the center point)
Sx, Sy, Sz	scaling factor in x, y, and z

POVCAD uses this format to represent light sources:

LTS 0.0 0.0 0.0 Tx Ty Tz Sx Sy Sz

where

0.0	not used
Tx, Ty, Tz	location of light source
Sx, Sy, Sz	scaling factor in x, y, and z (used only by POVCAD when drawing the light source symbols on the screen). Not used by Polyray.

Now compare the Session List with the content of the files TUTOR1.CAD and TUTOR1.TEX:

Contents of TUTOR1.CAD (geometry definition file)

```
"SPH .3 0.0 0.0 0.0 0 0 0 1 1 1"
"SPH .3 0.0 0.0 0.0 .5342 -.5342 0 1 1 1"
"SPH .3 0.0 0.0 0.0 -.5296 -.5296 0 1 1 1"
"LTS 0.0 0.0 0.0 5 5 -5 .25 .25 .25"
"LTS 0.0 0.0 0.0 -5 5 -5 .25 .25 .25"
```

Contents of TUTOR1.TEX (texture definition file)

```
"reflective_grey"
"white_marble"
"sapphire_agate"
" "
" "
```

Notice first that the content of the TUTOR1.CAD file is identical to the Session List. Then notice that each line in the TUTOR1.TEX file corresponds to the same line in the geometry file (*.CAD). Light Sources did not have any color associated with them so their entries are left blank.

This is a very complicated way of determining whether each object has a texture associated with it. An easier way is to use the scroll bar found at the bottom right corner of the screen. When you click the scroll bar, all of the objects available in the Session List are shown in the box labeled "Object" and the respective texture appears on the box labeled "Texture." If this box is blank, it signals that the current selected object has no texture associated with it. Notice that in figure 7.3 the Object box shows the string "SPH .3 0.0 0.0 0.0 –.5296" and the Texture box is empty. This image was generated before the textures were defined. If you wish to see the rest of the Object box string, click on it and use the right arrow from the keyboard to scroll through it.

The Polyray Scene File

Before you ray trace the image, take a look at the file TUTOR1.PI (see Listing 7.1).

Listing 7.1. First scene created with POVCAD (TUTOR1.PI).

```
//PROGRAM:   TUTOR1.PI GENERATED WITH POVCAD 2.0b (c) Alfonso Hermida 1993
//Created on 8/1/93 7:21:11 PM

include "colors.inc"
include "texture.inc"

viewpoint {
  from       <0.0, 1.0, -5.0 >
  at         <0.0, 0.0, 0.0 >
  up         <0.0, 1.0, 0.0 >
  angle      45
  hither     1.0e-3
  resolution 100,100
  aspect     1.0
  yon        1.0e5
  max_trace_depth 5
  aperture        0
}

// SPHERE
object {
  sphere < 0.0,0.0,0.0>, 0.3
    reflective_grey
}
// SPHERE
object {
  sphere < 0.5342,-0.5342,0.0>, 0.3
    white_marble
}
// SPHERE
object {
  sphere < -0.5296,-0.5296,0.0>, 0.3
    sapphire_agate
}
// LIGHT_SOURCE
  light < 5 ,  5 , -5  >

// LIGHT_SOURCE
  light <-5 ,  5 , -5  >
```

The file TUTOR1.PI is generated by POVCAD using the files TUTOR1.CAD and TUTOR1.TEX. The objects are generated in the same order they were created. The light sources are at the end of the file. An important point:

The coordinates of the spheres may vary a little from the coordinates that you saw in the Horz and Vert boxes. This is due to the SNAP function being disabled. If you need precise location of objects click on the SnapOff icon to enable it. Coming back to the scene file, another interesting feature is that the viewpoint definition has a lot more information than you used in the previous chapters. This is the viewpoint generated (with my modifications):

```
viewpoint {
from      <0.0, 1.0, -5.0 >
at        <0.0, 0.0, 0.0 >
 up       <0.0, 1.0, 0.0 >
 angle    45
 //hither      1.0e-3
 resolution 100,100
 aspect    1.0
 //yon         1.0e5
 //max_trace_depth 5
 //aperture        0
}
```

Normally, I delete `hither`, `yon`, `max_trace`, and `aperture` (it's a personal choice; you don't have to). You can also comment them out using the `//` symbol as shown. This brings up an important point: Is the scene perfect once it is generated by POVCAD? The answer is, "Maybe." If you ray trace the image as it comes out you will not have any syntax errors, but the definition of the viewpoint could be improved. The objects are not centered and they look rather small. The screen is not used completely. You'll have to modify the file by hand using a text editor. After some experimentation, I made two additional changes to center and maximize the size of the objects:

```
from      <0.0, 1.0, -2.0 >
at        <0.0, -0.2, 0.0 >
```

If you include these two changes, the objects will be in the center of the screen and their size will be as large as possible.

Before you ray trace this scene, remember to copy the TUTOR1.PI file to the directory where POLYRAY resides or else you will get errors.

Figure 7.6 shows the final ray-traced TUTOR1.PI image.

Figure 7.6

TUTOR1.PI ray-traced image.

Using POVCAD Primitives (Tutorial #2)

In this session, you create a scene using a few of POVCAD's primitives. First, you create a plane to use as a floor. Then you create a sphere, an ellipsoid, a box, and a cone, each with a different texture or color. Finally, you define the light sources and viewpoint.

Floor:

1. From the Object menu, select Plane_Y.

2. Select Xform and type the following values, clicking OK when done:

    Scale x = 100, y = 100, and z = 100

3. Click Texture and select Stone1

At this point, the plane is not visible, since the world limits are (–1, –1, 1, 1) and the plane has limits in (–100, –100, 100, 100).

Sphere:

1. From the Object menu, select Sphere.

214

2. Enter the following values, pressing Enter after each input:

Radius	0.5
x	0.0
y	0.5
z	0.0

3. Double-click the out button to zoom out.

4. Select Texture and pick reflective_cyan. You don't have to select the sphere since it's the last object you created.

Ellipsoid:

1. From the Object menu, select Ellipsoid.

2. Enter the following values (press Enter after each input):

x Radius	1.0
y Radius	0.5
z Radius	0.5

3. Click Xform and type the following values, clicking OK when done:

Rotate	y	45.0
Trans	x	1.5
Trans	y	0.5

4. Select Texture, Stone13.

Box:

1. From the Object menu, select Box.

2. Enter the following dimensions (press Enter after each input):

x Length	0.5
y Length	0.5
z Length	2.0

3. Select Xform.

Trans	x	−1.5
Trans	y	0.5

4. Texture menu, reflective_gold.

Cone:

1. From the Object menu, select Cone.

2. Enter the values:

   Radius   0.5

   Height   1.0

3. Xform menu:

   Trans   y   1.0

   Trans   z −2.0

4. Select the Colors command, SkyBlue.

Torus:

1. Select Torus from the Object menu.

2. Enter the values:

   Minor Radius   0.3

   Major Radius   4.0

3. Xform menu:

   Trans   y 0.3

4. Texture menu, reflective_white.

At this point you should save the file, in case something goes wrong. To save the current session, from the File menu select the Save As command. Enter the name TUTOR2 and press the Enter key. The only objects missing on the scene are the light sources and the viewpoint definition.

Light Source:

1. From the Misc menu, select Light.

2. Enter the location:

   x position   −10.0

   y position   5.0

   z position   −10.0

Light Source:

1. Create another light source and enter the location:

         x position   10.0

         y position   5.0

         z position   −10.0

Save the session again, this time use the Save command (in the File menu) since the session already has a name. Figure 7.7 shows the screen displayed in POVCAD.

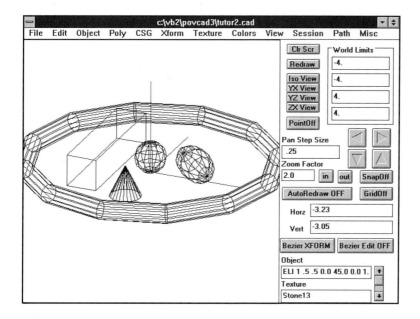

Figure 7.7

The TUTOR2 session in POVCAD.

Now create the viewpoint:

1. From the Misc menu, select viewpoint.

2. Enter the following parameters:

         from   <0, 5, −10>

         resolution   100,100

         aperture   0

3. Click the radio button labeled "include viewpoint."

4. To leave, click OK.

217

You don't have to save the scene again, since the viewpoint information is not saved by POVCAD. The final step is to create a Polyray file using the Export command. From the File menu, select Export and then Polyray. Replace the name POVCAD.PI with TUTOR2.PI and press Enter or click OK. You can exit POVCAD at this point.

If you try ray tracing TUTOR2.PI, Polyray reports that there is an error in line 25. A closer look at TUTOR2.PI (see Listing 7.2) shows that Polyray does not understand the texture name Stone1. This occurs because the file `"stones.inc"` was not included at the top of the scene file. After including it, I ray traced the image and found that the scene could use more light and the viewpoint was too near for my taste (you may have a different opinion). The next step was to edit the viewpoint definition and add an additional light source at the end of the scene. The light source was positioned at <0, 30, 0>. Figure 7.8 shows the results after ray tracing.

Listing 7.2. TUTOR2.PI.

```
//PROGRAM:    TUTOR2.PI GENERATED WITH POVCAD 2.0b (c) Alfonso Hermida 1993
//Created on 8/2/93 4:20:03 PM

include "colors.inc"
include "texture.inc"
include "stones.inc"                        // Added by hand!

viewpoint {
  from      <2.0, 5, -12.0 >                // Modified by hand!
  at        <0.0, 0.0, 0.0 >
  up        <0.0, 1.0, 0.0 >
  angle     45
  hither    1.0e-3
  resolution 100,100
  aspect    1.0
  yon       1.0e5
  max_trace_depth 5
  aperture        0
}
// PLANE (Polygon)
object {
// normal in Y direction
  polygon 4, <-1,0,1>, <-1,0,-1>, <1,0,-1>, <1,0,1>
    scale < 100.0,100.0,100.0>
    Stone1
}

// SPHERE
object {
  sphere < 0.0,0.5,0.0>, 0.5
```

```
      reflective_cyan
}
// ELLIPSOID
object {
 sphere <0.0, 0.0, 0.0>, 1
    scale <1.0, 0.5, 0.5>
     rotate < 0.0,45.0,0.0>
     translate < 1.5,0.5,0.0>
    Stone13
}
// BOX
object {
    box <-1, -1, -1>, <1, 1, 1>
     scale < 0.5,0.5,2.0>
     translate < -1.5,0.5,0.0>
    reflective_gold
}

// CONE
object {
    cone <0.0, -1.0,0.0>, 0.5, <0.0, 0.0, 0.0>, 0.0
     translate < 0.0,1.0,-2.0>
 texture { surface {color SkyBlue}}
}

// TORUS
object {
    torus 4.0,0.3, < 0.0, 0.0, 0.0>, <0.0, 1.0, 0.0>
     translate < 0.0,0.3,0.0>
    reflective_white
}

// LIGHT_SOURCE
  light <-10 ,  5 , -10  >

// LIGHT_SOURCE
  light < 10 ,  5 , -10  >

// LIGHT_SOURCE                          // Added by hand!
  light < 0 ,  30 , 0  >
```

219

Figure 7.8

Ray trace of TUTOR2.PI.

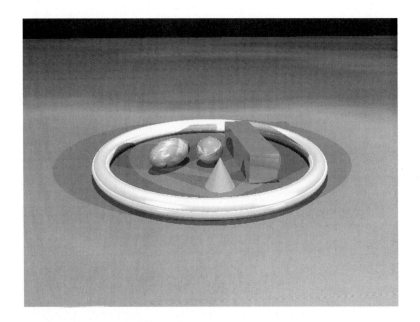

Creating Multiple Copies of Objects (Tutorial #3)

Looking back at figure 3.7, you can see the usefulness of having a function that creates multiple copies of an object. In this session, you have the opportunity to create an image similar to figure 3.7.

Center Torus:

1. Select Torus from the Object menu, and enter the values:

minor radius	0.1
major radius	1.0

2. To zoom out, double-click the out button.

3. Select Xform:

Rotate X	90

4. Select the YX View.

5. Select Texture, reflective_blue.

6. From the Object menu select Torus, enter the values:

   minor radius   0.1

   major radius   1.0

7. Click the SnapOff button (it should flip to SnapOn).

8. Click the GridOff button (it should flip to GridOn).

   At this point, the grid should appear on-screen. The Snap function forces the mouse to select only points which are located at the intersection of the grid lines. This method is used to select precise locations.

9. Locate the mouse at Horz = 1.6 and Vert = 0.0. Press the right mouse button.

10. Select Move (the second torus should move to the new position).

    You have created the center torus and one of the tori which will be copied and rotated through 330 degrees. In order to apply the rotation follow the next steps.

11. Move the mouse to the origin Horz = 0.0 and Vert = 0.0 (this will be your pivot point for the rotation). Press the right mouse button.

12. Select Copy/Rotate and enter the following values (Figure 7.9 shows the image that should appear on your screen.):

    rotation angle   30

    # of copies   11

13. If you wish to see other views of the image do so now by clicking on Iso View, YZ View, or ZX View. When done, return to YX View.

    The next step is to attach textures to each torus. You do this by simply selecting each torus and then defining the texture. To select a torus, click the mouse near the center of the torus. The torus selected will change colors.

14. Select one torus and attach a texture. Since the first torus already has a texture, you might want to start on torus #2 (the first copy). These are the textures I used for each one (all textures are of the type reflective_?):

221

1	blue	6	green	11	white
2	brown	7	grey	12	yellow
3	coral	8	orange	13	blue
4	cyan	9	red		
5	gold	10	tan		

Figure 7.9

POVCAD's display after creating multiple copies of the tori (Iso View, Grid Off).

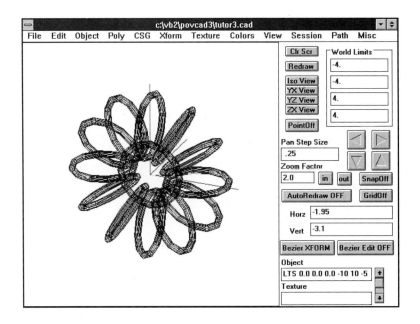

15. To check that each torus has a texture, use the scroll bar located at the lower right corner of the screen. To go back to the first object, press the scroll bar button with the arrow pointing up. If the texture box is empty, stop and select a texture for that object. Another way of checking the textures is to click on each one and check the texture box to see if it's empty. If it is, select a texture for it.

16. Save the image using the Save As command. Use the name TUTOR3 and press the Enter key.

Create two light sources with the following locations:

17. Light source #1 located at <5, 0, -10>.

18. Light source #2 located at <-10, 10, -5>.

19. Use the Save command to save the light source information.

20. Create the viewpoint (remember to click "include viewpoint"):

from	<1, 3, –5>
resolution	100,100
aperture	0

21. Generate the Polyray file using Export. Save the file as TUTOR3.PI.

Listing 7.3 presents the file generated by POVCAD for the TUTOR3 session. The viewpoint from vector was modified slightly to have a better view of the scene. Figure 7.10 shows the final ray-traced image.

Listing 7.3. TUTOR3.PI Polyray Scene File.

```
//PROGRAM:   TUTOR3.PI GENERATED WITH POVCAD 2.0b (c) Alfonso Hermida 1993
//Created on 8/2/93 9:45:15 PM

include "colors.inc"
include "texture.inc"

viewpoint {
  from      <1.0, 3.0, -7.0 >        // Modified by hand!
  at        <0.0, 0.0, 0.0 >
  up        <0.0, 1.0, 0.0 >
  angle     45
  hither    1.0e-3
  resolution 100,100
  aspect    1.0
  yon       1.0e5
  max_trace_depth 5
  aperture         0
}

// TORUS
object {
    torus 1.0,0.1, < 0.0, 0.0, 0.0>, <0.0, 1.0, 0.0>
    rotate < 90.0,0.0,0.0>
  reflective_blue
}
```

continues

223

Listing 7.3. Continued.

```
// TORUS
object {
    torus 1.0,0.1, < 0.0, 0.0, 0.0>, <0.0, 1.0, 0.0>
    translate < 1.6,0.0,0.0>
    reflective_brown
}

// TORUS
object {
    torus 1.0,0.1, < 0.0, 0.0, 0.0>, <0.0, 1.0, 0.0>
    rotate < 0.0,0.0,30.0>
    translate < 1.385641,0.8,0.0>
    reflective_coral
}

// TORUS
object {
    torus 1.0,0.1, < 0.0, 0.0, 0.0>, <0.0, 1.0, 0.0>
    rotate < 0.0,0.0,60.0>
    translate < 0.8,1.385641,0.0>
    reflective_cyan
}

// TORUS
object {
    torus 1.0,0.1, < 0.0, 0.0, 0.0>, <0.0, 1.0, 0.0>
    rotate < 0.0,0.0,90.0>
    translate < 0.0,1.6,0.0>
    reflective_gold
}

// TORUS
object {
    torus 1.0,0.1, < 0.0, 0.0, 0.0>, <0.0, 1.0, 0.0>
    rotate < 0.0,0.0,120.0>
    translate < -0.8,1.385641,0.0>
    reflective_green
}

// TORUS
object {
    torus 1.0,0.1, < 0.0, 0.0, 0.0>, <0.0, 1.0, 0.0>
    rotate < 0.0,0.0,150.0>
    translate < -1.385641,0.8,0.0>
    reflective_grey
}

// TORUS
object {
    torus 1.0,0.1, < 0.0, 0.0, 0.0>, <0.0, 1.0, 0.0>
    rotate < 0.0,0.0,180.0>
    translate < -1.6,0.0,0.0>
    reflective_orange
}
```

```
// TORUS
object {
    torus 1.0,0.1, < 0.0, 0.0, 0.0>, <0.0, 1.0, 0.0>
    rotate < 0.0,0.0,210.0>
    translate < -1.385641,-0.8,0.0>
    reflective_red
}

// TORUS
object {
    torus 1.0,0.1, < 0.0, 0.0, 0.0>, <0.0, 1.0, 0.0>
    rotate < 0.0,0.0,240.0>
    translate < -0.8,-1.385641,0.0>
    reflective_tan
}

// TORUS
object {
    torus 1.0,0.1, < 0.0, 0.0, 0.0>, <0.0, 1.0, 0.0>
    rotate < 0.0,0.0,270.0>
    translate < 0.0,-1.6,0.0>
    reflective_white
}

// TORUS
object {
    torus 1.0,0.1, < 0.0, 0.0, 0.0>, <0.0, 1.0, 0.0>
    rotate < 0.0,0.0,300.0>
    translate < 0.8,-1.385641,0.0>
    reflective_yellow
}

// TORUS
object {
    torus 1.0,0.1, < 0.0, 0.0, 0.0>, <0.0, 1.0, 0.0>
    rotate < 0.0,0.0,330.0>
    translate < 1.385641,-0.8,0.0>
    reflective_blue
}

// LIGHT_SOURCE
  light < 5 ,  0 , -10  >

// LIGHT_SOURCE
  light <-10 ,  10 , -5  >
```

Figure 7.10

Ray-traced image of TUTOR3.PI.

You can simplify the file TUTOR3.PI generated by POVCAD if you consider that each torus can be created by a simple rotation statement. You can use the second torus you created and convert it into a primitive. Then all the remaining objects can be created by rotating the primitive. Listing 7.4 presents TUTOR3M.PI, a modified version of TUTOR3.PI.

Remember the steps taken to create the rotating torus objects. First, create a torus and displace it in the x axis by 1.6 units. Then, select the pivot point for the rotation at the origin. Select the Copy/Rotate command by pressing the right mouse button. The rotation angle is 30 degrees and the number of copies to make is 11. Therefore, every 30 degrees a torus is created (a total of 11 copies, not counting the original).

From this, we can create a primitive called OuterTorus located at <1.6, 0, 0>.

```
define OuterTorus
object {
    torus 1.0,0.1, < 0.0, 0.0, 0.0>, <0.0, 1.0, 0.0>
    translate < 1.6,0.0,0.0>
}
```

The first (original) and the second copy would be

```
// TORUS
object {
```

226

```
      OuterTorus
      reflective_brown
}

// TORUS
object {
      OuterTorus
      rotate < 0.0,0.0,30.0>
      reflective_coral
}
```

In other words, the object definition could be generalized as

```
// TORUS
object {
      OuterTorus
      rotate < 0.0, 0.0, Rx >
      ...texture...
}
```

where Rx varies from 0 to 330 degrees.

Listing 7.4. Improving TUTOR3.PI by defining a primitive.

```
// TUTOR3M.PI
// HAND SIMPLIFIED VERSION

include "colors.inc"
include "texture.inc"


define OuterTorus
object {
      torus 1.0,0.1, < 0.0, 0.0, 0.0>, <0.0, 1.0, 0.0>
      translate < 1.6,0.0,0.0>
}

viewpoint {
  from      <1.0, 3.0, -7.0 >        // Modified by hand!
  at        <0.0, 0.0, 0.0 >
  up        <0.0, 1.0, 0.0 >
  angle     45
  hither    1.0e-3
  resolution 100,100
  aspect    1.0
  yon       1.0e5
  max_trace_depth 5
  aperture        0
}

// TORUS
object {
      torus 1.0,0.1, < 0.0, 0.0, 0.0>, <0.0, 1.0, 0.0>
      rotate < 90.0,0.0,0.0>
      reflective_blue
}
```

continues

227

Listing 7.4. Continued.

```
// TORUS
object {
    OuterTorus
    reflective_brown
}

// TORUS
object {
    OuterTorus
    rotate < 0.0,0.0,30.0>
    reflective_coral
}

// TORUS
object {
    OuterTorus
    rotate < 0.0,0.0,60.0>
    reflective_cyan
}

// TORUS
object {
    OuterTorus
    rotate < 0.0,0.0,90.0>
    reflective_gold
}

// TORUS
object {
    OuterTorus
    rotate < 0.0,0.0,120.0>
    reflective_green
}

// TORUS
object {
    OuterTorus
    rotate < 0.0,0.0,150.0>
    reflective_grey
}

// TORUS
object {
    OuterTorus
    rotate < 0.0,0.0,180.0>
    reflective_orange
}

// TORUS
object {
    OuterTorus
    rotate < 0.0,0.0,210.0>
    reflective_red
}

// TORUS
```

```
object {
   OuterTorus
   rotate < 0.0,0.0,240.0>
   reflective_tan
}

// TORUS
object {
   OuterTorus
   rotate < 0.0,0.0,270.0>
   reflective_white
}

// TORUS
object {
   OuterTorus
   rotate < 0.0,0.0,300.0>
   reflective_yellow
}

// TORUS
object {
   OuterTorus
   rotate < 0.0,0.0,330.0>
   reflective_blue
}

// LIGHT_SOURCE
   light < 5 ,   0 , -10  >

// LIGHT_SOURCE
   light <-10 ,  10 , -5  >
```

Both TUTOR3.PI and TUTOR3M.PI define the same geometry. POVCAD is helpful in the sense that it lets you create prototypes quickly. You will have many cases like this, where you will decide that the scene can be made simpler and more readable by modifying it yourself.

Using CSG Operations (Tutorial #4)

POVCAD supports the use of Boolean operations to create primitives. The following session creates an object we'll call Elbow. Elbow is created by intersecting a torus and a box. Two cylinders are attached at the ends of the torus section. The three objects together have a shape similar to a piece of metal tubing bent 90 degrees. The bend is round and smooth. Creating this object requires two Boolean operations: intersection (*) and union (+), which can be written as

```
(torus * box) + cylinder#1 + cylinder#2
```

229

After you create the Elbow primitive, you'll develop a second scene by hand that will use the Elbow extensively.

POVCAD follows a special approach in order to define Boolean operations. As an example, we'll take the expression (torus * box) + cylinder#1 + cylinder#2 and explain how it will be developed using the program. First, the sub-expression (torus * box) is composed of two objects but the result is just one: a section of the torus. You can then simplify the initial expression to

```
torus_section  + cylinder#1 + cylinder#2
```

where torus_section is (torus * box). POVCAD uses the format

```
UNION
torus_section
cylinder#1
cylinder#2
ENDF
```

to represent the operation (this is shown in the Session command when the scene is created). This can be described as "create a union of the objects torus_section, cylinder#1, and cylinder#2." The expression ENDF indicates that the UNION operation is completed, in other words ENDF flags POVCAD that this CSG operation is complete—ENDFinal.

The next step is to work on the expression torus_section, which we said was the same as (torus * box). POVCAD represents this operation as

```
INTRS
torus
box
ENDF
```

This can be described as "create an intersection between a torus and a box." The expression INTRS represents the intersection operation. If you substitute one into the other, you have

```
UNION
INTRS
torus
box
ENDF
cylinder#1
cylinder#2
ENDF
```

POVCAD understands that the first ENDF closes the INTRS operation and not the UNION, so it replaces it with END. In other words, END is used to complete partial CSG operations while ENDF denotes that the complete CSG operation is now finished.

```
UNION
INTRS
torus
```

```
box
END
cylinder#1
cylinder#2
ENDF
```

This is roughly the format used by POVCAD to generate a CSG object. Take a look at the TUTOR4.CAD file that you will be creating shortly:

```
"UNION"
"INTRS"
"TOR .2 .1 90.0 0.0 0.0 0.5 0.5 0.0 1 1 1"
"BOX 0.0 0.0 0.0 0.7 0.7 0.0 .2 .2 .2"
"END"
"CYL .1 .5 0.0 0.0 90.0 0.25 0.7 0.0 1 1 1"
"CYL .1 .5 0.0 0.0 0.0 0.7 0.25 0.0 1 1 1"
"ENDF"
"LTS 0.0 0.0 0.0 5 5 -5 .25 .25 .25"
"LTS 0.0 0.0 0.0 1 5 -5 .25 .25 .25"
```

Observe that it follows the same logic that was just explained. The main point to remember is to create the objects and select CSG commands in this same order. The command to create the END and ENDF words is Close and can be found in the CSG menu. The CSG menu has the following commands:

CSG Menu:

>   Union

>   Difference

>   Intersection

>   Composite (not used in Polyray)

>   Close

Based on the TUTOR4.CAD output, here are the steps to create such a scene in POVCAD:

Session List Display	Operation Performed By User
UNION	CSG menu, click Union
INTRS	CSG menu, click Intersection
TOR ...	Object menu, click Torus
BOX ...	Object menu, click Box
END	CSG menu, click Close
CYL ...	Object menu, click Cylinder

continues

231

Session List Display	Operation Performed By User
CYL ...	Object menu, click Cylinder
ENDF	CSG menu, click Close
LTS ...	Misc menu, click Light
LTS ...	Misc menu, click Light

The sequence is intuitive, and after this tutorial you will be able to create objects with any amount of complexity. The following session will take you through the complete steps. (The parameters following the keywords were omitted for simplicity.)

To start constructing the scene, select the YX View and follow these steps:

1. CSG menu, select Union

2. CSG menu, select Intersection

3. Objects menu, Torus:

Minor Radius	0.1
Major Radius	0.2

4. Xform:

Rotate x	90
Trans x	0.5
Trans y	0.5

5. Object menu, Box:

x Length	0.2
y Length	0.2
z Length	0.2

6. Xform:

Trans x	0.7
Trans y	0.7

7. CSG menu, select Close (this step closes the intersection operation but the union remains open).

Now, let's create the cylinders:

1. Object menu, Cylinder

Radius	0.1
Length	0.5

2. Xform:

Rotate z	90
Trans x	0.25
Trans y	0.7

3. Object menu, Cylinder

Radius	0.1
Length	0.5

4. Xform:

Trans x	0.7
Trans y	0.25

5. CSG menu, select Close (This step closes the union operation.)

   To define a texture for the object as a group, select the Sessions command from the main menu and pick ENDF. Click Texture and choose reflective_gold.

6. Save the session as TUTOR4 with the Save As command.

Figure 7.11 displays the screen generated by POVCAD.

Figure 7.11

Display of the Elbow primitive in POVCAD.

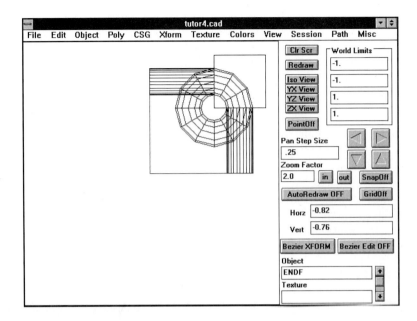

As always, create the light sources and the viewpoint:

1. Light source #1 located at <5, 5, –5>.

2. Light source #2 located at <1, 5, –5>.

3. Define viewpoint:

from	<0.5, 0.5, –2>
at	<0.5, 0.5, 0.0>
resolution	100, 100
aperture	0

Also click on "include viewpoint."

To complete the session, use the Save command, then Export to a Polyray file: TUTOR4.PI. Figure 7.12 is the ray-traced image of TUTOR4.PI. Listing 7.5 shows TUTOR4.PI.

Listing 7.5. Using CSG operations (TUTOR4.PI).

```
//PROGRAM:   TUTOR4.PI GENERATED WITH POVCAD 2.0b (c) Alfonso Hermida 1993
//Created on 8/3/93 9:52:34 AM

include "colors.inc"
include "texture.inc"

viewpoint {
 from      <0.5, 0.5, -2.0 >
 at        <0.5, 0.5, 0.0 >
 up        <0.0, 1.0, 0.0 >
 angle     45
 hither    1.0e-3
 resolution 100,100
 aspect    1.0
 yon       1.0e5
 max_trace_depth 5
 aperture         0
}

// CSG START
object {
// TORUS
object {
    torus 0.2,0.1, < 0.0, 0.0, 0.0>, <0.0, 1.0, 0.0>
    rotate < 90.0,0.0,0.0>
    translate < 0.5,0.5,0.0>

}

*
// BOX
object {
    box <-1, -1, -1>, <1, 1, 1>
    scale < 0.2,0.2,0.2>
    translate < 0.7,0.7,0.0>

}

+
// CYLINDER
object {
    cylinder <0.0, -0.25,0.0>, <0.0, 0.25, 0.0>, 0.1
    rotate < 0.0,0.0,90.0>
    translate < 0.25,0.7,0.0>

}

+
// CYLINDER
object {
    cylinder <0.0, -0.25,0.0>, <0.0, 0.25, 0.0>, 0.1
    translate < 0.7,0.25,0.0>

}
```

continues

Listing 7.5. Continued.

```
    reflective_gold
}
// CSG END

// LIGHT_SOURCE
  light < 5 ,   5 , -5  >

// LIGHT_SOURCE
  light < 1 ,   5 , -5  >
```

Figure 7.12

*Ray-traced
Elbow primitive
from TUTOR4.PI.*

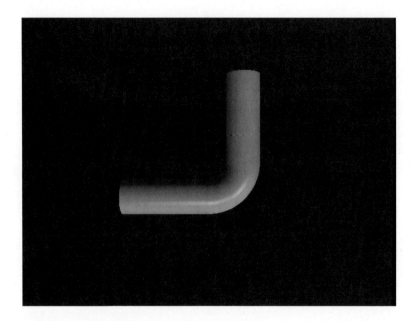

The scene file TUTOR4.PI only creates the Elbow primitive. Now that it's available, we can use it to develop more complex objects. Listing 7.6 presents a scene (TUTOR4M.PI) which expands on the Elbow object. The scene consists of a plane made of wood, with a tube on top of it that has been bent four times—roughly resembling the letter "P." This is done by making multiple copies of the Elbow.

Listing 7.6. Creating a letter "P" (TUTOR4M.PI).

```
//TUTOR4M.PI
//HAND MODIFIED

include "colors.inc"
include "texture.inc"
```

```
background grey

define Plane_XZ  object {
                 polygon 4, <-5,0,5>, <-5,0,-5>, <5,0,-5>, <5,0,5>
                }
//background grey


viewpoint {
  from      <1.0, 3, -9.0 >
  at        <0.0, 0.0, 0.0 >
  up        <0.0, 1.0, 0.0 >
  angle     45
  hither    1.0e-3
  resolution 100,100
  aspect    1.0
  yon       1.0e5
  max_trace_depth 5
  aperture        0
}

// LIGHT_SOURCE
  light < 5 ,  5 , -5  >

// LIGHT_SOURCE
  light < 1 ,  5 , -5  >


define Elbow                    // Create A Primitive

// CSG START
object {
// TORUS
object {
    torus 0.2,0.1, < 0.0, 0.0, 0.0>, <0.0, 1.0, 0.0>
    rotate < 90.0,0.0,0.0>
    translate < 0.5,0.5,0.0>
}

*
// BOX
object {
    box <-1, -1, -1>, <1, 1, 1>
    scale < 0.2,0.2,0.2>
    translate < 0.7,0.7,0.0>
}


+
// CYLINDER
object {
    cylinder <0.0, -0.25,0.0>, <0.0, 0.25, 0.0>, 0.1
    rotate < 0.0,0.0,90.0>
    translate < 0.25,0.7,0.0>
}


+
// CYLINDER
```

237

continues

Listing 7.6. Continued.

```
object {
    cylinder <0.0, -0.25,0.0>, <0.0, 0.25, 0.0>, 0.1
    translate < 0.7,0.25,0.0>
}

    reflective_gold
}
// CSG END


define DoubleElbow          // Create Another Primitive
object {
 object {
   Elbow
 }
+
 object {
   Elbow
   rotate <180, 0, 0>
 }
 reflective_gold
}

// Construct A New Object

object {
    Elbow
}

object {
  Elbow
  rotate<0, 180, 0>
  translate<-1, 0, 0>
}

object {
    cylinder <0.0, -0.5, 0.0>, <0.0, 0.5, 0.0>, 0.1
    rotate <0, 0, 90>
    translate < -0.5, 0.7, 0.0>
    reflective_gold
}

object {
    cylinder <0.0, -1.0, 0.0>, <0.0, 1.0, 0.0>, 0.1
    translate < -1.7, -0.7, 0.0>
    reflective_gold
}

object {
    DoubleElbow
    rotate<0, 0, -90>
}
```

```
object {
   Plane_XZ
   translate<0, -3, 4>
   wooden
}
```

In TUTOR4M.PI, two primitives are created: Elbow, which is the object created on TUTOR4.PI, and DoubleElbow, which is the Elbow object in union with another copy of itself, rotated 180 degrees about the x axis. It resembles an inverted letter "C":

```
define DoubleElbow
object {
 object {
   Elbow
 }
+
 object {
   Elbow
   rotate <180, 0, 0>
 }
 reflective_gold
}
```

Finally, figure 7.13 presents the ray-traced scene.

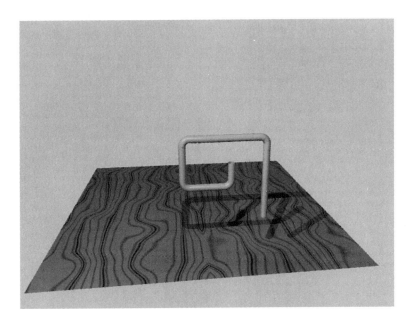

Figure 7.13

Bent tubing forming a letter "P" (TUTOR4M.PI).

239

Sweep and Extrude Objects (Tutorial #5)

POVCAD can create Sweep and Extrude objects. In Polyray, a Lathe object is the same as a Sweep object in POVCAD. Extrude objects are the same in both. For convenience, I'll use Sweep when referring to Lathe objects, and I'll call Extrude objects by their name.

In this session, you draw contours in POVCAD and rotate them 360 degrees to create a Sweep object. In addition, you Extrude a curve in the z axis. Both objects are created with two different methods: using POVCAD to generate flat triangles, and through the use of Polyray's Lathe and Extrude objects. As you see at the end of the session, there is no comparison between POVCAD's and Polyray's method. POVCAD generates a very rough object since the triangles are flat, but Polyray smooths the surface. To create the Lathe object, you use the program LATHE.BAS presented in Chapter 3. The Sweep object in Polyray is created by hand.

Let's start by creating the Sweep object:

1. Start POVCAD and click the YX View.

2. Click SnapOff (it should flip to SnapOn—Snap feature is ON).

3. Click GridOff (it should flip to GridOn—Grid feature is ON).

4. Click PointOff (it should flip to PointOn—Point creation is ON).

5. From the View menu, select Grid Spacing. Enter the value 40.

   At this point you're ready to start creating points on the screen. The grid lines are increased from 20 to 40, to increase the detail.

6. Click the following locations on the screen:

Horz	Vert
0.2	0.75
0.15	0.65
0.15	0.55
0.35	0.35
0.4	0.15

Horz	Vert
−0.35	−0.05
0.2	−0.1
0.35	−0.15
0.35	−0.2

If you make a mistake, select Del Points from the Edit menu and start over. Every time you create a point, the location of it is saved into a buffer in memory. You can execute other commands, like changing views, then continue creating other points. As long as the Del Points command is not used, they remain in memory (most of the commands in the Path menu also erase the point buffer).

Once the points are created, there are two ways to create a Sweep object: either by sweeping the current points, or by saving the points to a file and then sweeping them. We will use the second (file) method on the Sweep object and the first (points) method on the Extrude object. Saving the data is convenient since there are various commands that can read data files and either display them like the Load command inside of the Path menu or the B-Spline Data File also inside the Path menu. The B-Spline command smooths out a data file and saves it to a different file. This way, the original data is not lost.

7. Select the Path menu.

8. Pick the Freehand command.

9. Save the data as VASE.DAT.

Initially, the Path menu was developed to aid in the creation of animation files. It is convenient to create data files that would represent different locations of the viewpoint or an object. These could then be used to generate a series of frames that could be merged together later to produce an animation. Interestingly enough, you can use data files (or path files, as POVCAD refers to them) to produce curves and contours in Sweep or Extrude objects. Also, they are very handy when creating letters, as you see later in the chapter. The Path menu consists of the following commands

Path Menu:

Load   Loads a data file into POVCAD

Save   Applies transformations to current data files and saves as *.PTH

Freehand   Saves the point buffer to a data file

Linear   Divides a line into sections and saves to a data file

Circular   Creates an arc with line segments and saves to a data file

Parabolic   Creates a parabola with line segments and saves to a data file

Helix   Creates a helix with line segments and saves to a data file

B-Spline   Smooths the point buffer data and saves to a file

Merge Outer/Inner   Given an outer and an inner curve, converts both into an outer curve and saves to a data file

Join 2 Curves   Patches two data files together and saves to a data file

Flip Data File   Rotates the data so the beginning point becomes the end point and vice-versa

B-Spline Data File   Smooths the data from a file and saves to a data file

A data or path file is basically a file that contains a list of points that define a curve. Steps 8 and 9 take the points in the buffer and save them to a file.

Let's now create the Sweep object:

1. From the Object menu, select Sweep and then Data File.

2. A file selection box will appear. Pick the file VASE.DAT. When prompted for a name, use VASESWP.RAW.

   The Sweep command creates flat triangle information that is saved as a RAW data file. You do not have to use the *.RAW extension, but it becomes a good reference later.

3. The sweep angle is 360 degrees and the # of segments is 12.

4. Click the Iso View (see fig. 7.14).

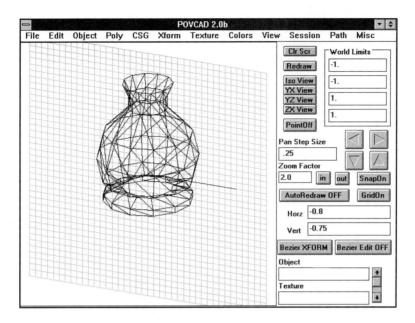

Figure 7.14

Sweep object created with VASE.DAT.

5. Click Session, select the first object and click OK.

6. Move the mouse to the drawing area and press the right mouse button. When the window appears, select Delete. Answer YES.

   This step has deleted the VASE.DAT file from memory but not from the hard drive.

7. Click Redraw to refresh the screen.

8. Select the YX View.

9. Click Session and select the SWP object (Sweep) and click OK.

10. Xform:

    Trans   x –0.8

    Trans   y   0.2

11. Select Texture, white_marble.

You have completed the creation of the Sweep object. Our next step is to create the Extrude object:

1. Click the PointOff button to turn on points creation.

2. Create the following points on the screen:

243

Horz	Vert
0.15	0.8
0.5	0.7
0.15	0.65
0.15	0.25
0.5	0.15
0.55	–0.05

3. This time you will not save the points but use them directly to create the Extrude object. From the Object menu select Extrude, Points; use VASEEXT.RAW as the filename. The extrude length is 1.0.

4. Zoom out by clicking on the out button, then change to the Iso View (see fig. 7.15).

5. Select Texture, reflective_red.

Figure 7.15

Sweep (left) and Extrude (right) objects.

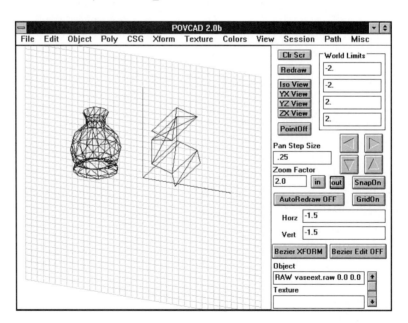

6. Create two light sources:

light #1	<10, 2, 1>
light #2	<0, 2, –10>

7. From the File menu select Save As and use the name TUTOR5.
8. Create a viewpoint:

from	<1, 1, –4>
resolution	100,100
aperture	0

   Click on "include viewpoint."
9. Use the Export function to create a Polyray file and create TUTOR5.PI (see Listing 7.7 and fig. 7.16).

Listing 7.7. Sweep and extrude object tutorial (TUTOR5.PI).

(Note: Listing was truncated due to its large size.)

```
//PROGRAM:   TUTOR5.PI GENERATED WITH POVCAD 2.0b (c) Alfonso Hermida 1993
//Created on 8/3/93 7:32:55 PM

include "colors.inc"
include "texture.inc"

viewpoint {
 from      <1, 1, -2.0 >
 at        <-0.1, 0.4, 0.0 >
 up        <0.0, 1.0, 0.0 >
 angle      45
 hither     1.0e-3
 resolution 100,100
 aspect     1.0
 yon        1.0e5
 max_trace_depth 5
 aperture        0
}

// RAW DATA
object{
 object {
   polygon 3,
    <0.15,0.65,0.0>,
    <0.2,0.75,0.0>,
    <0.1732,0.75,-0.1>
 }
+
```

continues

Listing 7.7. Continued.

```
object {
  polygon 3,
    <0.1299,0.65,-0.075>,
    <0.15,0.65,0.0>,
    <0.1732,0.75,-0.1>
 }

// This section was deleted to reduce the size of this listing

+
object {
  polygon 3,
    <0.35,-0.2,0.0>,
    <0.3031,-0.2,0.175>,
    <0.35,-0.15,0.0>
 }
   translate < -0.8,0.2,0.0>
   white_marble
}


// RAW DATA
object{
 object {
  polygon 3,
    <0.5,0.7,0.0>,
    <0.15,0.8,0.0>,
    <0.15,0.8,1.0>
 }
+

// This section was deleted to reduce the size of this listing

 object {
  polygon 3,
    <0.55,-0.05,1.0>,
    <0.55,-0.05,0.0>,
    <0.5,0.15,1.0>
 }
   reflective_red
}
// LIGHT_SOURCE
  light < 10 , 2 , 1 >

// LIGHT_SOURCE
  light < 0 , 2 , -10 >
```

The complete TUTOR5.PI is roughly 32 pages long! Keep the length in mind when you create the same scene using Polyray's Lathe and Sweep object definitions.

Figure 7.16

Ray-traced image of TUTOR5.PI created with POVCAD.

In order to create a Lathe object for Polyray, I used the data file VASE.DAT with the program LATHE.BAS, used in Chapter 3 to create Listing 3.16 and figure 3.13. I renamed TUTOR5.PI to TUTOR5M.PI and in it I deleted the original objects and added the Lathe and Sweep objects using Polyray's format (see Listing 7.8).

Listing 7.8. Simplifying TUTOR5.PI (TUTOR5M.PI).

```
//TUTOR5M.PI
//Modified by Hand

//Lathe Object Created With LATHE.BAS
//08-03-1993 19:54:30

include "colors.inc"
include "texture.inc"


define LatheTexture white_marble
define ExtrudeTexture reflective_red

viewpoint {
  from      <1, 1, -2.0 >
  at        <-0.1, 0.4, 0.0 >
  up        <0.0, 1.0, 0.0 >
  angle     45
```

continues

Listing 7.8. Continued.

```
hither      1.0e-3
resolution 100,100
aspect      1.0
yon         1.0e5
max_trace_depth 5
aperture         0
}


object {
    lathe  2 , <0, 1, 0>,  9 ,
          <   0.200,    0.750,    0.000>,
          <   0.150,    0.650,    0.000>,
          <   0.150,    0.550,    0.000>,
          <   0.350,    0.350,    0.000>,
          <   0.400,    0.150,    0.000>,
          <   0.350,   -0.050,    0.000>,
          <   0.200,   -0.100,    0.000>,
          <   0.350,   -0.150,    0.000>,
          <   0.350,   -0.200,    0.000>
    translate <-0.8, 0.2, 0.0>
    LatheTexture
}

object {
    sweep  2 , <0, 0, 1>,  6 ,
          <   0.15 ,    0.80 ,    0.0  >,
          <   0.50 ,    0.70 ,    0.0  >,
          <   0.15 ,    0.65 ,    0.0  >,
          <   0.15 ,    0.25 ,    0.0  >,
          <   0.50 ,    0.15 ,    0.0  >,
          <   0.55 ,   -0.05 ,    0.0  >
    ExtrudeTexture
}


// LIGHT_SOURCE
  light < 10 ,   2 ,   1  >

// LIGHT_SOURCE
  light < 0  ,   2 ,  -10  >
```

Listing 7.8 is the complete version! Compare it to POVCAD's 32-page version of the same scene. The file TUTOR5M.PI lets Polyray do all the hard work while the POVCAD version breaks the objects into polygons. Figure 7.17 displays the image generated with Listing 7.8.

Figure 7.17

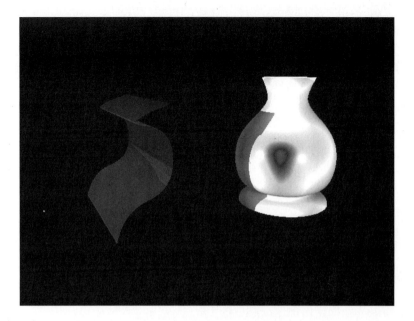

Using Polyray's lathe and sweep objects.

In symmetric objects like the vase created in POVCAD, Polyray does a great job. POVCAD has an advantage in that it can read a RAW data file which may not represent a symmetric object or a solid of revolution, such as a RAW data file of a plane or a face. Here, POVCAD can read the file and generate a set of polygons to model it. You may even want to use the program SMOOTH.BAS (from Chapter 3) to create smooth triangles. To read a RAW data file, use the RAW command in the Object menu. Polyray, on the other hand, can't use the Lathe or Sweep object on irregular RAW data files.

Creating Bézier Patches (Tutorial #6)

Being able to control Bézier patches is extremely interesting. POVCAD supports various Bézier patch based objects. These are the commands available under the Object menu, Bézier submenu:

Bézier SubMenu:

Load A File	Reads files that were created with POVCAD (*.BEZ)
Flat	Flat sheet
Cylinder 2 patch	Cylinder composed with 2 patches
Cylinder 4 patch	Cylinder composed with 4 patches
Ellipsoid	Ellipsoid
Cone	Cone
Torus	Hemi-Torus

In this session, you learn how to deform the Ellipsoid object. POVCAD generates a control mesh that defines the boundaries of the patches. The control mesh has nodes you can select and translate on any axis. The technique is to use the Iso View to select the control node and then change to a different view to displace it. The Iso View is good for picking a point from the screen but not for displacing them. The other views are ideal for doing translations on one plane at a time. Let's get started with the Bézier patches:

1. Select the Iso View.

2. From the Objects menu, select Bézier and then Ellipsoid.

   POVCAD generates a file with the control data. You must give it a name and it is suggested that you use the BEZ extension. Only files ending in BEZ can be later read by the Load A File command in the Bézier menu. Enter the name ELLIP.BEZ.

3. From the Misc menu, select Bézier Setup.

   In this window, you can select to see the control grid, the Bézier patch surface, or neither. In addition, you can specify how many divisions per side to make on the surface. The higher the number, the better the image it produces in POVCAD, but the program runs slower due to the increased amount of redrawing that has to be done. Set the number of divisions at 13, and select both the control grid and the surface patch.

4. Click SnapOff and GridOff.

5. To start deforming the Bézier object, click Bézier Edit Off (this enables editing).

POVCAD draws the control grid in black while the Bézier surface is drawn in blue. To deform the surface, click any of the intersections of the black lines (the nodes). Then click in a new location again to tell POVCAD the new position of the node.

6. Click the mouse at Horz = 0.0 and Vert = 0.5.

7. A red circle appears on the node that has been selected.

8. Select the YX View.

9. Click a point at Horz = 0.5 and Vert = 0.7 (the surface must deform at this point).

10. Click at Horz = 0.0 and Vert = –0.5 (selecting a node).

11. Click at Horz = 0.5 and Vert = –0.8 (deformation).

12. Click at Horz = –0.5 and Vert = 0.0 (selecting).

13. Click at Horz = –0.8 and Vert = 0.0 (deforming).

14. From the Misc menu, select Bézier Setup. Disable the control grid and set the number of divisions to 13 (maximum).

15. Click Redraw to refresh the screen.

16. Change to the Iso View (see fig. 7.18).

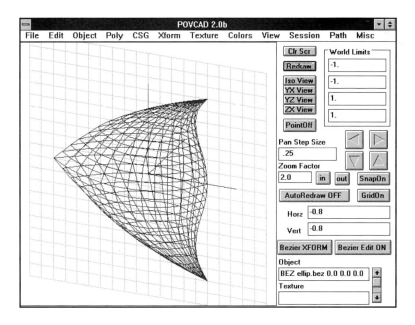

Figure 7.18

Deforming a Bézier patch.

17. Select Texture, steely_blue.

18. From the Object menu select Plane_Y.

19. Xform:

    Scale x, y, z   3 (all of them)

    Trans y   −1.5

20. Select Texture, mirror.

21. From the Object menu, select Plane_Z.

22. Xform:

    Scale x, y, z   3 (all of them)

    Trans y   2

23. Select Texture, mirror.

24. Create two light sources:

    light #1   <0, 5, −10>

    light #2   <5, 3, −10>

25. From the File menu, select Save As: TUTOR6

26. Create a viewpoint:

    from   <1, 3, −5>

    resolution   100,100

    aperture   0

    Click on "include viewpoint."

27. Export to Polyray: TUTOR6.PI (see Listing 7.9).

Listing 7.9. Polyray format file for TUTOR6.PI.

```
//PROGRAM:   TUTOR6.PI GENERATED WITH POVCAD 2.0b (c) Alfonso Hermida 1993
//Created on 8/3/93 11:35:02 PM

include "colors.inc"
include "texture.inc"

viewpoint {
  from   <1, 2, -7 >                          // modified by hand
  at     <0.0, -1.0, 0.0 >
  up     <0.0, 1.0, 0.0 >
  angle    45
```

```
 hither      1.0e-3
 resolution 100,100
 aspect      1.0
 yon         1.0e5
 max_trace_depth 5
 aperture        0
}


object{
// BEZIER PATCH
object{
    bezier 2, 0.05, 3, 3,
      <0.5,0.7,0.0>, <0.28,0.5,0.0>, <0.5,0.28,0.0>, <0.5,0.0,0.0>,
      <0.5,0.7,0.0>, <0.14,0.5,0.242>, <0.25,0.28,0.433>, <0.25,0.0,0.433>,
      <0.5,0.7,0.0>, <-0.14,0.5,0.242>, <-0.25,0.28,0.433>, <-0.25,0.0,0.433>,
      <0.5,0.7,0.0>, <-0.28,0.5,0.0>, <-0.5,0.28,0.0>, <-0.8,0.0,0.0>
   steely_blue
}
+
// BEZIER PATCH
object{
    bezier 2, 0.05, 3, 3,
      <0.5,0.7,0.0>, <0.28,0.5,0.0>, <0.5,0.28,0.0>, <0.5,0.0,0.0>,
      <0.5,0.7,0.0>, <0.14,0.5,-0.242>, <0.25,0.28,-0.433>, <0.25,0.0,-0.433>,
      <0.5,0.7,0.0>, <-0.14,0.5,-0.242>, <-0.25,0.28,-0.433>, <-0.25,0.0,-0.433>,
      <0.5,0.7,0.0>, <-0.28,0.5,0.0>, <-0.5,0.28,0.0>, <-0.8,0.0,0.0>
   steely_blue
}
+
// BEZIER PATCH
object{
    bezier 2, 0.05, 3, 3,
      <0.5,-0.8,0.0>, <0.28,-0.5,0.0>, <0.5,-0.28,0.0>, <0.5,0.0,0.0>,
      <0.5,-0.8,0.0>, <0.14,-0.5,0.242>, <0.25,-0.28,0.433>, <0.25,0.0,0.433>,
      <0.5,-0.8,0.0>, <-0.14,-0.5,0.242>, <-0.25,-0.28,0.433>, <-0.25,0.0,0.433>,
      <0.5,-0.8,0.0>, <-0.28,-0.5,0.0>, <-0.5,-0.28,0.0>, <-0.8,0.0,0.0>
   steely_blue
}
+
// BEZIER PATCH
object{
    bezier 2, 0.05, 3, 3,
      <0.5,-0.8,0.0>, <0.28,-0.5,0.0>, <0.5,-0.28,0.0>, <0.5,0.0,0.0>,
      <0.5,-0.8,0.0>, <0.14,-0.5,-0.242>, <0.25,-0.28,-0.433>, <0.25,0.0,-0.433>,
      <0.5,-0.8,0.0>, <-0.14,-0.5,-0.242>, <-0.25,-0.28,-0.433>, <-0.25,0.0,-0.433>,
      <0.5,-0.8,0.0>, <-0.28,-0.5,0.0>, <-0.5,-0.28,0.0>, <-0.8,0.0,0.0>
   steely_blue
}
}


// PLANE (Polygon)
object {
// normal in Y direction
  polygon 4, <-1,0,1>, <-1,0,-1>, <1,0,-1>, <1,0,1>
    scale < 3.0,3.0,3.0>
```

continues

Listing 7.9. Continued.

```
  translate < 0.0,-1.5,0.0>
    mirror
}

//  This plane was commented out by hand

/*
// PLANE (Polygon)
object {
// normal in Z direction
  polygon 4, <-1,1,0>, <1,1,0>, <1,-1,0>, <-1,-1,0>
    scale < 3.0,3.0,3.0>
    translate < 0.0,0.0,2.0>
    mirror
}
*/

// LIGHT_SOURCE
  light < 0 ,  5 , -10  >

// LIGHT_SOURCE
  light < 5 ,  3 , -10  >
```

Listing 7.9 presents the modified version of TUTOR6.PI. One of the planes was commented out and the viewpoint was also reworked (see fig. 7.19).

Figure 7.19

A Bézier patch object.

Using the Polygon Decomposition Technique (Tutorial #7)

Polygon decomposition refers to the technique used to convert a close curve into a flat surface. The surface will be composed of triangles. In this session, you create a 3-D letter "A" by creating the contours of it. First you create the outer contour of the letter and then the hole in the middle. Save them as data files. Then you extrude the contours. Finally, you use the Poly menu on the outer and inner contours to create a flat surface which will represent the "face" of the letter. Again, we'll compare this method with the use of Polyray's sweep objects.

An important point: The polygon decomposition method always assumes that the curves are created in the YX plane. The routines might work in other planes, but I can't guarantee it. You can always start in the YX plane then Xform to the final location.

Start by creating curves that define the contours of your letter "A":

1. Select the YX View.

2. Enable SnapOn and GridOn.

3. From the View menu, select a Grid Spacing of 40.

4. Enable PointOn.

5. Create the following points on the screen:

Horz	Vert
−0.2	0.5
0.2	0.5
0.55	−0.35
0.25	−0.35
0.15	−0.05
−0.15	−0.05
−0.25	−0.35
−0.55	−0.35
−0.2	0.5

6. From the Path menu, select B-Spline. Input AOUTER.DAT file and input 50 points.

7. From the Edit menu, select Del Points. Enable point creation by clicking on PointOff.

8. Create the following points on the screen:

Horz	Vert
–0.1	0.3
0.05	0.3
0.1	0.1
–0.05	0.15
–0.2	0.1
–0.1	0.3

9. Disable points creation, click on PointOn.

10. From the Path menu select B-Spline. Input AINNER.DAT file and input 18 points. Now erase the points by selecting the Edit menu and clicking on Del Points.

   At this point, both contours should be smooth on the screen after doing a redraw (see fig. 7.20).

   Take the next steps to extrude the curves:

11. From the Object menu select Extrude, Data File. Pick AOUTER.DAT, Save As AOUTER.RAW and use an extrude length of 0.5 units.

12. Select the Iso View.

13. From the Object menu select Extrude, Data File. Pick AINNER.DAT, Save As AINNER.RAW and use an extrude length of 0.5 units (see fig. 7.21).

   The sides and hole of the letter "A" are done. The remaining piece is the "face" of the letter.

14. From the Poly menu select Perforated. The file box appears. Pick the files AOUTER.DAT (which is the outer curve), then when the file box appears again select AINNER.DAT (the inner curve). If you're not sure,

read the title in the file box. It tells you which curve (outer or inner) is needed at that time.

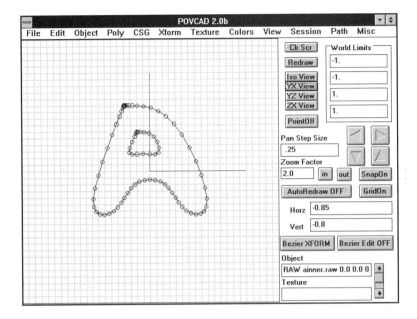

Figure 7.20

Smooth contours of the letter "A."

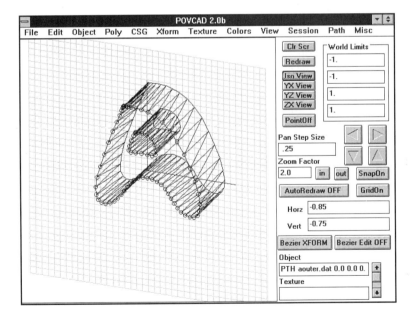

Figure 7.21

Extrusion of contours.

15. The output filename is AFACE.RAW.

16. Select the YX View (see fig. 7.22).

Figure 7.22

Polygon decomposition applied to face of letter "A."

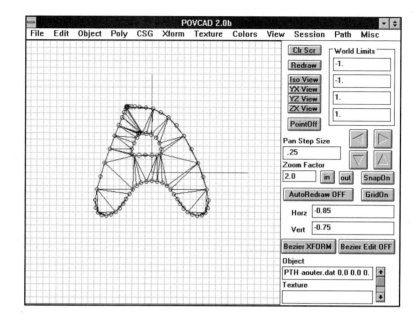

17. Using the Session command, select the objects

> RAW aouter.raw
>
> RAW ainner.raw
>
> RAW aface.raw

After each selection, attach the texture reflective_grey to the current object.

18. From the File menu Save As TUTOR7.

19. Create two light sources:

> light #1   <1, 2, –5>
>
> light #2   <0, 1, –10>

20. Save the scene using the Save command.

21. Define the viewpoint

> from   <1, 2, –5>
>
> resolution   100,100

aperture   0

Click on "include viewpoint."

22. To complete the process, Export to Polyray as TUTOR7.PI (see Listing 7.10 and fig. 7.23).

Listing 7.10. Creating the letter "A" (TUTOR7.PI).

(Note: file was truncated due to the length of the file)

```
//PROGRAM:   TUTOR7.PI GENERATED WITH POVCAD 2.0b (c) Alfonso Hermida 1993
//Created on 8/4/93 1:25:07 AM

include "colors.inc"
include "texture.inc"

viewpoint {
 from       <1, 1, -1.4 >
 at         <0.2, 0.2, 0.0 >
 up         <0.0, 1.0, 0.0 >
 angle      45
 hither     1.0e-3
 resolution 100,100
 aspect     1.0
 yon        1.0e5
 max_trace_depth 5
 aperture        0
}

// RAW DATA
object{
 object {
   polygon 3,
    <-0.1997,0.5,0.0>,
    <-0.2,0.5,0.0>,
    <-0.2,0.5,0.5>
 }

// File truncated due to length


+ object {
   polygon 3,
    <0.253009,0.277006,0.0>,
    <0.066667,0.141667,0.0>,
    <0.360417,0.075,0.0>
 }
   reflective_grey
}
// LIGHT_SOURCE
  light < 1 ,  2 , -5 >

// LIGHT_SOURCE
  light < 0 ,  1 , -10 >

// LIGHT_SOURCE
  light < 0 ,  3 , 5 >
```

Figure 7.23

Ray-traced letter "A" generated with POVCAD.

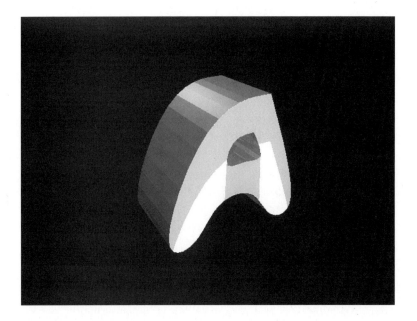

Listing 7.10 was extremely long and had to be shortened. In order to compare the geometry created with POVCAD and Polyray's features, I decided to make AOUTER.DAT and AINNER.DAT sweep objects. This shortens the file and creates a smoother surface than using flat triangles. Listing 7.11 presents a modified version of TUTOR7.PI named TUTOR7M.PI and figure 7.24 displays the resulting image of TUTOR7M.PI.

Listing 7.11. Using sweep objects in Polyray.

(Note: part of the file was truncated due to the length.)

```
//PROGRAM:    TUTOR7.PI GENERATED WITH POVCAD 2.0b (c) Alfonso Hermida 1993
//Created on 8/4/93 1:25:07 AM

include "colors.inc"
include "texture.inc"

viewpoint {
  from       <1, 1, -1.4 >
  at         <0.2, 0.2, 0.0 >
  up         <0.0, 1.0, 0.0 >
  angle      45
  hither     1.0e-3
  resolution 100,100
  aspect     1.0
  yon        1.0e5
```

```
 max_trace_depth 5
 aperture        0
}


object {
    sweep  2 , <0, 0, 0.5>,  61 ,
          <   -0.200,     0.500,      0.000>,
          <   -0.200,     0.500,      0.000>,
          <   -0.198,     0.500,      0.000>,
          <   -0.192,     0.500,      0.000>,
          <   -0.180,     0.500,      0.000>,
          <   -0.161,     0.500,      0.000>,
          <   -0.133,     0.500,      0.000>,
          <   -0.095,     0.499,      0.000>,
          <   -0.047,     0.495,      0.000>,
          <    0.007,     0.482,      0.000>,
          <    0.067,     0.458,      0.000>,
          <    0.129,     0.418,      0.000>,
          <    0.192,     0.358,      0.000>,
          <    0.253,     0.277,      0.000>,
          <    0.310,     0.180,      0.000>,
          <    0.360,     0.075,      0.000>,
          <    0.401,    -0.030,      0.000>,
          <    0.429,    -0.127,      0.000>,
          <    0.442,    -0.208,      0.000>,
          <    0.437,    -0.268,      0.000>,
          <    0.419,    -0.306,      0.000>,
          <    0.391,    -0.326,      0.000>,
          <    0.356,    -0.330,      0.000>,
          <    0.319,    -0.320,      0.000>,
          <    0.283,    -0.300,      0.000>,
          <    0.252,    -0.271,      0.000>,
          <    0.225,    -0.237,      0.000>,
          <    0.200,    -0.200,      0.000>,
          <    0.175,    -0.163,      0.000>,
          <    0.148,    -0.129,      0.000>,
          <    0.117,    -0.100,      0.000>,
          <    0.081,    -0.079,      0.000>,
          <    0.041,    -0.067,      0.000>,
          <    0.000,    -0.062,      0.000>,
          <   -0.041,    -0.067,      0.000>,
          <   -0.081,    -0.079,      0.000>,
          <   -0.117,    -0.100,      0.000>,
          <   -0.148,    -0.129,      0.000>,
          <   -0.175,    -0.163,      0.000>,
          <   -0.200,    -0.200,      0.000>,
          <   -0.225,    -0.237,      0.000>,
          <   -0.252,    -0.271,      0.000>,
          <   -0.283,    -0.300,      0.000>,
          <   -0.319,    -0.320,      0.000>,
          <   -0.356,    -0.330,      0.000>,
          <   -0.391,    -0.326,      0.000>,
          <   -0.419,    -0.306,      0.000>,
          <   -0.437,    -0.268,      0.000>,
          <   -0.442,    -0.208,      0.000>,
```

continues

Listing 7.11. Continued.

```
              <   -0.429,   -0.127,    0.000>,
              <   -0.403,   -0.030,    0.000>,
              <   -0.369,    0.075,    0.000>,
              <   -0.330,    0.180,    0.000>,
              <   -0.292,    0.277,    0.000>,
              <   -0.258,    0.358,    0.000>,
              <   -0.234,    0.418,    0.000>,
              <   -0.217,    0.458,    0.000>,
              <   -0.207,    0.482,    0.000>,
              <   -0.202,    0.495,    0.000>,
              <   -0.200,    0.499,    0.000>,
              <   -0.200,    0.500,    0.000>
       reflective_grey
}

object {
    sweep  2 , <0, 0, 0.5>,  22 ,
              <   -0.100,    0.300,    0.000>,
              <   -0.099,    0.300,    0.000>,
              <   -0.093,    0.300,    0.000>,
              <   -0.075,    0.300,    0.000>,
              <   -0.043,    0.299,    0.000>,
              <   -0.004,    0.290,    0.000>,
              <    0.033,    0.267,    0.000>,
              <    0.060,    0.225,    0.000>,
              <    0.073,    0.178,    0.000>,
              <    0.067,    0.142,    0.000>,
              <    0.040,    0.128,    0.000>,
              <   -0.001,    0.130,    0.000>,
              <   -0.050,    0.133,    0.000>,
              <   -0.098,    0.130,    0.000>,
              <   -0.138,    0.128,    0.000>,
              <   -0.158,    0.142,    0.000>,
              <   -0.155,    0.178,    0.000>,
              <   -0.137,    0.225,    0.000>,
              <   -0.117,    0.267,    0.000>,
              <   -0.105,    0.290,    0.000>,
              <   -0.101,    0.299,    0.000>,
              <   -0.100,    0.300,    0.000>
       reflective_grey
}



// RAW DATA
object{
 object {
   polygon 3,
     <-0.094792,0.499344,0.0>,
     <-0.133333,0.5,0.0>,
     <-0.16142,0.5,0.0>
 }

// FACE of Letter A data was truncated to reduce the size of the listing.
```

```
+
  object {
    polygon 3,
     <0.253009,0.277006,0.0>,
     <0.066667,0.141667,0.0>,
     <0.360417,0.075,0.0>
  }
    reflective_grey
}
// LIGHT_SOURCE
  light < 1 ,  2 , -5 >

// LIGHT_SOURCE
  light < 0 ,  1 , -10 >

// LIGHT_SOURCE
  light < 0 ,  3 , 5 >
```

In TUTOR7M.PI, both the outer and inner contours were converted into Polyray's sweep objects. The smoothness of the outer surface and hole can be seen in figure 7.24.

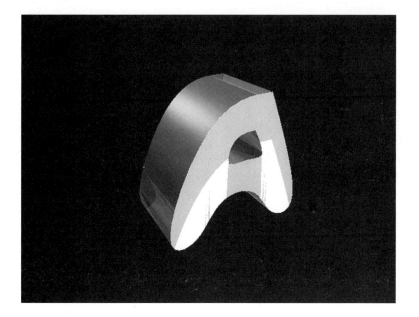

Figure 7.24

Using Polyray's sweep object definition.

Summary

This chapter presented you with a series of seven tutorials demonstrating all the major features of POVCAD. POVCAD is a 3-D wireframe-based modeler

that can help you create scenes for the Polyray ray tracer. After you create the scene in POVCAD, you can generate Polyray-compatible files.

The first tutorial presented a simple scene with three spheres. You learned how to create simple objects and position them in the coordinate system. In addition, you attached textures to each primitive and created light sources. Finally, you prepared a viewpoint definition and generated a Polyray compatible scene file using the Export command.

In Tutorial #2, you saw some of the different primitives available: the cone, torus, box, sphere, and plane.

Tutorial #3 covered the technique of creating multiple copies of objects using the Copy/Rotate command.

Tutorial #4 dealt with CSG objects. You saw the creation of a primitive Elbow, consisting of the intersection of a torus and a box. The resulting object was a union with two cylinders forming a tube-like shape, bent 90 degrees.

Tutorial #5 was dedicated to POVCAD's Sweep and Extrude objects, called Lathe and Extrude/Sweep in Polyray. You saw these objects compared to equivalent definitions using the Lathe and Sweep objects in Polyray. The quality of the surface using Polyray's objects was outstanding.

In Tutorial #6, you studied the creation and deformation of Bézier patches. You deformed an ellipsoid made with Bézier patches. POVCAD has the option of drawing the control grid, the generated surface, and changing the number of divisions in the surface.

Finally, Tutorial #7 presented polygon decomposition, a technique to create surfaces by subdividing them into triangles. Again, you saw the results compared with Polyray's, and the surface finish using Polyray's objects was better.

In the next chapter, you'll learn how to create animation using Polyray's built-in features. Various techniques will be covered that will discuss how to plan and model an animation with the help of POVCAD.

Animation

You are now at the point where you can take ray tracing a step further. The previous chapters were dedicated to understanding the different tools available in Polyray. The scenes used in the examples were all still images. The next step is to combine multiple still frames into an animated sequence or movie. Polyray's ray tracing features, combined with its built-in animation support, make the program ideal for modeling everything from bouncing spheres and orbiting planets to robots and cartoon figures. Let's start with the basics of animation, then cover Polyray's animation features, and finally show various examples of animated sequences, or animations.

The Basics of Animation

Animation can be broken down into some basic concepts: applying transformations, different types of motion that can be modeled, converting a sequence of frames into a movie, and the effect of image resolution in the animation. The next sections discuss these concepts in detail.

Transformation Operations

Transformations such as scaling, rotation, and translation are the key to object animation. In the previous chapters you used transformations to position objects, create multiple copies, or resize them. In animation, you have to be aware of how the order of the transformations can affect the position and orientation of an object. As an example, take a cone and position it at the origin (see fig. 8.1a). Applying a translation of <1, 0, 0> gives you figure 8.1b. Finally, apply the rotation <0, 0, 90> (see fig. 8.1c). Now, compare this result with the same operations in different order (see fig. 8.2a,b and c). Obviously, the results are not the same. In order to create figure 8.1c using a rotation and then a translation, you would have to apply the rotation <0, 0, 90> and then the translation <0, 1, 0>. This gives you the same result.

Figure 8.1

Applying a translation and a rotation to an object.

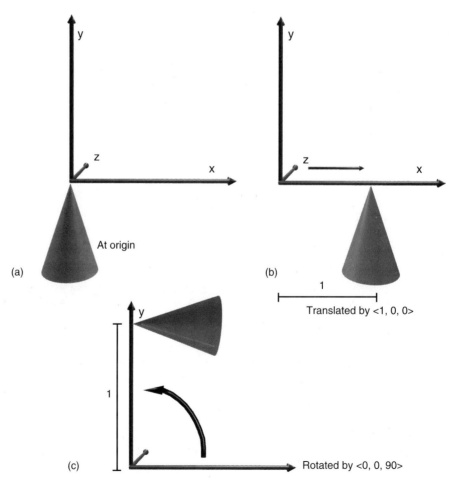

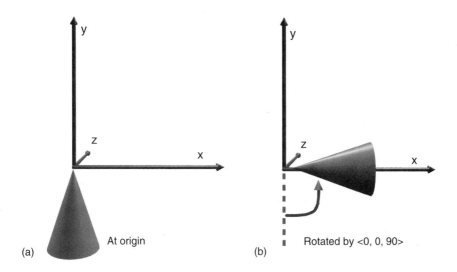

Figure 8.2

*Applying a
rotation and a
translation to an
object.*

(a) At origin

(b) Rotated by <0, 0, 90>

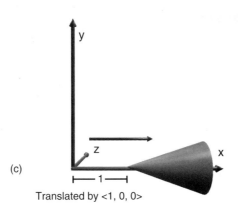

(c)

Translated by <1, 0, 0>

The main point to remember is that rotations are applied about a pivot point located at the origin. In animation, it is useful to create the object at the origin, rotate it, then apply the translations to locate the object in its final position.

Sometimes it is necessary to rotate an object using a pivot point located outside the origin (see fig 8.3a). In this example we want to rotate sphere S1 about the pivot point C by an angle "ang" about the Z axis. The pivot point C is located at <xo, yo, 0> and the sphere is located at <xo + xr, yo + yr, 0>.

Figure 8.3

Rotation of an object about a pivot point.

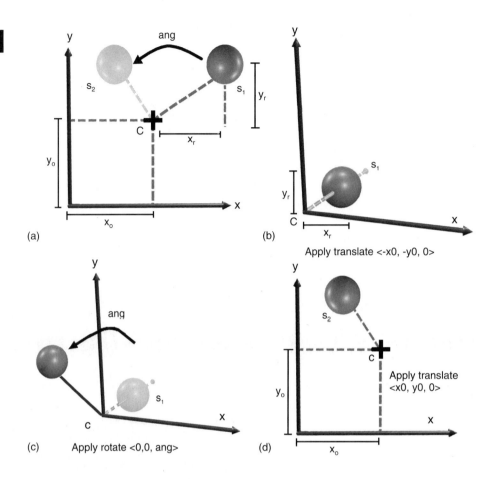

(a)

(b)

Apply translate <-x0, -y0, 0>

(c) Apply rotate <0,0, ang>

(d)

Apply translate <x0, y0, 0>

The first step is to move point C to the origin (see fig. 8.3b). Next, apply the rotation about the z axis (see fig. 8.3c). Finally, locate point C back to it's original place (see fig. 8.3d). As you can see, it's easy to bring the pivot point back to the origin, apply the rotations, then locate it back to its original place. In Polyray, the operations would be written as it is presented in Listing 8.1.

Listing 8.1. Figures 8.3a, b, c, and d in Polyray format (partial listing).

```
define xo ...
define yo ...
define xr ...
define yr ...
define ang ...
define radius ...
```

```
define S1
    object {
        sphere <xo + xr, yo + yr, 0>, radius
    }
define S2
    object {
        S1
        translate < -xo, -yo, 0>
        rotate <0, 0, ang>
        translate <xo, yo, 0>
    }
object {
    S2
    shiny_red
}
```

By leaving most of the numbers as variables, you only have to modify the top section of Listing 8.1.

Viewpoint Motion (Flyby)

Flyby motion is widely used in animating scenes of satellites passing near a planet and cockpit views as seen from inside an airplane or jet. This type of motion can be accomplished by modifying the vectors "from" and "at" from the viewpoint definition. In other words, the objects being looked at are stationary while the observer moves (see fig. 8.4).

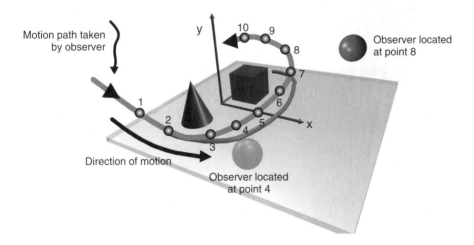

Figure 8.4

Path motion of an observer looking at the origin (flyby).

In figure 8.4, the observer follows a motion path. At each point, the point being looked at is the origin. A variation on this technique is to define the

269

motion of the observer plus the motion of the point being looked at (see fig. 8.5). In other words, there would be two motion paths: one for the observer's position and another for the "look at" point (see fig. 8.6). Figure 8.6 displays the motion paths without the objects.

Figure 8.5

Path motion of an observer looking at different points (flyby).

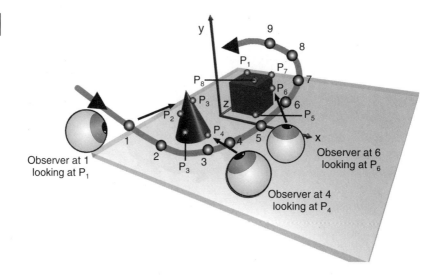

Figure 8.6

Path motion of the observer and the "look at" points.

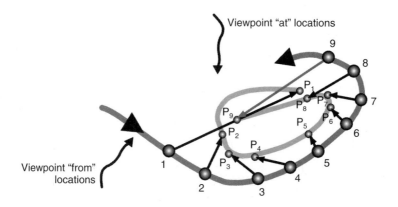

The light sources normally remain stationary in a flyby, but you can also create a light source that moves with the observer. This technique guarantees that at least one light source will be illuminating the point being looked at. If we assume that the "from" vector of the viewpoint definition is "from <x, y, z>," the light source can follow the observer by using the definition "light <x + dx, y + dy, z + dz>" where x, y, and z are the current coordinate locations of the observer and dx, dy, and dz are constant offset values.

As an analogy, the light source following the observer can be compared to the lamp on a miner's hat, which always follows the motion of the head.

Object Motion

The motion of objects can be modeled by applying transformations directly on the objects. An object can have simple translation (hockey puck—see fig. 8.7a), rotation motion in x, y, and z or a combination of both. A spinning top is a good example of an object that combines rotation and translation (see fig. 8.7c). Figure 8.7 also presents two kinds of rotations: about an axis away from the object (pendulum—see fig 8.7b) and about an axis that passes through the object (spinning top—see fig. 8.7c).

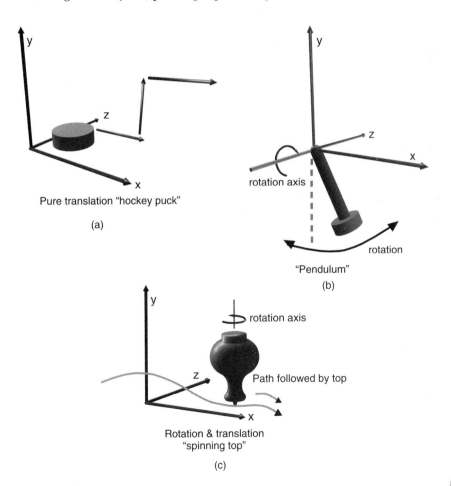

Figure 8.7

Examples of simple translation, rotation, and combined motions in objects.

It might be interesting to know that objects can appear to move if the viewpoint is not stationary. This technique requires that the viewpoint move in a way that makes the object look as if it is in motion. For example, to a person driving a car all the people on the street appear to move, even the people who are just standing on the sidewalk. The driver is a moving "viewpoint."

Finally, both the flyby and the object motion can be combined into one scene. For example, you can simulate a person walking as another person rides a bicycle and passes near him. Parts of the bicycle (gears, pedals) move, as does the observer.

Virtual Animation

If you've never heard the expression "virtual animation," it's because I just made it up! I use virtual animation to refer to a stationary scene that simulates the "double exposure" effect of cameras. You can create one image that shows where the object is in terms of location and orientation at each step in the motion path. The trick is to add transparency to all of the objects except the last one. The final scene appears as a group of "ghost" objects following the last one. For example, if a sphere animation has 20 steps, the first object can be made almost completely transparent. The second object can have less transparency than the first, but more that the third, and so on. The final object is not transparent (opaque).

What are the advantages and disadvantages of such a technique? With normal animation, you have to create 20 files (as an example) and then generate a movie with them. To see if the animation came out as expected, you must watch the movie. In virtual animation, only one file is ray traced, but this scene consists of 20 objects, each one in a different position. All of the objects are ray traced at the same time, and computation time increases with the number of objects. With the normal animation, if you only have one object per scene, ray tracing is fairly quick. In addition, if your virtual animation scene has a large quantity of objects, it may become too difficult to distinguish between them.

Figure 8.8 depicts the virtual animation of a pendulum. Initially, the pendulum is positioned at point A. At different time steps, it is shown as it swings towards point B. By looking at the variation of the transparency, we can determine the initial and final positions as well as the direction of the motion.

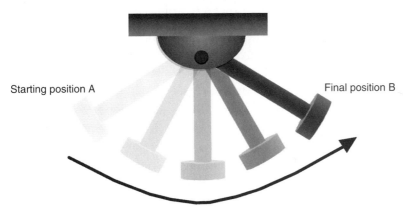

Starting position A

Final position B

Rotation direction

Figure 8.8

*Virtual anima-
tion of a
pendulum.*

Texture Variation

If you review the example scene files presented in previous chapters, you might note that the texture declaration is always applied after the transformations. For example,

```
object {
    sphere .....
    rotate ...
    scale ...
    texture...
}
```

This implies that the rotations are only performed on the geometry itself and not on the texture. In animation, this is not advisable. When an object moves, the texture should move correspondingly. This can be accomplished by applying the texture *before* applying the transformations you use to animate the object. When you apply the texture first, all the transformations that follow will apply to the texture as well as to the object:

```
object {
    sphere <0, 0, 0>, 2
    white_marble
    rotate <0, 45, 0>
}
```

In this example, a white_marble texture is applied to a sphere located at the origin. After this is done, both the sphere and the texture will be rotated 45 degrees about y. Since the sphere is symmetrical, you only see the texture rotate.

273

Polyray's Animation Features

Polyray has some powerful yet easy-to-use features to support animation. A *frame* is an image file that displays how the objects are positioned in a given time. Polyray can create a set of frames based on one scene file, and use conditional expressions to determine which objects are created at a given time. By using its built-in math and array support, you can modify the position and texture of an object on a given frame.

Frame Generation

If the position of the objects and the viewpoint is constant at each frame, the scene is referred to as "stationary." In animation, you want to do the opposite: change the position and orientation of the objects, the viewpoint, or both on each frame.

To create a set of frames with Polyray, you must indicate the number of frames to be generated, the starting number for the first frame, and either the ending number for the final frame or the total number of frames to be created. The syntax for frame creation is

start_frame	*value*	(variable) number of the first frame to be created
end_frame	*value*	(variable) number of the last frame to be created
total_frames	*value*	(variable) total number of frames to be created
frame		(variable) holds the current frame being ray traced
outfile "*filename*" or outfile *filename*		filename is the name of the frames to be created.

The name must be five letters or less since Polyray appends three digits to the end of this name.

Example: If the filename is TEST and you need 3 frames, starting at 1, Polyray will create:

TEST001.TGA

TEST002.TGA

TEST003.TGA

The default name is OUT.

All the variables used for creating frames can be used in mathematical expressions.

Listing 8.2 presents a sphere that increases its radius as a function of the frame number. The sphere is inside a unit box and an intersection operation is applied to both. As the sphere starts increasing in size beyond the box, the box acts as a clipping object; any part of the sphere that goes beyond the box is discarded. Figure 8.9 presents the four frames generated by ANIMCLIP.PI.

Listing 8.2. A sphere that increases in size(ANIMCLIP.PI).

```
//ANIMCLIP.PI
start_frame 1
end_frame 4
include "colors.inc"
include "texture.inc"
viewpoint {
  from      <0.0, 3.0, -6.0 >
  at        <0.0, 0.0, 0.0 >
  up        <0.0, 1.0, 0.0 >
  angle     45
  resolution 100,100
  aspect    1.0
}
// LIGHT_SOURCE
  light < 10 ,  10 , -20 >
// LIGHT_SOURCE
  light <-10 ,  -1 , -20 >
// LIGHT_SOURCE
  light <1 ,  10 , 0  >
background white
object {
    object {
        box <-1, -1, -1>, <1, 1, 1>
    }
*   object {
        sphere <0, 0, 0>, 0.5*frame
    }
    rotate <-17, 15, 0>
    wooden
}
```

Frame 1   Frame 2

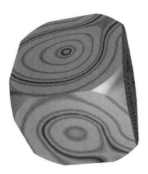

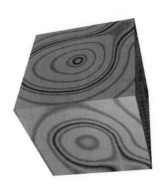

Frame 3   Frame 4

In Frames 1 and 2, the sphere is still smaller than the box. The radius of the sphere is

```
frame 1: 0.5 * frame = 0.5 * 1 = 0.5
frame 2: 0.5 * frame = 0.5 * 2 = 1.0
```

In Frame 3, parts of the sphere are clipped away and the shape appears more like a box. The radius in this frame is `0.5 * frame = 0.5 * 3 = 1.5`. Finally, Frame 4 presents a box with the texture used in the sphere. The sphere's radius is `0.5 * frame = 0.5 * 4 = 2`.

Notice that in Listing 8.2 the variable `total_frames` and the output file declaration were not used. Therefore, `total_frames = end_frame + 1`, and the filename defaults to OUT.

Conditional Processing

Conditional processing gives you the ability to define objects or token names based on the status of a conditional expression. For example,

276

```
if (frame == 0)
    define Radius 0.5
else
    define Radius 1.0
```

In this example, the token name `Radius` has a value depending on the current frame being ray traced. If `frame` is equal to zero, the `Radius` will be equal to 0.5, otherwise it will be equal to 1.0. You can also create objects in the same manner:

```
if (Radius == 1.0)
    object {
        sphere <0, 0, 0>, Radius
        shiny_red
    }
```

In this example, a shiny red sphere will be created on the current frame if `Radius` is equal to 1.0. If `Radius` is different from 1.0, the sphere will not appear on the scene. The syntax for conditional processing is

```
if (cexper) {
    [definition #1a]
    [definition #2a]
    ...etc...
}
else {
    [definition #1b]
    [definition #2b]
    ...etc...
}
```

where   *cexper*   is a conditional expression (refer to Chapter 6, Conditional Expression Section)

              definition   can be of the type:

                                       object {...}

                                       light ...

                                       define ...

The curly brackets are used only if there is more than one definition inside the `if` or the `else` statements.

You can also nest conditional processing expressions:

```
if (cexper #1) {
        ...etc...
}
else  if (cexper #2) {
        ...etc...
    }
```

```
    else {
    ...etc...
    }
```

As a final note, you can have complete control over objects in animation by combining conditional processing, conditional expressions, and special surface textures.

Static Definitions

As you know, conditional processing can create objects depending on a conditional expression:

```
if (frame == 0)
    object {
        sphere <0, 0, 0>, 2
        shiny_red
    }
```

The only problem with this expression is that the sphere will only be seen when frame = 0. On the remaining frames, the sphere will not appear. In other words, if you wish the object to appear on all of the frames you must replace the conditional expression with frame >= 0:

```
if (frame >= 0)
    object {
        sphere <0, 0, 0>, 2
        shiny_red
    }
```

or simply discard the conditional processing expression

```
    object {
        sphere <0, 0, 0>, 2
        shiny_red
    }
```

The static keyword is used to declare that once an object is defined, it does not have to be redefined on all the remaining frames; it will remain static. The declaration

```
if (frame = 0)
        static define MySphere
        object {
                sphere <0, 0, 0>, 2
                white_marble
        }
    object {
        MySphere
        rotate <0, 10*frame, 0>
    }
```

indicates to Polyray that the sphere called MySphere will be created once at the beginning (frame = 0) and will stay in memory throughout the creation of all the remaining frames. Using this on a sphere doesn't make much sense, but if you have a large quantity of objects, or those objects require lots of computation time (height fields, for example), Polyray will do the computation only once and save the objects to memory. In other words, all the tough computations are done once and then the remaining frames will just use the objects available in memory.

A static define can also be used to save and modify the values of variables from frame to frame:

```
if (frame == start_frame)
        static define radius 1.0
else    if (frame == start_frame + 1)
                static define radius (radius - 0.5)
        else
                static define radius (radius - 0.3)
```

In this example, radius is given the value of 1.0. In the next frame, radius = radius -0.5 and the value is saved in memory. For the remaining frames, radius = radius -0.3.

Arrays

Arrays are a powerful tool in animation. A typical example is the use of a path data file that contains the locations of the object on each frame. The frame number can be used as the index of the array to extract the current position:

```
start_frame 0
end_frame 3

define Location       [<0, 0, 0>,
                       <0.3, 5.5, 2.1>,
                       <0, -5, 3>,
                       <-6, 4, -1>]

object {
        sphere Location[frame], 2
        shiny_red
}
```

where, as an example, Location[0] = <0, 0, 0> and Location[1] = <0.3, 5.5, 2.1>.

Listing 8.3 presents a program that reads a data file and converts it into a Polyray array. The program is compatible with QBasic and Quick Basic 4.5.

Listing 8.3. Program to read a data file and create a Polyray array.

```
' ARRAY.BAS
' PROGRAM TO READ A DATA FILE AND CREATE AN ARRAY FOR POLYRAY
'
' This Program reads a data file that consists of 3D points in the form
' p1.x p1.y p1.z
' p2.x p2.y p2.z
' ...etc...
DIM inf AS STRING, outf AS STRING, an AS STRING
DIM x AS SINGLE, y AS SINGLE, z AS SINGLE
CLS
INPUT "Enter Name of Data File [TEST.DAT]"; inf$
IF inf$ = "" THEN inf$ = "TEST.DAT"
PRINT
INPUT "Enter Name of Output File [ARRAY.OUT]"; outf$
IF outf$ = "" THEN outf$ = "ARRAY.OUT"
PRINT
INPUT "Enter Token Name for Array [MyArray]"; an$
IF an$ = "" THEN an$ = "MyArray"
OPEN inf$ FOR INPUT AS #1
OPEN outf$ FOR OUTPUT AS #2
PRINT #2, "// Array ["; an$; "] created with ARRAY.BAS"
PRINT #2, "// from data file ["; inf$; "]"
PRINT #2, ""
PRINT #2, "define "; an$; " ["
DO
 INPUT #1, x, y, z
 PRINT #2, "           <"; x; ", "; y; ", "; z; ">";
 IF NOT EOF(1) THEN
 PRINT #2, ","
 END IF
LOOP UNTIL (EOF(1))
PRINT #2, ""
PRINT #2, "          ]"
CLOSE #1
CLOSE #2
```

The program asks the name of the data file to be used as input, the name of the output file to be created, and the token name for the array. The file can the be added to your scene files with a text editor or using an `include` statement.

To test the program, create an ASCII file with your text editor and type in the following data as it appears (press Enter after each line). Save the file as TEST.DAT:

```
1 1 1
2 2 2
3 3 3
4 4 4
5 5 5
```

Run ARRAY.BAS and press enter to accept all the default values. Listing 8.4 presents the output generated by ARRAY.BAS.

Listing 8.4. Output generated by ARRAY.BAS (ARRAY.OUT).

```
// Array [MyArray] created with ARRAY.BAS
// from data file [TEST.DAT]

define MyArray [
        < 1 ,  1 ,  1 >,
        < 2 ,  2 ,  2 >,
        < 3 ,  3 ,  3 >,
        < 4 ,  4 ,  4 >,
        < 5 ,  5 ,  5 >
    ]
```

The output file ARRAY.OUT presents the name of the array [MyArray] and the data file used as input [TEST.DAT]. To refer to this file in your scene, use the statement `include "array.out"`.

Creating the Animation File

The animation file is created by an external utility called DTA (Dave's .TGA Animator) written by David K. Mason (check the Introduction of this book for bulletin boards where you can find DTA). DTA creates Autodesk Animator-compatible files with the .FLI extension. The program accepts a series of command line parameters that define the files to be used in order to create the animation file, the speed of the animation and the output file name. DTA does not play the animation file after it generates it. You'll need another program called AAPLAY (Autodesk Animator Player) to view it.

For our purpose, DTA can be executed simply as

    DTA NAME*.TGA

where NAME is the 5 letter name given to the frames created by Polyray. Since Polyray will generate the frames in numerical sequence (NAME000.TGA, NAME001.TGA, NAME002.TGA, and so on) using the wildcard symbol (*) will tell DTA to select all the files that start with the word NAME and have the extension TGA. DTA will sort the files in the correct order. Since we didn't define a name for the output file, the default "ANIM.FLI" is used. If you wish to change this name, execute DTA as

    DTA NAME*.TGA /OFILENAME.FLI

where FILENAME is the name for the output file. The animation files should always end with the FLI extension.

Once the animation file is created, run AAPLAY and select your animation file from the menu to execute it.

Resolution Issues

There are two important issues concerning the resolution of the images to be ray traced and animated. First, creating multiple frames may consume plenty of time and hard drive space. As a suggestion, use low resolution in your viewpoint definition, for example, resolution 100,100 with an aspect ratio of 1.0. This reduces computation time and space requirements. Generate the animation file and preview it for correctness. If all is well, change to a higher resolution. Second, the highest resolution for a FLI animation is 320 by 200. If you wish to generate higher resolutions, use DTA to create FLC files (but you'll need an FLC player to view the animation, plus a good graphics card and a fast machine!).

When generating the final animation, use anti-aliasing, since aliasing is more noticeable at low resolutions (320 × 200).

Animation Examples

In the following section you'll have the opportunity to apply the different types of animation techniques presented in the previous sections: flyby, object, virtual, and texture variation.

Flyby

One of the easiest examples of flyby animation is to follow the path of a satellite as it orbits a planet. In order to compare the cases of the viewpoint when it's stationary and when it's in motion, you'll develop an animation that consists of two parts. The first part will have a planet with its own moon orbiting around it. The observer will remain stationary. In the second part, both the planet's moon and the observer are in motion.

To understand the motion of the moon and the observer, refer to figure 8.10.

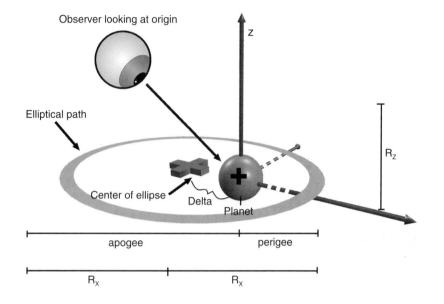

Figure 8.10

Elliptical orbit.

Figure 8.10 presents an elliptical path for the orbit. The smallest distance between the observer and the planet is called the *perigee,* and the largest distance is called the *apogee.* The *delta* is the difference between the center of the elliptical orbit and the center of the planet. The ellipse can be described by

    x = Rx * cos(2pt)

    z = Rz * sin(2pt)

    where   p = 3.1415....

               t varies from 0 to 1

               Rx = (perigee + apogee)/2

When Rx = Rz, the functions describe a circular path. (A good exercise is to use grid paper and calculate at least 4 points. Use t = 0, t =0.25, t = 0.5, t = 0.75, and connect them with lines.) In order to locate the center of the ellipse to the left of the planet (as it is in figure 8.10), the x value must be modified to

283

```
x = Rx * cos(2pt) - delta
```

where `delta = ¦Rx - perigee¦`

Since you will be using the variable frame as the increment, you can replace the expression `2pt` with `(2p/sections)*frame` where `sections` is the number of divisions of the `2p` (360 degrees). For example, to divide the orbit into 15 sections, write `(2p/15)*frame`. When `frame = 15`, the observer has completed one full orbit. In this scene, define `div = (2p/15)`.

Listing 8.5 presents two orbits. The first is the orbit of a moon around its planet and the second is the orbit of the observer around the planet (the moon is also orbiting the planet). Figure 8.11 displays four frames of the moon's orbit, and figure 8.12 displays four frames of the observer and the moon orbiting.

Listing 8.5. Flyby example (ORBIT.PI).

```
//ORBIT.PI
start_frame 1
end_frame 45
include "colors.inc"
include "texture.inc"
// Do not Modify
static define Pi 4*atan(1.0)      // Pi = 3.1415....
static define TwoPi 2*Pi          // 2*Pi
// Modify the following (if necessary)
static define perigee  1
static define apogee   3
static define Rz          2

// Do not modify
static define Rx          (perigee + apogee)/2
static define delta       fabs(Rx - perigee)
static define div         (TwoPi/15)
static define FirstCycle    <Rx - delta, 0, Rz>        // Stationary
static define SecondCycle   <Rx*cos(-div*frame) - delta, // Orbit Motion
                            0,
                            Rz*sin(-div*frame)>

if (frame<= 15) {
       viewpoint {
       from        FirstCycle
       at          <0.0, 0.0, 0.0 >
       up          <0.0, 1.0, 0.0 >
       angle       45
       resolution 100,100
       aspect      1.0
       }
}
else {
viewpoint {
       from        SecondCycle
```

```
        at          <0.0, 0.0, 0.0 >
        up          <0.0, 1.0, 0.0 >
        angle       45
        resolution 100,100
        aspect      1.0
        }
}
// LIGHT SOURCE THAT FOLLOWS THE OBSERVER
if (frame<= 15)
        light FirstCycle
else
        light SecondCycle

// LIGHT_SOURCE
  light <-10 ,   -1 , -20  >
// LIGHT_SOURCE
  light <0, 20, 0>

// PLANET
object {
    sphere <0, 0, 0>, 0.3
    white_marble
}
// MOON
object {
    sphere <0.5*cos(div*frame),0, 0.5*sin(div*frame)>, 0.05
    shiny_yellow
}
```

ORBIT.PI uses some interesting techniques. First, it has two viewpoint definitions depending on the number of the frame. This is accomplished through the use of conditional processing. If the frame number is less than or equal to 15, it keeps the observer stationary; otherwise it moves it in an elliptical path:

```
if (frame <= 15) {
        viewpoint {
        from        FirstCycle
        at          <0.0, 0.0, 0.0 >
        up          <0.0, 1.0, 0.0 >
        angle       45
        resolution 100,100
        aspect      1.0
        }
}
else {
viewpoint {
        from        SecondCycle
        at          <0.0, 0.0, 0.0 >
        up          <0.0, 1.0, 0.0 >
        angle       45
        resolution 100,100
        aspect      1.0
        }
}
```

The at vector remains constant in both cases.

Figure 8.11

*Orbit animation
(ORBIT.PI).*

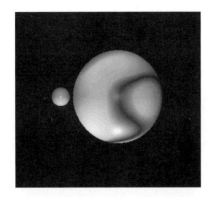 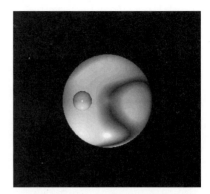

 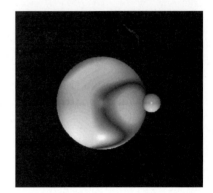

Another feature is the motion of one of the light sources. It follows the observer:

```
if (frame<= 15)
        light FirstCycle
else
        light SecondCycle
```

As I mentioned before, attaching a light source to the observer guarantees that at least one light source is illuminating what the observer is looking at.

Finally, the moon follows a circular orbit around the planet (Rx = Rz = 0.5), and it is continually in motion throughout the animation

```
object {
    sphere <0.5*cos(div*frame),0, 0.5*sin(div*frame)>, 0.05
    shiny_yellow
}
```

Can you distinguish a difference between figure 8.11 and figure 8.12? In the first four, the moon is the only object in motion. Since the planet is stationary, the texture doesn't rotate. In the four frames of figure 8.12, the observer is in motion, so you are able to look at different parts of the planet and the texture appears to rotate—not because the planet is in motion, but because the observer is.

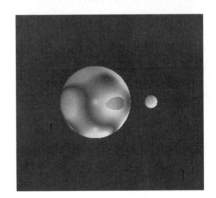

Figure 8.12

Orbit animation (ORBIT.PI).

Texture Animation

The next example provides a more explicit representation of what happens when transformations are applied after the texture. Listing 8.6 presents a sphere mapped with an alpha_yellow_marble texture. This texture was used in Chapter 4, "Layered Texture" section, and consists of a marble-like finish with some areas being transparent.

To animate the texture, the sphere and textures are rotated from 0 to 360 degrees about the y axis in 10 degree increments:

```
object {
   sphere <0,0,0>, 1.3
   alpha_yellow_marble
   rotate <0, 10*frame, 0>
}
```

Figure 8.13 displays the first four frames of AXISORBT.PI. To find out what happens when a transformation is placed before the texture, I suggest you modify Listing 8.6 by moving the statement rotate <0, 10*frame, 0> to before alpha_yellow_marble

```
object {
   sphere <0,0,0>, 1.3
   rotate <0, 10*frame, 0>
   alpha_yellow_marble
}
```

and generate the animation again.

Listing 8.6. Rotating the texture (AXISORBT.PI).

```
// AXISORBT.PI
start_frame 0
end_frame  36
include "texture.inc"
include "colors.inc"
background white
define alpha_yellow_marble
texture {
   noise surface {
      color white
      position_fn position_objectx
      lookup_fn   lookup_sawtooth
      octaves 3
      turbulence 3
      ambient 0.3
      diffuse 0.8
      specular 0.3
      microfacet Reitz 5
      transmission white, 1,1
      color_map(
      [0.0, 0.2, yellow, 0,    yellow, 0]
      [0.2, 0.5, yellow, 0,    black, 0.2]
      [0.6, 1.0, black, 0.2, black, 1]
      )
      }
}
viewpoint {
 from      <-2, 3, -7 >
 at        <0.0, -0.2, 0.0 >
 up        <0.0, 1.0, 0.0 >
 angle     45
```

```
 resolution 100,100
 aspect      1.0
}
// LIGHT_SOURCE
directional_light < 0 ,  5 , -7  >
object {
   sphere <0,0,0>, 1.3
   alpha_yellow_marble
   rotate <0, 10*frame, 0>
}
```

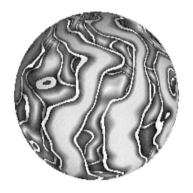

Frame 1

Frame 2

Figure 8.13

*Texture
animation
(AXISORBT.PI).*

Frame 3

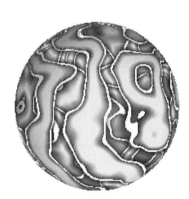

Frame 4

Object Animation

The following example models a robot hand and presents an animation of it
catching a ball. This is a good example of how the position and orientation of
objects can be dependent on the position and orientation of other objects. Take
your own right hand for example. The index finger is divided into three parts:
the base of the finger, the middle part, and the tip. If you can bend the tip, the
other two sections of the finger stay put. If you bend the middle part, the tip
will follow. And if you move the base of the finger, the middle part and the tip
will follow (figure 8.14 presents all the steps described). In other words, the base
of the finger depends on one angle for motion, the middle section on two
angles, and the tip on three angles (see fig. 8.15). Listing 8.7 presents the scene
file for the animation of a robot hand.

Listing 8.7. Robot hand animation (HAND.PI).

```
// HAND.PI
start_frame 0
end_frame 45
include "colors.inc"
include "texture.inc"
define HandTexture reflective_grey
define BallPath [                          // MOTION OF THE BALL
            < 0 ,   0 , -19.2 >,
            < 0 ,   3.2 , -14.4 >,
            < 0 ,   3.2 , -11.2 >,
            < 0 ,   3.2 , -9.6 >,
            < 0 ,   1.6 , -8 >,
            < 0 ,   0.1 , -7.1 >,
            < 0 ,  -1.3 , -6.4 >,
            < 0 ,  -2.9 , -5.6 >,
            < 0 ,  -5 , -4.7 >,
            < 0 ,  -4 , -4.1 >,
            < 0 ,  -2.8 , -3.4 >,
            < 0 ,  -1.7 , -2.8 >,
            < 0 ,  -0.6 , -2.3 >,
            < 0 ,   0.2 , -1.9 >,
            < 0 ,   1 , -1.5 >
        ]

define ThumbAngley     frame*2        // USE FRAME AS THE ANGLE.
define ThumbAngle2x    -frame         // START AT 0 AND END AT
define ThumbAnglez     -frame         // 45 DEGREES, EXCEPT THUMB
define FingerAnglex123 -frame
define FingerAnglex23  -frame
define FingerAnglex3   -frame
define FingerAnglez    0

define Plane_XZ
object { polygon 4, <-20,0,20>, <-20,0,-20>, <20,0,-20>, <20,0,20> }
// LIGHT_SOURCE
```

```
light < 10 ,  10 , 0  >
// LIGHT_SOURCE
light < -1 ,  5 , -20  >
viewpoint {
 from      <2.0, 5.0, -10.0 >
 at        <0.0, 1.5, 0.0 >
 up        <0.0, 1.0, 0.0 >
 angle     45
 resolution 100,100
 aspect    1.0
}

// OBJECT TO GRASP  - BALL STARTS MOTION AT FRAME #31
if (frame>30)
object {
    sphere BallPath[frame - 31], 1
    shiny_red
}
// FLOOR
object {
     Plane_XZ
     translate <0, -6, 0>
     matte_brown
}
// DEFINE THE PALM
// BOX
object {
    box <-1, -1, -1>, <1, 1, 1>
    scale < 1.35,1.5,0.5>
    HandTexture
}

//DEFINE THE THUMB
define ThumbPart
object {
    box <-1, -1, -1>, <1, 1, 1>
    scale < 0.3,0.5,0.5>
}
object {
// BOX THUMB 1
    object {
        ThumbPart
        translate<0.0, 0.5, 0.0>
    }
+
// BOX THUMB 2
    object {
        ThumbPart
        translate<0.0, 0.5, 0.0>
        rotate<ThumbAngle2x, 0.0, 0.0>
        translate< 0.0, 1.0, 0.0>
    }
    rotate < 0.0, 0.0, ThumbAnglez>
    rotate < 0.0, ThumbAngley, 0.0>
    translate < 1.75,0.0,0.0>
    HandTexture
}
```

continues

Listing 8.7. Continued.

```
// DEFINE A GENERIC FINGER
define FingerPart
object {
    box <-1, -1, -1>, <1, 1, 1>
    scale < 0.3,0.5,0.5>
}
define WholeFinger
object {
// FINGER PART 1  (NEAREST TO THE PALM)
object {
    FingerPart
    translate<0.0, 0.5, 0.0>
}
+
object {
// FINGER PART 2  (MIDDLE SECTION)
object {
    FingerPart
    translate<0.0, 0.5, 0.0>
}
+
// FINGER PART 3  (TIP)
    object {
        FingerPart
        translate<0.0, 0.5, 0.0>
        rotate<FingerAnglex3, 0.0, 0.0>
        translate<0.0, 1.0, 0.0>
    }
    rotate<FingerAnglex23, 0.0, 0.0>
    translate < 0.0 , 1.0, 0.0>
}
    rotate<FingerAnglex123, 0.0, FingerAnglez>
}

// CREATE INDIVIDUAL FINGERS
// INDEX
object {
    WholeFinger
    scale <0.9, 0.8, 1>
    translate < 1.1, 1.75,0.0>
    HandTexture
}
// MIDDLE
object {
    WholeFinger
    scale <0.9, 1, 1>
    translate < 0.3, 1.75,0.0>
    HandTexture
}
// RING
object {
    WholeFinger
    scale <0.9, 0.9, 1>
    translate < -0.5, 1.75,0.0>
    HandTexture
```

```
}
// PINKY
object {
   WholeFinger
   scale <0.9, 0.75, 1>
   translate < -1.3, 1.75,0.0>
   HandTexture
}
```

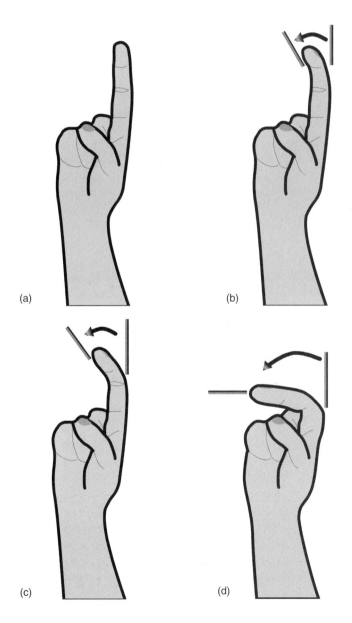

(a)

(b)

(c)

(d)

Figure 8.14

*Bending
different
sections of a
finger.*

293

Figure 8.15

The relationship between angles in the fingers.

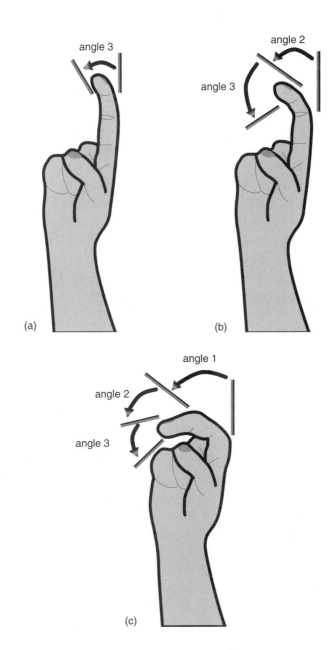

(a)

(b)

(c)

In HAND.PI, a set of angles are defined that correspond to the different angles in the fingers and in the thumb (the thumb's motion is different from the rest of the fingers). For orientation purposes, we will assume that the palm of the open right hand is facing the -z axis and the fingers, when stretched, are pointing in the +y axis. When the thumb is stretched out completely, it points in the +x axis (see fig. 8.16).

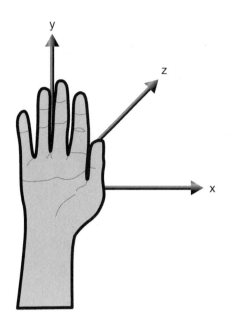

The angles defined for the hand are

Thumb Angles:

ThumbAngley	Rotation of thumb about y axis
ThumbAngle2x	Rotation of thumb tip about x axis
ThumbAnglez	Rotation of thumb about z axis

Finger Angles:

FingerAnglex123	Rotation of whole finger about x axis
FingerAnglex23 about x axis	Rotation of middle section and tip of finger
FingerAnglex3	Rotation of finger tip about x axis
FingerAnglez	Rotation of whole finger about z axis

Let's study how the thumb is modeled. The thumb is composed of two sections: tip and base (nearest to the hand). Start by defining a generic piece of thumb with a box:

295

```
define ThumbPart
object {
    box < -1, -1, -1 >, < 1, 1, 1 >
    scale < 0.3,0.5,0.5 >
}
```

The unit box is located in the origin, and a scale factor of <0.3, 0.5, 0.5> is used. If you look at your thumb, the pivot point for each section is at the base of that section, so a translation of <0.0, 0.5, 0.0> is required to locate the bottom of the box in the origin. Recall that it's easier to locate the pivot point in the origin and apply the rotations, then translate it to its final location.

The section THUMB 1 refers to the base of the thumb. The only transformation applied is the translation of the pivot point to the origin.

```
// BOX THUMB 1
    object {
        ThumbPart
        translate< 0.0, 0.5, 0.0 >
    }
```

The section THUMB 2 is the tip of the thumb and it requires more work. First, translate the tip so the pivot point is at the origin. Next, apply a rotation about the x axis by the angle ThumbAngle2x. Finally, locate the tip of the thumb on top of THUMB 1.

```
// BOX THUMB 2
    object {
        ThumbPart
        translate< 0.0, 0.5, 0.0 >
        rotate< ThumbAngle2x, 0.0, 0.0 >
        translate< 0.0, 1.0, 0.0 >
    }
```

After constructing each section of the thumb, you still have some more transformations to apply. At this point, the pivot point of the section THUMB 1 is located at the origin, and THUMB 2 is on top of THUMB 1. When the thumb rotates about z, the whole thumb rotates. The transformation rotate < 0.0, 0.0, ThumbAnglez> is applied to the whole thumb. The next transformation rotate < 0.0, ThumbAngley, 0.0> is applied also to the whole thumb but it is done after the z rotation. To experiment, try swapping these to operations. You'll see that the thumb will rotate in a way that is not physically possible. After all the rotations have been applied, its time to move the complete thumb to its place in the hand. The transformation translate < 1.75,0.0,0.0> does this.

The same technique is used to model the finger. Since the finger is divided into three sections, modeling it is more involved, but still straightforward.

After one finger has been modeled, you can create multiple copies of it and locate them in their respective places in the hand:

```
// INDEX
object {
   WholeFinger
   scale < 0.9, 0.8, 1 >
   translate < 1.1,1.75,0.0 >
   HandTexture
}

// MIDDLE
object {
   WholeFinger
   scale < 0.9, 1, 1 >
   translate < 0.3,1.75,0.0 >
   HandTexture
}

// RING
object {
   WholeFinger
   scale < 0.9, 0.9, 1 >
   translate < -0.5,1.75,0.0 >
   HandTexture
}

// PINKY
object {
   WholeFinger
   scale < 0.9, 0.75, 1 >
   translate < -1.3,1.75,0.0 >
   HandTexture
}
```

Notice that since the fingers of a hand have all different lengths, a scaling operation is used on each finger to change its length. This is by no means an accurate model of a hand, but it's a good foundation from where to start more complicated hands.

The next step is to animate the hand. To make things more interesting, halfway through the animation, a ball comes bouncing from nowhere and gets caught by the robot hand. The section of the code that sets up the animation for the robot hand is

```
start_frame 0
end_frame 45

define ThumbAngley    frame*2
define ThumbAngle2x  -frame
define ThumbAnglez   -frame

define FingerAnglex123 -frame
define FingerAnglex23 -frame
define FingerAnglex3 -frame
define FingerAnglez 0
```

The animation will have a total of 46 frames (0 to 45). Each angle will be equal to the frame number except `ThumbAngley` which will always be twice the frame amount (`frame * 2`).

To animate the ball, I used POVCAD and created a set of points on the screen and saved them with the `FREEHAND` command (in the Path menu). These points describe the path of the ball. Then I used the program ARRAY.BAS to convert the points into an array named `BallPath`. There are only 15 points, so the motion of the ball starts sometime in the middle of the animation. The idea was to show the ball approaching the robot hand, first by the ball's shadow, then by its reflection in the palm of the robot hand, then by showing it as it enters the observer's field of view.

The ball starts the motion by means of a conditional processing expression:

```
if (frame > 30)
object {
    sphere BallPath[frame - 31], 1
    shiny_red
}
```

If `frame` is greater than 30, the ball starts its motion. The location of the sphere is taken out of the array `BallPath`. To select the correct location, the expression `frame - 31` is used. When frame is equal to 31, then `frame - 31 = 31 - 31 = 0` (recall that the first element in the array has the index 0). When frame is 45, then `45 - 31 = 14` (the last element's index is 14).

Figure 8.17 displays various frames of the animation.

Virtual Animation

As I mentioned earlier, in a virtual animation scene the object is shown in all of the locations at one time. Transparency is used as a means of distinguishing which is the sequence of the animation: the object in the first location will be the most transparent and the last object in the sequence will be totally opaque. Listing 8.8 presents a virtual animation scene.

Figure 8.17

*Robot hand
animation
(HAND.PI).*

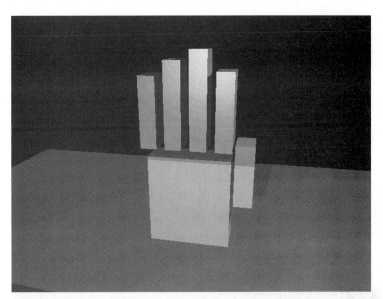

Frame 1

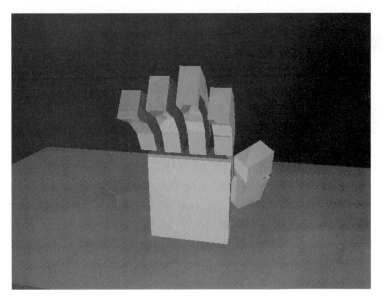

Frame 2

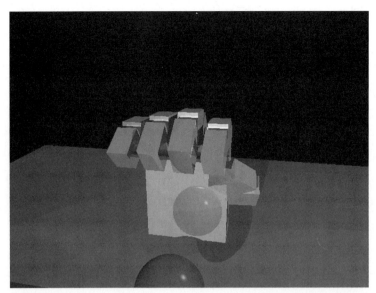

Frame 3

Frame 4

The scene VIRTUAL.PI has some interesting features. First, a set of textures *Tn* where *n* is a number indicating the location number, are defined:

```
define Transparent
   surface {
      color red
      ambient 0.1
      diffuse 0.7
      specular 0.2
      reflection white, 0.1
   }

define T1  texture {Transparent { transmission white, 1.00, 1}}
define T2  texture {Transparent { transmission white, 0.98, 1}}
define T3  texture {Transparent { transmission white, 0.96, 1}}
...etc...

define T19 texture {Transparent { transmission white, 0.00, 1}}
```

Since there are 19 spheres, the best way to reduce the amount of typing is by creating the surface definition "Transparent." Then each individual sphere will have its own transmission value.

The second feature is the use of an array to define the sphere locations. You saw this technique in the previous section where the robot hand catches a ball. This also considerably reduces the amount of typing. Figure 8.18 displays the final image.

Listing 8.8. Virtual animation of a bouncing sphere (VIRTUAL.PI).

```
// VIRTUAL.PI
include "colors.inc"
include "texture.inc"
background grey
define Transparent
   surface {
      color red
      ambient 0.1
      diffuse 0.7
      specular 0.2
      reflection white, 0.1
   }
define T1  texture {Transparent { transmission white, 1.00, 1}}
define T2  texture {Transparent { transmission white, 0.98, 1}}
define T3  texture {Transparent { transmission white, 0.96, 1}}
define T4  texture {Transparent { transmission white, 0.94, 1}}
define T5  texture {Transparent { transmission white, 0.92, 1}}
define T6  texture {Transparent { transmission white, 0.90, 1}}
define T7  texture {Transparent { transmission white, 0.88, 1}}
define T8  texture {Transparent { transmission white, 0.86, 1}}
define T9  texture {Transparent { transmission white, 0.84, 1}}
define T10 texture {Transparent { transmission white, 0.82, 1}}
define T11 texture {Transparent { transmission white, 0.80, 1}}
define T12 texture {Transparent { transmission white, 0.78, 1}}
define T13 texture {Transparent { transmission white, 0.76, 1}}
```

continues

Listing 8.8. Continued.

```
define T14 texture {Transparent { transmission white, 0.74, 1}}
define T15 texture {Transparent { transmission white, 0.72, 1}}
define T16 texture {Transparent { transmission white, 0.70, 1}}
define T17 texture {Transparent { transmission white, 0.68, 1}}
define T18 texture {Transparent { transmission white, 0.66, 1}}
define T19 texture {Transparent { transmission white, 0.00, 1}}
define BallPath [
                <-5.9184,  1.8992,  0>,
                <-5.5152,  2.3744,  0>,
                <-4.7856,  2.6304,  0>,
                <-4.1648,  2.448 ,  0>,
                <-3.77  ,  2.05  ,  0>,
                <-3.36  ,  1.3152,  0>,
                <-3.032 ,  0.4384,  0>,
                <-2.6   ,  0.95  ,  0>,
                <-2.0096,  1.5344,  0>,
                <-1.4608,  1.7904,  0>,
                <-0.8032,  1.7904,  0>,
                <-0.2928,  1.2784,  0>,
                < 0.0736,  0.74  ,  0>,
                < 0.4384,  0.4016,  0>,
                < 1.1696,  0.9136,  0>,
                < 1.7168,  1.2416,  0>,
                < 2.3744,  1.2048,  0>,
                < 2.9216,  0.9136,  0>,
                < 3.3968,  0.4016,  0>
            ]

define Plane_XZ
object { polygon 4, <-20,0,20>, <-20,0,-20>, <20,0,-20>, <20,0,20> }
// LIGHT_SOURCE
light < 10 ,  10 , 0  >
// LIGHT_SOURCE
light < -1 ,  5 , -20  >
viewpoint {
 from      <0.0, 2.0, -15.0 >
 at        <-1.0, 1.5, 0.0 >
 up        <0.0, 1.0, 0.0 >
 angle     40
 resolution 200,200
 aspect    1.0
}
// FLOOR
object {
    Plane_XZ
    matte_brown
}

object {
   sphere BallPath[0], 0.4
   T1
}
object {
   sphere BallPath[1], 0.4
   T2
```

```
}
object {
  sphere BallPath[2], 0.4
  T3
}
object {
  sphere BallPath[3], 0.4
  T4
}
object {
  sphere BallPath[4], 0.4
  T5
}
object {
  sphere BallPath[5], 0.4
  T6
}
object {
  sphere BallPath[6], 0.4
  T7
}
object {
  sphere BallPath[7], 0.4
  T8
}
object {
  sphere BallPath[8], 0.4
  T9
}
object {
  sphere BallPath[9], 0.4
  T10
}
object {
  sphere BallPath[10], 0.4
  T11
}
object {
  sphere BallPath[11], 0.4
  T12
}
object {
  sphere BallPath[12], 0.4
  T13
}
object {
  sphere BallPath[13], 0.4
  T14
}
object {
  sphere BallPath[14], 0.4
  T15
}
object {
  sphere BallPath[15], 0.4
  T16
```

continues

Listing 8.8. Continued.

```
}
object {
    sphere BallPath[16], 0.4
    T17
}
object {
    sphere BallPath[17], 0.4
    T18
}
object {
    sphere BallPath[18], 0.4
    T19
}
```

Figure 8.18

Virtual animation of a bouncing ball.

Summary

In this chapter, you studied different types of animation: by moving the viewpoint and the "look at" you can create the effect of a flyby. Textures can be animated by applying transformation in an object after the texture has been defined for it. Another type of animation called "virtual animation" is used to produce a static scene that would represent how an object moves in a sequence. This is accomplished by creating multiple copies of the object as it travels from one location to another. The effect is completed by varying the amount of transparency in the object's surface.

Now that you're done with the book, where do you go from here? My suggestion to you is this: take some time to experiment changing different parameters in the scenes included with this book. This teaches you how small changes in the parameters affect the final image. In terms of animation, try modeling different objects: a pair of scissors, a spinning top, a person walking, and so on. Some of these aren't easy, but you can model them by carefully observing which features are the most outstanding and then modeling those to give the animation the effect of reality. Finally, go to your nearest bookstore and get a couple of books on animation. I suggest the book *Advanced Animation and Rendering Techniques*, by Watt and Watt, as an excellent reference.

Where Can I Find Ray Tracing Software?

Here's a list of bulletin boards where you can find the latest and greatest in ray tracing software and utilities:

- Pi Squared BBS (Maryland)
  Alfonso Hermida (SysOp)
  (301)725-9080 running at 14.4K bps, 24 hours

  This is the home of POVCAD and the book that you are now reading. You can download the latest versions of POVCAD, POLYRAY, and other utilities from this BBS. Feel free to leave any comments or suggestions on the book and my program. Try selecting the [C]hat command...I might be around!

CompuServe
(614)-457-8650
(800)-848-8990
GraphDev Forum
Alfonso Hermida, ID# 72114,2060

The GraphDev forum in CompuServe is *the* place where people interested in computer graphics development, ray tracing, fractals, animation, and image processing meet. There are various message areas depending on the topic of your interest and file areas with utilities to aid you. There is also an extensive image file area inside GraphDev full of GIF files for you to download (these image files are created by people like you who enjoy sharing them with others).

You Can Call Me Ray BBS (Illinois)
Bill Minus/Aaron Collins (SysOps)
(708)358-5611

The Graphics Alternative BBS (California)
Adam Shiffman (SysOp)
(510)524-2780

Monsoon BBS (Maryland)
Sunil Gupta (SysOp)
(410)235-2365

In Europe:

Raytech BBS
Paul Smith (SysOp)
+44 862 88340

Digital Imagery BBS
Philip Harris
+44 295 272881 V32 MNP 5

CIX (UK equivalent of CompuServe)
ECS conference, POVCAD topic
+44 081 390 1255

Index

313

T

319

GO AHEAD. PLUG YOURSELF INTO PRENTICE HALL COMPUTER PUBLISHING.

Introducing the PHCP Forum on CompuServe®

Yes, it's true. Now, you can have CompuServe access to the same professional, friendly folks who have made computers easier for years. On the PHCP Forum, you'll find additional information on the topics covered by every PHCP imprint—including Que, Sams Publishing, New Riders Publishing, Alpha Books, Brady Books, Hayden Books, and Adobe Press. In addition, you'll be able to receive technical support and disk updates for the software produced by Que Software and Paramount Interactive, a division of the Paramount Technology Group. It's a great way to supplement the best information in the business.

WHAT CAN YOU DO ON THE PHCP FORUM?

Play an important role in the publishing process—and make our books better while you make your work easier:

- Leave messages and ask questions about PHCP books and software—you're guaranteed a response within 24 hours
- Download helpful tips and software to help you get the most out of your computer
- Contact authors of your favorite PHCP books through electronic mail
- Present your own book ideas
- Keep up to date on all the latest books available from each of PHCP's exciting imprints

JOIN NOW AND GET A FREE COMPUSERVE STARTER KIT!

To receive your free CompuServe Introductory Membership, call toll-free, **1-800-848-8199** and ask for representative **#K597**. The Starter Kit Includes:

- Personal ID number and password
- $15 credit on the system
- Subscription to CompuServe Magazine

HERE'S HOW TO PLUG INTO PHCP:

Once on the CompuServe System, type any of these phrases to access the PHCP Forum:

GO PHCP   **GO BRADY**
GO QUEBOOKS   **GO HAYDEN**
GO SAMS   **GO QUESOFT**
GO NEWRIDERS   **GO PARAMOUNTINTER**
GO ALPHA

Once you're on the CompuServe Information Service, be sure to take advantage of all of CompuServe's resources. CompuServe is home to more than 1,700 products and services—plus it has over 1.5 million members worldwide. You'll find valuable online reference materials, travel and investor services, electronic mail, weather updates, leisure-time games and hassle-free shopping (no jam-packed parking lots or crowded stores).

Seek out the hundreds of other forums that populate CompuServe. Covering diverse topics such as pet care, rock music, cooking, and political issues, you're sure to find others with the same concerns as you—and expand your knowledge at the same time.

Let Que Help You with All Your Graphics Needs!

Improve with Hot Tips!

These unique guides teach readers shortcuts as well as powerful techniques—improving the proficiency of both novice and experienced users.

Count on Que for the Most Up-to-Date Information on Integrated Packages

**Using Microsoft Works
for Windows, Special Edition**
Douglas Wolf

This book provides plenty of timesaving tips and hints on sharing information between Works' modules. A comprehensive reference and tutorial, this book will give you everything you need to know about Microsoft Works.

Version 1

$24.95 USA
0-88022-757-5, 550 pp., 7³/₈ x 9¹/₄

**Using Microsoft Works:
IBM Version**
Douglas Wolf

Through Version 2

$22.95 USA
0-88022-467-3, 444 pp., 7³/₈ x 9¹/₄

Using Q&A 4
David Ewing & Bill Langenes

Version 4

$27.95 USA
0-88022-643-9, 550 pp., 7³/₈ x 9¹/₄

Q&A 4 Quick Reference
Que Development Group

Latest Version

$9.95 USA
0-88022-828-8, 160 pp., 4³/₄ x 8

Q&A 4 QuickStart
Que Development Group

Version 4

$19.95 USA
0-88022-653-6, 400 pp., 7³/₈ x 9¹/₄

Que's Using Enable
Walter Bruce

All Versions Through Enable/OA4

$29.95 USA
0-88022-701-X, 700 pp., 7³/₈ x 9¹/₄

Using Lotus Works 3.0
J. D. Watson

Release 3.0

$24.95 USA
0-88022-771-0, 500 pp., 7³/₈ x 9¹/₄

Using PFS: First Choice 4.0
Katherine Murray

Through Version 4.0

$27.95 USA
0-88022-969-1, 600 pp., 7³/₈ x 9¹/₄

Using PFS: WindowsWorks 2
Deanna Bebb

Through Version 2

$29.95 USA
1-56529-073-9, 500 pp., 7³/₈ x 9¹/₄

**To Order, Call: (800) 428-5331
OR (317) 581-3500**

Root Solver Declarations (for Blobs, Polynomials, Splined Lathes, and the Torus)

(You may include any of these statements inside the object to improve computations.)

- root_solver Ferrari   (fastest, but numerically unstable)
- root_solver Vieta   (default)
- root_solver Sturm   (slowest, but best quality)

Object Modifier Statements

```
translate <tx, ty, tz>
rotate <rx,ry,rz>
scale <sx,sy,sz>
shading_flags shading_flag1+ shading_flag2+...etc...
u_steps u
v_steps v
bounding_box <x0,y0,z0>, <x1,y1,z1>
```

Shading Flags

Value	Flag
1	Shadow_Check
2	Reflect_Check
4	Transmit_Check
8	Two_Sides
16	Cast_Shadow
32	Check Primary Rays

Texture Declarations

```
surface { [ surface declarations ] }
noise surface { [ surface declarations ] }
special surface { [ surface declarations ] }
checker texture1, texture2
hexagon texture1, texture2, texture3
layered texture1, texture2, ..., textureN
```

Surface Declarations

```
color <r, g, b>
ambient scale
ambient color, scale
diffuse scale
diffuse color, scale
specular color, scale
specular scale
reflection color, scale
reflection scale
transmission color, scale, ior
transmission scale, ior
microfacet kind angle
```

Kinds of Microfacets

```
Blinn, Cook, Gaussian, Phong, Reitz.
```

Special Surface Declarations Add the Following to Surface Declarations:

```
normal vexper
```

Noise Surface Declarations Include All Surface Declarations Plus

```
color_map([index0, index1, Color0, [start_alpha0,] Color1[, end_alpha1]]
          [index2, index3, Color2, [start_alpha2,] Color3[, end_alpha3]]
             ...
          [indexx, indexy, Colorx, [start_alphax,] Colory[, end_alphay]])
bump_scale fexper
frequency fexper
phase fexper
lookup_fn index
normal_fn index
```

-d *p*	Dither objects with probability *p* (the number must be between 0 and 1). Use this parameter to reduce image generation time. Quality is also reduced.
	Example: -d 0.5
-D *p*	Dither *p* percent of rays used (the number must be between 0 and 1).
	Use this parameter to reduce image generation time. Quality is also reduced.
-q *n*	Select shading options:

Flag	Option
1	shadows
2	reflectivity
4	refraction
8	highlighting on both sides of a surface
16	check if object casts shadows
32	primary (eyes) rays will be checked

To use, simply add the number of the features wanted, for example,

```
shadows + reflectivity = 1 + 2 = 3.
```

The parameter usage would be -q 3.

Render Flag	Default
–r 0	– q 63 (all ON)
–r 1	– q 8
–r 2	N/A
–r 3	N/A

-x	Set image x resolution, default 512.
	Example: -x 640
-y	Set image y resolution, default 512.
	Example: -y 480

-Q	Abort run by pressing any key.
-R	Resume an interrupted trace.
-t *n*	Display tracing information.

Value	Status
0	none
1	totals at the end of trace
2	line
3	pixel (slows program down!)

-v	Ray trace image from bottom to top.
-V *m*	Screen preview status.

Value	Mode
0	none
1	VGA 320 × 200
2	VESA 640 × 480 hicolor mode (use –t 0 also)

-P *n*	Use palette number *n*.

Value	Colors
0	gray
1	666
2	884

-W	Wait for a keypress to clear the screen.
-z *n*	Start ray tracing at line *n*. This feature is good for checking partial images.

POLYRAY.INI File

You may wish to set some of the options outside of the command line or the scene file. You can optionally create a file named POLYRAY.INI containing some or all of the following keywords followed by one of the corresponding values (this file must be accessible by Polyray):

```
      blob components are:
      sphere <x, y, z>, strength, radius
      cylinder <x0, y0, z0>, <x1, y1, z1>, strength, radius
      plane <nx, ny, nz>, d, strength, distance

  box <x0, y0, z0>, <x1, y1, z1>

  cone <x0, y0, z0>, r0, <x1, y1, z1>, r1

  cylinder <x0, y0, z0>, <x1, y1, z1>, r

  disc <cx, cy, cz>, <nx, ny, nz>, r

  disc <cx, cy, cz>, <nx, ny, nz>, ir, or

  function f(x,y,z)

  height_field "filename.tga"
  smooth_height_field "filename.tga"

  (expression is of the form y = f(x,z))
  height_fn xsize, zsize, min_x, max_x, min_z, max_z, expression
  height_fn xsize, zsize, expression
  smooth_height_fn xsize, zsize, min_x, max_x, min_z, max_z, expression
  smooth_height_fn xsize, zsize, expression

  lathe type, direction, total_vertices,
     <vert1.x,vert1.y,vert1.z>,
     <vert2.x, vert2.y, vert2.z>,
       ...etc...,
     <vertN.x, vertN.y, vertN.z>

  parabola <x0, y0, z0>, <x1, y1, z1>, r

  polygon total_vertices,
     <vert1.x,vert1.y,vert1.z>,
     <vert2.x, vert2.y, vert2.z>,
       ...etc...,
     <vertN.x, vertN.y, vertN.z>

  polynomial f(x,y,z)

  sphere <xc, yc, zc>, radius

  sweep type, direction, total_vertices,
     <vert1.x,vert1.y,vert1.z>,
     <vert2.x, vert2.y, vert2.z>,
       ...etc...,
     <vertN.x, vertN.y, vertN.z>

  torus r0, r1, <xc, yc, zc>, <nx, ny, nz>

  patch <vert1.x,vert1.y,vert1.z>, <norm1.x,norm1.y,norm1.z>,
        <vert2.x,vert2.y,vert2.z>, <norm2.x,norm2.y,norm2.z>,
        <vert3.x,vert3.y,vert3.z>, <norm3.x,norm3.y,norm3.z>
```

Conditional Processing

```
  if (cexper)
     [single declaration]

  if (cexper) {
     [object/light/... declarations]
     }
  else {
     [other object/light/... declarations]
     }
```

Boolean (CSG) Operations

object1 + object2	Union
object1 * object2	Intersection
object1 - object2	Difference
object1 & object2	Clipping
-object	Inverse

Keyword	Values (select one or use a number if the # symbol appears)
abort_test	true, false, on, off
alias_threshold	# (threshold value for adaptive anti-aliasing)
antialias	none, filter, jitter, adaptive
display	none, vga, hicolor
max_level	# (max level of recursion)
max_samples	# (number of samples to use with anti-aliasing, or focal blur)
pallette	884, 666, grey
pixel_size	8, 16, 24, 32
pixel_encoding	none, rle
renderer	ray_trace, scan_convert, wire_frame, raw_triangles
shade_flags	default, # (shading options similar to –q)
status	none, totals, line, pixel
warnings	on, off

Input File Components

There are two classes of expressions:

fexper—Floating point expression; a number or a mathematical expression that returns a number.

vexper—Vector expression; a vector <a,b,c> or a mathematical expression that returns a vector.

Adding comments in a scene file

1. Any lines starting with "//" will be treated as comments and ignored.

    Example: // This is a comment

2. Any text between /* and */ will be ignored.

    Example: /* This is a comment */

Viewpoint

The following is a list of parameters inside the viewpoint definition that may be used to set the observer. You can omit any of the keywords and values to use the defaults.

viewpoint {	Defaults
from *vexper*	<0, 0, –1>
at *vexper*	<0, 0, 0>
up *vexper*	<0, 1, 0>
angle *fexper*	117
resolution *fexper, fexper*	512, 512
aspect *fexper*	1.0
hither *fexper*	1E –3
yon *fexper*	1E5
dither_rays *fexper*	–
dither_objects *fexper*	–
max_trace_depth *fexper*	5
aperture *fexper*	–
focal_distance *fexper*	–
}	

Define Statement

token = the name to be used in place of the expression to its right.

```
define token expression
define token object {...declaration ...}
define token surface {...declaration...}
define token color_map( ...declaration...)
define token texture {...declaration...}
define token transform { ...rotate/translate/scale statements... }
```

```
ln(x)                log(x)                       max(x, y)              min(x, y)
noise(P, o)          pow(x, y)                    radians(x)             sawtooth(x)
sin(x)               sinh(x)                      sqrt(x)                tan(x)
tanh(x)              visible(vexper1, vexper1)    vexper1 . vexper2
¦x¦                  ¦vexper¦
```

Vector Operators

+	vector addition
-	vector subtraction
*	cross product between two vectors
*	number times a vector (scaling operation)
.	dot product of two vectors

Functions That Return Vectors

```
color_wheel(x, y, z)dnoise(P, fexper)
rotate(vexper, <xdeg, ydeg, zdeg>)
rotate(vexper1, vexper2, deg)reflect(vexper1, vexper2)
trace(location, direction)brownian(vexper)
```

Predefined Variables

u, v, x, y, z, P, W, N, I, start_frame, end_frame, total_frames, frame

Conditional Expressions

```
(cexper ? true_value : false_value)
```

where *cexper* has one of the following forms

Conditional Expression	Returns True if the Following Are True
!cexper	NOT(cexper)
cexper && cexper	cexper AND cexper
cexper ¦¦ cexper	cexper OR cexper
fexper < fexper	fexper LESS THAN fexper
fexper <= fexper	fexper LESS OR EQUAL THAN fexper
fexper > fexper	fexper GREATER THAN fexper
fexper >= fexper	fexper GREATER OR EQUAL THAN fexper
fexper == fexper	fexper IS IDENTICAL TO fexper
vexper == vexper	vexper IS IDENTICAL TO vexper

and *true_value, false_value* can be a floating point expression, a vector expression or another conditional expression.

Image Mapping

(Use with special surface textures.)

```
environment("file1.tga", "file2.tga", ..., "file6.tga")
image("filename.tga")
cylindrical_imagemap(image, vexper [, repeat #])        (vexper is usually P)
planar_imagemap(image, vexper [, repeat #])             (vexper is usually P)
spherical_imagemap(image, vexper [, repeat # ])         (vexper is usually P)
heightmap(image, vexper)                                (vexper is usually P)
environment_map(vexper, environment)                    (vexper is usually reflect(I,N))
```

Object Declarations

```
bezier subdivision_type, flatness_value, u_subdivisions, v_subdivision,
      <x0, y0, z0>, <x1, y1, z1>, ..., <x15, y15, z15>

blob threshold:
   blob_component#1,
   blob_component#2,
      ...etc...
```

Including External Files

```
include "filename.ext"
```

Built-in Color Table

Aquamarine	Black	Blue
BlueViolet	Brown	CadetBlue
Coral	CornflowerBlue	Cyan
DarkGreen	DarkOliveGreen	DarkOrchid
DarkSlateBlue	DarkSlateGray	DarkSlateGrey
DarkTurquoise	DimGray	DimGrey
Firebrick	ForestGreen	Gold
Goldenrod	Gray	Green
GreenYellow	Grey	IndianRed
Khaki	LightBlue	LightGray
LightGrey	LightSteelBlue	LimeGreen
Magenta	Maroon	MediumAquamarine
MediumBlue	MediumForestGreen	MediumGoldenrod
MediumOrchid	MediumSeaGreen	MediumSlateBlue
MediumSpringGreen	MediumTurquoise	MediumVioletRed
MidnightBlue	Navy	NavyBlue
Orange	OrangeRed	Orchid
PaleGreen	Pink	Plum
Red	Salmon	SeaGreen
Sienna	SkyBlue	SlateBlue
SpringGreen	SteelBlue	Tan
Thistle	Turquoise	Violet
VioletRed	Wheat	White
Yellow	YellowGreen	

Background Color And Haze Effect

```
background color
background planar_imagemap(image("filename.tga"),P)
haze coeff, starting_distance, color
```

Light Sources

```
light color, location
light location
spot_light color, location, pointed_at, tightness, angle, falloff
spot_light location, pointed_at
directional_light color, direction
directional_light direction
```

Mathematical Expressions

Operators

+	addition
-	subtraction or minus sign
*	multiplication
/	division
^	exponentiation

Functions That Return Numbers

acos(x)	asin(x)	atan(x)	atan2(x, y)
ceil(x)	cos(x)	cosh(x)	degrees(x)
exp(x)	fabs(x)	floor(x)	fmod(x, y)

```
octaves fexper
position_fn index
position_scale fexper
turbulence fexper
```

(The output of the following function is passed through the lookup function, then into the color map.)

```
index = pos * position_scale + turbulence * noise(P, octaves);
```

Valid Values for *position_fn* Are:

0	No position function used (default)
1	X coordinate in object space
2	X coordinate in world space
3	Distance from z-axis
4	Distance from the origin
5	Radial measure (counter clockwise) around y-axis

Valid Values for *normal_fn* Are

0	No modification made to normal (default)
1	Bumpy
2	Rippled
3	Dented

Valid Values for *lookup_fn* Are

0	No modification
1	sawtooth
2	sin function
3	cosine function

Defined Textures and Colors in TEXTURE.INC, COLORS.INC, and STONES.INC

blue_ripple	bumpy_green	cloudy_sky	dented_red
glass	matte_aquamarine	matte_black	matte_blue
matte_brown	matte_cyan	matte_green	matte_grey
matte_magenta	matte_orange	matte_red	matte_white
matte_yellow	mirror	mountain_colors	reflective_blue
reflective_brown	reflective_coral	reflective_cyan	reflective_gold
reflective_green	reflective_grey	reflective_orange	reflective_red
reflective_tan	reflective_white	reflective_yellow	sapphire_agate
shiny_blue	shiny_coral	shiny_cyan	shiny_green
shiny_magenta	shiny_orange	shiny_red	shiny_yellow
steely_blue	Stone1	Stone2	Stone3
Stone4	Stone5	Stone6	Stone7
Stone8	Stone9	Stone10	Stone11
Stone12	Stone13	Stone14	Stone15
Stone16	Stone17	Stone18	Stone19
Stone20	Stone21	Stone22	Stone23
Stone24	white_marble	whorl_texture	wooden
xz_wheel_texture			

Animation Support

Runtime Variables

```
start_frame startvalue
end_frame endvalue
total_frames totalvalue    (optional if start_frame and end_frame are used)
outfile "name" or outfile name     (filename must be 5 letters long max)
```

Polyray 1.6A Quick Reference

Controlling Polyray from the Command Line

The following table is a reference to all the command-line parameters available with POLYRAY. You can set many options of POLYRAY at the command line. The first column lists the parameter, and the second column describes the parameter's actions and uses.

NOTE: You can set up some of these parameters externally creating a file named POLYRAY.INI, the next section presents this method. Any parameter declared in the command line will override those inside the POLYRAY.INI file.

> Example: POLYRAY demo.pi – o demo.tga –A –T 0.01 –S 15

where demo.pi is the input file, demo.tga is the output (image) file, use the adaptive antialiasing method with a threshold of 0.01 and the number of samples 15.

Command Line Parameters:

Parameter	Action
Antialiasing Parameters	
-a	Performs a simple antialiasing method of averaging the neighboring pixel colors.
-A	Performs an adaptive antialiasing method. It is dependent on the threshold value (parameter -T) and the number of samples per pixel (parameter -S).
-J	Performs a random (jittered) method.
-T n	Sets the threshold value to force over sampling. Over sampling is active if the difference in colors is greater than n. **Example:** -T 0.1
-S n	Sets the number of samples per pixel (n) for the adaptive (parameter -A) method. **Example:** -S 6
File Output Operations	
-b n	Saves the image data after calculating n pixels. This feature acts as a buffer to reduce the number of times that the hard disk is accessed. **Example:** -b 1280
-B	Saves the image data after calculating every line. Use this parameter if you are concerned with saving as much data as possible in case something goes wrong.
-o f	Specify the output file name f. If the parameter is not used, OUT.TGA is assumed. **Example:** -o table.tga
-p n	Set the number n of bits per pixel on the output image file. Acceptable values are 8, 16, 24, and 32. Default is 16. **Example:** -p 24
-u	Use uncompressed TARGA format on the output file.
Image Quality and Size	
-r m	Select method m to generate the image (the lower the number, the better the quality).

Value	Method
0	ray trace [default]
1	scan convert (requires substantial amounts of memory)
2	wireframe (to screen only)
3	Scan convert image and save as RAW data to a file.

Use as:

Polyray [parameters] –r 3 >filename.ext

where filename.ext is the name of the output file.

The RAW data file will consist of one line per triangle. The first nine numbers are the vertex coordinates. The next nine numbers are the components of the normal vectors of each vertex point in the corresponding triangle. Finally, the next six values are the local coordinates u1 v1, u2 v2, u3 v3 of each vertex. The coordinates u and v are the latitude and longitude coordinates of the triangle.